The Monarchy
fifteen hundred years of British tradition

The Monarchy
fifteen hundred years of British tradition

Edited by Robert Smith & John S Moore

This publication has been made possible by the generosity of Patrick Hannigan of Dirleton

The Monarchy
fifteen hundred years of British tradition

Published by Smith's Peerage Limited, Heron Place, 3 George Street, London W1H 6AD
for the Institute for Constitutional Research

ISBN 0 9524229 5 6

British Library Cataloguing and Publication Data. A catalogue record for
this book is available from the British Library: Great Britain − History −
early medieval to present (R Smith and J S Moore, joint Eds).

This book originated at a Conference held by the Manorial Society of Great
Britain at Pembroke College, Oxford, in September 1993. *The Monarchy,
fifteen hundred years of British tradition*, is the last in a series of three
books about the British Constitution. *The House of Lords, a thousand years
of British tradition*, was published in November 1994; and *The House of
Commons, seven hundred years of British tradition*, was published in 1996.

Typeset and printed by Martins Printing Group Limited, Neptune Close,
Medway City Estate, Frindsbury, Rochester, Kent ME2 4LT, England

London 1998

LIST OF SUBSCRIBERS

THE PEERAGE

The Lord Alderdice
The Earl of Annandale and Hartfell
The Lord Biddulph
The Baroness Blatch CBE
The Viscount Brookeborough DL
The Lord Carnock
The Lord Carter
The Earl of Clarendon
The Lord Clark of Kempston KT PC
The Lord Clifford of Chudleigh
Lord Courtenay
The Viscount Cowdray
The Lord de Clifford
The Lord de Ramsey
The Marquess of Donegall LVO
The Lord Eden of Winton PC
The Lord Gray of Contin PC DL
The Lord Hill-Norton GCB Admiral of the Fleet
The Earl of Lincoln
The Lord Macfarlane of Bearsden KT DL
The Lord Martonmere
The Earl of Meath
The Lord Menuhin OM KBE
The Lord Mostyn MC
The Lord Nelson of Stafford
The Lord O'Neill TD
The Lord Peyton of Yeovil PC
The Viscount Portman
The Lord Prentice KT
The Lady Saltoun of Abernethy
The Earl of Shannon
The Earl of Shrewsbury and Talbot DL
The Lord Stratheden & Campbell
The Earl Temple of Stowe
The Lord Vivian
The Lord Waddington GCVO DL QC
The Lord Wakeham PC
The Earl of Wemyss and March KT
The Duke of Westminster OBE TD DL
The Lord Wigram MC DL
The Baroness Willoughby de Eresby DL

THE FEUDAL BARONS

Clifford Balkwell, Baron of Dundalk
Paul Beresford-Hill MBE, Baron of Granard
Nicolaas & Heather Bergsma, Baron & Baroness of Longford
Sydney Brewin, Baron Castlecoole
Stuart Crane, Baron of Cluny
Charles Eugster, Baron of Callan
David Hodge, Baron of Cavan
Peter Hurlstone, Baron of Carlingford
Cecil Johnson, Baron of Kilmaine
Emma Kirby, Baroness of Chirnside
J Peter Liddle, Baron of Gilsland
Dr Harry Lockett, Baron of Castleknock
Lewis Luk, Baron of Greencastle
Hermann Meyer, Baron of Newry
Colin Morgan, Baron of Askeaton
Harold Peerenboom, Baron of Abbotshall
Michel Pilette, Baron of Kinnear
Victor Podd, Baron of Newcastle
Lady Previn, Baroness of Tirerrill
Maurice Taylor, Baron of Portlethen
Trevor Prider, Baron of Ballintober
Stephen Shadix, Baron of Orior
Paul Sleigh, Baron of Carbury
Daniel Sharpe, Baron of Twyneham
Antti Vauhkonen, Baron of Arklow
Douglas Wagland, Baron of Pitcruivie
Robert Williamson, Baron of Ballumbie

THE MANORIAL LORDS

Jacqueline Albright, Lady of Ireby
Leroy Allen, Lord of South Brent
Anthony Appleton, Lord of Great Baddow
Jean Armitage, Lady of Knockaline
Gerald Andrews, Lord of Grayrigg
Janet Armstrong, Lady of Littleover
Richard and Marilyn Ayearst, Lord and Lady of Bothamsall
Rev Dr Donald Baker, Lord of Coltishall
David Balkwell, Lord of Sleaford
Zoe Balkwell, Lady of Bedcote
Henry Banham, Lord of Okenhill Hall
Michael Barratt, Lord of Toseland
Miriam Batts, Lady of Birch & Lyth
Hugo Bayer, Lord of Thuxton

Hermann Erwin Beck, Lord of Great Hallingbury
Peter Beer, Lord of Port Eynon
Jacques Bichsel, Lord of Hackford
Brian Boreham, Lord of Boreham
L L Brandt-Bull, Lord of Itton
John Burnett, Lord of Normanton on Soar
Kathleen Busfield, Lady of Earls Dallinghoo
Clifford Buxton, Lord of Tibenham Hastings & Bishop
Brian Callan, Lord of Athlone
Gillian Campbell
Peter Chancellor, Lord of West Hartford
Murray Chapman
Peter Chapman OBE, Lord of Dodford
Achille Chiorando, Lord of Brampton
Timothy Clark, Lord of Soham with Netherhall Wygorne & Fordham
Gary Clarke, Lord of Heywood
Peter and Edit Clarke, Lord and Lady of East Bridgford
Mervyn Cole, Lord of Knowstone
Robert Combes, Lord of St Winnow
Jack Connolly, Lord of East & West Cheam
Roy Cooper de Bretton, Lord of West Bretton
Janis Cunningham-Coneys, Lady of Barton Oratory
Arnold Davis, Lord of Barnham Broom
Jack Davies, Lord of Ravensthorpe
Jacqueline de Fonseca, Lady of Purse Caundle
Douglas Densmore, Lord of Stratford St Andrew
Desmond de Silva QC KStJ
William Dougan, Lord of Landkey
Elsie Downer, Lady of Crouch
Barry Drury, Lord of Wiveton
Ruth Drury
Carl Dunning Gribble, Lord of Marnhull
Thomas Dwyer, Lord of Falmer
N Elnagy, Lord of Wicklewood
Malcolm Falconer, Lord of Bere & Falconshall
Antony Farnath, Lord of Woodcote
John Fordham, Lord of Uffington
Andrew Forster, Lord of Mynchens
Raymond Franks, Lord of Barwick in Elmet & Thorner
Jack Garside, Lord of Sulby
David Garrison, Lord of Byng
Ole Georg, Lord of Sheldowne
G Gehlsen, Lord of Ovington
Isabella Gibson, Lady of Brackenthwaite
Peter Gibson, Lord of Culverthorpe
K K Gibson-Wynes, Lord of Bottitors
Patrick Gilbert, Lord of Cantley Netherhall

J Gillies Shields, Lord of Melbourne
K R Graf v Rothenburg, Lord of Winsley
John Grant, Lord of Walton Wood
Dr Richard Grayson, Lord of Mursley
Gillian Green, Lady of Alveton and St Buryan
Joseph Hardy, Lord of Henley in Arden
Walter Hall, Lord of Brimstage
James and Eileen Halsall, Lord and Lady of Renacres
Jacqueline Harris, Lady of Caldwell
Ivan & Evelyn Hawkey, Lord & Lady of Wilsthorpe
Anne Hayter, Lady of Duffield
Norbert Helleckes, Lord of Gelham Hall
Col P W Herring OBE, Lord of Berewyk Hall
James Hilton, Lord of Lytham
John Holland, Lord of Boyland
Paul Hooley, Lord of Hoole
Niall Horan
John Hornchurch, Lord of Hornchurch Hall
Geoffrey Horne, Lord of Wakes Colne
Brian Hornsby, Lord of Hornsby
John Hunt, Lord of Worksop
Sandro Iaria, Lord of Tillingdon
Peter Jennings, Lord of Thremhall Priory
Roy Jennings, Lord of Minterne Magna
Hopkin Joseph, Lord of Stormy
Siegfried Joussineau, Lord of Diss
Simon Kearey, Lord of Kersall
Steven Kellner, Lord of Blencogo
Audrey Kirby, Lady of Stockwith
William Kulesh, Lord of Brampton
Ernest de Kuthy, Lord of Worminghall
Elvin Lashbrooke, Lord of Duston
J E Laurie, Lord of Boylands
Raymond Lescott, Lord of Tilstock
John Longford-Lewis, Lord of More Malherbe & Cotley
Joost Majoor, Lord Arreton
J V Machin, Lord of Gateford
Russell Male
Sadie Marks, Lady of Shovelstrode
Antonio Mas-Perez, Lord of Elkesley
Eric Mayer-Schaller, Lord of Cannon Hall
Royston McCracken, Lord of Crofton & Whinnow
Patrick and Monique McKenna, Lord and Lady of Ashridge
Luisa Mendoza Martin, Lady of Burwash
Ernest Martin
John Moore, Lord of Hardwick
Thomas Moore, Lord of Bridestowe Sanctuary

Russell Morton, Lord of Walton cum Trimley
John Mulvihill, Lord of Abbas Hall
William Neale, Lord of Lyneal
Henry Neumüller, Lord of Sawbridgeworth
Richard Nokes, Lord of Middleton Cheney
David Nugent, Lord of Castletown Delvin
Dr Donald Olliff
Michael Pendred, Lord of Frithsden
Derek Pilgrim JP, Lord of West Anstey
E Polli, Lord of Wellow
Charles Poole, Lord of Upton Warren
William Pryor, Lord of Bramhall
Adrian Pyatt, Lord of Wood Hall
Gerald Rand, Lord of Lynford
Martin Randall, Lord Pishiobury
Arthur Rawl, Lord of Cursons
Roger Reed, Lord of Coffinswell
Leslie Retford, Lord of Pleshey
Cecile Robinson
L H Rosan, Lord of Haverhill
David Rosow, Lord of Godington
Rex Rozario, Lord of Bickleigh
Vladimir Rubinstein MBE, Lord of Garford
Terence Rutter, Lord of Ling Hall
Louis-Marc Servien, Lord of Quendon
Barry Sewell, Lord of Hardingham & Flockthorpe
Christopher Shadix, Lord of Dardinston
Bernard Shaw, Lord of Ballycashel
John Shazell, Lord of Didcot
John Sherringham, Lord of Talkin
Thomas van Schoonbeek, Lord of Lambrigg
Timothy Shorland, Lord of Hempton & Northwick
John Shute, Lord of Stanmer
Marianne Simon, Lady of Winthorpe
John Stedman, Lord of Irthington
Howard Steers, Lord of High Hoyland
Frances Stevenson
Robert Steventon, Lord of Thistleton
Ian Stewart, Lord of Lowertoft & Breck of Muness
Gunter Streib, Lord of Westhall
John Szepietowski, Lord of Ingestre
Barry Theobald-Hicks, Lord of Danbury
Alvin Thompson, Lord of Hinton
Michael Tupholme, Lord of Tupholme
R Turrall-Clarke, Lord of Overhall in Hildersham
Lloyd Van Syckle, Lord of Hamptonet
Albert Vidler, Lord of Lanhadron

Sir Humphry Wakefield Bart
W David Walker OBE, Lord of Castlerigg & Derwentwater
Keith Wallis
Dr Archibald Weems McFadden, Lord of Deopham
Robert Williams, Lord of Allerby
Denis Woodfield
Clifford Worthing

Contents

Foreword

By the Sponsor, Patrick Hannigan of Dirleton

I AM acutely aware of the difficulties connected with a publication consisting of specially commissioned articles, such as this, and I like to think that my involvement as sponsor, which stems from one meeting with the joint editor and publisher, Robert Smith, was probably the least complex of the publisher's many tasks.

Anyone reading the two earlier parts of this series, *The House of Lords*, and *The House of Commons*, will appreciate the distinguished and uniquely well informed contributions made by members of the peerage, politicians, historians, and constitutional experts. In this, the third and final book in a series on the Crown and parliament, the history of the Monarchy from the earliest times and the problems it faces today and in the future is dealt with by contributors with the same high standard and attention to detail.

I take great pride, therefore, in my association with this valuable and important source of information, and commend it to anyone interested in understanding the relationship between the monarch and people, the centre of our democracy.

Preface

I AM INDEBTED to Patrick Hannigan of Dirleton without whom this book would not have been possible. His financial backing has made it possible for me to produce a publication of its type, whose technical excellence is second to none: paper and colour pictures of the highest quality. He has also taken away the strain any publisher feels about sales before publication. I have not had to worry whether we sell enough copies to break even. That said, the magnificent advance support from members of the Manorial Society of Great Britain and of the Peerage, together with bookshop orders, means that we shall have a useful profit to put towards our next venture, a history of aristocratic finance.

After serving in the Royal Air Force, Patrick Hannigan, a Scot by blood, became a merchant mariner and 30 years ago settled in Brazil where he married. He established a thriving cosmetics business, with outlets throughout Latin America. His son now runs the business day-to-day, enabling Patrick to re-establish himself in Britain, where, besides supporting this book, he is able to indulge his interest in numerous charities, not least St John Ambulance, and his love of the sea with his ocean-going yacht. It is good to see Britons making it abroad and putting something back.

Patrick has also been a wonderful moral supporter, and has encouraged me at every turn. Indeed, the trilogy which I have published about the history of our constitution – Lords and Commons in 1994 and 1996, and now Monarchy – has been fortunate in its sponsors. Celia Lipton-Farris started us off with our history of the House of Lords. Ironically, Celia is, originally, a wee lassie from Edinburgh and made a great reputation during and after the Second World War as a singer on a par with Vera Lynn: her father was the great band leader, Sydney Lipton, who sadly died two years ago. She now runs a patent empire in the United States and, like Patrick Hannigan, supports many charities. It is entirely coincidental that two British-Scots, making their way in North and South America, have been our sponsors!

I cannot permit another paragraph to proceed without mentioning John Moore, who has assiduously co-edited all three books in the trilogy. I met John 14 years ago when I was planning the ninth centenary exhibition, with the Public Record Office, of Domesday Book, for which I published the catalogue in 1986. This book, like its two siblings, sprang from conferences held by the Manorial Society at Oxford, and John was a huge help in suggesting contributors and helping to chair sessions. As the papers arrived in typescript to form chapters, I was able to send copies down to John who dealt with all my queries and doubts, and – importantly for a series such as this – got the notes into an intelligible arrangement. It is satisfying for us both to know that *House of Lords* is now on the undergraduate recommended reading list of some universities.

I am grateful to Christine McCeoch, another Scot, for producing the index, as she did for *House of Lords* and *House of Commons*. She has also proved an invaluable backstop for *errata* which John and I and the contributors missed in the text.

I have been extremely fortunate again in bringing together a group of academics known nationally and internationally for their work in their several fields of historical research. Two authors have contributed to all three volumes, Dr David Carpenter and the Hon Adam Bruce. I welcome back in this book Professors John Miller, Jeremy Black, and William Doyle, and the Rt Hon J Enoch Powell. I have known the first three for some years and was introduced, as an undergraduate, to Mr Powell almost 30 years ago by the eminent, though (by his own wish) little published, American scholar, Keith Wallis, whom I persuaded to contribute to *House of Lords* – not without a certain sleight of hand.

Professor Rosamond McKitterick was published by Lord Sudeley and me in our book, *The Sudeleys, Lords of Toddington*, in 1987, after a lecture to the Manorial Society. It is good to see her back in this publication. I welcome Professors David Loades and A P Smyth, who have lectured to the Society in the past, though not been published by me until now. Dr Ann Williams and I worked together on the Domesday Exhibition and Catalogue in 1986 and I have known David Williamson, co-Editor of Debrett's *Peerage and Baronetage*, since we both took part in an American television programme some years ago. New contributors include Drs Graham Loud and Barry Coward, and Professor Anthony Goodman.

The death of Diana, Princess of Wales, occurred just before we were due to go to press which meant changes to two chapters and a "rush" chapter on her life and legacy. For the latter I am indebted to the noted biographer, Hugo Vickers, who produced copy in a fortnight. Finally, my friend, David Starkey, has provided a seminal chapter on the modern monarchy, showing that, far from being a continuous threat of inevitability, the history of the monarchy, like all history, has developed capriciously. Insofar as there is a thread, the most recent one begins in 1917 with the anglicizing of the dynasty and ends in 1992 with the separation of the Prince and Princess of Wales. The future of the monarchy, like its past, could still go in any direction and this will depend largely on the key players, the Queen and the Prince of Wales: just as, had George III not been mad, or the Prince Consort lived longer, the Victorian monarchy might well have developed along Bismarckian and subsequent Dutch models – with real power and influence in an age of mass democracy.

This book is published for the Institute for Constitutional Research, a new group of which I am the Chairman, comprising academics, peers, and politicians. Our aim is to study all aspects of the Constitution at a time when anything "old" is deemed in need of "modernization". It appears to me that those countries which fail most miserably as nation states, France, Germany, Italy, Greece seem to require a new constitution about every one and a half generations; while written constitutions like those of the former Soviet Union or the People's Republic of China – excellent on paper – are tyrannies in practice. The two most successful nation states, the United States and the United Kingdom and some Commonwealth countries, have rather old constitutions, grown from the same root, and both, with all their faults, have defended civilization in the 20th century with a success that no other country can equal.

Robert Smith
London, January 1998

Notes on Contributors

Professor Jeremy Black PhD FRHistS (chapter 10) is Professor of Modern History at the University of Exeter. Educated at Queen's College, Cambridge, he graduated with a starred first. He was subsequently at St John's and Merton Colleges, Oxford, and was from 1980 to 1995 Professor of History at Durham. He is a member of the Councils of the Royal Historical Society and the British Records Association. His 18 books include *Sir Robert Walpole and the nature of Eighteenth-Century Politics* (London, 1990), *Culloden and the 'Forty-Five* (Stroud, 1990), *War for America* (Stroud, 1991), *Pitt the Elder* (Cambridge, 1992), and *The Politics of Britain, 1688–1800* (Manchester, 1993).

The Hon Adam Bruce MA (chapter 12) read History at Balliol College, Oxford, where he was President of the Union. He then returned to Scotland, to study Law at Edinburgh University and now works for a firm of solicitors in St Andrews. He has contributed chapters on the Scottish nobility to *The House of Lords: a thousand years of British tradition* (London, 1994) and on the Scottish Parliament to *The House of Commons: seven hundred years of British tradition* (London, 1996).

Dr David Carpenter DPhil FRHistS (chapter 5) is a leading authority on English medieval history. He was educated at Westminster School and Christ Church College, Oxford. He has held lectureships at Christ Church and St Hilda's Colleges, Oxford, at the University of Aberdeen, and at Queen Mary and Westfield College, London. He is now Reader in Medieval History at King's College, London. His publications include *The Battles of Lewes and Evesham* (Keele, 1987), *The Minority of Henry III* (London, 1990) and *The Reign of Henry III* (London, 1995) as well as numerous articles in books and learned journals.

Dr Barry Coward PhD FRHistS (chapter 8) is Reader in History at Birkbeck College, University of London. He was educated at Rochdale Grammar School and was an undergraduate and post-graduate student at the University of Sheffield. His publications include *The Stanleys, Lords Stanley and the Earls of Derby, 1385–1672* (Manchester, 1983), *The Stuart Age: England, 1603–1714* (London, 2nd edn, 1994), *Social Change and Continuity in Early Modern England* (London, 1988), and *Oliver Cromwell* (London, 1991).

Professor William Doyle MA DPhil FRHistS (chapter 11) has been Professor of History at the University of Bristol since 1986. An Oxford graduate, he spent 14 years at the University of York, before becoming Professor of Modern History at the University of Nottingham in 1981. He has also held visiting appointments in Oxford, Cambridge, Paris, Bordeaux, and in the United States. A specialist in 18th-century history, his main publications include *The Old European order, 1660–1800* (Oxford, 1978, 2dn edn, 1992), *Origins of the French Revolution* (Oxford, 1980, 2nd edn, 1988), *The Ancien*

Régime (Basingstoke, 1986), the *Oxford History of the French Revolution* (Oxford, 1989) and *Venality. The Sale of Offices in Eighteenth-Century France* (Oxford, 1996). He is now editing (with Colin Haydon) *Robespierre: History, Historiography and Literature* (Cambridge, 1998) and is writing a volume *France, 1763–1848* for the *Oxford History of Modern Europe*.

Professor Anthony Goodman MA BLitt FRHistS (chapter 6) is Professor of Medieval and Renaissance History at the University of Edinburgh. His books include *The loyal conspiracy: the Lords Appellant under Richard II* (London, 1971), *A history of England from Edward II to James I* (London, 1977), *The Wars of the Roses: military activity and English Society, 1452–97* (London, 1981), and *The New Monarchy: England, 1471–1534* (Oxford, 1988). He has edited (with A MacKay) *The impact of humanism on Western Europe* (London, 1990), and (with A Tuck) *War and border societies in the Middle Ages* (London, 1992). His most recent book is *John of Gaunt: the exercise of princely power in fourteenth-century Europe* (London, 1992).

Professor David Loades MA PhD LittD FSA FRHistS (chapter 7) graduated from Emmanuel College, Cambridge, in 1958, and held posts in the Universities of St Andrews and Durham before moving to the Chair of History at the University of Wales at Bangor in 1980. He retired from his chair in 1996 and is presently Honorary Research Professor at the University of Sheffield. His books include *The Oxford Martyrs* (Bangor, 1970, 2nd edn, 1992), *Politics and the Nation, 1450–1660* (London, 1974), *The Reign of Mary Tudor* (London, 1979, 2nd edn, 1991), *The Tudor Court* (London, 1986), *Mary Tudor: a life* (Oxford, 1989), *The Tudor Navy* (Aldershot, 1992), *The Reign of Edward VI* (Bangor, 1994), and *John Dudley, Duke of Northumberland* (Oxford, 1996). He has been President of the Ecclesiastical History Society, and is a Vice-President of the Navy Records Society. He is presently Director of the British Academy Project for a new edition of John Foxe's *Acts and Monuments*.

Dr G A Loud MA DPhil FRHistS (chapter 4) is a Senior Lecturer in Medieval History at the University of Leeds, where he has taught since 1978. He is the author of *Church and Society in the Norman Principality of Capua, 1058–1197* (Oxford, 1985) and of an Introduction to the Alecto Facsimile Edition of the *Somerset Domesday* (London, 1989). He has also contributed nearly 30 articles to scholarly journals in Britain, the US, Italy, and Germany, largely on the history of the Normans in southern Italy during the 11th and 12th centuries. He has written three chapters on south Italian history, 900–1200, for the *New Cambridge Medieval History*; in collaboration with Professor Thomas Wiedemann, he has completed an annotated translation of *The History of the Tyrants of Sicily by Hugo Falcandus*, to be published in 1998. He is now working on a book about Robert Guiscard and the Norman conquest of Italy.

Professor Rosamund McKitterick MA PhD LittD FRHistS (chapter 1), is Professor in Early Medieval European History in the University of

Cambridge, and Vice-Principal of Newnham College, Cambridge, where she has been a Fellow since 1974. She gained her doctorate from the University of Cambridge in 1976 and has also studied at the University of Munich. Her numerous books include *The Frankish Church and the Carolingian Reforms, 789–895* (London, 1977); *The Frankish Kingdoms under the Carolingians, 751–987* (London, 1983); *The Carolingians and the Written Word* (Cambridge, 1989); *Books, Seats of Learning in the Frankish Kingdoms under the Carolingians* (Aldershot, 1994); and *Frankish Kings and Culture in the early Middle Ages* (Aldershot, 1995). She has edited a number of books, including *The Uses of Literacy in early medieval Europe* (Cambridge, 1990); *Carolingian Culture: emulation and innovation* (Cambridge, 1994); *The New Cambridge Medieval History, vol. II: 700–900* (Cambridge, 1995) and, with Roland Quinault, *Edward Gibbon and Empire* (Cambridge, 1996).

Professor John Miller FRHistS (chapter 9) is Head of the History Department, Queen Mary and Westfield College, University of London. He was educated at Jesus College, Cambridge, and was a Research Fellow at Gonville and Caius College, Cambridge (1971–5). Since 1975, he has been at Queen Mary College as Lecturer in History, subsequently Reader and Professor. His books include *James II: a study in Kingship* (Hove, 1978, repr. London, 1989); *Charles II* (London, 1991) and *An English Absolutism? The later Stuart Monarchy, 1660–88* (London, 1992), and he has edited *Absolutism in Seventeenth-Century Europe* (London, 1990).

John S Moore FSA FRHistS (Joint Editor; Introduction) was educated at Brighton Technical College and the Institute of Historical Research, London. He was awarded the Alexander Prize of the Royal Historical Society and the John Nichols Local History Prize of Leicester University. Since 1968 he has been a Lecturer in Economic History at Bristol University. His main research interests are in the economic and social history of medieval and early modern England; his books include *Laughton: a study in the evolution of the Wealden landscape* (Leicester, 1964), *The Goods and Chattels of Our Forefathers* (Chichester, 1976) and *Domesday Book: Gloucestershire* (Chichester, 1981), and he has also written articles in *Anglo-Norman Studies, Economic History Review* and *English Historical Review*. He is now writing a book on the population of Tudor England, and, with Dr Neil Stacy, is editing the *Glastonbury Abbey Estate Surveys, 1130–1201* for the British Academy's Records of Social and Economic History series.

The Rt Hon J Enoch Powell MBE (chapter 14) was a member of the House of Commons from 1950 until 1987, except for a few months in 1974. He served in the Cabinet of the late Harold Macmillan (Earl of Stockton). With many other books to his credit, he co-authored with Keith Wallis *The House of Lords in the Middle Ages* (London, 1968). He was educated at King Edward's, Birmingham, and at Trinity College, Cambridge (MA, 1937). He was Professor of Greek in the University of Sydney, NSW, but returned to England at the outbreak of war in 1939, joining the Warwickshire Regiment as a private soldier. He rose to the rank of Brigadier in 1944.

Robert Smith, OStJ BA (Joint Editor; chapter 17) read History at the University of Nottingham and graduated in 1969. He is the Chairman of the Manorial Society of Great Britain and Publisher of Smith's Peerage. The *Peerage, Baronetage and Feudal Title Holders* in four volumes is in the process of research. He is Chairman of the Institute for Constitutional Research. He edited, jointly with Professor H R Loyn, and published for the Public Record Office, London, *Domesday: 900 Years of England's Norman Heritage* (London, 1986); he has also edited and published *Royal Armada, 400 Years* (London, 1988) for the National Maritime Museum; and *Against the Odds: The 50th Anniversary of the Battle of Britain* (London, 1990) for the Royal Air Force Museum, and other historical exhibition catalogues. He jointly edited with John Moore and published *The House of Lords: a thousand years of British Tradition* (London, 1994) and *The House of Commons: seven hundred years of British tradition* (London, 1996). He edits and publishes the *Bulletin of the Manorial Society* of Great Britain, and edited and published, *The Sudeleys – Lords of Toddington* (London, 1987).

Professor Alfred P Smyth DPhil FSA FRHistS (chapter 2) is Professor of Medieval History and Master of Keynes College at the University of Kent. He graduated in Medieval History and Archaeology from University College, Dublin, and conducted postgraduate research at the Universities of Iceland and Oxford. His books include *Scandinavian Kings in the British Isles* (Oxford, 1977), *Scandinavian York and Dublin* (Dublin, 2 vols, 1976–9), *Warlords and Holy Men: Scotland, AD 80–1000* (London, 1984) and *King Alfred the Great* (Oxford, 1995). He has held visiting appointments at the American University in Athens and at the Institute for American Universities in Aix-en-Provence. He is currently writing a book on the history of the Anglo-Saxons.

Dr David Starkey MA PhD FSA FRHistS (chapter 13) graduated from the University of Cambridge and writes and broadcasts on constitutional affairs. He has written *The reign of Henry VIII: personalities and politics* (London, 1985) and has edited *The English Court from The Wars of The Roses to the Civil War* (London, 1987), *Rivals in power: lives and letters of the great Tudor dynasties* (London, 1990) and *Henry VIII: a European court in England* (London, 1991), as well as (with C Coleman), *Revolution reassessed; revisions in the history of Tudor government and administration* (Oxford, 1986). He is now editing *The Inventories of King Henry VIII*.

Hugo Vickers (chapter 16) is a biographer who has specialized in 20th century figures, including Gladys, Duchess of Marlborough, Cecil Beaton, Vivien Leigh, the Duke and Duchess of Windsor, and Greta Garbo. His most recent book, *The Kiss*, won the 1996 Stern Silver Pen for Non-Fiction. He is an acknowledged expert on the Royal Family and was much involved with

ITN during the coverage of the death and funeral of Diana, Princess of Wales. He is presently researching a biography of Princess Andrew of Greece, the mother of the Duke of Edinburgh.

Dr Ann Williams BA PhD FSA FRHistS (chapter 3) graduated from the University of London in 1960 and obtained her PhD in 1964. From 1965 to 1988 she was successively Lecturer and Senior Lecturer in Medieval History at the Polytechnic (now University) of North London, and is now retired. In addition to many articles in scholarly journals, her books include *Victoria County History of Dorset*, vol III (Oxford, 1969); (with D A Kirby and A P Smyth) *A Biographical Dictionary of Dark-Age Britain* (London, 1991); (with The Hon R W H Erskine, Professor H R Loyn, and G H Martin) *Domesday Book* (London, 31 vols, 1986–92); and *The English and the Norman Conquest* (Woodbridge, 1995). She is now writing *Kingship and Government in pre-Conquest England*. She has just been appointed Honorary Research Fellow in History at the University of East Anglia.

David Williamson FSA, FSA(Scot) FSG (chapter 15) is co-editor of Debrett's Peerage and Baronetage. His published works include *Debrett's Kings and Queens of Britain* (Exeter, 1986), *Debrett's Kings and Queens of Europe* (Exeter, 1988), *Debrett's Guide to Heraldry and Regalia* (London, 1992), and *Brewer's British Royalty* (London, 1996).

Picture Captions

A: Although entitled "Edwardus", this portrait, by an unknown artist, is of Henry III (1216–72) whose reign in many respects presaged the inauguration of parliament. The reign signalled an increasing "Englishness" about the monarchy, caused largely by the loss of the Angevin possessions in northern France, particularly Normandy, during the stewardship of King John. The king's chief subjects in the 13th century were still the baronage (as they were to remain for several more centuries), but the members of this magnate class felt themselves unable to commit the realm to the supply of the king's financial requirements on their authority alone. It was one of Henry's greatest noblemen, Simon de Montfort, Earl of Leicester, who summoned what has come down in history as the "first parliament" during the Barons' War of the mid-1260s, although elements of a "commons" had been summoned to "parliaments" earlier in the reign. Henry's son, Edward I, whose Scottish wars pushed that king to extreme financial measures, instituted a tradition that was to develop: the grant of supply in return for the laying of petitions before the king. *By courtesy of the National Portrait Gallery, London.* See David Carpenter, page 116.

B: "The English kill their kings" was an accusation levelled against the people of these shores (the Scots also killed their kings). This portrait shows Richard II (1377–99), the second king of England to be assassinated in the 14th century, Edward II being nurdered in 1327. In the next century, Henry VI was to be murdered in 1471 and Richard III to be killed in battle against rebellious subjects in 1485. While true, the accusation was not entirely fair: doubt surrounds the deaths of the last kings of the Capetian dynasty of France and the *Jacquerie* mid-century brought a dauphin of France to his knees. The 15th century saw an ineffectual royal power between 1400 and 1460, and parliament made many gains, not least in extracting from Henry IV (1399–1413) an account of his spending. This picture, by Randall, is in Westminster Abbey. *By courtesy of the Victoria and Albert Museum Picture Library.* See Anthony Goodman, page 132.

C: Henry Tudor: Henry VII (1485–1509) restored the monarchy's prestige after the civil wars of the 15th century ("Wars of the Roses") and laid the foundations of the power of his son, Henry VIII. Henry VII has sometimes been seen as inaugurating a "New Monarchy", more businesslike, less interested in display than the medieval monarchy which reached a sort of apotheosis in the reign of Richard II. In fact, many of the medieval structures remained, but were made more efficient and, far from being uninterested in literature and the arts, Henry spent as lavishly on them as did the gaudy Edward IV. The problems inherited by the Stuarts from the Tudors had much to do with the fact that royal administration had not really changed since the late Middle Ages. Unknown artist. *By courtesy of the National Portrait Gallery, London.* See David Loades, page 149.

D: Henry VIII liked to be thought of as a Renaissance prince and started his reign with a million sterling in the Treasury, which he quickly spent in trying (unsuccessfully) to regain his ancestors' possessions in northern France. The problem for kings of England then, as it still is for prime ministers of Great Britain today, is their failure to come to terms with the fact that England (or Britain) is a mediocre power, and always was. Accident, happy or otherwise, has periodically enabled monarchs or their governments to "punch above their weight" – hence the Victorian British Empire which looked a great deal stronger on paper than it actually was, as the First World War belatedly demonstrated. While of immense power himself – and psychotically murderous with it – Henry sowed the seeds of future discord between king and people by having parliament sanction everything from weights and measures to the succession and religion. Unknown artist, after Hans Holbein. *By courtesy of the National Portrait Gallery, London*. See David Loades, page 149.

E and F: Edward VI, Henry VIII's son by Jane Seymour, came to the throne in 1547 at the age of nine. It was to obtain a male heir that his father had undone the Roman Catholic Church, seized its assets, and had parliament authorize the succession. The reign marked a hardening of Protestant attitudes, but, unlike the preceding century, a minority did not lead to civil war. However, parliament was increasingly used to sanction government policy and it was parliament, after the brief interlude of Lady Jane Grey, that helped to bring about the peaceful succession in 1553 of Edward's half-sister, Mary Tudor, whose mother was Catherine of Aragon. She is still wrongly called "Bloody Mary" for the few hundred leading Protestants, including the Archbishop of Canterbury, Thomas Cranmer, whom she burnt to death. It has been estimated that her father, Henry VIII, executed at least 100,000 people during his 38 years on the throne, including four people who were boiled to death, such a shocking method of execution that even the blood-thirsty London rabble could not stomach it, and the Act of Parliament that brought in this form of punishment was repealed. Mary took some steps to restore Roman Catholicism and, had she lived, things might have been different, but she was careful not to alienate the gentry, many of whom were deeply attached to the new way of worshipping God and, at least as important, had done so well out of the confiscated lands of the monasteries. Both portraits by unknown artists. *By courtesy of the National Gallery, London*. See David Loades, page 149.

G: Elizabeth I (1558–1603) was completely different from her half-sister, Mary Tudor. Mary adored her mother and Elizabeth "gloried" in the memory of her father. During her reign, England became increasingly a "gentry commonwealth". The bishoprics of the medieval church had been filled by the scions of the nobility. The bishops in Elizabeth's reign were largely from urban or minor gentry backgrounds. By the 1580s, because of its greater frequency and longer sessions, parliament became not only the gentleman's forum in national politics, but also the social highpoint in the kingdom where the sons of gentlemen could round-off their characters, make valuable marriage alliances, and meet a cosmopolitan "set". Everyone in England paid tax and in the early Tudor period taxes fell heaviest on those best able to pay them. With the inflation of the 16th century and the increasing control of wealthy patrons over parliamentary boroughs, who assessed their own contributions to the subsidy, Crown revenues slowly but inexorably declined as the century wore on. At her death in 1603, England was not poor, but the Queen's government was. Elizabeth had mortgaged her authority to the gentry. Portrait by an unknown artist. *By courtesy of the National Portrait Gallery, London.* See David Loades, page 149.

H and I: James I of England (from 1603) and VI of Scotland (1567–1625) inherited two principal problems that threatened the stability of the monarchy: the financial mess left by Elizabeth I and the ideological (ie religious) divisions in England. James was remarkably adept at tacking with the wind and kept the lid on the pressure-cooker of English politics for 22 years. His son and heir, Charles I, was conspicuously unsuccessful. James kept a raucous court where the main factions were represented. Charles's court was decorous and almost private, confined to his friends and supporters. While James was at his best in his "beer-and-sandwiches" political role, Charles dealt with opposition head-on. "Thorough", his and his ministers' – Strafford's and Laud's – policy, was designed to assert the King's prerogatives against a fissiparous Commons, and to establish an episcopacy whose centrepiece was obedience to God's anointed and the "beauty of holiness" as revealed through the Anglican liturgy. That both policies were misunderstood, or deliberately misconstrued, by his opponents led to accusations that the King intended to do away with parliament and return to the Church of Rome. In fact, Charles's problem was the same as that of so many of his predecessors: while he could rule quite effectively in peacetime, especially during the "boom" of the 1630s, he was unable to raise sufficient money to finance war, and the beginning of his undoing was the "Bishops' Wars" at the end of his "personal rule". The civil wars of the 1640s did not resolve the conundrum of how to have effective government and to get parliament to pay for it, and king-in-all-but-name, Lord Protector Cromwell, was no more successful in winning consent in the 1650s than Charles had been in the 1630s. Both portraits by Daniel Mytens. *By courtesy of the National Portrait Gallery*, London. See Barry Coward, page 167.

J, K, L: Charles II (1660–85), James II (1685–88), William III (1689–1702): When the monarchy was restored in 1660, there was a great sigh of relief, in the political nation at least, that stability and continuity had returned. The fundamental problem for a governing monarchy, however, is when the crown may pass to an incompetent, or even a madman, or to some one whose policies were not in accord with the governing élite. The problem was by no means new to England, where Edward II had been deposed and murdered in 1327 – and where William Rufus may even have been murdered in 1100. The Balkan and Portuguese monarchies earlier this century, the Bavarian at the end of the last, were continuations of the same problem. Divine right theory – the policy of non-resistance to the king – enjoyed a recrudescence at the Restoration, partly emotional with the cult of the "royal martyr", but also strongly political as monarchy was seen as a bulwark against the disorder of the 1640s and 1650s. The Exclusion Crisis of the early 1680s only underlined the importance of legitimacy and led to the generally popular succession of Charles's brother, James II. But King James's brief reign also underlined monarchy's great "fault-line": his policies most certainly did not accord with those of the political élite. His flight in December 1688 left the Tories, the "legitimists", with a problem: how could they accede to the deposition of a king and the enthronement of his daughter and her husband at the invitation of a convention parliament? The difficulty was largely overcome by a legal fiction: James had, in fact, "left the throne vacant", he had abdicated. His daughter, Mary II, a Protestant, succeeded jointly with her husband William III, whose grandfather, anyway, was James I; while James II's son by his queen, Mary of Modena, was conveniently branded a changeling. But William's powers, though ample, were very different from those of his immediate predecessor. William could claim no divine right while, by a series of acts of parliament in the 1690s, the monarch's power to raise money and rule without parliament was ended by the Triennial Act; his power to maintain a standing army without the consent of parliament was ended by the Mutiny Act; and his power to sack judges was ended by the Act of Settlement, the bedrock piece of legislation for our present constitutional arrangements. Portrait of King Charles by John Michael Wright, those of James and William by unknown artists, all *by courtesy of the National Portrait Gallery, London*. See John Miller, page 182, and Robert Smith, page 288.

M and N: George I (1714–27) and George III (1660–1820): The Hanoverians were among the most successful monarchs in British history, although this does not fit in with our general image of them. There were no disputed successions, and no repeats of the 1640s and 1650s, or of the Glorious Revolution of 1689. Republicanism only succeeded in the American colonies and even there a form of elective monarchy was instituted and prevails to this day, President Clinton notwithstanding. The Act of Settlement (1701) had, once for all, settled the contest between king and parliament for the supreme role in the state which was to be, and still is "the king in parliament", although this is now being eroded by British membership of the European Union. Portraits by Sir Godfrey Kneller and Sir William Beechey, both *by courtesy of the National Portrait Gallery, London*. See Jeremy Black, page 203.

O and P: Queen Victoria (1837–1901) and King George V (1910–36): When Victoria came to the throne, the First Reform Act had been on the Statute Book for five years, and more or less brought to an end royal participation in elections to the House of Commons. The Queen, with the assistance of the Prince Consort, successfully brokered coalitions after the Peel defeat in 1846, but once her adored Benjamin Disraeli had enacted the Second Reform Act (1867), mass parliamentary democracy was not far away. Victoria said that she would never reign over a democracy and, although that privilege was to await her grandson, George V in 1918, she presided over the beginning of the re-modelling of the monarchy which survived until the 1990s. The Royal Family became the archetypal family, expressing the moral mores of the vast majority of the population from the 1920s to the 1980s, the apogee being the wedding of Lady Diana Spencer with the Prince of Wales in July 1981. The "People's Monarchy" is not an invention of Mr Tony Blair's New Labour. The House of Windsor not only survived, but thrived, in the 20th century by supplying a deeply-held need for continuity and reflecting the people's sense of morality. The outpourings of grief for Diana, Princess of Wales, took place outside royal palaces not just because she was a member of the Royal Family: where else does the English (no disrespect to Welsh, but less so Scottish) nation express its grief, or its joy? For a hundred years and more, the nation has expressed its tender emotions outside Buckingham Palace. It expresses its anger outside the Palace of Westminster. Portrait by Julia Abercromby and photograph by Vandyk, both *by courtesy of the National Portrait Gallery, London*. See David Starkey, at page 248, and Hugo Vickers, page 278.

Captions by Robert Smith

John S Moore

Introduction

THIS VOLUME presents the papers given at the Annual Conference of the Manorial Society of Great Britain, held at Pembroke College, Oxford, in September 1993, with a few exceptions. During the time between the Conference being held and the production of this book, the proceedings of the 1994 Conference were published first, as *The House of Commons: seven hundred years of British Tradition*, in 1995, to coincide with, and to celebrate, the 700th anniversary of the Model Parliament convened by Edward I in 1295. In the intervening period, Robert Smith and I were fortunate in persuading Professor Alfred Smyth and Dr Ann Williams to contribute two chapters covering the period from the departure of the Romans from Britain in 410 to the Norman Conquest. In addition, the Hon Adam Bruce, who has provided chapters on the Scottish dimension to *The House of Lords: a thousand years of British Tradition* and *The House of Commons: seven hundred years of British Tradition*, has produced a chapter on the Scottish monarchy, and the Right Hon J Enoch Powell and David Williamson have given us some provocative reflections on why Britain has a monarchy and why it will survive. Finally, Robert Smith, as Chairman of the Manorial Society, has expanded his necessarily brief introductory remarks at the Conference into a full discussion of the Royal Prerogative.

The delay in producing this volume has led to a more logical order of progression, for the House of Lords and the House of Commons, which together constituted the English Parliament, since 1707 the British Parliament, and from 1801 the United Kingdom Parliament, were in origin subordinate and advisory bodies to the Crown. The House of Lords originated as the *witenagemot*, the "assembly of wise men" who were appointed by kings to advise them in the late Anglo-Saxon period, a body which after the Norman Conquest became the *Magnum Concilium* or "Great Council", consisting of those nobles and others whom the king trusted to advise him and to run the expanding bureaucracy of Anglo-Norman and Angevin England. When, in the 13th century, the Great Council gave way to what became the House of Lords, its members were again appointed by the Crown: to this day, membership of the House of Lords is defined as consisting of those persons who have received an individual writ of summons from the Crown Office to attend (although, of course, nowadays the issue of such writs is determined, in the case of hereditary peers, by the strict rules of succession to peerage titles).[1] An important reason why the Great Council was superseded by the House of Lords in conjunction with the House of Commons was that it had become clear that the claim of the baronage to represent its subtenants, knights as well as peasants, by virtue of the vertical links of tenurial responsibility, was not valid, and that the larger towns, most of which were royal boroughs, and thus outside the network of feudal obligation, could not possibly be represented by barons. Indeed, that eminent medieval economic and social historian, the late Professor M M Postan, once called medieval towns "little islands of freedom in a feudal sea".

Similarly, therefore, the House of Commons was originally summoned by the Crown from Edward I's time onwards so that the rural gentry and the townsmen, through their elected representatives ("chosen" would be a better word for the medieval period, at least, but "elected" is sanctified by usage), the "knights of the shire" and the "burgesses in parliament", could be easily consulted by the Crown and could give their consent to measures which the Crown thought it politic should have the agreement of the representatives of the governed, in particular grants of taxation.[2] Only very gradually and with much hesitation did parliament, and in particular the House of Commons, begin first to assert its own wishes as a *quid pro quo* for agreeing to the Crown's wishes, and it was not until the eve of the Civil War in the 17th century that parliament began to oppose the Crown outright (and then only either because of Charles I's ineptitude in handling parliament, or in trying to dispense with it altogether). It was not until 1689, the year of the Glorious Revolution, that, in the words of Bertrand Russell, "[my] family and a few others gave one king notice and hired another", and parliament only became the senior partner in the governing business of "the Crown in parliament" in the course of the 18th century, especially during and after George III's periods of incapacity caused by porphyria, finally culminating in madness. It was not until the 19th and 20th centuries that British monarchs, like their earlier Polish counterparts, "reigned but did not rule".[3] With hindsight, we can perhaps see the 17th century, and in particular the period between the run-up to the Civil War and the success of the settlement after the Glorious Revolution, as the crucial period in the long process of change in the balance between Crown and Parliament in the constitution,[4] but this was not apparent to most contemporaries, who probably saw "pudding-time ... [when] moderate men looked big" (as the contemporary satirical song, *The Vicar of Bray*, memorably described the reign of George I), as a period of restored political stability under the Hanoverians, similar to that which their ancestors had enjoyed under the Tudors after the ending of the Wars of the Roses.[5] Before the Civil War, there can be no real doubt that monarchs, their favourites, and subordinates did rule England in normal circumstances. When monarchs or chief ministers failed to do so, anarchy ensued: the collapse of later Anglo-Saxon England under Æthelræd the Unready, the "nineteen winters when Christ and his angels slept", while Stephen and Matilda strove for the English Crown, the baronial rebellions against Henry III and Edward II, the Lancastrian revolt against Richard II, the weak rule of Henry VI culminating in the Wars of the Roses.

But the case for studying the history of the monarchy in England, and later in Britain, does not rest just on the chronological priority of kings over parliament, nor on the indisputable fact that both houses of parliament originated as subordinate, advisory bodies brought into existence by kings to further their royal will. The king was in a very real sense the centre of his kingdom, for which he was responsible only to God. Thus Professor J M Roberts, the editor of the *New Oxford History of England*, remarked in his preface to the series.

> Its aim is to give an account of the development of our country in time. Changing geographical limits suggest it is hard to speak of that solely as a history of England. Yet the core of the institutional story which runs from Anglo-Saxon times to our own is the story of the state structure built around the English monarchy, the only continuous articulation of the history of those peoples we today call British.[6]

That is the real justification for studying the history of the monarchy in England and Britain: the history of the monarchy is not just a history of individual monarchs, the scholarly equivalent of present-day journalistic outpourings by so-called "royal authors" (who are certainly not royal and often, one suspects, not even royalist), though the personalities and the actions of most individual monarchs have often contributed much to the history of the monarchy as an instituion, as the chapters of the majority of the contributors to this volume testify. There is also a most substantial point encapsulated in a recent remark by Martin Malia: "The normal path to the nation-state leads through the dynastic state."[7]

In a very real sense, England, and later Britain, *were* the creations of English and then British kings: the early kings who welded together separate small tribes whose names are recorded in the Tribal Hidage into the larger kingdoms of the Heptarchy (chapter 2), the unification of England by the later dynasty of Wessex after the Danish invasions (chapter 3), the beginnings of the conquest of Wales (chapter 4), the final conquest of Wales (chapter 5), the full absorption of Wales into the administrative system already developed in England (chapter 7), the union with Scotland (chapters 8 and 12).

Even so, the history of the British monarchy as an institution is only part of the total history of Britain: rather, the monarchy is a window through which we can see and, we hope, understand much of our own history, of our ancestors as much as the forebears of the monarchs. Governor and governed, monarch and people, are two sides of the same coin. The late King Farouk of Egypt remarked in 1948:

> The whole world is in revolt. Soon there will be only five kings left – the King of England, the King of Spades, the King of Clubs, the King of Hearts, and the King of Diamonds.[8]

This prophecy now appears unduly pessimistic, although the 20th century has admittedly seen the departure of many royal dynasties, including, in Europe, the imperial houses of Austria, Germany, and Russia and the kings of Albania, Bulgaria, Italy, Romania, and Yugoslavia, and, outside Europe, the emperors of China and Iran, the kings of Afghanistan and Iraq, the sultans of Turkey and the Indian princes. Nevertheless, the Scandinavian monarchies appear in good shape (those of Belgium and Holland perhaps rather less so) and the Spanish monarchy has been successfully re-established thanks to the ability, hard work, and conciliatory efforts of King Juan Carlos. In Asia, the Emperor of Japan and the King of Thailand seem secure, the kings of Saudi Arabia and Jordan and the sultans and emirs of the Persian Gulf appear fairly safe, as do the individual sultans in Malaysia, which has, moreover, acquired an elective monarchy, while the Sultan of Brunei flourishes. King Sihanouk's continued survival in Cambodia appears problematic. In North Africa, Morocco, in southern Africa Lesotho and Swaziland, and in the Pacific Tonga and Western Samoa, are still monarchies.

Monarchy as a form of government has appeared to most of the world's peoples to be part of the natural order of things, whether the leader was styled emperor, king, sultan, chief, or by some other title. Republics before and after the Roman Empire appeared to be systems fit to rule city-states, whether those of Ancient Greece or medieval and early modern Germany and Italy, but in almost every case, if the city-state began to expand outside its traditional local boundaries, it tended to become oligarchical and then monarchical in substance if not in form. This had been true, for example, of the Athenian Empire in the 5th century BC, of the Roman Republic in the first century BC (when the last century of its existence was punctuated by dictatorships from Sulla to Julius Caesar), of Renaissance Milan under the Viscontis and Sforzas, and of Florence under the Medicis and later the house of Piedmont-Savoy: only Venice, despite acquiring a large empire in Italy and the Levant, remained a republic with elected leaders, the doges, though even there strong doges assumed a quasi-monarchical position. Poland, though technically a commonwealth because it was a fusion of the old kingdom of Poland with the "republic" of Lithuania, was nevertheless ruled by elected kings. The British Republic set up after the execution of Charles I in 1649 lasted only a few years before becoming, in effect, a new monarchy ruled by the Cromwell dynasty, the result of which was to remove republicanism from the realm of practical politics in Britain for more than 200 years.

Apart from the German and Italian city-states, only two countries, inside or outside Europe, before the 18th century had a genuinely republican constitution: the first was the Swiss Confederation and its constituent cantons, which have remained republican. The second was the Dutch Republic founded as a result of the revolt of the Netherlands in 1572. This, however, had as hereditary stadtholders (military leaders) the Orange family who in the course of time became kings of Holland; the republic was formally abolished in 1795 and replaced in 1815 by a constitutional monarchy (yet again, territorial expansion had proved fatal to republicanism).[9] In the 18th century, after the American Revolution (in British English the American War of Independence) the United States of America, the federation and the member states, comprised the only large republic in the world. Despite the hopes aroused by the French Revolution, especially after the deposition and execution of Louis XVI, the French Republic lasted only a few years before being overtaken by dictatorship, first that of Robespierre, then of the Directory, finally of Bonaparte, who was then succeeded by the restored Bourbon monarchy in various guises, and then another period of Bonapartist empire. Not until after 1870 did France at last become a republic, and, in Professor Doyle's words:

> only then because another Bourbon, missing his chance according to an unerring family tradition, refused once again to compromise with the Revolution's legacy, even though a gesture would have given him the throne.[10]

Outside France, the satellite republics spawned by early republican expansion for the most part were later converted into satrapies for the Bonaparte family and Napoleon's marshals, whose conquests in Italy and, later, his dissolution of the Holy Roman Empire – "neither Holy, nor Roman, nor an Empire" as Voltaire had called it in his *Essai sur les Moeurs* of 1756 – also radically reduced the number of republics by abolishing the remaining German and Italy city-states that still then remained. Apart from the Swiss Confederation, the US, after 1870, France and, after 1911, Sun-Yat-Sen's China, no large republics existed until after the First World War, though most of the former colonies of Spain and Portugal in Latin America became republics in form if not always in reality (nearly all succumbed at some time in their history to military dictatorship, as did Haiti, the first black republic and Brazil became an empire).[11] In practice, until after 1900, whether in Europe or in Asia, emperors and kings, either native or European, ruled, and the collapse of the Portuguese monarchy in 1910 and of the Manchu (Qing) Empire in China in 1911 was the first portent of things to come after 1918. In Africa also, behind the façade of European rule, particularly after the "scramble for Africa" in the 1880s and 1890s, power continued to reside in the hands of strong men, either native kings and chiefs or colonial officials, or both governing in concert.[12] Republicanism only began to appear as part of the natural order of things in Europe and the Near East after 1918, with the break-up of the Hapsburg, Hohenzollern, Osmanli, and Romanov empires and the ending of the Spanish monarchy, perhaps because republics appeared to be more representative forms of govern in an "age of democracy".

But appearance and reality are so often different. Even when republics became more numerous, republican forms of government were too often unscrupulously manipulated by new strong men: Lenin and Stalin in Russia, Hitler in Germany, Franco in Spain, Horthy in Hungary, Salazar in Portugal, Peron in Argentina, Stroessner in Paraguay, are only the most notorious (Mussolini, to be different, used a monarchy as the screen behind which he could exercise power.). Before and after the Second World War, a republic was (and is) by no means necessarily democratic. In Africa and in Asia, the departure of European colonial powers too often was followed by the rise of native dictators such as Kwame Nkrumah of Ghana, Emperor Bokassa I of Central Africa and Presidents Mobutu and Mugabe of Zaire and Zimbabwe, with, often, their concomitant single party regimes, or military dictatorships as in Burma:

very few ex-colonial territories have maintained democratic and civilized regimes, the most being India. (Recently, we have seen what was a constitutional republic, but one built on the racist foundations of apartheid, transformed into a multiracial democracy in South Africa.) Within Eastern Europe, as in China to this day, the "People's republic" was an acknowledged euphemism for the "dictatorship of the proletariat", which would perhaps have been tolerable if this meant the rule of the majority *by* the majority, but it did not. "New Presbyter is but old Priest writ large", as John Milton once remarked,[13] and this can be rewritten in the 20th century as "New Party Leader is but Old King writ large", despotism without benevolence, but with an even more efficient secret police than the old regime. Entirely characteristically, the Chinese People's Republic replaced a democratically elected Legislative Council in Hong Kong with a legislature of official appointees on the transfer of power from Britain. The Marxist-Leninist October Revolution in 1917 was not only the biggest political confidence trick of this century, but also the biggest disaster for the people of Russia and, after 1945, of Eastern Europe, and it is a matter of shame that so many British "intellectuals", from the Webbs, Harold Laski, and John Strachey to Bertrand Russell, not only failed to see what was happening in Russia but even had the effrontery to applaud the Russian system, and to recommend its spread to the rest of the world as the "New Civilization".[14] Inspired by the Bolshevik revolution, the Webbs proceeded in 1920 to compile *A constitution for the socialist commonwealth of Great Britain*. George Bernard Shaw, another Fabian socialist, voiced little disapproval of Communism in his well-known political handbook.[15]

By contrast, Bertrand Russell had very early perceived the dictatorial and authoritarian tendencies of Russian communism,[16] though in old age his obsession with the possibility of nuclear warfare made him appear to be a "stooge" of Communist "peace movements". Communism too often exercised a curious but powerful attraction for British intellectuals,[17] though not all intellectuals on the left abandoned their belief in democratic socialism.[18] Some historians also, notably E H Carr and R W Davies, could see little or nothing wrong in what was later, and rightly, termed "the evil empire".[19] Only recently has Eric Hobsbawm publicly recognized his lifelong attachment "to a hope which has plainly failed: the communism initiated by the October Revolution."[20] Other ex-Communists had seen the true nature of Stalinism decades earlier.[21] It is an open question whether such leftwing thinkers were more bewitched by the word "Socialist" (*alias* Communist) or the word "Republic" in the title "Union of Soviet Socialist Republics": what is now not open to question is that the Russian people in 1913 were not only more free in political and religious terms, but were also more prosperous in material terms than they were to be for the 75 years following, though both these truths were sedulously denied by many intellectuals in the West when they were put forward by clear-sighted thinkers such as Robert Conquest who revealed the true nature of the Soviet system.[22] As one wag recently wrote, wryly, "Conquest has conquered." Republicanism is not an automatic recipe for human happiness, any more than is monarchy: both are fallible systems headed by fallible human beings.

Nevertheless, before the 20th century, especially in Europe, monarchy did appear to be the natural form of government in advanced countries, including a representative assembly or assemblies as democracy became fashionable: republics, as we have seen, only became more numerous than monarchies after 1918. Why should monarchy have appeared to be the natural form of government for most people in Europe in the past? One answer lies in a remark by Peter Laslett,

> all of our ancestors were literal Christian believers, all of the time …
> their world was a Christian world and their religious activity was
> spontaneous, not forced on them from above.[23]

This apparently self-evident truism in fact combines several unverifiable assertions and half-truths. For the blunt fact is that we simply do not know, and cannot know, whether "all of our ancestors were literal Christian believers, all of the time". Neither medieval and early modern Catholic inquisitors and their Protestant counterparts such as Topcliffe in Elizabethan England, nor modern psychologists, psychiatrists, and secret policemen could or can be absolutely certain that they have elicited the truth by intensive interrogation, aided, in the case of the secret policemen, by torture. There were and are some brave men and women who have and will remain silent even under torture; others understandably, under duress, will say whatever they think their interrogators wish them to say, as was demonstrated by the bogus "confessions" elicited during the Moscow "show trials" of the 1930s. Even written statements not extracted by force or fear, for example depositions in various law courts now and in the past, may not be "the truth" and not necessarily "the whole truth"; any modern policeman can tell tales of widely discrepant statements about the same occurrence even by honest witnesses.

Since the vast majority of our ancestors before the middle of the 19th century were not literate, and even fewer were habitually literate, the evidence to justify assertions even about what most of our ancestors said they believed is scanty or nonexistent. As for the statement "their religious activity was spontaneous, not forced on them from above," this is indubitably false: modern historians have shown, for example, how in the mid-16th century each swing of the theological pendulum, from the initial rejection of papal authority in 1534 to the final Anglican religious settlement in 1559, was obeyed as far as possible by parish clergy and their congregations in adapting ritual, ceremonial, and clerical apparell to the latest orders from London.[24] The same was true of the period of the Civil War, the rule of the Long Parliament, the Cromwellian Protectorate, and the years from 1660 to 1720, satirically but memorably protrayed in *The Vicar of Bray*. Whatever their inner beliefs, most of our ancestors, again quite understandably, were not the stuff of which martyrs were made: whether they knew it or not, they observed the old Roman

Law maxim "what pleases the prince has the force of law". What *is* true is that "their world was a Christian world", in the sense that the prevailing ideology and common practice in Europe down at least to the 17th century, and in most areas well into the 19th century, was Christian. Whether the English people in the past believed in Christianity, we simply do not know: what we can say is that, for good pragmatic reasons, they behaved as if they were believers: it would have been very unsafe for most of them not to behave in that way, when, for example, from 1572 to 1832, poor relief was administered by parish officials, overseers, and churchwardens, who were part of, and answerable first to, the Anglican vestry. And so, therefore, we need to investigate the historical links between Christianity and monarchy.

Let us start, as all Christians in the past started, with the Bible. The Bible was not, it should be be stated, a Protestant invention, despite the greater weight which Protestants, like their Lollard and Hussite predecessors, put on it after the Reformation. It formed an essential basis of pre-Reformation Catholicism, which, however, placed increasingly greater emphasis on the authority of the Church as a repository and interpreter of tradition.)[25] The Old Testament, which we know is at best a quasi-historical record of the Jews, but was accepted by most contemporaries as the "Word of God" (as was the New Testament even more so), put great emphasis on leadership, from Moses onwards, and especially on kingship.[26] Modern historians have confirmed from a variety of sources that ancient Israel, apart from the period of the Babylonian captivity, was a monarchy until Israel's independent existence was finally suppressed by Rome.[27] The Bible was the quarry for medieval and early modern thinkers wishing to justify, as God's Will, four linked concepts of monarchy, of patriarchy, of acceptance of the established political, economic, and social *status quo*, and of obedience to political and social superiors. God, indeed, was the supreme king,

> God of Gods and a Lord of Kings ... the King of Kings and Lord of Lords
> ... Lord of Lords and King of Kings.[28]

"Thine is the kingdom,"[29] and Heaven was sometimes "the kingdom of Heaven", especially for the Apostle Matthew,[30] but much more often the "kingdom of God."[31] Fairly obviously, "The Lord's throne is in Heaven" where "I saw the Lord sitting on his throne ... God sitteth upon his Holy throne", for "Heaven ... is God's throne ... Heaven is my throne."[32] Given the multiplicity of references to the monarchical theme, it would be extremely difficult for any reader or listener in the "age of faith" not to accept that God was the supreme king in his heavenly kingdom, and very easy for such a reader or listener to conclude that monarchy was indeed a divinely ordained system of earthly government. Such a conclusion was further supported by frequent biblical references to Israelite kings from Saul onwards as "the Lord's anointed" (or "anointed of the Lord"),[33] which led to the process of anointing a king being incorporated into every West European Coronation *ordo* (official liturgical programme) from Charlemagne's time onwards, as Professor McKitterick shows in chapter 1: this precedent was copied by English kings from Offa of Mercia and the kings of Wessex to the present, as Professor Smyth notes in chapter 2.

God was also the supreme father: "God the Father" was the first person of the Trinity, and there were numerous references in the New Testament to "God the Father" or "God our Father".[34] The faithful were exhorted to "glorify your Father which is in Heaven",[35] and the Lord's Prayer (in the more accurate Latin of the medieval Vulgate, the *Paternoster*) began with "Our Father which art in Heaven."[36] Jesus prayed to God, "Father, forgive them" and referred to Heaven as "my Father's house".[37] Again, it would be difficult for most readers of, or listeners to, such texts not to draw the further conclusion that patriarchy also was a divinely ordained institution, which was supported by yet more biblical passages: "Honour thy father and mother", the Fifth Commandment brought down by Moses, was reiterated in the Old and New Testaments, and St Paul underlined the injunction, "Children, obey your parents in all things".[38] To complete the self-evident and divinely ordained superiority of fathers and husbands, it was finally necessary to stress that women were, by nature, the inferior sex, "sprung from Adam's rib", responsible for leading Adam astray in the Garden of Eden, and, therefore, the cause of human sinfulness, Original Sin; hence, it was ordered, "Husbands, dwell with your wives … giving honour unto the wife, as unto the weaker vessel," while wives were ordered to "submit yourselves unto your husbands" and in another place, "let the wife see that she fears her husband," because "the husband is the head of the wife,"[39] Another New Testament text emphasized female inferiority:

> Let a woman learn in quietness with all subjection. But I permit not a woman to teach nor to have dominion over a man, but to be in quietness. For Adam was first formed, then Eve … but the woman, being beguiled, hath fallen into transgression.[40]

Servants also, as part of most pre-industrial households, from ancient Israel to 18th-century Europe, were also enjoined to "obey in all things them that are your masters."[41]

Christians were also required to obey secular authority as much as ecclesiastical authority: "Render therefore unto Caesar the things which are Caesar's; and unto God the things that are God's", since "the powers that be are ordained of God".[42] In other texts, Christians were commanded, "obey them that have the rule over you and submit to them", and this order was also elaborated:

> Be subject to every ordinance of man for the Lord's sake, whether it be to the king, as supreme, or unto governors as sent by him … For so is the will of God, that by well-doing you should put to silence the ignorance of foolish men … as bondservants of God. Honour all men … Fear God. Honour the King.[43]

Christian spiritual leaders were instructed to enforce secular obedience in their flocks: "Put them in mind to be in subjection to rulers, to authorities, to be obedient."[44] An earlier rationale already existed in the Old Testament: "By me kings reign, and princes decree."[45] All this might perhaps seem to be above the heads of the common people, most of whom before the 19th century were formally illiterate in the sense that they could not sign their own names, though more may have been able to read, especially to read print.[46] But the Protestant Reformation, with its ideas of "the priesthood of all believers" and its intense opposition to the traditional position of the Catholic priesthood as intermediaries between God and man, put increasing emphasis on the necessity of reading the Scriptures. Even though the Anglican Church rejected most aspects of extreme puritanism, it did favour greater access to the English Bible which had been placed in every parish church since Henry VIII's reign (apart from a brief interlude under Mary).[47] The Protestant Dissenters after 1660 continued to regard reading the Bible as an indispensable part of religious life.[48] The Anglican Society for the Propagation of Christian Knowledge and the charity schools whose foundation it stimulated in the 18th century,[49] and the massive building of parish schools by the National Society in the 19th century, emulated by the British Society for the non-conformists,[50] all conduced to greater knowledge of the Bible. (*Per contra*, conservatively minded politicians, from the Duke of Norfolk in the 16th century to Viscount Melbourne in the 19th, regarded literacy as a subversive vice, liable to give the lower orders ideas unsuited to their station in life). But knowledge of the Bible was not confined to those who could read it: those who could hear the words of homilists and preachers also had access at second hand to its contents.

Not surprisingly, these homilists and preachers in the medieval and early modern periods also used the Bible as the source for texts on which to base their exposition and justification of the same set of concepts in "a tongue … understand of the people", as the *Book of Common Prayer* was to put it.[51] Wulfstan II, Archbishop of York from 1002 to 1023, was a noted preacher who used the contemporary evils of Æthelræd's reign to point the need for reform of church and state based on strong kingship in his *Sermon of "Wolf" to the English* in 1014; in the closing years of his life, in his *Institutes of Polity* he elaborated on the duties to be performed by all members of society, secular and ecclesiastical, if reform were to be effective.[52] Pauline Stafford remarks of Wulfstan's contemporary, Ælfric, a monk of Cerne who became abbot of Eynsham in 1005, "it is no surprise, therefore, to discover an interest in the role of kings in the writings of Ælfric," and she shows the strong links between monarchs and the Church in the last century of Old English history.[53] What one scholar has called "the cult of kingship in Anglo-Saxon England" had a practical purpose and a very respectable intellectual basis.[54] This English position had its continental ancestry and its continental analogues and counterparts, which are elaborated by Rosamund McKitterick in chapter 1.[55] After the Norman Conquest, preaching declined because the higher clergy habitally spoke and wrote Latin and Norman-French and, if they knew the vernacular tongue as it evolved from Old English into Middle English, they were not usually fluent in its use. Not until the rise of the friars in the 13th century and the "triumph of English" in the 14th century did preaching again flourish,[56] and then we find kings and kingship are once more being discussed. A preacher in Henry V's reign, for instance, compared "the realm of England" to "a great ship which sailed for many a day in the sea of Prosperity", in which, once

> Virtue ceased and Vices began to reign, Fortune changed her countenance ... Our ship was so hurled and burled amid the winds and straits that she was in great peril ... Our ship was in so great a peril that unless our noble King [had] set hand on the rudder and steered our ship at the right time, our ship had sharply to go all to wreck.[57]

(It is ironic to see Henry V and Mao Tse-Tung sharing the title of "Great Helmsman").

A preacher in the early 14th century, also talking about vice, attributed the loss of the Angevin Empire by King John to the complicity of his father Henry II, in the murder of Thomas Becket.[58] A noted preacher, Bishop Brinton of Rochester in Richard II's time, tells the story of Anselm's vision of William Rufus' death as a punishment for his sins:

> Anselm saw in a night-vision how all the saints of England made bitter complaint of the said king. And the Lord said, "Let Alban, the Proto-Martyr of the English, come hither"; and he gave to him a fiery arrow, saying, "Behold the death of that man of whom you have made so great complaint!"[59]

In the 16th century, Thomas Lever opposed rebellion precisely because secular authority derived from God:

> It is God that maketh these evyl men to be ... rulers and officers in the countrey: it is the sinnes of the people that causeth God to make these men youre rulers. The man is sometymes evyll, but the authoritye from God is always good, and God geveth good authoritye unto evyll men, to punyshe the synnes of the evyll people.[60]

Under Elizabeth, the shortage of preachers who were suitably qualified and suitably conformist led very early in her reign to the cancellation of existing licences to preach[61] (a policy which, significantly, had previously been adopted by Edward VI's Protestant government) and to the reissuing and expansion of the official homilies, again first composed in EdwardVI's reign, to be read in parish churches on Sundays in place of sermons by clergy who were not qualified preachers.[62] More than 50 years ago, Alfred Hart proved that these homilies were an important source of the political ideas so well expressed by Shakespeare, through whose plays and other writings the biblical ideas on monarchy were presented in a fresh guise to Elizabethan and Jacobean audiences.[63] These ideas were, therefore, in no way original to Shakespeare who was merely expressing the accepted, wholly conventional political wisdom of his age, that kings represented authority given by God, that treason was therefore blasphemy, and that obedience was the subject's first day. Thus Richard II is addressed as

> God's substitute, His Deputy anointed in his sight ... the figure of Gods Maiestie, His Captaine, Steward, Deputie elect;[64]

King Claudius asserts: "There's such Divinity doth hedge a King, That Treason can but peepe to what it would;"[65] Bates tells the disguised Henry V the night before Agincourt,

> Wee know enough, if wee know wee are the Kings Subiects: if his Cause bee wrong, our obedience to the Kinge wipe the Cryme of it out of us,

to which the king replies, "every Subiects Dutie is the Kings ..."[66] Such examples could be multiplied, and have been.[67] Underlying these ideas was the organizing principle of Order, cosmic and human, in which all events, all phenomena, all beings, were ultimately regulated by links in the "great chain of being" originating in God as the "first cause".[68] The importance of preserving order was expressed by Shakespeare's Ulysses in a classic passage:

> The heavens themselves, the planets, and this centre
> Observe degree priority and place
> Insisture course proportion season form
> Office and custom, in all line of order;
> ... But when the planets
> In evil mixture to disorder wander,
> What plagues and what portents, what mutiny,
> What raging of the sea, shaking of earth,
> Commotion in the winds, frights changes horrors,
> Divert and crack, rend and deracinate
> The unity and married calm of states
> Quite from their fixure. Oh, when degree is shak'd,
> Which is the ladder to all high designs,
> The enterprise is sick. How could communities,
> Degrees in schools and brotherhoods in cities,
> Peaceful commerce from dividable shores,
> The primogenitive and due of birth,
> Prerogative of age, crowns sceptres laurels,
> But by degree stand in authentic place?
> Take but degree away, untune that string,
> And hark, what discord follows. Each thing meets
> In mere oppugancy ...
> This chaos, when degree is suffocate,
> Follows the choking.[69]

Not surprisingly, the Catechism in the *Book of Common Prayer* required the newly confirmed person to swear "to do my duty in that state of life, unto

which it shall please God to call me", and understandably, *The Vicar of Bray*
declared:

> In good King Charles's golden days,
> … Unto my flock I daily preached
> Kings were by God appointed,
> And damned was he that durst resist
> Or touch the Lord's anointed.[70]

So much were such themes taken for granted that they were only articulated
as a rational political philosophy of divine right in their final form when
they came under attack in the 17th century from parliamentary opponents
of "Stuart despotism".[71]

But the Bible and its later expositors, down to the homilists of the 16th
century, were not the only source for the "cult of kingship". In addition to the
practice of the revived Western Empire of the Carolingians, there was also
the practice of the surviving Byzantine Empire, where the Emperor was not
only a divinely appointed ruler of the state, but was also the ruler of the
Eastern Orthodox Church.[72] Since numerous Englishmen served in the
Varangian guard of the Eastern Empire in the later 11th century,[73] there
was an open channel through which knowledge of Byzantine ideas and practice
could percolate back to England. The Normans in Italy and the Balkans as
well as in England provided yet another possible channel.[74] It is, therefore,
interesting and possibly a significant result of such ideas flowing back to
England and Normandy that the writer known to historians as the Norman
Anonymous or the Anonymous of York (or Rouen) was putting forward a
theoretical justification for the concept of royal control over the Church in
the early 12th century, describing the king as "by nature an individual man,
by grace a *christus*, that is, a God-man".[75] Such ideas certainly had an influence
on English kingship: Abbot Hugh of Fleury dedicated his *Tractus de regia
potestate et sacerdotali dignitate* to Henry I.[76] There was the practice also of
the medieval papacy, which, especially after the Gregorian Reform movement
of the later 11th century, became in the next two centuries increasingly
authoritarian in tone and monarchical in substance, so that modern scholars
refer to the "papal monarchy".[77] By the 13th century, the earlier claim of the
(Western) Catholic Church to be separate from, and independent of, secular
rulers, Pope Gelasius' theory of "the two swords", had developed into a claim
that the pope, as Vicar of Christ (a title first used by Innocent III, 1198–1215,
who asserted that "Christ left to Peter not only the whole Church, but also
the whole world to govern"), was superior to other earthly rulers, a claim
which directly impinged on the history of the English monarchy when King
John first opposed the papacy and was then forced to seek its protection as
feudal overlord.[78]

In addition, the 12th century experienced an intellectual renaissance sparked-
off by, first, the increasing rediscovery of Greek ideas and thought, including

political philosophy, and, secondly, their incorporation into what can now be called medieval political thought.[79] England fully shared in this movement, Henry II's reign seeing the appearance of the first example of English political thought since Archbishop Wulfstan's *Institutes of Polity* (and one of the first works of medieval European political thought) in John of Salisbury's *Statesman's Book (Policraticus)*.[80] (Admittedly, this was, so far as England was concerned, a flash in the pan: the next significant English political writer was to be Sir John Fortescue in the 15th century). The main Greek political thinker engaged by medieval theorists was Aristotle (partly because he wrote on so many different topics), whose *Politics* became the source for justifying theories of "mixed" (what we would call constitutional) monarchy.[81] Plato was less well known, and although *The Republic* had advocated rule by "philosopher-kings" as the ideal, it had also admitted the practical difficulty of finding and training such rulers, hence Plato's later work, *The Statesman*, had favoured a more moderate "mixed constitution"[82] Even in the 16th century, Machiavelli's highly authoritarian book *The Prince* was far better known to contemporaries than his more moderate *Discourses* (this is still largely true today). It was not until after Machiavelli that political thinkers seriously began to consider the problems of controlling an unjust secular ruler, and if necessary, deposing him,[83] although the Western Church had been forced to face this problem, after the Great Schism in the 11th century, when Church councils had been required to adjudicate on the claims of several persons all claiming to be the one true pope.[84]

The 17th century was, therefore, a crucial period for monarchy in England and in Europe. In practice and in theory, monarchy was for the first time since the Classical period being subjected to opposition as a system rather than being confronted with the simple problem of replacing one monarch by another. Nevertheless, despite the revolts in, *inter alia*, France (the Fronde), in Spain (the revolts in Catalonia and later in Portugal), Russia (the Time of Troubles), and Britain (the Civil War and then the Glorious Revolution), monarchy survived, and in Europe in the 18th century, the age of the benevolent (or enlightened) despots, became ever more absolutist. By contrast, in Britain, government was increasingly dominated by a parliament controlled, in the main, by the landed aristocracy and its allies in the urban, mercantile classes.[85] For this reason, among others, Britain survived the French Revolution and the Napoleonic wars in better shape than any other European monarchy, and continued to adapt to democracy in the 19th and 20th centuries.[86]

The English (later British) monarchy thus has an enviable record of survival, perhaps equalled in the world in terms of continuous longevity only by the Japanese monarchy (neither could compete in the number of centuries of their existence with the Chinese empire, but that came to an end in 1911).[87]

How did the monarchy in Britain originate? "Before the Romans came to Rye, or out to Severn strode," as G K Chesterton wrote, Celtic Britain was already divided into tribal territories ruled by chieftains who were often named as kings by foreign observers, such as Julius Caesar, and on the coins issued under the authority of the kings themselves.[88] These territories were, of course, absorbed into the provinces of Roman Britain after the Roman conquest was begun in earnest by the Emperor Claudius in AD 43, and many were transformed into self-governing regions (*civitates*) focused on tribal centres or on newly built Roman towns. (The Dobunni, for example, originally had their tribal capital at Bagendon, Gloucs; this was replaced by Cirencester, which progressed to become one of the provincial capitals of late Roman Britain). It is not known if any of the old tribal dynasties survived the period of Roman occupation, and such survival does seems rather unlikely on grounds of demographic probability alone, quite apart from Roman policy. Nevertheless, the units survived, and so did the provincial aristocracies who governed them. But when the Romans finally relinquished power in Britain in AD 410, effective authority again devolved to the regional aristocracies in the *civitates*, to whom the Emperor Honorius wrote bidding them to look after themselves, as a result of which a contemporary continental historian, Zosimus, recorded that

> the British people took up arms, bore the brunt of the attack [by Irish and Saxons], and freed their cities from the barbarian threat.[89]

Within a few years, aristocratic oligarchy, as represented by the "council" mentioned by both Gildas and Nennius, had given way to monarchy in the person of a "proud tyrant", unnamed by the sixth-century homilist Gildas but who is named as Vortigern in the *Anglo-Saxon Chronicle* and in apparently contemporary British materials collected by a ninth-century compiler, Nennius, who confessedly "made a heap of all he had found."[90] Native monarchy as a governing system thus soon returned to post-Roman Britain, although, as Professor Smyth shows in chapter 2, British monarchies were to be replaced within the next century and a half by Anglo-Saxon monarchies ruling most of lowland Britain and much of the highland zone, from the Firth of Forth to the English Channel.

After the victory at Dyrham, Glos, in AD 577 of Ceawlin, King of the West Saxons, over "three kings, Conmail, Condidan, and Farinmail", and the capture of "three of their cities, Gloucester, Cirencester, and Bath", the Celtic areas of Devon and Cornwall were separated from Wales by a wedge of Saxon territory in what later became Gloucestershire and Somerset.[91] The record of the "three kings" of the Britons shows that monarchy had persisted in the areas still controlled by native Britons. Some of these native monarchies, such as Elmet and Reged, long survived, while the Scots, having emigrated from Ireland to Dalriada, formed what was to be the basis of the Scottish monarchy (see chapter 12). In about AD 616, Æthelfrith of Northumbria

> led his army to Chester and there killed a countless number of Britons ... Their leader was called Brocmail,

and this drove a similar wedge of Anglian territory, the later Cheshire and

Lancashire, between Wales and the Britons of Cumbria-Strathclude.[92] By about AD 600, therefore, "England" was beginning to assume a recognizable outline, though its area was to remain divided between several kingdoms until Kent and Sussex were absorbed into Wessex and the remaining kingdoms were finally eradicated by Danish conquest. Wales became the core of the 'Celtic fringe', Cornwall and Devon in the south-west (the kingdom of Dumnonia) and Cumberland and Westmorland in the north-west being conquered by the English. (Cumbria was later conquered by the Scots and was only finally assimilated into England after its reconquest by William Rufus in 1093.) The Anglo-Saxons themselves (actually a mixture of Angles, Franks, Frisians, Jutes, and Saxons, with, in the West Saxon dynasty, some British blood), were ruled by kings,[93] like their Germanic ancestors in their homeland.[94] "Hengest and his son Æsc" are stated in the *Anglo-Saxon Chronicle* to have "succeeded to the kingdom [of Kent]"; later "Æsc succeeded to the kingdom and was king of the people of Kent for 24 years"; "Ælle and his three sons Cymen, Wlencing, and Cissa" who landed near Selsey are known to have founded the dynasty of Sussex, and Ælle was regarded by Bede as the first 'Bretwalda'; to the west, "Cerdic and Cynric succeeded to the kingdom of the West Saxons."[95] In the north, "Ida, from whom the royal family of the Northumbrians took its rise, succeeded to the kingdom".[96] Even when the invading leaders were not already kings - Cerdic and Cynric were first described as "chieftains" - they became kings before they died.[97] All these Anglo-Saxon kings shared another defining quality of kingship, namely the claim to legitimacy which was justified by reference to their descent from other kings or, even better, from gods.[98] The Chinese and Japanese emperors also claimed divine descent, and to this day one of the lesser titles of the Emperor of Japan is still 'Son of Heaven'.

But no claim, then or since, to royal legitimacy would be effective on its own: there were, after all, many such claimants to descent from kings or gods, and the claim could only be made good by demonstrably kingly action and behaviour. As Professor Smyth reminds us, kingship in the Anglo-Saxon kingdoms was elective, though the pool of candidates was normally restricted to those of close royal kin.[99] Thus the *adventus Saxonum*, the beginning of the English conquest of what became England, was achieved by, among other qualities, the good leadership of kings, as was the near-restoration of British rule circa AD 500 under "King Arthur", who was probably not a king himself but was certainly regarded as possessing kingly qualities, hence the title bestowed on him by posterity (aided by Geoffrey of Monmouth). By contrast, the initial failure of the Britons to defend and retain their lands was equally a failure of kingly leadership: of grave miscalculation by Vortigern, of cowardice and treachery hinted-at in the British sources which again reflect lack of firm royal control and leadership. By the third quarter of the fifth century, many British aristocrats and accepted that their cause was already lost and had migrated in such numbers to the Gallic province of Armorica that it was later renamed Brittany. John Morris also argued that many of the modern French place-names starting in "Bret(t)" throughout northern France, such as Breteuil

and Bretteville, originated in this migration of Britons to the continent.[100]
The later British failure in the sixth century can again be attributed mainly
to poor leadership and general demoralization, as the contemporary Gildas
emphatically states. Admittedly, Britain suffered severely from bubonic plague
in about AD 547, but it is difficult to see why Britons should be more vulnerable
to that disease than Anglo-Saxons. There can be no question that the Britons
were for long superior to the Anglo-Saxons in terms of numbers and resources,
even if we allow for some Germanic mercenaries already in Britain before
AD 410, as archaeology would suggest. (There is, therefore, no ground for a
neo-Marxist explanation of the success of the Anglo-Saxons: the Britons
inherited from the Romans a governing structure, a local military machine,
a functioning road-system, an efficient agriculture, all of which ought to have
ensured success against the Anglo-Saxons). But the Saxons were, there is
no real doubt, well led by kings who knew what they wanted and were prepared
to fight for it. As Professor Smyth demonstrates in the rest of his chapter,
once the Britons had been effectively eliminated - the last Welsh ruler of
stature was Cadwallon of Gwynedd, Penda of Mercia's ally against Northumbria
- Anglo-Saxon kings were able to indulge in the luxury of striving for mastery
among themselves, some being accorded the title of 'Bretwalda', which,
whatever its meaning, indicated acknowledged supremacy for the time being.
Mastery, it seemed, over the English was increasingly passing from
Northumbria to Mercia, with Wessex very much a second-rate power on the
sidelines. But, despite the apparent military superiority of the armies of
Northumbria and Mercia over those of Wessex, both collapsed before the
Danish onslaught, which, given the previous achievements of these armies,
can only really be attributed to poor tactics and worse leadership. By contrast,
Alfred of Wessex, rather like the Roman general Quintus Fabius *Cunctator*
(delayer) fighting against Hannibal, learnt in time the value of guerilla
warfare and of not fighting pitched battles until he was sure he could win.
Of course, Alfred was lucky (the supreme military virtue, according to
Napoleon): the Danes had disposed of every other English kingdom but
Wessex; this enabled Alfred

> to present himself, not only to West Saxons but to all English people,
> as the saviour of England in the face of a brutal and heathen enemy.[101]

Alfred was also lucky in another way: as the youngest son of his father, he
succeeded four brothers, three of whom were apparently childless, while the
two sons of his brother Æthelræd I, his immediate predecessor, were clearly
too young to rule in 871, so that he himself did not have to cope with problems
arising from a disputed succession. When Alfred died, though both these sons
had been mentioned in his will of *circa* 885, the elder, Æthelhelm, had
presumably died, and the revolt of the other son, Æthelwold, against Edward
the Elder, with some Danish assistance was crushed in 902. Soon after his
accession, Edward married his cousin Ægflæd, the daughter of Æthelhelm,
had her crowned as queen, and thus removed any threat to his position from
his immediate family.[102]

At this point Dr Ann Williams takes up the story (chapter 3). Alfred's success was not due simply to luck or even to the avoidance of pitched battles where possible, though, as she says,

> Alfred's victory over Guthrum's 'great summer army' at Edington in 878 is rightly regarded as a turning-point.[103]

The long-term achievement of Alfred and his successors was based not just on their personal character and ability - which only Eadwig (possibly) and Æthelræd II (certainly) lacked - but even more on their policies. Three of these policies are particularly noteworthy. The first was the adoption by the Wessex dynasty of the Mercian programme of building fortifications (*burhs*), initially to defend and then to extend the area of their rule as first Mercia, then East Anglia, and finally Northumbria were brought back under English rule in the first half of the 10th century. The second policy, the civilian counterpart to the first, was the extension and consolidation of a coherent and nationwide structure of local administration based on the shire and its sub-units, the hundreds and (in former Danish areas) the wapentakes, signalized in the division of reconquered territory into shires centred on a *burh* (the later county town) and the adoption on a national level of the *Hundred Ordinance*. This structure was regulated by new royal officials, the shire-reeves (the later sheriffs) who were in turn responsible to royal regional officers originally termed ealdormen, but in the 11th and succeeding centuries earls. So successful was this structure that hundreds and wapentakes were only superseded as local government units by poor law unions and rural districts in the 19th century, while the shires and counties established by the later Anglo-Saxon kings lasted with remarkably small changes in boundaries until the Local Government Reform Act of 1973.[104] As judicial units, the courts of hundreds and wapentakes, supplemented after the Norman Conquest by manorial courts, were only superseded in the 17th and 18th centuries by petty sessional districts which in most counties consisted of groups of hundreds or wapentakes.

The third policy was the increasing royal use of the Church for political purposes. This started with the policy of deliberate conversion of Danish and Norse kings and leaders to Christianity, from Guthrum onwards, to strengthen royal control over them and to ensure their loyalty to the kings of England. But from the revival of monasticism under Alfred and his successors and particularly after the monastic reform movement associated with St Dunstan and St Æthelwold in the mid-10th century the foundation of new monasteries was also being used by the kings to extend their patronage into outlying areas and to act as a check on the local authority of earls and other magnates. Finally, the Church was the main, though not the sole, source of literacy and of literate men able to serve the kings, hence the duality in modern English of "cleric" (a clergyman) and "clerk" (a secular administrator), both deriving from the same origin, the Latin *clericus*.[105] Monasteries served as royal archive offices, Winchcombe being the recognized depository in the ninth century for the old Mercian kingdom,[106] and the royal chapel at Winchester serving as the embryo chancery of the later Wessex kings.[107] Down until the 12th century, it was still common for monasteries, which were to receive grants of lands from kings or magnates, to prepare for the donors' attestation the charters which served as evidence of such grants. (This also enabled such monasteries, among them Westminster Abbey, to forge many charters).[108] Indeed, the mid-12th century *Liber Eliensis* incorporated a tradition that three abbots, of Ely, St Augustine's, Canterbury, and Glastonbury, had served the office of chancellor in rotation for four months of every year in late Anglo-Saxon England.[109] All in all, the later Old English kings provided firm foundations for the development of monarchy and of royal administration in the post-Conquest period.

The Norman Conquest, therefore, was not quite as revolutionary as some historians have supposed. It certainly replaced a native dynasty with a foreign dynasty whose chief interests lay outside England, but that was hardly a novelty to Englishmen in 1066, whose fathers had seen Cnut succeeding Edmund Ironside in 1016. For the following quarter-century, England had been part of the Danish empire, but when Cnut was absent from England, its affairs had been left to English earls, notably Earl Godwin, who had continued to be the power behind the throne after the accession of Edward the Confessor in 1042, apart from a brief period of exile in 1051-2. It would be difficult for any native Englishman to argue that the coming of foreign kings in 1066 would necessarily be injurious to English interests. Indeed England's part in a foreign empire also meant increased opportunities for Englishmen to share in the larger commercial opportunities to be made from an extended area of trade.[110] Equally, the Norman Conquest opened up new trading possibilities for north-south trade with Normandy and the rest of France, including the import of Caen stone (widely used in church buildings of all kinds after 1066) and wine from southern France and beyond.[111] Our putative Englishman in 1066 might regret the death of Harold Godwineson (who had proved himself an able war-leader against the Welsh and the victorious slayer of the feared Harold Hardrada of Norway) but he would not assume that a new, foreign king would necessarily be damaging to English interests: Cnut had by any standards been a considerable improvement on Æthelræd. Moreover, in 1066, the other English earls, Edwin, Morcar, and Waltheof had accepted the Norman duke as king of England.

The Norman Conquest certainly led to a radical replacement of about 4,000 English thegns as the landed aristocracy by about 200 Norman, Breton, and French barons,[112] but below this top level many English thegns survived, especially in northern England, and modern historians are increasingly finding examples of "Normans" who are recorded as holding land in 1086 not by right of conquest but because they have married the widows or daughters of Englishmen who held land in 1066. Two examples must suffice. Richard "the young man" is recorded in the Gloucestershire section of Domesday Book as having held lands in that county because he had married the widow of

Alwin, the last Old English sheriff; he must have married her very soon after 1066 since he was dead by 1086 when his son William held his lands. Wigot of Wallingford, the English thegn who saved William the Conqueror's life at the battle of Gerberoi in 1078, was succeeded by his daughter and heiress Ealdgyth who married Robert D'Oilly; their daughter Maud in turn married Miles Crispin, which explains how in 1086 Wigot's extensive estates, the later Honour of Wallingford, are held either by Miles Crispin or by Robert D'Oilly.[113] That is not to say that there was no illegal expropriation of Englishmen after 1066 - Robin Fleming has produced numerous examples of this happening[114] - but overall there was much continuity, as is shown above all by the assumption in Domesday Book that the landholders of 1086 normally had lawful predecessors in 1066 (*antecessores*), whose rights they were taking over.[115] Again, there were historical precedents in the recent past, notably the purge of the Old English aristocracy that occurred in the later part of the reign of Ætheræd II and the earlier part of Cnut's reign. In any case, there is no reason to suppose that such changes in manorial lordship affected the peasants who tilled the soil: whether the landlord was old or new, he still required the land to yield rent.

The Norman Conquest certainly introduced military novelties: castles, knights, and knight service, but of these only the castle, a private stronghold taking the place of the Old English public fortification, the *burh*, was to have long-term military and political significance, and even then for less than 200 years: after King John's successful siege of Rochester Castle in 1215, the contemporary chronicler Walter of Coventry recorded that "few cared to put their trust in castles."[116] Castles in the later medieval period declined into superior aristocratic residences, and in the 15th century some "mock" castles, such as Bodiam, were simply indefensible.[117] Knights as cavalrymen were without doubt a novelty to Englishmen after 1066, but only because they were cavalrymen, fighting on horseback in battle (the English and the Vikings had ridden horses between battles). The Old English huscarls and king's thegns had been just as professional a warrior class as the knights, whose name, as Ann Williams has recently reminded us, is pure English.[118] Moreover, it is not possible, by looking at arms and armour alone in the Bayeux Tapestry, to decide who is English and who is Norman: one needs either the running headnotes or the depiction of a ridden horse to make the distinction. Hence also, much to the annoyance of some modern textbook-writers, the Domesday "satellite" text known as the Exon Domesday refers apparently at random to "French thegns" and "English knights", hybrids who according to the textbooks should not exist.[119] Cavalry itself was not quite the important military innovation that earlier historians thought it was: the English infantry continued to be the backbone of Anglo-Norman armies after 1066, and frequently Norman knights were ordered to dismount and fight as infantrymen alongside the English *fyrd*.[120] As for knight service, no sooner was it elaborated in the 12th century than it began to decline into a device for kings to extract money from the landed class, partly by means of the tax known as scutage, because the kings increasingly preferred to hire mercenaries instead of having to rely on feudal levies, partly by means of the "incidents of feudal tenure" (wardship, marriage, heriots, entry-fines, and fines to alienate) which continued, divorced from any actual military obligation after 1327, until they were finally abolished, along with knight service itself in 1660 as part of the Restoration settlement.[121]

Finally, there was "feudalism" itself, a term not known to contemporaries (it was coined in the 18th century). But dependent land-tenure was well known in Anglo-Saxon England and the practical link between land tenure and military duties was, as we have just seen, short-lived: knight service survived as a type of land tenure to bedevil relations between Crown and the landed nobility down to the start of the Civil War in 1642. As a political system, a state ideally consisting of decentralized and effectively independent local authorities, feudalism was utterly pernicious to the ruler and to most of the ruled: its fissiparous tendencies were to hold back the complete reunification of post-Carolingian France until the French Revolution; it increasingly destroyed the authority of the German emperors; and exported to Palestine in the baggage trains of the Crusaders, ensured that the kings of Jerusalem had so little real power that their kingdom lasted less than a century (and only lasted that long because of Arab disunity).

In England alone did feudalism not have its usual disastrous effects: here strong kings, with their machinery of effective central government and a coherent and ubiquitous system of local administration, both inherited from their Anglo-Saxon forerunners, kept the barons in check: their counties did not become independent petty princedoms as in France and Germany, but were absorbed into English shires; their subordinate official, the *vicomes*, was assimilated by the English sheriff, and the king continued to rule over all. The importance of a strong monarchy was still further emphasized by the contrast with conditions when the king of England was not strong, in the "anarchy" of Stephen's reign, in the baronial revolts that afflicted England in the reigns of Henry III, Edward II, Richard II, and Henry VI. As Graham Loud remarks in chapter 4, this royal achievement had its dark side: medieval kings were only respected when they were feared for their harsh rule: "good kings" were usually, and necessarily, "bad men", and the kings who were, or appeared to be, "good men" (Edward the Confessor, Henry III, Henry VI) were invariably poor rulers unless (and so long as) they had strong ministers behind them (Earls Godwin and Harold, William Marshal and Hubert de Burgh, the Dukes of Suffolk and Bedford, chronologically).

Another result of the Norman Conquest was that until 1204 the kings of England were also, and primarily, dukes of Normandy, counts of Maine and later of Anjou, later also dukes of Aquitaine: until the loss of Normandy in 1204 most of the Norman and Angevin kings regarded their continental lands as more important than England itself, and spent much of their reigns on the continent rather in England. England gave them the title of "king" (useful when opposing their overlord, the king of France), and it provided the bulk of the money needed to defend the continental territories, but it was otherwise not the most highly regarded part of the Anglo-Norman structure. (The only obvious exceptions were the reigns of the weak King Stephen, who was ejected from Normandy by Geoffrey of Anjou in 1144, and of King John after 1204, though neither King John nor his son Henry III ever gave up hope of reconquering Normandy.) The practical result of the absence of English kings from England for years on end, coupled with their continuing need for English men and even more English money to defend their continental lands, was to force the further development of governmental institutions building on their strong Anglo-Saxon foundations. If the king was absent from England, there was need of a substitute king - initially and *ad hoc* appointment, such as an archbishop (Lanfranc), a queen (Edith-Matilda), a bishop (Odo of Bayeux or Roger of Salisbury) – but in the long run this led to the rise of the justiciar, the forerunner of the modern regent or viceroy.[122]

Behind this lay the continued evolution of the central machinery of government. The Anglo-Saxon kings had bequeathed to their successors an advisory council, the *witenagemot*, a central writing-office headed by a chancellor (which it seems reasonable to call a "chancery") and a central treasury; the Norman kings added an auditing body, the "Exchequer", and began to differentiate between the judicial court, the *Curia Regis*, and the advisory *Magnum Concilium*, though the membership of these bodies overlapped and continued to do so for centuries.[123] The Chancery developed into an institution permanently located at Westminster and began to devise a judicial function, particularly to rectify injustices, which could not be corrected quickly by the Common Law, by means of "equity", natural justice supplied by authority of the Royal Prerogative. Because of the immobility of the later medieval Chancery and its increasingly rigid administrative practices, its executive functions passed to other bodies closer to the king and more flexible in their operations, the Chamber of the Royal Household, later the Privy Council. Once the royal Treasury and the Exchequer (the original auditing body which eventually absorbed the Treasury) also settled permanently at Westminster in the late 12th century, some financial functions were exercised by subordinate treasuries in royal castles and by the Wardrobe of the Royal Household.[124] The *curia regis* diversified in the 13th century, with the King's Bench specializing in criminal matters and Common Pleas in civil cases, especially those affecting land. The effectiveness of central government was greatly enhanced by the beginning of the process of enrolment in the 1190s, in which all royal letters, whether charters, letters patent (for public consumption), letters close (for private communication between king and subject), or orders for payment (fines or writs of *liberate*), were copied at Westminster before being sent out. As part of the same trend, the decisions of the *curia regis* were also being enrolled for safe-keeping and better administration. It was not long before landholders perceived the value of getting their private deeds enrolled at Westminster, especially on the Close Rolls, for reasons of security: the lawyers were busy devising collusive law-suits, leading to "final concords" (fine) and to "recoveries", to give greater authority to their conveyancing.

At local level, royal power was made ever more manifest: from Henry I's reign onwards, sheriffs had to account at the Exchequer twice yearly, and thus became more amenable to royal control, as Dr David Carpenter shows in chapter 5; royal judges, local justiciars in Henry I's time, assize judges and itinerant justices on eyre under the Angevins and Plantagenets, were increasingly involved in the administration of justice in the counties, supplementing but not replacing the old county and hundred courts which were to continue into the early modern period, being strengthened by the county justices of the peace from the 13th century. Behind all these administrative and procedural developments there was the more fundamental evolution of what became known as the Common Law, in which judgment was more and more controlled by rules of procedure, in which even the king was increasingly seen not to be above the law (hence Magna Carta and Charter of the Forest, and their frequent reissues in the 13th century), and in which one uniform law prevailed throughout England, in royal and private courts.[125] By contrast, on the continent, most local and private courts enforced *la loi feodale*, the seigneur's law rather than the king's law (one result of this was that, despite persistent myths to the contrary, English law, precisely because it was royal law, not feudal law, did not allow English manorial lords to sleep with the new brides of their tenants, since it did not recognize the *droit de seigneur* or *ius primae noctis*, which was offensive to the law of God as well as the law of the king).

The evolution of kingly power in the Norman and Angevin periods thus had notable benefits for the English people, because this evolution entailed the development of law and administration which more and more regularized the conditions of life for the English people. One final example may be given. The feudal lawyers in the 12th and 13th centuries were trying to develop out of the existing feudal chain of tenure, linking king to tenants-in-chief, tenants-in-chief to knightly subtenants, and these subtenants or their subtenants ultimately to peasants, a generalized condition of subordination in which not only the peasant's land but also his personal property was assumed to be his lord's. Had these ideas been successfully embodied in practice, the English peasantry (who still constituted nine-tenths of the English population as late as the 16th century) would have been reduced to the state of legal servitude accompanied by economic depression which characterized their continental counterparts until the late 18th century in western and central Europe and until 1861 in Russia. But the underlying concept was abruptly controverted by the Crown in England in the early 13th century because it wished to tax the lower orders, including peasants, itself: in 1204 and again from 1275, customs dues were levied by the Crown on foreign trade handled by merchants, and from 1225 onwards the Crown began to tax the peasantry direct by means of lay subsidies of tenths and fifteenths of moveables; the Crown also insisted from Henry III's reign that all adult males, unfree as well as free, should bear arms.[126] Out of immediate royal need came long-term benefit, a process to be repeated later in the 13th and 14th centuries as parliament, and in particular the House of Commons, came into being.[127] All these developments are considered by Dr Loud in chapter 4 and by Dr Carpenter in chapter 5. With the Tudor "New Monarchy" (chapter 7) came the final abolition of the "franchises" and "regalities" (areas outside the normal system of county administration) and also the extension of the shire-system to Wales in 1536. In the meantime, personal serfdom and villeinage tenure, still the paradigms of English peasant life in 1300, had become antiquarian relics - where they survived at all - in 1500.

Thus the intervening later medieval period was one of marked contrasts: as Professor Anthony Goodman remarks, it

> starts with the deposition of one king, Edward II, and ends with deposition of another, Henry VI: it is neatly divided by the deposition of Richard II in 1461. It is hard to find precedents in English medieval history for these abasements of monarchy.[128]

As Dr Carpenter in chapter 5 and Professor Goodman in chapter 6 demonstrate, the loss in 1204 of Normandy (apart from the Channel Isles), Anjou, Maine, and Touraine had a radical long-term effect on the English monarchy, although this would become clear to contemporaries very gradually. On the failure of King John's anti-French alliance at the Battle of Bouvines in 1214, England was thrown back on its own resources: effectively, the kings of England were only that, and Gascony, the rump of Aquitaine, alone remained to them in France. Admittedly, they had acquired the lordship of Ireland (which was given to Henry II by the Pope to civilize), but this in no way compensated for the loss of most of the Angevin continental dominions. Edward I was to gain Wales after a long struggle, but his unsuccessful attempt to conquer Scotland too bedevilled Anglo-Scottish relations down to the 16th century.

Being confined to the British Isles had considerable repercussions on royal rule and kings' relations with their subjects. In particular, kings had to learn to live with the nobility, who could no longer be diverted from discontents at home by the promise of profits and glory abroad, a trend magnified by the effective ending of the crusades after the Third Crusade (1190). By contrast, but partly explaining the success of most kings of England in dealing with the nobles and the classes below them - the burgesses in the towns and the franklins/yeomen in the countryside - kings and their nobility were becoming more English. England was now the core of the realm, and the greater nobility had been forced, after the loss of Normandy, to decide whether to support the Angevins or the Capetians, whether to retain their estates in England or those in Normandy. The growth of parliament (equally useful to the kings, nobles, and commons for different reasons) helped to create a political community partly cutting across social barriers, for the electoral franchise introduced for the countryside in 1429, that of the 40 shilling freeholder, was fairly wide even in the 15th century and became wider still as its value was lowered by inflation after 1500.[129] Except in Gascony or during the Hundred Years' War, the French connection dwindled: spoken French, as

Chaucer noted, was becoming the French of "the scole of Stratford at the Bowe For Frenssh of Parys was to hire [the Prioress] unknowe"; English was now becoming the common language of all English men and women, high as well as low, in his time.[130] As Professor Goodman also shows in chapter 6, in other aspects too, the influence of foreigners declined: "Edward III was the last English king before James I who conspicuously gave office to, and ennobled, foreigners."[131] By the mid-16th century, the alien share in English foreign trade, once nearly half the total, had been virtually eliminated.[132] But the growth of parliament (whatever its long-term results were to be) was the result of royal action because of the royal need for money which could only come from taxation. Another consequence of the expansion of the royal administration from King John's time was that the doings of all Englishmen, lay or cleric, rich or poor, were increasingly being recorded by royal officials and preserved in the national archives, and thus preserved for posterity. The medieval English kings thus made possible, unwittingly no doubt, the modern reconstruction of the history of the English people in a fullness of detail which cannot be equalled at national level anywhere in Europe before the 16th century.

With all its faults, the later medieval monarchy bequeathed to the "new monarchs" of the 16th century a reasonably well-organized governmental and administrative system at central and local levels, a system which was to be fully deployed in Wales and the hitherto semi-autonomous palatinates of Chester, Durham, and Lancaster after 1536. As Professor Loades demonstrates in chapter 7, there were new developments in the 16th century, especially but not exclusively at the centre, associated with the so-called "Tudor revolution in government", which had important repercussions for monarchs and people. The power of the executive under the control of able and trusted ministers such as Thomas Cromwell, Earl of Essex, and William Cecil, Lord Burghley, certainly increased dramatically, and the system evolved by Cromwell survived his downfall in 1540.[133] As a result partly of this expansion of government power, and partly of the increasing complexity of the problems which confronted government, its operations became more expensive (the period from the accession of Henry VIII in 1509 to the end of the first Civil War in 1646 was marked by what was to contemporaries novel and persistent price-inflation). Inflation was not confined to England; it was prevalent throughout Europe in the 16th and 17th centuries, but the response of English governments differed from that of continental governments, and this marked the beginning of what was to prove an increasing divergence between England (and later Britain) and the continental powers not only in financial but also in constitutional and political aspects.

English rulers, from Henry VIII onwards, relied more and more on parliament (and the House of Commons was already the crucial part of parliament) to grant them revenues from taxation, initially only in time of war − the medieval belief that the king should "live of his own" (ie maintain himself from the yield of the royal estates and from hereditary Customs dues) still lingered-on, despite its unreality in the conditions of the 15th and 16th centuries - but from the mid-16th century also in peacetime. This need for parliamentary approval of taxation immediately required the Crown and its ministers to be able to manage the House of Commons, which was normally possible in the Tudor period, but the early Stuarts found increasingly difficult. In the long run, indeed, parliament, and the House of Commons in particular, became more assertive and more inclined to insist on "redress of grievances" before granting supply, as Dr Coward and Professor Miller stress in chapters 8 and 9. In part, this resulted from a definite political desire for change, but it was also an unintended result of the more frequent calling of parliaments in the 16th and 17th centuries, which gave its members in both houses increasing confidence and experience in political affairs. Parliaments had been exceptional at the end of the 15th century; they had become a normal, indeed indispensable, part of the apparatus of government by the time of the Union in 1707. For most of the 18th century, the Crown could normally control parliament, albeit with greater difficulty as time went on (see Professor Jeremy Black in chapter 10), but by Queen Victoria's accession in 1837, parliament had become the real power in the land, with the Crown's power becoming nominal. William IV was the last king to dissolve parliament of his own will: Queen Victoria had to put up with ministerial interference even in appointments to the Royal Household. All these political changes reflected the increasing confidence and assertiveness, *vis à vis* the Crown and its ministers, of the "political nation" - not just the landed aristocracy in the countryside but also its allies in the towns, the commercial, professional, and managerial classes who were assuming greater economic importance as Britain became the first industrial country in the world.[134] This concurrence between government and the most influential sections of the governed in turn had further benefits: the "financial revolution in government" meant that British governments were able not only to tap the wealth of the Crown's subjects by means of more effective taxation (notably the Excise, indirect taxation, and the direct Land Tax) but also to rely on borrowing from these subjects long-term at low rates of interest. Government bonds became the safest form of investment in the 18th century, a far cry form the stop on the Exchequer in 1672.[135]

On the continent, however, with the significant but singular exception of the Netherlands, the reaction on the part of most governments to the same set of circumstances - inflation, more expensive warfare, greater governmental ambitions, all leading to accumulating financial pressures - was quite different. All the great continental powers - France, Spain, Austria - and many of the lesser states in Germany relied on raising revenues without consent. Representative assemblies were increasingly sidelined and finally ignored. Symptomatic of this process was the history of the French Estates-General, last summoned (before the French Revolution) in 1614: when it was decided to resurrect this antique assembly in the early stages of the Revolution, archivists and historians had to be set to work to find out how it had functioned nearly two centuries earlier. This might seem to be not too relevant to the history of monarchy, but in fact it highlights the very close connection I mentioned earlier between rulers and ruled. The concomitant of a ruler not dependent on any form of assent by a representative assembly is his or her (Maria Theresa, Catherine the Great) effective absolutism, since the ruler is not subject to any explicit check other than a sense of what is possible. Some dynasties, notably the Bourbons, as Professional Doyle remarks in chapter 11, were almost entirely bereft of such political sense. Consequently, all sections of the population, deprived of any real participation in decision-making were increasingly alienated from government. The French monarchy was, therefore, an easy prey for the enthusiasms aroused by the French Revolution, however illusory these proved to be in the long run. If the ruler was all-powerful, there was no rule of law, since the law was "what pleases the prince"; the nobility became useless drones resident for years on end at Versailles, divorced from the regions they owned and from the resident population of these regions, most of whom were depressed and impoverished peasants suffering under the restrictions of serfdom. Lacking leadership from above - save that of (mostly not very) enlightened despots - and enterprise from below, it was hardly surprising that the continent of Europe, which had regarded the British Isles in the late 15th century as an unimportant, primitive, economically backward area, had been overtaken by Britain 300 years later. Without the rule of law, without representative government, there could be no political stability and no real economic growth.

Foreign visitors to England in the 18th century were amazed and often appalled by what they observed: the ordinary Englishman well-clothed and well-shod (when most continental labourers dressed in rags and went bare-foot), eating white bread (when the French ate brown bread and the Germans and Russians black bread) and meat (for high days and holidays on the continent, if then), drinking strong ale and tea sweetened with sugar and smoking tobacco (all far more expensive on the continent, if indeed obtainable by the majority), living in cottages or houses, mostly with glazed windows, but above all with security (whereas the continental peasantry lived in equal fear of the seigneur's steward and the king's tax-gatherer). Compare the situation of the English labourer as described by William Pitt the Elder in 1763:

> The poorest man may in his cottage bid defiance to all the force of the Crown. It may be frail; its roof may shake; the wind may blow through it; the rain may enter - but the king of England cannot enter; all his forces dare not cross the threshold of the ruined tenement.

Nor was it an exaggeration when, two years later, William Blackstone pointed with pride to the manifest constitutional and legal contrasts between Britain and continental Europe:

> The idea and practice of this political or civil liberty flourish in their highest vigour in these kingdoms ... the laws of England being peculiarly

adapted to the preservation of this inestimable blessing even in the
meanest subject. Very different from the modern constitutions of other
states, on the continent of Europe ... which in general ... vest an arbitrary
and despotic power, of controlling the actions of the subject, in the prince,
or in a few grandees.

As I remarked when I first cited these two passages,

Georgian and early Victorian England ... was still a better place for the
"common man" to inhabit than almost anywhere else in Europe. One
of the reasons, paradoxically, is that it was also a better place for noblemen
to inhabit.[136]

The transformation of Stuart "despotism" into the partnership of Crown and
parliament of the 18th century and the further and continued development
into parliamentary democracy (chapters 9 and 10) were, therefore, not simply
matters that concerned the monarchy alone, or even the monarchy and the
political nation: they affected the entire British people to their great benefit.

In earlier centuries, the king needed to be at least respected, and preferably
feared, if he were to be effective as a ruler. If, until the late 18th century, the
personality of the monarch was the principal factor determining his
effectiveness as a ruler, this requirement for a strong and capable personality
was bound, sooner or later, to conflict with another essential condition for
monarchical survival, namely legitimacy. In the nature of things, it was not
common for the sons or daughters of kings to inherit their father's merits (or
demerits), any more than it was for non-royal fathers (hence the tag "from
rags to riches to rags" about modern industrialists). The landed aristocracy,
faced with the same problem, evolved legal strategies such as the entail, the
use, and the settlement to overcome such difficulties, but these were not
available to the Crown.[137] A succession of effective monarchs could not be
guaranteed. Not all kings were succeeded by heirs who were of age or of the
male sex, both of which requirements proved necessary before the 16th century.
In Scotland, as Adam Bruce remarks, "The six James ... all succeeded as
minors", which helps to explain the very different evolution of the Scottish
monarchy which he outlines in chapter 12. An incompetent royal father could
nevertheless produce a competent or more than competent son. It is a tribute
to the monarchy and the Tudor revolution in government that England in
the 16th century experienced without real trouble a minority followed by two
queens regnant, all single events, let alone a series, which in earlier centuries
would have led to severe difficulty.

The new political circumstances and the new constitutional conventions that
evolved in reaction to the changed conditions of the 19th and 20th centuries
necessitated a changed role for the modern monarchy. The ritual element,
as Dr David Starkey emphasizes in chapter 13, became more evident, as
real power receded from the Crown, and the monarch became an icon embodying

the imperial destiny of Britain in the late 19th and early 20th centuries, notably at the Golden and Diamond Jubilees of Queen Victoria, the coronations of Edward VII and George V, and the Indian Durbar of 1911. A the sun finally did set on the Empire, and as a fully democratic system of government finally evolved in Britain between 1918 and 1945,[139] the monarchy developed a new role and a new style. It represented national unity in adversity, notably when George VI and Queen Elizabeth (now the Queen-Mother) stayed in Buckingham Palace during the war and shared the experience of the blitz with Londoners. It became more audible and visible to its subjects, first with the Christmas broadcasts on the radio from the 1930s, which were televized from the 1950s, as was the Coronation of Elizabeth II in 1953, but also with increased attention from the popular press. This probably made the Royal Family, especially George VI and the Queen, better known to, and probably better loved by, most of the people. It converged with another developing aspect of modern royalty, namely the Royal Family as the ideal, model family, setting the "tone" for the bulk of its subjects. As society changes, so has the British monarchy these past 150 years. According to Dr Starkey, it now needs to rethink its role which on experience it is likely to do.

Footnotes to the Introduction may be found on pages 319–30.

NORSEMEN

NORTHUMBRIA

SAXONY

MERCIA

THURINGIA

WESSEX

AUSTRASIA

FRANCIA

● Aachen

NEUSTRIA

● Paris

BRITTANY

CARINTHIA

BURGUNDY

BAVARIA

RHAETIA

AQUITAINE

Venice
●

LOMBARD KINGDOM

DALMATIA

GASCONY

SEPTIMANIA

SPANISH
MARCH

PAPAL
PATRIMONY
Rome
●

BENEVENTO

250   KMS
250   MILES

THE FRANKISH EMPIRE AT CHARLEMAGNE'S DEATH, 814

1: Rosamond McKitterick

Charlemagne and the western monarchical inheritance

EINHARD, protégé and biographer of Charlemagne, writing in about 817,[1] provides us not only with an account of the Frankish ruler's political achievements at home and abroad, his personal habits and enthusiasms, his administrative methods and his death, but also with a description of what he looked like and how he behaved:

> The Emperor was strong and well built. He was tall in stature, but not excessively so . . . the top of his head was round, and his eyes were piercing and unusually large. His nose was slightly longer than usual, he had a fine head of white hair and his expression was gay and good humoured. As a result, whether he was seated or standing, he always appeared masterful and dignified. His neck was short and rather thick, and his stomach a trifle too heavy, but the proportions of the rest of his body prevented one from noticing these blemishes. His step was firm and he was vigorous in all his movements. He spoke distinctly, but his voice was thin for a man of his physique. His health was good, except that he suffered from frequent attacks of fever during the last years of his life and towards the end he was lame in one foot. Even then, he continued to do exactly as he wished instead of following the advice of his doctors . . . he spent much of his time on horseback and out hunting . . . he took delight in steam baths at the thermal springs at Aachen . . . and was an extremely strong swimmer. He would invite not only his sons to bathe with him, but his nobles and friends as well . . . so that sometimes a hundred men or more would be in the water together. He wore the national dress of the Franks . . . he was moderate in his eating and drinking . . . during his meal he would listen to a public reading or some other entertainment. Stories would be recited to him or the doings of the ancients told again. He took great pleasure in the books of Saint Augustine and especially those which are called the *City of God*. . . When he was dressing and putting on his shoes, he would invite his friends to come in. Moreover, if the Count of the Palace told him that there was some dispute which could not be settled without the Emperor's personal decision, he would order the disputants to be brought in there and then, hear the case as if he were sitting in tribunal, and pronounce a judgment. If there were any official business to be transacted on that day, or any order to be given to one of his ministers, he would settle it at the same time. . . He learnt Latin so well that he spoke it as fluently as his own tongue; but he understood Greek better than he could speak it. . . He paid the greatest attention to the liberal arts; and he had great respect for men who taught them, bestowing high honours upon them. . . Charlemagne practised the Christian religion with great devotion and piety, for he had been brought up in this faith since earliest childhood. . . He took the greatest pains to ensure that all church ceremonies were performed with the utmost dignity. He was most active in relieving the poor.[2]

Such a physical description and moral portrait of an emperor had its precedents in Suetonius' *Lives of the Twelve Caesars,* a work which did, in fact, serve as a direct model for Einhard's own creation, even though Einhard added much that is peculiar to Charlemagne. Einhard was, after all, writing for an audience that was in principle as knowledgeable about his subject as the author himself. Great stress is laid on Charlemagne's specific military conquests, on his relations with his family, on his legislation and on his own education, and, most obviously diverging from the Suetonian model, there is a long account of Charlemagne's last years and death. Charlemagne's will, complete with witness list, is included in the Life and supplies essential authenticity to the high moral purpose of Einhard's plot. Nevertheless, Einhard's account of Charlemagne is in many respects a composite of the characteristics of the Twelve Caesars of Suetonius. Those who knew Suetonius might, therefore, recognize that Charlemagne was a super-emperor, by implication better than any one of his illustrious predecessors.

Other parallels were drawn by the court poets of Charlemagne's household. Theodulf, later Bishop of Orleans, for example, described Charlemagne, in a verse epistle to the King, thus:

> Charlemagne whom, by God's grace, I shall soon see. The sight of you is more brilliant than thrice-smelted gold, and he who can always be near you is fortunate indeed, who can gaze upon that forehead, so worthy of its weighty crown, which throughout the entire world has no peer; or set eyes upon that excellent head, chin or lovely neck, those golden hands which take poverty away.

> None surpasses you, for your skill and judgment are so widely famed that there is, I think, no limit to them.

> What wonder is it if the eternal shepherd made so great a man His pastor to tend His flocks. Your name recalls your grandfather, your noble understanding Solomon's, your strength reminds me of David and your beauty is Joseph's own. Guardian of treasure, avenger of crimes, dispenser of honours – because this is what you are, all these good things are granted to you.[3]

Theodulf adds Old Testament rulers to Einhard's Roman emperors as the fit comparisons for the Frankish King; he substitutes an explicitly Christian role for the ruler in place of Einhard's classicizing emphasis on the moral character of the monarch, though both stress his role as lawgiver and dispenser of justice.

Einhard's biography and the Carolingian court poetry nevertheless serve to remind us of what is a serious problem for historians when assessing a monarch or the monarchy, namely the fact that in biography, praise poetry, and historical narratives, we see kings always through the eyes, and in the words, of those who wished either to extol their virtues or to exaggerate their vices in order to justify the current political position of the author and his intended audience. Thus Einhard, for example, writing in 817, three years after the death of Charlemagne, provides an agenda for emperorship and a strong moral claim for the succession of Charlemagne's son Louis when such political support for Louis was vital.[4]

History writing and royal biography in such a context become part of contemporary political polemic, or panegyric. Nevertheless, the images biographers and historians created, however remote from reality they might have been, proved both powerful and enduring. They served as inspirations and warnings for their successors and provided an ideal around which Carolingian political thinkers could spin their theories.[5] Such royal image-making is reflected, moreover, in contemporary art. Let us consider a few examples.

In his own lifetime, Charlemagne apparently made little effort to promote a particular royal iconography. In line with Roman imperial coinage and some of the types struck in the early Germanic kingdoms of western Europe, one might have expected a portrait bust on his coinage. Following in the footsteps of his father Pippin III, who had been the first to assume royal control of the coinage, Charlemagne reorganized the mints and in 794 instituted a wholesale reform of the coinage. The so-called Class 3 coinage was produced. The coins' weight was increased and new types issued. Neither Pippin III's coinage, nor these early issues of Charlemagne's, however, portrayed the ruler. The obverse was generally the ruler's name in some form, and the reverse usually a mint name with sometimes a cross or RF (*rex francorum*). In the 794 Class 3 coinage, the *Karolus* monogram and mint signature were on the obverse and, usually, cross and CARLUS REX FR on the reverse. Only with the issue of his rare Class 4 coinage from 812-814 onwards, that is, 12 years after the famous Coronation as *imperator Romanorum et gubernans imperium* (Emperor of the Romans and governing the Empire) in Rome on Christmas Day 800, is there a portrait bust of Charlemagne. In what looks like a serious attempt to provide a likeness, the coin depicts Charlemagne as a Roman emperor, in bust profile, with laurel wreath and *paludamentum* (military cloak), and the inscription KAROLVS IMP AUG (*Karolus Imperator Augustus*) (Charles August Emperor) or a variation of this on the obverse.[6]

It was quite otherwise under Charlemagne's son Louis the Pious and especially so under his grandson Charles the Bald, King of the West Franks, for then an elaborate imagery of kingship developed, rich in symbolism, that was to endure for centuries to come.[7] In due course, this royal iconography became linked with the legend and the achievement of Charlemagne.

The surviving manuscript painting of the image of the Emperor Louis the Pious, in Hraban Maur's work *De laudibus sanctae crucis* (in praise of the Holy Cross), emphasizes his role as a warrior of Christ. The acrostic poem behind the King's figure makes an explicit connection between Louis' role as defender of the faith and his responsibility and authority as emperor.[8] The gold *solidus* (shilling) issued by Louis, perhaps for some ceremonial function, and representing Louis with a laureate profile bust on the obverse, makes the same point.[9] The portrait of Louis' eldest son Lothar is just as straightforward, for it is similar in its imagery to medallions of the Roman Emperor Constantine; he is enthroned and flanked by two bodyguards.[10]

The eight ruler portraits of Lothar's youngest brother, Charles the Bald, on the other hand, are full of symbolism. The most famous portrait is the dedication picture from the First Bible of Charles the Bald, produced in the scriptorium of St Martin of Tours and presented to him in about 846.[11] Here we see depicted the relationship between the King, his nobles, and the Church in a portrayal of the presentation of this very Bible to the King. Count Vivian, lay Abbot of Tours, presents it to his ruler. Charles is enthroned, flanked by two bodyguards and two noble attendants, and wears a hooped crown (very like that of his brother Lothar). The brethren of Tours, direct recipients of the King's beneficence, process towards the King and three of them (it is a large and heavy volume) bear the Bible. The other additions emphasize the King's royalty. Two female figures offering crowns are thought to personify royal virtues. The Hand of God indicates the divine source of royal authority. The association of rulership with the Old Testament kings is made explicit elsewhere in this manuscript (fol 215v) with the portrait of King David the Psalmist, crowned with a Carolingian crown like that of Charles the Bald and Lothar, and in the four corners the four cardinal secular virtues: prudence, justice, fortitude, and temperance.[12]

Other aspects of rulership are brought out by the representation of Charles the Bald in his personal prayer book, now in the Schatzkammer der Residenz in Munich. There he is depicted in an attitude of humility, abasement, and supplication before Christ on the Cross.[13] In a Mass book prepared for his coronation as King of Lotharingia in 869, a youthful king is crowned by two bishops with the help of the Hand of God, again signifying the essential relation of the King with the Church and the Christian faith as well as his God-given authority.[14] These themes are further reinforced in the portraits in Charles the Bald's Psalter, and in Charles' Third Bible, with the significant addition of his consort, Queen Richildis, the earliest representation in art of a Frankish queen.[15]

The magnificent ivory throne presented to the Pope in 875 to mark Charles' coronation as Emperor makes further associations. It is richly adorned with ivory panels, carved with scenes from the labours of the pagan hero Hercules. A recent study of this throne has argued that the use of Hercules was to provide a measure against which a Christian ruler could define himself and chart his proper course; it acted as a specific warning in the context of the creation of Charles as Roman emperor.[16]

In the *Codex Aureus* (Golden Book) portrait in Charles the Bald's Gospel Book, produced *circa* 870 by the group of artists Charles himself had gathered together to create fine books for his personal use, there is again the enthroned ruler, with his crown, sceptre, orb, the Hand of God, the military attendants, and the female figures, this time labelled to indicate that they are personifications of "Francia" and "Gotica", that is, the territories over which Charles ruled. Charles in this manuscript is gazing at the celestial vision opposite the Adoration of the Lamb. Thus heavenly and earthly rule are juxtaposed.[17] This pair of pictures, moreover, represents an earlier reality. When Charlemagne sat on his throne in the palace chapel at Aachen, he too would have been able to gaze at the mosaic representation of the Adoration of the Lamb.[18]

Later rulers were to draw on this imagery. Portraits of the Saxon and Salian emperors, for example, as in the Gospel Book of Otto III, represent the German emperors in the Carolingian tradition. The portrait of Henry II, completed between 1002 and 1014, is in fact virtually a replica of the picture of Charles the Bald from the *Codex Aureus*.[19] Later portraits of the Anglo-Saxon kings, such as in the Charter of King Edgar for New Minster (966-975), also draw on this imagery, with its stress on territorial power, the support of the Church, military strength, and divine authority.[20]

Thus in historical writing and in works of art, a particular and idealized image of a monarch is presented. It was complemented in the political thinking and the liturgical ritual of the period. In his tract on Christian rulers, for example, Sedulius Scottus cites the examples of Solomon, David, and Constantine the Great, and emphasizes how a king is "notably raised to the summit of temporal rule when he devotes himself with pious zeal to the Almighty King's glory and honour".[21] Jonas of Orleans summarizes the proper office of the king "to govern the people of God, to rule with equity and justice, and to exert himself so that they might have peace and concord".[22]

The most dramatic liturgical expression of ideas of kingship was in the prayer *Prospice* (Look Down) included in the rite of royal consecration in the ninth century, and afterwards widely used throughout western Europe. Indeed, it was in the Carolingian period that the medieval and later rituals of royal inauguration, masterminded in particular by Archbishop Hincmar of Rheims, were first composed and elaborated. It is also the case that there is a Frankish element in the English royal coronation *ordo* (order), even down to the consecration of our own Queen Elizabeth II, though the early English development of an *ordo* independent from that of the Franks is also clear.[23] In the prayer *Prospice,* there is a repeated use of the words *potestas* (authority) and *potentia* (power) and the prayer asks God:

> Grant him, Omnipotent God, to be a most mighty protector of the fatherland, and a comforter of churches and holy monasteries with the greatest piety of royal munificence, and to be the mightiest of kings, triumphing over his enemies so as to crush rebels and heathen nations; and may he be very terrible to his enemies with the utmost strength of royal potency.

> May he also be generous and lovable and pious to the magnates and the outstanding leaders and faithful men of his realm, that he may be feared and loved by all.
>
> May kings come forth from his loins through succession of future times to rule this whole realm. And after glorious and happy times in this present life may he be worthy to have eternal joys in perpetual blessedness.[24]

The essential point to make about Carolingian political thinking is that it is king-centred. The dominant idea is that political power comes from God and the king acts as his deputy in securing justice and peace for a Christian people. Further, as Janet Nelson has stressed, there is a hegemonial idea of empire, that is of an emperor ruling many peoples and realms, which arose directly from the political experience of the eighth century. Kingdoms emerged within this empire which were territories and social entities, with a lay and clerical élite sharing power and responsibility with the king.

If the apprehension of monarchical rule is created by deliberate image-making in many different spheres, the practice of the ruler still set the agenda for the commentators. Whether the exercise of justice was fair or arbitrary, a king was a lawgiver and judge. Whether he were a brilliant strategist or a hopeless ditherer in the field of battle, his was still the role of warleader. Even if his personal morals and piety were less than exemplary, he was still the defender of the faith and the supporter of the Church. From such a text as Einhard's *Vita Karoli* (Life of Charles) or the other historians of the time, therefore, we can gain a list of royal criteria or attributes and expected activity within a general theoretical understanding of a monarch's function.

From non-literary sources, moreover, the actuality of Charlemagne's rulership is demonstrable. Thus from the succession of royal capitularies (edicts published in clauses or *captula)* we can establish the range and ingenuity of Charlemagne's administrative organization and his attention to the proper administration of justice throughout his realm. From the reorganized royal household, with its chapel and chancery officials, based from the end of the eighth century at the newly-built palace complex at Aachen, to the counts and the *missi dominici* (King's agents) in the localities, governmental oversight was direct, reinforced by the constant itinerancy of the monarch, holding court, hearing petitions, presiding over the annual assemblies of his faithful men, attending the synods and Church councils of the bishops and abbots. Royal legislation for the most part intermingled secular and ecclesiastical matters. The Synod of Frankfurt in 794, for example, decided on the imposition of uniform weights and measures, reformed the coinage by introducing a new standard heavy penny, and pronounced on the Frankish position on the theological issues of iconoclasm and Adoptionism.[25] Rulings of canon law were placed alongside practical requirements for the protection of widows and orphans, the education of boys, the behaviour of the clergy, and the functions of the count in the programmatic capitulary known as the *Admonitio*

Generalis (General Admonition) of 789. In the first and most savage capitularies concerning Saxony of 782-5, the forced imposition of Christianity and Frankish rule on the Saxons is recorded, though the measures were considerably softened by 797.[26] The programmatic capitulary of 802 inaugurated administrative reorganization on a massive scale, notably in establishing and defining the districts and judicial duties of the newly commissioned *missi dominici*. Such capitularies as that for the mobilization of the army in 808 provide a clear indication of the means by which an army was to be recruited from the free farming men of the realm and how they were to be assembled and equipped for a military expedition.[27] Einhard's reference to Charlemagne's lawgiving is thus entirely backed up by the king's extant legislation.

One might wish to argue that such legislation, essentially normative in character, is as much part of the image-making of a monarch as the biographies written about him. Explanatory prefaces abound for many capitularies and are self-conscious proclamations of the royal role. In the *Admonitio Generalis,* for example, the king proclaims himself to be "by the grace of God and the gift of His mercy King and *Rector* (Ruler) of the Franks and devout defender and humble adjutant of the Holy Church". His decisions are reached with the help of his *sacerdotes* (priests) and advisers and he relies on them to see that his provisions are carried out, with the added support from the *missi* who "with the authority of our name may correct together with you, those things which ought to be corrected."[28] Yet this image-making is done by the king himself.

Nevertheless, the laws also had a practical function. In innumerable instances – the activities of particular officials, written reports, court proceedings noted in charters, the survival of many law books from the ninth century as a consequence of the stipulation that judges should reach their decisions on the basis of written law rather than on their own opinions, the extensive organization of the Church, the creation of schools, and the efflorescence of learning – we can observe how much of the legislation was acted upon.[29]

Besides being a brilliant administrator, Charlemagne's more glamorous undertakings as warleader were spectacular and earned him lasting fame as a warrior and conqueror worthy of the title of emperor. His first campaign on his accession to the throne in 768 was to consolidate his father's subjugation of Aquitaine. He conquered the Lombard kingdom of Italy in 774, annexed Bavaria in 788, destroyed the Avars between 791 and 793, invaded northern Spain (though with mixed success and one notable defeat at Roncesvalles celebrated in later legend in the *Chanson de Roland)*, subdued the Bretons, forced the Beneventans to capitulate (for the time being, at least) to his authority, negotiated successfully with the Byzantines and Venetians, exerted Frankish suzerainty over the Croats in Dalmatia, and, after a protracted series of campaigns and harsh retaliation, hammered the Saxons into submission by 797. Such a dry catalogue of successful military conquest should not neglect to mention, however, the slaughter, the pillaging, and the rich booty brought back to Francia (such as the fabulous Avar treasure).

Nor should it be forgotten that some of these campaigns were not simply aggression; in the cases of Spain in 778 or of the Lombards in 773-774, they were the result of appeals for assistance. Other conquests, moreover, such as that of Bavaria, were not accompanied by destruction. Charlemagne simply deposed his cousin Tassilo, Duke of Bavaria, and took over the government of the region.

Thus by the time he received the honorific title of emperor, Charlemagne ruled a vastly extended territory. It was a prodigious achievement. Although subsequently it was rare for this whole area to be ruled by one man, these conquests had the effect, nevertheless, not only of enriching the Carolingians, but also of introducing Frankish culture, Frankish administrative practice, Frankish ecclesiastical organization, and Frankish methods and principles of rulership over much of the territory we now recognize as western Europe. This was to have far reaching consequences, for it was a legacy of an ideal and an actuality of monarchy drawn on for centuries thereafter. It was also an idea of monarchy wedded to the fortunes of a unified Europe. Charlemagne earned his epithet *Europae pater* (father of Europe) before the end of the eighth century; even now he symbolizes the concept of Europe in that the Charlemagne Prize is awarded for services to European unity.

In ecclesiastical and monastic reform, Charlemagne was no less active in initiating policies and appointing men likely to see them through. He concerned himself with the larger schemes, such as the reorganization of ecclesiastical provinces and the convening of reform synods, as well as with the content of sermons and the provision of correct and authoritative texts of all the principal books required for the Christian faith.[30] His patronage of culture and learning, alluded to by Einhard, is even more richly documented than Einhard would have led us to suppose. Not only did Charlemagne possess a remarkable library of his own, including many rare classical works: he also promoted scholarship, patronized scholars by assembling them at his court and subsequently endowing them with rich abbeys and bishoprics, poured wealth into the creation of works of art, and legislated to promote education and learning in his kingdom.[31]

Charlemagne was, of course, far from being the first ruler to patronize learning and culture. Indeed, such activity could be regarded as one of the obligations of royalty from Antiquity onwards. What distinguished Charlemagne and his immediate successors in their patronage of culture, however, was their motives, for patronage was inextricably bound up with the themes of *correctio* and *emendatio,* that is, reform, the removal of error, the provision of correct texts, and the enhancement of Christian learning, that are so striking a characteristic of the Carolingian Renaissance of the late eighth and the ninth centuries. Authoritative texts of the Mass Book, canon law, the Homiliary, the Gospels, the Bible, the Rule of Benedict, and the secular laws of the people under Frankish rule were produced under the auspices of Charlemagne and Louis the Pious. They also encouraged the dissemination of correct liturgical music. As a consequence of the scholarly activity Charlemagne stimulated, there was what appears to have been a concerted attempt to gather the works of the great classical and late Antique authors and copy them. Certainly, the contents of Charlemagne's library, the activities of scholars such as Einhard and Lupus of Ferrières in the mid-ninth century, and the fact that of the surviving classical manuscripts that have come down to us, the greater majority of the earliest manuscript copies of any classical Latin author date from the ninth century, witness to this.[32] Rather than acting as occasional benefactors, moreover, or accumulating merely selfish collections of treasures, Carolingian rulers sustained groups of artists, scribes, and craftsmen over a long period to create artefacts for their particular objects. Their patronage was ultimately towards the same goal as that of their conquests and ecclesiastical and administrative reforms, namely, the promotion of their royal power as Christian kings and the consolidation of the Christian faith by disseminating the key texts on which that faith was based.[33]

We need, therefore, to ask how such a manifold role for a monarch had developed. How much of it was the particular contribution of the early Carolingian rulers and especially Charlemagne? How in particular was the association of secular and divine authority made? In any consideration of Frankish kingship before Charlemagne, a crucial source of information is the *Historiae* of Gregory of Tours, written between 578 and 594. Gregory, however, tells us that in his own day, many people did not know the names of the first kings of the Franks nor whether they were kings or not. We are no better off than Gregory's contemporaries on the origins of Frankish kingship. The earliest ruler of the Franks known with any certainty is Childeric, the father of Clovis, who died in 481 and whose probably pagan grave at Tournai was discovered in 1653. Found with Childeric was his signet ring bearing his name, a purse of 100 gold and 200 silver coins, a bracelet, a Roman military buckle of gold, a cloak embroidered with 300 gold cicadas (imitations of which were sewn on Napoleon's imperial coronation cloak in order to make an explicit connection with the ancient rulers of France), a bull's head of gold, and the severed head of a warhorse.

The Franks appear gradually to have replaced Roman authority in northern Gaul in the later fifth century, being recognized as rulers in due course by Romans and Franks. Further, they do not appear to have gone through a long period of alienation from the Catholic Gallo-Roman aristocracy and ecclesiastical hierarchy, but were converted directly from paganism to Catholic Christianity. From the end of the fifth century, therefore, there was a close integration of Franks and Gallo-Romans in the secular and ecclesiastical spheres to a degree not encountered in the other independent Germanic kingdoms of the time. In particular, the famous letter which Archbishop Remigius of Rheims wrote to Clovis indicates that the support of the Gallo-Roman episcopate would make Clovis' task much easier, though it would probably be a mistake to assume that such episcopal support was essential to Clovis' success.[34]

The rulership of the early Merovingian kings has much of the Roman military governorship about it, as well as that which is commonly associated with a "Germanic warleader". Certainly, Clovis embarked on a ruthless series of military campaigns. By his death in 511, he was in control of much of Roman Gaul. The Franks were the only Germanic rulers who succeeded in maintaining royal succession according to hereditary principles and favouring filial succession (though not primogeniture).[35] All other kingdoms – of the Ostrogoths, Vandals, Visigoths, Lombards, and possibly the Anglo-Saxons in the fifth, sixth, and seventh centuries – remained in principle elective, though particular leading families seem to have provided an eligible group from which rulers might be chosen, and some fathers were succeeded by one of their sons, or, in some Lombard cases, sons-in-law.[36]

Many features of Frankish kingship, moreover, were established from the very beginning. Christian rulership, marked by the baptism of Clovis, was something learnt from the Christian emperors of Rome from the fourth and fifth centuries in the aftermath of Constantine's conversion. The role, as elucidated in Augustine's *De civitate dei* (City of God), was based on a *ministerium* (ministry) of the people, with the ultimate source of authority being God. The king thereby was seen to have a special relationship with the Church. The bishops saw to it that the kings' position in relation to the Church and his obligations to the Church and clergy were carefully defined by the clergy themselves so as to ensure and enhance their position. Such a theoretical position had its practical expression in the Frankish kings' contacts (however limited) with the papacy, their convening of some Church councils, their endowment of monasteries, and interest in the appointments to bishoprics. On the Church's side, the bishops and clergy counted on the king's physical protection and material support; they offered him spiritual enhancement and prayer in return.[37] Kings were now buried in churches; some even acquired the attributes of saints and the ability to heal. *Iustitia, pietas, ministerium* (justice, piety and service) were stressed within a Christian emphasis on rulership which increased markedly from the seventh century onwards. In the Gallican liturgy of the late seventh century, provision for the ruler is made for the first time and it is significant that the most prominent is the prayer for the king as he goes out to battle.

Yet the observable actual practice of the Merovingian kings is as important as the hopeful expectations of rulership. Succession practice, for example, although hereditary, was also partible, so that Clovis handed on his hard-won kingdom to his four sons and it was divided between them. Such filial partitions remained a feature of the Frankish monarchy throughout the Carolingian period as well, even though in some cases the death of all but one son before the father's death simplified the succession. Many solutions were sought for the problem of providing a continuity of authority, but difficulties remained. The potential conflicts and political and territorial alignments of the partition of the Empire of 843, agreed between the sons of Louis and Pious by the Treaty of Verdun, for example, in which the West

Frankish, Middle (Lotharingian), and East Frankish kingdoms were defined, were not finally settled formally until 1919, after the First World War.

When the Carolingian mayor of the palace, Pippin III, removed the last Merovingian king, Childeric III, from the throne in 751, and had himself anointed by Frankish bishops as king in Childeric's place, therefore, he inherited a well-developed monarchical tradition. From the position of mayor of the palace, or general factotum in the palace in the Merovingian period, the office of mayor had become, from the early seventh century, one in which an increasing amount of executive power was *de facto,* and sometimes *de jure,* invested. The mayors in the old kingdoms of the Merovingian polity – Neustria, Burgundy, and Austrasia – had, by the early eighth century, consolidated their position as leading magnates. The Carolingian mayors were among several powerful individuals whose interests and ambitions within these kingdoms sometimes clashed.[38] The Carolingians, on coming to power, were able to take advantage of some of the political adjustments of the previous few decades. On the one hand they benefited from Merovingian royal traditions and practices in terms of adminstrative organization, wealth, and legislative practice. On the other, their rule was based far more obviously on the *consensus,* that is, agreement, of their lay and ecclesiastical magnates than had apparently been the case under the Merovingian rulers.[39] It is significant, moreover, that the office of mayor of the palace simply ceased to exist.

Loyalty thus played a key role in the ethos of rulership and government. Charlemagne himself demanded oaths of loyalty from his *fideles,* (faithful men). That is the oath was not a custom of a particular class of men but an obligation imposed by the king. The annual accounts are full of references to particular groups, Franks and conquered peoples, coming to the king and swearing oaths of fidelity to him. In 775, for example, the royal Frankish annals report that the Saxon *Austreleudi* under the leadership of Hassi came to him with hostages and swore oaths that they would be faithful to the king.[40] After political crises or great changes, these oaths apparently had to be renewed. Between 786 and 793, for example, a capitulary was issued explaining the necessity for the oath of fidelity on the basis not only of ancient custom (*ex antiqua consuetudine* – a usefully vague reference), but also arising from the fact that recent rebels against Charlemagne had provided as their excuse that they had not sworn an oath of fidelity to him. The oath: "I promise that I am and shall be faithful to my Lord Charles the King and his sons all the days of my life without deception of deceit",[41] therefore, was to be sworn by all bishops, abbots, counts, royal vassals, vicedomini (high-ranking clerics), and canons.[42] Further, in 802, Charlemagne required that all men in his realm, whether lay or cleric, who had previously sworn an oath of fidelity to him as King were now to make that promise again to him as Emperor. All men of 12 years and over who had not yet sworn such an oath were now to do so. The oath of fidelity on this occasion was glossed, so that the obligations inherent in the oath should be fully understood. These obligations concerned not only military and political loyalty to the Emperor, but also service to God, to the land, and to the maintenance of justice, to maintain the legal rights of the royal fisc and those who worked upon his land, to protect the Church, widows, orphans, and pilgrims, not to neglect the proper care of a benefice granted to a *fidelis* by the Emperor or to alienate land from it for his own purposes, to obey the summons to military service and do nothing to prevent anyone else from obeying it. The proper proceedings of justice in the courts were in no circumstances to be corrupted or prevented.[43] An oath of loyalty to the Carolingian king, therefore, was also an oath of loyalty to the institutions and public morality for which he was responsible.

In the practical sphere, the advent of the Carolingians strengthened the force of some of the Merovingian territorial conquests and extended the areas under Frankish rule. A new relationship with the Church was established by means of extensive and politically-oriented monastic patronage and reform of the organization of the Church. The system of ecclesiastical provinces and metropolitan archbishops was overhauled and some new provinces created, both within the ancient Gallo-Roman ecclesiastical organization and to take account of the establishment of new sees beyond the Rhine.[44] Clerics were called upon to serve in the royal administration and writing office, headed by a *cancellarius* (chancellor) and a prominent bishop acting as archchaplain of the palace chapel and adviser to the King. Charlemagne, indeed, even went to the extent of requesting a papal dispensation so that his chosen *cancellarius* and archchaplain, Archbishop Hildebold of Cologne, could be absent from his diocese for long periods in order to assist the King. The Carolingians located a new focus of power in the Mosan region and created new centres and royal residences, adding their own family lands to those they took over from the Merovingians as well as what they had won through conquest and confiscation. Their wealth was prodigious; they could also impose on the Church land for hospitality and renders of food and drink (*fodrum, gistum, et servitium regis*). The full extent of the royal demesne is not known, though estates and residences were scattered throughout the area under Frankish rule, from Paris to Regensburg, and Aachen to Rome. Any distinction we might wish to make between private land and that pertaining to the office of king is blurred and difficult to disentangle from the contemporary accounts of royal donations and alienations of property to monasteries, bishoprics, and lay magnates. Such accounts nevertheless make it clear that the role of king as giver of gifts, favours, patronage, and offices was a marked feature of Carolingian rule.

A number of important differences between Merovingian and Carolingian kings and kingship can be observed. The imperial title added in 800, of course, introduced a conscious emulation of the Christian Roman emperors of the fourth century, even if its strength was in its evocation of the past and enhancement of prestige rather than in any practical augmentation of the Carolingians' position. There was the introduction of new names, such as Pippin, Charles, and Carloman, into the customary royal names, though it is also significant that ancient Merovingian names such as Clovis and Chlothar

(*Chlodovechus, Chlotarius*) were preserved in slightly modernized forms as Louis and Lother (*Hludowicus, Lotharius*). There was also a change in sacral attributes, in that the Carolingians abandoned the long hair of the Merovingian kings and appear to have deliberately substituted anointing at the hands of a bishop. There was thus now a specific role for the Church in king-making. As a parallel development, and as indicated earlier, *consensus* on the part of the lay magnates was far greater an element of political stability and decision-making than hitherto. In documentary practice, the royal monogram was introduced as a symbol of royal authority on charters and then applied to the coinage as well. The type and range of legislation was dramatically innovative, as was the promotion of education and learning, and the patronage of scholarship. Further, under the Merovingians there had been no central royal control or even royal monopoly of the production of coins. It was the Carolingians who exerted central control of the mints; initial changes were made by Pippin III, and his son Charlemagne undertook important coinage reforms, transforming the conditions of production as well as the type of coin produced. Most of these changes were initiated by Pippin III, who in his turn built on the material and political base provided by his father Charles Martel and grandfather Pippin II.

In the practical achievements of their monarchy, the Carolingians contributed substantially to the creation of a monarchical tradition.[45] They were consciously emulated by the Saxon and Salian rulers of Germany and by the Capetian kings of France.[46] Their methods of government and their political ideals were direct continuations of those of Charlemagne and his successors.

But what of England? From the sixth century, there is evidence of close contact, assistance, rivalry, and even political interference between the various rulers of the separate kingdoms of Anglo-Saxon England. Certainly, in the eighth and ninth centuries, the power and the legend of Charlemagne had made themselves felt. Frankish episcopal legates had come to England in 786 and Charlemagne had a somewhat acrimonious exchange with Offa, King of Mercia.[47] The latter has been discussed by modern historians in a measure out of proportion to its (or Offa's) importance if only because it is one of the few direct pieces of evidence of political contacts across the Channel before the mid-ninth century.

The relevance of the European monarchical inheritance as far as the medieval English monarchy is concerned is to be acknowledged in a number of different, sometimes indirect, spheres. In the first place, of course, it sprang from similar intellectual roots, with an elaboration of theories of kingship after the Anglo-Saxons' conversion to Christianity on exactly the same Roman, biblical, and patristic bases as on the continent. It was coupled with similar traditions of war leadership and judicial responsibility, and formed by a process of conquest and settlement that we can no longer recover in any detail.[48] In the post-Conquest period, moreover, we should acknowledge the difference, as Graham Loud has emphasized below, the Conquest made to the Anglo-Norman monarchy in comparison to its continental contemporaries.[49]

One of the most important of the influences the Franks exerted on the English was in the range of royal involvement or interference in the affairs of the kingdom. It is remarkable, for example, how closely Offa's coinage reforms followed those of Charlemagne. News of Frankish ecclesiastical reform under the aegis of the ruler rapidly reached England and prompted concerted activity on the part of the English bishops and the Mercian ruler from the middle of the eighth century onwards.[50] In the creation of a royal image, Frankish example was no less potent, for Asser in writing his life of Alfred the Great was obviously influenced by Einhard's life of Charlemagne, just as Alfred himself may have been prompted in some of his thinking about his royal responsibilities as ruler by the portrait Einhard presented. Establishing the influence of Einhard is, frustratingly, by verbal echo only, for no other evidence survives of knowledge of the *Vita Karoli* in Anglo-Saxon England. The manuscript dissemination of Einhard's text was wide in the ninth and 10th centuries, and it is possible that a north Frankish manuscript of the *Vita Karoli* might have been made available to Asser or Alfred in some way through the connection with Grimbald of St Bertin. Nevertheless, no pre-Conquest copy of Einhard's *Vita Karoli* with an attested English origin or provenance is extant.[51] A further powerful influence exerted on Alfred's political thinking was the work of the sixth-century Italian philosopher, Boethius, whose *Consolation of Philosophy* Alfred himself translated into English.[52]

If continental ideas and examples played a role in the ideology of Anglo-Saxon kingship, it would not appear to be the case that there was any influence in matters of practical government in anything but the most general sense. Helen Cam long since offered many suggestions and rejected many possibilities for there being any specific instances of pre-Conquest influence of Frankish governmental practice on the Anglo-Saxon rulers of Wessex, despite the fragmentary evidence of constant contact between England and Francia between the eighth and 10th centuries.[53] It is arguably in the late ninth, the 10th, and the early 11th centuries that the English monarchical tradition became so firmly established, and of which the Normans were able to take such advantage after 1066. The Normans also, no doubt, brought with them elements of their own practice and assumptions about rulership which in their turn were influenced by those of the Carolingians. In this way, we may be able to posit indirect Frankish influence on England and the development of the English monarchy, though the extent of Frankish influence on the early development of the Normans before their arrival in England is itself disputed. Yver, for example, has argued that Norman institutions were based on Carolingian ones, and that there was marked continuity in the Normandy region with Frankish administrative structures.[54] An alternative view is that the Normans of the late 10th century revived contemporary Carolingian institutions which they observed in use by their Carolingian neighbours. There is, in fact, some indication of the survival of local administration from the ninth century onwards; Norman administration, though modified, was essentially Carolingian in its origins. If the Norman rulers had themselves inherited something of the Carolingian traditions of their French overlords, and if their own histories made an explicit connection between them and the Charlemagne portrayed in Einhard's *Vita Karoli,* they nevertheless appear to have learnt more from the sophisticated English practice of royal administration and government they encountered in their conquered territory than they brought with them from Normandy.[55]

In the creation of a European, no less than of an English monarchical inheritance, therefore, we have always to reckon with the interweaving and interdependence of ideal and reality, and thus the inspiration for later monarchs' actions as well as for their political ideologies that the historical and the idealized Charlemagne had provided.[56]

Footnotes to this Chapter may be found on pages 330–33.

2: Alfred P Smyth

The earliest kings: from Arthur to Alfred

THE Anglo-Saxons were a Germanic people who formed part of the *Völkerwanderung* or "Wanderings of People" – the barbarian invasions which helped to topple the Roman Empire in the West in the fourth and fifth centuries. As such, they shared a common heritage with their continental Frankish and other Germanic cousins. Rome's continental empire was firmly based on all sides of the Mediterranean basin, and as soon as that empire came under lasting threat from barbarian invaders,[1] the will to defend the province of Britain – with its Celtic sub-Roman population – was found to be conspicuously lacking. Not only was Britain an offshore island from the continental empire, but Rome only controlled a section of that island, with all of its wilder northern regions in the hands of barbarians, Picts and Scots, and with dissident Celtic tribes still surviving even in the more inaccessible mountainous regions within the Roman province itself. Already by the 380s, Rome had withdrawn its garrisons from the Pennines, while the entire Roman army was withdrawn altogether from Britain in about 407. In 409, the writer Zosimus reported that the Britons had expelled their Roman officials and were organizing their own defences against barbarian attack.[2]

That attack came from several different quarters – Picts and Scots from the north, Irish from the West, and a new Germanic menace from across the North Sea. Those Germanic peoples – the earliest English settlers – came into Kent, the Thames valley, East Anglia, the Wash, the Humber, and up along coastal Northumbria. Scattered communities were already in place from AD 400 onwards. A Gallic chronicler could record that by 441-2, the Saxons had taken over the provinces in Britain, although by then such invaders could scarcely have had any more than a foothold in the eastern lowlands.[3] These English warriors and settlers were led by kings – or at least they were led by powerful and adventurous warriors who took upon themselves the role of kingship as they had experienced it in their Germanic homelands. The territories they took over were probably based either on the Roman *civitates* they had overrun, or on Celtic kingdoms which they found in place when they arrived. So the English kingdom of Kent was based on the Roman *civitas* of the Cantiaci based on Canterbury. Bede believed that the men of Kent and their kings, as well as the conquerors of the Isle of Wight, were Jutes, and since Bede's continental *Angli* had lain between the Saxons and the Jutes, he seems to suggest that the men of Kent had their origin in Jutland. The Kentish kingdom was different in some respects from other Anglo-Saxon groups, but however "Jutish" Bede believed it to have been, it also had a strong Frankish and Rhineland dimension in its archaeological culture and social organization. Bede identified the conquerors of the greater part of the south as Saxons – a Germanic people who were located not only in north-central Germany, but who occupied lands from Schleswig-Holstein across modern Holland. The Saxons who invaded Britain may have included a significant Frisian element. Hence, the sixth-century Byzantine historian, Procopius, informs us that in addition to the (Celtic) Britons, Britain was inhabited by Angles and Frisians.[4] While Bede saw the Saxons as the main group who conquered the south of post-Roman Britain, he labelled the northern English as *Angli,* or Angles, whose name is linked with the modern Angeln in Holstein. It is from the word *Angel* that the "English" or *Angel-cynn* take their name. Their territory became known as *Engla land* or "England" and their language – *Englisc* or "[Old] English" – was the parent tongue of that language which is now spoken and understood across the world.

Bede's distinction between Saxons and Angles is still useful. There is no doubt that the ethnic or tribal labels of West Saxons (Wessex), South Saxons (Sussex), East Saxons (Essex), and Middle Saxons (Middlesex) show the southern colonizers to have considered themselves as being predominantly Saxon.[5] On the other hand, Bede's distinction between Angles and Saxons was too rigid. English writers from the seventh and eighth centuries as well as neighbouring peoples such as Irish and Franks, together with the more distant papacy, all showed that English people could be referred to as either "Angles" or "Saxons" regardless of whether they hailed from north or south of the Humber or from north or south of the Thames.

In the early eighth century, when Anglo-Saxon historians and genealogists were trying to piece together the oral traditions of their people, Oisc was remembered as a supposed son of Hengest and founder of the Oiscingas dynasty of Kentish kings. Similarly, Wuffa was designated the first of the Wuffingas to rule East Anglia, Icel as the founder of the Mercian dynasty, while a relative latecomer, Cerdic, was supposed to have landed on the shores of Wessex in 495, where he founded the West Saxon royal line.[6] But Cerdic's name was Celtic (*Ceretic)* as were the names of his dimly remembered successors, Cædwalla and Ceawlin, suggesting that there was a strong native British in-mix present in the West Saxon royal house. It is not impossible that in certain circumstances, some post-Roman British rulers may have won acceptance as kings over invading English war-bands. The account in the Anglo-Saxon Chronicle of the initial landing of Cerdic and his son Cynric at *Cerdicesora* on the Wessex coast (perhaps near Totton at the head of Southampton Water) in 495 takes no account of archaeological evidence which shows early focal points of Saxon settlement based on the upper Thames valley as well as along the Icknield Way – suggesting entry points for Saxon migrants from the Wash and from the East Anglian coast. It may be that Wessex began life from the initiatives of two separate groups of invaders – one which settled first in the Dorchester-on-Thames, Bensington, and Wallingford areas, and a second group which entered from the south and occupied the Winchester region. One of those groups may have been composed of a Saxon people called the *Gewisse* a people known to Bede in the early eighth century, but who by his time had been merged with the West Saxons proper. Founding kings, such as the West Saxon Cerdic or earlier heroes such as the Kentish Hengest and Horsa, may indeed have been dimly

remembered historical figures, or they may have been originally part of the
mythology of their people and were later assigned the roles of mortal men
and leaders of migrating bands. At all events, by the time St Augustine
arrived in Kent in 597, English kings were an integral part of the English
political and social landscape, leading their people in war and issuing laws
in consultation with their counsellors in times of peace.

Historical sources from the seventh and eighth centuries provide us with a
view of England ruled over by a series of provincial kings in Wessex, Sussex,
Essex, Kent, East Anglia, Mercia, and Northumbria – the Heptarchy of our
conventional history books. But Essex and Sussex lost their own independent
kings early on, and there were several other smaller kingdoms such as the
Hwicce (Warwickshire, Worcestershire, and Gloucestershire), the Middle
Angles (East Midlands) and the men of Lindsey – all of whom were soon
absorbed within the greater kingdom of the Mercians. So there were once
many more than seven kingdoms in Anglo-Saxon England, and within each
kingdom in turn, there may have been several rival dynasties.[7] Besides,
when the middle of the ninth century was reached, there were only four royal
houses left – Wessex, Mercia, East Anglia, and Northumbria. The notion of
a rigid Heptarchy of Anglo-Saxon kings was reinforced by Bede's list of
Bretwaldas or "Rulers of Britain" in the *Ecclesiastical History of the English
People* where Bede listed a series of overlords who exercised an *imperium*
over their fellow kings south of the Humber.[8] These seven rulers came,
according to Bede, from Sussex, Wessex, Kent, East Anglia, and Northumbria.
While he assigned three *Bretwaldas* to Northumbria, Bede did also grudgingly
accept that Æthelbald (716-57), who was King of Mercia in Bede's own time,
was also an overlord of the English south of the Humber. So when we include
Mercia in Bede's formal list of *Bretwaldas,* and with the exception of Essex,
we arrive at the traditional Heptarchy or seven kingdoms, however schematized
it may have been.

On the side of the native Britons, too, heroes who stemmed the tide of the
Anglo-Saxon onslaught were dimly remembered in later centuries and
fused together in the collective memory to produce a super-king, Arthur,
who protected the sub-Roman population from the invaders. Arthur began
life as an historical figure in *The History of the Britons* by the early ninth-
century Welsh historian, Nennius. There he is introduced as a "leader of
battles" where he is portrayed as a commander with authority perhaps over
several "kings of the Britons".[9] Nennius associated Arthur with a victory
over the English at Mount Badon. Arthur was remembered in the 10th
century Welsh Annals as having died in a battle at *Camlann,* dated perhaps
arbitrarily to AD 537.[10] Arthur's association with placenames and with
archaeological sites which have been located as far apart as Scotland and
South Cadbury in Somerset is suggestive of his unhistorical and "composite"
nature. For although the historical figure or figures which lie behind the
Arthur of Nennius seem to have a southern location, some battle sites point
to associations much further north. Two of Arthur's supposed "twelve battles"

may refer to Chester and to the Caledonian Forest, and Arthur's last battle at *Camlann* has been tentatively identified with Birdoswald, north of Hardians Wall. Geoffrey of Monmouth who wrote his *History of the Kings of Britain* in 1136, worked over legendary material which had accumulated around the figure of Arthur within Wales from the ninth century onwards, and it was Geoffrey who gave to the world the chivalric heroes of Arthurian romance.[11] Gildas, writing his *Ruin of Britain (De excidio Britanniae)* probably in the mid-sixth century, claims that a British ruler, "the proud tyrant", employed Anglo-Saxon or Germanic mercenaries in an attempt to keep other northern barbarians (Picts and Scots) out of Britain. This tyrant was later identified by Nennius with the British king, Vortigern, who supposedly handed over the island of Thanet to the earliest invaders. These newcomers were led by the brothers, Hengest and Horsa. Hengest supposedly sent his son, Octha, north to fight the Picts and settle on the Pictish border. These earliest English leaders later invited in more warriors from their homeland and then attacked and overran the British.[12] Gildas' "proud tyrant" (*superbus tyrannus)* could well be a Latin word-play, if not a translation, of *Vortigern* whose Celtic meaning is "Great or Superior Lord".

Gildas then goes on to describe the overthrow of urban civilization in Britain and the flight of the sub-Roman population either overseas or up into the hill country – "steep, menacing, and fortified". Gildas has no mention of Arthur. Instead, he tells us of Ambrosius Aurelianus, a British leader who was the "last" or "alone of the Romans" and who led the counter-offensive against the Anglo-Saxons in *circa* 500. Gildas implies in his description of Ambrosius' parents that they wore "the purple" and that Ambrosius may have been the descendant of one of the imperial usurpers in Britain at the end of the Roman period *circa* 407.[13] According to Gildas, Ambrosius won a victory over the Anglo-Saxons which was followed by a series of battles – with the victory sometimes going to one side, sometimes to the other – culminating in the "siege' (*obsessio)* of Mount Badon (*mons Badonicus)* which was a significant British victory. The defeat of the English at Mount Badon halted their advance and ushered in a prolonged era of peace. The place of this British victory has been variously identified as Badbury Hill Camp, an Iron Age Hillfort west of Faringdon (Berkshire), or as Liddington Castle (Wiltshire), another hillfort not far from the White Horse at Uffington. But other *Badbury* placenames – and even the less likely Bath – jostle for the historian's attention. Nennius ascribes the victory at Mount Badon to Arthur, and he lists that victory as the last of Arthur's 12 battles against English. Nennius introduces that battle roster by telling us that on the death of the English invader, Hengest, his son Ochta came down from the north of Britain to found the kingship of the men of Kent and as a result of the increase in the ranks of the English

> Arthur fought against them in those days, together with the kings of the British. But he was their leader in battle.

Already, however, even in the account of Nennius, it is clear that by the early eighth century, Arthur had become a folk hero whose name had acquired legendary associations with ancient monuments in the Welsh landscape. Geoffrey of Monmouth was later to synthesize and add to such legends. The world of Guinevere and Bedivere, and of the otherworld, Avalon, and the sword Excalibur, all belong to 12th-century fiction. By the time of Stukeley in the 18th century, antiquaries could point to South Cadbury hillfort as the site of Arthur's Camelot, where local tradition claimed that King Arthur and his men rode forth on moonlight nights on horses shod with silver shoes.[14] But behind such tales and the gallery of heroic knights in a mythical landscape that provided a backdrop to them, lay a shadowy historical world of the fifth and sixth centuries when the Britons struggled on their own without Roman help to preserve their land and their Celtic civilization.

However obscure the careers of rulers such as Vortigern, Ambrosius Aurelianus, or Arthur may be, they remind us that the Anglo-Saxon advance from the east and south coast into the British interior was a slow process. Wansdyke, a remarkable earthwork built in the fifth or sixth century, was clearly designed to exclude an invader who was coming from the north and threatening British-held territory in south Wiltshire and Somerset. This impressive monument stretching from south of Hungerford almost to the Bristol Channel, suggests that native opposition in the south to Saxons on the upper Thames was not only well organized but was most probably in the hands of one overall commander of exceptional ability. As late as the early seventh century, an independent British kingdom of Elmet was still holding out in the region of Leeds; the British of Dumnonia still dominated what was later Devon and Somerset past the middle of the seventh century. A continuous band of Celtic kingdoms stretched from the Cornish peninsula through Wales and up through Lancashire and Cumbria to join up with the Northern British of Strathclyde and their Celtic cousins, the Gododdin in Lothian south of the Forth. We know from the Old Welsh poem *The Gododdin* that Britons from Lothian mounted an attack on English Catterick (North Riding) at the opening of the seventh century, while up to the time of King Æthelfrith (592-617) of Northumbria, the English of Bernicia were clinging on to their stronghold at Bamburgh more like a pirate host than confident settlers in a new kingdom.[15]

The common Germanic heritage of Anglo-Saxon kings and their aristocracies is nowhere more apparent than in the language of the earliest English settlers who came to Britain in the fifth and sixth centuries, and whose descendants in later times established Old English or Anglo-Saxon as the dominant language, in this island.[16] To this new people the indigenous Britons, with their strange Celtic language and culture, were *Wealh* or "foreigners" – hence "Welsh", and the word also meant, significantly, "a slave". We have only to look at the names of early Anglo-Saxon kings or their supposed ancestors to recognize at once their common culture with royal namesakes in continental Europe. The royal house of Essex claimed descent from the continental Saxon god, Saxneat, and the poet of the Old

English epic, *Beowulf,* not only celebrates the exploits of Scandinavian heroes from the migration age, but he makes a special point of highlighting the prowess of a king, Offa of Angeln in Holstein, who was known to the English audience of the poem as an ancestor of the English Angles and of King Offa of Mercia (757-96) in particular.[17] Or take, for instance, *Eormenric,* the name of the father of King Æthelberht, the first Christian ruler of Kent. Eormenric, who died about AD 580 shared the same name as Ermaneric that famous fourth-century King of the Goths whose deeds were immortalized by the historian, Ammianus Mercellinus, and by the sixth-century Jordanes. The first element *Eormen-* ("immense" or "universal") in the Kentish King Eormenric's name also appears in several of the names of his royal descendants and successors, and while in England that element was a characteristic of the Kentish dynasty, it does recur across the Channel among the Franks. So, too, the name *Sigeberht* ("Bright Victory"), borne by English kings of Essex and by others of East Anglia in the seventh century is also to be found among the Merovingian Frankish kings of the sixth and seventh centuries. The element *Æthel-* ("Noble") to be found in the names of Alfred the Great's father, brothers, and many descendants is cognate with the modern German word *adel* meaning "noble" and occurs in aristocratic personal names throughout the medieval continental Germanic world from Lombardy through Germany and France.

The names of King Alfred (871-99) and his royal brothers and kinsmen, tell us much, too, about the warrior nature of early English kingship and remind us that Anglo-Saxon rulers were warrior kings whose heroic and rural ways of life take us nearer to warrior societies among the Plains Indians of 19th-century America than they do to the advanced technological and urbanized societies of our own time. Alfred's grandfather was King Ecgberht of Wessex (802-39) whose name means "Glinting (Sword's) Edge", and his son in turn was King Æthelwulf ("Noble Wolf"), who fathered not only Alfred ("Elf's Counsel"), but also a series of older sons – all of whom ruled as kings either of Kent or of Wessex – Athelstan ("Noble Stone"), Æthelbald ("Noble Courageous One"), Æthelberht ("Noble Bright One"), and Æthelred ("Noble Counsel"). Alfred's own son, Edward, had a name meaning "Happy Guardian", who in turn had a son Edmund ("Happy Protection"), who was in his turn the father of the great 10th-century King Edgar ("Happy Spear"). Such Germanic elements as *-bald* in the name *Æthelbald* could be grouped in different combinations to give a form such as *Baldwin,* the name of several counts of Flanders from the ninth to the 12th centuries – as well as of several kings of the Crusading kingdom of Jerusalem – and meaning "Courageous Battle".

Early English kings were leaders of their warband, who claimed descent from the Germanic gods and who ruled through the support and unyielding loyalty of their great magnates. These kings led from the front, taking their place in the shield-wall and being seen to risk life and limb in defence of their people. It is said of the hero-king, Hrothgar, in *Beowulf:*

> That famous leader never failed to be in the van where the dead fell thickest[18]

and of King Alfred's grandsons, the 10th-century kings Athelstan and Edmund, we are told:

> It was natural to men of their lineage to defend their land, their treasure, and their homes, in frequent battle against every foe.[19]

In *Beowulf* yet again, we read of what a king's leading warriors expected of their lord:

> They counted on him as a help against misfortune, they hoped the prince would uphold the honour of his house and prosperously govern the people, [his] stronghold and [his] treasury.[20]

The earliest English kings had almost certainly a priestly function in their role as leaders of their people in war. So crucial was the magical presence of the king on the field of battle that the warriors of King Sigeberht of East Anglia refused to fight the Mercians without him, even though he had abdicated to become a monk. Sigeberht's warriors begged him "to go into the fight with them in order to inspire the army with confidence". When he refused

> they dragged him to the fight from the monastery, in the hope that the soldiers would be less afraid and less ready to flee if they had with them one who was their most vigorous and distinguished leader.[21]

It was not as though the East Angles lacked a king to lead them against the Mercians. They already had their new king, Ecgric. Nor is there any mention of Sigeberht's possible help as a monk. He was needed for his earlier kingly successes in battle. When the reluctant Sigeberht was dragged out of monastic retirement, he entered the fray carrying only a staff and, not surprisingly, he was cut down and slain by the foe.

The magnates of the king were pledged in their turn to support their lord to the death in war, and to help him to administer his territories in peace. These were the *thegns* ("thanes") or nobles of early England, the top echelons of whom included the *ealdormen* who ran the shires and the *witan* or "Wise Men" – who were the most senior magnates who advised the king in peace and war, and who elected his successor from among a wide selection of candidates in the royal kindred. Although early English kingship was hereditary – and indeed was viewed as a sacred office in pagan and Christian times – primogeniture was not practised before the ninth century and probably any *ætheling* ("a man of royal blood") whose great-grandfather or even more distant ancestor had been a king, was eligible for election. While the English king's power was immense, he could on occasion be deposed or assassinated by his own followers, as happened to the unfortunate King Æthelbald of Mercia in 757 and Oswulf his royal colleague in Northumbria two years later.

A more genteel way of retiring from the brutal obligations of warrior kingship was offered by retreat to a monastery or to set off on pilgrimage after injury in battle or in old age. So Æthelwulf, the father of Alfred the Great, and his son-in-law, Burgred of Mercia, both set off on their separate ways to Rome in the ninth century, while a succession of Mercian and Northumbrian kings withdrew to local monasteries. English kings may have been at their best in war, but even in those awkward times of peace they were surrounded by no small amount of pomp and ceremony. Bede describes King Edwin of Northumbria (617-33) progressing through his kingdom and being preceded along the road by a Roman-style standard-bearer.[22] King Alfred the Great describes a royal farm when the King is in residence and holding an assembly of his nobles:

> Some [of the King's men] come from afar and have a very long and very bad and very difficult road. Some have a very long and very direct and very good road. Some have a very short and yet hard and difficult and dirty one. Some have a short and smooth and good one. . . Some are in more honour and more ease than others. So, in every king's court [when his men arrive], some dwell in the inner chamber, some in the [the king's] hall, some on the threshing floor, some in prison.[23]

We get a fleeting glimpse of King Alfred himself from a legal document which shows him in informal mood in a similar *bur* or inner bed-chamber as that which the king described in the above passage. It was while he stood washing his hands in the royal inner chamber at his hall in Wardour in Wiltshire, that King Alfred gave a hurried audience to litigants in a lawsuit in about 890.[24]

Royal halls have been brought to light by archaeological excavation showing substantial wooden aisled buildings where kings entertained their warriors and great men, and where poems such as *Beowulf* were read aloud, praising the virtues and valour of the ruler and reminding him and his warriors of the heroic deeds of their ancestors. Feasting and gift-giving from king to right-hand-man were the order of the day. In *Beowulf* a fabulous hall of an idealized king is described:

> Orders were given for the decoration of the interior of Heorot, and a large number of men and women made the banqueting hall ready. Golden tapestries gleamed along the walls, and there were many wonderful objects to be seen by those with an eye for such things. . . Men of note took their seats on the benches and regaled themselves with the abundance set before them. Hrothgar and his valiant nephew Hrothulf toasted one another with bumpers of mead in the banqueting hall. Heorot was filled with friends.

> Hrothgar gave Beowulf an embroidered banner of gold, a helmet and a corselet, in reward for his victory. Multitudes saw the jewel-studded sword of honour presented to the hero. Beowulf drank a ceremonial cup in the banqueting hall for the gifts were so costly that in accepting

> them he need feel no shame before the fighting men. Few men have presented four such treasures of gold over a banqueting table with such good will.

The halls of real-life kings in the historical period may not have matched all the fantasies of *Beowulf,* but they were nonetheless impressive by the standards of those primitive times. What is probably the royal hall of Edwin of Northumbria (616-33) was uncovered at Yeavering by archaeological excavation in the 1950s, revealing a great building, some 80 feet long and 40 feet wide. The Yeavering complex is also thought to have included an open-air "grandstand" seating about 300 people and facing a podium. The two most important halls of the early Northumbrian kings, however, now lie under centuries of subsequent buildings – one at York, and the other high on the rock of Bamburgh facing out to Lindisfarne and looking over the North Sea. The powerful Offa, King of the Mercians, fortified his royal settlement at Tamworth in Staffordshire in the eighth century, but in the earliest period an English king's hall may have been a simple wooden structure located on a royal farm. Such farms dotted about the kingdom made up the royal estates which provided the king and his many retainers with food and shelter as they moved constantly through the countryside governing their people. A royal villa might consist of a farm and an enclosure (*tun)* around the king's dwelling, or it might have locked gates as at the West Saxon hall at Wimborne in Dorset. Alternatively, the king might reside in a strongly fortified *burh.* Royal estates acted as administrative centres for the king, where his taxes and food renders might be collected from the surrounding population and where he might hold his court during a visit to the region. It is no coincidence that when the Vikings overran England in the ninth century, they massed their armies around these royal centres.

The history of England and of its Anglo-Saxon kings begins with the earliest historical documents at our disposal and so we depend on those Roman missionaries who introduced written records into England in 597 for our first glimpse of English royalty. The magnate to whom we are then introduced is Æthelberht, King of Kent, who was also acknowledged as overlord or *Bretwalda* of the many other Anglo-Saxon kingdoms which went to make up England, the land inhabited by the *Angel cynn* – "The People of the English". King Æthelberht received Augustine, who arrived as head of an evangelizing Christian mission dispatched by Gregory the Great, one of the most remarkable popes in the whole of the Middle Ages. Their first meeting took place on the Isle of Thanet and we are told by the historian Bede that Æthelberht feared to enter the same house as Augustine, lest the power of the foreign magician might overcome that of the English King.[25] England was a pagan land in 597, and the principal reason for Augustine's landing on Thanet and his eventual setting up his infant bishopric at Canterbury (rather than at London) was because King Æthelberht was at that very time enjoying the vague and tenuous title of overlord or *Bretwalda* among his fellow kings. Another reason for Augustine's establishing his headquarters at Canterbury – which was seen then as a temporary operation even if it were destined to endure into the third millennium – was that Æthelberht, King of the men of Kent, was already married to a Christian princess, Bertha, daughter of the Frankish King, Charibert of Paris. So Æthelberht – perched out on the Kentish peninsula – already had close ties with his Christian continental neighbours, and English history began – as it continues today – with a strong European dimension in its politics. Despite his Christian connections, Æthelberht did not immediately abandon his pagan gods and plunge headlong into baptism. But he did allow Augustine to preach his novel message of salvation and he did eventually become a Christian. Meanwhile, in Essex, Æthelberht's nephew, King Sæberht – the son of Æthelberht's sister Ricula – was also persuaded to join the Christian club. Æthelberht under the influence of the new literacy of his Roman guests, issued the first written Law Code of any English king. Æthelberht's Code – like those of other English king's after him – shows a central concern for the protection of the king's person and makes provisions to discourage violence and wrongdoing either in the king's presence or on his estate or against those who enjoyed his protection. A later Kentish law code of the kings Hlothhere and Eadric dating to *circa* 680 reveals the inward-looking nature of early Anglo-Saxon society in so far as it discouraged the harbouring by Kentish men of

> a stranger, a trader or any other man who has come across the frontier, for three nights in his own home, and then supplies him with his food.[26]

Anyone who befriended such a stranger in that way became responsible for any misdeeds he might later commit. Æthelberht died in about 618 and was buried in St Augustine's Abbey (SS Peter and Paul) in Canterbury – a foundation of Augustine's where the site of his tomb may still be seen. He was succeeded by his son, Eadbald, who had resisted baptism and who in pagan fashion married his stepmother when he became king. Eadbald did eventually become a Christian, thereby salvaging the Roman mission, and his sister Æthelburh, who married Edwin of Northumbria, introduced a Christian mission under Paulinus to the Deiran kingdom based on distant York. When the York mission collapsed on the slaying of King Edwin in 633, Æthelburh was forced to flee back to Kent, but she felt obliged to send King Edwin's son and grandson further on overseas, to the notorious Merovingian King, Dagobert. Even Kent was not a safe place for Northumbrian refugees escaping the long arm of the new northern overlord, King Oswald. Paganism at the royal Kentish court may have taken longer to die than is often appreciated. It was not until the time of Eadbald's son, King Eorcenberht, that a royal decree was issued ordering the destruction of idols throughout the whole kingdom. In Essex also, there was a reversion to paganism under the sons of King Sæberht between 616 and 623.

When the earliest Anglo-Saxon kings did embrace Christianity, they did so with an intensity which for them turned the new religion into a veritable family business. The wives, sisters, and daughters of the earliest Christian kings of England founded monasteries which grew in reputation over later centuries and which acted not only as powerhouses of prayer, but as public manifestations of royal piety and royal power. Eanswyth, daughter of Eadbald, King of Kent and granddaughter of King Æthelberht, founded the earliest nunnery in England at Folkestone. Her brother, King Eorcenberht, married Seaxburh of East Anglia, who eventually went on to found Minster-on-Sheppey, where she retired as a nun on the death of her husband in 664. Seaxburh later succeeded her own sister, St Æthelthryth, as Abbess of Ely, and Seaxburh's daughter, Eormenhild, who was widow of Wulfhere, King of the Mercians, succeeded her mother as abbess of Minster-on-Sheppey. If royal women were remembered as saints, their warrior fathers and brothers managed to get on with the business of butchery and slaughter even against their own kindred. King Ecgberht of Kent (664-73), son of Eorcenberht, murdered two of his cousins at Eastry who were in danger of posing a challenge to his rule. Ecgberht took out fire insurance for the Christian afterlife by granting land to Eafa, sister of the murdered princes, who, in her turn, founded a monastery at Minster-in-Thanet. That same King Ecgberht was also the founder of Reculver Abbey, whose ruins as part of a Roman fort can still be seen crumbling into the North Sea, to the east of Herne Bay.

Travel in early medieval England was safer and quicker by water rather than by dry land, where roads and bridges were poorly maintained and where strangers might be set upon by brigands as soon as they left the relative safety of their own tribal territories. It is not surprising, then, to find that Kentish kings had many ties with neighbouring royal houses to the north, including distant Northumbria, which could be reached by sailing up the east coast of England. We learn from Bede that Æthelburh of Kent, the Queen of the northern *Bretwalda,* King Edwin, travelled by sea to Northumbria. Seaxburh, the daughter of Anna, King of the East Angles, was married to King Eorcenberht of Kent, and that marriage together with others between the Kentish and Essex royal houses were also facilitated by contact between these regions across the Thames estuary.

The Kentish overlordship which happened by chance to coincide with the introduction of Christianity was not to last for long. Bede tells us that already before the death of King Æthelberht of Kent, the overlordship of the English kings was passing into the hands of Rædwald, King of East Anglia. Rædwald became a major player in the power struggle between Northumbria and Mercia in the period from 600 to 625, befriending the young Edwin of Northumbria who had been forced into exile from his Deiran (York) kingdom. In 617, Rædwald defeated King Æthelfrith of Northumbria – that Bernician king who had driven Edwin into taking refuge at Rædwald's court. That victory, gained over the Northumbrians at the river Idle, meant that Rædwald had established himself as *Bretwalda.* He was already the leading king south of the Humber, and however powerful Edwin of Northumbria might become, he would always owe his succession as king to the crucial assistance of Rædwald. Ealdwulf of East Anglia who died in 713, remembered seeing as a boy, a temple established by King Rædwald in which there was a Christian and pagan altar. Rædwald had become a Christian while visiting Kent, but neither his Queen nor his magnates was enthusiastic about the new religion and entire kingdom of the East Angles reverted to paganism after his death in *circa* 625. The Sutton Hoo ship burial discovered near Rendlesham in Suffolk in 1939 – an important centre of East Anglian royal power – must be connected with the House of Rædwald, if it is not the actual tomb of Rædwald himself. This immense treasure surely constitutes a royal horde and even if it had belonged to a more locally-based chieftain than Rædwald or his heirs, Sutton Hoo provides ample evidence for the power and prestige of East Anglian rulers at *circa* 625. Far-flung trading and other cultural contacts between the kings of the East Angles and southern Sweden is indicated by the details of the great Sutton Hoo boat – almost 90 feet long and 14 feet wide amidships – and of the armour it contained – helmet, shield, and gold belt-buckle.[27] This southern Swedish element at Sutton Hoo is so strong as to prompt the notion that East Anglia's royal dynasty was founded by Swedish kings at the opening of the sixth century.

Beowulf's central hero was a king of the Geats who inhabited southern Sweden (but who were enemies of the Swedes proper) and he could scarcely have been immortalized through the patronage of English kings if some of their ancestors had not come from that world.[28] Not only does *Beowulf* deal with a Scandinavian theme, but its images bring the archaeological evidence from Sutton Hoo back to life, with its battle-harness and weapons of high status for its fallen king:

> Bloodstained corselets, iron helmets with golden boar-crests, and numbers of dead chieftains were plainly to be seen upon the pyre, for many notable men had fallen in battle. . .

> The huge flames swirled to the clouds. They roared before the grave-mound, while heads melted, wounds burst open, and blood spurted from gashes in the bodies. Fire, the greediest element, swallowed up the dead on both sides, and their glory perished.[29]

Mercifully for archaeologist and historian alike, cremation was not the rite followed at the Sutton Hoo obsequies. That treasure reveals more than just Germanic tribal connections across the North Sea. Thirty-seven Merovingian gold coins, dating as a hoard to *circa* 625 reveal that seventh-century Frankish contacts with England were not confined to the men of Kent and remind us that King Rædwald's son, Sigeberht, lived as an exile in Francia prior to his becoming king in about 630. When he did return to East Anglia, Sigeberht established the Burgundian Felix as Bishop of the East Angles and he also set up the Irish Christian missionary (and famous visionary), Fursa, in Burgh Castle in Suffolk. Three remarkable hanging bowls found in Sutton Hoo may well have an Irish connection. A great silver dish was made in distant Byzantium between 491 and 518, while two possible silver christening spoons inscribed with the names *Paulos* and *Saulos* may have been a baptismal gift to either Rædwald or his pious son. Here then was treasure – some old, some new – fit for an English king at a time when England's warlords were at the crossroads between Christianity and their ancient paganism. Sutton Hoo reminds us that even in the early seventh century, the English were still a pagan people who had only just abandoned their migratory past, and that to have been an English warrior aristocrat at this time must have embodied a strong awareness of the heroic Germanic world which had only just been left behind in Northern Europe. *Beowulf,* the greatest Old English epic, after all, is a tale not of Englishmen, but of swashbuckling Danish and "Southern Swedish" heroes. Yet that great tale which delighted audiences for centuries in royal halls across pre-Norman England, later became so neglected by modern and more insular Englishmen that we find a first mention of it only in 1705. It was not until 1815 that the first edition of this extraordinary poem was printed – not in England, but in Denmark, and by the Danish scholar, G J Thorkelin. An English translation at last emerged in 1837 – only a century before that great 1300-year-old ship burial was dug out of the Suffolk ground at Sutton Hoo.

In the historical period – from about 700 onwards – the Northumbrians are seen as a distinct and separate English people, who, as their name implies, lived "north of Humber". The Northumbrians likewise viewed their southern English cousins as "South Humbrians" – a name which failed to establish itself in later centuries. King Alfred the Great, writing in the 880s and 890s, described the Northumbrians of his day as a distant people about which he knew little.[30] It is clear, however, from Bede and other early writers that the Northumbrians were Angles and therefore part of the same confederacy of peoples as the East Angles and Mercians. Furthermore, the concept of "North" – as opposed to "South Humbrians" – may have replaced a more general earlier population label of "Humbrians" which referred to those Angles who colonized lands north and south of Humberside, and which would have included some Mercians as well as the men of Lindsey in Lincolnshire. It is possible, as Nennius vaguely suggests, that the earliest English settlers of eastern Northumbria were warriors invited north from East Anglia or even from Kent by British tribes such as the Votadini (or Gododdin) who were desperate for help against encroaching Picts and Scots pushing south across Lothian. Two warrior societies of early English settlers established themselves north of the Humber – one based on York (the kingdom of Deira) and the other much further north at Bamburgh Rock and on Lindisfarne (the kingdom of Bernicia). The earliest Bernician king about whom we know a good deal is Æthelfrith, who transformed the Northumbrian colony from its precarious status as a pirate warband into an over-kingdom controlling the whole of the north-eastern lowlands from the Humber to Edinburgh. Æthelfrith was probably the English king who smashed the power of the northern British Gododdin when they attacked Catterick in the early years of the seventh century. He followed through with a victory over the Welsh at Chester when he slaughtered unarmed British monks from Bangor who were praying for a Welsh victory. Bede, pious Christian that he claimed to be, could not contain his racial dislike of the Welsh when writing up that incident. He justified the actions of the pagan Æthelfrith on the grounds that the recalcitrant Welsh clergy deserved to be slaughtered because they refused to submit to the authority of St Augustine of Canterbury – head of an English mission. Æthelfrith also repulsed an invasion by the Scots King, Áedán Mac Gabhráin, probably at Dawston in Liddesdale in 603, when Áedán tried his fortune in seeking a slice of the kingdom of Gododdin which was then being dismembered by the English of Bernicia.

When Æthelfrith had pushed back his British and Scottish enemies, he set about uniting the two Northumbrian kingdoms of Deira and Bernicia, and in doing this he found Edwin, heir to the southern Deiran kingdom, in his way. Edwin was driven out by Æthelfrith in 604, and Æthelfrith then married Edwin's sister, Acha. Such marriages between conquering kings with women of defeated royal houses were powerfully symbolic of the claims to power made by new rulers. Edwin fled for protection to the court of Rædwald, King of East Anglia, and when Rædwald refused to be bribed by Æthelfrith into delivering up Edwin, Rædwald and Æthelfrith fought a battle on the east bank of the river Idle where Æthelfrith lost his life.

The death of Æthelfrith left the way open for Edwin to return to the kingship of Deira and to the overlordship of all the Northumbrians. It also meant that the family of the fallen Æthelfrith found themselves in imminent danger and were forced to flee north into the lands of the Picts. Edwin may have been a Northumbrian overlord, but his Anglian connections with the south were in no doubt. We have seen how he had lived as a fugitive at the East Anglian court, and in 625 he chose his Queen, Æthelburh, from among the daughters of King Æthelberht of Kent – that *Bretwalda* who had played host to St Augustine. That marriage was to have a dramatic effect on Edwin's pagan court, for Æthelburh was a Christian who introduced Bishop Paulinus, a member of St Augustine's mission, into the Northumbrian kingdom. Bede provides a celebrated account of how the pagan Edwin conferred with his *witan* or royal councillors in his hall to debate the pros and cons of the new religion. According to Bede, one of the magnates of King Edwin delivered this eloquent harangue which powerfully evokes the atmosphere in the hall of an Anglo-Saxon king:

> This is how the present life of man on earth, King, appears to me in comparison with that time which is unknown to us. You are sitting feasting with your ealdormen and thegns in winter time; the fire is burning on the hearth in the middle of the hall and all inside is warm, while outside the wintry storms of rain and snow are raging; and a sparrow flies swiftly through the hall. It enters in at one door and quickly flies out through the other. For the few moments it is inside, the storm and wintry tempest cannot touch it, but after the briefest moment of calm, it flits from your sight, out of the wintry storm and into it again. So this life of man appears but for a moment; what follows or indeed what went before, we know not at all. If this new doctrine

brings us more certain information, it seems right that we should accept it.[31]

For all Bede's fine imagery here, an alternative British tradition claimed that Edwin had been baptized at the court of the northern British king, Rhun son of Urien of Rheged (whose territory was based on Carlisle, the Eden Valley, and coastal Cumberland). Whenever Edwin became a Christian – whether during his years of fosterage or exile among the Britons, or whether at the hands of the Roman Paulinus, it is clear that the Roman mission from Kent initially made many converts at Edwin's court and among the people of Deira. Edwin built the earliest version of York Minster – in wood – and Paulinus became its first Bishop. Bede shows us Paulinus preaching at the royal palace at Yeavering for 36 days when he baptized crowds of converts in the nearby river Glen.

Edwin went on to conquer the British kingdom of Elmet (based on the Leeds region) and his war-machine made its presence felt among his enemies as far as Anglesey in north-west Wales. But Edwin's most dangerous enemies came from among the ranks of his own English nation. The family of the rival of Æthelfrith plotted against him in exile, and even distant enemies in Wessex could cause alarm. Cwichelm, King of the West Saxons, dispatched an assassin called Eomer to Edwin's court. This man arrived with a "short sword, double-edged and smeared with poison" to make sure the job was properly done. He presented himself at Edwin's hall, located "near the Derwent" on Easter Day, 626. As the assassin struck, one of Edwin's loyal thegns interposed his own body to receive the blow. The poisoned blade pierced the body of the thegn and lunged yet further to wound the king – though not fatally. Such was the loyalty expected by an English king from members of his warband who were sworn to defend him to the death. Edwin's luck finally ran out on Hatfield Chase on 12 October 633 when an alliance between Penda, King of English Mercia, and Cadwallon, the Welsh King of Gwynedd, slew him in battle. Now it was the turn of Edwin's royal house to take the road to exile. His Kentish Queen fled south with several royal offspring and in their company was Bishop Paulinus who now deserted his infant church.

After the overthrow of Æthelfrith in 617, his royal children, including his son and successor, Oswald, had fled into exile among the Scots. The Scots were a Celtic people who (unlike the Welsh) were of Gaelic or Irish descent. Their ancestors had moved out of north-east Ireland in the fifth century to found the kingdom of Dál Riata in what is now Argyll. The Scots of Dál Riata were led by an expansive warlike aristocracy which had made successful inroads into the northern regions of Roman Britain during the death throes of the Roman Empire and their ever-expanding colony in Argyll was rapidly built up at the expense of the older Pictish inhabitants. The destiny of Dál Riata, however, was transformed with the advent of Columba, an aristocratic holy man from the Irish mainland who arrived in Scotland in 563 and who founded a monastery on Iona – in the heart of Scots territory. Columba and his foundation at Iona gave cohesion and purpose not only to an infant Scottish church, but also to the ambitions of the warrior kings of Dál Riata.[32] Columba was personally associated with the kings of Dál Riata and he is said by his biographer, Adomnan, to have chosen and consecrated Áedán Mac Gabhráin – that enemy of King Æthelfrith of Bernicia – as King of Scots. This powerful Scots warlord campaigned from the Orkneys to the Isle of Man and was a major player in Irish as well as Pictish and Anglo-Saxon dynastic politics. After campaigning against the southern Picts or *Miathi* who occupied lands between Angus and the Mearns and south of the Forth to the Antonine Wall, the Scottish Áedán inevitably came into hostile contact with Æthelfrith of Northumbria. Áedán led a coalition of warriors from Ireland and Scotland against Æthelfrith's kingdom in 603. He was repulsed with heavy losses at *Degsastan* or Dawson, and after that defeat, the Scots did not renew their interest in Lothian until late at the 10th century.

It was among these old northern enemies of their own people, then, that the children of Æthelfrith sought refuge when their father was slain in 617. The royal fugitives included the future kings, Oswald, and his brothers, Eanfrith and Oswiu, together with their sister Æbbe. Their choice of exile was to have immense consequences for the history of the Northumbrians and their English kings. While living among the Scots, the children of King Æthelfrith were introduced to Christianity on Iona and when Oswald eventually established himself as overlord of the Northumbrians, he introduced a Christian mission into his kingdom led by the saintly Bishop Aidan, a monk from Iona. That moment came when the powerful Edwin was slain by Penda in 633. Eanfrith, first of Æthelfrith's sons, then seized the kingship of Bernicia, but he was slain within a year by the Welsh warlord, Cadwallon of Gwynedd. It was now Oswald's turn to attempt to restore the fortunes of his father's house by confronting Cadwallon at Heavenfield, near Hexham. Cadwallon was bent on exterminating the English colony in Northumbria. According to Adomnan, Oswald had a vision of Columba – who had died on Iona in 597 – in which he saw that saint enfolding the entire English war camp under his mantle on the eve of the fateful battle.[33] Next day, Oswald led his Northumbrians to glory. Cadwallon was slain and his army overthrown. This victory gave Oswald the kingship not only of Bernicia, but also of Deira – the southern kingdom centred on York – as well. Soon the influence of this King was being felt throughout the whole of England, where he was recognized (in later times by Adomnan and by Bede at least) as *Bretwalda*. Oswald took as his Queen, Cyneburh, daughter of King Cynegils of distant Wessex. Cynegils and his son and co-ruler Cwichelm were, like Oswald, the enemies of Edwin of Deira and of Penda, King of the Mercians. The West Saxon kings found a natural ally in Oswald, and it is an indication of Oswald's huge influence at this time that he was able to persuade Cynegils of Wessex to accept Christian baptism and become his godson. It was as a result of that conversion that Cynegils established Birinus as the first Bishop of the West Saxons at Dorchester-on-Thames in about 640. King Oswald's greatest contribution to English Christianity, however, was his invitation to Aidan from Iona to establish his bishopric and monastery at Lindisfarne – an island off the Northumbrian coast, which lay very close to Oswald's palace fortress at Bamburgh. It was from that mission station on Lindisfarne that Aidan and his followers set out to evangelize, first the Bernicians and later all of the Northumbrians and countless southern English peoples besides. Lindisfarne itself became a centre of piety, learning, and artistic achievement which became the envy of the Christian West. Those heroic early days of Aidan's mission are described by Bede, who tells us that King Oswald, because he had become proficient in the Irish language during his exile, would sometimes act as interpreter for Bishop Aidan as he preached to the pagan Northumbrian nobility.[34]

But Northumbria's enemies to the south had not gone away. The irascible Penda – still clinging to the paganism of his Old English gods – struck again in 642 when King Oswald fell in battle before Penda's host on the field at Oswestry. Earth from the spot where the Northumbrian hero-king had fallen was claimed to have cured an ailing horse and Oswald was hailed as a saint and martyr of the Northumbrian church. His mangled body was first buried in Bardney Abbey by his niece Osthryth. King Alfred's daughter, Æthelflæd, Lady or Queen of the Mercians, later removed Oswald's bones out of the track of the heathen Danes in 909 and placed them in the safety of St Oswald's at Gloucester. The head of the fallen English King was preserved at Lindisfarne where it eventually came to rest in the same coffin with the relics of St Cuthbert, one of Bishop Aidan's saintly successors in the bishopric of Lindisfarne. Because the bishopric of Lindisfarne was eventually moved to Durham in the 10th century, the relic of King Oswald's head is now interred in Durham cathedral. Oswald's death was a setback to Northumbrian overlordship, but within a year of the disaster at Oswestry, Oswald's brother Oswiu, who had shared the exile of the family in Scotland, now established himself in the kingship. Oswiu consolidated his hold over Northern England and tried to heal old wounds caused by an endless cycle of assassination and exile, by marrying Eanflæd, the daughter of Bernicia's inveterate enemy, King Edwin of Deira. This marriage alliance did not altogether solve the problem of Deiran separatism. Oswiu's experiments to hold the southern part of Northumbria in check by assigning them to under-kings were not successful. His first choice fell on Oswine, a kinsman of Oswiu's Deiran Queen, but that ended in the murder of Oswine by Oswiu in 651. Then Æthelwold, Oswiu's own nephew, was put into the kingship of Deira only to rebel against Oswiu in 655. Finally, Alhfrith rebelled against his father, Oswiu, during his time as under-king and disappears from the records after 664. The politics of Deira in many ways determined the events of Oswiu's eventful reign. Æthelwold's rebellion against Oswiu in 655 formed part of an alliance between Æthelwold and the notorious Penda of Mercia – always anxious to take advantage of Northumbrian disunity. But Oswiu and his son, Alhfrith, met the combined forces of Penda and the Deiran Æthelwold at *Winwæd* in 655. Penda was defeated and slain and his powerful Mercian war machine was routed. Oswiu by this victory had avenged the humiliation and death which Penda and the Mercians had inflicted on Oswald, and the Northumbrians under Oswiu were now the most powerful people of all the English.

But Deiran and Bernician separatism which would dog Northumbrian royal politics until the final collapse of that English kingdom before the Vikings in 866, reared its head yet again in Oswiu's reign – this time in the guise of a celebrated ecclesiastical dispute. On the death of King Edwin in 633, that Christian Roman mission which he had welcomed under the leadership of Paulinus all but collapsed. Paulinus and most of his followers abandoned their infant flock in the face of an onslaught by the victorious and pagan Penda, and only a deacon, James, remained in the Catterick region to serve the needs of the Christians who survived there. That crucial presence of a Roman missionary helped to keep mainstream Roman Christianity alive in the Northumbrian kingdom. In 642, King Oswiu married Eanflæd, the daughter of his old enemy Edwin, who had been brought up in her mother, Æthelburh's, Kentish homeland and who therefore also followed the Roman rite of Christian worship. Bede tells us how King Oswiu and his Queen, Eanflæd, celebrated Easter at different times because Oswiu, following the Celtic rite of Iona – into which he had been baptized in his youth – accepted a different reckoning for the date of Easter from that then laid down by Rome.[35] Other differences existed between Roman and Celtic ecclesiastical ways – such as in the form of tonsure for monks, the rite of consecration of bishops, rites of baptism, and disputes relating to the authority of bishops. The King and Queen of the Northumbrians might have gone on indefinitely celebrating Easter at different times and following their own preferred Christian practices, were it not that Oswiu's son, Alhfrith, who ruled as under-king of Deira from 655, began to support the Roman party which had survived under Deacon James at York. James was probably unlikely to have caused Oswiu difficulties over church matters, but the flames of dissent were fanned by Wilfrid, an ambitious cleric who followed Roman ways and who won the backing of Alhfrith, under-king of Deira. Oswiu now felt under pressure from the dissident sub-kingdom of Deira where political unrest had now spilled over into sensitive Church matters. A synod was convened at Whitby in 664 to decide whether the Northumbrians should follow the liturgy and discipline of Lindisfarne and Iona or abandon that Celtic route in favour of mainstream Roman orthodoxy. King Oswiu presided over the proceedings, and he was a devotee of the Celtic rite as was his kinswoman, Abbess Hild of Whitby who, although baptized by Paulinus, was greatly influenced by Aidan of Lindisfarne. Yet the decision went in favour of the Roman party. Clearly, Oswiu could not afford to back a provincial church – whose roots lay beyond his kingdom in distant Ireland – as against the prestige and political clout of Roman Christianity.[36]

Oswiu's own influence as *Bretwalda* was already waning by 664. Wulfhere, King of the Mercians, was establishing his overlordship of the English south of the Humber, and by the time of Oswiu's death in 670, although his dynasty would still preside over a great flowering of cultural achievement and political domination of the North, it was losing its grip on political affairs in southern England. Ironically, by accepting Roman forms of Christianity and by excluding the rites of his old Christian allies on Iona, Oswiu opened the door not only to Roman ways, but to the eventual dominance of Canterbury and its archbishop in the affairs of northern English Christianity. No one could have foreseen the consequences of that decision in the 660s, but three centuries later, the kings of Wessex would use the Church of Canterbury as an ally in their conquest of Northumbria and in the unification of all England under the descendants of King Alfred. But for now, all that happened was that Celtic clergy and their English followers were required to relinquish their posts unless they conformed to Roman ways of doing things in the Northumbrian church.

On the death of Oswiu, the Northumbrian kingship passed to his sons – first to the warrior – King Ecgfrith (670-85), and then to the scholarly Aldfrith (685-705). Ecgfrith began his reign by having to assert his supremacy against the Mercians. Ecgfrith had himself once been a hostage of the notorious Penda of Mercia when that ruler led his "thirty legions" against Northumbria in 655. Penda was slain then by the Northumbrians under Ecgfrith's father, Oswiu, at *Winwœd,* but Ecgfrith, remarkably, survived his Mercian captivity and eventually succeeded to the overlordship of Northumbria. When Ecgfrith became king, his younger brother, Ælfwine, served under him as King of Deira, Ecgfrith at first repulsed the Mercian threat, led by their King, Wulfhere, in 674, but five years later, the Mercians under a new king, Æthelred, routed Ecgfrith's army on the Trent and slew his brother, King Ælfwine. This defeat marked the end of Northumbrian dominance in the affairs of southern England. Neither Ecgfrith nor his warband could yet be written off, however, and from 679 onwards they concentrated on expanding into northern Britain at the expense of all their northern neighbours – the Britons of Rheged (north-west of the Pennines), the Scots and especially the Picts. The armies of Rheged were routed and their warriors driven into exile in Ireland, while Church lands of their Celtic monks were seized and handed over to Bishop Wilfrid's monastery at Ripon. Wilfrid had earlier benefited from the expulsion of Irish and Scots clergy from Lindisfarne by being granted a bishopric based on York. But Wilfrid quarrelled first with King Oswiu and later with his son, Ecgfrith. He encouraged Ecgfrith's first wife, Æthelthryth, to leave the King and become a nun at Coldingham in 672. This affair, together with the hostility between Wilfrid and Ecgfrith's second wife, Iurminburg, eventually led to Wilfrid's expulsion from Northumbria in 678.

In 684, Ecgfrith launched an expedition against coastal areas of eastern central Ireland – an attack condemned by Bede who described the Irish as a "harmless people who had always been most friendly to the English." The raid may have been in retaliation for harbouring the warriors of Rheged, or it may even have been directed against those Irish kings and their monasteries who were harbouring Ecgfrith's half-brother and potential rival – the future King Aldfrith. Almost certainly under Bishop Wilfrid's promptings, Ecgfrith began an offensive against the Southern Picts with whom he shared a border in Lothian. Sometime after 680, an English bishopric was established at Abercorn (West Lothian) with a view to extending Northumbrian Christianity and political and cultural domination among the Picts. Ecgfrith's hold over this borderland had been established as early as 672 when his armies carried out such a massacre of the Picts that, in the battle-route, the Northumbrians crossed two rivers dry-shod by treading on the corpses of their retreating enemies. Ecgfrith, however, had either never learnt of, or else failed to understand, the problems facing those Roman commanders who had tried to conquer the Picts. The Romans wisely – with a few notable exceptions – held back from any attempt to conquer or colonize the Pictish enemy in his own land. But in 685, King Ecgfrith went a glen too far. Leading his warriors ever further north towards Angus and the Mearns he was confronted by a Pictish army led by their King, Bruide Mac Bili, at Nechtanesmere. Ecgfrith lost his life, and his Northumbrian war machine which had dominated England throughout the seventh century, was virtually annihilated. The Picts pushed south again and regained their old territories around the Firth of Forth.

In the chaos which followed news of the death of Ecgfrith and the massacre of his warriors in the heart of Pictland, Ælfflæd, Abbess of Whitby, who was a daughter of King Oswiu, played an important role in bringing her half-brother, Aldfrith, to the kingship of Northumbria. In this, she was supported by Cuthbert of Lindisfarne, one of the holiest men in the whole of Anglo-Saxon England. Aldfrith was a son of Oswiu of Northumbria and an Irish princess of the leading Uí Néill dynasty which also supplied abbots to the monastery of Iona. During his time as a young man in Ireland, Aldfrith became an accomplished scholar studying under Adomnan – later a celebrated writer and abbot of Iona – as well as under the West Saxon, Aldhelm of Malmesbury, the leading scholar in southern England. Aldfrith inherited a badly bruised and much weakened Northumbrian realm from his warrior brother Ecgfrith, but Aldfrith's style of kingship had its own strengths. This king presided over a cultural flowering of English art and learning which was the envy of western Europe. It was during Aldfrith's reign that the great Northumbrian crosses at Bewcastle and Ruthwell were commissioned, while at this time too, Eadfrith, Bishop of Lindisfarne, commissioned the magnificent illuminated Lindisfarne Gospels (now housed in the British Library). Meanwhile, at Jarrow, Abbot Ceolfrith commissioned the *Codex Amiatinus* (now in Florence) which survives as the oldest complete text of the Latin Bible. In Jarrow, also at this time, the young Bede was receiving his grounding in Latin scholarship which would result in his becoming one of the greatest scholars in the Medieval West. Bede's celebrated *History of the English Church and People* provides – along with the Anglo-Saxon Chronicle – the main framework of Anglo-Saxon history. Bede's literary output was prodigious. In addition to his monumental *History* he also wrote two *Lives* of St Cuthbert; a History of the abbots of Monkwearmouth and Jarrow; numerous works on biblical scholarship and two works on the all-important business in the Middle Ages on the reckoning of time. Bede and later Alcuin of York (*circa* 796-804) may be said to represent the pinnacles of the Northumbrian golden age, which was launched on the world under the kingship and patronage of Aldfrith. That scholar-king befriended scholars and holy men and promoted learning throughout his life. He received a copy of Adomnan of Iona's book on the Holy Places of Palestine in return for releasing those Irish captives taken back to England in 684 by his belligerent brother, King Ecgfrith. He also received books from his former teacher, Aldhelm, and he made a gift of land to the monastery of Jarrow in return yet again for the present of a precious scholarly book. He chose as his Queen, Cuthburh, sister of King Ine of Wessex – a choice of partner which indicates the continued importance of Northumbria under Aldfrith's rule. Alcuin of York regarded this great English king as,

> a man from the earliest years of his life imbued with the love of sacred learning, a scholar with great powers of eloquence, of piercing intellect, a king and a teacher at the same time.'[37]

In an age when most of Europe was ruled by illiterate barbarian warlords, this was a fine epitaph for an English king from another English scholar who was himself a leading light at the court of the Emperor Charlemagne.

The earliest historical king who consolidated his hold over lesser English tribal territories stretching from the Welsh marches to the Wash and from the Humber to the Thames was Penda of Mercia. This ruler came to power in about 610 and although his career as king coincided with the first 40 or 50 years of Christianity among the English, he remained a pagan to the end. It was Penda who stood out against the supremacy of the Northumbrians and it may have been this king who first confined Northumbrian territory to the north of that Humber estuary which gave Northumbria its name. There is some evidence to suggest that Northumbrian rulers once ruled over lands in Lindsey, Lincolnshire, and their frontier with the Mercians then ran along the river Idle (between Nottinghamshire and South Yorkshire). As late as 829, it would seem that the Northumbrian frontier came as far south as Dore, to the southwest of Sheffield. Penda was Northumbria's implacable foe and in his determination to destroy its overlordship he even allied himself with the hated "foreigner" (*wealh*) – Mercia's traditional Celtic enemies in Wales. It was with the help of Cadwallon, King of Gwynedd, that Penda succeeded in slaying King Edwin in 633, and his next victim was Oswald who fell before Penda and his Welsh allies at Oswestry in 642. Once during the time of Bishop Aidan's episcopacy on Lindisfarne (635-51), Penda's warriors penetrated the heart of the Northumbrian kingdom, setting fire to the royal citadel at Bamburgh. Penda did not have it all his own way in prosecuting his feud with the Northumbrian *Bretwaldas*. It is true that this pagan had slain two of their Christian kings and was instrumental in providing Northumbria with its saint and martyr, King Oswald, but Oswald had slain Penda's ally, Cadwallon, near Hexham in 634 and Oswiu finally slew Penda himself in the battle of the *Winwœd* in 655. Penda also pushed his frontiers south and west across Gloucestershire, Worcestershire, and parts of Warwickshire – the territory of the ancient Hwicce – which he wrested from the kings of Wessex in a battle at Cirencester. He put together a formidable alliance of the kings of East Anglia and dissident kings within Northumbrian Deira, and he placed his sons as sub-kings in older tribal territories within Mercia. His son Merewahl ruled over parts of Hereford and Shropshire, while another son, Peada, was king of the Middle Angles. Although Penda remained a pagan all his life, his sons and successors were all Christian and several of his daughters became nuns. Christianity eventually came to the Mercians through the influence of Peada, who received baptism at Wallbottle from the hands of Bishop Finan of Lindisfarne. Peada, with his father Penda's assent, introduced Bishop Cedd from Northumbria into his kingdom to evangelize the Middle Angles. Penda's reign conformed to the heroic ideals expected of an Old English king – to be leader of his warband, to expand his frontiers, enrich his loyal followers, and finally to fall in the heat of battle. It was this king who laid the foundations for his descendants and successors to give direction and firm rule to the heartlands of England.

Penda's successors eventually ousted Northumbria from the overlordship of the English and the centre of gravity of English political and cultural power moved slowly southwards from Northumbria, away from Irish and Scots influence, and towards the far south of England and continental Francia. Mercia languished for three years under Northumbrian domination after Penda's defeat at *Winwœd,* but Penda's son and successor, Wulfhere, rallied his kingdom and went on to become over-king of Essex, thereby extending Mercian control south-eastwards to embrace the lucrative town of London. Wulfhere also dominated Surrey and Sussex and much of Wessex, conquering the Isle of Wight. His marriage to the daughter of the king of Kent was an early indication of Mercia's ambition to reach the English Channel and control the lucrative trade across the Straits of Dover. But that was still some time in the future. Wulfhere finally made a move to avenge the defeat and death of his father by invading Northumbria in 674. That expedition ended in disaster and Wulfhere died in the following year. His brother, Æthelred, succeeded as king of the Mercians in 675 and it was this king who finally ended Northumbrian supremacy among English kings with his victory over Ecgfrith of Northumbria in the battle of the Trent. Although married to Ecgfrith's sister, Osthryth, the enmity between Mercia and Northumbria continued unabated with the slaying of Ecgfrith's brother, Ælfwine on the Trent in 679 and with the murder of Queen Osthryth by Mercian nobles in 697. Things were worsened by Æthelred's harbouring of the troublesome Northumbrian bishop, Wilfrid, who fled into Mercia during the kingship of Aldfrith of Northumbria, in about 700.

The once pagan Mercian rulers now became conspicuous for resigning their warrior kingships in favour of the cloister in old age. So Æthelred retired to Bardney in 704, a monastery he had founded with his wife; and his nephew and successor, Coenred, set off to Rome to become a monk in 709. The moral tone of the Mercian court took a serious turn for the worse, however, with the advent of Æthelred's son, Ceolred, and his successor Æthelbald (716-57). Both rulers were regarded by St Boniface as notorious fornicators. Ceolred was said to have gone suddenly mad during a drinking bout, and Æthelbald was accused of fornicating with nuns. Whether a fornicator or not, King Æthelbald took Mercia to new heights of greatness. He is styled in one of his charters as "king not only of the Mercians but also of all the provinces which are called by the general name 'South English'". He also, on occasion, sported the title of "King of Britain" and even if his authority were unknown as well as nonexistent in Scotland, he may have extracted tribute from neighbouring Welsh kings. The Northumbrian Bede, because of his dislike of the age-old Mercian enemy, could never bring himself to include Æthelbald in his list of *Bretwaldas,* but he did concede that in 731, Æthelbald of Mercia was overlord of all the southern English. Æthelbald was set upon and slain by his own warband at Seckington in 757 and his body was buried at Repton, a royal monastery of the Mercian dynasty associated with the holy man and hermit, Guthlac. Not only was St Guthlac a kinsman of King Æthelbald, but this seducer of virgins was in turn a great promoter of the cult of St Guthlac.

Æthelbald's successor, the mighty Offa, brought Mercian power to its greatest heights in the second half of the eighth century. Offa had to fight his way to the kingship in the crisis which followed the assassination of Æthelbald in 757. Offa built up the Mercian war machine and continued the policy of his predecessors in pushing south-east towards London and Kent in a bid to secure cross-Channel and overseas trade for the magnates of middle England. It was Offa who brought about the collapse of the embattled Kentish dynasty, now reduced from their days of greatness in the time of King Æthelberht and St Augustine, to the level of petty tribal kings. Offa had conquered the men of Kent by 764 and the numerous coins of the Mercian overlord which have been discovered near the busy Anglo-Saxon port of Sandwich testify to the economic dimension which drove the Kentish conquest. But local feeling in Kent was deeply rooted, and the location of the successor of St Augustine – the archbishop of all the English – in his metropolitan see at Canterbury, lent political clout to a region which was otherwise in decline. Kent was also a difficult territory for a Midland king to annex – surrounded as it was on three sides by sea and separated from its northern neighbours by the Thames estuary and from the west by the impassable forest of the Weald. The men of Kent rose up against their Mercian oppressors in 776 and from their victory then at the battle of Otford (north of Sevenoaks) until 785, they managed to regain their independence. Even when Offa seized control in Kent again, he was still opposed by Archbishop Jænberht of Canterbury.

It was then that Offa demonstrated his ability to negotiate with the world powers of his day in a way in which no other Old English king had ever done – not even Alfred the Great a century later. Offa persuaded Pope Hadrian

I to elevate the Mercian see of Lichfield to the status of an archbishopric in 787. He sidelined the power of Canterbury at a stroke and when Hygeberht, the new archbishop of Lichfield, anointed Offa's son Ecgfrith, king in the same year, it was an action which must have been seen as a studied slight to the power of Canterbury. The idea of royal anointing, or consecration of a king by the English archbishop was new to Anglo-Saxon England. The earliest English kings, like their Germanic cousins, were elected by their leading warriors and inaugurated or "made" kings by ancient pagan rituals such as shield-raising – being raised aloft on a shield in front of their whole army. Other more unsavoury pagan fertility rituals associated with continental kingship involved copulation with a mare which was then sacrificed and eaten. Whatever pagan practices had existed in England would have been outlawed by Christian clerics in the seventh century. New ecclesiastical rituals for the making of English kings almost certainly reached King Offa's court from the contemporary Carolingian world, where Charlemagne, and his father Pippin before him, had benefited from ecclesiastical consecration. It is just possible, but less likely, that the Mercians borrowed the idea of hallowing their kings from the Scots and Irish where ecclesiastical anointing was long established. From the eighth century onwards, however, English kings were no longer ruling with a mandate from their pagan ancestor gods, but instead ruled by the grace of the Christian Almighty. So King Alfred the Great began his more solemn decrees with the phrase: "I, Alfred, king by the grace of God. . ." – that phrase *gratia Dei rex* surviving in British royal titles to this day. It is not known when crowns first came to be worn on English royal heads, but Offa is clearly portrayed on his coins wearing a fillet or diadem signifying his royal status. By the time of King Edgar's (great-grandson of Alfred) coronation at Bath in 973, crownings of English kings, together with elaborate coronation ceremonies, had become the order of the day. The splendid portrayal of the crowning of King Harold in Westminster Abbey in the Bayeux Tapestry shows how impressed men of William the Conqueror's generation were with Anglo-Saxon coronation rites.

Even though Lichfield was returned by the papacy to its original position in 803, Offa's success in persuading the papacy to elevate its status in 787 was a remarkable coup. The papacy was in effect altering a pattern which had been established some two centuries before, and it was never an institution known for its flexibility in tinkering with long-established procedures. Yet another sign of the respect in which Offa was held by the papacy was the fact that the papal legates, George of Ostia and Theophylact of Todi, were sent to his court in 786, and the Church council which they convened was held in Offa's kingdom and not at Canterbury. Offa was remarkable for his ability to be taken seriously by Charlemagne, King of the Franks and future Emperor of the Christian West. The two rulers corresponded on a range of matters and negotiated a trade agreement in 796. Even more remarkably, a marriage alliance between Charlemagne's daughter and Offa's son was discussed. The marriage never came off, probably because of the unstable and violent nature of Offa's rule which were well known at Charlemagne's court because of the presence there of the shrewd Northumbrian scholar, Alcuin. Yet never before or since in pre-Conquest England had such a prestigious marriage alliance been mooted. Offa's reform of the coinage on Carolingian lines is also an indication of the ability of this king to see beyond the tribal horizons of his Mercian kingdom. He gave England the first issue of silver pennies which lasted in its essentials until the 13th century. Offa's coinage ranks among the finest in early medieval Europe.[38] His mint at London supplied a need for coin in a thriving port, while that at Canterbury answered the needs of a region close to Frankish trade. Offa or one of his immediate predecessors was most probably responsible for *The Tribal Hidage,* a survey of territories required to yield tribute (assessed in hides) to the Mercian king. The hide was a unit of taxation and was reckoned as the amount of land required to sustain one peasant household. It varied from about 40 to 120 acres depending on the quality of the land. *The Tribal Hidage* sheds a flood of light on the smaller tribal or territorial units which existed within Mercia, and whose names and relative size would have remained otherwise unknown to us. Offa's Dyke, if it were constructed by that ruler, would testify to his power and ability to carry out such a colossal work, involving as it did the employment of thousands of labourers over many years. The dyke is found sporadically along a frontier with the Welsh for almost 150 miles. It is the largest archaeological monument of its kind in medieval Europe and is longer than the total distance involved in the Hadrianic and Antonine Walls in northern Britain.[39]

Offa aspired to the title of "King of the English", and of all kings before the time of Athelstan in the 10th century – including Alfred – Offa is the one outstanding figure who dominated early English politics. This conqueror of Kent was also overlord of Sussex and Essex, and his protégé, Beorhtric of Wessex, who came to power in 786 was married to Offa's daughter, Eadburh. Offa has been overshadowed for too long by his image as a ruthless warrior, whose hand was raised against all neighbouring kings. That in part at least is due to the paucity of the sources which survive for his reign – and to sources too often compiled by his enemies. Because Bede was a Northumbrian, his detailed account of Northumbrian overlords can obscure the fact that Offa was a king of equal if not greater stature than, say, Oswald or Oswiu. Offa may have been no less a patron of the arts than his Northumbrian counterparts. In later times (in the 880s) when King Alfred the Great sought scholars to help him with his ambitious writing programme, he was forced to seek help outside his own Wessex kingdom and invite in scholars from Mercia. That would suggest that Mercia had a long-standing tradition in learning which is likely to have gone back to Offa's time. It is likely, too, that the Old English epic, *Beowulf,* was written down in Mercia during Offa's reign. There is a significant digression in the poem inserted after the narration of Beowulf's triumph over the monster in the lake and immediately before the hero's return to the hall of Hygelac, King of the Geats in southern Sweden. This irrelevant insertion into the poem tells a tale in summary of a difficult and evil princess, Thryth, who became a reformed woman renowned for her goodness, after her marriage to another Offa, a fourth-century king of Angeln. Not only is this Offa from the Germanic past described as

> a notable solder [who] ruled his native land wisely and was famous for his victories and generosity[40]

but that same Offa turns up in the English royal genealogies as an ancestor of his namesake, the eighth-century king of Mercia.

The early history of Wessex will never be properly pieced together, largely because when Alfred the Great consolidated his hold over that kingdom in the 880s, either he or his clerks set out to rewrite the history of their people to their own liking. An immediate consequence of that rewrite was to weld together diverse traditions relating to the origins of Wessex and to present it to the world as a continuous annalistic and genealogical record beginning with the founding father, Cerdic, and ending with Alfred himself. As part of that process, a collection of early kings who may originally have belonged to quite separate Saxon dynasties – such as the Gewisse and the West Saxons proper – were presented in a direct line of succession from father to son. In that process two quite distinct rulers of the same name were sometimes fused into one individual. Because not even King Alfred's persuasive powers enabled him to claim direct descent from the famous West Saxon King Ine (688-726), Alfred had himself traced back in a direct line to Ine's supposed brother, Ingild. But Alfred's dynasty in truth can scarcely be traced with much certainty beyond the time of his grandfather, King Ecgberht (802-39).

The first king of the West Saxons for whom there is contemporary historical documentation is Cynegils who ruled from 611 to 643 and who supposedly shared the kingship with his son, Cwichelm. But there may have been as many as three kings by the name of Cwichelm in Wessex during this era and it would be hazardous to try to disentangle their poorly understood identities. These rulers had to contend with hostility from the expanding kingdom of Penda of Mercia and even from more distant Northumbria, whose king, Edwin, one of the Cwichelms tried to assassinate in about 625. When Edwin took his revenge on the West Saxons in 626, he slew no fewer than five kings who were then ruling among them – kings about whom the Alfredian Chronicle is otherwise silent. When the powerful Oswald regained his position within Northumbria in 634, things took a turn for the better for the West Saxons. Oswald married Cyneburh, the daughter of Cynegils of Wessex, and as part of the deal, the West Saxon king agreed to baptism and he also founded the first bishopric in Wessex at Dorcester-on-Thames *circa* 640. Cynegils was succeeded by his son, Cenwealh, in 643 who at first refused to become a Christian and who also fell out with his wife who was a sister of the notorious Penda of Mercia. This marital upset resulted in Cenwealh having to spend three years in exile at the court of Anna, King of the East Angles, where he did eventually accept Christianity. On returning to Wessex in 648, he quarrelled with the Frankish bishop who then ruled from Dorchester-on-Thames because the English king, who understood only Old English, grew weary of the foreign bishop's "barbarous speech". So Cenwealh divided the only existing West Saxon diocese and established an Englishman, Wine, as first bishop of Winchester. Bede's naive explanation for the origin of the bishopric of Winchester[41] and the curtailment of the jurisdiction of the earlier bishopric at Dorchester-on-Thames may conceal a tale of deeper dynastic and tribal divisions within the kingdom of greater Wessex. The Dorchester bishopric had been established within the heartland of that upper Thames region where archaeological evidence points to the earliest Saxon settlement established by colonists who had entered England from the Wash, and along the Icknield Way. That colony would seem to have been originally independent of another large Saxon enclave based on Hampshire and Wiltshire, whose origin legends took their founding fathers into England at Southampton Water. It was to cater for the needs of this southern section of the West Saxons – be they Gewisse or otherwise – that Wine was established as bishop of Winchester in about 660. Winchester would grow in importance as the centre of King Alfred's kingdom, becoming ever more important in the reign of his grandson Athelstan (924-39) and regarded as the capital of England by the reign of Cnut (1016-35).[42]

Cenwealh's West Saxon warriors pushed south and west against the British kingdom of Dumnonia which was forced to yield up Somerset to West Saxon control after Cenwealh's victory at Posbury in 661. Unusually in an early medieval society, Cenwealh's queen, Seaxburh ruled in her own right over Wessex for a whole year after her husband's death in 672. According to Bede, the West Saxon kingdom was divided among sub-kings at this time, which suggests that Cenwealh had managed to exert a temporary overlordship over the whole of Wessex during his reign, but that several tribal kings still survived within the local regions. This diversity of tribal kings in Wessex continued down to the time of Ine if not for longer, and the chronology of West Saxon history cannot be taken as accurate until we reach the end of the seventh century. Centwine, the brother of Cenwealh, eventually took the kingship of the West Saxons in 676, and continued his brother's push against the Britons, conquering parts of Devon and putting the Britons "to flight as far as the sea" in 682.[43] Meanwhile, as the West Saxons pushed westwards, their dangerous and powerful Mercian neighbours to the north were pushing south against Wessex so that the earliest West Saxon see at Dorchester-on-Thames became engulfed within the Mercian kingdom. Cædwalla who became king of the West Saxons in 685 devoted his energies to expanding West Saxon power eastwards into Sussex and Kent. He overran the Isle of Wight and destroyed its traditional line of kings, giving half the island to the restless Bishop Wilfrid during one of that prelate's enforced exiles from Northumbria. Wilfrid was also capable of doing business earlier with Æthelwalh, King of Sussex, who was slain by Cædwalla of Wessex in 685. Cædwalla also forced his way into Kent, but the Kentishmen retaliated by burning to death his brother Mul in 687. After being seriously injured while harrying the Isle of Wight (or perhaps because of some illness), this warlord's days were numbered and he set off for Rome where he was baptized on Easter Day 689, with no less a dignitary than Pope Sergius I acting as his godfather. What is remarkable is that this powerful English king, who virtually founded the greater kingdom of Wessex, had remained a pagan until so late into the seventh century.

Cædwalla was succeeded in the West Saxon kingship in 688 by Ine, famous for his earliest West Saxon law code and for his continued campaigns against the Britons of Dumnonia who were defended by their King, Geraint. Ine's fortress at Taunton may suggest that part of Somerset was still near the front line with the Cornishmen or "West Welsh", although the fact that this fortress was demolished by Ine's Queen, Æthelburh, may also point to serious strife within the royal family itself. Ine's rule was challenged by rival royal factions at the end of his reign. He followed in the footsteps of Cædwalla in 726 when he resigned his kingship and headed off on the Rome pilgrimage where he died. Meanwhile, the Mercians, now ruled by Æthelbald, one of their greatest warrior kings, were bent on pushing south to the English Channel. That push was not directed exclusively at their newly acquired hold over London and ambitions further afield in Kent. As Æthebald of Mercia gained in strength, he overran all of Berkshire and even succeeded as overlord in annexing Wiltshire to the Mercian kingdom. The very heartland of Wessex was now at risk, and the West Saxon dynasty was in danger of total collapse as had happened to dynasties which had ruled smaller territories such as Sussex, the Isle of Wight, and (soon after this) Kent. It was not until the assassination of Æthelbald in 757 that a clear picture emerges of the West Saxon kingship in the 30 years after the death of Ine. When we do get a clearer picture, it has to be said that Cynewulf, who ruled Wessex from 757 until 786, did so under the shadow of the mighty Offa. Offa's victory over Cynewulf at Bensington in 779 was but part of a wider issue involving Mercian domination of the south. But we note that Offa's victory over the West Saxons at Bensington took place only a few miles south of Dorchester-on-Thames – in that erstwhile heartland of West Saxon power – and in a region which would remain disputed borderland for a long time to come. A detailed account of the assassination of Cynewulf of Wessex by his own kinsman Cyneheard is preserved in the Anglo-Saxon Chronicle. The deed[44] was done at *Merantun* (perhaps Martin, in south-west Hampshire) where the king was surprised while visiting his mistress at that fortified royal farmhouse. Wessex was plunged into even greater dependence on Mercia with the accession of Beorhtric to the kingship in 786. This ruler came to power with Offa's active support, and his marriage to Offa's daughter, Eadburh, consolidated that dependency. A later and doubtful legend in the *Life* of *King Alfred the Great* would remember Eadburh as a malicious queen who poisoned her husband and who ended her days penniless as an exile in Pavia.

The future of Wessex, however, lay not with the Mercian puppet, Beorhtric, but with Ecgberht, a rival magnate who claimed descent from Ingeld, the brother of Ine. Having failed in his bid for kingship against Beorhtric in 786, Ecgberht was forced into exile and spent three years at the court of

Charlemagne. His time at the Carolingian court may have coincided with those momentous days when Charlemagne was crowned emperor in Rome on Christmas Day 800. Ecgberht's experiences in Francia at this crucial time must have shaped his ambitions and his plan for the future of Wessex. He returned to Wessex on Beorhtric's death in 802 to find a very changed political situation. Offa had died in 796 and Ecgberht seized his opportunity in the political mayhem which followed on Offa's departure from the Mercian stage. For Ecgberht there were personal as well as tribal scores to settle. He had been forced into exile overseas because of Mercian backing for his former rival within Wessex, and in 825 Ecgberht defeated King Beornwulf of Mercia at *Ellendun* or Wroughton, near Swindon, where he finally brought Mercian supremacy over Wessex to an end. Ecgberht next moved against Kent and against the Mercian domination of that kingdom. Ecgberht's son, Æthelwulf – father of Alfred the Great – was dispatched as under-king to conquer the south-east for Wessex. Æthelwulf drove Baldred, the last of the Kentish kings, from his kingdom and annexed Surrey, Sussex, and – more remarkably – Essex, to his father's overkingdom. The final victory over Mercia came in 829 when Ecgberht's armies overran Mercia and Ecgberht qualified as the first West Saxon king to merit the title of *Bretwalda*. West Saxon power had reached its greatest limits in that year, when Ecgberht received the submission of the Northumbrians at Dore, near Sheffield.

In the midst of these successes, a new menace had appeared in Britain – pagan Northmen – bent on piracy and eventually on the colonization of the whole of England. Danish pirates descended on the exposed Isle of Sheppey, off the north Kent coast, in 835. Sheppey, with its famous royal minster, like Thanet and Lindisfarne, were offshore islands which hitherto gave protection to holy places venerated by England's Christian warrior aristocracy. For pagan Northmen, such royal sanctuaries appeared as shop windows crammed with the unprotected loot of centuries. King Ecgberht of Wessex may have been able to overcome his age-old Mercian enemies, but he was not quite so successful against Scandinavian raiders. He was defeated at Carhampton by 35 ships' crews in 836 and in 838 the Cornish Britons made common cause with the Northmen, but were defeated by Ecgberht at Hinston Down, north-west of Plymouth. Ecgberht, as well as tightening his hold over the shires and former kingdoms of the south-east, had also renewed the push against the Britons of Dumnonia, and it was this king who confined the Britons behind the boundary of modern Cornwall.

When Ecgberht of Wessex died in 839, leaving his kingdom in the hands of his experienced son, the former sub-king, Æthelwulf, the fortunes of Wessex had been transformed. The West Saxons now dominated the whole of the south of England. The men of Kent had finally been deprived of their own kings and had been annexed to Wessex, thereby opening up lucrative and safer ways of reaching Frankish trading ports. The annexation of Essex had secured both sides of the Thames estuary, although London was still in Mercian hands. The Cornishmen, if still holding out defiantly in the extreme west of their peninsula, were now most probably in a tributary position to Wessex. Mercia, although rallying under the rule of the tenacious Wiglaf, was never to regain its supremacy and would henceforth be forced to treat with Wessex on equal terms if not as a subordinate. Burgred, King of the Mercians (852-74), was married to Æthelswith, daughter of King Æthelwulf of Wessex and sister of Alfred the Great. The new alliance between erstwhile enemies in Mercia and Wessex now worked in favour of the West Saxons. In 853, for instance, Burgred sought Æthelwulf's help in a joint expedition against the Welsh and as the Viking fury gathered pace, Mercia was forced to move ever closer to the rising power of Wessex. It was also about this time in 853 that Berkshire was returned from Mercian to West Saxon control.

During the 850s, Viking inroads against England became ever more serious. The Mercians failed to repulse an assault on London in 851, while in 865 the entire country came under threat from an invading "Great Army of Danes" which first landed in East Anglia and then under treaty with the East Angles moved north against York. The leaders of this Scandinavian invasion were themselves kings of an ancient north Germanic line – remembered in later legend as the Sons of Ragnar Lodbrok, a notorious Danish sea-king.[45] Three royal brothers, Ivar, Halfdan, and a third brother, probably named Ubbe, were to transform English politics and redraw the map of England in the 13 years from 865 to 878. Their agenda was to destroy every native dynasty in England, before colonizing the Old English kingdoms with their own followers or their English clients. That they had singled England's kings out for personal attack is clear from the fate of so many of those rulers and from the Danish tactic of entering a kingdom and first seizing a royal estate before challenging the native rulers to pitched battle. The early successes of Ivar and Halfdan were indeed staggering. Three of the great Old English kingdoms which had stubbornly held out against each other for centuries were wiped off the map without any sustained resistance being offered to the invaders. When the Great Army of Danes arrived in York on the Feast of All Saints, 1 November 866, they found the Northumbrian kingdom locked into a civil war between two rival kings – no doubt a perpetuation of the age-old animosity between Bernicia and Deira. It was not until March before the rival Northumbrian kings were able to join forces against a formidable Danish foe whose army may have exceeded 5,000 men. The Northumbrians attacked York with disastrous results. Both the kings were slain in a massacre which occurred within the old Roman walls of the city and the kingdom that once dominated all England militarily, and dazzled the Christian West with its learning, now lay at the feet of a heathen invader. One of Northumbria's two rival kings, Ælle, was remembered in Norse poetry from about the year 1000 as having a bloody eagle carved on his back by Ivar who was nicknamed "the Boneless". Later sagas record how King Ælle's mangled body had its rib-cage torn apart and its lungs pulled out to evoke the spectre of a bloody eagle, offered to the Norse wargod, Odin, as a sacrifice for victory. Such lurid tales of pagan conquerors had replaced overnight Bede's narrative of that sparrow flying through the hall of the Christian Edwin. A Northumbrian golden age, underpinned by an army which once kept Scot and Pict as well as Mercians at bay, was now replaced by illiterate Scandinavian warlords who set the cultural clock back more than two centuries.

The Danes next moved south to Nottingham, where Burgred of Mercia, fearful of acting alone in the wake of the Northumbrian tragedy, summoned help from his two brothers-in-law in Wessex – King Æthelred I and his younger brother, Alfred the Great. But not even West Saxon help was sufficient to dislodge the Danes from Nottingham. Their next move after a brief return to York – where they had set up an English king of their own choosing – was to attack Edmund, King of the East Angles, who had so far been in a state of truce with the invaders. Edmund was captured in battle in November 869 and like Ælle, he too was dismembered,

> his ribs laid bare by numberless gashes, as if he had been put to the torture of the rack, or had been torn by savage claws

as well as being shot full of arrows "like a hedgehog".[46] Edmund was soon revered by his own people and even by his Scandinavian killers as a saint and martyr. But his East Anglian dynasty and kingdom – once ruled by heroic figures such as Rædwald and Anna, and which boasted the royal treasures of Sutton Hoo – was now no more. The Great Army of Danes next moved against Wessex, seizing the town of Reading on its northern border with Mercia. King Æthelred and his brother Alfred made the near-fatal mistake of trying to dislodge the invaders from Reading and were repulsed with heavy losses. Apart from one significant West Saxon victory over the Danes at Ashdown near the Ridge Way in Berkshire, the first phase of the Danish wars in Wessex ended badly for the West Saxons. King Æthelred had died a young man in 871 and Alfred unexpectedly found himself in the kingship of his people at a time of greatest crisis.[47] As Æthelwulf's youngest of five sons – all of whom preceded him in kingship – it was only chance which brought the youthful Alfred to the throne of Wessex. To make matters even worse, while Alfred was attending his brother's funeral at Wimborne in Dorset, news came of a second "Great Summer Army" of Danes which had joined those invaders already holed up at Reading.

Only a miracle could have saved Wessex and that miracle materialized in the form of a Northumbrian revolt against the invaders which induced the Great Army to withdraw temporarily from Reading and London in 871. After putting down the northern rebels in 873-4, Halfdan and his followers set about colonizing the old Northumbrian kingdom of Deira, while his fellow kings, together with a newcomer, Guthrum, moved south again to finish off Wessex and to challenge Alfred's brother-in-law who was still clinging on to Mercia by means of a tenuous peace agreement with the Danes. The Great Army took Repton in northern Mercia – that cult centre and base of royal power since the days of St Guthlac. The Danes, deposing Burgred, established Ceolwulf II from a rival Mercian line, as their puppet in his place. Burgred, mindful of the fate of his fellow kings, Ælle and of Edmund, fled along with his Queen, Æthelswith. They headed for Rome where Burgred ended his days. Æthelswith – who was the sister of King Alfred the Great – survived for another 14 years, dying an exile in Pavia in 888. The Mercian war machine – that pride of Penda, Æthelbald, and Offa, which had once overrun Northumbria, Wessex, and Kent – yielded to the overwhelming Danish threat without striking a single blow. Alfred alone of all the Old English kings still survived to mount resistance to the Danes. His kingdom of Wessex – shorn now of Essex and under attack on all fronts – was all that survived of the lands of an independent English people. The *Angel cynn* were now in serious danger of losing their English identity altogether in the face of this Danish onslaught.[48]

The Danes under King Guthrum returned to finish off Wessex by directing an attack by land and sea – first on Wareham in Dorset and then against Exeter. After several abortive peace treaties with Alfred, they suddenly attacked him from western Mercia as he spent Twelfth Night (6 January) 878 at Chippenham in north Wiltshire. Alfred mercifully escaped into the Somerset marshes where he changed his tactics from fighting pitched battles to attacking the Danes as a guerilla commander. The invaders were now masters of Wiltshire and in imminent danger of overrunning all Wessex and Kent. But Alfred surprised his enemy at Edington, some 12 miles south of Chippenham, and won a resounding victory over his tormentors. That victory and a subsequent siege of the whole Danish army resulted in the forced baptism of Guthrum and his pagan chiefs together with their withdrawal to East Anglia. Wessex had been saved, and Alfred alone of all the kings of the old Heptarchy survived to found a dynasty which would soon unite all England under its rule. Gone forever now were the great houses of Edwin, Oswald, Penda, and Offa who had jostled for supremacy and the vanity of that nebulous title of *Bretwalda*. From 878 onwards there were only two powers left in England – the House of Alfred the Great, and the Scandinavian kings of the *Danelaw* who ruled from York in the north and from the Five Boroughs of Lincoln, Leicester, Nottingham, Derby, and Stamford in the south. The Danes had achieved what other English kings had only dreamt of for centuries. Alfred, partly by default and partly out of sheer tenacity and his own personal courage, found himself in a position where he could present himself not only to West Saxons but to all English people, as the saviour of England.

Footnotes to this Chapter may be found on pages 333–36.

Diagrammatic pedigree charts of the many royal houses are found at pages 311–318.

3: Ann Williams

The West Saxon kings, 978–1066

THE DYNASTY which held power in the 10th and 11th centuries was one of the most remarkable ever to reign over the English. At the end of the ninth century, its founder, King Alfred, not only defended Wessex against the Vikings, but also laid the groundwork for his successors to bring all England under their control, creating a united kingdom of the English. This process is often described as a "reconquest", but the conquered lands had never before been under West Saxon control. At the same time, the rulers of Wessex were claiming lordship over the British princes of Wales and the north-west, and the Scottish kings. In the 11th century, the West Saxon kings were forced to defend their realm against repeated invasions from abroad. That they were ultimately unsuccessful does not detract from their achievement, for they bequeathed to their conquerors a kingdom more united and more firmly governed than any other in contemporary Europe.

The making of England, 878–973

Alfred's victory over Guthrum's "great summer army" at Edington in 878 is rightly regarded as a turning-point. Two years later, Guthrum and his men settled in East Anglia, which Guthrum ruled in his baptismal name of Athelstan until his death in 890. Though Viking raids and campaigns did not cease, Alfred was never again forced back into a purely defensive position; his victory gave him a breathing-space to reorganize his forces. A significant part was played in Alfred's campaigns by the burhs and their garrisons. The word *burh* is the ancestor of modern English "borough", but had no urban connotations in the 10th century; it means only "a fortified place", and could be used of defended manor houses as well as fortresses and walled towns. The idea of creating a series of fortified defensive centres was not new; in the early ninth century, the Mercian kings had ordered the construction of fortifications against the Vikings, and the destruction of similar strongpoints built by the Vikings themselves.[1] Alfred, however, was the first West Saxon ruler to use fortification on a large scale, and by the time of his death, Wessex was ringed by a series of strongpoints. The *Burghal Hidage,* which dates from Edward the Elder's reign (899-924), describes the basis on which the West Saxon *burhs* were maintained and manned from their dependent territories, and similar fortresses were built by the Mercian rulers.[2]

It was Alfred who took the first steps towards the annexation of the kingdom of Mercia, now partitioned between the English, who held the west midlands, and the Danes, who held the east. Ceolwulf II, who died in 878 or 879, was the last King of Mercia.[3] By 883, he had been succeeded by Æthelred, whom contemporary sources style ealdorman or (more frequently) "Lord of the Mercians". Æthelred married Æthelflæd, Alfred's first-born child, in or before 886, the year in which Alfred captured London from the Danes, and (according to the *Anglo-Saxon Chronicle)* "all the English people that were not under subjection to the Danes submitted to him". Alfred entrusted the formerly Mercian city to Æthelred, but it is from this time that he began to use the title "king of the Angles and Saxons". His law code, promulgated in the late 880s or early 890s, drew upon earlier Mercian and Kentish codes as well as the laws of Ine, and was clearly intended to express his authority over all the English, and his successor, Edward, was crowned as king of both peoples.[4] Alfred's recognition as king in Mercia may have been what encouraged the kings of south Wales to seek his protection; Asser presents them as "driven by the might and the tyrannical behaviour of Ealdorman Æthelred and the Mercians".[5]

In the warfare of the 890s, described in detail in the contemporary *Anglo-Saxon Chronicle,* the "English army" is shown defending a single realm, to the extent of suppressing the role of Æthelred, and even that of Alfred's own son Edward.[6] But Mercia was not yet a province of Wessex. The Mercian council *(witan)* was still separate from that of the West Saxons, and Æthelred issued charters in his own name, though usually acknowledging Alfred's consent.[7] Indeed, the late 10th-century chronicler Æthelweard (himself a descendant of the West Saxon royal house) calls Æthelred a king and Mercia his kingdom.[8]

When Alfred died on 26 October 899, the frontier between English and Danes was defined (roughly speaking) by the line of Watling Street. To the north was the Danish kingdom of York, and to the east that of East Anglia, while the lands of what had once been eastern Mercia (the north and east Midlands) were dominated by individual Scandinavian jarls (military commanders), supported by their warbands. Outside Wessex and western Mercia, the only English enclave to survive was the ancient kingdom of Bernicia, governed by a line of rulers established at Bamburgh.

It was Alfred's son, Edward the Elder, crowned on 8 June 900, who overran the Danish settlements of the east midlands. He had the full support of his sister, Æthelflæd, whose role grew in importance as her husband Æthelred became incapacitated by illness; after his death in 911, she ruled alone as Lady of the Mercians. The first step was to incapacitate the Danish kingdom of York and in 909 the territory of "the northern army" was harried by West Saxons and Mercians. The Danes of York retaliated the following year with a raid deep into Mercia, but were caught by the combined army of West Saxons and Mercians at Tettenhall, Staffs. The English force destroyed the Danish army and killed its leaders, including two kings.[9] The result was to cripple the York Danes, and allow the English rulers to begin operations against the southern settlements.

Edward directed his attack towards East Anglia and the east Midlands, while Æthelflæd concentrated on the north and north-east.[10] The means to hand were the *burhs,* which (like later castles) could be used to defend and control territory already won and to launch fresh attacks into the lands of the enemy. Many were "double boroughs", like that built at Hertford in 912, which included "the northern borough . . . between the Maran, the Beane and the Lea" and another "on the south side of the Lea". Their purpose was to control rivers navigable by Viking ships. The building of such fortifications was often sufficient in itself to bring about the capitulation of the local forces. In 914, for instance, "King Edward went to Buckingham with his army, and stayed there four weeks, and made both the boroughs, on each side of the river, before he went away", with the result that the local jarl, Thurcetel, submitted to Edward as did "all the *holds* and principal men who belonged to Bedford, and also many of those who belonged to Northampton".[11]

Æthelflæd's *burhs* are recorded in the *Mercian Register,* which probably emanates from a source close to her court.[12] Its record of the fortification of the ancient centre of the Mercian kings, Tamworth, in 913, sounds a note of especial pride:

> In this year, by the grace of God, Æthelflæd, Lady of the Mercians, went with all the Mercians to Tamworth, and built the borough there in the early summer.

It is clear that brother and sister were acting in concert: the military strongpoints on the eastern frontiers of Mercia helped to put pressure on the Danish army at Bedford and eventually secured its submission in 915, and, conversely, Edward's successful campaigns against the armies of Northampton and Leicester in 917 allowed Æthelflæd to take the Danish fortress at Derby.[13]

Æthelflæd's northern fortresses at Eddisbury (914) and Runcorn (915), both in Cheshire, were directed against the threat of Viking fleets operating in the Irish Sea. The killing of the Danish rulers of York at Tettenhall had opened up a power vacuum in southern Northumbria, soon filled by the grandsons of Ivar the Boneless, whom the Irish had expelled from Dublin in 902; indeed, Ragnall, the eldest, may have first established himself at York in the immediate aftermath of Tettenhall.[14] In 918, however, he was back in Ireland, reestablishing his family's kingdom of Dublin. Æthelflæd organized an alliance against him, which included the King of Scots, the rulers of Northumbria, and even some of the York Danes, who, in 918, promised "that they would be under her direction"; but soon afterwards, on 12 June, she died at Tamworth.[15] On hearing of her death, Edward immediately "occupied the borough of Tamworth, and all the nation of the Mercians which had been subject to Æthelflæd submitted to him".[16] In 919, as the *Mercian Register* bitterly records, Æthelred's daughter Ælfwynn "was deprived of all authority in Mercia and taken into Wessex, three weeks before Christmas". It is noticeable that the main text of the *Anglo-Saxon Chronicle* has nothing to say of the Mercians' role in the subjugation of the Danish settlements; all the glory is attributed to Edward the Elder.

In 919, Ragnall returned from Ireland to seize York, leaving his brother Sigtrygg *Caech* ("the squinty") in control of Dublin. Edward strengthened the defences of north Mercia and in 920 moved into the Peak District and fortified Bakewell. At this point, according to the *Anglo-Saxon Chronicle,* he received the submission of the Scots King (Constantine II), Ragnall himself, Ealdred, Lord of Bamburgh, and his brother Uhtred, and the King of the Strathclyde Britons (Donald, Constantine II's brother). Ealdred of Bamburgh may already have been an adherent of Edward, but it is unlikely that either Ragnall or Constantine II saw themselves as dependants of the West Saxon King, and their "submission" was probably more in the nature of a mutual definition of spheres of influence.[17]

Ragnall of York died before the end of 920 and was succeeded by his brother Sigtrygg *Caech. En route* from Dublin (left in the hands of a third brother, Gothfrith), Sigtrygg sacked Davenport (Cheshire), and Edward's construction of the *burh* at *Cledemutha* (on the River Clwyd, near Rhuddlan) in 921 was perhaps a response to this raid, but no other hostilities are recorded.[18] There was trouble of an unspecified kind at Chester in 924, and it was while dealing with this that Edward died, at Farndon, on 17 July 924.[19] Ælfweard, the elder son of Edward's second marriage, died soon afterwards, the the kingship passed to Athelstan, son of Edward's first wife, Ecgwynn, who was consecrated and crowned at Kingston-on-Thames, on 4 September 925. Edward bequeathed to his son the makings of a unified kingdom – Wessex from Cornwall to Kent, western Mercia, the east and north midlands (except Lindsey, which was controlled by York) and East Anglia; he could also claim overlordship over the kings of the Welsh, the Danish kings of York, the Northumbrians, and the Scots. But it was a kingdom which still had to be secured and consolidated, and much of Athelstan's reign was occupied in making his theoretical suzerainty a reality.

On 30 January 926, Sigtrygg of York met Athelstan at Tamworth and concluded an agreement, cemented by the marriage of Sigtrygg with one of Athelstan's sisters.[20] When Sigtrygg died in the following year, Athelstan drove out his brother Gothfrith and seized York. This show of power brought him the (temporary) allegiance of Constantine II, King of Scots, who "established peace with pledge and oaths" at *Eamot* ("watersmeet"), possibly the Roman fort of *Brocavum* (Brougham Castle) at the confluence of the rivers Eamont and Lowther near Penrith (Cumbria).[21] Later in the same year, a similar meeting at Hereford secured the allegiance of the Welsh kings, led by Hywel Dda ("the Good"), King of Deheubarth, and in 928 Athelstan received the submission of the "west Welsh" (the Britons of Cornwall) at Exeter.[22]

Constantine, however, was merely playing for time. The scanty sources for Athelstan's reign do not reveal the details, but in 934, in response to some challenge, "King Athelstan went into Scotland with both a land force and a naval force, and ravaged much of it".[23] The effect was to drive Constantine still further into the arms of the Dublin Vikings. By 937, Olaf Gothfrithson, who succeeded his father in 934, had established control in Dublin, and was ready to claim his father's kingdom of York. Olaf and Constantine harried deep into Mercia, until they met the West Saxon and Mercian armies at the still unidentified site of *Brunanburh*.[24] The entry for this year in the *Anglo-Saxon Chronicle* consists of a specially-composed poem, which describes how Athelstan and his half-brother Edmund "clove the shield-wall, hewed the linden-wood shields with hammered swords", and drove their enemies from the field. Olaf and Constantine escaped, but Constantine left his son among the slain, along with five kings, one of whom was probably his cousin Owen, King of Strathclyde, seven of Olaf's jarls, and "a countless host of seamen and Scots".[25] Athelstan returned to Wessex, leaving behind him

> the dusky-coated one, the black raven with his horned beak, to share the corpses, and the dun-coated, white-tailed eagle, the greedy war-hawk, to enjoy the carrion, and that grey beast, the wolf of the forest.

His kinsman, Æthelweard, writing towards the end of the century, says the engagement "is still called the 'great battle' by the common people".[26]

The *Anglo-Saxon Chronicle* has no more to report of Athelstan but his death, on 27 October 939, when he was about 45 years old. But Athelstan was more than a great warlord. His capture of York in 937 made him the first king of all the English peoples. The verse panegyric which records it speaks of *perfecta Saxonia*, "England [now] made whole", and it is at about this time that Athelstan's coins begin to bear the legend *rex totius Britanniae*, "King of all Britain".[27] At Malmesbury, where he was buried, he was remembered as one who excelled his predecessors by his piety as well as his prowess, a just and learned King, famed throughout Europe for his "nobility of lineage and greatness of mind".[28] The counts of Flanders and Boulogne were his cousins, and his half-sister Eadgifu was married to Charles the Simple, King of the Franks.[29] When her husband was deposed in 923, she fled home with her young son Louis (b 920), who was reared at Athelstan's court. In 926, Athelstan betrothed Eadhild, Eadgifu's full sister, to Hugh the Great, Count of Paris, and 10 years later the brothers-in-law negotiated the return of the young Louis to his father's throne. In 929, another sister, Eadgyth, married the future emperor, Otto I, initiating a long and mutually profitable relationship between the kings of the English and the German emperors.[30]

Athelstan was succeeded by Edmund, the elder son of Edward the Elder's third wife, Eadgifu of Kent, then in his 18th year.[31] He had to fight to retain the kingdom. Athelstan's dominance had been based on military force and his own formidable reputation. His death encouraged Olaf Gothfrithson to make a second, successful attempt on York, which had accepted him as king before the end of 939. Olaf's ambition to recreate the York-Dublin axis, destroyed by Athelstan, is symbolized by the coinage minted for him at York; one of the designs included the figure of a raven, recalling the "Raven banner" captured by the English from his grandfather's brother in 878.[32] In 940, his armies overran the north-east Midlands as far as Northampton. Edmund counter-attacked, besieging the Danish forces at Leicester, but there was no decisive engagement, and a truce was arranged, in which the north-east Midlands, so laboriously won by his father and aunt, were conceded to Olaf.

Olaf's death in 941 allowed Edmund to retrieve the position. In 942, he recaptured the lost territories and even succeeded in detaching Lincoln and Lindsey from the control of the York kings. The *Anglo-Saxon Chronicle* breaks into alliterative verse at this point, celebrating Edmund's victory as a "redemption" of the Danes of these parts, hitherto "subjected by force under the Norsemen". The poem was probably composed some time in the late 950s, and it is debatable whether Edmund's contemporaries, especially among the Danes, shared these views.

Olaf Gothfrithson was succeeded at York by his cousin, Olaf Sigtryggson, called *Cuaran* ("Sandal") by the Irish.[33] In 943, he was baptized, with Edmund as his godfather, which suggests some temporary acknowledgment of West Saxon authority. Olaf Sigtryggson had rivals in York, including Olaf Gothfrithson's brother Ragnall, and it was perhaps some internal dispute that enabled Edmund to expel Olaf and Ragnall in 944.[34]

Edmund was an able and energetic ruler, who "might have been remembered as one of the more remarkable of Anglo-Saxon kings" but for his early death; he was stabbed in the course of a brawl at the royal vill of Pucklechurch (Gloucs), on the 26 May 946.[35] He left two young sons, the children of his first wife, St Ælfgifu, but the kingship passed to his brother Eadred, who was consecrated at Kingston-on-Thames on 16 August 946.

Eadred stepped into the same preeminence among the rulers in Britain which his brother Edmund had enjoyed, but (like Edmund) he had to fight to retain it. In the north, he was challenged by Olaf Sigtryggson, and by the Norwegian prince, Erik Bloodaxe (d 954). The position was complicated by the existence of rival factions in York itself (one led by Archbishop Wulfstan I), and by the rivalry between the Anglo-Scandinavians of York and the English of Northumbria beyond the Tyne, led by Osulf, son of Ealdred of Bamburgh, a supporter of the West Saxon kings.[36]

The chronology of Eadred's reign is confused, but it seems that Olaf Sigtryggson was established at York by 947, possibly with Eadred's acquiescence.[37] In 949, however, Olaf was expelled by the York faction led by Archbishop Wulfstan, who submitted to Eadred; but within the year "they were false to it all, both pledge and oath", and accepted Erik Bloodaxe as their king.[38] Eadred responded with a punitive raid. On his return southward, his rearguard was badly cut up by Erik's forces at Castleford; but when Eadred threatened to return in force to York and "destroy it utterly", the leading men of York submitted to him and expelled Erik. The date was probably 952, the year in which Eadred deposed and arrested Archbishop Wulfstan, presumably for supporting Erik.[39] Erik himself survived until 954, when he was ambushed and killed at the Rere Cross on Stainmore. It is said that he was betrayed to his enemies by Osulf of Bamburgh, whom Eadred chose as the first earl of all Northumbria after Erik's fall.[40]

Erik's death marked the end of the independent kingdom of York, though this may not have been apparent at the time. In his will, Eadred left £1,600 of silver "for the redemption of his soul and for the good of his people, that they may be able to purchase for themselves relief from want *and from the heathen army* if they have need".[41] In the event, it was to be another quarter of a century before such a need arose, and then the threat came not so much from the colonies in Ireland as direct from Scandinavia.

Eadred died on 23 November 955, an able and even energetic king, much hampered by debility; he had some digestive problem which prevented him from swallowing his food, so that he was reduced to sucking the juice out of it and spitting what remained back onto his plate: "a nasty practice which turned the stomachs of the thegns who dined with him".[42] His physical frailty may be the reason that he never married, and his heirs were his nephews, Eadwig and Edgar.

Estimates of Eadwig, who can have been no more than 20 when he died in 959, vary widely. For the earliest biographer of St Dunstan, writing between 995 and 1005, Eadwig was a foolish young man "endowed with little wisdom in government". This estimate is coloured by Eadwig's poor relations with Dunstan; Dunstan's biographer gives a vivid picture of how, on the night of his coronation feast, Dunstan discovered the young King in bed not merely with his future wife, but also with the lady who subsequently became his mother-in-law. Dunstan's friend and contemporary, St Æthelwold, who was on better terms with the King, also criticizes Eadwig's folly, but attributes it to his youth. Only Eadwig's kinsman and brother-in-law, Æthelweard the Chronicler (the only lay commentator) is wholly favourable; Eadwig was named "All-fair" because of his great beauty, and "deserved to be loved".[43]

Much is still obscure about the politics of Eadwig's reign. The year 956 is marked by the issue of an unprecedented number of royal charters, which might suggest that the King had to buy support, but too little is known of the background to be sure. In 957, Eadwig's brother Edgar became King of the Mercians. Dunstan's biographer presents this as a coup; Eadwig, because of his foolishness, "was wholly deserted by the northern people". Æthelwold, however, says merely that Eadwig "dispersed his kingdom and divided its unity", whereas Æthelweard claims that "he held the kingdom continuously for four years".[44] It is not impossible that the division was made by mutual agreement between the brothers or even that it signalled Eadwig's acceptance of Edgar as his heir; and it is noticeable that, though Edgar issued his own charters in 958, usually as "King of the Mercians", Eadwig retained throughout the title "King of the English".[45]

Whatever the precise circumstances, Edgar succeeded to the whole kingdom on Eadwig's death on 1 October 959. His patronage of the Benedictine reformers was amply repaid in the favourable portrait of the King which appears in their writings. As a result, we are well informed of Edgar's ecclesiastical dispositions, but have few indications of his secular career. The *Anglo-Saxon Chronicle* has little to record apart from his consecration, on 11 May 973, at Bath, and his meeting immediately afterwards with the other rulers of Britain at Chester. Here Edgar was rowed on the Dee, "from the palace to the monastery of St John the Baptist", by six (or eight) kings, including Kenneth II, King of Scots, Donald of Strathclyde and his son Malcolm, and Iago, King of Gwynedd.[46]

The ramifications of Edgar's consecration at Bath and the meeting at Chester have been much discussed.[47] Bath was not the usual place for royal inaugurations, and there is a further problem, that of the delay between Edgar's accession in 959 and the consecration in 973; was 973 a second inauguration, and if so, to what? It has been seen as an "imperial" coronation of Edgar as Lord of Britain, the culmination of previous West Saxon claims to overlordship of all other British rulers. No doubt it seemed very different to the British and especially to the Scots. Kenneth II had his own reasons for allying with Edgar, notably to secure Edgar's acceptance of Scottish control in Lothian, which had once been part of Bernicia, but it is highly unlikely that he saw himself as in any way subordinate to Edgar.[48]

Edgar and his brother Eadwig were the first kings of their line who did not have to fight to maintain their kingdom; hence Edgar's later byname of *pacificus* ("the Peacemaker"). It is important, however, to appreciate the basis of this "peace". The verses recording Edgar's death not only claim that many kings paid homage to him "as was his due by birth", but hint at the reason: "there was no fleet so proud, nor raiding army so strong, that fetched itself carrion among the English race, while the noble king governed the royal seat".[49] Edgar ruled, as his predecessors had done, by force as well as by diplomacy. Yet rule he did; and his "imperial" coronation in 973 was the culmination of all that his forebears had striven for, the united kingship of all the English.

Having conquered their kingdom, the West Saxon kings had to devise ways of governing it. The legislative tradition revived by Alfred was continued by his successors.[50] Edward issued laws at Exeter, referring back to other legislation which had not been properly enforced; Athelstan issued at least three codes, and there are three from the short reign of Edmund. No code in Eadred's name is known, though he may have been responsible for the *Hundred Ordinance;* and there are three codes from Edgar's time, four if the *Hundred Ordinance* is to be attributed to him.[51] Edgar's last code (IV Edgar) orders that copies are to be made and circulated by the leading ealdormen "that this measure may be known to both the poor and the rich".[52] From the eighth century (and perhaps earlier) Wessex had been divided into shires, each presided over by an ealdorman, who represented the king's interests. Similar regions can be found in all the pre-Alfredian kingdoms, but as the West Saxons absorbed England north of the Thames, they swept away the existing subdivisions and replaced them with shires, based on the *burhs* established by Edward and Æthelflæd.

By Athelstan's time, the ratio of "one ealdormen, one shire" was no longer practical. It is likely that three ealdormen were responsible for eastern, central, and western Wessex and three more for northern, central, and south-east Mercia. The best known of Athelstan's ealdormen is his namesake, Athelstan Half-king, whose huge ealdordom comprised not only East Anglia, but also the territories which had been eastern Mercia.[53] Naturally, the Half-king needed subordinates to govern this vast swathe of land and some can be identified: Thurferth, who was perhaps ealdorman of Northampton, Scule, whose territory was probably in Suffolk, and Halfdane, possibly in Hertfordshire.[54] This pattern, of lesser ealdormen within the districts of greater ones, was to become general over the next half-century. After 954, the ealdordom of Northumbria covered not only York and the north Midlands, but also Bamburgh, which nevertheless retained its own line of high-reeves (later earls); and by the 960s, the ealdordom of Mercia stretched from Cheshire to Gloucestershire. In the reign of Cnut, Wessex itself became an earldom (the title of earl replaces that of ealdorman in Cnut's time). It is important to notice, however, that there was no unit of local administration higher than the shire, which, by the middle of the 10th century, was the special responsibility of the shire-reeve (sheriff), a royal official appointed not by the ealdorman, but by the king. The greater ealdormen never became provincial governors; they remained royal officers, overseeing the king's rights in the territories to which he had appointed them.

By the middle of the 10th century, the shires were subdivided into hundreds, themselves further divided into tithings; the structure is described in the *Hundred Ordinance*.[55] Hundreds could be grouped together for special purposes, like the three hundreds of Oswaldslow, held by the Bishop of Worcester in return for supplying a ship to the king's fleet.[56] As for the tithing, its purpose was essentially to provide surety; the members of the tithing (10 men in all) were jointly to ensure each others' performance of their legal duties, and if one of their number failed to answer to any charge, the rest could be fined in the hundred court.[57] In the Danelaw (York and the north-east Midlands) the wapentake replaces the hundred, and the term "hundred" is applied (confusingly) to a smaller unit comparable to the tithing.[58] Local variation in custom was only to be expected in a kingdom made up of such disparate regions, each with their own traditions.[59]

Triumphs and disasters, 975–1066.

The successes enjoyed by the Benedictine reformers in Edgar's time gave rise to disturbances after his death. The key figure was Æthelwold, Abbot of Abingdon, who was made Bishop of Winchester in 963. Æthelwold was the most thorough-going of the reformers and his arrival at the Old Minster, Winchester, produced a transformation:

> Now at that time in the Old Minster, where the episcopal seat is situated, there were evil-living clerics, possessed by pride, insolence, and wanton behaviour, to such an extent that several of them scorned to celebrate Mass in their turn; they repudiated wives whom they had married unlawfully, and took others, and were continually given over to gluttony and drunkenness. The holy man Æthelwold by no means put up with this, but when King Edgar's permission had been given, he very quickly expelled the impious blasphemers of God from the minster, and bringing monks from Abingdon, placed them there, being himself both their abbot and their bishop.

It was not only Æthelwold's personal charisma which achieved this end; he was accompanied by the King's emissary, Wulfstan of Dalham, who "commanded the clerks by the royal authority speedily to give place to the monks or to accept the monastic habit".[60] Of course, all the accounts of the reform movement are written by the winners; the unfortunate clerks have left no record of their side of the argument.

Æthelwold was a great patron of monasteries, especially in the Fenland, where he founded or refounded Ely, Peterborough, Thorney, and Crowland. The new abbeys had to be endowed, which caused tension with the lay landholders in their vicinity. In the first place, the scale of the benefactions was unprecedented. Domesday Book reveals that in some southern shires, up to a third of the taxable land belonged to the Benedictine houses, the greater part of it acquired in the latter part of the 10th century. It is clear, moreover, from the records actually made by the reformers, that their methods were not beyond question; there are complaints of force, and of under-payment for estates given or sold to the new establishments.[61] The increasing prominence of the reformers themselves in the councils of the king and in the local courts also set up tensions between individual lay and ecclesiastical magnates, and similar rivalries existed within the ranks of the lay magnates.[62]

All these tensions erupted after Edgar's sudden death, on 8 July 975, in his 31st year. He had been married at least twice, and left sons by two wives: Edward (the Martyr) by his first wife Æthelflæd *eneda* ("the White Duck") and Æthelred by his second (or third) wife and queen, Ælfthryth.[63] Byrhtferth of Ramsey, in his *Life* of St Oswald, says that Edward (who can have been no more than 16) was a violent and evil-tempered youth who "inspired in all not only fear but even terror"; nevertheless, he had the support of Dunstan, Archbishop of Canterbury, and Æthelwine, ealdorman of East Anglia.[64] The

Queen, Ælfthryth, urged the cause of her own son Æthelred, a boy of eight or nine; she was supported by Bishop Æthelwold and by Ælfhere, ealdorman of Mercia.[65] The participation of the two leading magnates south of the Humber lent an edge to the proceedings; both were arming their followers, and civil war was only narrowly averted. Edward was crowned before the end of 975, but on 18 March 978, he was murdered at Corfe, Dorset, by adherents of his half-brother.[66] The corpse was concealed, and only after its discovery and translation to Shaftesbury in February 979 could Æthelred be consecrated and crowned, at Kingston-on-Thames, on 4 May 979.[67]

Æthelred has become known as the "ill-counselled" (unræd) king whose vacillation allowed the Danes to conquer England. Though his byname (a pun on Æthelred, "noble counsel") is recorded only from the 12th century, the picture of his incompetence is already found in the Anglo-Saxon Chronicle, in the 'C', 'D', 'E' and 'F' texts, all of which draw upon an account written between the years 1016 and 1023 by an author who was probably working in London.[68] This chronicler, however, wrote his account of the King's reign in the knowledge of its disastrous outcome, which affects his presentation of events; and this in turn has affected the attitudes of later historians, from the 12th century to the present day.[69] Though it ended in defeat, there was more to Æthelred's reign than a catalogue of disasters, but even his most recent biographer, who has done most to salvage his reputation, concedes that "he was a poor judge of men".[70]

Since Æthelred was at most 12 years of age when he became king, his early years were dominated by those who had advised his father, notably his mother Ælfthryth and her close associates, Bishop Æthelwold of Winchester, and Ealdorman Ælfhere of Mercia. Ælfhere died in 983 and Æthelwold in 984, and it seems to have been after Æthelwold's death that the young King, now of age, began to assert himself; his mother ceases to attest his charters in 984, reappearing only in 993. It seems that the period between 984 and 993 was one which Æthelred came to regret, when ambitious men took advantage of his youth and inexperience to further their own ends (one may, of course, suspect some special pleading here). The main recorded complaints centre on the spoliation of various churches, whose lands and rights the repentant King now restores, but there were clearly political troubles as well. In 985, Ælfric cild, who succeeded his brother-in-law Ælfhere as ealdorman of Mercia, was exiled for treason of some unspecified kind, and in 986, "the King laid waste the diocese of Rochester", apparently in the course of disputes between the bishop and one of the royal favourites.

It was in these years also that the Viking fleets returned. Southampton was sacked in 980, and Thanet and Cheshire were ravaged. In 981, the church at Padstow was burned down, and the coasts of Devon and Cornwall harried; in 982, it was the turn of Portland in Dorset; and in 988 Watchet (Somerset) was raided. These raids seem fairly localized, and were probably launched not from Scandinavia, but from the Viking colonies in Ireland, Man, and the Western Isles.

In the year 991, a much more serious threat appeared. In this year (according to the 'A' text of the *Chronicle)*

> Olaf came with 93 ships to Folkestone, and ravaged round about it, and then from there went to Sandwich, and so from there to Ipswich, and overran it all, and so to Maldon. And Ealdorman Byrhtnoth came against him there with his army and fought against him; and they killed the ealdorman there and had control of the field.

It is not quite certain that Olaf Tryggvason was, in fact, at Maldon, and even if he was, he was not the only commander.[71] What is significant is that the raid was launched from Scandinavia itself, and its leaders were the warlords of the emergent Scandinavian kingdoms, intent on gaining the fame and treasure which would enable them to win political power at home. Olaf's force roamed the coasts of England for the next three years, from East Anglia (in 992) to Northumbria (993) and back again (in 994) to besiege London (unsuccessfully) and raid all round the south-east coast as far as Hampshire. Since force of arms could not stop them, the King opened negotiations. As the winter of 994 drew in, they made camp at Southampton "and they were provisioned throughout all the West Saxon kingdom, and they were paid £16,000 in money".[72]

Æthelred has been much criticized for paying Danegeld, but so did Alfred, and no one has called him "ill-advised". Indeed, even the contemporary chronicler, so critical of much of the King's policy, complains not so much of the payment of tribute *per sé,* but that it was never offered in time, but only "when they had done most to our injury was peace and truce made with them".[73] In Olaf's case, the pay-off was successful; he was baptized at Andover, with Æthelred as his godfather, and took himself off with his winnings to establish his brief kingship in Norway.[74]

We do not know who led the army which operated in England between 997 and 999, when it removed to Normandy, only to return in 1001; in 1002, it was bought off with a tribute of £24,000.[75] It may have contained a significant element from the north-west, for in 1000, Æthelred personally led his army to ravage the Norse colonies in Cumbria, and at the same time the English fleet raided the Isle of Man.

It was perhaps to detach Normandy from its Scandinavian allies that Æthelred married Emma, sister of Duke Richard II, in 1002. She was his second wife, and he already had a clutch of children (six sons and at least three daughters) by his first wife Ælfgifu.[76] On 13 November in the same year, he attempted to rid himself of the Danish merchants and mercenaries in England, of whose loyalty he was becoming suspicious; this is the infamous St Brice's Day massacre, in which "all the Danish [as opposed to Anglo-Danish] men who were in England" were to be slaughtered.[77]

In 1003, Swein Forkbeard, King of Denmark, appeared on the scene. It was not his first visit; he was one of Olaf's allies in 994, and had been raiding in East Anglia and Essex even earlier.[78] His chief motive was probably plunder, to consolidate his power in the nascent kingdom of Denmark. Swein's campaigns caused great disruption and damage until 1007, when a temporary halt was bought by a tribute of £36,000. In the breathing-space thus obtained, Æthelred began an overhaul of the English fleet. The chronicler records that in 1008 "the King ordered that ships should be built unremittingly over all England, namely a warship from 310 (or from 300 hides) and a helmet and a corselet from eight hides".[79] In 1009, a great fleet was assembled at Sandwich (Kent) but dispersed (according to the chronicler) because of a quarrel between two of the King's commanders.[80] This was particularly unfortunate because in August of the same year there arrived "the immense raiding army which we called Thorkell's army".[81] Its leader, Thorkell the Tall, was one of Swein's opponents, but this did not help the English. He and his men remained in England, raiding and harrying, until in 1012, Canterbury itself was sacked. Among the hostages was the Archbishop, Ælfheah (St Alphege), and when he refused to allow a ransom to be raised for him, he was murdered by the Danish host. This act seems to have shocked even Thorkell, who was probably at least a nominal Christian, for he immediately led 45 of his own ships to join Æthelred's service. The rest of his force was paid a massive tribute (£48,000) and then (as the chronicler says) "dispersed as widely as it had been collected".[82]

In his account of these years, the chronicler's complaints intensify: bad or conflicting counsels, inability to plan or carry out plans once made, treachery, lack of coordination so marked that "in the end no shire would even help the next".[83] Thorkell, though a Dane, was in no sense Swein's man (it may, indeed, have been Thorkell's alliance with Æthelred that provoked Swein's invasion of 1013), but the disastrous performance of the English must have come to the ears of the Danish King.[84] In 1013, his fleet appeared off Sandwich, and moved up the east coast to the Humber, and thence up the Trent to Gainsborough; and here, without a blow struck, "Earl Uhtred [of Bamburgh] and all the Northumbrians submitted to him, as did all the people of Lindsey, and then all the people belonging to the district of the Five Boroughs, and quickly afterwards all the Danish settlers north of Watling Street". Only when he crossed Watling Street did Swein's men begin to ravage; and thus he secured the submission of Oxford, Winchester, and Wallingford, until finally, at Bath, the south-western thegns submitted to him, "and all the nation regarded him as full king". The Londoners, who had held out until this point, capitulated. Queen Emma had already fled to her brother in Normandy, and her children were sent after her. Thorkell remained faithful to his new lord, and his ships bore Æthelred from London, first to the Isle of Wight, where he spent Christmas, and at last to join his family in Normandy.[85]

All that prevented the establishment of Danish rule at this point was the death of Swein on 3 February 1014. His young son, Cnut, left at Gainsborough, was chosen king by the Danish army, but the English councillors sent to Æthelred in Normandy, saying that "no lord was dearer to them than their natural lord if he would govern them more justly than he did before". Æthelred for his part promised "that he would be a gracious lord to them, and reform all the things which they all hated", and returned, to universal rejoicing, in the spring of 1014. Soon after Easter, he personally led his army north to dislodge Cnut from Gainsborough and expel him from the country.[86]

By 1014, Æthelred had reigned for 36 years, longer than any of his predecessors, and the strains were beginning to show; his last years were racked by internal dissension as well as external invasion. He died on 23 April 1016, having (in the chronicler's words) "held his kingdom with great toil and difficulties as long as his life lasted". He was succeeded by his eldest surviving son, Edmund "Ironside".

Swein, meanwhile, had been succeeded in Denmark by his elder son Harald, but the younger, Cnut, had already been proclaimed King of the English, and was not about to give up his prize without a fight. Moreover, he had allies there, for he had probably already married the English noblewoman, Ælfigifu of Northampton, daughter of Ælfhelm, ealdorman of Northumbria from 993 to 1006.[87] Cnut's fleets returned in 1015, and found a ready ally in the ealdorman of Mercia, Eadric *Streona* ("the Grasping"), a protégé of Æthelred who had fallen out with Edmund. In 1016, Cnut and Edmund locked horns for the final prize: the kingdom of the English. King Edmund called out the full muster no less than four times, and fought five general engagements, at Penselwood (Somerset), Sherston (Wilts), Brentford (Middx), Otford (Kent), and finally *Assandune* (Essex). This was the last battle, in which "Cnut had the victory and won for himself all the English people".[88] At Olney near Deerhurst (Gloucs), the kingdom was partitioned; Edmund retained Wessex, but ceded Mercia (and probably Northumbria) to Cnut.

When Edmund died, on 30 November 1016, Cnut succeeded to the whole kingdom.[89] He was probably crowned as early as 1017, but the surviving English æthelings had to be disposed of; in 1017, Edmund's brother Eadwig was exiled, and probably killed, and Edmund's infant sons were smuggled abroad to save them from the same fate. In the summer of the same year, Cnut married Æthelred's widow Emma, presumably to forestall claims by her sons, exiled in Normandy.[90] Finally, in 1018, an agreement was reached at Oxford, by which Cnut promised to observe the laws of King Edgar. He was not merely King of the English, for on his brother's death in 1019, he became King of Denmark as well as overlord of Norway; and by the late 1020s, he was claiming suzerainty over some part of Sweden too.[91] His desire to promote himself and his line is shown by his visit to Rome in 1027, to attend the coronation of the Emperor Conrad II, and towards the end of his reign, he made a closer alliance with the Emperor by the betrothal of Gunnhild, his daughter by Emma, to Conrad's son, the future Henry III.[92] Cnut's enthusiastic self-publicity perhaps derived from the fact that his dynasty, even in Denmark, was not very old; despite the attempts of Cnut's Scandinavian court poets to make him a descendant of Ivar the Boneless, his historical ancestry goes back only to his great-grandfather, Gorm the Old, who probably died in 958.[93]

Cnut was concerned to show himself as a legitimate English king, and his law codes repeat and enlarge those of his English predecessors; indeed, they stand as the last great statement of English custom before the Norman Conquest.[94] It has been claimed that the Danish conquest transformed pre-Conquest England from an Anglo-Saxon to an Anglo-Scandinavian society, but the Danish elements in Cnut's administration seem fairly superficial. The Scandinavian title "earl" (jarl) replaces English "ealdorman", but the powers of the 11th-century earls were little different from those of their 10th-century predecessors. Certainly, Cnut introduced men of his own into the hierarchy of the English administration. Thorkell the Tall, Æthelred's former commander, was made Earl of East Anglia, and Erik of Hladir (in Norway), Cnut's staunchest ally, received Northumbria. Mercia, however, was entrusted to the Englishman Leofwine, who had been ealdorman of the Worcester region under Æthelred, but Cnut placed a a check on his authority by appointing Danish earls to the shires of Worcester (Hakon, son of Earl Erik), Gloucester (Eilaf Thorgilson, Cnut's brother-in-law), and Hereford (the otherwise unknown Ranig). Few of these earls lasted long, and by the 1030s, Englishmen held the dominant posts; Earl Leofric (son of Ealdorman Leofwine) in Mercia, and Earl Godwine in Wessex. It was this last office which marked a genuine departure from previous practice; no English king would have allowed Wessex itself to become an earldom.[95]

Much has been claimed for the royal housecarls ("men of the household"), who have been described as a kind of military guild, or even as a standing, paid army. This interpretation depends on later Danish sources, which have more to say about 12th-century Denmark then 11th-century England. All great lords, English or Danish, laymen or ecclesiastics, kept military retainers. Once Cnut's Danish followers received land and married into the local English nobility, they became indistinguishable from thegns, to the extent that the terms "housecarl" and "thegn" could be used interchangeably of the same man.[96] Even the royal fleet, stationed at London, with its paid ships' crews, the lithesmen, was an innovation not of Cnut, but of Æthelred II; its origins lie in the ships which Thorkell brought to Æthelred in 1012, and the tax which paid for its upkeep, the heregeld, was raised from that year until 1051, when it was abolished by Edward the Confessor.[97]

In contrast to the laity, the ecclesiastical establishment of Æthelred's day continued into that of Cnut. He patronized the cults of the West Saxon royal saints, Edward the Martyr and his half-sister, Eadgyth of Wilton, and was a generous benefactor of the Church.[98] Bury St Edmunds, indeed, regarded him as its founder; an interesting choice for a Dane, and especially for Cnut, given that it was dedicated to the memory of the East Anglian king martyred by the Viking army of his alleged ancestor, Ivar the Boneless. Cnut's patronage of Bury illustrates his desire to reconcile his English subjects and rehabilitate his Danish ancestors. This desire also underlies the translation of the relics of St Ælfheah, murdered by Thorkell's army in 1012; in 1023 his body, which had been buried at London, was removed to Canterbury by his former community, attended by a bodyguard of royal housecarls.[99] The success of this policy is shown by the high reputation of the Danish kings in the east midlands, where by the 12th century Cnut occupied the place given, in southern and western England, to Edgar the Peacemaker.[100]

Cnut's "northern empire", impressive though it looked, collapsed on his death in 1035. His son Swein, who had been sent to govern Norway, was expelled by the Norwegians, who, flushed with this success, attempted to drive Harthacnut, Cnut's son by Emma, from Denmark itself. As a result, Harthacnut was unable to return to claim his English inheritance. Instead, the English nobles vested power in his half-brother, Harold son of Ælfgifu of Northampton. The 'E' text of the Anglo-Saxon Chronicle says that Harold was made regent "for himself and for his brother Harthacnut", but this was clearly a pretext, and in 1037, "Harold was chosen as king everywhere and Hardacnut was deserted because he was too long in Denmark".[101]

All versions of the *Chronicle* make it clear that the real power did not lie with these young princes, but with the great earls who had risen under their father, Leofric of Mercia and Godwine of Wessex. Indeed, it was the defection of Earl Godwine from Hardacnut's cause that tipped the balance in favour of Harold. Why he changed sides we do not know; but change he did, in 1036. It was in this year that the exiled æthelings in Normandy, the sons of Emma and Æthelred II, decided to play their hand. The younger brother, Alfred, assembled a force in Flanders and Boulogne, and landed in Wessex, intending to go to his mother at Winchester, but Godwine intercepted him and delivered him to Harold I. The 'C' text of the *Chronicle* even makes Godwine responsible for the subsequent murder of Alfred, though 'D' blames Harold, as does the *Encomium* of Alfred's mother Emma.[102]

Harold completed his coup by expelling Emma, who fled to Bruges in 1037. He himself died in 1040, and as the *Chronicle* says, "they sent to Bruges for Hardacnut, thinking that they were acting wisely".[103] He was perhaps the obvious choice; but he made himself immediately unpopular by raising the rate of the *heregeld* to maintain a fleet much larger than that of Cnut and Harold I. By 1041, his stock had fallen so low that when Edward, Emma's elder son by Æthelred, arrived in England, Harthacnut was forced to recognize him as his heir. Since he was no more than 24 and Edward rising 40, this probably did not seem too great a matter; but it was Hardacnut who died first, in 1042, while drinking at the marriage feast of one of his thegns.

Edward the Confessor, the last king of the West Saxon line, acquired a posthumous reputation for sanctity, largely manufactured by the monks of his favoured abbey, Westminster.[104] The anonymous *Life* of Edward, despite its title, deals not so much with the King as with his chief rivals, Godwine of Wessex and his sons.[105] The work was commissioned about 1065 by Edward's Queen, Edith (Eadgyth), and the earliest sections, written in 1065 or 1066, form a kind of collective biography of her family; only after the disaster at Hastings on 14 October 1066 was the work recast as a eulogy of her deceased husband. Edith's family came, on her father's side from Sussex; her paternal grandfather was Wulfnoth *cild,* whose quarrel with another of Æthelred's thegns had so hampered the English fleet in 1009.[106] Wulfnoth's son Godwine was married, probably in 1023, to Gytha, sister of the Danish jarl, Ulf, who had married Cnut's sister Estrith, and of Eilaf, to whom Cnut had given an earldom based on Gloucestershire.[107]

By 1042, when Edward came to the throne, Godwine's elder children were reaching their maturity. In 1043, the eldest, Swein, was given an earldom centred on Hereford; in 1044, Harold, the second son, became Earl of East Anglia, and in 1045, an earldom in the east Midlands was bestowed on Gytha's nephew, Beorn Estrithson.[108] It was in 1045 also that Edward married Godwine's eldest daughter Edith. The King's favour to Godwine was probably always a matter of expediency rather than choice. Edward's long exile in Normandy had given him little opportunity to build up a following in England, and Cnut's purge of the West Saxon æthelings had deprived him of any close kin. Yet throughout the 1040s, Edward was creating his own faction, mainly drawn from the Normans and Frenchman who had accompanied him on his return to England.

Godwine's position was not helped by the behaviour of his eldest son. In 1046, Swein abducted the Abbess of Leominster, and left the country when he was refused permission to marry her. His lands and offices were distributed between his brother Harold and his cousin Beorn, who were none too pleased when he was reconciled to the King in 1049. Swein in revenge murdered Beorn, a crime for which he was outlawed, though once again he was pardoned and allowed to return to his lands and earldom in 1050.

By this time, Edward felt able to oppose the ambitions of his most powerful earl. The archbishopric of Canterbury was vacant, and the monks of Christ Church chose Godwine's kinsman Ælric, but the King overruled the election and gave the see to his Norman favourite, Robert of Jumièges. Moreover, he bestowed the earldom of the murdered Beorn not on one of Godwine's younger sons, but on his own nephew, Ralph.[109] In 1051, another Norman follower, Osbern Pentecost, was allowed to build a castle in Herefordshire, in Swein's earldom, and about the same time, Robert fitzWymarc erected a castle at Clavering, Essex, within Harold's territory.[110]

It appears that a third castle was projected, at Dover, within the territory of Earl Godwine himself.[111] This seems to be the reason for the visit to England of Count Eustace of Boulogne, Edward's one-time brother-in-law, in the summer of 1051.[112] The fullest account is in the 'E' text of the *Anglo-Saxon Chronicle,* then being compiled at St Augustine's, Canterbury:

> Then Eustace came from overseas . . . and went to the King and told him what he wished, and then went homewards. When he came east to Canterbury, he and his men took refreshment there, and went to Dover. When he was some miles or more on this side of Dover, he put on his mail-shirt, and all his companions did likewise.[113] So they went to Dover. When they got there, they wished to lodge where it suited their own convenience. Then one of Eustace's men came and wished to stay at the home of a householder against his will, and he wounded the householder, and the householder killed him. Then Eustace got upon his horse and his companions upon theirs, and went to the householder and killed him upon his own hearth.[114] And afterwards they went up towards the town and killed, within and without, more than twenty men. And the townsmen killed nineteen on the other side and wounded they did not know how many. And Eustace escaped with a few men, and went back to the King, and gave him a prejudiced account of how they had fared, and the King grew very angry with the townsmen. And the King sent for Earl Godwine and ordered him to carry war into Kent towards Dover. . . And the Earl would not consent to this expedition because he was reluctant to injure his own province.

Godwine and his sons gathered the men of their earldoms at Godwine's estate of Beverstone, Gloucs. The King in turn ordered the levies of Earl Leofric and of Siward, Earl of Northumbria, to come to him at Gloucester. The King's counsellors urged caution, saying that

> it would be a great piece of folly (*unræd*) if they joined battle, for in the two hosts was most of what was noblest in England, and they considered that they would be opening a way for our enemies to enter the country and to cause great ruin amongst us.[115]

A council was called to meet at London on 25 September. Godwine and Harold were summoned to attend but, perhaps because of his past record, Swein was exiled and his earldom of Herefordshire was given to the King's nephew, Ralph; at the same time, all the thegns of Earl Harold were transferred to the King's allegiance. It is clear that Godwine's support was ebbing fast and when he was refused safe conduct to attend the London meeting, he and most of his kin rode for Bosham, Sussex, where their ships were lying, and fled overseas to Bruges. Earl Harold, with his brother Leofwine, made for Bristol and took ship to Ireland. Edward repudiated his wife Edith, Godwine's daughter, and imprisoned her in the nunnery at Wherwell, where his half-sister was abbess.[116]

In Bruges, Godwine made alliance with Count Baldwin V of Flanders, cemented by the marriage of his third son, Tostig, to the Count's half-sister Judith; while in Ireland, Harold collected a fleet with aid from Diarmid, King of Leinster. In 1052, the family returned in force, and compelled the King to restore their lands and earldoms, and expel their chief enemies, notably

Robert of Jumièges, Archbishop of Canterbury. Only Swein did not return. From Bruges he set off on the pilgrimage to Jerusalem, compelled either by family pressure or genuine remorse. He is said to have walked barefoot all the way, and died on his return journey, at Constantinople, on 29 September 1052.

Earl Godwine soon followed his eldest son to the grave. On Easter Sunday, 1053, (11 April) he was dining with the King at Winchester, when,

> he suddenly sank towards the footstool, bereft of speech and all his strength. Then he was carried to the King's private chamber, and they thought that it was about to pass off. But it was not so. On the contrary, he continued like this without speech or strength until the Thursday [April 15] and then lost his life. And he lies there in the Old Minster, Winchester.[117]

It might be thought that Earl Godwine's death would give King Edward a second chance to diminish the family's standing, but, in fact, the King seems to have lost interest in public affairs after the humiliation of 1052. He occupied his later years in hunting, which he greatly enjoyed, and in the building and endowment of his abbey at Westminster. After 1053, the governance of England was largely in the hands of Harold Godwineson.

Harold succeeded to his father's earldom of Wessex in 1053, relinquishing East Anglia to Ælfgar, son of Leofric of Mercia. It was now the turn of his younger brothers to prosper. In 1055, Earl Siward of Northumbria died and his young son Waltheof was passed over in favour of Tostig Godwineson. In 1057, Earl Leofric died, and his son Ælfgar succeeded to Mercia, but East Anglia was given to Godwine's fourth son, Gyrth. In the same year, Earl Ralph, the King's nephew, died. Ralph's earldom in the east Midlands was divided between Earl Tostig and his brother Leofwine, who also became an earl, and his earldom of Hereford went to Harold.

The earls of Hereford were responsible for the defence of the Welsh border, where the chief enemy was Gruffudd ap Llewelyn, King of Gwynedd. In 1055, Gruffudd invaded Herefordshire and was met by Earl Ralph and his forces, but "before any spear was thrown, the English army fled, because they were on horseback, and many were killed there – about four or five hundred men – and they killed none in return".[118] It was Harold and the levies of Wessex who saved the day, and from this time he probably exercised the functions of earl in the west. It was in the wars against Gruffudd ap Llewelyn that Harold made his name as a military commander. In 1063, a joint land and sea expedition was launched against Gwynedd, Harold leading the fleet and Earl Tostig the land army. In the course of the fighting, King Gruffudd was killed by his own men and his half-brothers allied with Harold.[119] It was perhaps about this time that Harold married, as his second wife, Gruffudd's widow Ealdgyth, daughter of Earl Ælfgar of Mercia.[120]

Edward's last years were dominated by the problem of the succession. For whatever reason, his marriage with Edith was childless, and when, in 1051, he repudiated his wife, he turned to his maternal kin in Normandy, and offered the succession to his cousin, Duke William. The return of Godwine in 1052 nullified this arrangement, but an heir still had to be found. In 1054, a mission, led by Ealdred, Bishop of Worcester, an adherent of Harold, was dispatched to find the two sons of Edward's half-brother, King Edmund Ironside, who had been smuggled, as babies, out of England to save them from being murdered by Cnut. It was not until 1057 that one of these lost æthelings, Edward, returned to England. He himself died, before he even met his kinsman the King, but he left a wife, Agatha, two daughters and an infant son, Edgar. The 'D' text of the *Anglo-Saxon Chronicle* implies that Edward ætheling's death was the result of foul play ("we do not know for what reason it was brought about that he was not allowed to see the face of his kinsman, Kind Edward") and the finger of suspicion has been pointed at Earl Harold. But it was not in Harold's interests to arrange the death of the ætheling, who was the best insurance against a Norman succession, and his death must remain a mystery.

By this time, King Edward was in his mid-50s and did not come of a long-lived family. It was highly unlikely that he would live to see his great-nephew, Edgar, reach manhood. Perhaps for this reason, the King renewed his promise of the succession to Duke William, and in 1064, according to the Norman sources, Harold visited the Duke, and pledged support with an oath of fealty.

The year 1065 saw the second great crisis of Edward's reign, the Northumbrian rebellion. Soon after St Bartholomew's Day (24 August)

> all the thegns of Yorkshire and of Northumberland came together and outlawed their earl, Tostig, and killed his bodyguard, all they could get at, both Danish and English, and took all his weapons in York, and gold and silver, and all his treasure. . . And they sent for Morcar, son of Earl Ælfgar, and chose him as their earl.[121]

Harold prevailed on the King to ratify the Northumbrians' choice of Morcar as their earl. There was probably little else he could do, since the feeling in the north against Tostig was such that any attempt to reimpose his authority would have led to full-scale war. But Tostig was outraged at what he considered his brother's treachery (and it probably did not help that Earl Morcar was Harold's brother-in-law). He publicly accused Harold of inciting the Northumbrians to rebel against him, and, getting no satisfaction, left England for Flanders. The author of the *Life of King Edward* sees this quarrel between Harold and Tostig as the cause of the downfall of them both.

By Christmas 1065, the abbey church of Westminster was finally complete. It was dedicated on 28 December. On 5 January 1066, King Edward died, and on his deathbed, chose Harold as his successor.[122] He was buried next day, in the choir of his new church, and the funeral was followed immediately by the consecration of Harold II as King of the English, the first coronation to take place in Westminster Abbey. The ceremony was performed by Harold's friend, Ealdred of Worcester, now Archbishop of York; and, as the chronicler says, "he met little quiet in it as long as he ruled the realm".[123]

It did not need the appearance of Halley's Comet on 24 April to presage trouble. As soon as he could move his ships from their winter base at London, King Harold

> assembled a naval force and a land force larger than any king had assembled before in this country, because he had been told as a fact that Duke William from Normandy, King Edward's kinsman, meant to come here and subdue the country.[124]

The first comer, however, was Tostig, in late April or early May. Having gathered men and supplies from the Isle of Wight, a large part of which belonged to him, he began to raid along the south coast. At Sandwich, he encountered his brother's fleet, which drove him away northwards. After a descent on the Humber, where he was opposed by Earl Morcar and his brother Edwin, Earl of Mercia, he went to Scotland, where he spent the summer at the court of Malcolm III Canmore.

Throughout the summer of 1066, from May to September, the English host stood to arms in the southern shires, while the fleet, under the King's command, patrolled the Channel from a base on the Isle of Wight. By 18 September, this combined land and sea force had been maintained for nearly four months – a formidable feat for a medieval army – and could be supported no longer. The land army was stood down, and the fleet returned to London. As King Harold disembarked, he learnt that a huge Norwegian fleet, 300 ships strong, had arrived on 15 September in the Humber.

Tostig had received help from an unexpected direction. Harald Sigurdson Hardrada ("Hard-counsel"), King of Norway, was one of the most formidable warrior-kings of Scandinavia. His intervention in 1066 seems, despite the later saga traditions, purely opportunistic; countries suffering from political instability had always been regarded by Viking leaders as potential venues for the picking up of unconsidered trifles. Hardrada made rendezvous with Tostig off the Northumbrian coast, and their joint fleets landed at Riccall and made for York. On 20 September they met the brother earls, Morcar of Northumbria and Edwin of Mercia, at Gatefulford, and there, after a bitter struggle, the English were put to flight. York perforce opened its gates to the Vikings and its citizens made peace with Hardrada.

Harold Godwineson received news of the Norwegian landing on or just before 18 September. "Then," as the 'C' text of the Chronicle says, "he went northwards day and night as quickly as he could assemble his force". Harold's march from London to York is justly famous. He left London on or just before 20 September; on 24 September he and his host were at Tadcaster, nine miles south of York. On the next day, 25 September, he launched his troops through York to Stamfordbridge, where Hardrada was encamped, a distance of 16 miles. In the ensuing battle, Harald Hardrada and Tostig were killed, and a great slaughter was made of the Norwegian host; only 24 ship-loads survived to return to Norway under Hardrada's son, Olaf "the Peaceful".[125] Harold Godwineson's victory at Stamfordbridge was one of the most decisive battles ever won by an English army over a Viking host, recalling Alfred's triumph at Edington in 878, which forced the host of Guthrum to sue for peace and leave Wessex.[126]

As Harold and his men rested at York, celebrating their victory, news came that Duke William had landed at Pevensey and was ravaging along the south coast. Harold set out for the south. He reached London on or about 7 October and spent five days there gathering fresh troops. On 12 October, he left with what men he had been able to raise, and his own élite bodyguard; his brothers Leofwine of the east midlands and Gyrth of East Anglia were with him. Harold has been charged with rashness for challenging Duke William so soon after the exhausting battle at Stamfordbridge, but he had little choice: Sussex was the heartland of Godwineson power, and he could not abandon it to the ravaging of the Norman army.

It is clear too that Harold was trying to repeat the tactics which had brought him victory in the north. The rallying point for which he was aiming was "the hoary apple-tree", a landmark on Caldbec Hill, just north of the present town of Battle. Thence he expected to launch an attack on Duke William in his newly built castle at Hastings, seven miles to the south. Duke William's intelligence service was, however, better than that of the defeated Harald Hardrada. He got wind of King Harold's approach, and advanced to meet him. After a night march, Harold arrived at his rendezvous on 14 October to find the Norman army, not at Hastings, but on Telham Ridge.[127] Battle was joined at the third hour (about 9 am) and raged all day, until, as the light waned, the Norman cavalry broke through the English shield-wall and cut down the King. Gyrth and Leofwine had already fallen, and the remnant of the English host fled into the thick woodland of the Sussex Weald.

William of Poitiers, Duke William's panegyrist, relates that the final struggle around the English standard, the White Dragon of Wessex, was so fierce that the English dead were unrecognizable; Harold's corpse was so mutilated that it was identified "not by his face but by certain indications", with his brothers lying beside him. William also says that the dead King's mother, Gytha, offered Duke William its weight in gold for her son's corpse but that the Duke refused the ransom; another source even claims that the body was interred on the sea cliffs near Hastings, wrapped in a cloak of royal purple.[128] The 12th-century historian, William of Malmesbury, believed on the other hand that Duke William accepted the ransom, and allowed Harold to be buried by the canons of Waltham Holy Cross, the church of which he was patron. The history of this community was written soon after 1177, by one of the canons who entered the church as a boy in about 1124. The author asserts that the corpse was identified by Harold's first wife, Eadgyth Swanneck, "by certain tokens known only to herself", and claims to have heard the older men describe how "they touched with their hands the marks of the wounds visible on the very bones" of the dead King. He had, moreover, as a boy, seen the translation of King Harold's remains into the choir of the new church, built in the 1120s.[129] The battered tomb, still visible within the foundations of the Romanesque choir at Waltham, may thus be the final resting place of King Harold II.

The last image that we have of pre-Conquest royalty is of Harold, crowned, anointed, and enthroned on the Bayeux Tapestry. His pose may be compared to those on the seal of Edward the Confessor, on the obverse of which the crowned and enthroned King bears the orb and sceptre, while on the reverse he holds a sword and a long rod of office. The crown is now so familiar an object that it is easy to forget that the earliest kings were not crowned, but wore instead a ceremonial royal helmet (a *cynehelm)*. The first representation of a crowned king appears on the coinage of Athelstan, and the first coronation *ordo* to prescribe the use of a crown in the ceremony is the *Second English Ordo,* composed for the coronation either of Athelstan, or his father Edward the Elder.[130] It was under the West Saxons that all the traditional trappings of royalty – crown, orb, sceptre, rod, and sword – came together in a single image of the royal lord *(cynehlaford, dominus rex),* as warrior, protector, benefactor, and judge. This image they bequeathed to the Norman kings who supplanted them. The "formidable authority of the royal majesty", which the author of the 12th-century legal tract, the *Leges Henrici Primi (Laws of King Henry I),* praised "for its continual and beneficial preeminence over the laws", was based upon the achievements of the West Saxon kings.[131]

Footnotes to this Chapter may be found on pages 336–44.

4: G A Loud

The English monarchy, 1066–1199

THE KING of England in the later 12th century cut an impressive figure. As one of his bishops wrote to the exiled Archbishop Thomas Becket in 1165: "He is a great, indeed the greatest of monarchs, for he has no superior of whom he stands in awe, nor subject who may resist him . . . those who have reason for dispute with him prefer to come to terms, even though they know these to be unfavourable, rather than rush to uphold their rights, since the scale of his riches, the size of his forces and the extent of his power is so much the stronger".[1]

We may, if we like, take some of this with a pinch of salt; we are dealing after all with a courtier writing to one of the few people who did oppose the king, and who had created a public scandal by doing so. The writer was not surprisingly trying to convince the archbishop of the hopelessness, and indeed the wrong-headedness, of his cause, and persuade him to seek a settlement with the king. But we do have other evidence which backs up Arnulf of Lisieux's high opinion of Henry II.

One of the most striking illustrations of this theme comes in an anecdote which occurs in two different, though not necessarily independent works, concerning the contemporary King of France, Louis VII. The earlier of the two versions comes in one of the most fascinating of the 12th-century literary texts, Walter Map's *On Courtiers' Trifles*. Walter describes a conversation which he himself claims to have had with King Louis, only a very few years before he was writing in the early 1180s, in which the king compared the respective wealth of various contemporary rulers. The king's remarks concluded with a comparison between himself and Henry II of England. "Your lord . . . wants for nothing, he has men, horses, gold, silk, jewels, fruit, game, and everything else. We in France have nothing but bread and wine and gaiety".[2] A generation later, the story was repeated, with embellishments, by a friend of Walter Map's, and fellow-Welshman, Gerald, Archdeacon of Brecon, more usually known as Gerald of Wales.

Gerald indeed developed the story as part of a wider argument, in a work called *About the Instruction of Princes*. England, he had the king say, was noted for the number of its parks, filled with beasts of the chase, and its wealth in precious metals, wealth which had been extorted by the power of the Normans from the subject English. Louis then repeated his "bread, wine, and gaiety" quip. Gerald does imply that Louis VII was overdoing his modesty in playing down the resources of his own kingdom, but he went on to develop at some length the admirable qualities of the French royal family, and implicitly criticize the lack of such virtues in the Angevin dynasty which ruled England. The French kings were pious, modest, moral, did not indulge in adultery – this was certainly a dig at Henry II – they even avoided bad language. And in particular they did not gain power by violence. Rather than acting as "lions and bears" among their subjects, they were invariably affable and kindly to all, and because they acted in a manner pleasing to God their power was enhanced. The lands of tyrants and the wicked would come into the hands of such pious princes.[3] Given that this passage was written after the French conquest of Normandy in 1204, the application of these comments to the Angevins, if coded, was unmistakable.

Of course, we have here a very clerical view of kingship, and indeed one penned by an ambitious, bitter, and disappointed man who was no admirer of Henry II and his sons. His picture of the French rulers was idealized to an almost ludicrous extent. The modesty and piety might well fit Louis VII, most of whose reign had in fact been a tale of frustration and lost opportunities – to quote Sir Richard Southern "Louis VII was a modest man, and modern historians have generally thought that he had a good deal to be modest about".[4] But it sits very badly with the character of his son, Philip II, "the hammer of the Normans" as Gerald himself described him, a subtle and devious schemer, always on the lookout for means to enhance his authority, and no moral paragon in his private life either. However, what is significant about this passage is not what it says about the French monarchy, which is anyway not our concern here, nor even whether the anecdote is actually true (and neither Walter nor Gerald could ever resist a good story), but what by implication it says about the English crown and those who wore it in the century or more before 1204. The kings of England were wealthy and powerful; they were also harsh and aggressive rulers, whose subjects knew the smack of firm government, and the burdens which such government placed upon them. England in the 12th century was an "over-governed" country, liable to be exploited by a predatory and acquisitive royal administration. *Why* that was the case is the theme which will be developed here.

Contemporary writers, all of whom were clerics (a point which is certainly significant), tended to have pretty mixed feelings about the kings of England after 1066. On the one hand, they were powerful and formidable, and generally had a good record in preserving law and order (always a desirable but fragile state of affairs in the Middle Ages). On the other hand, they were for the most part not only prone to exploit the Church for their own financial benefit, something of which no clerical writer could really approve, but they were almost all personally harsh and dislikable men (a verdict which modern scholarship has undoubtedly confirmed). William Rufus was, we are told, described by his uncle as a man "fastidiously reared, ferocious in spirit, whose scornful look discloses his overbearing nature, who would risk all in defiance of faith and justice".[5] Rufus was loathed by the writers of his time, nearly all of whom were monks, for his open and brutal exploitation of the Church and for his fondness for blasphemous jokes, and probably too for his homosexuality, although this is only hinted at by the chroniclers. But the personalities of his father and younger brother, as depicted by his contemporaries, are little more appealing. *The Anglo-Saxon Chronicle* described William I as "stronger than any of his predecessors had been . . . stern beyond all measure to people who resisted his will", and concluded that "in his time, people had much oppression and very many injuries".[6] At the death of Henry I in 1135, one contemporary summed up his character and achievements. King Henry, he said, was believed to possess three virtues, wisdom, success in war, and wealth, and three vices, avarice, cruelty, and lust. (Given the king's 20 or so known bastards, one might suggest that this last characteristic was proven fact).[7] A perceptive modern student of his administration comments, "as an individual, Henry I was complex, and in many respects highly unpleasant".[8]

To enforce their rule, these kings resorted unhesitatingly to acts which to 12th century eyes seem barbarous in the extreme. William the Conqueror laid Yorkshire waste during the winter for 1069–70 as punishment for rebellion, killing those of the inhabitants he could get his hands on and undoubtedly condemning many of the survivors to death by starvation. After the rebellion of 1075, he imprisoned for life the son of his cousin and closest associate William Fitz Osbern (whose own father had saved William's life when he was a child) and had his niece's husband executed, even though the latter's crime was at worst guilty knowledge of, rather than an active part in, the revolt. William I later imprisoned his own brother, intending to leave him there for the rest of his life, but was persuaded on his deathbed to order his release.[9] William Rufus had a count whom he distrusted blinded and castrated when he lost a judicial duel into which he had been forced.[10] After his victory at Tinchebrai in 1106, which gave him possession of Normandy, Henry I imprisoned his elder brother and his cousin, and unlike Odo of Bayeux, William I's half-brother, neither of these was ever released. Duke Robert of Normandy spent his last 28 years in captivity, Count William of Mortain was incarcerated for more than 30 years before he was allowed to become a monk.[11] The same king later responded to complaints by his mercenaries that they were being paid in debased coinage by ordering that all the moneyers of England should have their right hands cut off and be castrated. No doubt, as Miss Prism would have said, it was a lesson to them. (Or, as a monastic chronicler put it, less flippantly, "from this great good resulted at once to the whole kingdom"). But the problem may in fact have been caused not so much by deliberate dishonesty as by a shortage of silver available to be minted, and the hapless moneyers were, therefore, little more than scapegoats.[12] Even rulers who were considered to be of generally kinder disposition than Henry I could on occasion perpetrate the most appalling atrocities. King Stephen had the entire garrison of the rebel castle of Shrewsbury summarily hanged in 1139, all 94 of them, despite pleas from his own men to spare them, and Henry II responded to the failure of his Welsh expedition of 1165 by mutilating 22 entirely innocent hostages.[13]

Yet appalling as such deeds may seem, we must be careful not to judge them simply by modern liberal values. (The 20th century can anyway hardly boast an unblemished humanitarian record itself). Contemporaries might regret such instances of royal brutality, but they did not necessarily condemn them out of hand, nor did the kings of England have a monopoly of such violent action. Even the ostentatiously pious French rulers, Louis VI and VII, could at times act with considerable savagery to enforce their rule, as indeed did any medieval ruler, not least because contemporaries expected them to do so.[14] Those who did not display such harsh qualities were simply not respected, nor were they capable of enforcing peace. Take, for example, the verdict of Orderic Vitalis on William the Conqueror's eldest son.

> All men knew that Duke Robert was weak and indolent; therefore, trouble makers despised him and stirred up loathsome factions where and when they chose . . . being merciful to suppliants he was too weak and pliant to pass judgment on wrongdoers.[15]

Henry I was a very different kettle of fish, but his severity had a purpose: "He always devoted himself to preserving peace, and after he had secured the lasting prosperity he desired he never declined from his early power and strict justice . . . he always attempted to give peace to his subject peoples, and strictly punished law-breakers according to severe laws."[16] A contemporary French view of Henry I was very similar, and equally approving: "He set his land in order, imposed peace by force, promising nothing less to those who stole than the loss of their eyes or a high gallows."[17] Henry II was considered to be less severe than his grandfather, but "he condemned those accused of treason to exile, punished plunderers with a death sentence, terrified thieves with the gallows and levied financial penalties from those who oppressed the poor".[18] Law and order were so fragile that drastic action was necessary to ensure their continuance, and however much modern criminology may deplore the idea of exemplary punishment to deter crime, medieval men had no doubts whatever about its effectiveness.

This is not to say that all medieval commentators automatically approved any barbarous royal act simply because it was royal, and therefore upholding the *status quo*. Orderic Vitalis, whom I have been quoting at some length, was the most interesting of Anglo-Norman chroniclers precisely because, as the child of a French father but an English mother, he had distinctly ambivalent views about the Norman Conquest. It may have been God's judgment on the sins of the English, and especially the perjured King Harold, but it also led to much suffering, of innocent as well as guilty. Orderic generally regarded William the Conqueror as a "good thing", a stern but pious ruler forced to disagreeable actions by necessity, but he condemned the ravaging of Yorkshire precisely because most of those affected by it were innocent of any wrongdoing. It was, therefore, as we would say, a war crime.[19] Many other harsh actions were, however, more justifiable. Orderic reported one such deed in the course of the Norman rebellion against Henry I in 1124. The king condemned three captured nobles to be blinded, but the Count of Flanders, who was visiting his court at the time, "moved by compassion" protested at this decision, saying that it was quite wrong to exact such a penalty on men who were only serving their lords. The king's reply, while pitiless, was entirely logical. Two of the men had sworn fealty to him, and then broken their word by fighting against him. The third had admittedly never done homage to him, but had previously surrendered and been released unharmed, and promptly fought against the king once again, compounding his offence by denigrating him with scurrilous songs. "Other men who learn how his rash folly was cut short may mend their ways".[20] Disloyalty, and breaking agreements, was a cancer which had to be cut out, and kings could not afford to be merciful twice over. Another contemporary, William of Malmesbury, commented on the imprisonment of Count William of Mortain: "While he was worthy of praise for his intelligence and youthful vigour, because of his treachery he deserved his hard fate".[21]

The paradigm of the good and decent man who was by those very qualities unfitted for kingship was King Stephen. His biographer described him as "rich and at the same time unassuming, generous and courteous . . . good-natured and agreeable to all . . . affable and amenable to whatever age" – all these admirable qualities, but not necessarily in a ruler.[22] Stephen was, in the words of the Peterborough chronicler, "a mild man, and gentle and good, who did no justice", and the result was "nineteen years when God and his saints slept".[23] A very similar view was recorded during the reign of his successor by the chronicler of Battle Abbey: "King Stephen succeeded, and in his time justice seldom prevailed. He who was strongest prevailed".[24] Even those rare moments when Stephen did abandon his habitual good nature and behave brutally must be seen in this context. Hence Orderic's view of the execution of the garrison of Shrewsbury which the king ordered "because unruly men regarded his gentleness with contempt and many great lords scorned to come to his court when summoned". And, at least for a time, it worked. "When their rash accomplices heard of the king's ruthlessness they were abjectly terrified, within three days they came to the king trembling".[25]

Fear was a key weapon for any medieval king. A great king like Henry I was feared, and because he was, his rule was effective. Indeed, a king's very physical presence had to have its effect. In 1126, Henry, who was already well into his fifties, took steps to arrange the succession after his death. His only legitimate son had drowned in the Channel six years before, and while the widowed king had remarried within three months of his son's death his second marriage was barren. So he took what was for the time a revolutionary step, by designating his daughter as his heir. Not surprisingly this was a somewhat unpalatable pill for his barons to swallow, in a world where women were important only for the provision of heirs (male) and the transmission of property. However, we are told, the king commanded them to swear to support her succession, "with that loud commanding voice that nobody could resist he rather compelled than directed the leading men of the whole kingdom", and the only dispute thereafter was about who was to swear first.[26] Such was the stuff of personal kingship.

So too were the notorious temper tantrums of the Angevin kings. Most notorious of all was the one on Christmas Day 1170 which was to lead to the Church acquiring a new martyr in Canterbury cathedral four days later. But while the consequences of that outburst were, to say the least, embarrassing, royal anger was a potent political weapon. Witness Count John of Mortain (the future king's) fury when crossed by his brother's chancellor in 1191.

> Wrath cut furrows across his forehead; his burning eyes shot sparks; rage darkened the ruddy colour of his face. I know not what he would have done to the chancellor if in that hour of fury he had fallen like an apple into the hands of the raging count.[27]

Such outbursts, like those of Henry II where he flung off his clothes and chewed the rushes on the floor, might today suggest a need for psychiatric counselling, but to contemporaries they were fearsome exhibitions to be appeased, not pitied.[28] Royal *ira et malevolentia* might blight a man's prospects for ever. Those who incurred Henry II's wrath made desperate attempts to regain his favour. After blotting his copybook by suspected involvement in the rebellion of 1173, Bishop Arnulf of Lisieux wrote desperately not only to the king, who refused to see him, but to anybody whom he thought might be able to persuade Henry to absolve him, protesting his long service and innocence of any wrongdoing; "my working towards and eagerness to return takes up almost all the power of my being". But, as Gerald of Wales wrote, Henry II "never forgave a man he once disliked".[29] Disloyalty was indeed unforgivable, as Becket found out, and the really effective king was one whose anger men feared to incur. Richard I was so formidable that, we are told (and by one of the more sober and restrained of contemporary writers), when his return to England in 1194 was announced the rebellious castellan of St Michael's Mount in Cornwall died of fright.[30]

But necessary as such personal qualities were, there was more to kingship than strong character or ruthlessness alone, or indeed personal courage. Duke Robert of Normandy and King Stephen were both widely known as gallant soldiers; both were utter failures as rulers. Even successful warfare in the 12th century needed more than an inspiring example or good generalship. It needed money; and to raise money successfully required an administrative infrastructure of some complexity, even at this early date. Furthermore, to concentrate upon the personal qualities of individual monarchs, or their lack of them, would not explain our central problem, why the rule of the kings of England was seen as qualitatively different, and that much harsher, than that of other monarchs of the same era, most notably their French counterparts. Decisive and ruthless as William I or Henry I may have been, were they any more so than contemporaries such as Louis VI of France, or the German Emperors Henry V and Frederick Barbarossa, let alone perhaps the ablest of all 12th-century politicians, Roger II of Sicily, or that monster of cruelty the Emperor Henry VI, the man alleged to have had an iron crown nailed to the head of a rival for the throne of Sicily?[31]

What above all marked out the monarchy in England was the Norman Conquest. It was this which dictated why the government of England was different, and that the administrative structure was much more precocious, and the burden of government heavier, than in continental kingdoms. Combined with this was the accident of geography which made England smaller and thus potentially more coherent and easy to govern, given the primitive communications of the time than, for example, Germany, and to a lesser extent France. The German and French kingdoms were arguably too large to be effective political units – it was not indeed until the reign of Louis XIV that the French king was ever really in effective control of the deep south of his kingdom. England by contrast was small enough to be effectively governed. But it was William the Conqueror's victory of 1066 that was really crucial. The kings and almost all the aristocracy were foreigners, although this was not in itself the decisive factor. (One should not, however, forget that, even though many may have been bilingual, French remained the principal language of the upper-class until the second half of the 14th century, and the official legal language right up to the Commonwealth of 1649). Henry II, we are told, "had a knowledge of all the tongues used from the French sea to the River Jordan, but spoke only French and Latin".[32] That the rulers were foreigners was not in itself important, just as it was not after 1714, nor can one see the English as necessarily groaning under the yoke of foreign tyranny, galling as it must have been to have to learn French to communicate with one's overlords. An Englishman saved William the Conqueror's life at the Battle of Gerberoi in 1078, and English troops supported William Rufus against the rebellion of 1088 and helped Henry I to conquer Normandy in 1106. Indeed, if we are to believe Orderic Vitalis, it was the English in particular who urged Rufus to punish the rebels severely.[33] What was really important was the continuance of the connection with Normandy up to 1204.

During the hundred and thirty-eight years between the Conquest and 1204, England and Normandy were ruled by the same man for all but 25 of those years. Henry II and his sons after 1154 ruled not only Normandy, but virtually the whole of western France – Anjou, Touraine, Poitou, and Gascony, as well as being overlords of Brittany. Two very important consequences followed. First, and most significantly, the King of England was almost invariably an absentee landlord. Of the kings between 1066 and 1204, only Stephen was a permanent resident in England, visiting Normandy only once, in 1137 (and his reign did not perhaps commend this residence as a precedent). Henry I and Henry II ruled for almost exactly the same time, 35 years. Henry I spent less than half his reign in England, his grandson only about a third. Richard I, famously, passed only some six months in England during the nearly 10 years of his reign. Richard, indeed, was the least English of these decidedly un-English "English" kings (the adjective is entirely a misnomer at this period), for although born in England he was brought up on the continent, and as an adult had only made two very brief visits to England before he became king.[34] Appropriately enough, he lost his life in April 1199 besieging a petty castle in the Limousin. The Angevin kings in particular were far too migratory to have a capital; indeed there was no real concept of a capital city at this period, but if the Norman and later Angevin empires had a political centre it was undoubtedly Rouen, not Westminster or Winchester.

Not only were the kings more usually on the continent than in England, but their absences were often prolonged. William the Conqueror, who after his early years, spent progressively less and less time in England, was, for example, in Normandy for four continuous years between 1076 and 1080. Henry I's absences there included four continuous years between 1116 and 1120, three years from 1123 to 1126, two years from 1127 to 1129, and just over two years from August 1133 until his death on 1 December 1135. Henry II was notorious for the speed with which he travelled round his far-flung dominions, and given their size he visited England relatively frequently, but his periods on the continent still included some long spells, notably four and a half years between August 1158 and January 1163, and a further four years between 1166 and 1170. Given absences like these, some sort of provision had to be made for the governance of England without the king.

Of course, the Channel was a means of communication as much as a barrier. Petitioners, litigants, and officials from England could and did cross it to find their ruler, and English business was often settled on the continent.[35] Yet the king's absences often imposed long and frustrating delays, which litigants in particular found galling and expensive. The experience of Battle Abbey early in Henry II's reign was probably not unusual: "The king would now be crossing to Normandy, and now returning to England on his own affairs. Therefore, although the case was over a long period brought before the justices who presided over the court in the king's place . . . never could the issue be satisfactorily settled".[36] Nor was the Channel entirely safe or always speedy as a communications route. William the Conqueror had been kept waiting by contrary winds in the summer of 1066, just as Henry II was at Portsmouth from January to mid-Lent in 1182.[37] Henry I's son and heir, and all but one of his shipmates, had drowned after their ship had been carelessly sailed onto an uncharted rock in 1120.[38] The chancellor of Henry the Young King (Henry II's eldest son) drowned in the Channel in 1177, as did an ex-Master of the Knights Hospitaller in 1183. Much of the treasure confiscated from the estate of England's richest moneylender, Aaron of Lincoln, was lost at sea in 1187.[39] Henry II himself was once in imminent danger of death during a Channel storm, and was allegedly only saved by invoking the spiritual assistance of the Carthusian Hugh of Avalon.[40] Sometimes the king's presence might be desperately needed on both sides of the Channel. In 1173, Henry II faced rebellion in England and Normandy, and preferred to stay south of the Channel to deal with matters there – a good reflection of his sense of priorities – and left his representatives in England to deal with matters as best they could. Despite a number of successes, his lieutenants could not stamp out the rebellion entirely, and a series of increasingly desperate embassies were sent, asking the king to return. Finally, the Bishop of

Winchester, one of the king's most trusted servants, crossed to Normandy. One of the best of the contemporary chroniclers records here a rare instance of a medieval joke. "The Normans said, 'when the English have sent so many envoys and now send this man, what else could they send to call the King back to England except the Tower of London'".[41] But the situation in 1173-4, by far the most greatest political crisis of Henry II's reign, made especially serious because the leader of the continental rebels was the king's eldest son and designated heir, Henry the Young King, was very far from being a joke, and illustrated the potential pitfalls of cross-Channel rule.

Some sort of provision had, therefore, to be made for the governance of England in a king's absence. Royal relatives were one solution, assuming that they could be trusted, and indeed they did on occasion act as the king's representative, notably Odo of Bayeux under William the Conqueror, until his disgrace and imprisonment in 1082; Queen Matilda under Henry I, until her death in 1118; and Henry the Young King under Henry II, until his rebellion in 1173. But this was at best an *ad hoc* solution – where queens were concerned their role was largely as a figurehead (in Queen Matilda's case there is some evidence of independent action, but not a great deal), and teenage princes like the young Henry were apprentices, learning on the job so to speak. Some more settled arrangement was needed, and thus in the reign of Henry II there emerged the Justiciar, invariably a great nobleman of proven loyalty, but not just the vicegerent but also the overall head of the royal administration, even when the king was present in England. The precursor of this arrangement was Bishop Roger of Salisbury under Henry I. But while the bishop was the administrative head, and almost certainly the creator, of the great financial office known as the Exchequer, he held no formal office as the king's deputy, and indeed may only have functioned as this during the king's absence between 1123 and 1126. Contemporaries were clearly groping for the correct word to describe his functions – they used terms like the *provisor* or *procurator* of the realm – but the provision of an institutional deputy for the king had to wait for the rule of Henry I's grandson.[42]

The powers conceded to the Justiciar were considerable, acting as the king's representative in judicial matters, as the overall supervisor of the Exchequer and thus of royal finance, and as the political representative in the king's absence. In 1173, for example, Richard de Luci was not only responsible for the suppression of rebellion, but also presided over an assembly of the clergy at Westminster in which elections were made to fill the six episcopal sees then vacant. In the same year, he was present at the election of Richard of Dover as Becket's successor at Canterbury, although it was the other bishops who had the final say in the choice of candidate.[43] All this was on the king's instructions, and there were occasions when the king might countermand the Justiciar's orders or disregard his advice, as when Henry II insisted on punishing infringements on the royal forest after the 1173-4 rebellion, despite Richard de Luci's protests.[44]

Nonetheless, the emergence of the Justiciar was symptomatic of the development of a royal administration that had its own independent existence, separate from that of the king's household. The beginnings of this process date from the reign of Henry I. The first reference by name to the Exchequer comes in 1110. Even by 1135, the Exchequer may not have been entirely separate from the royal household, and there was a considerable overlap or interchange of personnel.[45] But by 1130, and probably a good bit earlier, annual accounts of royal income were being drawn up, on a regular pattern, and very little different from that which was to be the case under Henry II.

The Exchequer was not the only part of this development of government, and one should draw attention to the growth of both central and local courts (though the evolution of the former, in particular, was by no means complete by 1200), legislation and the emergence of a cadre of professional administrators. But the Exchequer and royal finance was at the heart of the process, and here the development was at its most precocious. At the end of Henry II's reign, the author of the treatise *On the Laws and Customs of England,* ascribed (almost certainly wrongly) to the King's last Justiciar Ranulf Glanvill, could say that the laws had never been written down, and could not be wholly reduced to writing because of their "confused multiplicity", although, by the very act of producing his treatise, he showed how the standardization of procedure was gathering pace.[46] But the *Dialogue of the Exchequer,* written a decade earlier than "Glanvill", shows a bureaucratic institution long since emerged from its chrysalis and in full and effective working order, in which routine and regularity were all. The Exchequer was above all the institution which gave continuity and pattern to the administration, and which was least affected by the periodic interventions of Henry II, a monarch whose besetting sin was his tendency to energetic but erratic meddling – a man of great ability and decisiveness, but not one of nature's systematizers.[47] Furthermore, its function was at the heart of government, for 12th-century governments were just as much in need of finance as those of any other age, and England was above all the financial heart of the Norman and Angevin empires.

Once again, the link with Normandy was crucial. If the kings raised the bulk of their cash in England, they spent it in Normandy. The defence of Normandy was the fundamental problem with which all the kings of England had to grapple. This was why they spent so much time there, and so relatively little in England. The Norman frontier was always, or almost always, under threat. The county of Maine was disputed with the rulers of Anjou from the 1060s until Geoffrey of Anjou conquered Normandy in 1144-5. The Vexin region remained in dispute with the King of France right up to 1204. Claims to overlordship of Brittany were a fruitful source of difficulty throughout this period. The loyalty of the Norman border lords was always fragile – even Henry I never fully resolved his problems with the Vexin aristocracy.[48] Henry had to fight to gain Normandy from his feckless elder brother in 1104-6, and then fought three further wars to retain it in 1111-13, 1116-9, and 1123-4.

All were successful, but all needed money in large quantities; to support the royal *familia* or military household which was the core of the king's army, to pay the stipendiary knights who provided most of the rest of the troops, and to build and repair the castles which consolidated the victories secured on the battlefields of Tinchebrai (1106), Brémule (1119), and Bourgthéroulde (1124).[49] It was the military burdens in Normandy which made the kings of England so anxious for money and gave them their more or less universal reputation for avarice. The Exchequer officials and the sheriffs were the agents who made the defence of Normandy possible. But to raise money, all sorts of expedients were needed, and royal rights and prerogatives were exploited to the limit, and often beyond. As the king demanded the ruthless exploitation of his financial and judicial rights (and justice was not simply the maintenance of order, but a source of money in itself), it was not surprising that his officers were equally ruthless in feathering their own nests whenever they could.

Thus it was the link with Normandy which explained the precocious administrative development of the English kingdom, and the reputation which England rightly "enjoyed" (!) as a country burdened with an oppressive and aggressive government. England was a wealthy country, certainly in the estimation of contemporaries, and therefore ripe to be exploited to finance the defence of the king's other dominions.[50] The accession of Henry of Anjou to the English throne in October 1154, with the scale of the continental commitments that much greater, and certainly little or no financial surplus to be derived from Anjou or Aquitaine, only enhanced England's role as the treasure house – or milch cow – of its rulers' empire.

There are, of course, other factors to consider. England in 1066 already possessed a more advanced and centralized administrative system than any other kingdom or state in western Christendom; and certainly more developed than that of the duchy of Normandy. There was, for example, no ducal writing office before 1066 – the duke's charters were written by the scribes of those for whom they were destined.[51] England was the only kingdom of the 11th century to have a national tax, the geld, even if it was only sporadically levied. Domesday Book, the supreme administrative achievement of the Anglo-Norman kingdom, could never have been compiled on the scale it was and with the speed it was without a mass of written material (most of it pre-1066) on which to draw.[52] But it was above all the financial needs of the Norman kings, and especially Henry I, which led to the development and exploitation of these beginnings. That William Rufus and Henry I had succeeded to the throne in the teeth of fierce opposition, and in consequence had to alienate some of the royal lands in return for support, made the search for other sources of revenue that much more determined.[53]

Secondly, one must consider, albeit briefly, the anomaly that the one surviving royal account from the reign of Henry I, the Pipe Roll of 1130, shows the King enjoying an income more than twice that of his grandson in the early years of his reign. That the King's income did not reach the 1130 figure again until 1184 certainly shows how hard Henry I's government was turning the financial screw. However, the sharp drop in royal income must be attributed to the ravages and administrative disruption of Stephen's reign (and to the alienation of resources to attract or retain supporters during this period), not to any royal change of heart or circumstance. The Exchequer was probably still working under Stephen, even after the crisis of 1141, but its operations may only have covered the six or seven counties firmly under his control, and it took a long time for royal revenue to recover after 1154, particularly since the levying of the geld was abandoned after 1162.[54] But from the 1180s onwards, royal financial exploitation was probably every bit as oppressive as under Henry I, because any lingering effects of the problems of Stephen's reign had long since disappeared, and because the situation in the French lands was becoming more urgent, with a new and more ambitious Capetian king, Philip II, seeking to exploit the weakness in the Angevin empire.[55] The consequences of this, and the unpopularity of such pressure, can be seen from the posthumous reputation of Richard I, as recorded by a chronicler writing, at the latest, in the early 1220s.

> He oppressed the English who redeemed him from imprisonment with greater debts and more frequent exactions than any other previous king had inflicted upon them. He spared no one, whatever their rank or station, whether of the secular power or ecclesiastical dignity... Every day he devoted all his efforts to thinking up devices through which he could swindle money from everyone and carry it away to be heaped up in his treasuries. No other age records, nor is authority given in any history, that any of the previous kings, even those who had reigned for a long time, had demanded so much from their kingdom, and had received as much money, as this king exacted for himself and heaped together in the five years after his return from captivity.[56]

Then there is the question of the royal officials. These enjoyed an unsavoury, and well merited reputation for the abuse of their position for their own private gain. We may, if we like, dismiss the Canterbury monk Eadmer's description of the riotous and disorderly household of William Rufus, the very approach of which led people to flee into hiding, as monastic denigration of a notoriously Godless king. Anyway, we are told that Henry I put a stop to the worst excesses.[57] However, the *curiales* of that monarch may have been less violent, but they were every bit as greedy. The *Gesta Stephani* described, somewhat rhetorically, how Henry I's officials were afraid after his death to attend the court of the new king "lest they should be overwhelmed by the cries of the poor and the complaints of the widows whose lands they had appropriated".[58] Before we assume this also to be a chronicler's exaggeration, we must point to the testament of Nigel d'Aubigni, one of King Henry's principal lieutenants in northern England, on what he thought was his deathbed in 1118, giving a long list of churches and laymen to whom he asked his brother to make restitution.[59] But, although members of the king's personal household had set allowances laid down, other royal officials did not receive fixed salaries, nor indeed were they to do so for many centuries to come. Even as late as the 17th century, it was hard to draw the line between the customary perquisites of office and out and out corruption. The real payment for all royal officials came in favours from the king. Sometimes, especially early on in the reign, this might be land confiscated from rebels; Henry I was remembered as being "close with his own substance, lavish with other people's".[60] But there were plenty of other benefits available: the provision of heiresses as wives, or wives for sons, geld exemptions, a share in judicial profits, and in the opportunity to exploit favour and position at the expense of others – in what was little better than a system of legalized plunder. That the chroniclers complained about the rise of "men from the dust" should not be taken as an accurate reflection of the social status of royal officials, who were generally from minor baronial families (many of them from Henry's lands in the Cotentin peninsula which he had possessed before he became king). It does, however, reflect how much these *curiales* profited from their role as royal servants.[61]

Henry II's officials would probably not have won many popularity contests either, although the sources are not quite so vocal in their dislike. Ralph of Diceto, however, records the king's difficulty in finding judges who could not be bribed, and William of Newburgh that Henry himself was widely disliked.[62] Leading royal administrators like Ranulf Glanvill, Geoffrey Fitz Peter, and William Brewer still rose from relative obscurity to baronial status (and in Geoffrey's case eventually to an earldom).[63] If there was not quite the volume of complaint that there had been earlier, this may perhaps be attributed to the profits of office becoming steadier and less spectacularly at the expense of other people, with landholding more stable than in the early part of the century. By now, the king was more likely to impose financial penalties rather than complete confiscation on those who opposed him (the 1173 rebels, for example, nearly all recovered their lands in the end).[64]

There was thus a strong element of royal favour, indeed caprice, in how the administration worked. Justice was by no means impartial. The *Dialogue of the Exchequer* noted that: "To some he [Henry II] does full justice for nothing, in consideration of their past services, or out of mere goodness of his heart, but to others (and it is only human nature) he will not give way for love nor money".[65] Those whom the king disliked or distrusted might find all sorts of obstacles placed in their path, their title to property questioned, their legal cases going astray, payment of long-forgotten debts suddenly demanded, royal officials digging up all sorts of petty infractions for which fines might be levied. At worst, someone might have to pay, either in money or in land, to recover the king's *benevolentia* – if they could.[66] We are told of the hapless Bishop Arnulf of Lisieux that "he preferred to abandon his episcopal duties rather than to suffer the king's hatred any longer", although a decade earlier, in happier days, he was so much in favour that he had been able to beg a substantial cash present from the king to pay his debts.[67] But even in cases like this, the king's attitude might be arbitrary and unpredictable. A Northamptonshire baron who slyly tried to take advantage of the Earl of

Leicester's involvement in the 1173 rebellion to escape his obligations of vassalage towards the earl found himself not only still saddled with the latter's overlordship, but also punished with a thousand mark fine "that the king remits his anger towards him and for the confirmation of his charters"[68]

What may we conclude, therefore, about the nature of royal rule in 12th-century England? It was harsh, it was oppressive, it was exploitative, especially financially, *and it worked*. Its agents were correspondingly unpopular. That they exploited their positions to their own advantage was in the nature of any pre-modern governmental system. That they had such opportunity to do so reflected the growth of the system. If, Exchequer apart, the "system" was still haphazard and often based on expedients, and was to develop much further during the 13th century, it was, however, more developed and more systematic than anywhere else in Christendom, except for the kingdom of Sicily (where law and administration drew heavily on Byzantine and Arab precedents).[69]

The reign of Richard I, absent for almost the whole of his reign either on Crusade, in captivity in Germany, or fighting in France, showed how far this development of a governmental apparatus, not so much without the king as alongside the king, had come. Three aspects of this need briefly to be mentioned. First, there was the extraordinary administrative effort needed to organize and finance Richard's Crusade, spurred on by the king's enthusiasm but carried out by royal officials and co-opted churchmen. That a large fleet could be raised and equipped, sailors paid a year's wages in advance, food purchased in huge quantities, almost certainly an enlarged *familia* of household troops subsidized, discipline maintained and the king still have sufficient cash to sustain his Crusade once he got to the Holy Land, even to lend money to other leaders, despite the long delays on the way, was a striking testimony to the efficiency of English royal administration.[70] Second, despite factional dispute and great problems, especially with the recalcitrant Count John, the government could be maintained even while Richard was a prisoner, and a large ransom was speedily raised to free him. Third, during his reign, and more specifically during the justiciarship of Archbishop Hubert Walter (1194-8), there was a very considerable development and specialization of the central administration: the Exchequer was finally divorced from the judicial activity of the *Curia Regis,* a separate financial department was set up to deal with Jewish debts, and experiments were made with new methods of raising revenue. There was at the end of the 12th century a veritable explosion in record keeping (although some of this may date back to the last years of Henry II). Separate rolls were in future to be kept of debts owed to the crown, legal agreements made in the royal courts, royal grants, both in formal charters and in writs, and fines and amercements imposed by royal judges.[71]

This plethora of written record is testimony to how far the divorce of administrative activity from the direct action of the king had already gone by 1200. This is, or course, not to say that the king was, therefore, unimportant.

He still made the ultimate political decisions, led his army in war, took, if he chose, a personal role as judge, convened assemblies, personally appointed bishops (despite papal protests) and officials, and – probably the most difficult task of all – managed and balanced the touchy susceptibilities of his leading subjects. But in the 12th century, he ruled an empire, not just a single kingdom. Because of this, and the problems which it engendered, there developed in England an administration which could work in the king's absence, while he grappled with the much greater difficulties of ruling his continental dominions. Normandy and England at least had certain ties bringing them together, not least baronial families who possessed estates on both sides of the Channel.[72] But otherwise, the Angevin empire after 1154 was little more than a heterogeneous collection of disparate lands, held together only by the person of the king. To rule them he had to be forever on the move, whatever the weather or time of year, "travelling in unbearably long stages . . . merciless beyond measure to the household which accompanied him". Henry II's restless energy, his chronic inability ever to sit still, even in Church, "perpetually wakeful and at work", was a positive advantage here.[73]

Let us end, as we began, with another of the alleged *obiter dicta* of Louis VII of France (a king perhaps more memorable for striking words than deeds). On Henry's return to the continent in 1172, he exclaimed with wonder: "Now Ireland, now England, now Normandy, the King of England seems rather to fly than to travel by horse or ship".[74] But, however rapidly he travelled, Henry II could only continue this itinerant monarchy because for much of the time England could be left to its own devices, because it had an administration which could work without the king's daily presence, and because it served as the financial prop supporting the whole edifice of the Angevin empire. In the end, that burden was to prove too much, and King John was to reap the fruits of his father's and his brother's exploitation of the kingdom they only sometimes (in Henry's case) or rarely (in Richard's) saw.

Footnotes to this Chapter may be found on pages 344–49.

5: David Carpenter

The thirteenth-century kings

ON 28 NOVEMBER 1871, a strange gathering took place in Edward the Confessor's chapel in Westminster Abbey. It was led by the Dean of Westminster, The Very Rev Arthur Penhyrn Stanley, and comprised ecclesiastics, antiquaries, and workmen. Its purpose was to open the coffin and examine the body of King Henry III. The purpose was unachieved. As Stanley later recorded, after the marble slabs above the coffin had been lifted, "a feeling was found to prevail that there did not seem, upon historical grounds to be sufficient motive to warrant the opening of the coffin".[1] According to the story preserved at the abbey, Queen Victoria had not been amused at plans to tamper with the bones of her predecessor and had ordered Stanley to desist.[2] So Henry III still rests undisturbed, his body probably perfectly preserved. Stanley did, however, measure the coffin and found it 6 feet 1 inch long. Assuming that body length was considerably shorter than coffin length, Henry was, therefore, a man of middle height, just as stated by the chronicler Trevet.[3] Perhaps he stood about as tall as his father, King John, whose body was examined in 1797 and measured 5 feet 5 inches.[4] John and Henry, therefore, were considerably shorter than Henry's son, Edward I. His corpse, inspected in gruesome detail in 1774, measured a magnificent 6 feet 2 inches.[5]

Eighteenth- and 19th-century antiquaries were able to indulge their fascination for kings and corpses partly because of the continuities of English history. There had been no revolutionary sacking of royal tombs in England like those suffered in France at Fontevrault and St Denis. The antiquaries were also lucky that all three 13th-century kings had died and been buried in England. John died at Newark on 17-18 October 1216 and was buried in Worcester cathedral; Henry died on 16 November 1272 at Westminster and was buried there; Edward died on 7 July 1307 at Burgh-on-Sands by the Solway Firth and was brought back to Westminster to lie beside his father. These English deaths and burials were not mere coincidences. They reflected a momentous change in the whole nature of the Plantagenet dynasty which had taken place in the early 13th century.

The 12th-century kings had spent roughly half their time in England and half in their dominions on the continent. In 1189, Henry II died at Chinon in the Touraine; Richard I died 10 years later at Chalus Chabrol in the Limousin; both were buried at Fontevrault abbey under massive self-confident effigies. Here, far more than England, was home. The loss of Normandy and Anjou in 1203-4 altered the pattern completely. Although the dynasty retained Gascony, the duchy's lack of revenues and castle-palaces precluded living there. Henry III might leave his heart to Fontevrault, but he created a new mausoleum for his family in the great abbey church at Westminster. It was there that he and Edward were buried beside their sainted Anglo-

Saxon predecessor, Edward the Confessor. It was there the dynasty now belonged.

The Englishness of the dynasty was also reflected in its military activities, or at least in those activities at their most successful. John's victory at Mirebeau in Anjou in 1202 was the last Plantagenet triumph on the continent before Edward III's at Crécy in 1346. After 1202, John's efforts to recover the Angevin empire, like those later of Henry III, were abject failures. In 1259, in the Treaty of Paris, Henry acknowledged that Normandy, Anjou, and Poitou were gone. Within the British Isles, the pattern was very different. John campaigned successfully in Wales in 1211 as did Henry III in the 1240s. Both seized from the princes of Gwynedd the lands between the rivers Conwy and the Dee. These successes foreshadowed Edward I's Welsh wars of 1277 and 1282 which finally brought to an end the long history of independent Wales, in the process remodelling the whole political shape of Britain and providing the dynasty with significant compensation for its losses on the continent. By 1305, two years before Edward's death, the shape of Britain appeared even more profoundly changed. For Edward, in a series of campaigns since 1294, seemed also to have conquered Scotland. More than any monarch before the Act of Union in 1707 he was truly king of Britain. That was not, to be sure, how Edward looked at things. He remained King of England, and Wales and Scotland became *lands* annexed to the English Crown; a fact which helps to explain the eventual Scottish revolt under Robert Bruce, the triumph at Bannockburn (1314) and the survival of the Scottish kingdom down to the 18th century.[6]

The reduction of Wales and Scotland to the status of lands reflects something else about Edward's success: it was founded on force, not consent, and thus depended crucially on money, money, which "gives power. . . Those who are lacking in it become a prey to their enemies, while those who are well supplied despoil their foes". These were the words of the *Dialogus de Scaccario,* the great book written about the working of the exchequer in 1176.[7] Edward's conquests were, indeed, made possible by a transformation in the whole basis of English royal finance. The forces necessitating that transformation were a combination of inflation and a decline in the Crown's income from land.[8] Between 1180 and 1220, many prices doubled or tripled: the wages of a knight, for example, rose from 8d a day to 2s. Lay and ecclesiastical magnates, deriving the great bulk of their income from land, could profit from this situation. They took their estates in hand, and produced corn to sell on the market, thus taking advantage of the rising prices. But the king was unable to do this on the same scale since much of his income came from non-landed resources. In this respect, there had been a great change during the course of the 12th century as the vast royal estates acquired by the Norman Conquest were given away to provide patronage for servants and supporters.[9] In the early 12th century, more than half the king's income came from land; a hundred years later perhaps only a third did so. The shortfall was made up from other sources: from judicial amercements; from amercements for offences against the royal forest; from reliefs (the tax paid by a baron to inherit his estates); from the exploitation of wardships; and from extortions from the Church. The trouble was that these sources bore heavily on individuals and institutions in a way income from selling corn did not. Such revenues could only by expanded at the cost of political discontent. King John did expand them with remarkable efficiency and ruthlessness. At its height, his income from England was in real terms larger than that enjoyed by any of his predecessors.[10] The result was Magna Carta, for the Charter, more than anything else, was designed to limit the king's financial exploitation of the kingdom.

The civil war which followed John's rejection of Magna Carta destroyed the financial resources of the Crown far more effectively than the Charter would ever have done.[11] King Henry III lived with the consequences throughout his reign and had no solution to them. In the 1240s and 1250s, he struggled to live within his means and build up a treasure, a treasure saved in gold (the currency of the East) in order to finance a crusade. Visually, the result did not look very impressive for, at its height in 1253, the gold treasure would still have fitted into a large suit case. But gold's bulk, of course, has no relation to its value. The treasure was worth some £20,000, not far short of a year's annual income. The trouble was that it had taken nearly a decade to save. Even when he was trying hardest, Henry had been able to put by only a few thousand pounds a year.[12] The lesson was clear. In the mid-13th century the King of England could live within his means, but he could not fight a sustained and major war – for which far more than £20,000 was required. Lack of money as much as lack of martial ardour explains why Henry III neither recovered his lands in France nor made permanent conquests in Britain.

Edward I transformed this situation.[13] He introduced Italian bankers, the Riccardi of Lucca who funded a large number of royal activities, most notably the wars in Wales in the 1270s and 1280s.[14] They were repaid from an entirely new source of revenue: the customs. From 1275, Edward levied 6s 8d on every exported sack of wool, thus increasing his annual income by about £10,000. Finally, to meet the monumental costs of the wars in Scotland and France in the 1290s, Edward resorted to general taxation. The form of such taxation dated back to at least 1207; every individual, save the very poor, paid a percentage of his movable property, essentially his corn and cattle. But Edward was the first king to secure such taxation on a regular basis, thus tapping the wealth of the country which had risen throughout the century with a growing population. Between 1294 and 1307, six taxes brought in some £270,000, with another £224,000 coming from taxation levied on the Church.[15] In real terms, given that inflation had continued, if at a slower pace after 1220, Edward had exceeded the income of King John[16] without provoking the same level of political protest.

That is not to say there were no political consequences. John's exploitation of the kingdom produced Magna Carta; Edward's established the Commons in parliament. Constitutional limitations were the final way in which English kingship was transformed in the 13th century. John had rejected the Charter within a few months of its concession in 1215. He had seen it merely as a tactical device to gain time. The government of his young son, however, (Henry III was only nine on his accession in 1216) performed the greatest U-turn in English history. They issued new versions of the Charter in 1216, 1217, and 1225 to divide the rebels during the war and to secure support and taxation during peace. The 1225 Charter and its companion Charter of the Forest became definitive and were formally accepted by all subsequent English kings. Some of the Charter's clauses were highly successful, notably that which limited the relief of a baron to £100, where kings before 1215 had sometimes charged thousands. Others proved vague or unenforcible. Still a principle had been asserted: kings were subject to the law; their capacity for arbitrary, tyrannical conduct was more limited as a consequence.[17] In the long run, however, it was the development of parliament which proved more significant. In the sense of a great assembly of the realm, parliament had existed since the time of the Anglo-Saxon witan. But more happened in the 13th century than simply a new name for an old institution. First kings became dependent, as we have seen, on general taxation, taxation which needed parliamentary sanction if it was to be collected. Second, during the course of the century, the great barons in parliament felt that they alone could no longer give that sanction. In 1225, 1232, and 1237 they had done so; but all the taxes levied by Edward I were voted by representatives sent from the counties and the boroughs. (Usually each county sent two knights and each borough two burgesses). Here then was the beginning of the House of Commons. In 1301, it was a knight of the shire, Henry of Keighley, who presented a petition highly critical of royal government at the Lincoln parliament.[18] This was the shape of things to come.

The powers and conditions of kingship had, therefore, changed very greatly during the course of the 13th century. In 1200, a king, more Angevin than English, had lived off his own, ruled without constitutional restraint, and dealt politically with a smallish group of great barons. A hundred years later, a very English king could no longer live, or at least no longer fight, off his own but needed general taxation; he had to steer within or around Magna Carta, negotiate with parliament and deal with a political community which embraced knights, esquires, burgesses, freemen, and peasants as well as bishops and barons. The business of kingship had thus become more complex and conditional. If a king failed to meet the conditions he became weaker than any of his predecessors. That was the fate of Henry III. But when the king could meet the conditions, as Edward I did on occasions, he could generate more power from England than ever before. It was Wales and Scotland which suffered the consequences.

In dealing with these changing circumstances, the personality of the individual kings was of central importance. What were they like? John, it has been said, was "energetic, licentious, cruel, impious, suspicious, cunning, and graceless".[19] Henry seems the exact reverse. He was indolent, chaste, merciful, trusting, naive, and sometimes at least, charming. Edward differed from Henry just as Henry had from John. Perhaps in each case, the reaction was conscious. Edward shared his father's chastity and (if with less ostentation) his piety but his military expertise, tightfistedness, political grasp, and iron determination were utterly unlike. To his barons he must often have seemed, in the memorable words of Professor Lionel Stones, "the stern headmaster".[20]

The character sketches proffered above may well provoke scepticism. How can we know what the kings were like? There are two principal sources to draw on. The first of these are chronicles.[21] In terms of volume, the 13th century was the great age of the monastic chronicle. At St Albans, Roger of Wendover wrote extensively about John and about Henry III down to 1235. The *Chronica Majora* (Greater Chronicle) of his successor, Matthew Paris, runs to more than 1,600 printed pages for the years from 1236 down to Matthew's death in 1259.[22] Chronicles were also produced at the houses of Barnwell, Coggeshall, Bury St Edmunds, Dunstable, Dover, Guisborough, Norwich, Osney, Waverley, Tewkesbury, Burton, Winchester, and Worcester to name just a few. There were also chronicles written by the occasional layman, notably the London alderman, Arnold fitz Thedmar.

From one point of view, the yield from these works is disappointing. No chronicler writing about King John matched William of Newburgh's long, balanced assessment of Henry II.[23] Even the Barnwell chronicler, the most intelligent in the reign, contented himself with the true but obvious verdict that John was "a great prince but unlucky, like Marius experiencing both types of fortune; he was munificent and liberal to aliens but a despoiler of his own people . . . wherefore he was deserted by them before the end".[24] For the rest, the chroniclers do little more than berate John for his cruelty, licentiousness, and tyrannical extortions. All that may be true, but it scarcely takes us far inside the character.

With Henry III, things are little better. The chroniclers praised him for piety and lamented the favours he showed to his foreign relatives, but not a single contemporary chronicler, not even the voluminous Matthew Paris, provided a serious set-piece examination of his character.[25] The fullest sketch of King Henry comes in the chronicle of the Franciscan friar, Nicholas Trevet:

> The king was considered to be as little prudent in secular affairs as he was great in devotion to the Lord. For he was accustomed to hear three sung masses a day, and, wishing to hear more, he assiduously attended masses celebrated privately. Indeed, it happened that St Louis, King of the French, when discussing this with him, said he should not always spend his time at mass, but should listen to sermons more often. To whom [Henry] wittily replied that he preferred to see his friend more often than to hear him speak, although uttering good things. [Henry] was of medium height, of compact build, with the lid of one eye drooping so that it hid part of the black pupil; he was strong in build but rash in

behaviour, but since he had happy and fortunate endings, many thought
him the lynx, penetrating all things, prophesied by Merlin.[26]

This is an engaging portrait, yet it is one assembled by a later historian, not
painted by a contemporary. Trevet was born in about 1258, but did not write
his chronicle till 1330, nearly 60 years after Henry's death. The initial sentence
which balances Henry's imprudence and his piety was essentially borrowed
from an earlier chronicler, Walter of Guisborough (who wrote about 1300).[27]
Although, as we have seen, Trevet may have been right about the King's
stature, his statement about hearing three masses a day, although true to
the spirit of Henry's devotion to the mass, is false to the facts when tested
against the actual records of his household.[28] What price then the widely
quoted anecdote about St Louis?

Trevet also provides by far the fullest description of Edward I. We learn of
his fame as a knight; his passion for hawking and hunting; his great height;
his long thighs; his protruding stomach; his lisp; his broad forehead and
regular features marred only by his father's hanging eyelid. Here Trevet is,
of course, more nearly a contemporary source; yet while he presents a splendid
outward picture of the King, on Edward the politician he offers merely that
"he was a man of tried prudence in affairs of state".[29] The 12th-century
chroniclers did rather better. Here, for example, is William of Malmesbury's
description of King Stephen where every word is weighed to illumine the
strengths and weaknesses of his character:

> He was a man of energy but little judgment, active in war, of extraordinary
> spirit in undertaking any difficult task, lenient to his enemies and easily
> appeased, courteous to all; although you admired his kindness in
> promising, still you felt his words lacked truth and his promises
> fulfilment.[30]

If we ask why the 13th century chroniclers compare badly to the 12th, the
answer lies partly in inclination, partly in ability. The Barnwell chronicler,
writing of John's reign, and Thomas Wykes at Osney Abbey, writing of Henry
III and Edward I, had the ability to paint sensitive portraits of their monarchs,
but not the inclination. Matthew Paris, by contrast, sometimes wrote
formal obituaries of prominent people, and might have attempted one of
Henry III, had he lived long enough; but he lacked the ability to make such
obituaries particularly illuminating. Matthew's judgment was blurred by
his hostility to foreigners and his detestation of any form of taxation. He
was also unperceptive. These traits together could produce passages of
considerable confusion. In the 1250s, for example, Matthew was aware that
Henry III was joining native nobles and foreigners together at court. But he
could not believe that Englishmen could do anything but hate foreigners
and so, in an extraordinary passage, Paris has the English despairing at
themselves.

> The prelates and magnates of England were terrified and thrown into
> an abyss of despair because the King, having surrounded himself with
> aliens, now, with ineffable cunning, attracted to himself and allied with
> many and nearly all the best men of England . . . and also a good many
> other nobles.[31]

One need not, however, despair of the 13th-century chroniclers. If they are
short on analysis and set-piece description, they do provide a magnificent
amount of information. Paris, for example, records in detail his own
conversations with the King as well as many other of Henry's speeches and
remarks. The central question here is that of Paris's accuracy. It is a question
to which we shall return.

First, however, a word about the second main source for the 13th-century
kings, namely the records produced by their own government. This is a source
which hugely increased in scale and importance at the beginning of the 13th
century. It then became the practice to record on a series of rolls, nearly all
of which survive, the letters written by the chancery in the king's name. From
the same period, we have the first surviving memoranda rolls of the Exchequer
which, among other things, record the king's intervention in matters of finance,
and the first records of the judicial bench and the court *coram rege* which
recorded his interventions in law cases. There are problems with using these
sources. When, for example, a royal letter on the chancery rolls expressed
the king's anger or astonishment, was he really angry or astonished, or were
these simply conventional words of the chancery clerks?[32] For much of the
13th century, the chancery was with the king so he almost certainly had much
to do with many letters on the rolls; the problem is to decide which ones.
Which letters are personal, which merely routine? Even when one can feel
confident that letters and memoranda are personal, there is still the difficulty
of interpreting what exactly is meant. If, however, these difficulties can be
overcome, then remarkable light may be shed on the king's personality and
his intimate relations with his courtiers.

The difficulties and the possibilities are illustrated from two entries on the
chancery rolls, one from the rolls of King John, one from those of King
Henry. Sometime in 1204-5 the chancery clerk made the following entry:

> The wife of Hugh de Neville gives the King 200 chickens so that she
> can lie one night with her lord, Hugh de Neville. Pledges: Thomas of
> Sandford for 100 chickens and Hugh himself for 100 chickens to be
> delivered by the beginning of Lent and any then outstanding are to be
> delivered by the following Easter.[33]

Historians have long puzzled over the meaning of this. Hugh de Neville was
John's chief forester and constable of Marlborough.[34] Thomas of Sandford
was constable of the nearby castle of Devizes and another royal intimate.
Perhaps the most likely explanation is that Hugh's wife, Joan, was John's
mistress and that John was setting fanciful terms for her return for one night

to the matrimonial bed.[35] If so, it suggests the cruel sense of humour with which John teased and tormented his intimates. The chickens, of course, were part of the joke. Their value was about 16s 8d, considerably less than the King might lose in a game of dice.[36] That was all, John implied, a night with Hugh was worth. And if the chickens were not delivered by Lent, Hugh might have to wait till Easter for the brief resumption of his marital rights. No wonder in 1216, at the crisis of John's fortunes, Hugh deserted and handed Marlborough over to the rebels. The example from Henry III's rolls also records a debt owed to the King. It runs as follows:

> Memorandum that the Lord King playing a game[*ludendo*] with Peter the Poitevin in the ship when he crossed back from Gascony to England [in 1243] ordered all the following things to be enrolled so, however, that with Peter not seeing they should be immediately cancelled.

> Memorandum that Peter the Poitevin owes the Lord King 3 marks which he received from the Abbot of Margam and which the Abbot ought to have delivered to the King.

> Item. The same owes 60 capons for a transgression in the ship.

> Item. The same owes the Lord King 24 casks of wine for the arrears of the wines which he bought for the use of the King at Mussak where he dreamed that he had seen the Emperor Otto.

> Item. The same owes the Lord King £100 which he promised him in the ship the day after the octave of the nativity of the Blessed Mary.

> Memorandum that Peter the Poitevin is in arrears for £71 for 71 casks of wine which cost £154, which wines he sold by order of the King, each cask for £3, and he ought to pay the wine merchant all the money save the foresaid £71 which he pays the king.[37]

The background to this entry, unlike the one about Joan de Neville, is clear for it is stated: Henry was having a game with Peter, one of his household clerks.[38] He was pulling his leg by saddling him with a whole series of ridiculous debts.[39] It was fairly innocuous stuff, for it seems highly unlikely that Peter ever thought he would really have to pay the debts even though the joke was prolonged by concealing the cancellation from him. John and Henry, therefore, were each having fun at the expense of one of their servants. But whereas John's jest was cruel and humiliating, Henry's was playful and harmless; a contrast which reflects the very different characters of the two kings and the differing atmospheres of their domestic circles. It would be nice to conclude this section with an equivalent episode featuring Edward I; but examples of Edward's humour are unknown.

The records of government can, therefore, take us close to the personality of the king. They also help to control the evidence obtained from chroniclers. When government and chronicle evidence are used together they can be particularly fruitful. An example of such a conjunction is Henry III's speech at the Exchequer in October 1256[40] Here the accuracy of Matthew Paris' account can be checked against the official version on the memoranda roll of the Exchequer. The two sources can throw new light on Henry's strengths and weaknesses as a king.

To understand Henry's speech a word of background is necessary. Since the 12th century, each sheriff had been required to appear at the Exchequer on the day after Michaelmas and the day after the close of Easter to make his "proffer", that is to pay in the money he owed for the farm of his county and for all the debts (many arising from amercements) which the Exchequer had summoned him to collect from individuals. Various towns, boroughs, and manors, which enjoyed the liberty or privilege of a direct relationship with the Exchequer, were required to do the same.[41] Henry's pronouncement dealt with this practice or rather with the breach of it. Matthew Paris recites it as follows.

> What the King did then at the Exchequer
>
> In the same year, the Lord King came to the Exchequer on the fourth day before the day of St Edward [9 October], and sitting there with the barons, pronounced with his own mouth that each sheriff, who did not appear each year in the octaves of Michaelmas with his proffer of the king's money from farms, amercements, and other debts, should be amerced on the first day at five marks, on the second day at ten, on the third at fifteen, and on the fourth if still absent, he should be held to ransom. The king made a similar pronouncement against the cities which have liberties and answer at the Exchequer through their own bailiffs; so namely that on the fourth day if they did not appear in the same way as the sheriffs they should lose their liberties.[42]

Here next is the official record on the memoranda roll of the Exchequer.[43]

> Provision of the Lord King
>
> It has been provided by the Lord King that each sheriff of England shall come to the Exchequer on the day after Michaelmas and the day after the close of Easter in his own person both with his farms and his summonses to make his proffer as he ought to according to the ancient custom of the Exchequer. And unless they come, as aforesaid, within the fifth day on the foresaid terms they shall be amerced on the first day at £5, on the second day at £5, on the third day at £5 on the fourth day at £5 and on the fifth day at the King's will.
>
> And all the sheriffs are ordered by the King to proclaim in their counties that all who ought to answer at the Exchequer by their own hand for cities, boroughs, and other demesne manors of the King shall be at the Exchequer at the said terms in their own persons to answer for their farms and for other debts of the King for which they ought to answer by their own hand under the liberty conceded them by the King. And

unless they are there as aforesaid, each mayor of each city and each
keeper both of boroughs and other demesnes of the Lord King, shall be
amerced on the first day at 5 marks, on the second day at 5 marks, on
the third day at 5 marks, on the fourth day at 5 marks, and on the fifth
day the city, borough, or other demesne shall be taken into the King's
hands, not to be returned save by the grace and will of the King.

And if there is any other bailiff or keeper of the King who ought to
answer at the Exchequer for debts of the King by his own hand and has
not come to the Exchequer at the foresaid terms to answer, then, as said
before, he shall be amerced each day within the fifth day at £5 as with
the sheriffs.

Matthew Paris' account is characteristically undiscerning in failing to explain
either the background or the success of the King's pronouncement, points to
which we shall return. Here, however, the question is that of Matthew's
factual accuracy. It is easy to point to the omissions and errors. He failed
to note that the sheriffs were to appear at Easter as well at Michaelmas.[44]
He said they were to be amerced 5 marks a day for the first three days whereas
in fact it was £5 a day for the first four days.[45] He said the cities and boroughs
were to be amerced at the same rate as the sheriffs whereas it was they who
were to be charged the 5 marks. Although some of the details may be shaky,
Paris has got the gist of King's pronouncement right. He knows the ruling
covered sheriffs and cities; he knows the aim was to secure the personal
appearance of the officials with their proffers; he has the size of the penalty
nearly accurate and knows that it would be repeated over several days until
the sheriffs were amerced at the King's will[46] and the cities lost their liberties.
More generally, it is impressive that Paris simply knows about the episode
at all. No other chronicler mentions it. This confirms, what other evidence
also shows, that Matthew was in close and unique touch with events at the
Exchequer.[47] Paris, moreover, records the facts fairly accurately, even though
they touched on one of his main obsessions: the financial exactions of the
Crown.[48] Indeed, by making the monetary penalty 5 marks rather than £5
he made the level of those exactions rather less than they were.

What then of the two of pieces of information Paris supplies which are not
in the official record. The first is the date, namely 9 October; the second the
priceless statement, if true, that Henry sat with the barons of the Exchequer
and made the pronouncement "with his own mouth". The date is precisely
the type of detail one might expect Paris to get wrong, yet there is confirmation
that he was right, or very nearly so. Having concluded his account of the
King's appearance, Paris continued by saying that *on the same day* all the
sheriffs were amerced 5 marks for disobeying an order to distrain all those
with lands worth £10 a year to become knights. Again we have an official
record of this measure attached to a chancery roll which dates it to Tuesday
before the Feast of St Edward, that is Tuesday 10 October.[49] Either, therefore,
the King's pronouncement took place on 10 October not the 9th or Paris was
mistaken about it taking place on the same day as the measure about distraint

of knighthood. Either way we may feel that Paris has got the date very nearly right. By that token, he is unlikely to have been mistaken about the much larger point, namely that Henry made the pronouncement in person. A study of the King's itinerary supports that conclusion: it was precisely on 8 or 9 October that Henry reached Westminster on a journey back from Canterbury where he had been earlier in the month.

This impression of substantial accuracy mixed with the occasional shaky detail is confirmed by Paris' account, just mentioned, of the amercement of the sheriffs for disobeying the order for distraint of knighthood. Paris was wrong to say that all those with £10 a year were to be knights; the level was £15,[50] and, as we have seen, he may have been slightly out with the date. But this time he was right about the size of the penalty – 5 marks – and he was right too about the story as a whole: all the sheriffs were indeed amerced.[51]

It would be wrong to extrapolate with total confidence from Paris' success on these occasions. There are other episodes where his account, tested against the records, appears far less satisfactory.[52] Clearly, however, Paris can never be ignored. There must always be a good chance that his accounts of speeches, remarks, and conversations are tolerably accurate. Indeed, his versions of Henry's speeches at the parliaments of 1244 and 1248 and his account of his quarrels with the Countess of Arundel and the Earl of Norfolk all find confirmation from record evidence. Paris is, in short, a far better source than he is often given credit for. He was prejudiced and unperceptive. He rarely showed much insight into people and events. But he also provided a vast amount of essentially trustworthy information which enables the history of the years from 1236 to 1259 to be written in a detail unparalleled for any other period in the Middle Ages.

Returning to Henry's speech at the Exchequer in October 1256, what light does it throw on his kingship? At first sight, it is surely a favourable one. Henry appears very much a "hands on" king, determined to control his officials and increase his revenues. Admittedly, one can devalue the fact that Henry spoke for himself. Perhaps he was told what to say by his councillors and even then made a hash of it, muddling up pounds and marks, hence the discrepancy between the Paris version and that of the Exchequer with the former reflecting what Henry actually said and the latter, Hansard fashion, what he was supposed to have said. The story of Henry's gold treasure, however, shows his interest in the strategy and detail of financial policy;[53] it seems unlikely that he did not, at the very least, have a great input into the provisions of October 1256. He may even have conceived them. Henry came to the Exchequer alone, or at least Paris does not mention surrounding councillors; he acted as soon as he arrived at Westminster from Canterbury, so there cannot have been lengthy discussion with the Exchequer officials. Indeed, as we shall see, they may even have disapproved of the initiative, at least in the form it took.

From one point of view, there was every reason for Henry to take action. The ruling had two immediate objects: first, to make the sheriffs turn up on time on the day after Michaelmas and the day after the close of Easter; second, to make them turn up in person and not through deputies.[54] With respect to punctuality, the memoranda rolls appear to suggest that nothing much was wrong. In 1256, almost all the sheriffs are recorded as appearing, in person or by proxy, on the day after Michaelmas.[55] The pattern is much the same in previous years at the Michaelmas proffer and the Easter. There are reasons for thinking, however, that the record of appearances on the memoranda rolls was on some occasions fictional. According to the roll, the citizens of York appeared through a deputy on the day after Michaelmas 1256 and brought £23. Yet elsewhere on the roll, in fact immediately after the text of the King's ruling, an entry states that the mayor and bailiffs of York had neither come in person nor sent deputies with money either on the day after Michaelmas or on the three subsequent days.[56] It was not till 7 October that the receipt roll records money received from the citizens.[57] The fact that only York was singled out for individual comment (and punishment) in 1256 might suggest that only York had failed to turn up. On the other hand, perhaps the Yorkists were made an example of because they were unlucky or because they had done nothing to palliate or excuse their offence. It may well be that the memoranda roll record was misleading in other cases also. Thus the proffers it records as brought on the day after Michaelmas (Saturday 30 September) do not begin to appear on the receipt roll until Monday 2 October and continue to come in over the next days and weeks.[58] Now it is possible that the sheriffs whose money was received on or soon after 2 October did indeed appear in person or through deputies on 30 September, for it would have taken some time for the money they brought to be counted and thus formally received into the Exchequer.[59] But can this still be true of the sheriffs whose money was received as late as 14 and 17 October and indeed, in one case, on 4 November?[60]

Just how many sheriffs or deputies defaulted at Michaelmas 1256 is, therefore, impossible to say, but quite probably there were enough to make Henry feel there was a serious problem. Clearly, the failure of the mayor and bailiffs of York to appear caused particular outrage. Henry could feel equally concerned about the use of deputies. At Michaelmas 1256, just before his demarche, eight sheriffs had appeared in person at the Exchequer; 16 sheriffs had sent deputies.[61] That made it difficult, on the face of it, if the proffer was inadequate to pin responsibility where it belonged. The Michaelmas 1256 proffer was indeed inadequate, or so it appeared. It produced a mere £1447 as against £2486 the year before.[62] Henry's financial difficulties at this time were almost overwhelming.[63] He had every reason to get his money in on time and punish those responsible for delay and shortfall.[64] His action had plenty of precedent. In 1237, the Exchequer had amerced 16 sheriffs £5 each for failing to appear in person on the day after the close of Easter;[65] indeed, the £5 a day penalty for failure to appear and the ultimate threat of direr penalties at the King's will were mentioned by the *Dialogus de Scaccario* as early as 1176.[66]

What then were the results of Henry's impressive provision? There were
some immediately. The mayor and bailiffs of York were first amerced £20
for their failure to appear on the first four days after Michaelmas and then
the city was taken into the King's hands.[67] The real test, however, would
come at the Easter Exchequer of 1257, the first at which the new ruling
requiring the sheriffs and bailiffs to appear on time and in person, would be
in force. It was a test which was failed comprehensively. Just how many
sheriffs did not appear on the day after the close of Easter itself we cannot
know. But fail some almost certainly did if we may judge from the dates at
which the money they brought was received into the Exchequer. The day
after the close of Easter was 16 April; it was not till 25-28 April that the
proffers of the sheriffs of Lincolnshire, Bedfordshire-Buckinghamshire, and
Northumberland were received into the Exchequer. Other receipts were later
than that.[68] The continuation of deputies was even more blatant. Eight
sheriffs appeared in person and 15 sent deputies, almost exactly the same
as at the previous Michaelmas.[69]

Now was the moment for punitive action and the Exchequer prepared to take
it. "Concerning the sheriffs who have not come personally to the Exchequer
on the day after the close of Easter as accustomed," wrote the clerk in the
margin of the memoranda roll. Against this entry was added, "The sheriff
of Lincoln has not come on the first day, the second day nor the third. The
sheriff of Bedfordshire and Buckinghamshire similarly".

The clerk then left about three inches blank and drew a bracket in the margin
to embrace the names which would follow.[70] But none ever did. There is no
sign that the sheriffs of Lincolnshire, Bedfordshire-Buckinghamshire or
any one else were amerced for failing to turn up punctually and/or in person.[71]
The whole scheme was abandoned. At the following Michaelmas proffer of
1257, eight sheriffs came in person and 15 sent deputies, almost exactly the
same as the year before.[72] The pattern of punctuality likewise seems much
the same.[73] Nor is it clear that the initiative had done much to improve the
general efficiency of the sheriffs and other bailiffs. The £1489 proffered at
Easter 1257 was still some £200 less than the previous Easter.[74] Admittedly,
the Michaelmas proffer of 1257 raised £2722, £1275 more than at Michaelmas
1256, when the low amount may have prompted Henry's initiative. But the
figure in 1256 was explained neither by the use of deputies, whose numbers
were much the same at Michaelmas 1255, 1256, and 1257, nor by the sheriffs'
general delinquency. It was explained by the way Henry had issued writs
ordering the sheriffs to pay their money direct into his wardrobe rather than
into the Exchequer, itself a reflection of the hand to mouth state of his finances.
The Exchequer was perfectly aware of this and under its record of the
Michaelmas 1256 proffer, noted for the first time the amount authorized by
such writs alongside the amount brought in in cash.[75]

The trouble was that Henry was trying to reverse a very well established
practice. He claimed in his speech that the sheriffs were to appear on time

and in person with their proffers "as they ought to do according to the ancient custom of the Exchequer". But the custom he referred to, if it had ever existed, was so ancient that it had long since fallen into desuetude. The first chronological receipt roll to survive, that for Michaelmas 1236, already shows that the shrieval proffers were paid in over a period of time.[76] Throughout Henry's reign, the memoranda rolls of the Exchequer show a good proportion of the sheriffs making their proffers through deputies. The same had been true in the reign of John. At the Easter proffer of 1208, the only one of which we have a record, eight sheriffs came in person and 14 through deputies.[77] Admittedly, nine of the 14 had the best possible excuse, they were with the King, or so their deputies claimed. But it would be wrong to conclude that the absence from the proffer was otherwise punishable in the way Henry had envisaged. The Exchequer took no action against the five remaining absent sheriffs and also accepted that the others were with John on the sole say so of their deputies. In other words, no formal writ from the King was required to excuse absence from the proffer. This was already established practice in 1176. In that year, the *Dialogus de Scaccario* acknowledged that the sheriffs could excuse themselves on many grounds from personal appearance, provided they sent a deputy with the money. It was only if they wished to account through a deputy that they needed a writ of authorization from the king.[78]

From one point of view, Henry's attempt to overturn this long established custom had some merit for the shrieval office had changed a great deal since John's reign, making the personal appearance of the sheriff at the proffer far more important, or so it could be argued.[79] A considerable proportion of John's sheriffs were great men, close to the King, as the numbers with him at Easter 1208 showed. Their counties were usually run for them by under-sheriffs, at least eight of whom had turned up for their masters at the 1208 proffer. In effect, therefore, the Exchequer was still dealing with the *de facto* sheriff. By the 1250s, by contrast, great men rarely held sheriffdoms, formal under-sheriffs had disappeared, and the sheriff himself ran the county. Thus the deputies appearing at the proffers were no longer, as they had sometimes been in John's reign, the men responsible for the county. Many were simply sheriffs' clerks, although that trend too was already evident by 1208. It was, therefore, far more important to get the sheriffs to appear personally at the proffers in the 1250s, when they were really administering their counties, than in the 1200s when they were not.

Yet looked at from another point of view, to do so was impractical and pointless. There was one essential reason for this: the increasing time lag between the sheriff's proffer and the sheriff's account. In the early 12th century, when the business of the Exchequer was comparatively slight, all the sheriffs could turn up for the Michaelmas proffer, remain around and render their individual accounts within the next few weeks. A hundred years later that was no longer possible. The hearing of the accounts lasted from Michaelmas through to the following summer. A few sheriffs could be dealt with in the days immediately after Michaelmas, but the great majority would have to return home and come up again at later dates, dates which could not always be coordinated with the second compulsory personal appearance at the Easter proffer. Some sheriffs would have to make three journeys to the Exchequer in the course of the year: twice to proffer, once to account.[80] With the administrative burdens of the office increasing by leaps and bounds, this was verging on the absurd, especially when the sheriff had to come from outside the home counties.

The same delay also made it increasingly unnecessary for the sheriffs to come to the proffer. If they were there, perhaps Henry hoped to saddle them with responsibility when the proffer was inadequate. Certainly, a grossly substandard performance would be detected; but, in many cases, adequacy or inadequacy was something only the process of account, often months away, would establish. This was why, as the *Dialogus* already recognized, it was far more important to have the sheriff at the account that at the proffer. The person who brought up the money was little more than a postman. Nor was there much point in insisting that he arrived on the day after Michaelmas and the day after the close of Easter. The amount of money brought mattered far more than the delay of a few days or even a few weeks.

If all this is true, however, how does one explain the Exchequer initiative of 1237 when, as we have seen, it amerced 16 sheriffs £5 each for failing to appear in person on the day after the close of Easter; or indeed explain a parallel action in 1290 when the Exchequer amerced nine sheriffs 5 marks each for not arriving personally with their proffers that Easter.[81] If Henry was wrong in trying to enforce personal appearance, he was in good company. Or was he? In 1237 and 1290, the Exchequer made no grand pronouncements, but took punitive action. In 1256, Henry pronounced grandly, but took no action at all. He threatened penalties far more severe than in 1237 and 1290, but never executed them. Whether the earlier and later initiatives were really designed to secure personal appearance is an open question; if they were, they were failures.[82] But what they did do was to impress the sheriffs with the power of the Exchequer and keep them on their toes. Henry's pronouncement had precisely the reverse effect. It showed that his threats would not be implemented. He was a paper tiger.

In 1256, Henry should have settled for something less grand and more practical. He could, following the advice of the *Dialogus de Scaccario*, have insisted that the deputies should not be clerks "since it is improper for them to be arrested for matters of money or account";[83] he could have reinstated the practice of John's reign, revived briefly in the Minority, of recording on the memoranda roll the reasons for the sheriffs' absence;[84] he could have anticipated the Cowick ordinance of 1323 which accepted that the proffer might last several days, maintained the principle of personal appearance, but allowed excuses "according to the usages of the Exchequer", and solved the problem of not knowing how good the proffer was by linking it, where necessary, to a preliminary view of the sheriff's account.[85] Henry, however, liked to think big: hence Westminster Abbey. A dramatic entrance, a sweeping set of provisions appealed to him; forcing the policy through against hostile sheriffs and a tepid Exchequer was another matter. By the time the Exchequer opened after Easter in 1257, Henry had left Westminster and withdrawn to the company of the emollient monks at Merton. He was still thinking about money, but now another grand and improbable scheme filled his head: that of setting aside £13,333 a year (a far larger sum than required) for the expenses of the royal household.[86] Until the sum was collected, the treasurer, poor man, was to resist Henry's orders for the diversion of money elsewhere even when given with Henry's own mouth. This scheme too was soon abandoned. So too was the gold coinage, launched later in the year, after the mayor and citizens of London had come to the Exchequer and told Henry how useless the whole thing was. At least a few of the splendid gold pennies survive to show Henry, as he doubtless wished to be shown, sitting regally on this throne. Henry was certainly a king with ideas. What he lacked was the ability to judge their viability.

It would be wrong to be too critical, however. In his ruling at the Exchequer, as in saving his gold treasure, Henry was grappling with the central problem of 13th-century kingship: the inadequacy of the ordinary revenues of the Crown. The time it took to save the gold treasure out of ordinary revenues and the difficulty of increasing them through tighter control over the sheriffs suggested the necessity of new solutions. It was Edward I who found them by securing general taxation from parliament. With all its constitutional consequences that was the future for English kingship.

Footnotes to this Chapter may be found on pages 349–54.

6: Anthony Goodman

Edward III to the Battle of Barnet

THE PERIOD starts with the deposition of one king, Edward II, and ends with the deposition of another, Henry VI: it is neatly divided by the deposition of Richard II in 1399. It is hard to find precedents in English medieval history for these abasements of monarchy. Richard, when a prisoner in the Tower of London, said at dinner on 21 September 1399, "My God. A wonderful land this is, and a fickle – which has slain, exiled, destroyed or ruined so many kings, rulers, and great men, and is ever tainted and toileth with strife and variance and envy".[1] For examples of kings maltreated in these ways, Richard would have had to cast his mind back to times long before Edward II – indeed, to before 1066.[2] However, his own dramatic fate gave his thesis some currency. The theme that the English people had from ancient times demonstrated that they were fickle and treacherous by nature, and inclined to turn against their kings, was elaborated by French writers, eager to belabour the enemy in the 15th century.[3] The pro-French Castilian noble, Dies de Games, writing in the 1430s, illustrated the supposed viciousness of the English by describing how Richard was ceremonially divested of the symbols of regality – a scene which appears to have been invented, but one which dramatized English faithlessness.[4]

Anti-English propagandists naturally avoided seeking parallels with the toils of kings in their own principalities. In this context, it is worth recalling a few of the notable scenes of royal degradation elsewhere in our period, putting the harsh treatment of some English kings in perspective. In 1357, there was the spectacle of the Dauphin Charles, Regent of France (the future Charles V) being forced to witness the slaughter of his friends by a Parisian mob which had invaded his apartments, and which forced him to don a hood in their colours of red and blue.[5] In 1437, there occurred the assassination of James I of Scots in his bedchamber at the Blackfriars in Perth by a faction of the nobles, who battered the queen who frantically tried to defend her husband.[6] Another unpopular king, Henry IV of Castile, managed to die peacefully in his bed, but in 1465, a seated effigy of him had been set up outside Avila, from which the nobles solemnly removed the crown, sword, and sceptre, finally toppling the figure from its throne.[7] One 15th-century English writer perceptively interpreted the travails of English monarchy in his day as part of an historic European phenomenon. Sir John Fortescue in the 1460s, at an age when chief justices hoped to be living in slippered ease on their estates, endured the rackety, threadbare existence of an exile, plotting in Scotland and the duchy of Bar for the restoration of Henry VI, and grooming his son Edward for the succession. Fortescue, in his little treatise on *The Governance of England,* developed the thesis that monarchs were threatened with deposition by "overmighty" subjects when the latter came to dispose of more income than the former. In such circumstances, a noble might aspire to the king's estate and gain the support of subjects in his designs, since, as

Fortescue argued, with a cynicism worthy of Machiavelli, "the people will go with him that best may sustain and reward them".[8] Fortescue's analysis of the problems of the Crown was fundamentally based on the circumstances in which Henry VI's government had been challenged and eventually overthrown by Richard, Duke of York (d 1460) and his kinsmen and allies. He also instanced historic and contemporary "overmighty subjects": for instance, James II of Scotland (d 1460) "put out of the same land the Earl Douglas, whose livelihood and might was nearly equivalent to his own, moved thereto by no other cause, save only dread of his rebellion".[9]

Though Fortescue's implicit, and sometimes explicit, criticisms of important aspects of Lancastrian public finance and policy are devastating, he certainly does not exude a terminal pessimism about the future of the English monarchy. Despite the hard knocks the elderly judge took in royal service, culminating in his capture by Edward IV in the bloody battle at Tewkesbury in 1471, his historical perspective of the English monarchy remained an upbeat one: *The Governance* provided a blueprint for the restoration of kingship. Indeed, when we consider what have been generally regarded as the high points of English medieval monarchy, some of the flashier successes occurred in our period. The presentational skills of the chronicler, Jean Froissart, projected memorable scenes of the victorious Edward III at the battle of Crécy (1346) and the siege of Calais (1347), and of his son, the Black Prince, at the battle of Poitiers (1356) – scenes which were to form part of the historical landscape of generations in the English élites, through the medium of Lord Berners' stirring 16th-century translation of the *Chroniques*.[10] Henry V's early biographers gave what were to be, indirectly, influential accounts of his triumph at the Battle of Agincourt and his conquests in France. Public and official opinion, even under the Yorkists, accepted this Henry of Lancaster as an embodiment of regal ideals.[11] Yet, since Henry was cut down in his prime, another ruler from our period long continued to be regarded as England's most successful king since William the Conqueror – Edward III (ruled 1327–77), whom Lancastrians, Yorkists, and Tudors all revered. It is not surprising that his reign was considered to have marked seminal public developments.[12] For instance, accounts of events in the "Good Parliament" of 1376 show that parliaments (and, notably, the Commons) had by the end of Edward's reign established habits and modes of business, areas of public concern, and the determination to exercise powers and influence, which were to be of historic significance in the government of the realm. In earlier parliaments of Edward III, statutes had been passed which were the basis of future regulation and legislation for generations in areas such as control of labour and wages, curtailment of papal jurisdiction, the grant of judicial powers in the shires to the keepers of the peace, and the maintenance of hierarchy in the wearing of apparel. Edward established the claim of English (and subsequently British) kings to the French crown, a claim given up in 1803, as well as direct English rule over the port and March of Calais, conquered by the French in 1558. On the grounds of his claim to the overlordship of Scotland, he ruled parts of southern Scotland, long-held remnants of which were the castles and burghs of Roxburgh (lost in 1460) and Berwick-upon-Tweed (incorporated into England in 1974). In the 15th century, supposed features of his rule were held up as exemplary. His protection of English overseas trade was praised by the author of *The Libelle of Englyshe Polycye,* a notable political poem of about 1436.[13] The royal councillors who in about 1476 compiled *The Black Book,* a model for the organization of Edward IV's household, took Edward III's household as their exemplar.[14] Moreover, as subsequent generations appreciated, Edward III had notably remodelled the physical and mental environment of monarchy: his handiwork was stamped all over Westminster Palace until the fire of 1834 (and can still be seen in the Jewel Tower), and he extensively rebuilt Windsor Castle, especially to provide ceremonial settings for his Order of the Garter, one of the first secular orders of knights.

How, then, can we account for the extremes of monarchical success and failure in the period? Firstly, let us glance at the lifestyles and roles of kings in our period, with an eye to underlying changes. The offices and routines of the royal household continued along well established lines, providing stable settings for the king's performance of public acts, such as the customary crown-wearings on the great feast days, and for business and private life in the apartments of the chamber. Great nobles, as well as the knights and esquires of the chamber, were prominent among the king's customary companions on ceremonial occasions, in private pleasures, and, in varying degrees, in the discharge of public business, such as in giving counsel and in witnessing royal charters.[15] However, it seems to have been unusual for nobles to reside semi-permanently at court: it may have been exceptional that Richard II's bosom companions, such as the earls of Oxford and Nottingham, had their own suites in some of the palaces in the 1380s.[16] Public opinion was highly sensitive about the issues of the king's household expenses, and of courtiers lining their pockets; Richard's eldest uncle, John of Gaunt, Duke of Lancaster, was allegedly criticized for residing long at court in the 1390s.[17] Yet the chamber did not become an ivory tower, isolating the king with his boon companions, fixers, and "gofors", insulated from critical opinion among the élites. The chamber was the place where many of the most important people in the realm met regularly to socialize, and to give their opinions on policy. In some circumstances, gatherings of nobles elsewhere might be regarded as suspect: in 1394, John of Gaunt felt it necessary to write to Richard in order to convince him that the party which he was holding for his kinsmen at his castle of Pontefract in Yorkshire was a leave-taking one, innocent of politicking.[18] Refusal by a noble to obey a royal summons to come and give counsel was possibly a breach of allegiance; illness, diplomatic or real, was not always accepted as a valid excuse. In 1395, at Eltham Palace (Kent), Richard II was consulting his magnates in the chamber, when the most awkward of his uncles, Thomas of Woodstock, Duke of Gloucester, abruptly walked out, going into the hall, the public part of the palace, where he ordered an early dinner. After he had eaten, he took leave of the King, and rode from court before the council ended. This was considered untoward behaviour.[19] One cannot say, then, that in this period king and nobles in general became literally or metaphorically distanced. Frictions arose or were magnified because regular occasions of familiarity might produce antipathy or excessive cordiality. In some cases, the relations of king and noble probably originated in shared education, in childhood play, and schoolroom tensions.

The Council at Eltham in 1395 reveals Richard II being the very model of a working monarch – opening proceedings at eight o'clock in the morning, and presiding for more than four hours over a difficult session. He presided over an afternoon session too.[20] Four of the five kings in our period had the good health and stamina necessary to perform a demanding role in government for the whole or most of their reigns. The exception was Henry IV, who, after being an acclaimed international sportsman, a peerless and enthusiastic jouster, became an invalid in his late 30s.[21] Edward III's health had given way in his early 60s: from *circa* 1372, he favoured rural semi-retirement in the company of a mistress, Alice Perrers, who proceeded to give birth to a brood of children of dubious parentage.[22] Henry VI was the only king who early on developed a settled aversion to important facets of the business of kingship.[23] This was, indeed, a potentially disastrous dereliction of duty. From an early age, kings were trained for their office. They were taught reading and grammar as well as military and courtly skills. Henry VI's love of sacred literature shows that he had been taught literate skills very well: his tutor was a former master of the grammar school at Bury St Edmunds (Suffolk).[24] Kings were also instructed, in a vein which leaned more to the didactic than the practical, in the duties and functions of governor. The poet Thomas Hoccleve presented the future Henry V, in about 1408, with his composition *The Regement of Princes,* heavily based on standard hoary text of advice on ruling. Yet Hoccleve was a clerk in the principal administrative clearing houses of central government, the Privy Seal Office: he did not think it appropriate to instruct Henry on the workings of government, and how they might be reformed.[25] In our period, the literary interests of some of these well educated kings loom large. Henry IV seems to have been the first English king to have a royal study erected. This was at Eltham Palace: it had seven windows and two desks, one of which had a shelf on which he could keep the books he was consulting.[26]

It would be wrong to give the impression that the kings of this period were essentially well educated businessmen who held frequent conferences, and threw the best parties. Characteristically, they were leading sportsmen too. If we knew more about the sporting abilities of kings, nobles, and chamber knights, and about the relative prestige of their livestock, hunting, and hawking establishments, we would have a much more rounded view of politics. Leicester Abbey basked in royal favour in the later 14th century partly because Abbot William Cloune was reputed to be the best hare-courser in the realm. Edward III and his sons eagerly beat paths to his door.[27] Henry IV's cousin, Edward Duke of York, put his love of hunting and skill at the game to political use. When in royal disfavour and imprisoned, he translated and augmented a French hunting treatise, with the object of presenting it to the Prince of

Wales.[28] Kings pursued leisure strenuously in the summer vacation, if there was not a war on. The French invasion of Flanders in 1383 and the rapid disintegration of the English army there wrong-footed the government: the youthful Richard was on holiday, making an East Anglian progress. On receiving news of the emergency across the Channel, he rode through the night from Daventry (Northamptonshire) to London, borrowing a fresh horse on the way from the Abbot of St Albans, which, the abbey's chronicler sourly remarked, he failed to return. The King's Council was summoned for the following morning: the King announced to it his intention to confront the French forthwith, a brave but impractical intention from which the Council dissuaded him.[29] More congenially, kings often kept a low profile in the summer, disappearing from court with a restricted staff of attendants: the king then became a mysterious, private figure, whom legend might credit with disguised and almost magical appearances among his humbler subjects. Richard II had a house built as a retreat for himself, his Queen, Ann of Bohemia, and a select household group on an island in the Thames near his palace of Sheen (later, Richmond). His bathroom was sumptuously paved with 2,000 painted tiles.[30]

The aspects of royal behaviour discussed above were basically traditional: there were, however, significant changes in the royal environment in the period. One was the decline in the number of foreigners who won favour. Edward III was the last English king before James I and VI who conspicuously gave office to and ennobled foreigners. His marriage into the ruling house of Hainault, his alliances against the French crown, and his eclectic taste for chivalrous companionship all inclined Edward this way. He and his sons led armies into France whose captaincies were more international than Henry V's were to be. A good example of a recipient of Edward's favour is Walter, Lord Manny, KG, who was one of the many Hainaulters (including the chronicler Froissart) who sought their fortunes at the English court. Young Manny was the Queen's page: in 1331, he was yeoman of Edward's chamber, and he campaigned strenuously in his service in Scotland and France. He received the great privilege of marriage to a close kinswoman of the King, a grand-daughter of Edward I. He received personal summons to sit as a lord of parliament. In 1947, his remains were identified during excavations on the site of the London Charterhouse: he was the founder of this distinguished monastery. Lord Manny was one of the last foreign males to be exaltedly accepted into the English royal establishment in the Middle Ages.[31]

Why were aliens squeezed out? One reason may be that since the later 13th century, kings of England had come to rely more exhaustively and exclusively for support in war on their subjects in England, and that these subjects, because they bore these as well as older common responsibilities to royal government, were defining themselves more clamourously as being Englishmen. The kings themselves edged fitfully towards asserting their English identity. Henry III was the last one who strongly stressed his Angevin roots, willing that, while his chief burial place should be in Westminster

Abbey, his heart should be interred at Fontevrault Abbey in Anjou. That was where his mother, Isabella of Angoulême, was buried, and his paternal grandparents Henry II (Plantagenet) and Eleanor of Aquitaine, besides his uncle Richard I. His embalmed heart was apparently taken to Fontevrault.[32] Subsequent members of the royal family alluded to their Angevin ancestry and historic ties in France. The emblems of the broom plant (*planta genista*) embroidered on Richard II's tomb effigy in Westminster Abbey may allude to this. Henry V revived this interest by making the claim, dropped by Henry III in 1259, to his Angevin ancestors' lost inheritances in France. His tenure of the duchy of Normandy, alluded to in his tomb inscription in Westminster Abbey, had an antiquarian as well as a practical flavour – and he too left part of his body to be buried in France (less importantly than Henry III, his viscera).[33] Henry VI's propaganda in France laid stress on his descent through his Valois mother from the Capetians rather than the Angevins, but his kinsman, Richard, Duke of York, was to sign himself "Plantagenet", presumably as an oblique way of stressing his English royal descent.[34] Nevertheless, kings of our period made much greater play with their English royal antecedents, though this was not entirely novel. Richard II adopted the (mythical) coat of arms of St Edward the Confessor. In *The Wilton Diptych* at the National Gallery, the King is introduced to Christ by St John the Baptist, St Edward, and another royal English saint, Edmund the Martyr, and Christ invests the King not with the royal banner, but that of St George, the patron saint of England.[35] In 1416, the ruler of the Holy Roman Empire, Sigismund, knowing how Henry V prized the cult of St George, brought the saint's heart to England as a present for him.[36]

Such royal gestures are a manifestation of a sense of Englishness which was becoming, in the 14th century, a political force, a sense of nationality which some prejudiced foreigners alleged had a distinctive and distasteful stridency. Dies de Games wrote that the English "liked no other nation, and sought to dishonour valiant knights who visited England to seek a livelihood, perform feat of arms or on diplomatic missions".[36] Curtailment of alien jurisdictions and exercise of patronage in England had been enshrined in the Statute of Provisors, enacted in 1351, which restricted papal freedom to provide either foreigners or natives to benefices within the English Church. Such papal provision, especially of aliens, was a staple grievance voiced by the Commons in parliament. In parallel, gentlefolk were touchy about competition from aliens for places in the royal household and administration, and for the rewards of royal patronage. There were criticisms of the foreign servants of Richard II's and Henry IV's queens, Ann of Bohemia and Joan of Navarre. Critics of Richard's favourite Robert de Vere, Earl of Oxford, were particularly angered when in 1387 he deserted his royally born English wife and ran off with one of the Queen's Bohemian maids.[38] It is unlikely that Edward III's successors were consciously bowing to political pressure in recruiting fewer foreigners: they were touchy about criticisms in parliament about household finances and personnel. Rather, recruitment of English personnel may have seemed the best means of dealing with domestic problems of government.

Moreover, some of these kings, as we have seen, may have been personally tinged with their English subjects' prejudices.

During the course of the 14th century, the character of the English monarchical establishment not only became more English: in notable, though not in all respects, it became southern and midland English. In the late 1330s, Edward III effectively gave up the attempts by his predecessors for nearly 40 years to dominate Scottish affairs, which had led them to base their government of England frequently in the north: after Edward III, English kings seldom went north of the Trent in normal circumstances. A network of royal residences on the way north came to be neglected: as the relative sums spent on the king's domestic works from the later 14th century onwards demonstrate, kings spent much more time in their residences in or near the Thames Valley.[39] Contemporaries came to expect this. Chroniclers' remarks reflect southern disquiet when Richard II took his household to itinerate in distant parts of the midlands in the summer of 1387. When, in 1392 he transferred not only his household, but courts and institutions which habitually functioned at Westminster, to York, there was dismay in London, as he intended. Yet a few generations back, it had been a matter of relative indifference about where the king governed from.

However, it was not pressure of public opinion that led kings to reduce their circles of itinerary: this stemmed from changes of emphasis in their own interests. Since some of the principal administrative and judicial institutions of government were now more firmly based at Westminster, the proximity of the royal household eased the work of government. Members of the King's Council (an institution growing in authority in the period), sitting in their Westminster boardroom, the Star Chamber, could more easily communicate with the king, and any of their fellow councillors and other chief royal officers staying with him when the court was at the palace, across the Thames at Kennington, or not far out in the country at Windsor, Eltham, or Langley. However, the main reason for these royal preferences was the convenience of being near London, long the main English resort of alien merchants and craftsmen, but whose own merchants were gaining an ever increasing dominance in domestic and overseas trade.

Londoners could now most conveniently supply many of the luxury goods, furnishings, and foodstuffs whose importance in defining and projecting majesty and nobility was receiving new emphasis in the 14th century. Londoners could best supply, too, the bulk consumption demands of the royal household, which when fully functioning had the largest personnel of any institution in the realm.[40] Moreover, by the last decade of Edward III's reign, London had replaced Florentine banks as the main source of royal loans, increasing financial contact between royal officials and merchants. The Crown was becoming heavily dependent on the prosperity of the City and the cooperation of its élite. London could be plausibly referred to as "the king's chamber": the young Richard II was sneered at as "king of the Londoners'. In the mid-

1430s, a well informed and well connected pamphleteer, the author of *The Libelle of Englyshe Polycye,* argued that the best foreign policy for England was one primarily aimed to protect and promote the interests of its traders, more specifically, those of an influential section of London exporters. The City became the setting for princely processional entries, which in 14th-century Europe were developing into lavish displays of majesty. These were, indeed, very occasional events, principally marking the coronation and royal funerals, but they doubtless made a great impression. We have detailed accounts of Richard II's entry into London in 1392, to mark his restoration of the City's recently suspended liberties of self-government. On his way from London Bridge to St Paul's Cathedral, the King was greeted by displays of Biblical characters and by angelic choirs, notably at the principal symbol of royalty in the city, the Eleanor Cross in Cheapside, transformed for the occasion into an elaborate and brightly painted castle, housing sacred persons. Figures, verses, and song expounded the theme of the pageant, which likened the King to Christ entering Jerusalem.[41] In 1415, Henry V, after his victory at the Battle of Agincourt, went along the same processional way, to be received with similar plaudits.[42]

Such celebrations idealized relations between Crown and City: the reality was somewhat different. Both sides had their own agenda. Relations might be worsened by the physical juxtaposition of Court and City: disputes over jurisdiction were intensified when there were brawls between courtiers and apprentices. The highest in the land might become embroiled when the issue of curtailing the City's privileges was raised. In 1377, John of Gaunt, dining on oysters at the London house of one of his knights, hastily jumped up from the table in order to flee from a mob, escaping by boat across the river.[43] His brother, Thomas of Woodstock, lying abed at his house in Cornhill, was rudely disturbed by rioters banging on his front door.[44] The presumption of wealthy merchants as well as that of the populace sometimes irked nobles. In 1388, a group of them (led by Thomas) procured the execution of the leading grocer Nicholas Brembre, former mayor, who had had the temerity to become a companion of the king and an unofficial councillor, member of a hated "kitchen cabinet". The Commons in parliament enthusiastically supported Brembre's condemnation for treason, while his fellow citizens keenly distanced themselves from a colleague who had imprudently embraced the Court.[45]

Royal associations with London and Londoners did not habitually alienate nobles and provincial élites from king or Court: they too appreciated how crucial the City's financial power was to the strength of the kingdom – as well as, in many cases, to their own financial health. Gentlefolk staying in London often shared courtiers' exasperations with the affronts of noisome rubbish, the licentiousness, dishonesty, and crime which they believed to be all too prevalent there. Nevertheless, they were irresistibly drawn to the City. Litigants attended the courts meeting in Westminster Hall during law terms, others on summons for examination by the Chancellor, the King's Council, or the barons of the Exchequer. By the later 14th century, gentlefolk were acquiring the habit of sending their sons to be educated and groomed at the Inns of Court. The phenomenon appeared of the gentleman who preferred London life to vegetation in the shires: a conspicuous example is the landowner and poet John Gower, whose tomb is, appropriately, in Southwark Cathedral, in whose shadow he spent many years in lodgings of what was then a wealthy house of Augustinian canons. Lords attending Court, enlarged meetings of the King's Council, or parliament, and elected members of parliament up from the country needed lodgings in and near the City, when such gatherings, as was often the case, were at Westminster. After John of Gaunt's suburban residence, the Savoy, was burnt down during the Peasants' Revolt of 1381, he seems to have eventually taken a long lease on Ely Place, the Bishop of Ely's fine house in Holborn.[46] In 1382, the two MPs for Suffolk, Sir William Wingfield and Sir Richard Waldegrave, were both staying during the parliamentary session at an inn in Fleet Street, *The Sword of the Hoop*. Waldegrave's lodgings were broken into, and two coffers containing valuable jewels and his seal were stolen.[47] Despite City hazards, the holding of parliaments elsewhere was unpopular, because of accommodation problems.

The frequent and regular intermixing of provincial lords, knights, esquires, and burgesses with London merchants and with the Westminster coteries of civil servants and lawyers, which became so marked in the 14th and 15th centuries, gave an enhanced metropolitan flavour to national politics. This is reflected in the development of the writing of chronicles by and for London citizens, often as continuations of earlier histories of England which had originally been written for clerics and gentlefolk. The "London chronicles" of the 15th century, written now in English, were histories of recent events in the City and in the realm at large. As Denys Hay pointed out, the writing of history from provincial viewpoints had practically died out in England – in contrast to France. Country landowners purchased copies of "the chronicles" on their visits to London, and learnt their English history from them, history which had a strong bias in favour of the exercise of strong, just, and warlike kingship. Provincially based movements of protest against the Crown had to project themselves within this historical context: they lacked the sustaining cultural bedrock found within some French provinces.[48]

Such "natural" bases of resistance to the exercise of central power were relatively feeble in later medieval England. Instead, there had come into existence a metropolitan political hothouse where a widely based consensus might be forced into a dominant, if often ephemeral, blooming of opinion. This could boost royal policies with formidable support, when there was a coincidence between them and the convictions of magnates, gentry, London merchants, and provincial citizens and burgesses. Conversely, such a head of opinion might isolate king and councillors. This occurred notably in the Good Parliament of 1376, when the Commons boldly impeached Edward III's courtiers and their business associates in the City, who, they believed, had been milking royal resources and patronage excessively, to the detriment of the realm. Clearly, country knights and squires sitting as MPs would not have set in train what they saw as the reform of government with such assurance, vigour, and clarity had they not been cheered on by disgruntled magnates, and supplied with "classified information" by disaffected former ministers and London bankers. Popular excitement about the crisis was reflected in the sale by ballad hawkers of poems in praise of the Commons' spokesman, Sir Peter de la Mare, who had pressed charges with eloquent tenaciousness. Not just country knights, but street folk, wanted to make their opinions known about high policy.[49]

To sum up: though in our period the routines of the king's public and official functions, and of his daily living, continued along highly traditional lines, there were changes in the cultural ambience and physical settings of monarchy in the 14th century which made it more "English", and stimulated a dialogue between kings and a formidable new nexus of opinion. Expectations about royal policy were precise and vociferously expressed. Yet the views of kings and subjects about the principal functions and powers of monarchy generally continued to coincide.

The period saw no challenge to the traditional orthodoxy that English kings derived authority and freedom to govern from God. Their right to exercise customary prerogatives flowed from the anointing at the coronation, and was made manifest throughout their reigns by the continual exercise of miraculous healing gifts. With the exception of Richard II (an overemotional man of poor judgment, who became convinced that his prerogatives were vitally threatened), kings did not feel the need for the exaltation of majesty through a strong enhancement of religious symbolism. Their piety, in its public and private aspects, tended to be staid, decorous, and conservative, apart from the increasing elaboration of funeral rituals, tombs, and chantry chapels characteristic of the later Middle Ages. Henry VI was the only king who had an interesting spiritual life, from which was to flow the burgeoning of the Crown's role as an educational patron, with his foundation of Eton College and King's College, Cambridge.

The common reverence for monarchy is reflected in the "popular" canonization of kings who had not been shown due reverence by their subjects. Edward II and Henry VI, long after their unhappy decease, remained forgivingly active as miracle-workers among their subjects, both of them posthumously revealing a hitherto unremarked practicality. Henry at least retained some shreds of his mortal husk. His apparition was easily recognized by the distraught and the delirious, on account of its shabby raiment.[50] Would Richard have been disappointed that his soul was not similarly employed? He had, after all, shown considerable aversion to many of his English subjects: the thought of tending their sores till doomsday might have seemed a particularly nasty purgatory. It was, indeed, Henry IV's good fortune that a Ricardian cult failed to develop. Some individuals cherished Richard's memory. The brass of his former standard-bearer, Sir Simon Felbrigg, in Felbrigg Church (Norfolk) depicts Sir Simon holding aloft the arms of St Edward which

Richard adopted as his own. Then there was the unknown person who mysteriously spirited away (perhaps in the turmoil of 1399) that intense mystical vision of Ricardian kingship, *The Wilton Diptych,* which was clearly looked after with reverence in the Lancastrian period.[51] However, a cult needs authentic and accessible remains. Many people were not convinced that the corpse largely encased in lead, which was exhibited as Richard's in St Paul's Cathedral in 1400, was genuine. it was buried within the palings of a royal residence, at the friary of King's Langley (Hertfordshire). Nevertheless, for several years, there was were persistent rumours that Richard was alive and well, though probably living in what most Englishmen would have regarded as a living purgatory – in Scotland. There was a "pseudo-Richard" died in 1419, and was buried with royal honours at Stirling.

As well as religion, political theory inclined opinion to accord supreme personal authority to kings. The most popular political handbooks, apart from the Bible, emanated from the Aristotelian schoolmen of the later 13th and early 14th centuries. They were concerned to demonstrate that monarchy was the form of political authority best suited to fulfil the common good of Christian society. A favourite later medieval text was the *Secretum Secretorum,* which purported to be advice given by Aristotle to Alexander the Great on methods of governing, among other things. Another was *De Regimine Principum,* by Aegidius Colonna, who was better known in England as "Giles of Rome'. In the third part of this treatise, written *circa* 1277–8 for Philip IV of France, Giles was concerned to teach the prince his responsibilities under God, and to distinguish between rule for the good of the republic and tyranny.; Writing in a milieu of authoritarian ideas about kingship, Giles had no truck with suggestions that the king should set limits to his prerogative, or that subjects should threaten to impinge on royal authority by attempting to reform government.[52]

Giles's book was regarded as suitable for the education of English princes. Sir Simon Burley, who was in charge of Richard II's education, possessed a copy of it, and Hoccleve used it extensively in the tract which he wrote for the future Henry V. Many English laymen as well as clerics possessed such political works in the later Middle Ages. It was an age when noblemen were expected to be able to read French and English; many read Latin too. Thomas, Lord Berkeley, was more comfortable with works in English, for, at his behest, his chaplain John Trevisa in 1387 translated *De Regimine* from Latin into the vernacular. Richard II's saturnine uncle, Thomas of Woodstock, Duke of Gloucester, possessed two copies of the treatise, one of them, in Latin, his library copy at his country seat, Pleshey Castle (Essex); the other, in French, was bequeathed by his widow in 1399 for the education of his son and heir Humphrey.[53] Thomas of Woodstock had led a rebellion against Richard's rule in 1387, and may have attempted his deposition then. Yet he apparently approved of the sentiments of this royalist tract, as was widely the case. However, one must remember that in this period, nobles and other laymen were starting to gloss Biblical texts in sometimes highly unorthodox ways, inspired by the teaching of John Wycliffe (d 1384), the English heresiarch. One devout and thoroughly orthodox contemporary writer, William Langland, bewailed the fact that sacred theology had become a subject for noble table talk.[54] Is it not possible that, in the same critical spirit, nobles were scrutinizing Giles' rules for royal duties and obligations, and using them to monitor the king's performance? In this spirit, the articles justifying the deposition of Richard by the assembled estates in 1399 do not attack the concept of royal prerogative, but award the King a series of "fail marks" for his conduct in office, some for allegedly serious attacks on the public good – but others simply for bypassing normal administrative procedures.[55] Thus, the King's attitudes and actions had been picked over by men who expected him to behave in ways rigidly prescribed by precept and precedents.

How was it that the English political élites could fervently subscribe to ceremonies and theories which exalted royal authority, and yet on occasion felt justified in imposing checks on it, even to the point of coercing kings? Such ambivalence was not, indeed, new, but rooted in the historic development of kingship in conjunction with noble power in England. Since the Norman Conquest, the Crown had developed a remarkable continuity of administrative and judicial control over most of the realm. Consequently, subjects' expectations of redress and reward were more narrowly focused on the Crown in England than on princes in many other parts of Europe. The inhabitants of Fife or Dumfriesshire, of Burgundy and Béarn, were living in more enclosed and inward-looking political cultures than those, say, of even remote and peripheral Northumberland, over whose assizes royal justices habitually presided at Newcastle. Great regional powers, like the Percy family, did, indeed, gather large parts of the local élites under their patronage, but their dependants looked to them in part to act as intermediaries to procure royal favour and redress. It was a delicate task for kings to satisfy a multitude of expectations, on the fulfilment of which the standing of magnates depended – and to calm the rivalries of them and their followers, intent on dominating the regional operations of royal government and common law. These political and social imperatives fashioned the governing roles of nobles: they were propelled towards dissent if they considered that the king was thwarting them from playing the roles which they perceived as necessary in order to maintain the honour and profit of their families. In our period, there were opportunities for them to harness the concerns of the "community of the realm" in opposition to royal policies.

Developments in foreign relations were particularly fraught with hazards for the unchallenged exercise of the King's will. The realm was in an almost continuous state of formal war with Scotland from 1335 to 1502, with the Valois kings of France from 1337 to 1492, and with Castile from 1369 to 1467. For most of these periods, indeed, there was truce with these opponents, but truces were hard to enforce (especially at sea). On land, in the north and in France, they often needed a high level of expenditure on border fortifications, garrisons, and cross-border conferences to deal with infractions of truce and to negotiate extensions. Warfare had a considerable impact on the king's lordships outside England. The duchy of Gascony had come to the future Henry II in 1152 with his bride, Eleanor of Aquitaine. He had first asserted his lordship over Ireland in 1169. The Norman and Angevin kings insisted on their suzerainty over Welsh princes, and over the Norman lords who carved out Marcher lordships in Wales: in the early 1280s, Edward I conquered the last Welsh principality, Gwynedd, and set up his own principality of Wales. The English had a settled view by the 14th century that all these lordships were inalienably annexed to the English Crown, and that they were adjuncts of the realm.[56] The status of some of Edward III's new acquisitions was ambiguous. The Scottish Border shires which he ruled from the 1340s were held by virtue of his lordship over Scotland, a claim manifestly difficult to implement. The March of Calais was occupied from 1347 on the grounds of Edward's claim to the French throne, but while it was in English hands it was always administered from Westminster, and regarded as an outpost of England. Like Ireland and Gascony, it was customarily governed by Royal lieutenants who were English (or sometimes, in Ireland, Anglo–Irish lords who were regarded by the English as "one of us"). In Gascony, however, though the English held a few key administrative posts, government was otherwise in the hands of privileged communes and *noblesse*. Few English settled in Gascony: there were traders domiciled at Bordeaux. There was surprisingly little Anglo-Gascon intermarriage, despite close and historic trading ties, and knightly comradeship in the Hundred Years' War – the Battle of Poitiers was as much a triumph for the Gascons as for the English. In Ireland, where there had been a large immigration from England in the 13th century, England's rapidly evolving governmental and judicial institutions had been successfully transplanted. The Dublin administration was modelled on Westminster's, and the city's government and culture, like that of other south-eastern Irish ports, was similar in nature to that of English towns. However, there remained large areas where a distinct and vigorous Gaelic society flourished, lacking feudal lordships and shires, whose chiefs honoured the English king as their overlord with little more than fine words.

Edward's Scottish lordship retained its own institutions, albeit ones akin to England's. In the Border shires, Scots law continued to function under the watchful eyes of local English lieutenants, whose main task was the maintenance of castles and garrisons. There were English burgesses in Berwick and, living precariously on the cliffs further up the coast, monks from Durham Priory at its cell of Coldingham. Some northern English squires picked up estates forfeited by Scots who had refused to accept English allegiance. By the end of the 14th century, the areas under English control were much reduced – only one important family, the Percys, had a substantial landed stake in the occupied region. The town of Calais did not have a conspicuously English character: it bore some resemblance to later European trading posts across the oceans. Its skyline was filled with ships' masts, formidable fortifications, and warehouses; its markets were thronged by a polyglot and largely transient crowd of traders, soldiers, and sailors. It was a place where people went to make money.

In Ireland and Wales, those who were not manifestly of immigrant stock were distrusted and discriminated against by incoming English officials, and by descendants of settlers who exploited their separate legal status. Edward I's conquest of Gwynedd had involved some "ethnic cleansing": in the face of determined resistance, a harsh regime was imposed on the Welsh. They were forbidden to reside in boroughs, an abode of the English in Wales, and they were for long unable generally to progress far up the ladders of ecclesiastical and secular preferment in their own country. In official documents, they could be referred to as "mere Welsh". Not surprisingly, the bitterest reaction to English rule occurred in Wales, in the revolt of Owain Glyn Dŵr. In 1401, he imaginatively proposed an alliance between his fragile independent principality of Wales, the king of Scots, and Irish chieftains: nothing came of this alternative programme for the development of the British Isles.[57] The only English lordship where English rule came to be regarded generally with cordiality was Gascony, whose inhabitants saw the king-duke as the guarantor of their privileges. The Gascons were the only lieges of Henry VI in France who revolted (1452) in favour of the restoration of his rule after the French conquest.

The king's foreign subjects found few opportunities for advancement in England. There were Welsh and Irish students at Oxford, and Scottish ones too, until the Great Schism of 1378 put England and Scotland into different papal allegiances. There were few openings for their preferment: high office in the English Church and state was overwhelmingly held by Englishmen. Irish clerks might aspire to the nominal eminence of suffragan bishoprics. There were Scottish labourers north of the Tees: further south they risked suspicion and arrest because of their accents. Some Gaelic Irish and Border Scots served in English armies abroad: only the Welsh were recruited frequently in large numbers. The Black Prince provided uniforms for his Welsh soldiers, tabards and hats in green and white, presumably so that a watch could easily be kept on them.[58] However, some Welsh captains so distinguished themselves fighting in English armies in France that they were treated as honorary Englishmen, and acquired estates in England.[59]

Elites and groups of English settlers in Wales and Scotland were not sufficiently numerous or united to have a powerful voice at Westminster. By contrast, the Anglo-Irish were substantial in numbers: their sense of community was in some respects enhanced by edgy relations with Englishmen sent to rule them, by the threats from their Gaelic neighbours, and their need for more military support from the English Crown. There were few Anglo-Irish magnates in this period with the resources to uphold their interests on both sides of the Irish Sea. In 1394–5, when Richard II was in Ireland, he very reasonably tried to reverse this trend, encouraging English nobles to develop Irish estates, but they concluded that profitability was too uncertain in the fragmented and depopulated frontier society which rural Ireland had become. They complained, according to Froissart, that the island was full of bogs, and that its inhabitants were uncouth and did not fight chivalrously.[60]

So the English did not empathize with their fellow subjects, except for the Gascons. They were wearied by the often rugged and barren terrain they had to traverse in Ireland, Scotland, and Wales, and repelled by what they considered to be the outlandish habits and treacherous nature of many of their inhabitants. They were not drawn sympathetically thither by internationally prestigious shrines. The main destinations abroad for English pilgrims lay in Germany, Spain, Italy, and Palestine. Those Englishmen who visited their king's "empire" usually did so on short contracts and commissions as rulers, administrators, soldiers, and sailors. Officials and military men often served in their careers in different lordships, but seldom put down roots in any of them. In contrast, the duchy of Normandy, conquered by Henry V between 1417 and 1421, provided offices, military commands, and hereditary lordships which had an appeal. English nobles and gentlefolk regarded the duchy as rich and civilized – some could trace ancestral roots there. Henry V gained lasting admiration for providing the English with a lordship where there were superior opportunities, albeit one that remained an apanage of the French Crown.[61]

There were other reasons why the English élites valued the lordships attached to the English Crown. They added honour to the king and realm; more tangibly, possession of them might be seen as necessary for the security of England. Indeed, remarkably little concern was shown about holding Ireland securely: there had been no noteworthy foreign invasion there since Edward Bruce's ill-fated one in the 1310s.[62] However, as a result of the ancient conflicts with the Welsh, and the more recent ones with the Scottish and French crowns, there was an awareness of the vulnerability of the west midlands, the most northerly shires, and the long eastern and southern coastlines. The border with Scotland was not a good line of defence. There were bitter memories of how, in Edward II's reign, Robert Bruce's armies had harried the English Borders, and ranged as far south as Yorkshire. By the later 14th century, the economy and manpower resources of the far north had declined so drastically that defence was heavily reliant on aid from further south. The maintenance of a garrisoned buffer zone in Scotland, and the subsidizing of defence forces maintained and controlled by wardens of the Marches seemed a worthwhile price to pay to the well informed who, for the most part, like Geoffrey Chaucer, would have probably professed only a hazy knowledge of northern geography.[63] The largely unexcavated remains of Roxburgh Castle, a formidable site, bear witness to the fact that it was one of the English Crown's prime fortifications.[64] Just beyond another vulnerable extreme of the realm lay the March of Calais, one of the most heavily fortified areas of Christendom. The revolt of Owain Glyn Dŵr revived memories of the insecurity of England's western border. In 1405, his French allies advanced to within eight miles of Worcester.

Along with an appreciation of the importance of the royal lordships to the English polity, there developed an ideology of English nationality with imperial overtones. This was stimulated by royal propaganda, which sought to give the community a sense that it had a stake, ideological as well as practical, in upholding the Crown's exterior claims. Edward I had used supposed historical precedents to justify his claims of *imperium* over Britain, projecting his rule as a revival of an ancient British empire, whose finest ruler had been King Arthur. The precedent of Arthur also had a relevance to the claims of Edward III and his successors in France, since Arthur had supposedly invaded Gaul. The evident modern *translatio imperii* from the Britons to the English nation was, for the later medieval nobility, a matter of pride, and a justification for them to rule their neighbours. The link with a sense of nationality was articulated in debates at the General Council of the Church in sessions at Constance in 1417. There England's opponents argued that the English were not a separate nation, but part of the German nation. One English counter-argument rested on the evident or claimed lordship of the English Crown over some of its neighbours – in, under, and part of the renowned English nation there had been of old and still were many kingdoms, England, Scotland, Wales, and four Irish kingdoms.[65] This concept of a multiple English polity was one which particularly exalted its kings. An iconographical change was made in Henry VI's reign which reflected this view of them. The ancient crown of St Edward the Confessor was altered from an open one to a closed crown, in imitation of Charlemagne's.[66]

Outstanding military leadership and fortunate circumstances enabled Edward III and Henry V to appear to their subjects as worthy successors of King Arthur, making the historic English *imperium* more secure, and extending it spectacularly in France. Yet these successes spelled danger for kings. Their authority and prestige had come to rest in part on the successful defence of an overstretched empire. The monarchy lacked the domainal resources to pay fully for the heavy defence costs in times of truce, let alone open war. Kings had repeatedly to call on the resources of their English subjects: the economy of England was much smaller than that of its principal opponent, the French crown. The lordships, for the most part, contributed little to the costs of this main struggle; their own defences had to be subsidized by the English. Apart from Gascony in the first half of the 14th century, the empire was a source of loss rather than profit to the Crown, though its English subjects reaped benefits from trade with Gascony and Ireland, and through Calais. So the financial underpinning of the empire remained precarious;. The great gains in France were soon wiped out – the extended duchy of Aquitaine of 1360 in little over a decade, the conquests of Henry V within 30 years or so of his death in 1422. The other lordships tended to shrink. The Anglo-Irish government's effective rule was reduced to a few coastal enclaves. In the Scottish Borders, English rule was completely whittled away between 1384 and 1461, though Berwick was recovered in 1482. Long before Gascony was finally lost in 1453, effective rule was confined to the regions around Bordeaux and Bayonne. The new Lancastrian dynasty had one crucial success: Glyn Dŵr's revolt was defeated. In the later 15th century, other new dynasties, the Yorkists and Tudors, appreciated that it was vital for their prestige to maintain control of Calais. By the second half of the 15th century, however, much of the English empire had disappeared.

The crumbling of empire, most conspicuous in the later 14th and mid-15th centuries, rocked the personal prestige of kings, but did not undermine the authority and powers of the Crown. A strong force of English public opinion had developed, which exalted monarchy, but expressed, too, strident and often narrow expectations of how kings should behave, and what measures they should take to foster the interests of the commonwealth. The defence of the realm's imperial outliers was one main area of concern. The king who was fortunate and skilful enough to harness these forces of opinion could be formidable to his domestic and foreign opponents. Royal failure to measure up led to domestic strife and even deposition. There were, indeed, underlying problems for the monarchy which made it peculiarly dependent on the support of the élites, and which made success in defending their security hazardous. Though royal prerogatives were generally reverenced, and supported by a remarkable administrative system, the Crown's domainal resources were unimpressive. The defence of its foreign lordships was often difficult to sustain: this was an empire which was scattered, with components which were vulnerable to attack or disintegration, and which were unprofitable. England's patchy wealth was needed, to the exasperation and often to the misery of its inhabitants. These were some of the factors which created fickleness to kings.

Footnotes to this Chapter may be found on pages 354–56.

7: David Loades

A new Monarchy: Henry VII and the Tudor achievement

FASHIONS in historiography change. When I was a student in the 1950s, the idea that the Tudors established something called the New Monarchy was yesterday's fashion. It had been the orthodoxy of the 1930s and 1940s, propounded by such great historians as AF Pollard and Kenneth Pickthorne. But the rising young revisionists of the post war years, GR Elton, RL Storey, and JR Lander, who were the teachers of my generation, seemed to have consigned it to the scrap heap.[1] Now it is staging a comeback, and Anthony Goodman has written a book with that very title. So the reign of Henry VII is once again in the front line of controversy. Was the first Tudor (as I have been teaching my students for 30 years) a good king of a typically medieval kind, who used the ideas and machinery which were in place at his accession, and invented nothing? Or was he after all an innovator, although perhaps in rather more subtle ways than was once supposed? It has been normal in recent years to link Henry VII with Edward IV, as two examples of successful late medieval kingship, to emphasize the continuities of policy, and even of personnel, between the two reigns and to suggest that if there was anything new about the monarchy in the late 15th century, then it began in 1470 and not in 1485.[2] However, this may well be questioned. There were many ways in which the styles and personalities of the two kings contrasted, and we should not make too much of the fact that many of Edward's councillors also served Henry, or that both (eventually) used the treasury of the chamber in preference to the Exchequer. It is important to remember that the brief reign of Richard III had come between, and that loyal Edwardians such as John Morton, were only too happy to support the man who had defeated their *bête noir*. Once they were convinced that Edward V was dead, he represented the best prospect for political stability.

Perhaps we should begin by questioning how successful Edward IV had really been. Like Henry VII, he was a usurper, but unlike Henry, some of the rebellions against him were successful, at least temporarily. He was imprisoned briefly by the Earl of Warwick in 1469, and was driven into exile in 1470–71. Moreover, his regime disintegrated on his death, and within two years his dynasty had been dispossessed. He was the first English king for many years to die solvent, but he did not manage to bequeath a stable realm to his son. Edward restored "good government" in the sense that he reestablished the personal ascendancy of the monarch over his peers.[3] He was recognized as a good lord in ways which Henry VI had never been able to achieve – accessible and impartial in judgment – but he was still responsible for the political circumstances which destroyed his heir. This came about not because he created a "Woodville faction", nor even because he failed to make adequate provision for a minority, but because he failed to transcend the limitations of "magnate politics". The Woodvilles were not a powerful or coherent political faction in 1483. Their strength lay almost entirely in the close personal ties which bound the young King Edward V to his uncle, Earl Rivers. Richard of Gloucester, as the late King's only surviving brother, was the obvious man to act as Regent, whether Edward had left specific instructions to that effect or not.[4] The problem did not lie in irreconcilable private animosities, but in Edward's failure to build up the institutional strength of the Crown. He was very conscious of the status and culture of nobility, and only too willing to see himself as *primus inter pares,* with the realm of England as his lordship. He was a great subscriber to the Burgundian cult of chivalry, reorganizing the ceremonial of the Order of the Garter along the lines of the Toisant d'Or, and building the magnificent Garter Chapel at Windsor Castle. In consequence, he ruled through noblemen, particularly his brother Richard, his Chamberlain, Lord Hastings, and Henry Stafford, Duke of Buckingham.

Each of these men was given extensive powers, almost matching those of a French provincial governor. The Courtenay earls of Devon and the Percy earls of Northumberland similarly ruled their "countries" in the King's name, but on a very loose rein from the centre. All these peers served Edward well as long as he was alive, but only Hastings transferred that loyalty unequivocally to his son. Henry VI had ruled through favourites whom he was unable, or unwilling, to control – the Duke of Suffolk, the Beaufort dukes of Somerset, and his Queen, Margaret of Anjou. Edward had not made so obvious or so elementary a mistake, but he had failed to look beyond his own lifetime. His magnate servants were controlled, not by laws, nor by constitutional checks, nor by other forces in society, but only by himself. When he died unexpectedly and they fell out among themselves, there was no referee capable of imposing rules in the subsequent power struggle.

Henry VII's whole approach was quite different, and the old view of a "new monarchy" recognized that fact. Unfortunately, the wrong language was used to describe it. Henry was described as a "middle class" king, a man with a liking for merchants and civil servants and an animosity towards the nobility, particularly the old nobility. He became in the popular mind the Scrooge-like figure portrayed by Rudyard Kipling;[5] a man with the mind of an Income Tax inspector and a style to match. The revisionists of the 1950s and 1960s pointed out quite rightly that this was nonsense – mythology rather than history. Henry's favourite companions were selected noblemen, such as the Earl of Oxford, and most of his peers served as councillors at one time or another. He could no more have governed his realm without the support of the nobility than without the Church. Noblemen held office in Court and state. John de Vere, Earl of Oxford, was Lord Great Chamberlain throughout the reign; John Radcliffe, Lord Fitzwalter, and George Talbot, Earl of Shrewsbury, served as Lord Steward, while John, Lord Dinham, and Thomas Howard, Earl of Surrey, divided the reign between them as Lord Treasurer. Noblemen also kept their "countries" in order, as they were traditionally expected to do. Moreover, Henry knew how to keep a good court. Nothing could be further from the truth than an image of parsimony. He spent generously on building, particularly at Richmond, on court entertainments, on plate, jewellery, and books. His taste in amusement seems to have been boisterous and simple, and there are many references in the household accounts to tumblers, jugglers, acrobats, and dancing girls – one of the latter being given the enormous reward of £30.[6] He employed the best tennis and jousting instructors for his sons, and his library was famous, being larger and far more varied than that of his predecessor. Magnificence was an aspect of a king's power; it attracted honour and service and could not be neglected in the fiercely competitive world of Renaissance diplomacy.

Nevertheless, Henry did not distribute wealth or power with a free hand. He created fewer peers than Edward, and far fewer than his son was to do. Nor were there any satraps in Tudor England, not even his trusted uncle Jasper, Duke of Bedford, who was made strictly accountable for the power which he exercised as a Welsh marcher lord.[7] The nearest to a traditional magnate was probably the fourth Earl of Northumberland, but he was killed in mysterious circumstances at Cocklodge in 1489, and his heir was a child. Henry was calculating in his distribution of money and trust. "Seek to serve me, and I will seek to enrich you", he told one of his lesser favourites, Sir Henry Wyatt. Small responsibilities well discharged led to small rewards and greater responsibilities to follow. Trust and wealth had to be earned, and the rewards of loyal service were secure, if not particularly generous. A good example is provided by the career of Thomas Howard, Earl of Surrey. Howard had served Edward IV and Richard III, being wounded and captured at Bosworth. He began the reign attainted and imprisoned, but within a year had been released and pardoned. Part of his property was then restored, and he entered a bond for his loyalty and good behaviour. Three years later, having satisfied the King that his reconciliation was genuine, he was appointed Warden General of the Northern Marches, in succession to the Earl of Northumberland. His title and the balance of his estates were then restored. He served with distinction at the time of the Scottish incursion in 1496, and in 1502 succeeded Lord Dinham as Lord Treasurer. After Henry's death, in 1513, he won a great victory over the Scots at Flodden, and in the following year his father's Dukedom of Norfolk was conferred upon him.

Two devices were typical of Henry's style of government, and he did not invent either of them. The first was the bond, or recognizance. This was used typically in two types of situation. On appointment to office, the new holder would be required to enter into a bond with the King for the loyal and faithful discharge of his duties. If the King was satisfied, then the bond remained dormant, and might eventually be cancelled altogether, at which point the office holder would also be rewarded. If, on the other hand, he was not satisfied, then the bond might be declared forfeit, and the sum specified would then be owed to the Crown. Since the preferment was likely to be lost as well, this was a formidable sanction. The second situation was more obviously penal. A person who had committed an offence, or who had earned the King's distrust in some other way, would be required to enter into an obligation whereby a specified sum would become forfeit to the King if he failed to discharge the conditions of his bond. This might be to obey the decision of a court, to surrender a piece of property unlawfully held, to make restitution to an aggrieved party, or simply to keep the peace towards a named person or group of people. Fines imposed by the King's Council were often secured in this way, and the sums involved were sometimes quite unrealistic – even as much as £10,000. Out of 62 peerage families in existence between 1485 and 1509, 46 were at one time or another subject to bonds of this kind, and many families carried more than one, the record being held by Lord Mountjoy with 23.[8] Such burdens were not specifically aimed at the peerage; any person of wealth or established local power might be nailed in this way. The victims were frequently resentful, but they were effectively prevented from undertaking any political action which the King was not prepared to sanction.

The other device was the commission. Commissions were instruments under the Great Seal, delegating certain aspects of the King's authority to named people for a specific purpose. They took many forms, but two examples will suffice. A commission of oyer and terminer was a judicial commission to hear certain cases (or perhaps a single case) within a specified area. Edward had used such commissions, but they became much commoner after 1485, having the great advantages of authority and flexibility. A commission of the peace was judicial and administrative, and was standing rather than *ad hoc*. It normally covered a single county and empowered a group of noblemen and gentlemen with residences or substantial interests in the county to hold courts and impose discipline in the King's name. The great advantage of this type of commission was that it represented a mutually advantageous partnership. The King recruited the direct service of men of substance in the locality, which gave additional weight to the decisions which they made on his behalf, and the local worthies gained extra prestige, and probably patronage, by becoming in a special sense the King's men. The commission of the peace had existed since the 14th century, but it was Henry VII who, by making greatly increased use of it, began to turn it into the cornerstone of Tudor local government, which it had become by 1547.

Broadly speaking, Henry's style of government could be described as distributive. Instead of working through a small number of very powerful men, he deliberately worked through a very much larger number of lesser men. This did not exclude the nobility, but it brought the next rank down, the knights and esquires, much more directly into contact with the Crown. In due course, this had the effect of lessening their dependence upon the nobility, and changing the pattern of "good lordship". This may not have been Henry's intention, and it was certainly not completed in his lifetime, but it represented an important shift of emphasis. In the words of Professor Lawrence Stone, even the gentlemen of Lancashire in time discovered that "... the King was a better lord than the Earl of Derby".[9] Similarly, in the Northern Marches, a number of prominent local gentlemen were taken directly into royal service.

Known as the King's "fee'd men", they introduced a direct royal presence into an area which had for centuries been dominated by the retinues of the great marcher lords. The same pattern can also be seen in the Council and in the Court. More than 220 men were designated as councillors during the 24 years of the reign. They included the majority of the peerage, and a substantial number of bishops, but well over half were knights, gentlemen, and lesser clerics. These were not necessarily prominent in an advisory capacity, but formed the executive and administrative team which carried the King's wishes into effect. At Court, Henry deliberately attracted the sons (and sometimes daughters) of the provincial gentry into household service, thus building bridges to their home areas. A friend or relation at Court became a necessary prerequisite for success in local politics, and the Court thus became a centre of communications as well as a pace-setter in style. There was nothing innovatory about this as an idea – a medieval court was supposed to be a means of access to the king, but Henry VI had failed conspicuously in that respect, and Edward had made no very conscious attempt to widen the circle of access, which was naturally dominated by the nobility.

Henry is probably best known for his fiscal policy, and in that respect he was least an innovator. He made the traditional revenues from land, customs dues, and the profits of justice more profitable, but by stricter administration, not by devising new exactions. A classic example of this is provided by the income from the royal estates, which averaged £3,000 a year in 1487–9, £11,000 a year in 1492–5, and £40,000 a year in 1502–5.[10] This was not the result of any huge increase in the size of the royal demesne, but simply of stricter estate management. It is sometimes said that he made huge sums from bonds and recognizances, and that this was a new departure, but neither statement is quite true. Henry certainly used bonds far more extensively than his predecessors, and in theory they produced an income of nearly £220,000 between 1504 and 1507. However, the bulk of this was purely notional. About £30,000 actually came in cash; of the rest, much was forgiven, and some which was due was never paid.[11] If we believe that the essence of Henry's success was that he was rich, then the argument for continuity is at its strongest. "New and strange exactions" were part of the legend created for Henry in his own lifetime. He made a calculated policy of threatening penal fines, but the sums he received by such methods were comparatively modest.

Similarly, if a new relationship with parliament is deemed to be a part of the "new monarchy", then the term does not apply to Henry VII. He used parliament in a strictly traditional way, and only when he needed to. Between 1485 and 1497, while he was still building up the security of his regime, he called six. After that, when his position was established and his revenue system working efficiently, he called only one. It was not until the following reign that the traditional limitations of legislation were transcended. Nor did Henry innovate in his Council. He called a total of about 230 men to Council at different times, and at any given moment there would be 50 or 60 councillors, of all ranks, including most of his peers. However, in this case, the obvious picture is slightly misleading. The inner ring of trusted office holders and advisers usually numbered no more than a dozen, and apart from the Duke of Bedford and the Earl of Oxford, consisted of prelates like John Morton and gentlemen such as Sir Reginald Bray, rather than noblemen. Henry relied far less than Edward had done upon the advice of his peers in important issues of policy. He also made considerable use of what would later be called "Council committees" for specialist business – the Council in the Star Chamber, for example.[12] These groups mainly comprised lay officials and men of business, and were essentially executive agencies. Such groups had existed before, but on a less regular basis, and with a lower profile.

Where Henry did make important changes, they tended to be of emphasis rather than structure. He is well known for his Statute of Liveries (1504), but in most respects this act had been anticipated by Edward IV, and even by Henry VI. What was different was that the emphasis was placed, not upon prohibition but upon licensing A nobleman was not forbidden to retain men outside his household, but he had to have the King's permission to do so. This was realistic and enforceable, because it recognized the King's need to depend upon such noble retinues in time of war. His use of wardship as a means of controlling aristocratic families showed a similar initiative. The feudal right of wardship had existed for centuries. The kings had often exploited the resources of their ward's estates, or endeavoured to do so, but Henry sold or granted wardships for the express purpose of imposing political control, often using his mother's household for that purpose.[13] A similar point might be made about his intelligence service. There was nothing new about kings employing spies, but Henry's agents were particularly thorough and effective. In 1469 and in 1470, Edward had been taken unawares by rather obvious conspiracies which any ruler of reasonable prudence should have been able to anticipate. In 1495, Henry was able to break Perkin Warbeck's plot, and arrest those involved, even a man so close to him and high in his confidence as Sir William Stanley, before any overt action had been taken. When Warbeck made his landing at Deal in July, the King knew where he would land, and how many men he would have with him. As a result, the "invasion" was a fiasco which could be defeated by the local militia.

Geoffrey Elton said in 1955 that Henry restored, but did not innovate. The observation was made of conciliar control in the north and the Marches of Wales, and in that context it remains valid. There was no innovation in establishing a youthful prince of Wales with a council at Ludlow, or a lieutenant in the north. Nor did Henry create new machinery in any of the principal branches of government. On the other hand, in certain specific areas, a change of pace or emphasis does not adequately express the nature of what happened. At Court, after the execution of Sir William Stanley, the King withdrew increasingly from the public life of the chamber. His confidence in his natural companions had been seriously undermined, and he sought to establish "private space" in a manner very unusual for a medieval king. While remaining politically accessible, at certain times of the day, and even more at night, he began to withdraw into what soon became known as his "privy chamber".[14] This consisted of a suite of rooms beyond the chamber, which was staffed only by menial servants, and to which access was very tightly controlled. These servants did not at first form a distinct department, and were not in any sense the King's companions, but their unique opportunities for access to him soon made their places much sought after. By the time Henry died, the potential of this situation was beginning to be appreciated, and in the following reign the privy chamber was to become the political and social hub of the Court. Similarly, important steps were taken to redefine the status of the King's ships. Edward had reestablished the office of clerk of the ships as recently as 1480, and there were only five vessels in the clerk's care in September 1485. In 1509, there were seven, but the figure is extremely misleading, because two of those seven were large, custom built warships of a kind which were entirely new to England. These ships represented a new policy of "keeping the seas", and two more had been laid down at the beginning of 1509, one of which was the revolutionary *Mary Rose*. To maintain and repair these great ships, a new dockyard had also been built at Portsmouth, and the harbour there fortified.[15] It would be an exaggeration to describe Henry VII as the "founder of the Royal Navy", but it would be equally mistaken to argue that he did no more than continue the policy of his immediate predecessors. His innovations in shipbuilding, and experiments with guns gave his more bellicose and adventurous son a flying start in the process of naval development.

It could be argued that, without creating any new law, or new institutions, Henry nevertheless founded a new system of government, with different priorities from those of his predecessors. I think that would be an exaggeration. With the benefit of hindsight, his real originality can be seen to lie in his "distributive" style, and in building bridges directly to the gentry.[16] Perhaps William I had done no less with his Oath of Salisbury in 1087, but on this occasion the change of direction proved permanent. Henry VIII and Wolsey picked up the same policy, and the Tudors thereafter consistently pursued it. Where Henry failed, and it could have been fatal, was in not giving his nobility quite enough to do to identify them with his system. The distributive policy could have carried the seeds of its own destruction. That did not happen because his successor added another dimension to his activity – war. Henry VIII encouraged his nobles to return to the battlefields from which his father (for good reasons) had withdrawn them. This gave them a rewarding and honorific function which enabled them to accept their diminished role in government. If you compare the Earl of Warwick in 1470 with the Duke of Buckingham in 1520, the relative strength of king and magnate tells its own story. If you compare Buckingham with the Earl of Essex in 1601, then the development of a "new monarchy" in some sense becomes an unavoidable conclusion. But I would certainly not attribute the lion's share of that advance to Henry VII.

Henry VIII was virtually compelled to start his reign as though he intended to be a new broom. His father's government in its latter days had accumulated too many cobwebs for him to have any choice; but in many respects the appearance was deceptive. Richard Empson and Edmund Dudley were arrested with a display of righteous indignation, but most of the old King's councillors retained their positions, and their ascendancy. William Warham, the Archbishop of Canterbury, remained Lord Chancellor until December 1515. Richard Cox, the Bishop of Winchester, was only replaced as Lord Privy Seal after his death in 1516; and Thomas Howard, who became Duke of Norfolk in 1514, stood down as Lord Treasurer two years before his death in 1524. The atmosphere of the Court was transformed, but many of the personnel remained the same, at least for the time being. Nevertheless, Henry was his own man, as he demonstrated within weeks of his accession by marrying his sister-in-law, to the astonishment of his Council and in the teeth of much contrary advice.[17] The real, but unarticulated, political question was whether the nobility would succeed in taking advantage of his inexperience in government to recover the ground which they had lost over the previous 20 years. His boisterous athleticism, chivalric dreams, and love of congenial company suggested a return to the days of his maternal grandfather. That did not happen for two reasons, both probably unintentional. The first was the King's compulsive urge to cut a dash on the European stage, which meant, in effect, reopening the Hundred Years' War and the second was the rise of Thomas Wolsey.

The war, which began in earnest in 1512, cost a great deal of money, but it also gave the rising generation of young nobles a chance to spread their wings at a safe distance from the centre of power. The Marquess of Dorset made a fool of himself in Guienne, and the victor of Flodden was the ageing Earl of Surrey, but it was a war in which honour and reputation could be won. Nor was Henry afraid to distribute titles with a generous hand. In 1514, the Earl of Surrey became Duke of Norfolk, and the King's jousting companion, Charles Brandon, Viscount Lisle, became Duke of Suffolk. Even more significant in some ways was a creation which owed nothing to the war, that of Margaret Pole as Countess of Salisbury in her own right. Margaret was the daughter of George, Duke of Clarence, and consequently first cousin to Henry's mother, Elizabeth of York. Henry VII had married her safely to his trustworthy servant and remote kinsman, Richard Pole, who had died in 1505. Margaret never showed an inclination to remarry, but her three sons constituted a potential challenge to the Tudor succession.[18] Her elevation to the title of her maternal grandfather, therefore, constituted a political signal that Henry was no longer afraid of the White Rose, and considered his state to be secure. The war came to a not particularly glorious end in 1514, but the rewarded and decorated gallants who flocked back to a brilliant Renaissance court did not take over the reins of power. While they had been away, the King had found his own man. Thomas Wolsey was not a dashing gallant, but a middle-aged cleric. Born in 1472, his career had advanced slowly to a royal chaplaincy by 1505, but he had caught the eye of the young Duke of York, as Henry was, and became Almoner shortly after Henry's accession. By 1512, he was an important councillor and a regular channel of communication between the King and his ministers. He was extremely competent, and there was also a bond of personal friendship between them. In 1513, he was given the task of organizing the army which Henry led to France, and so successful was he that by the end of that year he surpassed all but Richard Fox in the King's confidence.[19] He became in rapid succession Bishop of Tournai, Bishop of Lincoln, and Archbishop of York. By the end of 1515, he was also Lord Chancellor, and the most powerful man in England after the King.

Wolsey was a man with a firm grasp of political reality. He knew that the young King was in a stronger position than his father had been, and could afford, up to a point, to indulge his bellicose fancies. But he also appreciated the merits of Henry VII's distributive system. Noblemen were fine at Court or on the field of battle, but in the Council chamber, and above all in local government, they needed to be watched and curbed. The power of the Crown was his dominant consideration, because it was only by that power that the peace and stability of the realm could be protected. Consequently, when the Duke of Buckingham, a magnate whose rank and wealth owed nothing to the Tudor dynasty, and who had a remote claim to the throne, began to show indiscreet signs of *hubris* in 1520, Wolsey used all his resources of ingenuity to undermine him. It was, of course, the King who destroyed the Duke, not the Chancellor, but it was Wolsey who aroused Henry's volatile suspicions, and whose discreet management enabled him to dispose of one of his greatest subjects without a ripple of resistance.[20] The execution of Buckingham on an insubstantial charge of treason was another signal, because due process of law was observed, and he was properly condemned by his peers. The King was, and intended to remain, master in his own house. Wolsey built up the Crown's equity jurisdiction through the Court of Star Chamber, and maintained the system of fee'd men in the north. He also extended his own and the King's authority by persuading Henry to send his daughter Mary to the Welsh marches, and his illegitimate son, Henry FitzRoy, to the north, each with a substantial council largely selected by the Chancellor. Mary was 10 and FitzRoy six, so their personal involvement presented no challenge. Wolsey's relations with the nobility were usually bad. His influence with the King made many of them his clients from time to time, but they despised him for his humble origins, and blamed him for their lack of political power. It was only after his fall that they were forced to recognize the King as the true source of their discontent.

Unlike his father, Henry did not use financial pressures to control his nobles. The Duke of Suffolk, who owed him large sums of money, was freely forgiven.[21] He used the totally different tactic of creating a service nobility. There were exceptions, like the Countess of Salisbury and the Earl of Devon, promoted to the Marquessate of Exeter in 1525, but the great majority of Henry's generous creations were soldiers or men of business. Thomas Boleyn, Viscount Rochford 1525, Earl of Wiltshire 1529; Thomas, Lord Burgh 1529; Thomas, Lord Cromwell 1536, Earl of Essex 1540; Edward Seymour, Viscount

Beauchamp 1536, Earl of Hertford 1537; and many others. Years later, the
Princess Mary was to berate her brother's Council, declaring "my father made
the most part of you almost from nothing . . ." and there was an element of
truth in the jibe.[22] Wolsey's fall made no difference to this policy, but its
corollary, the destruction of the old nobility, became more marked after
1530, largely because of the controversial paths which the King was then
treading. Political pressure forced the sixth Earl of Northumberland to
disinherit his brother, and when he died in 1537 the King became his heir,
extinguishing his great marcher lordship for a generation. In 1538, the
Marquess of Exeter was executed, like the Duke of Buckingham, on a flimsy
charge of treason; and the great house of Howard was ruined by similar
charges only weeks before the King's death. Thomas Cromwell, the chief
minister from 1532 to 1540, was frequently blamed by his contemporaries
for this policy, but that is a bit like blaming Edmund Dudley for the financial
policies of Henry VII. Cromwell, like Wolsey, could see the benefits of such
a policy and was happy to promote it, but it was Henry who had to make
that sort of decision. By 1547, the nobility was largely service-based, and
even "old" nobles like the Earl of Arundel depended upon the Court for their
political power. Henry was being over-confident when he declared in 1545
that he would not be bound to be served by nobles, but by such men, whatsoever
their status, that he should appoint to office.[23] He had not quite reached the
position where the King's authority on its own was sufficient for all purposes,
but it was a declaration of policy which was beginning to seem realizable.

The commissions of the peace continued to grow in value and authority, not
as a result of any specific decision, but because the King and his advisers
appreciated the immense value of a service gentry for a crown which could
not afford an elaborate professional bureaucracy. However, Henry VIII's claim
to have invented a new monarchy does not rest upon the changing roles of
nobles and gentlemen in the broad context of government, but in the sharp
institutional focus of the parliament. This assembly of King, Lords, and
Commons had existed upon an occasional basis since the 13th century for
the purpose of voting taxes and letting off steam about grievances which
might otherwise have driven an engine of revolt. Because of its representative
nature, it had by the 14th century acquired the right to make pronouncements
upon some issues which were accorded the authority of law. This presented
no conceptual difficulties for a customary law which was in any case supposed
to have been evolved by the community rather than handed down by authority.
But it was a strictly limited function, and could not be extended to such
matters as the royal succession or the jurisdiction of the Church. Indeed,
when appealed to upon the succession issue in 1460, the Lords of the parliament
had disclaimed any competence in so high a mystery of state.

However, between 1529 and 1536, Henry VIII was confronted with a crisis.
He had no son and his wife Catherine was passed the childbearing age. The
King was convinced that this state of affairs was a punishment from God for
having married his brother's widow, and nothing could shake that conviction.

He was determined to set her aside and marry again; the Pope, within whose jurisdiction such matters lay, was determined for a variety of reasons to allow him to do no such thing. By a series of adroit manoeuvres, Thomas Cromwell, acting on the King's behalf, and with his full authority, forced an unwitting, but not entirely unwilling, parliament into resolving the issue for him. In a series of statutes between 1533 and 1535, it declared that the supreme ecclesiastical jurisdiction in England rested, and always had rested *de jure,* with the King.[24] Flying in the face of canon law and practical experience, it asserted that the authority of the Pope was a usurped power of corrupt human origin, and that God's intention was, and always had been, to rule his Church in its various locations through the appropriate temporal magistrates. It is clear enough why Henry should have wanted to force the issue in this way, but much less clear why the Lords and Commons, many of whom did not believe a word of what they were saying, should have been willing to abet him. A rather short sighted anti-clericalism may have played a part, although that now seems a less plausible explanation than it used to. The Church undoubtedly needed reform, and Wolsey's failure, in his capacity as papal legate, to bring that about, persuaded some that the King would make a better job of it. However, the most probable explanation is that everyone appreciated the King's determination to end his marriage, and sympathized with his reasons, however much they may have disliked Anne Boleyn. They also believed that the Royal Supremacy was a mere ploy to bring that about, and that when Henry had consoled himself with a son or two, relations with the papacy would be renegotiated, and the *status quo* restored. In other words, they did not take his pretension seriously, and saw no reason why they should risk the fate of Thomas More for the sake of resisting a temporary aberration.

By the time they had discovered that they were wrong, it was too late to go back. In whatever frame of mind he had started out, by 1536 Henry had convinced himself that his ecclesiastical jurisdiction was lawful in the sight of God, and even when Catherine and Anne were both dead, rejected the opportunity to reconsider his position.[25] At the same time, his subjects were finding good reasons why they should continue to support him. The destruction of the great pilgrimage shrines in 1535, and the dissolution of the lesser monasteries in 1536 gave the nobility and gentry more than a scent of plunder. All ranks comforted themselves with the thought that obedience to the King was a religious duty, which absolved them of all responsibility. If the King was leading them astray, he would be answerable for the sin, and not them. By 1547, the Royal Supremacy had won general acceptance, and the authority of parliament had been transformed. If the High Court of Parliament could terminate the Pope's jurisdiction, dissolve monasteries which had stood for a thousand years, and lay down new standards of doctrinal orthodoxy, was there anything which it could not do? Some scholars have argued that the Royal Supremacy did not, in fact, give Henry much more power over the Church than his predecessors had been able to wield when they chose, but that is a very narrow view.[26] Henry interfered, not only with ecclesiastical property to an unprecedented extent, but also with liturgy, the calendar, and even doctrine in a way which had never been attempted before. Although not all lawyers were to admit it for some time, it was no longer possible in practice to traverse a statute on the grounds that it was *ultra vires*. Provided an act had been properly made, it had the force of law unless or until it was repealed. Sir Thomas Smith was able to write in 1565

> The most high and absolute power of the realm of England consisteth in the parliament . . . (a statute) is the prince's and the whole realm's deed whereupon no man can justly complain but must accommodate himself to find it good and obey it. That which is done by this consent is called firm stable and *sanctum,* and is taken for law. The parliament abrogateth old laws, maketh new, giveth order for things past and for things hereafter to be followed, changeth rights and possessions of private men, legitimateth bastards, establisheth forms of religion, altereth weights and measures, giveth forms of succession to the crown. . . And the consent of the parliament is taken to be every mans consent.[27]

Very little of this description could have been applied in 1485. The medieval estates, with their recognized but very limited function, had become in effect a sovereign legislature.

It is very unlikely that this had been Henry VIII's intention, and doubtful whether it had been Thomas Cromwell's. It was a development which greatly enhanced the authority of the Crown, but also restricted it in ways which only gradually became apparent over the following century. In Henry's own hands, parliament continued to be a biddable instrument, hardly ever denying him what he wanted, but his successors were to find it recalcitrant from time to time, and ultimately unmanageable. By chance, Henry was succeeded by a child, and the whole of his, and his father's achievement was put to the test. There were good precedents to establish that a regent, or a regency council, could exercise the full authority of the Crown during a minority but no precedents for a minority in the Royal Supremacy.[28] Moreover, the success of the Tudors had been built upon the ability of two adult men to control their servants and agents effectively over a period of more than 60 years. Would the habits of obedience which had become established survive a minority of eight or nine years? Remarkably, they did. There was a revival of aristocratic power, but it was frustrated by a number of fortuitous circumstances. Edward Seymour, Duke of Somerset, the King's maternal uncle, became Lord Protector with the backing of a noble faction, but his insistence on maintaining the traditional Tudor hostility to enclosure and the spread of sheep ranching, alienated him from most of his aristocratic colleagues. In 1549, they overthrew him and installed a regime more to their own liking, which certainly maintained a common aristocratic front against social revolt, but it also produced a leader, in the person of the Earl of Warwick, whose policies were equally divisive in other ways. Warwick was unpopular with those who had welcomed Somerset's social policies, but that hardly mattered because they had little political influence. More importantly, his decision to increase the pace of religious change, probably based on a shrewd judgment of where the King's convictions were likely to settle, alienated many of his more cautious and conservative peers. Fear of renewed popular revolt kept nobles and gentlemen firmly in line between 1550 and 1553, but it did not make the Earl of Warwick loved, and certainly did not permit any recovery of influence by the old nobility. The men who ran England during Edward VI's minority were the service nobles of his father's reign.

Despite vociferous objections from affronted conservatives, such as the Bishop of Winchester, the Royal Supremacy was successfully assumed by the Council. This was made possible by parliament. The doctrine and worship of the English Church was shifted onto a Protestant basis by a series of statutes, particularly the two Uniformity Acts of 1549 and 1552. By effectively controlling the Lords and Commons in the King's name, the Council was able to carry out a legislative programme whose validity it was impossible to deny without calling the whole basis of the Supremacy in question; and that no one, not even Winchester, was willing to do. The only person who openly denied the validity of these statutes was the Princess Mary, who described them as "... a late law of your own devising . . . not worthy to have the name of law";[29] but since she was trying to defend her father's settlement rather than to overturn it, her argument had little logic or force. What she had identified in making this protest was the movement of the Royal Supremacy from a personal function to an institutional one, or rather the completion of that process. England became Protestant because that was what the law prescribed. A number of scholars have recently and plausibly argued that there were actually very few Protestants in England in 1552, and most people, including the nobility, disliked the new settlement intensely.[30] Respect for lawful authority did not keep them silent, but it did prevent them from taking effective action to protect what was left of the old faith. It was a very effective demonstration of the constitutional revolution which had taken place since 1530.

So far, the Earl of Warwick and his supporters had worked with the grain, using the changes which Henry VIII had brought about to effect their purposes, but when the King fell sick in the spring of 1553, the Duke of Northumberland (as Warwick had then become) was confronted with a different kind of problem. The heir to the throne, declared by the Succession Act of 1543 and by Henry VIII's will, authorized in that Act, was Mary. Both the King and Northumberland, for somewhat different reasons, were determined that she should not possess the Crown. Edward declared, upon his own authority, that his heir should be his cousin, Jane Grey, recently married to Northumberland's son, Lord Guildford Dudley. The tortuous reasoning which dictated this choice need not concern us. Mary was the heir by law, and Jane by the King's clearly expressed intention. There was no time to repeal the 1543 Act, but the Council, under enormous pressure, endorsed Edward's decision. When he died at the beginning of July 1553 there was, therefore, a straightforward issue. Jane had the backing of the Council and, apparently, control over the resources of the state. On the other hand, her mentor, Northumberland, had many enemies, and Mary had many friends. The contest lasted only 10 days, and did not come to a military arbitration. Jane's position collapsed and Mary was proclaimed amid general rejoicing. There were, of course, a number of factors which contributed to that outcome, but the most important was the overwhelming authority of statute law. Had Edward succeeded *mere moto suo* in traversing his father's Succession Act, it would have seriously undermined the recent constitutional developments, and opened the way to an untrammelled absolutism. Significantly also, Mary's success was achieved, not by the support of conservative magnates anxious to teach the service nobility a lesson, but by the support of the gentry.[31] Those who moved first to proclaim her, in East Anglia and elsewhere, were the county élites; men such as Sir Thomas Wyatt in Kent and Sir Peter Carew in Devon, who had appeared to be sympathetic to the previous regime. Foreign observers were bewildered. They were accustomed to noble factions and to palace revolutions; they were also familiar with peasant revolts, but what had happened in England was none of those things. Diplomats, like the Imperialist Simon Renard (who was delighted with the outcome), shrugged their shoulders and declared that the islanders were unstable and unpredictable. They should have come to exactly the opposite conclusion.

In most respects, Mary was a total contrast to her brother. But there was at first one similarity. She was the first woman to rule England in her own right, and no one knew exactly what her authority should be; least of all in respect of the Royal Supremacy, which was no more designed for a woman than it had been for a child. The first issue was settled, predictably, by a statute, which declared her power to be identical with that of a male ruler.[32] The second was resolved, in the first instance, by the fact that the Supremacy had become part of the constitutional authority of the Crown. No attempt was made in England to disqualify the Queen from ecclesiastical jurisdiction on the grounds of her sex. The only person to argue along those lines was her cousin, Cardinal Reginald Pole, to whom the whole concept of the Royal Supremacy was a blasphemy. Mary had no difficulty in persuading parliament to revert to her father's settlement by repealing her brother's legislation; but it is significant that she insisted upon the repeal of statutes which she had earlier described as "no true laws". Even more significantly, having decided that her father's whole position had been deluded, she undertook the prolonged and extremely difficult task of securing the repeal of the Acts of Supremacy, although she must have regarded those Acts as invalid *ipso facto*. After 1555, neither Protestant nor Catholic could deny that the settlement of the Church of England was a matter for the parliament of England, and that was a notion which sat much more easily with the reformers than it did with the Romans.

It was not only in religion that Mary was conservative. Many of the service nobility paid for their involvement in the Edwardian regime. Few lost their heads, but many lost their offices and the confidence of the ruler. The old noble families which Henry had destroyed were rehabilitated – Howard, Courtenay, and above all Percy.[33] It would be an exaggeration to say that they recovered their old ascendancy, but the signal was unmistakable and much might have changed if Mary had lived longer. Mary was not deliberately reactionary, either in politics or religion, but her confidence was bestowed in ways which caused justifiable unease. In the first year of her reign, she paid more attention to the Imperial Ambassador, Simon Renard, than she did to any of her own councillors. In the second year of her reign, she was, understandably, much influenced by her husband, Philip of Spain, and his advisers, and thereafter chiefly by the Cardinal Legate, Reginald Pole. Pole was an Englishman and an aristocrat, but he had been out of the county for 20 years, and his priorities bore little relation to those of the resident governing class. The Queen had neither the knowledge nor the will to set about a deliberate policy of unravelling the political and adminsitrative changes which had taken place over the previous two generations. She relied on administrators who had been trained under Thomas Cromwell, perforce used experienced councillors whom she did not fully trust, and accepted the newly acquired status of parliament. On the other hand, the steady advance of the service nobility was checked. All the great titles conferred by Mary were restorations, and she failed to build the kind of *rapport* with the county élites on which her sister was to set such great store. Perhaps with experience, the momentum would have been resumed, but in the event, Mary's main service to the development of Tudor monarchy, apart from her recognition of statute, came in the preservation of a lawful order of succession. In 1553, she did that by insisting upon her own claim, and in 1558 by recognizing, no matter how reluctantly, the right of her half-sister Elizabeth.

The last of the Tudors seems to have set out to be as different as possible from her predecessor. The two women had disliked each other intensely, for obvious reasons. Mary had been devoted to her mother; Elizabeth "gloried" in her father, and a well informed observer noted within a few days of her accession ". . . she gives her orders and has her way absolutely in all things, as her father did".[34] It was an exaggeration, but a significant one. When conspirators were murmuring against Mary in 1556, one of them had expressed the wish that "my neighbour of Hatfield" (Elizabeth) might secure the throne ". . . for then would gentlemen of service be regarded".[35] Rightly or wrongly, Mary had given the impression of being more interested in clergy and in members of the old noble families, than in the service gentry. This was probably caused, not by any positive preference of that kind, but by the fact that so many of the county élites had cooperated willingly, if not enthusiastically, with the Henrician and Edwardian regimes, and were therefore compromised in her eyes. Those who had suffered imprisonment or dispossession for resisting the new ways, on the other hand, automatically commended themselves. Mary's favourites were consequently the first to feel the chill wind of the new Queen's disfavour. The privy chamber was completely reshaped, and only the Lord Treasurer, the Marquess of Winchester, survived among the high officers of state. The Court and the Council became markedly secular in tone. Unprecedentedly, no prelate sat on the Privy Council until Archbishop Whitgift was appointed in 1583. The new Acts of Supremacy and Uniformity, as well as reestablishing the Edwardian Church, signalled a return to insular priorities. The Queen described herself as "mere English", and was observed to court the popular acclaim of her subjects – even the humble ones. Unlike her father, she did not maintain a service nobility. Some titles were given for that reason – the barony of Burleigh and the earldom of Lincoln for example – but most were conferred for political reasons which had little to do with the mechanics of government. As the reign progressed, titles of all kinds became scarce, and in that Elizabeth resembled her grandfather. She also resembled him in bonding directly with the gentry. By the 1580s, William Lambarde was complaining of the "stacks of statutes" which the justices of peace were being called upon to administer, and the military reorganization of the 1570s conferred upon some of the same men the duties and authority of the deputy lieutenancy, the mustering and leadership of the trained bands in every county.[36]

Despite the social prestige and wealth which the nobility still retained, Elizabethan England became increasingly a "gentry commonwealth". This was reflected in a number of aspects of the national life. The medieval Church had been run by bishops who were, in effect, ecclesiastical noblemen; in some cases they were scions of noble families, such as the Beauforts and the Nevilles. The bishops of the Elizabethan Church were mostly of urban or minor gentry backgrounds, and, although they continued to sit in the House of Lords, ranked for social and political purposes with the greater knights and esquires. The number of peers declined slightly during Elizabeth's reign, but gentlemen increased dramatically, both in absolute numbers and as a proportion of a rising population. There were a number of reasons for this. The English gentleman, unlike the minor nobleman of France or Spain, was not debarred by law or custom from gainful employment. Gentlemen traded, commanded ships, and above all monopolized the thriving legal profession. Education became increasingly a gentleman's prerogative. Even in 1540, Archbishop Cranmer had been forced to resist pressure for his newly founded school in Canterbury to be opened to the sons of gentlemen only.[37] Many nobles had profited greatly from the dissolution of the monasteries, but the greatest quantity of the land sold on by the Crown between 1540 and 1560 had ended in the hands of gentry families. Every county could show families which had risen from obscurity to wealth by the acquisition of former monastic lands. So powerful was the vested interest that Pope Julius III had been forced to yield to it in 1554 in order to recover his jurisdiction. The gentry had put Mary on the throne, and most of them continued to support her, but they were not going to do so unconditionally. At the same time, the House of Commons became the gentleman's forum in national politics. The rise of parliament, and the frequency of sessions, brought the knights and burgesses to London more often, and for longer periods. Business and marriage networks grew up, and by the 1580s only the largest and most populous cities retained control over their own representation. The majority of boroughs had conceded their seats to neighbouring gentlemen, or to the younger sons of noblemen expecting, usually rightly, to benefit from the concession. At the death of Henry VII, 296 members sat in the House of Commons of whom 222 represented boroughs. By 1603, the comparable figures were 460 and 370. Over the same period the membership of the House of Lords had declined from a little over 100 to about 75,[38] and the days were fast approaching when a speaker could claim that the lower house could buy out the upper several times over.

Elizabeth welcomed this situation, and took every opportunity to promote it. When the rebellion of 1569 cost the heads of the Earl of Northumberland and the Duke of Norfolk, and the estates of the Earl of Westmorland, the beneficiaries, apart from the Crown, were the loyal gentry of the north and East Anglia. After 1572, there were no more dukes in Tudor England. Elizabeth liked her noblemen where she could see them, around the court or in safe offices. One of the reasons for her dread of war, apart from the expense, was that war was the nobleman's natural ground, where he flourished and she could not follow him. It is not surprising that she favoured gentleman commanders like Sir Francis Drake and Sir John Norris. Noble favourites were a different matter, but Leicester and Essex were kept in leading strings, and the latter was never allowed any serious political power. In return for this favour, the Queen enjoyed the enthusiastic support of the great majority of the county élites; they even backed her Church when they did not much like its teaching. But there was a price to pay, and it may be doubted whether Elizabeth ever realized how high that would turn out to be. Contrary to what was once argued, she did not surrender any significant political initiative to the House of Commons, and it is now recognized that the word "opposition" can only be used in that context with grave reservations.[39] Elizabeth's parliaments cooperated in the process of government, just as Henry VIII's had done, sharing the Queen's strategy and disagreeing mostly about tactics. The really damaging aspect of the Queen's *entente* with her gentry did not involve power directly, but money. Put very simply, the gentlemen who served on the commissions of the peace, and in countless other local offices, did not see why they should pay for the government as well as staff it. No one in England was exempt from taxation, and one of the features of the early Tudor subsidy had been that it had fallen most heavily upon those best able to pay. After 1560, that became progressively less true. In a period of inflation, and of steadily increasing gentry wealth, the subsidy assessments remained the same, or even declined. Apart from exemptions, England was probably the most lightly taxed country in western Europe. Because the Tudors had involved the parliament so closely in the processes of government, they had been unable to emancipate themselves from the medieval custom of consent to taxation. Elizabeth, realizing the extent of her dependence upon the cooperation of parliament and the gentry, did not feel inclined to disrupt those relationships by asking for a realistic level of financial support. This was never admitted, but assessments were either left untouched or revised by the gentlemen themselves, until Sir Walter Raleigh could admit in a moment of candour that the Queen's books showed "not a hundreth part" of the real wealth of himself and his friends. England was not poor in 1603, but the Crown was. Elizabeth became notorious for allowing her courtiers and officers to help themselves, through monopolies and other devices, at the expense of her subjects at large because her lack of political courage left her without enough money to reward them. Like her grandfather, her parsimony became notorious, but unlike him she was not applying financial sanctions where they could be effective.

There can be no doubt that by the time Elizabeth died in 1603, the English monarchy was very different from what it had been in 1485. In some respects it was much stronger. Neither the Church nor the nobility, those two great curbs on medieval monarchy, exercised any real political power. On the other hand, no one could have described James I as an absolute king, even in the limited sense that Henry IV of France or Philip III of Spain were absolute. For better or worse, and probably without conscious intention, the Tudors had mortgaged their authority to a gentry commonwealth. This had not come about suddenly. Rather it had been a continuous thread, running through their policies from one generation to the next. It had started with the distributive strategy employed by Henry VII and continued by Wolsey, but its greatest single advance came during the Reformation parliament, which revolutionized the authority of statute. Neither the dominance of the service nobility under Edward VI nor the partial recovery of the old nobility under Mary, had been long enough or deliberate enough to reverse the trend. Elizabeth was happy enough to protect a system which enabled her to overcome the numerous problems of the early part of her reign, and to build a national regime with a solid basis of support and a growing sense of identity. In the long run, the gentry commonwealth was to prove much stronger than the Crown, and had converted it into a constitutional monarchy by the 18th century. The Tudors cannot be credited with the whole responsibility for that, but they did develop a style of government which was not medieval, and was significantly different from the *ancien régime* monarchies which were growing up at the same time in most of England's continental neighbours.

Footnotes to this Chapter may be found on pages 357–58.

8: Barry Coward

The early Stuart monarchy: James I to the Commonwealth, 1603–49

IN THE 1640s, Sir Anthony Weldon published *The Court and Character of King James,* which contains a very famous description of the man who, in 1603, became James I of England as well as already being James VI of Scotland. "He was", wrote Weldon,

> a man of middle stature, more corpulent through his clothes than in his body, yet fat enough, his clothes ever being made large and easy, the doublets quilted for stiletto-proof, his breeches in great pleats and full stuffed. He was naturally of timorous disposition, which was the reason of his quilted doublets; his eyes large, ever rolling after any stranger that came into his presence, insomuch that many for shame have left the room, as being out of countenance. His beard was very thin: his tongue too large for his mouth, which ever made his speech full in the mouth, and made him drink very uncomely, as if eating his drink, which came out of the cup of each side of his mouth... His walk was ever circular, his fingers in that walk fiddling with that codpiece; he was very temperate in his exercises and in his diet, and not intemperate in his drinking ... [he was] in his apparel so constant as by his goodwill he could never change his clothes until worn out to very rags. . . .[1]

This venomous pen-portrait of James VI and I by Weldon is one that reflects and has shaped the strong image of James that has lasted for centuries: an image of a shambling, dirty old man, a buffoon, whose incompetent hands (when they were not fiddling about his codpiece) took over the reins of the English state in 1603 from the more than capable hands of Gloriana, Good Queen Bess, who put England onto the High Road to Civil War.

The verbal image of James's son, Charles I, who succeeded his father as King of Britain in 1625, that has been almost as influential in shaping popular perceptions of the second Stuart monarch, is the account of Charles I at his trial in 1649. Here is part of the trial proceedings, from the second day, 22 January 1649, when John Bradshaw, the president of the court, tried to get the King to answer the charges against him, which the King consistently refused to do. Instead, Charles said this:

> It is not my case alone, it is the freedom and the liberty of the people of England, and, do you pretend what you will, I must justly stand for their liberties. For if power, without law, may make laws, may alter the fundamental laws of the kingdom, I do not know what subject he is in England can be assured of his life or anything he can call his own.[2]

In this extract, I think that we have one of the origins of the popular image of Charles I as the Martyr King, the constitutionally-minded monarch, strong and principled, standing up for English liberties. I am fairly certain that both these images of James I and Charles I are very misleading indeed, and in what follows I want to show why I think that there are other, more accurate historical interpretations of these two early Stuart monarchs.[3]

My first priority needs to be to clear away a huge pile of myths and misleading assumptions that have grown up over the years about the early Stuart monarchy. To do that I need a metaphorical bulldozer to carry out some drastic ground-clearing, sweeping some historical myths into an historical dustbin, or indeed something larger, perhaps a large and capacious waste disposal skip.

My first target for demolition and disposal is Weldon's "codpiece" pen portrait of James I. What helps to destroy it is the fact that Weldon was hardly fitted to be an objective commentator on the Scottish King. For one thing, Weldon was violently prejudiced against Scotland and all things Scottish. In a book that Weldon wrote after visiting Scotland as part of James's entourage on a royal tour of the northern kingdom in 1617, he wrote that Scotland

> is too good for those that possess it, and too bad for others to be at the charge to conquer it. The air might be wholesome, but for the stinking people that inhabit it. . . There is [he continued with a horrible pun] a great store of fowl too, as foul houses, foul sheets, foul linen, foul dishes, and pots, foul trenchers and napkins.[4]

Not surprisingly, after reading this, the Scottish James was furious and sacked Weldon from his Court office, after which Weldon had no reason not to turn his bitter pen against James as well as his fellow countrymen. His book, *The Court and Character of King James* with its codpiece portrait is the result. That clearly is not the piece of objective historical evidence that it is often assumed to be. It is instead a piece of typical rabid English anti-Scottish rhetoric. As the hostile Weldon-type view of James topples and its pieces are swept into my historical waste disposal skip, what emerges is a different image of a king who was not devoid of good political sense and who possessed a vast reservoir of tact and an ability to rule well.

The second target for demolition by my metaphorical bulldozer is the image of Charles I as a defender of the fundamental laws. What I want to show is that there are powerful reasons for doubting the validity of such an image and for portraying instead, at best, an inept, stupid, and foolish king, and, at worst, a monarch who was capable of stooping to unconstitutional and sometimes illegal action. It is possible to claim (and I do) that Charles I was the most disastrous English monarch since Henry VI in the mid-15th century and a king who did not have Henry VI's excuse that he was mad. In place of the image of Charles I as a principled monarch, I want to erect another: of a king whose incompetence ensured not only his own execution, but also the abolition of the institution of monarchy in Britain in 1649.

But before I start the work of construction, while I have got my metaphorical bulldozer running, could I also clear away two other myths that are prevalent about early 17th-century monarchy. The first is that monarchy in England by this stage was very different from medieval times. I do not think that it was. There had been no Tudor revolution in government in the 16th century that transformed government from personal monarchy to a bureaucratic state.[5] At the beginning of the 17th century, English monarchs still held immense personal political power. The king was in a very real sense still "the government". Although monarchs often sought advice from members of the Privy Council, either formally or informally, privy councillors were advisers who were appointed by and who owed their positions solely to the Crown. Consequently, monarchs were not bound to follow the advice they received. They could, moreover, obstruct parliamentary legislation by veto or by dissolving parliament. They had the power to dispense individuals from the law and, above all, they made all the key decisions of government. The foreign policy of James I was quite literally that. This being the case, the quality of government depended very much on the character and the abilities of the monarch for the time being, which is why historians of monarchy in this period have a very powerful justification for peering into the private lives of monarchs. What kings and queens did in their palaces, indeed in their bedrooms, is of more consequence for historians of the 17th-century monarchy than it is for those who write about monarchy in the later 20th century. This being the case, too, in the early 17th century, the centre of government was where the king was, which is why the recent historical emphasis on the Court and the downgrading of parliament's place in the government process at this time is perfectly justified.[6] When the idea that the Tudors created a different type of monarchy from the medieval monarchy is jettisoned, then these kinds of continuities with the medieval past personal monarchy, the political importance of the Court, and so on are revealed. In the early 17th century, monarchs still ruled as well as reigned.

This leaves one final target for me to demolish, and this task I approach with some trepidation, given its popularity. This is the legend of the greatness of Elizabeth I. My view of the Virgin Queen is a different one from that manufactured at the time by a government propaganda machine that churned out images of Elizabeth I, including stylized portraits, that showed a divinely-ordained queen, totally in control of her kingdom and ruling over a stable state: an image that future generations perpetuated and which was developed into an historical orthodoxy in Sir John Neale's books on Elizabeth I.[7] When you take away that image, you see a different kind of reality, as will be explained later. What skills Elizabeth possessed were those of a short-term political fixer, at best papering over deep cracks in the body politic. When she died in 1603, she left the country in a mess.

I think that is a good link to the point at which I can begin to present a view of early Stuart monarchy that is uncluttered by misleading assumptions. The best starting point for a reassessment of the abilities and achievements of James I and Charles I is an analysis of the problems of government that they inherited from Elizabeth I, since only by an appreciation of these problems can the extent of the success and failures of the early Stuarts be assessed. Among the many problems facing the early Stuart monarchy, three fundamental weaknesses of government stand out, weaknesses which Elizabeth I had done little to remedy. In fact, I think that as she aged and her political powers faded, she made these problems worse.

The first is a fairly familiar problem to people living nowadays. This is the government's financial weakness, which was largely rooted in the inflation which had been under way since the early 16th century. In peacetime, things were bad enough, but during wartime the existing system of public finance was simply unable to produce the vast sums of money necessary to fight a war. It is true that, in meeting this problem of falling income and rising expenditure, Elizabeth had some short-term success, largely by following expedients that are reminiscent of those used by governments recently, that is by cutting public expenditure to the bone. But, looked at from a long-term perspective, the consequences were less successful, because Elizabeth never tackled the root cause of the financial problems of the early modern English state: its inadequate revenue. The upshot was that in the late 1580s and 1590s, the Elizabethan government was forced to devise extraparliamentary emergency sources of income, such as forced loans, ship money, and the sale of monopolies, expedients that produced the bitter political tensions that erupted in Elizabeth's last two parliaments in 1597 and 1601, illustrating the way in which the Crown's financial problems could easily and rapidly escalate into constitutional opposition.[8] In the 1590s, and again in the later 1620s, the Crown's desperate search for new ways of raising money began to be interpreted as radical interference with the ancient constitution, a point that needs stressing. The unreformed and weak financial position of the monarchy at the beginning of the 17th century had the potential to produce constitutional opposition. Because the Crown seemed to be acting in novel constitutional ways, fears and anxieties about the future of parliaments emerged. Was the Crown intent on absolutism? My point quite simply is that the real danger to the stability of the state of the financial mess left by Elizabeth I was that it contained the seeds of dangerous ideological divisions in England.

The second governmental problem inherited by the early Stuarts in 1603 is (to us) a less familiar problem of government than that of financial weakness. This is the problem of religion, a problem that was rooted in the 16th-century changes associated with the Reformation. The English Church that was officially established in 1559 was a half-reformed Church: the Prayer Book services in the new Church were purged of most aspects of Roman Catholic liturgy, but they retained traditional ceremonies like bowing at the name of Jesus and the use of the sign of the Cross in baptismal ceremonies. Within the Church in the later 16th and early 17th centuries, the most controversial issues were whether the half-reformed Church of 1559 should be further reformed, whether the Calvinist predestinarian theology of the new Church should retain its dominant position, or whether it should be modified or replaced by a theology of free will. Elizabeth's reaction to these divisions within the Church was typical of her approach to most serious problems: she ignored them, or at least suppressed all discussions about them. What she did not do was attempt to heal these potentially explosive divisions within the Church.

In short, Elizabeth left for her successor the problem of a divided Church, as well as a financial situation that threatened to destroy the stability of the state. It may be going slightly over the top to write (as John Guy has done) that under Elizabeth I England "had quietly become ungovernable",[9] but what had happened during her reign made the task of governing England a very difficult one indeed. What made matters worse for the early Stuarts is that they were rulers, not only of England, Wales, and Ireland, but of Scotland as well. The European experience of monarchs in similar situations was not encouraging. The Spanish monarchy's rule of multiple kingdoms in the Iberian and Italian peninsulas and in the Spanish Netherlands was punctuated by rebellions in Catalonia, Portugal, Naples, and the Netherlands in the later 16th and early 17th centuries. The early Stuarts were faced with ruling multiple British kingdoms that were riven by as many fundamental differences of economic, social, and legal traditions as were the multiple Spanish monarchies. There were also serious religious differences: Roman Catholic Ireland, a half-reformed Protestant England, and a much more fully-reformed Presbyterian Scotland.[10] All this amounted to a potentially lethal cocktail for James I and Charles I to digest.

The traditional view of James I is that, when he became King of England in 1603, he failed totally to deal with these problems, that he simply lacked the ability to do that, and that the accession of the Wisest Fool in Christendom effectively put England on the High Road to Civil War.[11] This view is wrong. The reign of James I has got very little to do with the causes of the Civil War, let alone the total collapse of monarchy in Britain in 1649. James I as King of England between 1603 and 1625 effectively contained most of the problems I have just described. But it would be foolish to attempt to whitewash James I completely. So I shall qualify what is going to be my overall picture of a fairly successful monarch in two ways.

The first is by conceding that James I was clearly a complex, neurotic, dotty man. This is a king who, as the editor of his letters points out, could address a letter to an august courtier, George Keith, Earl Marischal of Scotland, as "my little fat pork", who would call Robert Cecil, Earl of Salsibury, in letters to him, "my little beagle" or "my little wiffe-waffe", and who could warn his son, Charles, when choosing a wife to think "as well upon the business of Christendom as upon the codpiece point".[12] Although that is good advice, the way James put it is typical of his rather crude, basic attitude to sex. He regularly visited the bedrooms of newly-married courtiers to interrogate them about the details of their first nights together. Some of his references to sex have a touch of the Benny Hill about them. At the Hampton Court ecclesiastical conference in 1604, one of the godly reformers there, John Reynolds, who was a bachelor, rather primly objected to the explicitly sexual nature of the words in the marriage service, "with my body I thee worship". To which James replied with a leer: "Many a man speaks of Robin Hood who never shot in his bow".[13] He would have been God's gift to the modern tabloid press, who would have had a field day with "sound bites" like that, or like his comparison of his homosexual relationship with George Villiers, Duke of Buckingham, to that between Christ and John the Baptist. "Christ had his John: I have my George," he said. There is a serious historical point to all this, which is that James' personality did not help (to say the least) in the essential task of presenting a monarch who was supposed to match the contemporary ideal of "God's lieutenant on earth". Moreover, it helped to get the Jacobean Court a reputation for sexual sleaziness and financial corruption that rebounded against the King.[14]

That is the first qualification to the picture of James, the successful ruler. The second is that some of James' actions inflamed the fears of creeping royal absolutism that I mentioned were already there when he became King of England. One of the main reasons for the failure of James' proposal to unite his two kingdoms of England and Scotland into one country early in his English reign was sheer fear that this might mean the end of English Common Law and traditional constitutional procedures. In April 1604, Robert Cecil told the King that

> all of the judges of the realm have joined with the opinion of three
> parts of the House [of Commons] that the first hour wherein Parliament
> gives the name of Greaty Britany there followeth necessarily . . . an
> utter extinction of all the laws now in force.[15]

James's infamous financial extravagance drove his ministers to seek extraparliamentary sources of money, like impositions, which were additional customs dues that had not been approved by parliament, and these were seen as direct threats to parliamentary liberties. All this led to periods of quite serious political tension between James and his parliaments. "If the power of imposing were quietly settled in our kings", forecast one MP, James Whitelocke, in 1610

> considering what the greatest use they make of assembling Parliaments,
> which is the supply of money, I do not see any likelihood to hope for
> often meetings in that kind because they would provide themselves by
> that other means.;[16]

But, while making these qualifications, what I want to argue next is that these periods of political tension, caused by issues like James's proposal to unite England and Scotland and raise money by extraparliamentary impositions, never reached the level of seriousness that characterized the rifts that developed between Crown and parliaments, between Court and country, very soon after the accession of James' son, Charles I, in 1625.

In explaining why this never happened in James's reign, the Court presided over by James is a good place to begin. James' Court might have lacked the decorum of that of Elizabeth I or of his son, but most powerful factions in the country were represented there, which was important in an age when, as pointed out earlier, the Court was one of the principal arenas of politics where debate and competition took place. In the 1980s, it became fashionable among some 17th-century historians to talk about the presence of political consensus in early Stuart England, but this is misleading.[17] In early modern England, there never was a time when politicians, statesmen, ministers, courtiers, or monarchs were in agreement with one another about everything. In these circumstances, it was essential that political differences – whether they were rooted in scrambling for office or royal favour, or in serious policy differences about peace or war – should be allowed to be voiced, but yet be contained and controlled. By and large, the Jacobean Court filled that function. James' long experience, approaching 20 years, as adult King of Scotland had made him particularly adept at coping with the factional politics of the English political jungle.

For one thing, James realized (as Elizabeth had not) that in order to be a successful monarch, he had to be bountiful. The cooperation of leading magnates and the Crown in government partially depended on monarchs dispensing royal bounty. Some of the political tensions of Elizabeth's later years grew out of the fact that the cost-conscious Elizabeth was not bountiful enough. She made few grants of land, money, or titles of honour. James may have gone over the top in the other direction, but political expediency dictated that on Elizabeth's death James filled the traditional royal role of bountiful patron – what in the Middle Ages was called the role of "the good lord".[18]

James' political skill in defusing political tensions also showed to good effect during parliamentary sessions, not so much on set-piece occasions, when he made long and pompous speeches, which have captured the attention more of historians than they did (I suspect) of his audiences, but during the nitty-gritty, behind-the-scenes sessions of political debate and negotiation. This shows up most clearly in that famous episode early in his reign over the case of the disputed Buckinghamshire election of 1604, about which James has had a lot of bad historical press for apparently making provocative speeches about royal rights. But what the historian, who has done a lot of work on the evidence thrown up by this case has found, is that a case that exploded out of local political rivalries in Buckinghamshire onto the parliamentary political stage was skilfully defused by James' behind-the-scenes negotiations, during which a successful compromise was reached. James always appears best and most successful in this "beer-and-sandwiches" political role rather than when he took part in formal political set-pieces.

What also helped him to keep the lid on political trouble was his determination to keep England out of the Thirty Years' War that began in Europe in 1618. It is true that James' negotiations with Spain, his attempts to secure a marriage alliance with Spain, rather than committing England to a war against creeping Catholicism in Europe, was condemned by his more militant Protestant subjects. But it is arguable that, given the limited financial and military resources available to him, England could not afford an interventionist foreign policy in Europe. This is surely supported by the history of England's role in international affairs from at least the days of Henry VIII's inglorious wars against France in the early 16th century. Financially, James' diplomatic, peaceful approach to international affairs was sensible as it did not involve his embarking on the financially ruinous and politically damaging expedients that Charles employed when he abandoned it after 1625. Undoubtedly, James' failure to enter a war to defend the Protestant interest in Europe aroused suspicions among anti-Catholic Englishmen and women.[20] James I was not the most popular king in English history, but it is likely that he did not open a wide gulf between himself and most of his subjects.

That is a conclusion that is amply reinforced by, arguably, James' greatest success, which is in the field of religion.[21] Here (as I explained) the growing divisions within the national Church at the beginning of the 17th century were great. They were rather like an unexploded bomb ticking away beneath the foundations of a state in which religious uniformity was rigorously enforced. However, whereas Elizabeth I had dealt with the situation by repression and confrontation (as far as she was concerned the religious settlement of 1559 was literally *the settlement*), James' response was conciliatory. Just as in international affairs he took the role of *rex pacificus,* so in the Church he adopted a similar role, attempting to keep a balance between factions within the Church and leaving open the possibility of further religious reform. The importance of the Hampton Court Conference in 1604, to which were invited leading theologians of varying Protestant views, is that it gave James an opportunity to act a part he liked most of all: as a mediator. It is true that he rather slipped up on one occasion when one of the speakers at the Conference appeared to favour a Presbyterian Church without bishops, which sparked off James' famous "No bishop, no King" outburst. Yet that outburst does not typify the conference. It is, writes Professor Patrick Collinson, "better described as a kind of round-table conference on a variety of topics than as a debate between two sides".[22]

Under James, as he made clear at Hampton Court and on other occasions, there was the possibility of further reform of the Church. For example, James and his bishops promoted a preaching ministry in the best Puritan tradition. Just as James' public parliamentary speeches are not the most accurate reflection of James the politician, so James' oft-quoted public outburst at Hampton Court is not the best indication of his ecclesiastical policy. His more successful role was again behind the scenes, keeping in check theological divisions within the intellectual élite of the universities and of the Church between the proponents of predestinarian and of free-will theologies, and putting his weight behind a package of moderate Church reforms that gained fairly broad support in the country. The way James brought about and maintained a period of religious harmony in England is arguably his greatest achievement.

Finally on James, this story of relatively successful Jacobean kingship can be extended to his rule of Scotland also. Ruling two different countries was not easy. Yet James straddled the two with a fair degree of success, largely because he knew Scotland intimately and, even when he was absent in England (as he was for much of his life after 1603), he employed Scotsmen, like the Earl of Dunbar, who shuttled to and fro from Scotland to England helping him to keep his finger on the political pulse of his northern British kingdom. James' religious policies in Scotland, as in England, are the most impressive illustration of his political skill.[23] Like his son, his ambition was to bring together two very disparate churches in his two kingdoms. But, unlike his son's approach, James' was slow and pragmatic, but not without some success, the most dramatic example being in his persuading fiercely Presbyterian Scots to accept a modified episcopal system – no mean achievement. Moreover, as in England, when he realized that his actions were producing serious disquiet – as over his attempt to force the Articles of Perth on the Scottish Kirk – James wisely back-pedalled and rode out political storms.

My argument so far has been that James with all his faults had two great strengths as a king, which enabled him to deal fairly effectively with the problems of government left by Elizabeth I. The first is his determination to act as a *rex pacificus* – a conciliator – at home in the Church and in international affairs. It is true that as the Thirty Years' War got under way after 1618, he found it harder and harder to maintain that conciliatory role and certainly there is some evidence that towards the end of his reign he wobbled slightly in the ecclesiastical sphere away from his mediatory stance, moving away from the faction in the Church which was increasingly critical of his failure to declare war on Spain and towards those who held what later became known as Laudian ecclesiastical views. But "wobbled" is the key word. He never totally abandoned his *rex pacificus* role in Church and international affairs.[24] That was his first strength. His second was his political shrewdness, which enabled him to ride out political storms in a way that was later a characteristic of Charles II.

Now I want to stress that in both these respects, Charles I contrasts almost totally with his father with dramatic, disastrous political consequences. Firstly, unlike his father, he adopted a strongly activist and partisan role in the Church and in international affairs, and secondly he was political inflexibility personified. He appeared to be unable to see viewpoints that differed from his own and he interpreted even the expression of slight differences from his own opinions as tantamount to sedition. He did not know the meaning of the word compromise and he adopted extreme (and in some cases blatantly illegal) positions. The result was to provoke confrontation and political polarization between Charles and a significant number of his great subjects on the key issues of finance, religion, and multiple kingdoms that I have identified. This is most clearly demonstrated in the later 1620s, in the early 1640s, which witnessed the greatest crisis faced by the English monarchy since the mid-15th century, and in 1648–9, which witnessed an even greater crisis, the abolition of monarchy itself.

In part, Charles' troubles stemmed from his decisions very early in his reign to declare war on Spain and on France. Why he decided to take on two of the world's leading superpowers at the same time is not easy to see, although his hatred of Spain undoubtedly originated in his (and George Villiers') tragi-comic visit to Madrid in 1623 to woo the Spanish Infanta and conclude the Spanish marriage treaty, a visit which ended in deep personal humiliation for him.[25] The consequences, however, are easy to see, and, given the financial weakness of the monarchy, fairly predictable. Given the unreformed state of the Crown's finances, Charles had to find money from expedients like forced loans and to resort to billeting troops in private houses. As in the 1590s, such measures produced very strong opposition on ideological grounds and caused the rumbling fears of royal absolutism that had been there since at least the 1590s to flare to great heights.[26]

Charles' reactions to this situation were politically inept. Unlike his father, he poured fuel on the political flames. In part, this happened because Charles did not follow his father's practice of distributing royal favour widely enough. On the contrary, he very quickly allowed George Villiers, Duke of Buckingham, to capture royal patronage and to use it for the benefit almost solely of the Villiers family clientage. This was disastrous, since, as it has been seen, it was politically essential, if the political system were to work smoothly, that monarchs used royal bounty and spread it widely in order to bind to them their powerful subjects. Because of Buckingham's dominance, this was not done in the later 1620s. Significantly, one of the Commons' charges when they impeached Buckingham in 1626 was that he had not allowed the King to do that. As they said, Buckingham had not allowed the King "to be master of his own liberality". The result was that in the later 1620s, as had happened in roughly similar circumstances in the 1450s during the reign of Henry VI, natural allies of the King, like Thomas Wentworth, looked to parliament rather than the Court as a forum to represent their own and their localities' interests.

This was serious enough, but far more damaging were the inflammatory ways in which Charles responded to parliamentary criticisms of the Court's policies. Unlike James, who back-pedalled in the face of criticism to good political effect, Charles refused to budge. His reactions to criticism were rigidly authoritarian, inflammatory, and (in at least one case) illegal. Given the rumbling fears of many MPs about the uncertain future of parliaments, it was the height of political folly to allow his secretary of state, Dudley Carleton, to make a speech in the House of Commons in 1626, which inflamed those fears by pointing to what had happened to troublesome representative assemblies that had once existed in countries elsewhere in Europe, where

> monarchs began to show their own strengths, and seeing the turbulent spirits of their parliaments, at length little by little began to stand upon their prerogatives . . . and at last withdrew their parliaments throughout Christendom, except here only with us.[27]

Given such an explicit threat to do away with English parliaments, as monarchs were doing elsewhere, it is not surprising that many feared that Charles had turned to "new counsels",[28] who were urging him to follow the example of continental monarchs.

But the most extreme lengths to which Charles was prepared to go to stifle opposition that I know of is what happened in the aftermath of the proceedings of the famous case of the Five Knights, who were imprisoned for refusing to pay a forced loan. It is a famous case because during it Charles claimed that he had the right to imprison people without giving any other cause than unspecified reasons of state. What is significant is that *that* is not what the King's Bench judges in that case decided. What they decided is that *in this one particular case* the five men should remain in prison. What they did not decide was that kings had a *general* right to imprison people without bringing them to trial. What happened next reveals Charles' utter contempt for the law, because he forced Sir Robert Heath, his attorney-general, to put pressure on one of the justices to alter (ie to falsify) the legal record, in effect changing the ruling in the case as though there had been a final judgment on a point of general principle.[29] Given all this, it is hardly surprising that, when this leaked out, the outcome was the Petition of Right, which was meant to be a legal restraint on the absolutist pretensions of the Crown. Whether Charles had such absolutist pretensions is not clear. What is clear is that his actions had *seemed* to suggest that he had been listening to "new counsels" who were urging him to adopt authoritarian measures. It is not difficult to see Charles himself as the main reason why opposition to the Crown had been brought to such a pitch by 1628–9 and why relations between Crown and parliaments had plummeted so drastically and dramatically in the short period since his accession in 1625.

Fortunately for Charles, however, this was not the point of no return that many have thought that it was. The Civil War sides were not formed in 1628. For many reasons (including a conservative reaction against some of the radical tactics used by some MPs in 1628–9, Buckingham's assassination in 1628, the end of the wars with France and Spain in 1630, and an economic upturn after 1631) the 1630s saw a lessening of political tensions. In short, everything moved Charles' way and the King was presented with a golden opportunity to take advantage of the situation by adopting tactics that Oliver Cromwell was later to call "healing and settling", at which, it has been seen, James I was a past master. But these were tactics which Charles failed to adopt. As a result, despite the recent efforts of Professor Kevin Sharpe to follow the Earl of Clarendon in portraying the 1630s as halcyon days, it is likely that the Personal Rule without parliament between 1629 and 1640 was marked by growing and fairly general dissatisfaction in the country, to which Charles contributed in two important additional ways.[30]

The first was the way in which he transformed the Court, so that, unlike the Jacobean Court, it was a much more civilized and orderly place, but one which was increasingly cut off from the country. As time went by, a narrowing range of interests came to be represented there. Partly, this was the result of Charles' introverted character. Partly, it was a result of his obsession with order and decorum. James' Court may have been chaotic at times, but people could get to the King to put their points of view. Just how suddenly things changed at Charles' Court is shown by a letter from John Chamberlain to Dudley Carleton only two weeks after Charles' accession: "the King shows himself very gracious and affable", Chamberlain wrote, "but the court is kept more straight and private than in former times".[31] "Private" is the key word here. Increasingly, the Court no longer played the vital public role of communication with the country, with the result that there was immense room for misapprehension about what the King was doing.

Moreover, what made this disastrous for Charles is that it coincided with what is no doubt his biggest mistake of all: his decision to break with James' support for a broad, comprehensive national Church and to commit himself to one faction within it, that led by William Laud, hence one of the many labels it has been given, Laudianism.[32]

The central aim of William Laud as he clambered up the ecclesiastical career ladder to become Archbishop of Canterbury in 1633 was essentially to bring order and unity in the Church. This is what probably attracted Charles to Laudianism, which, he believed, promised to bring to the Church the order and decorum he sought to bring to the Court. What is striking about what Laud attempted to do in the Church is his attempt to bring about sacramental and ceremonial uniformity, as much as uniformity of theology: bowing at the name of Jesus, the upgrading of the ceremonial roles of ministers, the emphasis on vestments, the downgrading of sermons and preaching, the raising and railing off of altar rails and so forth. There is a case for Laud's attempt to bring order into churches, to restore the fabric of churches, to ensure that the clergy received better financial support, and so on. But this is a case that not everyone appreciated at the time. It is difficult to exaggerate the ferocity with which Laud came to be hated by some people in Caroline England, and also in Scotland. In his northern kingdom in the late 1630s, Charles set about a headlong rush to impose the English Prayer Book on the Scots, that pushed Scotland into a great religious and national rebellion – the Scottish Revolution, led by the Covenanters – and war against England, another contrast between James' skilful approach in Scotland and Charles' utter ineptness.[33] South of the Border, things were only a little better: not everyone felt as strongly about Laud as did Lord Brook, who called Laud *excrementa mundi* – the turd of the world – and as did others who entered secret, treasonable negotiations with the Scottish Covenanters.[34] But hatred of Laudianism in England was widespread. Why?

The basic reason is that Laudianism came to be seen as something that it was not. It came to be identified with Popery, with a design to undo the Reformation. The real significance of Charles' adoption of Laudianism is not only that it broke the Jacobean unity of the Church, but that it also aroused fears of absolutism. These had been inflamed by the King's actions in the 1620s, and became linked with Popery because of his promotion of Laudianism. That Popery and absolutism went together became one of the most powerful political beliefs of the 17th century and Charles was instrumental in bringing down the full force of it against himself.

As a result, in the later 1630s, very slowly, the idea took root that the King was the victim of a popish plot: that unless he was mad, then the only rational explanation why Charles was acting in, as they saw it, such a radical and disruptive way was that he was in the grip of a gang of Jesuits and Catholics, who had brainwashed him to work in the interests of Antichrist and of Rome.[35] In May 1641, parliament decreed that every adult male in the country should take the Protestation Oath, into which its drafter, John Pym, had skilfully interwoven all the elements of the alleged popish plot. "The designs of the priests and Jesuits, and other adherents of the see of Rome", proclaimed the preamble to the Oath,

> have of late been more boldly and frequently put into practice than formerly, to the undermining and danger of the ruin of the true Reformed Religion. . . There hath been and . . . still are . . . endeavours to subvert the fundamental laws of England and Ireland, and to introduce the exercise of an arbitrary and tyrannical government by most pernicious and wicked counsels, practices, plots and conspiracies, and that the long intermission and unhappier breach of parliaments hath occasioned many illegal taxations . . . and that divers innovations and superstitions hath been brought into the Church, multitudes driven out of his Majesty's dominions, jealousies raised and fomented between the King and people, a popish army levied in Ireland, and two armies brought into the bowels of this kingdom, to the hazard of his Majesty's royal person . . . and . . . endeavours have been, are used, to bring the English army into misunderstanding of this Parliament, thereby to incline the army by force to bring to pass those wicked counsels.[36]

It is on the face of it a fantastic notion, but one that gained credibility in the context of what has been seen had emerged in the 1630s: an isolationist court, headed by a king who promoted practices in the Church that appeared to be as near to Catholicism as made no difference.

A striking illustration of how Charles' actions gave substance to the growing belief in a popish plot is the way that in the 1630s he surrounded himself with crypto-Catholic advisers, allowed Catholic masses to be said in London, and welcomed papal agents like Gregorio Panzani and George Con at Court. Moreover, in the 1630s his Catholic wife, Henrietta Maria, apparently increased her hold on him.

Charles' relations with his wife are a marvellous illustration of the close way in which the private and public lives of monarchs in this period were interwoven. Charles and Henrietta Maria married in 1624 when she was only 15, and, as far as one can judge, the two at best felt little affection for each other and at worst disliked each other fairly strongly. For the first few years of their marriage there were stories of violent quarrels between the two, in and out of bed. (In 1626, Charles vividly described in a letter a marital slanging match he conducted with his young wife in bed, which was followed by Henrietta Maria smashing her hand against a window and threatening to go home to France.) Then, in 1628, coinciding with Buckingham's assassination, this torrid relationship was transformed into one of deep love. What Charles and Henrietta Maria did in bed from that point onwards is fairly obvious from the series of royal pregnancies, resulting in May 1629 in a miscarriage, and the births of Charles (the future Charles II) in May 1630, Mary in 1631, James (the future James II) in 1633, Elizabeth in 1635, Ann in 1637, a stillborn girl in 1638, and Henry in 1640.[37] But that story of *private* bliss had disastrous *public* consequences, because Catholic Henrietta Maria's closeness to Charles was seen as fitting into and confirming the idea of a popish plot that, as a result, began to seem less and less fantastic.

Against that kind of background, the otherwise seemingly wild allegations that were made by John Pym and others in 1640 and 1641 in the Protestation Oath and other documents and speeches about Charles I and a popish plot become explicable, as do the increasingly radical efforts that were made to tie the King's hands by constitutional limitations when the Long Parliament first met in and after November 1640.

But what makes Charles' ineptness even starker than ever is not just that his action pushed his opponents into increasingly extreme positions in the early 1640s, as they had done in the later 1620s, but, as had also happened before, what is striking is the way that the radical extremism of his opponents in turn produced a backlash in the King's favour. Yet, as before, Charles failed to capitalize on it as fully as he might have done.

One of the strongest findings of recent research on the history of the 1640s is the way that, in that decade, support for Charles increased, while support for his opponents in parliament and in the army decreased. Paradoxically, growing conservatism was a dominant trend during the English Revolution of the 1640s.[38] It gave Charles enough support to fight a Civil War by 1642. It gave him massive political support even in the face of military defeat at the end of the Civil War in 1646. It ensured that even as late as December 1648, only a few weeks before his execution, a majority in the House of Commons voted to conclude a settlement with the King on very generous terms. Yet throughout the 1640s, Charles threw away every chance of a settlement and, as in the 1620s and 1630s, he maintained an uncompromising, inflexible stance, alienating his supporters and giving little help to his friends.

All that – the 1640s – is a complex story, of course, but what I am suggesting in broad terms is that Charles' role in that decade fits in well with his record since he became King in 1625. What I am suggesting is that, although there are many reasons for the outbreak of Civil War in England in 1642 and for the collapse of monarchy in 1649.[39] one of the most important explanations is the character of Charles I, a man who deserves much of the criticism that has often been unfairly heaped on his much maligned father.

Footnotes to this Chapter may be found on pages 358–61.

9: John Miller

From the Restoration to the Hanoverians 1660–1714

AT THE HEART of any hereditary, personal monarchy lies a potential tension, between legitimacy and competence. Following clearly understood rules for the transmission of the title to the Crown has the advantage of reducing (but not eliminating) the danger of a disputed succession, but the disadvantage that sooner or later the Crown is likely to pass to a child, an incompetent, or even a madman. The aura of divine approval conferred by royal blood and the anointing in the coronation ceremony, and expressed in the practice of the royal touch,[1] was never, on its own, sufficient to ensure the obedience of subjects. Even the most apparently absolute rulers had to maintain – even earn – the loyalty (or at least acquiescence) of those who mattered politically. In Russia, tsars were deposed and murdered by their own kin or the palace guard. In France, Louis XIV, learning from the experience of the Fronde, was careful not to antagonize the most powerful groups in society, above all the nobilities of sword and robe. And, of course, in England, Charles I was defeated in battle, tried, and executed in the name of his people.

The tension between legitimacy and competence can be illustrated by discussions of the nature of monarchy in later Stuart England. On one hand, the traditional concept of the divine right of kings not merely survived the civil wars but reemerged stronger than ever.[2] Far from the concept's being invalidated by the execution of Charles I, many saw the King's death as sacrilege and blasphemy. Indeed, Charles' projection of himself as a royal martyr, continued after his death by the publication of his alleged prison writings, *Eikon Basilike,* (embellished with appropriate iconography), contributed far more to the prestige of the monarchy than anything he had done in his lifetime. Besides, the upheavals of the 1640s and 1650s, the overturning of the traditional political, ecclesiastical, and (apparently) social order, made it clear to the ruling élite how crucial the monarchy was to the reestablishment and preservation of that order. There were thus political as well as emotional reasons for the resurgence of divine right theory, and it was stridently reaffirmed in the face of the perceived fear of civil war in the Exclusion Crisis.[3]

Two traditional features of divine right theory were strongly reinforced by the experience of the civil wars and Exclusion Crisis. First, non-resistance: the Tudor Church and state had stressed that resistance to lawful authority – "the most detestable vice of rebellion"[4] – constituted resistance to God and the events of the 1640s and 1650s confirmed the direst warnings of the chaos that such resistance could bring. Second, the hereditary transmission of the Crown: the Tudors had laid little stress on this – not surprisingly, given the weakness of Henry VII's title and the complications created by Henry VIII's matrimonial adventures. The Stuarts, however, laid great stress on the hereditary principle. James I's title depended on descent (in defiance of acts of parliament)[5] and Tories responded to demands to exclude the future James II from the throne by claiming that this was beyond parliament's power, as only God could determine the succession.

If the Interregnum and Exclusion Crisis gave new force to some traditional features of divine right discourse, they also added new elements. Restoration writers – and indeed legislation – insisted that parliament could neither make war against the king nor legislate without him.[6] Such an insistence would not have seemed necessary before the civil wars, because the issues had not arisen. To see divine right theory as purely negative or reactive would, however, be misleading. As we shall see, some writers (especially among the Anglican clergy) developed something much closer to a theory of royal absolutism. Moreover, divine right was by no means purely political or rational in inspiration. There was a strong emotional element too, seen in the cult of the royal martyr and above all in a final, doomed efflorescence in the reign of Anne.

By 1702, Tories knew that when the Queen died they would face the choice between a Catholic Stuart and a Hanoverian, whose hereditary claim was weak, but who was at least a Protestant. Most, when forced to choose, opted for Protestantism rather than descent in 1714 as in 1688–9, but in so doing they were ruled by their heads, not by their hearts. The hereditary principle was doomed as a major prop of Tory ideology: already damaged in 1688–9, it would logically disappear altogether when Anne died. Nevertheless, Tories, and above all Tory churchmen, wallowed once more in Cavalier nostalgia and devoured Clarendon's *History of the Rebellion,* now published for the first time. "Round the prosaic head of Queen Anne at her teatable this legitimist school picked out the halo of the Lord's anointed."[7] Such views may seem backward-looking and illogical, but they struck a strong chord among the largest and freest electorate England was to see before 1832. Tory clerics and politicians articulated a widespread resentment of the Glorious Revolution and all its works and a longing to get back to the days of Charles II, which now, in retrospect, seemed so golden; and the Tories fared far better than the Whigs in the general elections of Anne's reign.[8] Even after 1714, divine right emotion lived on, as seen in constant references in debate to the civil wars and in Jacobitism. It found expression not only in the drunken maunderings of disgruntled squires and parsons passed over for preferment, but also, among angry artisans and labourers, in the image of the Pretender as the embodiment of ultimate justice.[9]

Thus far, we have concentrated on divine right theory as a support for monarchy, but the idea that the king derived his power from God also implied that he would use that power according to God's moral laws. Most of those who supported Charles I in the civil wars, or James, Duke of York, in the Exclusion Crisis believed that the king was morally and legally obliged to respect his subjects' personal liberty and property rights, to rule with the advice and consent of his parliament and to follow policies broadly acceptable to his people. In other words, divine right theory was – or ought to have been – congruent with a basic axiom of 17th-century English constitutional thought – that the powers of the Crown and the rights of subjects were complementary and mutually supporting. This axiom was often expressed through the concept of the "ancient constitution": the origins of the monarchy, laws, and parliament were all buried in the mists of antiquity and the relationship between them, encapsulating the cumulative wisdom of innumerable generations, had evolved in a complex and mutually advantageous balance.

Now such ideals of harmony and mutual advantage might seem naive, but they had some basis in reality. By the reign of Henry VIII it was clearly understood that the king could not impose taxes or make laws without the consent of parliament. This was not necessarily a weakness, however: experience showed, throughout Western Europe, that it was easier for kings to get taxes paid and laws obeyed if they had secured the consent of a representative assembly. That consent was often forthcoming: indeed, the Tudor period saw an increase in the powers of monarch and parliament. The process of legislation placed great emphasis on consultation, especially as both Houses preferred to avoid votes and aimed for consensus. The enforcement of law in the localities depended heavily on the voluntary (and unpaid) cooperation of the king's subjects – county gentry and urban businessmen as magistrates, yeomen farmers as churchwardens and overseers of the poor, more or less any adult male as trial juror or village constable. If the monarch needed the subject's cooperation, the subject seemed willing to cooperate.

That willingness to cooperate was not unconditional, however. Indeed, the very practice of cooperation and consultation tended to develop assumptions about the ground-rules upon which that cooperation rested. Men could be expected to assist in the king's government only so long as the king did not seriously threaten their interests and principles, their personal liberty, property, and religion. If once the king seemed to be doing so, then men would have to face up to the problems that the cosy obscurantism of the "ancient constitution" enabled them to evade: what remedy did the subject have? Logically, there were two alternatives: resistance or submission, but the picture was not quite as simple as that, given the distinction between ordinances of man and of God. The 1547 Homily on Obedience, while stressing the subject's duty to obey the king's "laws, statutes, proclamations, and injunctions", added that "we may not obey kings . . . if they would command us to do anything contrary to God's commandments." In such cases, one must refuse to obey and suffer the consequences, "referring the judgment of our cause only to God".[10] Such, alas, was a counsel of perfection. The religious wars of the 16th century not only led to a blurring of the boundaries of the spiritual and the secular, but the increasing preeminence given to the former undermined this passive and fatalistic response to "tyranny". Calvinist and Jesuit writers developed theories of tyrannicide (although the latter soon abandoned the idea). The permissibility of resistance was now an issue for discussion and even monarchist writers were prepared to consider it, admittedly within strict limits. John Locke enjoyed a certain amount of malicious fun at the expense of Robert Barclay: how, he asked, could one "resist force without striking again" or "strike with reverence"?[11]

Not all were as remorselessly logical as Locke, however. Generations of indoctrination had encouraged the English political élite to see resistance as a sin. The English habit of seeking political legitimacy in the past, in precedent, left men ill-equipped to cope with unprecedented situations. Moreover, history and the events of 1641 showed members of the élite that resistance involved risks: what if an aristocratic challenge to royal authority was followed by a popular challenge to the authority of the aristocracy? Until 1640, the most immediate challenge to the liberty, property, and religion of the ruling élite had come from the king and the bishops: in 1640–1 it became only too clear that the élite's interests could also be threatened from below – by London artisans and apprentices, by peasant farmers determined to overthrow enclosures, by iconoclasts and sectaries. Only too aware of the weakness of the machinery of order, members of the élite trembled at the prospect that the "many-headed monster", the people, would become aware of its own strength.[12] Such fears helped to drive many erstwhile critics of Charles I to fight for him in the civil wars. They help to explain what may seem, to the modern mind, the extraordinary reluctance of parliament to assert a right of resistance and its eagerness to cling to the fiction that it was not resisting the king because the king, "deranged" by evil counsellors, did not know his own mind. They help to explain, too, why even when claiming a right of resistance by virtue of representing the people, parliamentary writers tried hard to rebut any suggestion that this implied that parliament was therefore accountable to the people.[13]

What happened subsequently, in the 1640s and 1650s, served to confirm the worst fears of anxious gentlemen and clerics and to convince even many parliamentarians that matters had got out of hand. The 1650s saw a growing cooperation between Royalists and moderate Parliamentarians (or Presbyterians) and the latter contributed significantly to the Restoration. More significantly in the long term, the civil wars and their aftermath served as an awful warning to members of the élite. If they still worried about the prospect of royal tyranny, they were also fearful of revolution from below. Many, indeed, were torn between the two fears, and apparent inconsistencies in behaviour can simply reflect a shifting perception of where the greater threat lay. In the 1660s, with a series of real or alleged plots and risings, moderate men worried most about the threat from below. In the 1670s, anxieties grew about Charles II's conduct and intentions, but during and after the Exclusion Crisis, such anxieties were overlaid, or outweighed, by renewed fears of civil war. Such conflicting anxieties help to explain the power and the defensiveness of Restoration divine right discourse.

A similar tension can be found even in those who came closest to expressing a truly absolutist ideology – the High Anglican clergy of the 1670s and 1680s. Even more than their Laudian forebears under Charles I, Restoration churchmen were convinced that the Church was tied to the Crown by principle and interest and looked to the monarch to crush nonconformity and vice. The problem was that, for much of his reign, Charles II seemed singularly disinclined to fulfil this role, while James II became openly hostile to the Church. Forced to choose between obeying the king and obeying God, these most outspoken proponents of divine right decided that their first loyalty was to the Church and in 1688, in refusing to read the Declaration of Indulgence in their churches, the clergy were responsible for the most comprehensive example of disobedience of the whole period.[14]

These various tensions – between respect for legitimacy and expectations of competence, between the threat from below and the threat from above, between loyalty to the Crown and loyalty to the Church – ensured that Charles II would have to earn his subjects' obedience and support, but also that there was a great fund of loyalty and goodwill upon which he would be able to draw. If the men who made the Restoration were careful not to give the king too much power, they were also careful not to give him too little. Indeed, I shall argue that they tried to reestablish the harmony, the balance between the powers of the king and the rights of the subject, which should have existed before the civil war. On top of this, there was a widespread acceptance that monarchy was not only traditional, not only instituted by God, but also functional. During the 1640s, parliament and its committees had taken over the executive functions of government. Some MPs had revelled in this: many clearly had not, as attested by the low attendance at committees. Many country gentlemen did not relish spending hours each day drudging over accounts, especially as many were not very numerate – and none was paid. One of the least trumpeted features of the Restoration settlement was that parliament quietly handed back to the king responsibility for the executive. The last important task performed by a Commons committee was paying off the New Model Army. Thereafter, MPs were able to revert to their traditional and more congenial role of advising, criticizing, and complaining.[15] The very fact that they were prepared to do so showed that they were prepared to trust the king to govern. His ability to do so, and his success in doing so, would depend on how far he could match up to their expectations and thus maintain their goodwill.

> On 29 May 1660, Charles II entered London with a triumph of above two hundred thousand horse and foot, brandishing their swords and shouting with inexpressible joy; the ways strewed with flowers, the bells ringing, the streets hung with tapestry, fountains running with wine; the mayor, aldermen and all the companies in their liveries, chains of gold, banners; lords and nobles, cloth of silver, gold and velvet everyone clad in; the windows and balconies all set with ladies; trumpets, music and myriads of people flocking the streets and ways as far as Rochester, so as they were seven hours in passing the City, even from two in the

afternoon till nine at night. I stood in the Strand and beheld it and blessed God. And all this without one drop of blood.[16]

John Evelyn's famous description of the King's return marked the climax of six months of popular pressure for the restoration of the monarchy, which had demoralized the New Model Army and persuaded General Monck that the recall of the King without conditions was feasible and necessary. The day of Charles' return, indeed, was marked by unanimity of a sort that had not been seen for at least 20 years and was rarely to be seen again. It was easier to agree that the monarchy should be restored than on the form in which it should be restored. Charles' Declaration of Breda, referring some of the most contentious issues to parliament, helped to persuade the Houses to delay decisions on the nature of the settlement until after his return, but such decisions could not be postponed indefinitely.

The constitutional settlement was enacted by the Cavalier Parliament, elected in the spring of 1661. It laid down that all legislation which had not received the royal assent was null and void, thus sweeping away the ordinances of the Long Parliament and its successors, but leaving in place the reforming legislation of 1641. Charles II would therefore be unable to raise money except in ways approved by parliament, nor (despite some debate) were the Houses willing to revive any of the prerogative courts. However, the legislation of 1641 had been seen then, by a majority in the Commons and a minority in the Lords, as offering insufficient safeguards against future misgovernment. Parliament therefore demanded, from 1641 to 1648, that the king share with Parliament two of his key prerogatives: choice of ministers and control of the armed forces. At the Restoration, no stipulation was made about the former, so that the King was able (as we have seen) quietly to resume his control of the executive. As for control of the armed forces, this was unequivocally vested in the King by the Militia Act of 1661.

It may seem odd that the Cavalier Parliament should do this, especially after experiencing Charles I's misrule. Charles II had no money, no army, and (one might add) no experience: whatever bargaining power he possessed depended on his popularity and the goodwill of his subjects. But there was calculation as well as goodwill behind these provisions, as the Militia Act explained with bald simplicity. It stated that the supreme command of the armed forces had always been vested in the Crown and that parliament had no claim to it, "nor lawfully may raise or levy any war against His Majesty; and yet the contrary thereof hath of late years been practised, almost to the ruin and destruction of this kingdom".[17] The fear of revolution from below, which was stated so starkly here, was apparent in other measures too. It was made illegal to call the King a papist or to petition "tumultuously": often in the 1640s, large crowds had accompanied petitions to Westminster, in order to intimidate the Houses. Most striking of all were acts empowering the King to censor the press – hitherto censorship had depended on the prerogative alone – and to appoint commissioners to purge corporate towns of those regarded as "disaffected'.

Erstwhile radicals were aghast at what seemed to them the Cavalier Parliament's servile determination to build up the power of the Crown to a point where Charles II could prove as "tyrannous" as his father. Such a view was understandable, but somewhat misconceived. For a start, on some key issues, King and Commons did not see eye to eye. Charles had to intervene repeatedly and decisively to prevent the Commons from unravelling the Act of Indemnity passed by the previous parliament, the Convention of 1660. If he succeeded in this case, on the issue of the Church settlement he was defeated: the Act of Uniformity ensured that the national Church would be rigorously Anglican, with no attempt to comprehend moderate Puritans within it.[18] On other matters, too, the Cavalier Parliament made it clear that it was not willing to trust the King too far. While vesting in him full control over the armed forces, it politely ignored pleas that he needed a substantial army: MPs preferred that he should rely on the militia, an essentially civilian force, officered by country gentlemen like themselves. The Corporation Act emerged in the form the Commons wanted: amendments proposed in the Lords, which would have allowed the King to intervene far more extensively in the towns' internal affairs, were firmly rejected.[19] The Licensing Act, which authorized press censorship, was only temporary: it was initially to be in force for two years only; it was twice renewed until the end of the next session of parliament; when in 1665 it was again renewed, this time until the end of the first session of the next parliament, few can have seen that this meant that it would remain in force until May 1679 (when it lapsed).[20]

The impression that the Cavalier Parliament wished the King to be strong enough to counter the perceived threat of revolution from below, but not strong enough to threaten the interests of the Cavalier gentry and Anglican clergy, is reinforced by the financial settlement. The legislation of 1641 left the Crown with insufficient revenue to rule the country, unless parliament voted more. All that remained to Charles I were the crown lands and income from wardship, but the former were confiscated after Charles I's execution and the latter was abolished by an Act of 1645.[21] Charles II thus had effectively no revenue when he returned. It would have been easy for the Commons to give him a revenue that was manifestly insufficient to support the government or a revenue that was adequate, but granted only for a limited period. Either way, Charles would have been forced to call parliament frequently and the Commons could have exploited his shortage of money to demand concessions – redress of grievances, changes of ministers or policies – in return for supply.

That this had been the Commons strategy in 1641 had been shown by their voting Charles I customs duties (tonnage and poundage) for short periods. Parliament's conduct at the Restoration could not have been more different. Even before Charles returned, the Commons debated how best to compensate him for the loss of revenue from wardship. In August 1660, the Commons considered an estimate of the necessary expenditure of the Crown and agreed in principle to provide him with revenues sufficient to meet that expenditure. This was the first time that the Commons had systematically considered how much the King needed, but even more striking was the resolution that these revenues should be voted for life or in perpetuity, not just for a fixed period – especially as the House of Commons in question, that of the Convention, was fairly evenly balanced between men of Royalist and of Parliamentarian backgrounds. By the end of 1660, Charles was assured of the customs and the excise.[22]

This grant of revenue seemed too good to be true and, in the short run, it was. If the calculation of necessary expenditure, at £1,200,000, was not unrealistic, calculations of likely income were decidedly optimistic, not least because one important item had been counted twice (and the King's treasury officials had not noticed). This over-optimism was nothing unusual. Many MPs were not very good with figures – they tended to use too many "noughts", or too few – but they were also eager to reduce the fiscal burden, after almost two decades of unprecedentedly high taxes, and wished to believe that the shortfalls reported to parliament were due to administrative inefficiency rather than inadequate grants: how much easier it was – and how much more acceptable to neighbours and constituents – to call for greater efficiency of collection rather than vote larger sums of money. Yet when all allowances are made, the Cavalier Parliament made only one addition to the permanent revenues voted by the Convention: the bitterly unpopular hearth tax, abandoned by William III as a goodwill gesture in 1689. Instead, the Commons again and again voted either one-off taxes on land, or poll taxes, or additional customs or excise duties for a period of years. These could be generous – the £2,500,000 voted in 1664 to enable the King to prepare for war against the Dutch dwarfed anything granted to the early Stuarts. But the fact remained that by voting money in this way the Commons could also choose not to be generous. They had given the King a series of revenues which were more or less sufficient – in the 1660s less rather than more – to support the day-to-day government and maintain his dignity as King. They had not given him enough to tempt him to rule without parliament: if he was not reduced to an utter supplicant, the fact that he was inclined to be short of money created the likelihood that he would be prepared to make concessions as "the price of money".[23] This was rarely stated crudely: politeness dictated that the King's concessions were seen as springing from his grace and goodness, the Commons' grants from their love and loyalty. Nevertheless, the fact that speakers of the Commons ostentatiously stressed that they were not linking supply with redress more than hinted that there was, in fact, a connection between the two. Even though the Commons on occasion loudly repudiated the idea of "compelling the King", the fact remained that, despite having granted Charles II revenues for life, they still possessed real financial power, and they knew it.[24]

How great that power was depended on the size of the King's revenue and his ability to live within his means. The Commons granted Charles, not a fixed sum, but a series of revenues to exploit as best he could. At first, this worked to his disadvantage: as we have seen, estimates of yield were over-sanguine and the King's income was badly hit by plague (1665), the Great Fire (1666), and the Second Dutch War (1672). He thus built up a burden of debt, which was exacerbated by his own undoubted extravagance. By the 1670s, however, trade was booming and collection was becoming progressively more efficient. By the last year of the reign, the revenue had climbed to about £1,400,000 – well above the estimate of 1660 – and that without recourse to the sort of fiscal measures that had made Charles I so unpopular. (Prices remained roughly stable during the reign.) Had Charles been prepared to curb his spending – and had he not embroiled himself in another war against the Dutch – he would have achieved solvency sooner than he did. As it was, by the 1670s, with the help of borrowing, Charles could in theory have got by without parliamentary grants – so long as he avoided war. But at that time, life without parliament did not seem a practical proposition: it would have necessitated severe retrenchment; it would have been politically extremely unpopular; and Charles was under great pressure from 1674 to 1678 to join the great coalition against France (which indeed he prepared to do in 1678). In 1679, with peace made and much of his army disbanded, Charles at last committed himself to retrenchment and, with his revenue continuing to grow, he was able to live out his last four years without calling parliament.[25]

If one seeks to assess the balance of financial power between Charles II and his parliament, then the picture is a complex one. Charles' revenue, for much of the reign, was insufficient for his needs, enlarged as they were by extravagance and debt. He did not have the option that his father had had of raising money without parliament: the notorious French subsidies brought in relatively little. On the other hand, borrowing could give him some leeway and when his needs were greatest – between 1660 and 1671 – the Commons tended to be more generous than they became later. Only in wartime could he be forced to make concessions that he really did not want to make – for example, withdrawing the Declaration of Indulgence in 1673. That said, his ability to extract supply from his faithful Commons depended heavily on his willingness to follow policies that they found acceptable.

Charles's prospects of working harmoniously with his parliaments might be threatened in one of two ways: either he might become embroiled in disputes among his subjects or his conduct might give rise to suspicions that he wished to overturn the constitutional balance reestablished at the Restoration to make himself "absolute".

The bitterness created by civil war long outlasted the Restoration. Royalist and Presbyterian had cooperated against the Protectorate and the army, but as soon as the King returned jealousies reappeared, "the Court and royal party grudging at every favour to the Presbyterian, and they on the other side thinking they have not enough.[26] Debates in the Convention on the bill of indemnity gave ample opportunity for Royalist spite; the Royalists denounced the Act as giving indemnity to the King's enemies and consigning his friends to oblivion – hence the attempt to reopen the issue in the Cavalier Parliament.

At the local level, where old Cavaliers regained office as JPs and militia officers, they used their power to harass their former enemies: the purges of boroughs under the Corporation Act (1661) continued a trend that had already begun in rural areas. The habits of thinking of the 1640s and 1650s could not be abandoned overnight: in 1664, an MP referred to "the old royal party" in the Commons; in 1670, when the Duke of Ormonde attended a race meeting in Staffordshire, there were 300 gentlemen present and "not a Roundhead among them".[27]

For much of Charles II's reign, political divisions were expressed largely in religious terms: the "Church" (or "loyal") party against the "fanatics" (or "disaffected"). This doubtless owed much to the fact that the Act of Indemnity forbade raking up the past (although this did not stop people doing it). Conformity to the restored Church of England created a new, post-Restoration criterion of loyalty – there was a comfortingly large overlap between Protestant dissenters and former opponents of Charles I. One reason why the terms of conformity were made so stringent was doubtless to lump in as many Presbyterians as possible with the other, sectarian denominations. Another, however, was that religious nonconformity was seen as *prima facie* evidence of political disaffection: scruples of "pretended conscience" and a stiff-necked refusal to conform in "things indifferent" seriously called into question a person's loyalty to the new regime. While there was strong and growing support for the restored Church of England, a whole generation of clergy and gentry had grown up in a non-Anglican church and it is difficult to see the Commons' animus against dissent in the 1660s as wholly religious in origin.[28]

Charles II, therefore, had a choice: either he could rule as a partisan king, relying on and supporting his old friends, the Cavaliers and Church party against the old Parliamentarians and dissenters; or he could try to rule as king of all his people, to forgive and forget and to try to heal the wounds opened by the civil wars. He chose the latter, not because it was the more statesmanlike option, but because he had an exaggerated impression of the power of political radicals and religious nonconformists: at times, indeed, he was persuaded that the latter made up more than half the population. Crude political calculation,then, impelled him to insist on maintaining the indemnity and to try repeatedly first to water down the Church settlement and then to allow a measure of toleration to dissenters.[29] In the terms in which he himself thought, however, this policy was misguided. Dissenters made up a small minority of the population, as the Compton Census of 1676 made clear.[30] Faced with the strongly partisan House of Commons elected in 1661, it might have been wiser for Charles to pursue the sort of partisan policies that MPs wanted. Charles, however, proved inept at reading the mood of the House. In 1668, his suggestion that the laws against dissent might be relaxed provoked the Commons to produce a new bill against nonconformist meetings, or conventicles. "The King if he pleases may take a right measure of our temper by this," remarked one MP, "and leave off crediting . . . [those] who persuade him that the generality of the kingdom and of our House too is inclined to a toleration."[31] The debates on dissent in 1668, indeed, produced an odd inversion of arguments, with Presbyterians and dissenting sympathizers implying that the matter should be resolved by the King, using his prerogative, while churchmen argued that he was strictly bound by acts of parliament.[32]

However irritated MPs may have been by the King's softness on dissent (not to mention the mismanagement of the Second Dutch War and the sordid public image of his court), their instincts of loyalty remained immensely strong. When, in 1670, Charles suddenly gave them the policies they wanted they responded with a glee that more than hinted at the release of pent-up frustration:

> The Speaker then went to the Parliament House and the members were so in love with His Majesty's gracious speech that in acknowledgment thereof they voted they would wait upon the Speaker all on foot, which we did, two and two, hand in hand, through King's Street to Whitehall, all the whole House. . . The Speaker told him the sense that the House had of His Majesty's most gracious speech did ravish them and he was commanded to return him their thanks. . .   All persons there present could not forbear their acclamations of joy and many did express it in tears. The King's servants then invited the Speaker and us all into the cellar. Old and young, grave and mad went . . . and each man drunk the King's health so long that many will want their own tomorrow.[33]

Thus wrote Richard Legh MP, for whom this was a special day, to be recalled with nostalgia in less happy times. Andrew Marvell, who had assisted Milton as Latin Secretary to the Protectorate, saw it very differently. He dismissed the "going into the cellar" as "a pretty ridiculous thing" and concluded: "The King was never since his coming in, nay, all things considered, no king since the Conquest, so absolutely powerful at home as he is at present. Nor any parliament, or places, so certainly and constantly supplied with men of the same temper."[34]

There was much to support Marvell's view. The parliamentary sessions of 1670–1 were the most harmonious of the reign. Ruling as a partisan king, it seemed, produced results. Yet at this very time, Charles was embarking on new policies which seriously undermined the trust upon which this new-found harmony was based. In May 1670, Charles signed the secret Treaty of Dover, in which he and Louis XIV of France agreed to make war on the Dutch and (in a clause which remained secret) Charles undertook to declare his conversion to Catholicism. I have considered elsewhere Charles' reasons for wanting the treaty (which I see as mainly diplomatic and geopolitical).[35] What concerns us here is the political reaction in England. The decision to join with the greatest Catholic absolutist ruler in Europe against the Protestant Dutch seemed particularly sinister when viewed in conjunction with two other developments. First, early in 1672, Charles issued a Declaration of Indulgence, in which he claimed the power, by virtue of his prerogative, to suspend the enforcement of the laws against dissenting worship – and allowed Catholics to worship in their own homes. Second, in the course of the same year, it became clear that the King's brother and heir presumptive, James, Duke of York, had become a Catholic. For 17th-century English Protestants, it was axiomatic that "popery" was inseparable from "arbitrary government" or absolutism. Worried contemporaries, therefore, seeking a link between these developments, came to fear a great conspiracy, whereby Charles would help Louis XIV to destroy liberty and Protestantism in the Dutch Republic and then Louis would help Charles to impose popery and absolutism in England.

With hindsight, and access to the French diplomatic archives, it is apparent that no such conspiracy existed, but repeated evidence of Charles' duplicity had led his subjects to suspect the worst. In 1671, Charles persuaded parliament to vote money to enable him to guard against the threat from France; the next year, it became clear that the French King was not his enemy but his ally. At the start of 1672, all payments out of the Exchequer were stopped and the money diverted to the war, an exercise in bad faith which wrecked the credit apparatus built up since 1665. In 1673–4 Charles undid some of the damage: he withdrew the Declaration of Indulgence, at the behest of an angry Commons, and, reluctantly, made peace with the Dutch. But the damage to his credit – political and financial – could not be undone so easily. Sir Edward Dering and Gilbert Burnet looked back on the events of 1672 as a watershed, bringing to an end 12 years in which (in Dering's words) "we lived in peace, plenty, and happiness above all nations in the world."[36] As one royal official remarked sadly in February 1674: "nothing is to be trusted to good nature in the future."[37]

Having failed to act as a partisan king in the 1660s, Charles (by provoking fears of popery and absolutism) now faced the danger that Cavaliers and Roundheads, churchmen and dissenters would unite against him. The suspicions which had developed in 1672–3 finally burst into the open in the attempts to exclude York from the succession between 1679 and 1681, on the grounds that, as a Catholic, he would be bound to try to impose absolutism. The conduct and arguments of the Exclusionists, or Whigs, raised unpleasant echoes of 1640–42, but in the end the perceived danger of civil war – and Whig attacks on the Church – worked in the King's favour. Anxious churchmen, or Tories, saw the threat of revolution from below as far greater and far more immediate than the possible threat of royal absolutism. They looked to the King to defend them – and the Church – and eagerly encouraged Charles's counterattack against the Whigs and their allies, the dissenters. The years 1681–85 saw the most severe religious persecution of the reign; Whigs were harassed into quiescence or submission; and town corporations, above all that of London, were brought under much closer royal control. With his revenue now well above the £1,200,000 judged necessary by parliament in 1660, Charles lived out his last four years without calling parliament.

In 1685, the power of the Stuart monarchy was at its zenith. Charles II may not have used his prerogative as widely as his father had done, but experience (especially that of 1639–40) had shown that to do so could be counter-productive: one of the monarchy's greatest strengths was the support and cooperation of the people.[38] However, the civil wars had left a legacy of political and religious division, exacerbated by the Exclusion Crisis, which made it impossible for the King to win the active support of *all* his people. In the last years of his reign, Charles did what he had been unwilling to do in the first: he committed himself to pursuing policies acceptable to his natural supporters – his "old friends", the "loyal party", the "Church and King men", the Tories. It was a spectacularly successful strategy, but only because it was in tune with political reality. Charles needed the Tories as much as they needed him and he was careful to give them Tory policies. His successor, James II, did not, with disastrous results for himself and the monarchy.

James II made reality what had only been a threat in 1672–73. Instead of exploiting the divisions within the political nation, he succeeded, if not in uniting Whig and Tory, at least in turning both – and particularly the Tories – against him. Despite later Whig claims that the Tories had been servile supporters of absolutism in the 1680s, most believed as firmly as the Whigs that the King should rule according to law and in the best interests of his subjects; they differed to some extent in their interpretation of the law[39] and much more on what constituted the subjects' best interests. They actively supported James' claim to the throne because they thought that to do so was morally right and because they thought that the Whigs were using James' Catholicism as a pretext to attack Church and monarchy. They accepted James' assurances, reiterated at his accession, that he would defend the Church of England and calculated that his own self-interest would lead him to rely on his "old friends".

There was, however, a certain amount of self-delusion on both sides. James declared: "I know the principles of the Church of England are for monarchy and the members of it have shown themselves good and loyal subjects; *therefore,* I shall always take care to defend and support it."[40] The Tories did not appreciate the conditional element in that assurance. James would support the Church only so long as the churchmen showed themselves loyal, and it transpired that James' definition of loyalty differed from theirs. He understood the Tory principle of nonresistance as implying absolute obedience and became incensed when Tories (and especially Tory clergymen) refused to obey him on the grounds that they were obliged to obey God rather than man.[41] The Tories, for their part, assumed that practical commonsense, honour, and gratitude would lead James to keep his Catholicism a private matter and to rule as if he were an Anglican. Their assumptions proved wrong. James was determined to promote his religion.[42] When the Tories failed to cooperate, he turned to dissenters for support and proclaimed his commitment to a general religious toleration. As such a toleration could be effectively established only by parliament, he set out to secure a House of Commons consisting of dissenters and of Anglicans committed to toleration. As this was clearly against the wishes of the bulk of the nation, he sought to achieve his ends by the use of his royal prerogative in two controversial ways.

First, he greatly extended the King's traditional power to dispense with the penalties of laws in particular cases. Traditionally, this had been used to temper justice with mercy, on a very occasional basis. Now, having secured a ruling (from a heavily purged bench of judges) that he possessed the power to dispense with the penalties of law, as he judged necessary, James dispensed thousands of dissenters from the laws against conventicles and allowed dissenters and Catholics to hold public office, despite acts of parliament to the contrary. In 1687, he went further: his Declaration of Indulgence suspended all laws requiring attendance at church and prohibiting nonconformist or Catholic worship.

Second, he used the powers over boroughs acquired by Charles II in his last years to install dissenters and Catholics as members of corporations – and as electors. Over four-fifths of MPs represented boroughs, the majority of them small; James hoped to mould, persuade, or intimidate the electorates of enough small boroughs to ensure the election of a House of Commons pledged to repeal the laws which denied dissenters and Catholics freedom of worship (the penal laws) and excluded them from public office (the Test Acts).[43]

In using his prerogative in this way, James does not seem to have believed that he was doing anything wrong. He thought in terms of simple polar opposites – right or wrong, legal or illegal. As far as he was concerned, the penal laws and Test Acts were morally wrong. He feigned ignorance of the law's subtleties – "I am obliged to think what my judges do is according to law" – quietly passing over his habit of sacking judges who did not share his views.[44] As far as he was concerned, he was just employing powers used by his royal predecessors; in intervening in the internal affairs of boroughs, he was merely following the precedent set by his brother.

Such reasoning was defective in two respects. First, whatever James' pretences, the difference of degree between his conduct and that of his predecessors was so extreme as to constitute a difference in kind. It was one thing to dispense one individual from the penalties of a law; it was quite another to dispense the whole country, as the Declaration of Indulgence did. As one of the judges remarked in 1688: "If this be once allowed of, there will need no parliament; all the legislature will be in the King."[45] Similarly, Charles had kept within the letter of the law when intervening in boroughs. Corporations were "persuaded" to surrender their charters and receive new ones, under which the King could remove members of the corporation whom he regarded as "disaffected" and require the borough to choose a replacement. James assumed that he could install his own nominees.[46] Moreover, Charles' intention was to support one large section of the political nation against another; James wished to secure a parliament that would endorse a measure that was anathema to the great majority of Tories and Whigs, the repeal of the penal laws and Test Acts. Had he succeeded, the House of Commons would have ceased to be representative in any meaningful sense and parliament would have been subjugated to the royal will.

The second way in which James' reasoning was defective was that it failed utterly to take account of the perceptions and principles of his subjects. He might feel justified in his interpretation of the laws and in turning against the Tories. They reacted with horror to what they saw as "torturing the laws to make them speak contrary to the intention of the makers" and to James' increasingly vindictive treatment of the clergy, culminating in the deprivation of the fellows of Magdalen College, the order to read the Declaration of Indulgence in parish churches, and the trial of the Seven Bishops on a charge of seditious libel.[47] Tories shared with Whigs the traditional Protestant identification of Catholicism with absolutism. In 1679–85 they had been prepared to give James the benefit of the doubt, trusting him to rule as if he were a Protestant. By 1688, they were coming to accept that the Whigs' forebodings had been justified. The clergy refused *en masse* to read the Declaration in their churches and some of the bishops even began to make overtures to the dissenters.[48]

James' alienation of the Tories might not have mattered had he won wholehearted support from Whigs and dissenters. Some – more, indeed, than would later admit it – were won over by James' offers of toleration.[49] Those offers, however, were trumped by James' heir presumptive, Mary, and her husband, William of Orange, who made it known that they favoured toleration without the price that James demanded, the admission of Catholics into positions of power.[50] By the summer of 1688, therefore, James II was politically even more isolated than his father had been in the summer of 1640. Even the long-awaited birth of a son and heir turned out to be a mixed blessing, as it reinforced William's determination to invade England.

The Whigs eagerly supported William's invasion, which offered them the prospect of power, after years in the political wilderness. The Tories, for their part, showed no eagerness to oppose it. Not only were they still smarting from the indignities heaped upon them by James, but they calculated that James would be forced to make concessions that would undo all that he had done since 1685 and reestablish the Tories in power. It was a reasonable calculation, but it rested on the premise that James would stand his ground. When he fled on the night of 10 December, making no provision for ordered government in his absence, the Tories gain felt betrayed. As William became more closely identified with the Whigs, the Tories also felt that they had been duped into aiding and abetting a rebellion, from which only the Whigs would benefit. When James was stopped and returned to London, some Tories looked to him to save their cause, but he proved a broken reed and fled again. Most Tories were not sorry to see him go. He had treated them badly, but there seemed little prospect that the all-conquering William would treat them any better. Bitter and disillusioned, the Tories gave vent to their frustrations in a largely negative contribution to the Revolution settlement, which nevertheless was profoundly and permanently to change the English monarchy.[51]

The Revolution settlement and the post-Revolution monarchy were shaped by a complex of forces. The first was a sense of exasperation with the Stuarts: they had been given the benefit of the doubt at the Restoration and had abused parliament's trust. Many Whigs argued that experience showed the need to restrict the royal prerogative; some of the Tories, having failed to prevent William from becoming King, did their utmost to limit his effective power; indeed, the Tories became more vocally suspicious of those in power as time went on and "Country" sentiment grew. There was no suggestion that parliament should take over effective control of the executive, but there was a widespread determination to make the monarch more accountable to the Commons for his conduct.

A second important, if negative, influence was the fact that the settlement was necessarily bipartisan. The Whigs had a majority in the Convention House of Commons, elected in January 1689, but the Tories had a majority in the Lords and until William became King he was unable to create new peers or appoint new bishops. Whig leaders in the Commons were, therefore, careful to avoid aggressively partisan measures and to justify their proposals in terms that the Lords might be willing to accept. This meant, on one hand, that the legislation of 1689 represented a lowest common denominator, broadly acceptable to both parties; on the other, that important issues of principle tended to be fudged and ideological divisions smothered in ambiguity.

A third, much less visible, factor was the influence of William. The need to avoid outraging English public opinion and his princely (and often Catholic) allies on the continent led him to mask his military conquest of England with the appearance of popular consent, expressed in a series of "invitations' – to invade, to come to London, to take on the government, to summon a parliament, and to become King. When the "invitations" were slow to materialize, or when they seemed likely to be accompanied by unacceptable conditions, William applied a little judicious pressure – above all, by threatening to return to Holland.[52] With much of James' army still in being – and extremely disgruntled – and with English rule in Ireland on the verge of collapse, such a threat was sufficient for William to get his way.

A final formative influence on the settlement and the post-Revolution monarchy was war. When William came to England, the Dutch were already at war with France. With James in exile in France and William King of England, it was inevitable that England would join in this great European war, in order to prevent James' being restored as a French puppet. Although Louis XIV recognized William as King in 1697, four years later he recognized James' son as James III of England, an action which helped to draw England into an even greater European war, that of the Spanish Succession. These two wars were the largest and the most costly that England had ever fought. They made necessary a massive increase in taxation and government borrowing. As the revenue and armed forces grew, so did the administration.[53] The impact of these developments was ambivalent. On one hand, the need for taxation and credit made the King more dependent on parliament than ever before. On the other, the growth of the state vastly increased the volume of patronage – places and pensions – at the Crown's disposal and thus its ability to buy support in parliament and in the country at large.

It is often claimed that the change of ruler in 1689 dealt a permanent blow to the hereditary descent of the Crown and so to the sanctity of monarchy: William's title, it is alleged, depended on parliament. He was, however, by no means the first king to win the Crown by conquest and then to receive the endorsement of parliament: the same was true of Henry IV, Edward IV, and Henry VII (and William's hereditary claim was certainly more plausible than Henry VII's). The question of the hereditary principle was important in 1689 only because it had become such a contentious issue in the Exclusion Crisis, but (whatever they might claim later) it was not resolved unequivocally in the Whigs' favour. On one hand, the Tories accepted the key Whig argument for exclusion: both Houses voted *nem con* that experience showed that it was inconsistent with the safety of a Protestant kingdom to be governed by a Catholic prince. This swept aside the claim of James' infant son (who would presumably be raised as a Catholic) and reestablished Mary as heir to her father, who (in deference to Tory sensibilities) was agreed to have abdicated rather than having been deposed. Any hope that William might be content with the role of a mere consort (as Philip II had been to Mary Tudor) was dashed by his insistence that he did not "think it reasonable to have any share in the government, unless it was put in his person and that for term of life". William's elevation to the throne alongside his wife was certainly a blow to the hereditary principle, but he was prepared to soften it: "he thought, that the issue of Princess Anne should be preferred in the succession to any issue that he might have by any other wife than the Princess [Mary]".[54]

Taken together, these provisions ensured that the damage to the hereditary principle was limited. If William was elevated from third place in the succession to first equal (if one ignored the Prince of Wales), the interruption to the hereditary succession was temporary: once James and William were dead, the succession would flow back into its proper channel. Indeed, the *transmission* of the claim to the throne was to be strictly hereditary: first Mary's children, then Anne's, then William's (by any subsequent marriage). Although Mary had no children, it seemed more than probable that Anne would: indeed, she was pregnant when the Convention met, so there seemed every prospect of a continuing Protestant Stuart line. Only when Anne's last surviving child died did the Tories have to choose between their legitimism and their Protestantism. In the Act of Settlement of 1701 they opted, reluctantly but

EDVARDVS :·

A

Anno ꜧ o ꜱ 29 octobʒ jmago henʒich vij ꞇʒaꞇuꞇʒ ꝛꞇgꝛ jlluꞇꞇꝛꝯmꞇ
oꝛꝺmaꞇa ꝑ hꝛꞇnꞇaꝑ ʒmck ℔o ʒꝛoꞇꝛ ... aꞇꞇoꞇmꞇ ·

C

E

ANNO DNI · 1 5

DI MARI   DOVGHTE
HE MOST   VERTVOVS
NG HENRI   THE EIGH

HE AGE OF   XXVIII

F

G

BEATI PACI

H

1

L

unequivocally, for Protestantism, vesting the succession after Anne in the House of Hanover. Even that did not completely kill Tory attachment to the hereditary principle: they continued to assert it – within the Protestant line.[55]

In practice, then, William III's accession did less harm to the hereditary principle than Henry VII's. If it seemed in retrospect seriously to have undermined that principle, this can be explained partly by the fact that Whig ideology (which placed the safety of the people before the rights of the royal family) played down that principle, partly because the personal power of the monarch declined after 1689. This decline owed little to the legislation of 1689. The need for bipartisan agreement, together with William's insistence that he should enjoy the same prerogatives as his predecessors, ensured that the Declaration (later Bill) of Rights was a relatively bland and uncontentious document, concerned mainly to restate what most people thought was the law. Only one clause was truly novel: the statement that "the raising or keeping of a standing army within the kingdom in time of peace, unless it be with consent of parliament, is against law".[56] More serious restrictions were added by subsequent legislation. The Triennial Act of 1694 forced the King to call a general election at least once every three years. The Act of Settlement (among other provisions) decreed that no future monarch could leave the country without parliament's permission and deprived the monarch of the power to dismiss judges. Yet while such legislation materially reduced the monarch's prerogatives, his basic powers remained intact. He still summoned and dismissed parliament, appointed ministers, directed the executive, commanded the armed forces, and made war and peace.

Or at least he did so in theory. In practice, the monarch's personal exercise of these powers was increasingly constricted, thanks to a variety of developments which stemmed directly from the Revolution, notably in relation to the revenue. William in 1689 had the power to block legislation which threatened his power. He did not have the power to force the Commons to vote him money. Most royal revenues having lapsed with James' "abdication", needed to be granted afresh and MPs were in no hurry to grant them. Even in the debates on the Declaration of Rights, some identified the revenue as the key issue. William Harbord told the House:

> You have an infallible security for the administration of the government. All the revenue is in your hands, which fell with the late King and you may keep that back. Can he whom the place on the throne support the government without the revenue? Can he do good or harm without it?

A year later, when William pressed to have the revenue settled, Paul Foley argued that they should not repeat the mistake of 1660, giving the King more than he needed: "If you settle such a revenue as that the King should have no need of a parliament, I think we do not do our duty to them that sent us hither." His call for caution was supported by Tories as well as Whigs. William was granted the customs for four years only. As he had already given up the hearth tax (and received nothing in return) his ordinary revenue was insufficient to cover the peacetime cost of government.[57]

But William's reign was not a time of peace. The war of 1689–97 made the Crown's financial dependence on parliament complete. Charles II had often been able to survive without parliamentary grants; William III never could. This meant that the Commons could either refuse supply to extort concessions or "tack" unpalatable conditions to revenue bills, leaving the Lords (who could not amend money bills) and the King with the choice of accepting the conditions or losing the money. William fought against this development – he vetoed far more bills than Charles II – but he had to accept some humiliating defeats. He was forced to revoke grants of Irish land to Dutchmen and to disband most of the forces raised for the war (starting with his own regiment of guards) after the peace of Ryswick (1697).

After 1689, then, the balance of financial power between Crown and Commons swung irreversibly in favour of the Commons. Given the strength of party, this created the danger that the leaders of the majority party would use their control over the Commons to extort from the monarch the policies and appointments they wanted. Under William and Anne, this happened less than one might expect. Backbench MPs were less interested than their leaders in constraining the King – and might indeed regard it as morally wrong to do so. Many also put winning the wars before partisan measures, as shown by the rejection in 1704 of the move to tack the occasional conformity bill to the money bill.[58] Moreover, not all issues were party issues. Throughout the 1690s, MPs were often animated by Country resentment of the misdeeds and corruption of those in office: the essence of "the Country persuasion" was suspicion of power, not a desire to exercise it.[59] This Country mentality was strong among the Tories, inhibiting them from developing clear policy objectives and making them difficult to lead and to organize. As a result, even though they were the natural majority party under Anne, they made less effective use of their numbers than the Whigs did. Last but not least, William, Anne, and their political managers – Sunderland, Marlborough, Godolphin, Harley – strove to preserve a measure of freedom of action for the monarch.[60]

After making all due qualifications, however, William and Anne had to struggle to retain control of decision-making. William was helped by the fact that for much of his reign party divisions were less sharply defined than they were to be under Anne. He was also able to make use of his Dutch advisers and the Dutch diplomatic corps, thus shutting English politicians out of some areas of policy. Anne, handicapped by her gender, poor health, and the revived "rage of party", found it hard to live up to her ideal of ruling as Queen of all her people. While Tory ministers might pursue partisan policies, they were far less ruthless and single-minded than the Whigs when it came to forcing one another into office. By 1708, Marlborough and Godolphin were arguing that the Queen's measures would not get through the Commons unless she dismissed Harley from office and gave more places to Whigs, including the lord lieutenancy of Ireland to the rakish Lord Wharton, whom she loathed. Anne was to reassert herself and bring Harley back into office in 1710, but the power to control the Commons (and with it supply) gave party politicians a leverage with the monarch which their forebears had not possessed.[61] As a result, even William saw the advantages of meeting trouble halfway – avoiding measures that would antagonize the Commons and taking pains to consult the House even when he was under no legal obligation to do so. Thus, while diplomacy was still a prerogative matter, by the end of his reign, William was laying treaties before parliament.[62]

If in some ways the Revolution had weakened the Crown, in others it had strengthened it. The problems created by the complex interrelationship between the Stuarts' three kingdoms had played a crucial part in bringing about civil war. By 1714, England and Scotland had been united as a single kingdom, while British rule over Ireland seemed secure. The state over which Anne presided was far more powerful than that of Charles II, with much larger armed forces and a greatly increased revenue. Between 1689 and 1714, as under the Tudors, in many ways one sees a strengthening of parliament and the Crown. Moreover, the Crown now possessed a much enlarged pool of patronage. If the prerogative of the Crown had been tamed, its "influence" (the ability to buy support) seemed to have grown to dangerous proportions. Anxious country spokesmen feared that a growing influx of placemen and pensioners would sap the independence of the Commons and promoted place bills (and the 1694 Triennial Act) in an effort to stem the tide.

Yet if "the Crown" was growing more powerful, at the same time there was an important shift of power within the government, away from the monarch and towards the ministers who acted in the monarch's name. Their most crucial task was to extract money from the Commons and they were chosen in part for their ability to do so; this meant that they were normally leading members of the majority party. But their power in the Commons gave them great bargaining power when dealing with the monarch. If he still possessed extensive prerogatives, he had to exercise them with the advice of ministers who in time became more and more answerable to parliament and, later, to the electorate. There developed a huge gulf between the theory and practice of the prerogative which had not existed before 1689. Nowadays, in theory, the Queen appoints the prime minister and summons and dismisses parliament; in practice, she appoints the leader of the party that has just won the general election and then acts on that leader's advice. The decline of the personal role of the monarch was a long, slow process, which began with the failure to grant William III a sufficient revenue in 1690.

To conclude, let us return to the point made at the start of this chapter, about the tension between legitimacy and competence. By 1714, the sense of legitimacy had been weakened. The accession of a German did little to reinforce the prestige of monarchy among a xenophobic populace; the unpopularity of the new dynasty is highlighted by the abiding strength of Jacobite sentiment. Even before 1714, however, the monarchy was losing some of its aura. William III was a foreigner, he spent much of his time abroad, and he was somewhat reclusive and unsociable. Anne made a real effort to return to a more traditional style of monarchy, consciously modelling herself on Queen Elizabeth. Yet despite the effusions of the proponents of divine right, despite her revival of ceremonial and of touching for scrofula, despite her obvious popularity with the people, Anne's influence with the political élite was limited and her Court was far less important politically than Charles II's had been. Party loyalties had cut across and to some extent superseded loyalty to the Crown.[63] In the future, popular esteem for the monarchy was to have its ups and downs – perhaps more downs than ups. Monarchs enjoyed their subjects' loyalty and respect, perhaps even affection – but no longer awe or reverence.

And yet the monarchy survived. The hereditary succession, interrupted in 1689, has been maintained since. This survival, as we have just seen, owed little to legitimacy, but much to competence. The enhanced financial power of the House of Commons meant that it could force the king to accept its interpretation of his prerogative. There was, therefore, little danger of a future king's provoking a crisis by misusing his prerogative in the way Charles I or James II had done. (Whig cries of "tyranny" at the start of George III's reign were far from ingenuous). If anyone was to suffer for the misdeeds of the government, it was the ministers, which was only right and proper, as they were the ones who wielded the real power: "ministers", declared George II (smiling), "are the kings in this country."[64] He exaggerated: kings still possessed considerable power. Decorum required that they be treated with deference and persuaded, rather than bullied, but in the last analysis politicians could prescribe the terms on which they were prepared to serve.[65] Conversely, kings could no longer presume simply to command. If they were to get their way, they had to learn to manage the politicians. As Britain edged towards mass democracy, the monarch's personal influence over the politicians was increasingly outweighed by their need to satisfy the electorate. The price that the monarchy has paid for survival has been the loss of power.

Footnotes to this Chapter may be found on pages 361–64.

10: Jeremy Black

The British Monarchy 1714–1837

ALTHOUGH IT scarcely fits with our general image of them, George I, II, III, and IV and William IV were among the most successful monarchs in British history, conspicuously so in contrast with the position since the late 14th century. This may seem a surprising assertion. These were not the most popular of monarchs. George IV ruled the country as Prince Regent between 1811 and 1820, while his father was incapacitated by porphyria, and as King from 1820 to 1830, yet when he died *The Times* remarked "Never was there a human being less respected than this late King...what eye weeps for him?" Strong words, but George I had scarcely been more popular in 1721, George II in 1744, or George III in 1763. They were not the most competent of monarchs. The British monarchy lost a large portion of its subjects when George III lost the Thirteen Colonies, while, more generally, the power of the monarchy has been seen as very limited after the Revolution Settlement, the constitutional changes of 1689–1701 that resulted from the Glorious Revolution of 1688.

Yet these kings were also successful. First, they were so in a dynastic sense. The succession was maintained in the Hanoverian line and there was no repetition in Britain either of the republican episode of 1649–60 or of the monarchical coup of 1688: republicanism was only successful in North America. This was a particularly important achievement because the Glorious Revolution of 1688–9 created a fundamental schism of loyalty in Britain, the Jacobite movement, which was a threat to the Hanoverians until crushed at Culloden in 1746. The extent of Jacobite support is a controversial topic among historians. It can be argued that compared to the political world of 1678–89 – the years of the Popish Plot, the Exclusion Crisis, the Monmouth rising, and the Glorious Revolution – the situation in England after the defeat of the Jacobite rising in 1715 and the consolidation, with George I's support, of Whig hegemony between 1716 and 1722 was less volatile. Yet the fundamental stability of the system was challenged by the existence of a Stuart claim to the throne, and there is an argument for including James VIII and III and his sons in any treatment of British monarchy in this period.

Two rival princes competed at Culloden: the heir to the Jacobite cause, Charles Edward Stuart (Bonnie Prince Charlie), and George II's second and favourite son, William, Duke of Cumberland. Thus, in the crisis of the Hanoverian state and monarchy, the royal family played a vital role. Cumberland took the leading role in 1745–6 and was an active general more akin among the royal generals of the 1740s to Frederick the Great of Prussia, his first cousin, than to Louis XV of France.

After Culloden, the Hanoverian monarchy was stronger, its legitimacy unchallenged. The crisis with North America did not lead to comparable problems in Britain, although from the early 1790s the example of France helped to encourage radicalism within Britain (radicalism had begun earlier, but increased markedly in the 1790s). Yet this again was a challenge that the British monarchy and state surmounted. Just as parliamentary unions – with Scotland in 1707 and Ireland in 1801 – reflected the crises of those periods, but also produced a more unitary state, so, in some measure, the monarchy likewise benefited from challenges. The challenge of the French Revolution helped to produce a rallying of the social élite and of much opinion, around country, Crown, and Church in the 1790s. The monarchy, although not the person of the monarch, served as a potent symbol of national identity and continuity especially after the execution of Louis XVI in January 1793. This led to a powerful reiteration of monarchical ideology in Britain, now part of the process by which the British were differentiated from the French.

On 30 January 1793, Samuel Horsley, Bishop of St David's and a supporter of William Pitt the Younger, gave the annual Martyrdom Day sermon in Westminster Abbey before the House of Lords. This marked the anniversary of the execution of Charles I, the individual elevated most closely to sainthood by the Church of England. In the first half of the century, 30 January had often been a focus for discontent, for riots, and a Jacobite challenge to the dynasty. Now it served to affirm, not the Stuart house but the institution of monarchy itself. In 1793, Horsley delivered a powerful attack on political speculation and revolutionary theory. He dismissed the notion of an original compact arising from the abandonment of a state of nature, and instead stressed royal authority. According to Horsley, the existing constitution was the product and safeguard of a "legal contract" between Crown and people, while the obedience of the latter was a religious duty. Horsley's forceful peroration linked the two executions:

> This foul murder, and these barbarities, have filled the measure of the guilt and infamy of France. O my Country! Read the horror of thy own deed in this recent heightened imitation! Lament and weep, that this black French treason should have found its example, in the crime of thy unnatural sons!

The congregation rose to its feet in approval. If the fate of religion and monarchy in Britain seemed clearly challenged by developments in France, that did not mean that all rallied to the cause of kings, but rather that the monarchy played a greater role in political ideology than it had done between 1689 and 1746. In the earlier period, an emphasis on monarchy had been compromised by serious differences over the legitimacy of the dynasty as well as the contentious nature of constitutional arrangements after 1688. No such problems hindered a stress on monarchy on the part of conservative elements from the 1790s: however much the failings and foibles of individual members of the royal family, not least George III's ill-health, were to pose difficulties, the role of the monarchy was one that conservatives could support.

This was an important part of the success of the Hanoverian monarchy. It was helped by the course of the Revolutionary and Napoleonic wars. The royal family did not win personal glory in these conflicts; nor indeed did they take as prominent a role as William III had done in Ireland and the Low Countries in the 1690s, or as Cumberland had done in Scotland and the Low Countries in 1744–8. The 1799 landing in Holland under George III's son, Frederick, Duke of York (now best remembered in the nursery rhyme for marching troops up and down hills), ended in failure; although York played a significant role in improving the army thereafter. His brother Ernest, who served against the French with Hanoverian forces in 1793–4, 1806, and 1813–14, did so without particular success, but he acquired a justified reputation for bravery.

Nevertheless, there were no disasters and humiliations akin to those that affected most of the European dynasties. French troops did not seize London as they did Berlin, Lisbon, Madrid, Moscow, Naples, Turin, and Vienna. The royal family was not obliged to accept a royal marriage with Napoleon as the Habsburg Francis I had to do. There was no forcible abdication to make way for one of Napoleon's relatives, as happened in Spain. A Napoleonic marshal did not gain the throne, as did Bernadotte in Sweden. Survival was not obtained by humiliating subservience as in the case of Bavaria, Prussia, and Saxony. In 1742, 1744 or 1782, the British monarchy had appeared one of the weakest in Europe, its rulers unable to sustain in office ministers who enjoyed royal confidence – Walpole, Carteret, and North; yet by 1810 it was the strongest in Europe after Napoleon's monarchical dictatorship, which lacked comparable legitimacy. Other European rulers, such as Louis XVIII, the rulers of Naples, Portugal, and Sardinia and the Prince of Orange, took shelter in Britain or behind the cover of British forces, particularly the Royal Navy. British ministers had to consider what would happen if Napoleon invaded – would they have an army in Dover or concentrate forces south of London – but it never happened.

In addition, Britain became *the* world empire in this period. In 1714, Britain was already one of the leading colonial powers with extensive territories in North America, valuable sugar islands in the West Indies, and important bases in West Africa, India, and the Mediterranean. Yet Britain was not yet the leading colonial power. If it had gained Gibraltar, Minorca, Newfoundland, Nova Scotia, and recognition of its claim to Rupert's Land to the south of Hudson's Bay at the Peace of Utrecht (1713) which had ended the War of the Spanish Succession, Britain's colonial territories were far less extensive, populous, and wealthy than those of Spain, while France was still an important colonial rival and the Dutch still an important colonial force. The British attempt to seize Quebec from the French in 1711 had been unsuccessful and there was little sign that the British would be able to gain colonies from other European powers, as opposed to seizing territory from often weaker non-European peoples as in North America.

By 1837, the situation was totally transformed. Spain had lost its empire in Latin America; and France had lost most of its 18th-century empire: Canada, Mauritius, St Lucia, and the Seychelles conquered by Britain; Louisiana sold to the United States. Britain had lost its Thirteen Colonies and the Old North-West beyond the Appalachians; and had failed in its expeditions to Argentina in 1806–7; but it was the strongest state in the world, the leading power on the oceans, and had the best system of public finance. Australia and New Zealand were British colonies, the colony of South Australia being founded in 1836. Canada was under British control. The British dominated much of India, particularly Bengal and the south, and also ruled Ceylon and parts of Burma. In the 1840s, the British were to annex Sind and Punjab. Cape Town had been acquired from the Dutch during the Napoleonic wars, while other gains at the Congress of Vienna (1815) included Trinidad, Tobago, St Lucia, Malta, Guyana, and the Ionian Islands. In the two decades after the Napoleonic war, British policy and power played a crucial role in securing Greek independence and that of Latin America.

If Britain was so successful during this period, it might fairly be asked how much was due to the monarchs. There is an apparent paradox in the unpopularity of the Hanoverian monarchy, at least under George I, II, and IV, and the success of the British state. In many ways, the connections between the growing capacity and status of the British state and the monarchy were indirect, but dynastic stability was a condition of the Hanoverian political settlement. When the reasons for the success of Britain in these years are discussed, they are generally those of economic growth, financial resources, naval capability, and such like. The kings do not feature, and indeed in so far as Britain's triumph owed much to military success, this was scarcely surprising. The martial qualities of the Hanoverians did not become more pronounced. George II was, at Dettingen in 1743, the last British monarch to take part in a battle. In 1793, Sir William Beechey painted a massive *George III Reviewing the Troops*, a work destroyed in the fire at Windsor Castle on 19 November 1992. This depicted an equestrian group of George, Prince of Wales, and the Duke of York, who became a Field Marshal in 1795 and Commander-in-Chief in 1798, reviewing the 10th Hussars and the 3rd Dragoons. It was at one with military poses struck by the Prince in this period; and that of his second cousin, William V of Orange who declared in December 1792, when the French were apparently about the invade the United Provinces (modern Netherlands), that "he would resist to the utmost, and die upon the spot". In fact, William survived the French invasion: dying heroically was more fashionable in Neoclassical and Romantic iconography than it was in practice for the monarchs of the period. George IV's military pretensions verged on the ridiculous: later in life, he used to tell people that he had been at Waterloo, and would seek confirmation from the Duke of Wellington, winning the tactful reply, "So you have told me, Sir".

The Duke of Clarence, later William IV, was made a rear-admiral in 1790, a vice-admiral in 1794, an admiral in 1799, and in 1811 admiral of the fleet, and thus commander-in-chief: it was not until 1821, when George IV promoted the Earl of St Vincent, a distinguished veteran, that there was a second such commander. In 1827, Clarence was made Lord High Admiral, a post created for him. These were years of British naval triumph and hegemony, but Clarence was not responsible for them. Whereas he had seen active service during the War of American Independence and commanded ships in peacetime in 1786–90, thereafter he did not serve afloat other than for brief ceremonial purposes. In 1814, Clarence commanded the escort of Louis XVIII when it was reviewed by the Prince Regent and the allied sovereigns at Spithead. In 1828, Clarence put to sea in command of the Channel Fleet despite the view of George IV, the Prime Minister, Wellington, and the head of the Admiralty Board, Sir George Cockburn, that his position as Lord High Admiral did not give him the authority to exercise military command. Their complaints led to Clarence's resignation. This was scarcely a career to match that of Nelson who served with William in the West Indies in the 1780s and was a friend. When Nelson was married, William gave away the bride, and Nelson praised his abilities as an officer; but there are no signs that he had the capability to be an effective admiral and he was never given a chance.

A lack of impressive military service is not the same as a neglect of military matters. The kings took their duties seriously, especially George I and II. George I and II promoted the principle of long service as the main way to advancement and did their best to counter the purchase of commissions. George II used his formidable memory for names to good effect in keeping oversight of the leading members of the officer class. He personally signed military commissions.

Even the unmartial George III took a keen interest. He exerted influence on military policy, especially after his son Frederick became Commander-in-Chief. George was portrayed in military uniform, for example by Zoffany in 1771, and this was clearly part of his self-image. He reviewed the fleet at Portsmouth in 1773 and off Plymouth in 1789. In 1780, George took a close interest in the suppression of the Gordon Riots, and pressed for firm action, "for I am convinced till the magistrates have ordered some military execution on the rioters this town will not be restored to order". In 1798, he wrote, with reference to the French invasion of Ireland, "I have received this Day the further letters that have been forwarded to the Admiralty relative to the Squadron on the NW Coast of Ireland; I flatter myself to hear tomorrow in Town some account for the four frigates not yet known to have fallen into the hands of some of our Cruisers".[1] All monarchs devoted great attention to military appointments.

Nevertheless, it cannot be said that the kings were great military administrators. None matched the aptitude or energy of Cumberland and his military career was brought to an ignominious close in 1757 when he failed to prevent a French invasion of Hanover and signed the humiliating and politically embarrassing Convention of Klosterseven to save his army from destruction. George III and IV were no Napoleons and the contrast between them exemplified different forms of monarchy. Napoleon personified meritocratic monarchy, but one of the main aspects of the success of the British state and of British monarchy was that there was no need for either George to be a great warleader. A system of hereditary monarchy deals with the basic question of legitimacy by providing a succession within a family; and by the 18th century the rules of succession were very clear. Monarchy is appropriate for a society structured around privilege and hereditary succession. Such a society, however, confronts the problems of the continual need for energetic and talented leadership and administrators. To a certain extent, talent will be found within its ranks, but it does not necessarily correspond to the hierarchies of society. It is notable how many of the talented leaders and ministers of Hanoverian Britain were not at the apex of society. A surprising number were not eldest sons – Henry Pelham, both Pitts, Wellington, Ilay, Henry Fox, and Charles James Fox – and many others were not born into the purple: Walpole, Jenkinson, Nelson.

Similarly, at the level of royalty, any system that requires a continuous level of talent poses problems. It is difficult to supply this in an hereditary system, while any alternative faces problems of legitimacy and stability. On the European scale, George IV might not have been an impressive rival to Napoleon, but it is difficult to regard Charles IV of Spain (1788–1808) as any more impressive. The Emperor Francis I (1792–1835) was more industrious than George, but he was also stubborn and fell out with the leading royal general, Archduke Charles. Like George, Frederick William II of Prussia (1786–97) was a follower of the politics of the boudoir, but he was also interested in mystical religion and his tergiversations made consistent policy making difficult. The same was true of Paul I of Russia (1796–1801), while his successor Alexander I (1801–25) was a less than impressive general. The difficulties of the dynastic system were also revealed within the Napoleonic family. Neither Louis, King of Holland (1806–10), nor Joseph, King of Naples (1806–08) and of Spain (1808–12), or Jerome, King of Westphalia, had the ability or determination of their brother.

The British system can be seen as a successful compromise that reflected the strengths and weaknesses of hereditary monarchy. Such an approach may seem complacent, indeed Whiggish, and it risks smoothing over detailed crises in favour of a more schematic approach. Nevertheless, the "limited" or "parliamentary" monarchy of the period was flexible, neither the constitution nor the political arrangements and culture so rigid that they were unable to adapt to the differing interests and abilities of individual monarchs, to changes in their responses to the political world, and to alterations in their position, for no monarch should be seen as an invariable feature of the political landscape, more particularly not monarchs who reigned for as long as George II (1727–60) and George III (1760–1820). The role of the Church and clergy in legitimizing the Hanoverian monarchy – all those clergy straining their sinews to inculcate obedience to their new masters – was also important.

So indeed were the personalities of the rulers. George I and II were particularly modest men. George I's diffidence, honesty, and dullness and George II's amiable lack of imagination produced a complacency with very practical consequences: they were pragmatists who did not have an agenda for Britain (unlike, for example, James II). These kings' place in politics was not of their choosing, but rather a consequence of 1688–9, the Act of Settlement (1701), and the Union of 1707. They were sensible enough to adapt and survive. Nevertheless, by driving the Tories into the political wilderness, the first two Georges weakened their own position: their attitude was very different from that of Charles II at the Restoration.

Much of the credit for Britain's constitutional monarchy rests with those who defined the royal position between 1689 and 1707, but, precisely because there was no rigid constitution, the attitude and role of individual monarchs were also crucial. Survival was all the early Hanoverians sought: George I and II did not have pretensions to mimic the grandiose palaces of the continental monarchies, and the same applies to their lifestyles and incomes. Both appeared in a relatively modest way in London society: at the parks, theatre, the opera. This was not a case of the vast charades of some continental monarchs. They were also accommodating, quite prepared to be prodded into levées, ceremonies, and public appearances that were alien to them. George III displayed a similar modesty in his lifestyle, although he did have a political agenda for Britain.

Clearly, there were moments when the political situation was less happy, when the absence of consensus extended from issues of place and policy to the very constitution. Such crises did not have to centre on the position of the monarch: as already suggested the radicalism and republicanism of the early 1790s onwards was less challenging because it threatened the entire system. In the early 1780s, however, George III was so outraged by the necessity to part with Lord North in 1782 and to accept the Rockinghamites in 1782 and the Fox-North ministry in 1783 that he talked of abdication. George was far from alone in seeing this as a crisis. John, 2nd Earl of Buckinghamshire, a former diplomat, when not admiring the scantily-clad bathing beauties at Weymouth, meditated on the crisis:

> This unhappily disgraced country surrounded by every species of embarrassment, and without even a distant prospect of establishing an Administration so firm and so respectable as to restore to England any proportion of her defeated dignity. The state is now circumstanced as a human body in the last stage of a decline. Whig as I am and sufficiently vain of my descent from Maynard and Hampden, it sometimes occurs to me that something might be obtained by strengthening the hands of the Crown.[2]

A clear sense of crisis, current or imminent, emerges from much of the political correspondence of the early 1780s, and it can be seen in the letters of politicians with very different ideas. The hostility of George III and the Fox-North ministry created a particularly serious political situation, and its resolution in 1784 in the form of a ministry under William Pitt the Younger winning electoral and parliamentary support, was far from inevitable. Yet, once Crown-élite consensus had been restored, at least in so far as was measured by the crucial criterion — the ability of George III to cooperate with a ministry enjoying the support of parliament — Britain was politically stable. This stability was a reflection of that ability; one that required a willingness to adjust, if not compromise, by both parties.

The competence, character, and interests of the monarchs were central to the workings of "parliamentary monarchy". Yet their evaluation faces problems with the sources. Whereas for George III there are 12 substantial volumes of correspondence, there is little surviving for George I and II. Although the fall of Walpole in 1742 is generally cited as a defeat for the Crown, it also testified to the importance of the royal family. Walpole had done badly in the general election of 1741, due less to any groundswell of popular opposition than to the defection of a number of important electoral patrons, most seriously Frederick, who, as Duke of Cornwall, controlled many boroughs in a county that was heavily over-represented in parliament. The refusal of Frederick to accept any political settlement with his father unless Walpole fell played a crucial role in the minister's decision to resign after his failure to deliver parliamentary majorities. Frederick was very much in the hands of superior political intelligencies and personalities, but the attitude of the immediate successor to the throne was a decided advantage to the opposition.

Although defeated politically on a number of occasions, George II was certainly no cipher. Contemporaries were with reason convinced that he played a central role in ministerial politics, as in 1742 when a prominent Tory, and sometime Jacobite, was kept out of the Admiralty Board:

> A list was drawn up; amongst them Sir John Hynde Cotton was put down; upon the scheme, as was before said, of placing the administration upon the broad bottom. This list was presented to the King. He struck out Sir J H Cotton with his own hand. This alarmed all people to a high degree. The seeds of a vehement and formidable opposition were sown anew.[3]

Aside from lacunae in sources and scholarship, there is also the question of how best to assess influence in a political culture in which so much was settled by word of mouth. The Court was essentially a political world of personal contact, not a bureaucratic sphere in which written communication was central and, as a consequence, it is very difficult to assess the course and impact of royal views. For most of the period, there is no source comparable to the memoirs of Lord Hervey, a Court insider fascinated by character, who left such a vivid, although without doubt slanted, account of George II's Court in the 1730s. George III had no Boswell and because he did not travel to

Hanover, as his grandfather and great-grandfather had done, there is no series of correspondence between ministers in London and Hanover to throw light on the King's opinions. His correspondence with Bute only covers a small portion of his reign.

The Court was a crucial political sphere, although it had declined under Queen Anne. There were, however, reasons for the decline of the Court under Anne. Leading politicians could not hope for the physical proximity to the monarch that was possible under a king. That drawback was eliminated after 1714, though George I's somewhat reclusive character and linguistic limitations posed problems. As long as the monarch was and remained the ultimate political authority, his Court necessarily remained the political centre, since it provided access to him. The indications are that the Court revived, but not in cultural terms, under the Georges, though, with no collections of royal correspondence or Lord Hervey to leave memoirs, the evidence for the 1740s and 1750s is admittedly inconclusive. Whig historiography in the following century sidelined the Georgian Court: instead parliament was seen as the Crown's dominant partner after the Glorious Revolution and the Court was presented as dropping out of the political picture. George II's Closet was not Henry VIII's Privy Chamber, but the insignificance of the Hanoverian Court has been greatly overdone. There is lots of evidence of competition for royal favour.

Furthermore, the parliamentary opposition can often be presented in terms of a rival court. If parliament as an institution did not have the confidence to thwart or bring down the king's ministers, opposition factions within it did – but they were arguably dependent on the heir to the throne. The events of 1717–20 sound very modern if presented in terms of parliamentary politics, but viewed as rivalry between two royal courts, they carry less contemporary resonance. Without Leicester House, where the courts of George II and III as heirs, and of Frederick Prince of Wales were based, to give opposition respectability, parliamentary opposition had little chance: the support of the heir helped to overcome early Georgian repugnance to "storming the Closet" – unacceptable politicians forcing their way into office (storming the Closet referred to gaining access to the private quarters in which the monarch discussed confidential matters) – and also to systematically opposing the king's government. The Prince of Wales was as crucial in Walpole's closet-storming of 1720 as the next Prince of Wales was in his fall in 1742. Leicester House's move into open opposition between 1755 and 1757 was a crucial element in the crisis that took Pitt the Elder to power. Though that crisis can be explained in terms of parliamentary followings and events outside parliament, it can just as plausibly be presented as a feud between Cumberland and Leicester House. Ministers had scant influence on such crucial quarrels within the royal family.

The crisis of 1746 was serious, but also showed the importance of the Crown. George II was totally responsible for creating an abnormal situation, resulting from his attitude to the Pelhams after they had refused to work with Granville. It could be contended that the crisis demonstrated the importance of the royal family because Bath and Granville could have been saved by the support of Prince Frederick, a notion that is difficult to credit, not least because of the weaknesses of Frederick's character. It can also be argued that the outcome emphasized the power of the Court in the Commons. By withholding his confidence from his ministers, George II undermined their position in parliament. Hence their desperate resignation at a time of war and rebellion, which left George little room for manoeuvre. George's self-imposed limitations contributed to the same end. He did not want to turn to the Tories to support the ministry; and wanted to employ favourites such as Granville and Bath, yet also regarded as essential the Old Corps Whigs who detested them. Having got himself into a difficult position, George II lacked the nerve to play his ace and dissolve parliament. The '45 was as good as over: Charles Edward Stuart had retreated to Scotland and the French had not landed. With a parliamentary majority, George II possibly could have cleared out the Old Corps as George III did in the 1760s and prefigured the displacement of the Fox-North ministry in 1783–4. The year 1746 was an extraordinary crisis, but it cannot be regarded as typical of the 18th-century constitution.

The thwarting of royal ministerial choice usually reflected abnormal divisions within the Court – or rather between two courts. When that happened, the monarch could lose his majority in parliament. There was nothing uniquely British about royal ministers needing a majority in whatever estates controlled supply, which it was their ministers' first duty to secure. What would have made Britain unique was the habitual inability of Court ministers to deliver such a majority. Unless there were two courts, the king's and his heir's, this was not the case. When it was, it can usually be attributed to old-style dynastic feuding rather than modern-style parliamentary politics.

Hatton's portrayal of George I as a figure of the early Enlightenment is very problematical and she failed to address his undoubted unpopularity in Britain. Whatever his cultural interests, George I preferred drilling his troops and hunting. He fought in 1675–8 in the Dutch war against Louis XIV, and against the Turks in Hungary in 1683–5, led forces into Holstein in 1700 and an invasion of Wolfenbüttel in 1702, and commanded on the Rhine against Louis XIV's forces in the War of the Spanish Succession. To contemporaries, George I was a distant figure. Unlike William III, who was familiar with English politics and politicians from earlier visits, marriage into the English royal family and extensive intervention in English domestic politics, George knew relatively little of England and his first experience of it was as an older man than was the case with William (or James I). George's failure to learn English and his obvious preference for Hanover further contributed to this sense of alien rule, while as an individual he was a figure of suspicion because of the incarceration of his adulterous wife and the disappearance of her lover, and because of rumours about his own personal life. Scurrilous ballads made much of the theme of the royal cuckold. *Sir James King's Key to Sir George*

Horn's Padlock dwelled on the theme, while an *Address to Britannia* included, "Pray let no Cuckold be still ruler over thee/Nor any German bastard begot in Privity". Another manuscript verse that circulated satirized George and his alleged mistresses, condemning their influence on him and their competition for his attention by contrasting them with the goddesses vying for the attention of Paris. As later with radical pornography in the 1790s and 1800s, humiliation was a powerful political weapon. To demystify the monarch and subject him to ridicule and abuse was part of a determined attempt to weaken his position. Royal popularity was, of course, difficult to gauge. The Swiss visitor, Cesar de Saussure, in 1725 and 1727 recorded the London mob cheering George I and mourning him, and celebrating George II's accession. It is unclear whether this was simply the fickle mob using any opportunity for an "event"; or a London phenomenon; or evidence that the unpopularity of George I and II has been overstated. They were the Whigs' monarchs, although it is unclear how much personal popularity this brought them.

It could be argued that the scurrilous ballads and verse that circulated provided an opportunity for popular expression about the monarchs, perhaps especially George I and IV, that helped to secure their position. Such expression was tolerated in marked contrast to the more repressive position in continental Europe. It also provided the monarchy with an identity that was not Hanoverian. It was far better for George I to be lampooned for human weaknesses than to be perceived as alien; although the latter critique was also advanced. His son was also to be criticized for sexual waywardness. Amalie Sophie Marianne von Wallmoden, whom George II made Countess of Yarmouth, became an influential political figure because of her access to the King. She was alleged to have recommended at least three peerage creations in return for bribes. George II's favour for her was not ignored by the populace. In December 1736, William Pulteney reported:

> One Mrs Mopp, a famous she Bone-setter and mountebank, coming to Town in a coach with six horses on the Kentish Road, was met by a Rabble of People, who seeing her very oddly and tawdrily dress'd, took her for a Foreigner, and concluded she must be a certain great Person's Mistress. Upon this they followed the Coach, bawling out, No Hannover Whore, no Hannover Whore. The lady within the Coach was much offended, let down the Glass, and screamed louder than any of them, she was no Hannover Whore, she was an English one, upon which they all cry'd out, God bless your Ladyship, quitted the pursuit, and wished her a good Journey.[4]

Aside from his personal life, George I's obvious preference for Hanover caused considerable complaint, among Whigs as well as Tories. Lady Anne Paulet was ready to believe a report that the King would not return to Britain for the winter of 1716–17 "for I fancy he is so much easier where he is that he will like to be from us as long as he can".[5] This was exacerbated by a sense that the preference for Hanover entailed an abandonment of British national interests, as resources were expended for the aggrandizement of the electorate and as the entire direction of British foreign policy was set accordingly. A reasonable critique of foreign policy was advanced on this basis, but George I and II were comparatively restrained in their Hanoverianism. The establishment in 1714 and 1727 was far more like the theory of the dual monarchy of 19th-century Austria-Hungary than the wholesale Hanoverian takeover that some feared. Despite periodic rows about Hanoverian interests, the kings did not swamp Britain with German ministers or systems. If anything they adapted admirably to British institutions. They conformed to the Church of England despite their strong Lutheranism. Even their dynastic disputes were fitted into a parliamentary framework with Court and Leicester House parties at Westminster.

Concern about Hanover contributed powerfully to the "Whig Split", a deep division among the Whigs in 1717–20 that led a large section under Robert Walpole to seek cooperation with the Tories to achieve the overthrow of the Whig government. This can be seen in a number of lights. The Split can be presented as a serious defeat for George I. In 1714, all the Whigs had welcomed him to the throne and had indeed been prepared to fight to achieve the Hanoverian Succession. The following year, the Whigs united in defence of the King (and themselves) when challenged by a dangerous Jacobite rising. Yet in 1717, George's policies helped to divide the government and to lead loyal Whigs to look for Tory support. They were opposed to the direction of British foreign policy and to George's handling of the struggle for influence between the leading Whigs.

On the other hand, George I was scarcely to blame for Whig divisions. Furthermore, his choleric quarrel with his son and heir, which interacted with and seriously worsened the political disputes, was an aspect of a classic feature of dynastic policies: the tension between ruler and heir and between those who looked to one or the other. If George I, II, and III clashed with their heirs so also did other dynasties. Peter the Great had his son Alexis murdered, while Catherine the Great and her son, the future Paul I, were rivals. Frederick William I of Prussia had very poor relations with his son the future Frederick the Great, as did Maria Theresa with her son and heir, Joseph II. Victor Amadeus II of Sardinia was imprisoned by his heir, Charles Emmanuel III, when he tried to retract his abdication, while Philip V of Spain had very poor relations with the future Ferdinand VI.

To note common problems is not, however, the same as to deny responsibility or blame. If the Hanoverians faced tensions in their family and divisions among their ministers, then part of the art of royal politics was the ability to tackle such problems. The assertion of royal will, without the creation or worsening of serious political divisions, was crucial whatever the formal constitutional powers of the sovereign. In 1717, George I proved unable to do so, and thus helped to precipitate a crisis.

A central problem was that of the degree to which the ruler would allow a minster or group of ministers in effect to deploy royal power or influence. In 1717, George lost the support of Walpole and Townshend because he was too closely associated with their rivals, Stanhope and Sunderland. The last wrote in 1717, "upon the whole, I don't doubt, the King's steadiness will carry it".[6] Once thus associated, it was, however, difficult to avoid the consequences of criticism and opposition from those against the minister, and, more particularly, to escape damage if the minister was weakened. Thus, George I had eventually to accommodate himself to the rise of Walpole: "The King is resolved that Walpole shall not govern, but it is hard to be prevented."[7] For ministers, it was essential to win the public support of the monarch to underline their own influence and stability. Thus, in 1724, one of Walpole's allies wrote to Sir Robert's brother:

> The King has not a thought with relation to his affairs either at home or abroad, that is not entirely agreeable to the sentiments of your friends ... he has certainly done more towards declaring his inclinations than the most sanguine man among us could ever hope for ... it was our misfortune last summer that His Majesty was apt to think he did everything that we could in reason expect from him, when in reality there was nothing essential done that could convince the world with whom he placed his credit and confidence.[8]

This state of anxiety if not tension over royal-ministerial relations was common to all 18th-century monarchical states and is a reminder against assuming that the British monarchy was particularly weak or peculiarly prone to foibles. If British rulers were constrained or at least affected by the need to find ministers who could manage parliament, this usual formula begs a few questions. In normal circumstances, by a mixture of patronage and moral support from the monarch and loyalty from most MPs, the king's choice *ipso facto* commanded a parliamentary majority. The crucial issue, as the Georges all saw, was the appointment of ministers, but, generally, it was only necessary for the monarch to find ministries acceptable to himself; acceptance by parliament would follow in normal circumstances. The different views of Charles James Fox have generated much confusion about contemporary views of the 18th-century constitution. His modernity in the eyes of late 19th-century historians, such as G O Trevelyan, commended his merits as a Hanoverian commentator. But his preference for parliamentary majorities rather than royal choice as the basis of ministries was more eccentric in the 1780s (or even, in Lord Blake's view, in the 1820s) than it seemed after 1867.

The relationship between monarch and ministers can also be viewed in two other lights. First, in the absence of unified parties with clear leadership on the modern pattern, it was possible for the ruler to seek to create a ministry around the most acceptable politician who might be able to manage parliament, and, conversely, to keep at a distance those whom he disliked. Secondly, even if the monarch had to accept ministers who were not his first choice, as in 1720, 1742, 1744, 1746, and 1757, it was possible to use a ministry that could manage parliament in order to win support for royal interests. George I and II were reasonably successful in this, but, thereafter, the situation changed. George III found that ministries he did not want – the Rockingham and Fox-North governments – sought to push through unacceptable policies.

There were three reasons for this shift, a shift that arguably marked a weakening in royal influence. First, whereas ministries had been bound to George I and II (and to a considerable extent to William III) by a fear of Jacobitism, this was no longer so from the late 1740s on. Indeed, the room for manoeuvre enjoyed by the elderly George II in the political crisis of 1754-7 was lessened by the impossibility of uniting Whigs on an anti-Jacobite-Tory platform.

Secondly, George I and II had concentrated their attention on foreign policy, and in particular on the details of German affairs. It was difficult to arouse public and sustained political interest in these questions, although the issue of subsidies for Hanover and the conduct of Hanoverian troops caused outrage in 1742–4. From the accession of George III, the Hanoverian issue receded as a source of contention, for George was not particularly associated with Hanover, most clearly because he never went there. In contrast, George III was more associated with domestic issues that were very contentious in their own right and in which the role of the monarch was especially sensitive. This was true of the matter of ministerial choice in the 1760s and early 1780s and of policy towards the North American colonies from 1765 until 1783.

Thirdly, and linked to the last, was the ability of some politicians to create a coherent political connection or party that focused much of its ideology and energy on hostility to what was seen as royal views; and even extended to a much more dangerous antipathy to monarchy as it was generally understood in 18th-century Britain. Thus, the theme of the king as a pernicious political force taking a malevolent role in British affairs was strongly revived in the 1760s after two reigns in which the negative image of the monarch arose largely from their Hanoverian concerns. John Brewer, in his *Party Ideology and Popular Politics at the Accession of George III*, argued that under George III constitutional conventions were a matter of fundamental disagreement, in effect between those who looked to the past and those who anticipated the future: a Whiggish interpretation. Apart from Fox and possibly the Rockinghams, however, there was little dissent from the belief that monarchs appointed ministers. Fox was a maverick who wanted to change the constitution and whose attitudes were widely rejected – hence the erosion of Fox and North's majority against Pitt the Younger in early 1784 and the verdict of the subsequent election. There was a whiff of republicanism about Fox and his friends which put them well outside the general run of politicians angling for power.

Politically, George III was the most interesting (and longest ruling) of the Hanoverians. He came young to the throne and had little earlier political experience: one of the most pernicious consequences of the bad relations between the Hanoverians and their heirs was that the latter had no real apprenticeship, and what they did have was a totem of opposition activity: scarcely the most helpful training for the commitments of the throne. George III was not the brightest of monarchs and he was certainly not the most sparkling. He had, however, several qualities that are worthy of note while, in addition, he matured in office becoming a practised politician and a man more capable of defining achievable goals. George's conscientious nature shines through his copious correspondence. It was not novel: both his predecessors were conscientious and hard-working monarchs and the same was true of each ruler since Charles II. As Prince of Wales, George II's son Frederick had given few such signs and indeed in his artistic interests, political opportunism, and self-indulgence had prefigured George IV, but as Frederick did not become king he left the task of recreating the monarchical habits associated with Charles II to his grandsons, George III's numerous progeny.

If George III was scarcely unique in being industrious, his energies were directed in different courses from those of his predecessors. In addition, he came to play a role in a political world that had grown accustomed during the last 14 years of his elderly grandfather, George II, to a monarch of lesser energy who accepted the direction of most domestic affairs by his leading ministers.

George III, in contrast to his predecessor, devoted considerable energy to domestic politics and the internal workings of his ministries. Whereas George I and II had been principally concerned with the army and foreign affairs, George III, although interested, particularly in the latter, had different priorities. His stress on domestic policy was an aspect of concern for a proper conduct of British government and society, a concern that also illustrated his committed Anglicanism, his determination to ensure the proper government of the Church of England, his interest in public morality and, not least, his desire that the royal family should set an example of appropriate behaviour. George's cultural preferences, particularly his interest in the work of Handel, were related to his moral concerns. Handel said of George: "While that boy lives, my music will never want a protector".

To further his goals, George III thought it necessary that he personally take a central political role. This was not only his constitutional role as one of the three elements in the constitution, but also his moral duty. The two fused in the potent idea of George as a "patriot king", a notion that stemmed from Viscount Bolingbroke's earlier discussion of such a concept in his *Idea of a Patriot King* (1749), which called for a monarch powerful enough to override parties. These were the ideas so beloved of Frederick, and which were inculcated in George as a youth. George was influenced by the concept of patriarchal government implicit in Bolingbroke's book. Thus, in maintaining his right to choose ministers and his ability to block legislation, George was ensuring that he could discharge his functions and, to use a concept that he understood, serve. The King was to act as a political redeemer, a notion that reflected a powerful optimistic element in the political iconography of kingship.[9]

For George, these roles were hindered primarily by the self-interest of others, more particularly by the willingness of politicians to group together for factional ends, most particularly the pursuit of office. As much as any continental ruler who did not have to face a powerful representative institution, George was determined to reject the objectives and politics of faction, to thwart the efforts of unacceptable politicians to force their way into office. The determination of his grandfather, George II, to pick his own ministers had played an important role in the instability of 1742–6 and 1754–7, but in the case of George III there was an additional problem: like other rulers, George found it most difficult to create acceptable relationships with senior political figures at his accession, when he had to persuade politicians who had enjoyed a good working relationship with his predecessor, and those who had looked for a dramatic change, to adjust to the wishes of a new monarch. This was largely responsible for the ministerial instability of the 1760s, and the anxieties, tensions, and hostile images of that period helped to colour subsequent views of the King.

George's opponents argued that he acted in an unconstitutional fashion, and Whig historians naturally believed them. It was, however, the assertion of royal will that was crucial. The real problem in the eyes of the politicians, whatever they alleged, was not George's unconstitutional tendencies, but the opposite – that for the first time since William III a monarch was determined to deploy to the full powers that could be seen as his. Except, perhaps, with George Grenville in May 1765, when George III climbed down, with particular respect to Stuart Mackenzie and control of Scottish patronage, George III was prepared for confrontation, although he frequently complained that it would ruin his health and endanger his mental stability. He displayed a cool nerve, total conviction of rectitude, and bloody-minded determination to have his way. Opponents were enraged, spiteful, and helpless. The myth of despotism was their only recourse.

George III found that he was expected by many politicians to obey a set of unwritten conventions that dictated his choice of minsters. The fourth Duke of Devonshire, a member of the inner Cabinet, argued that George should retain his grandfather George II's minsters:

> The Duke of Newcastle had united with him the principal nobility, the moneyed men and that interest which had brought about the [Glorious] Revolution, had set this Family [the Hanoverian dynasty] on the throne, and supported them in it, and were not only the most considerable party but the true solid strength that might be depended on for the support of government ... they were infallibly the people that the King must trust to for the effectual support of his government.[10]

George had different views. Having made his favourite Lord Bute first minister in 1762 and seen him fail to retain his position in the face of bitter criticism, George complained to the French ambassador in 1763 about the spirit of fermentation and the excessive licence which prevails in England. It was essential to neglect nothing that could check that spirit and to employ firmness as much as moderation. He was very determined not to be the toy of factions ... and his fixed plan was to establish his authority without breaking the law.[11]

Thus the ambiguity of a number of constitutional points, such as the collective responsibility of the Cabinet and the degree to which the monarch had to choose his minsters from those who had the confidence of parliament, exacerbated a political struggle that was essentially a commonplace of monarchical regimes, the efforts of a new ruler to take control of the government. It was not until 1770 that George found, in the person of Lord North, a satisfactory minister who could manage parliament.

George's earlier attempts to do so helped to spawn a critical political literature that condemned his alleged despotic attitudes and policies, a literature that influenced the American response to the government's plan to increase its American revenues. Failure in the subsequent war led to the fall of North and in 1783–4 George, in the eyes of his opponents, breached several fundamental political conventions in his attempt to create and sustain a new and (to him) acceptable ministry, but the subsequent political and popular effect was far less damaging than that created by George's support for Bute: the loss of America had been a cathartic experience and the particular circumstances of 1783–4 made it harder to present Fox-North as a "patriot opposition". Instead, the notion of a "patriot king" above party seemed to be fulfilled, and the royal-backed Pitt ministry achieved considerable success in the general election of 1784.

Some additional light upon George III's views is thrown by the Morgan-Grenville papers recently deposited in the British Library, a collection that includes letters of the King that are not published in the edition of his correspondence. The King took great pains with the choice of the governors of his sons.[12] In 1780, he appointed Colonel Richard Grenville as a governor for his son, Frederick, Duke of York, who was going to Germany to reside as Prince-Bishop of Osnabrück. In Grenville's instructions, George noted:

Though in this country I highly disapprove of masquerades, I do not put any injunction to his not frequenting them at Hanover, where the Officer of the Guard has power to prevent all irregularities, and in reality it is necessary from the established custom in Germany of not permitting the Bourgeoisie to mix with the Nobility but in Mask at Balls and Assemblies ... must attend Divine Worship in the Chapel of my Palace every Sunday Morning.

The following year, George wrote of "the anxiety I have for the success of my endeavours to fit my children for the various stations they may fill, and that they may be useful and a credit to their Family.[13] Aside from admonitions to read the classics and not to gamble, George revealed his sense that affairs in Britain were so disturbed that it was sensible for Frederick to be abroad: "though I miss him terribly, yet every hour convinces me that the sending him abroad has probably saved him from perdition".[14] Other letters reveal George as a caring or fussy parent, depending on one's perspective:

> I find you do not forsee any inconvenience in my permitting my son to sup at the houses of the first Class of Nobility and partake of the little balls that are sometimes given at this time of the year ... trust it will not diminish his inclination to pursue his studies. One great comfort I have is that I find by his letters that his attachment to me is visibly increasing which considering how much I love him is you may be certain a principal object with me.[15]

> I cannot expect to put an old head on young shoulders though I wish his love for reading was greater.[16]

As the political crisis deepened in Britain, George III became more convinced of the value of a German upbringing. In 1783, he wrote to Grenville about the future William IV:

> I hope speedily to send William to Germany not thinking this a safe place on many accounts for one of his age and not less so who by having been two years abroad must expect more liberty than I can approve on this side of the water ... Frederick had succeeded so well that his example cannot be too closely followed ... William is rather giddy and has rather too much the manners of his profession, polishing and composure are the ingredients wanting to make him a charming character.[17]

Aside from throwing vital light on George III's views about the upbringing of his children, often a crucial guide to character, his correspondence also offers valuable indicators about his constitutional views and political practice. In 1784, he wrote to William:

> I am glad to find you propose being more regular in your correspondence, it is impossible you cannot want for topics if you take pains to improve your mind; the natural attendance whilst at sea certainly was no advantage to your manners nor could your education be so closely followed as could be wished either in your station as a prince or as an officer for seamanship is but a very small part of the requisites necessary in superior commands and for want of which the service has on many opportunities most fatally suffered. The knowledge of the springs that actuate men is necessary to know how to turn them to the pursuits that are honorable to themselves or of utility to the state; that you may by diligence become what it must be your own desire as well as that of those who wish you well will ever by my objective.

His preference for stability was indicated by a letter of 29 July 1783 in which, writing of Frederick, he claimed "till things of *every kind* have taken a more solid turn here, he can neither acquire advantage nor comfort here". On 13

February 1784, he presented himself as the bulwark of the constitution, with a somewhat uncomplicated reading of a more complex situation:

> The present strange phenomenon, a majority not exceeding 30 in the House of Commons thinking that justifies the stopping the necessary supplies when the House of Lords by a majority of near two to one and at least that of the People at large approve of my conduct and see as I do that not less is meant than to render the Crown and the Lords perfect cyphers; but it will be seen that I will never submit to so degrading a situation.

George III's conservative and often moralistic conviction of his crucial constitutional role was, thanks to the signs of support for royal policy in early 1784, married to a greater awareness of the possible popular resonance of the Crown. Thus, George could feel in the 1780s that the monarch could reach out, beyond antipathy and factional self-interest on the part of politicians, to a wider, responsible, and responsive royalist public opinion. After the unsuccessful attempt by Margaret Nicolson to assassinate him in 1786, George wrote on 29 August about "the interposition of Providence on the late attempt on my life by a poor insane woman ... I have every reason to be satisfied with the impression it has awakened in this country, where perhaps my life is at present of more consequence than I could wish".

Thus, in the mid-1780s, George III was able to create a political world that accorded with his aspirations at his accession: royal proclamations could be used to galvanize public opinion on a range of issues. This contrasted greatly with the situation from 1763 on for the rest of that decade: his apparent unpopularity and his failure to create a stable effective ministry. The early 1770s had brought an improvement, although it was one that was to be swallowed up by the American crisis. In July 1773, Sir Joshua Reynolds wrote after his return from the review of the fleet:

> The King is exceeding delighted with his reception at Portsmouth. He said to a person about that he was convinced he was not so unpopular as the news papers would represent him to be. The Acclamations of the people were indeed prodigious. On his return all the country assembled in the Towns where he changed horses. At Godalming every man had a branch of a tree in his hand and every woman a nosegay which they presented to the King (the horses moving as slow as possible) till he was up to the knees in flowers, and they all singing in a tumultuous manner, God save the King. The King was so affected that he could not refrain shedding abundance of tears, and even joined in the Chorus.

Portsmouth arguably was a special case. Huge numbers were directly dependent on the Crown, and any association with the Royal Navy was popular. Aside from this evidence of royal popularity, which was to be repeated when the King visited Portsmouth in 1778, Reynolds' letter also sheds useful light on other aspects of George III:

When he came to Kew he was so impatient to see the Queen that he opened the chaise himself and jumped out before any of his attendants could come to his assistance. He seized the Queen, whom he met at the door, round the waist and carried her in his arms into the room; I trouble with these particulars as everything relating to Kings is worth hearing.

An instance happened today which shows to what an amazing degree of minuteness the King's knowledge extends in regard to the connections of men, one Echard a Dutchman was showing the King his inventions for draining land, and said he was in hopes of being employed to drain the Flats in Bedfordshire but that the Duke of Bedford's steward gave him but little hopes. The King turned to Sir William Chambers, you, says he, are going to Blenheim, the Duke of Marlborough's Steward (calling him by his name) is nephew to Palmer, the Duke of Bedford's Steward, perhaps if you will use your interest with him, he will persuade his uncle to employ Mr Echard. This is only one instance in a thousand which I mention more as it happened but today, his knowledge of this kind is incredible he knows the connections of very man that he has anything to do with, and every circumstance about them.[18]

This ability helped George in his political management. He had a good grip of the composition of both Houses of Parliament and of the interests and connections of peers and MPs. As a consequence, George was in no doubt about the results to be desired from particular electoral contests and his correspondence reflected this. In September 1780, George wrote to John Robinson, Joint-Secretary to the Treasury and a crucial informant: "There cannot be the smallest doubt that driving Sir Lawrence Dundas out of the Orkneys is a very desirable object. I am clear Mr Robinson ought to encourage the Lord Advocate of Scotland to manage this business.[19] Secret Service funds were indeed provided and the following month the government candidate won the election, having secured control of the head count; although in February 1781 he was unseated for his misconduct of the election.

The same letter, one only recently deposited in the British Library, also made it clear, however, that George's close interest in the mechanics of politics, an interest that he had somewhat shunned at the idealistic outset of his reign, was related to his determination to maintain his constitutional and political position. He wrote of the unsuccessful attempt to negotiate through Frederick Montagu a coalition with the opposition, "I never have seen any part of Opposition inclined to make the smallest concessions, and no power on Earth shall ever reduce me to deliver myself up into the hands of any of them".

Such obduracy created greater problems for his minsters when in the 1790s George III opposed the extension of rights to Catholics in Ireland or Britain. Arguing that such moves would breach his coronation oath, George stated that he would not give royal assent to such legislation. This helped to precipitate Pitt's resignation in 1801 and the fall of the Grenville ministry in 1807.

In some respects, George reflected the stronger emphasis on a monarchical, as opposed to a "balanced", constitution that characterized the 1790s.[20] George's attitude also made religious issues even more central in the politics of the early 19th century than they might otherwise have been. His firmness, not to say rigidity, contrasted with the more flexible attitude of his non-Anglican predecessors, George II, George I, William III and, arguably, Charles II; it also helped to focus the defence of order, hierarchy, and continuity much more on religion than would otherwise have been the case in a period of Revolutionary threats. The insistence upon religious uniformity as a qualification for full civil rights was undermined by, and in turn undermined, the Union with Ireland of 1801, and had the Thirteen Colonies remained part of the Empire this might also have been a source of renewed strife.

George was motivated not only by his religious convictions, but also by the argument that the position of the Church of England rested on fundamental parliamentary legislation. Any repeal would also thus challenge the constitutional safeguards that were similarly founded and secured. It is not therefore surprising that Edmund Burke's emphasis in his *Reflections on the Revolution in France* on continuity and the value of the Glorious Revolution found favour with George III. His duty was involved in resisting radicalsim at home and French atheism abroad. What might initially be more surprising is that his heir, George IV, came to share his father's concern about the constitutional importance of confessional privileges and to see the maintenance of the Revolution Settlement as part of his duty. As a young man, Prince George appeared flexible, sceptical, and in touch with the "progressive" intellectual notions which viewed denominationally defined civil rights as anachronistic. The enthusiasms of youth rarely last and in George IV's case there were potent additional reasons for him to change his opinion: the pressures that came from royal office and the anxieties that stemmed from the collapse of the old order in France.

Yet, whereas George III's resistance to Catholic Emancipation had been successful, George IV had, despite bitter hostility, to accept it. This reflected different political circumstances, but also a shift in the position of the monarchy, as well arguably as the contrasting character of the two monarchs. Long-term trends lessened the role of the monarchy despite George III's growing popularity from the 1783–4 crisis on. The growth of business and the increased scope of government lessened the ability of one man, whether monarch or minister, to master the situation. This helped to encourage the development of the Cabinet. The ministries of Pitt the Younger (1783–1801, 1804–6) and Lord Liverpool (1812–27) were especially important in this process. The discussions and decisions of the inner core of ministers, the Cabinet council, became more formal. Collective responsibility and loyalty to the leading minister increased, and this strengthened the Cabinet's ties with that minister and increased his power with reference to the monarch: Cabinet unanimity was a potential weapon against the Crown. When it could be obtained, most obviously with the mass resignations of 1746, such unanimity was effective, but, conversely, a lack of Cabinet unity could strengthen the king's position with respect to the Cabinet, as with the clash between George III and Pitt over Catholic Emancipation in 1801. George IV muttered against his ministries and ministers, but he was not strong enough to overthrow them. Liverpool was strongly supported by his Cabinet. Royal influence and patronage declined with the abolition of sinecures, the diminishing influence of Court favourites, and the growing accountability of parliament.

Personal factors were very important to this process: the breakdown of George III's health in 1788 and the consequent Regency Crisis of 1788–9, the subsequent slackening of his grasp, and his later illnesses; the lack of interest displayed by George IV; the impact of Pitt's longevity in office. As a consequence, greater Cabinet cohesion and influence, and consistent united Cabinet control of policymaking was more a feature from the 1790s on than of the 1780s. The monarchy, or perhaps the *image* of the monarchy, was reconstructed in important ways in the the later years of George III's reign. The peculiar patriotism of war and the King's virtual disengagement from day-to-day politics combined fruitfully to facilitate the celebration less of the reality and more of the symbol of monarchy.[21] The jubilee celebrations of 1809 were a case in point. In this sense, the precondition of the creation of a popular monarchy was the perceived decline in the Crown's political authority; although the somewhat paranoid Fox, who had never freed himself from ideas of royal conspiracies, felt able to tell his nephew Holland in 1804: "There is not a power in Europe, no not even Bonaparte's that is so unlimited", as monarchical authority in Britain.[22] J J Sack, however, has recently reexamined the question and argued that "ignoring seminal moments, such as royal jubilees or funerals, the glorification of George III or that of the rest of his family by the loyalist press, seems ... tinged with qualification and unease".[23]

Nevertheless, such authority was very much that of the government, rather than simply the monarch, and within the government the political role of the monarch, particularly in the initiation of policy, declined. This was an uneven, hesitant process, but it can be seen as beginning under George III; although Robert Bucholz has suggested that Anne "anticipated" the process.[24]

George IV was not a man able effectively to resist the trend towards a lesser political role for the monarch, however much he might spasmodically insist on his views of his own importance. He lacked his father's strong sense of duty, as well obviously as his moral concern, and the absence of both was reflected in his failure to follow George III's pattern of royal diligence. Fifty-seven at his accession, his stamina weakened by laziness, self-indulgence, and poor health, George IV's agenda was dominated by more immediate concerns. It was difficult for a monarch to speak convincingly about the constitution when he was perceived as more interested in the Civil List. At the outset of his reign, George sought to divorce his long-estranged wife, the allegedly disreputable Caroline, and to remove her royal status: the ministry introduced a retrospective Bill of Pains and Penalties in the House of Lords to dissolve the marriage and deprive her of her royal title. The press lapped up the sexual details and engaged in a vicious and personal debate about whether Caroline was a wronged woman or a disgrace to her sex. Her cause was taken up by the public, the debate lent focus and interest to political controversy, and the government felt obliged to abandon its campaign against her, although she was successfully denied a coronation.

The contrast with the domestic life of the uxorious George III was readily apparent. George IV could scarcely have issued a proclamation against vice and immorality as the pious George III did in 1787. George III set standards of prudence and austerity that have been characterized as "middle class". Cartoonists lampooned George III and Queen Charlotte for austerity and boring parsimony, while excoriating their sons for extravagance. In addition, George IV scarcely displayed the ability to manage scandal. Instead, there was much that was ridiculous as well as degrading about the Divorce Bill and the coronation of 1821. Fortunately for George, Caroline died in 1821.

The coronation was followed in 1821–2 by popular visits to Ireland, Hanover, and Scotland. George's wearing of Highland dress was particularly successful in courting popularity in Scotland.[25] Thereafter, he retreated from the public face of monarchy, and after 1823, bar the ceremonial opening and proroguing of Parliament, he made no public appearances in London. Instead, he spent most of his time in Brighton and Windsor: one of the reasons George showed himself so rarely in London was that he was very unpopular there. This was no longer the prince who had built so grandly[26] and strove in his own fashion to compete with Napoleon. The contrast with the restored Bourbons in France is striking. Philip Mansel's recent study *The Court of France 1789–1830* argues that the French court was used most successfully to strengthen the relationship between crown and élite, not under Louis XVI, Napoleon, or Louis-Phillipe, but under Louis XVIII (1814–24) and Charles X (1824–30). These two "achieved a synthesis ... their court was neither social and domestic [like that of Louis XVI] nor aloof and autocratic like that of Napoleon I. It was a mixture of both, accessible as well as splendid, official as well as aristocratic". Far from anxiously teetering on the brink of revolution, the restored Bourbons maintained an enormous and spectacular court and an elaborate social life during what Mansel sees as a golden age of energy and optimism. It was the restoration French court, not that of George IV, that set the tone and fashion for court life throughout Europe, whether in female dress in England, mourning in Naples, or receptions in Turin. The Hanoverian court has received less attention than that of the Bourbons and it is symptomatic that the main scholarly study is devoted to the situation a century earlier.[27] The Hanoverian court lacked the cultural presence and impact of its Tudor and Stuart predecessors. It was also less magnificent.

George IV might have been termed the "first gentleman in Europe", but as monarch he lacked charisma, and was widely believed to have no sense of integrity; his reign was a lost opportunity for assertive monarchy. In some respects, the history of the British monarchy has been often such. James I failed to unify England and Scotland, and his Stuart successors found it impossible to create a domestic consensus or to win glory abroad. The Glorious Revolution did not produce an uncontested succession, or lead to the accession of vigorous monarchs with children. George I, II, and III were not without success, but under George IV and William IV British monarchy lacked flair and George IV had a general and sustained unpopularity that was greater than that of his Hanoverian predecessors.

William IV's reign can be seen as beginning the process of revival that was to culminate in the development of imperial splendour under Victoria and Edward VII. Like his successors, William IV had to and could adapt to political reform. The hostility of the House of Lords to reform led Lord Grey, the leader of the Whig government, to remark that the situation was "too like what took place in France before the Revolution". Majorities in the House of Commons for reform and popular agitation, including riots in Bristol, Merthyr, and Nottingham, led to a political crisis, and William eventually felt it necessary reluctantly to agree that he would make enough new peers to create a majority reform in the Lords. This led the Lords to give way, and thus to the First Reform Act of 1832. In the cartoon *The Reformers' Attack on the Old Rotten Tree*, which advocated electoral reform, William was portrayed on "Constitution Hill" applauding the process of reform and surrounded by respectful figures representing England, Scotland, and Ireland. He was seen as wanting to be a "constitutional" monarch, which he indeed sought to be. William's (alleged) support for the Bill was used extensively, and to considerable effect, by supporters of Reform in the 1831 election. However, an assessment of the political role of William IV is complicated by his dismissal of Melbourne's Whig ministry in 1834, "the last time a British monarch dismissed his ministers and called on others to take their place".[28] Certainly, contemporaries saw parallels between 1783–4 and 1834–5; but crucially, the sequel was different: Pitt won the 1784 election, Peel lost the 1835 election. William was somewhat eccentric, his conversations going off on a tangent, but he was popular and seen as having integrity. William's service to the state was popular: mainly his naval service, but also (to a lesser extent) his (ultimate) flexibility over reform in the 1830s.

This was not the cause of the ultras. Indeed, from William's reign on, the British monarchy was not associated with the forces of political conservatism, as it would have been had his brother Ernest, Duke of Cumberland, been king. Whether Edward VIII would have led in that direction is unclear, but his abdication represented another failure of the possibility of assertive monarchy. Arguably, this is why Britain is still a monarchy – where are the other crowned heads of Europe who followed their own way now? – but any emphasis on successful adaptation to political change in Britain may appear complacent. It is only in hindsight that patterns appear clear. There was nothing predictable about political developments in 1827–32 and a different attitude on the part of the monarch, and indeed a different position for the monarchy, might well have been crucial. A fit George III would doubtless have provided such an alternative. That cannot, however, imply that the "wrong" course was followed; but simply that British political culture in the early 19th century was changed by the decline of the monarchy in the person of one of its most flamboyant, and in many respects pathetic, figures, the self-centred George IV, a man of more sensibility than sense.

Footnotes to this Chapter may be found on pages 364–66.

11: William Doyle

The French Revolution and Monarchy

THE FRENCH REVOLUTION is one of that handful of historical events that everybody knows, or thinks they know, something about, even if what they know is culled largely from *A Tale of Two Cities* or *The Scarlet Pimpernel*; and these days, not the books either, but rather the films of the books. One image dominates these snapshot perceptions: the guillotine, that uniquely gory, inhuman, mechanical decapitator, the chosen instrument of social resentment and class terror, surrounded by the screaming mob, and grim and vengeful lower-class harridans, knitting, and ticking off the aristocratic heads as they rolled into the basket. Everybody knows this. Everybody has seen a version, or several versions, of this lurid scene, and has never forgotten it, and recognizes it instantly when it recurs. It *is* the French Revolution. They also know, though perhaps rather more vaguely, that the most illustrious of the aristocratic victims of terror were a king and queen. They know it was a Louis, though probably not which one – there were so many. They probably do know that his queen was called Marie Antoinette, much more of a one-off name to remember. If they know that, they probably also know that she made one very silly remark: *let them eat cake*. Silly it undoubtedly was, but surely (so the thinking proceeds) not heinous enough to cost her her head. Such a terrible penalty for such an innocent quip. And so the word slips out: *innocence*. It is the catalyst that makes the drama of the guillotine work. Whatever its victims had done, they did not deserve *this*. What they did deserve never then enters into it.

A further mental leap follows: if the French Revolution killed the king and his consort, then the Revolution must have been in essence anti-monarchical. This was certainly the reflex of the Duke of Edinburgh who, explaining the Queen's refusal to attend the celebrations to mark the 200th anniversary of the fall of the Bastille in 1989, declared that a movement which murdered monarchs was not something to celebrate. President François Mitterand knew as well as anybody what dangerous associations the memory of the Revolution had: that was why he emphasized that the Bicentenary was celebrating 200 years of the Rights of Man, something that could be completely separated from the guillotine, and terror, and regicide. But it was no good. People refused to take the Revolution apart in their minds; and the most successful historians of the bicentenary year were those who most clearly proclaimed that the Revolution was all of a bloodthirsty piece, and could not be meaningfully disaggregated – François Furet in French, Simon Schama in English.[1]

But was the French Revolution anti-monarchical from the start? Only, it seems to me, in a very restricted sense, and one that constituted no necessary threat to the persons of Louis XVI and his Queen. What the French unquestionably were against in 1789 was *absolute* monarchy. They wanted representative government. They believed that they were overtaxed, over-governed, and misgoverned too. The crisis out of which the Revolution emerged, after all, arose because the state's finances were out of control, and ministers admitted as much. Now, in objective terms, much of this was Louis XVI's fault. As an absolute monarch, he took all the final decisions on every great matter of state. He was, therefore, directly, responsible for France's fateful involvement in the American War of Independence; and for the overspending that followed. Louis XVI's insistence that he understood finance (so clearly brought out in John Hardman's recent biography)[2] and his consequent refusal to surrender financial oversight to anyone else, was surely one of the more important precipitants of the old regime's final crisis. Yet his subjects do not appear to have blamed him for any of this. Hardly a note of criticism against the King personally is heard before July 1789. There was much joking and lampooning, of course, about his sexual incompetence; and historians recently have made a good deal of this, arguing for a decline in respect for the monarchy, if not a positive "desacralization".[3] But the sexual habits and personal inadequacies of French monarchs had been a subject for lampoons and popular jokes since at least the time of Henry III, back in the 16th century. Interestingly, it is historians born and brought up in republics who have made the most of the "desacralization" idea: those born subjects of a monarch know that sovereigns can take a huge amount of criticism and ridicule without monarchy itself ever coming remotely under threat. What is most striking about the atmosphere in France in the late 1780s is the almost touching faith that most of Louis XVI's subjects retained in their King's benevolence and good intentions. In a totally traditional way, they blamed ministers and courtiers for everything that had gone wrong, for misleading the King and abusing his credulity. If the King knew the facts, the message comes through again and again, he would not allow these things to happen; he would ensure that justice was done; he would protect his people. The appeal of representative government was that it would give him this true information. The purpose of representation was to control ministers, not the King; to outflank their control of access to the sovereign by putting him in direct touch with the concerns of his subjects. That was, after all, the historical role of the assembly which all opponents of the government were calling for from 1787 to 1789, the Estates-General. Elections to these bodies had traditionally been accompanied, as this one was, by the drawing-up of *cahiers*, grievances lists precisely intended to bring the complaints of his subjects directly to the King's ears. It is largely on the basis of these *cahiers* that these claims can be made about what the French thought of their monarch in 1789.

The original aim of the French Revolution, therefore, was not to destroy monarchy, but to change an absolute monarchy into a constitutional one. Popular antagonism throughout the struggles of 1788 and the first half of 1789 was directed against the nobility and clergy, the so-called "privileged orders", rather than against the King. Although Louis XVI was dismally ineffective in holding the ring in these conflicts, it was largely perceived that he *was* holding the ring rather than taking sides with the privileged. If the first suspicion about his conduct arose over the troop movements revoked after the defiance of Paris on 14 July, goodwill towards the King survived the crisis. Only three weeks later, the destruction of the old social order on the night of 4 August concluded to cries of *Vive le Roi* and the order that a commemorative medal be struck, proclaiming Louis XVI "Restorer of French Liberties".

It was only when the National Assembly turned, in the following weeks, to drafting the rules for a constitutional monarchy that the problems began. Almost the first question they confronted was that of whether the King should have a veto on legislation, and if so, whether it should be permanent or merely delaying. When the King appeared hesitant to accept the ultimate decision in favour of delaying power only, the result was the march of the Parisian women to Versailles in the first days of October. Scenes of riot in the palace were followed by the famous procession back to Paris, which, in terms of the impact of the French Revolution on monarchy in general, was one of its most decisive occurrences. For, whether they applauded the event or deplored it, all onlookers could agree with Richard Price's famous description of the procession back to Paris as subjects leading their king in triumph. The King had been taken prisoner in his own palace, and humiliated. He was no longer a free agent. He had not even, like Charles I, been defeated in battle. He had simply surrendered himself, and his power, to a mob.

These events broke the mystique of monarchy far more decisively than Louis' execution 39 months later. After all, French kings had been killed before: there was Henry III, and Henry IV, and as recently as 1757 a would-be assassin had stabbed Louis XV. Like mocking and lampooning the monarch, regicide was nothing new in French history. Louis XVI was not the first king to be put on trial either, of course. That dubious distinction belonged to Charles I of England – by whom (John Hardman has recently reminded us yet again[4]) Louis XVI was fascinated long before it was conceivable that he might one day share the same fate. Nor was Louis XVI the first monarch to be killed by his subjects even in the 18th century. Many suspected that that was what had happened to Charles XII of Sweden, although the issue remains open to this day.[5] Most people thought Catherine the Great had murdered her husband, Peter III; and in the spring of 1792, at a masked ball in Stockholm, Gustavus III was assassinated by dissident noblemen. Interestingly, however, with his dying words Gustavus placed the blame not on the aristocrats with whom he had been in conflict for a number of years, but on *Jacobins* – friends, or agents, of the French Revolution. At this moment, Louis XVI was still on the throne of France; but here was a dying king stating the conviction that revolutionary France was the natural enemy of all monarchs.

That conviction surely went back to Louis XVI's captivity in Paris which began on 6 October 1789. It showed how vulnerable kingly power could be, and that there was no necessity for ordinary people to be cowed by it. It made people think about the nature of monarchical authority, how it was best maintained, and how it might be lost; it made them think about what it was for, whether it was necessary, and if so, why. All these were questions scarcely addressed in the 18th century until then. Of course, there had been plenty of discussion about the nature of monarchical authority, and its legitimate limits, but nobody seriously thought of turning any monarchy into a republic. Republics, the orthodoxy was, could only work in small states, like the Greek cities of classical antiquity. Most contemporary republics were certainly of that sort. Even the biggest, the Dutch Republic, was in reality a loose federation of smaller units. So ingrained was this sense that large countries could not work as republics, that it took the intervention of an iconoclastic outsider, Tom Paine, to convince even the American rebels against George III, in his pamphlet *Common Sense*, that they could do without a king, and even then the experience of the Articles of Confederation convinced many Americans of the need for some sort of monarch – which in some senses the American president is during his term of office. Although the American republic worked well enough to secure its independence, as with so much about 18th century America, Europeans simply said, *it couldn't happen here*, and ignored the example, however interesting they found it.

It was, therefore, the captivity of Louis XVI in Paris, and the way the National Assembly recast the nation's institutions without reference to him, which convinced people that republicanism was a viable proposition for an important European state. Whether onlookers welcomed or deplored the prospect depended on how they viewed the circumstances which had brought about the captivity. Burke, launching a belated debate on the Revolution with his *Reflexions* of 1790, clearly abominated the idea. He was first stung into writing precisely by Price's celebration of the October Days, which Burke saw as the work of the swinish multitude. For Burke, the French monarchy was a natural growth, something to be improved, but treasured, rather than abandoned at the behest of a mob. He was outraged at the insult offered to a queen whose youthful charm had captured his imagination on a visit to Paris years before. Naturally, monarchs, with the possible exception of the Emperor Leopold II, were horrified by the prospect of Louis XVI marooned in what seemed a hostile capital, unable to influence in any way the fate of his country – or so at least they presumed, since after the October days he never raised the slightest demur at any piece of legislation put to him for sanction by the National Assembly. What Louis XVI himself thought also had to be presumed, since he said very little to anyone, as had always been his way. Most of the evidence we have for what he thought comes from Marie Antoinette, who had her own agenda, not necessarily the same as his. What finally dispelled the last doubts was his attempt to escape from his metropolitan captivity in the Flight to Varennes in June 1791. None could doubt, after that, that this king was unreconciled to what had happened to him and his power since 1789; and whereas what he really intended by the flight remains a matter for scholarly disagreement[6], everybody at the time, on all sides, thought his intention was to escape the country entirely, and only return accompanied by the armed cohorts of foreign monarchs. The capture, and the return of the fugitives to Paris, was the October days all over again, but (as it were) in technicolour. Popular republicanism in France now came out into the open, while rulers abroad began to talk about military intervention to restore the King of France to his rightful position and prerogatives.

From then on, the French monarchy was doomed. True, the fiction was elaborated that the royal family had been kidnapped, the King was reinstated, and accepted the new constitution. He remained on the throne until 10 August 1792. But hardly anybody by now believed that a constitutional monarchy with him at the head of it could work, or was even worth making work. He himself continued to dream, if no longer of escape, at least of rescue. He welcomed war in the spring of 1792 as the opportunity to bring that moment closer, even though he knew that his opponents only wanted it in order to bring him down. As a result, further humiliations were in store, even before the monarchy was overthrown. On 20 June, for instance, after he had refused to rescind vetoes on legislation against presumed traitors, a mob penned him in a corner at the palace, and amid much jeering and coarse insults, forced him to wear the red cape of liberty and to drink the Nation's health. With dignity and resignation, he did so: but refused to yield on the veto. At a late stage, he was beginning to acquire some stature in adversity, assets he would build on further at his trial. On that occasion, again with calm and dignity, he claimed either innocence or ignorance as each charge was read to him. These displays of stoicism in the face of mortal danger, carried through to his behaviour on the scaffold itself, did more for his reputation, and that of monarchy itself, than all the stumbles and fumbles, the gaucheries and the stupidities, that marked his public behaviour over much of his reign. As a reigning monarch, Louis XVI had always lacked the desirable presence and dignity. Faced with martyrdom for monarchy, he suddenly acquired it. Perhaps he had learned something from all that reading about Charles I.

By the time the execution happened, nobody outside France was surprised. It was all that could be expected from a movement that had consistently humiliated the King ever since October 1789. Once the monarchy had been overthrown, amid considerable bloodshed as the Swiss Guards attempted to defend the Tuileries Palace against the forces of the Paris Commune, the fate of the former King seemed a forgone conclusion. They would execute him. Nothing else seemed safe for the new republic. The people of Paris certainly thought that, as did large numbers of the members of the Convention now ruling France. Yet close inspection reveals that a large number of people were not in favour of executing him. While the Convention agreed at his trial almost unanimously that he was guilty of the charges brought against him, the decision to execute him passed, famously, by a single vote; and almost half the Convention subsequently voted for a reprieve.[7] Here were deputies who thought it would do no good to execute an adversary already defeated; that it would be needlessly provocative; that it would make the National Convention seem the tool of the bloodthirsty populace of Paris, which only three weeks after the fall of the monarchy had massacred hundreds of inmates of the capital's prisons; and that it would make it infinitely more difficult to restore a monarchy later. Nobody made this last point in their speeches on the question. In the atmosphere of late 1792, it would have been suicidal. But we can be certain that it was uppermost in the minds of many. This is the great paradox of the French Revolution's impact on monarchy. For every person whom it convinced that kingship could, and should, be dispensed with, there were many more (even if they were not in a majority in the Convention) who found that the whole experience demonstrated the *necessity* of monarchy.

Nobody at all had doubted it at the start. One wonders whether, if the King had been somebody other than the wooden and unimaginative Louis XVI, married to a lethally silly woman, it would ever have been called into doubt at all. The fatal problem was that a reluctant king, or more often, a king presumed to be reluctant, could only be made compliant by unleashing the Parisian populace against him; and that made mob rule seem the only possible alternative to monarchy. Once he had been brought to Paris, it was assumed that this ploy would not be needed again; and the National Assembly blithely continued drafting its constitution, assuming that Louis had learned his lesson and would not drag his feet again. It took him for granted; and only learned its mistake when he tried to escape. In the aftermath of Varennes, overt republicanism surfaced; and the mask it wore was that of the Parisian people, whom the constitution makers had planned to exclude from all say under their constitutional monarchy. Now they realized how right they had been: a king was the surest ally of men of property against the destructive envy of those who had nothing. He symbolized authority and hierarchy as nothing else could.

So the months after the *débacle* of Varennes had seen the first serious attempts to conciliate and win over Louis XVI to the virtues of the constitution, by men who saw that France could not do without a king. With the King they had, unfortunately, it was too late. He was beyond winning over, embittered by all that they had allowed to happen to him – thereby confirming all the worst suspicions that republicans had of him. So the country polarized into those who felt that the Revolution could never be safe so long as this king sat on the French throne, and those who believed that the gains of the Revolution would never be stably established without a monarchy to endow them with some permanence and continuity. If the execution of him whom his enemies loved to call Louis the Last was intended to settle this conflict, it signally failed to do so. Within two months of the execution, a royalist rebellion had broken out in the Vendée that would rumble on for a decade. If all that the persistence of royalism, and the support given to it by an ever-widening circle of foreign enemies, including the British, did in the short run was to provoke further gratuitous anti-monarchical gestures, like the execution of Marie Antoinette after a ludicrous trial and a range of farcical charges that nobody except Lynn Hunt could take seriously[8], none of this lent any real strength to French republicanism. The first two years of the French republic, after all, were marked by the horrific episode with whose imagery

I began: the Terror. Systematic massacre was scarcely an alluring advertisement for politics without a king. The moment the Terror was over, accordingly, men began to think of a restoration. It seems clear that among men of property at least, there was a heavy majority in favour of a monarchy from this time right down to Napoleon's seizure of power in 1799. The results of successive elections, and the measures taken by the Directory to annul them, show that plainly enough. Their only problem was their candidate. Louis XVII, Louis XVI's last remaining son, looked ideal. Still a child, and in captivity, he could be brought up as a copy-book constitutional monarch through a carefully controlled education. But he died in June 1795. That left Louis XVI's brothers, and within weeks the elder, in proclaiming himself Louis XVIII, had thrown his chance away with the Declaration of Verona, in which he pledged, if restored, to dismantle the entire work of the Revolution since 1789. Once again, the proverbial stupidity of the Bourbons had snatched defeat from the jaws of victory. In the face of Louis XVIII's intransigence, France's weary constitution-makers had no alternative but to go ahead with a republican form of government, whatever its unfortunate and bloodthirsty associations.

It never worked; but despite that Louis XVIII had to wait another 20 years before he sat securely on the throne of France. The reason was, of course, that Napoleon had captured that lost monarchist constituency which Louis had turned his back on at Verona. After four years in which a revamped republic, while avoiding further terror, signally failed to deliver the stability which royalists believed only a monarch could provide, the French propertied classes handed themselves over to a successful general who promised to impose order and respect the Revolution's gains, even if he offered no guarantees for representative government. Napoleon did all that a king was expected to do, leaving the only arguments of those who still preferred a Bourbon to him, as mere arguments of sentiment. When Louis XVIII was eventually restored, at the hands of foreign victors, only a handful of Frenchmen saw this primarily as a victory of some mystic legitimacy. It was simply that there was nobody else.

The French Revolution, therefore, though it showed for the first time that a republic in a large-European state was a practical possibility rather than a classical dream, failed to offer the prospect of such a republic working, except by Terror or (as between 1795 and 1799) repeated *coups d'état*. It was scarcely an encouraging prospect. The Revolution, therefore, though it consistently humiliated and then destroyed a king, did not destroy the appeal of monarchy. On the contrary, it reinforced that appeal with a terrifying spectacle of what life without one could be like. It was a lesson that the 19th century was to learn thoroughly. Many new states were established during the century after 1789, but hardly any were established as republics. It had become more axiomatic than ever that a viable state needed a monarch — even one, like Belgium or Italy, created with the help of insurrection. Republics in the 19th century were fleeting, and tumultuous, and therefore tended to underline the lessons of the 1790s. Only in France did a durable republic eventually established itself, almost a hundred years after the Revolution; and only then because another Bourbon, missing his chance according to an unerring family tradition, refused once again to compromise with the Revolution's legacy even though a gesture would have given him the throne.

So in the end, the French monarchy at least was destroyed by the Revolution; even if, as anyone who looks at the constitution of the Fifth Republic can see, the monarchical reflex in French political life remains powerful. Although it reinforced the case for monarchy as a general principle in Europe, the Revolution changed the sources of its strength. Monarchy now appealed not because it had always been there, and not because it was ordained by God, but because it was a symbol and guarantee of the social order. The French Revolution, and the fate of Louis XVI, largely destroyed its mystical appeal. Nineteenth-century monarchies flourished because they worked, not because they were right. Monarchy now had to earn the respect it received. It could no longer expect it as its due. Burke saw that as early as 1790 "never, never more, shall we behold that generous loyalty to rank... that proud submission, that dignified obedience, that subordination of the heart, which kept alive, even in servitude itself, the spirit of an exalted freedom." In the post-revolutionary age, one monarch could always be replaced by another; who needed a Louis so long as there was a Napoleon? Of course, new age monarchs tried to decorate themselves with traditional trappings. Napoleon gave himself a lavish coronation, and eventually, like Louis XIV and Louis XVI before him, married a Habsburg. He set up a court, created a nobility to people it. That was what people expected kings to do. The one thing they no longer expected them to do was take it all seriously enough to think that they ruled by divine right. When Charles X, who began his reign with a lavish traditional coronation at Rheims, looked like trying to revive the monarchy of the Old Regime, he did not last six years. The Revolution of 1830 summarily bundled him out, and installed another, less tradition-bound ruler in his place: Louis-Philippe, the umbrella-king, a new ruler for a new age.

But it was not simply mystical posturings that ruined Charles X. They were all of a piece with more profound misjudgments. His dream was not simply to restore the mystique of his murdered brother's monarchy, but also much of his power. What really triggered the Revolution of 1830 was the fear that the King and his friends wanted to take France back beyond the Revolution, to the absolute monarchy of the Old Regime. For the Revolution had destroyed that, too. Its original aim had been to substitute a constitutional monarchy for an absolute one. In the short term it failed: in the longer term, however, it made constitutional monarchy the only acceptable sort: that is, a monarchy that reigned in open, and, to one degree or another, institutional cooperation with its subjects. Napoleon, the first monarch to rule France after the death of Louis XVI, could afford to ignore this lesson, ruling as he did on the capital of having restored stability, and of military success – although even he had some carboard representative institutions.[9] But in all sorts of ways, he was exceptional. After 1789, other monarchs had to learn that they needed social allies, that the forces of order had to be conciliated with some say in how things were run. The age of absolutism was over. Kings who tried to perpetuate it did so at their peril.

It was not simply the example of what happened to Louis XVI, however, that taught these lessons. It was also the fact that every monarch in Europe saw his territory invaded, plundered, carved up, and often redistributed by the French, and sometimes several times over, between 1792 and 1814. Crushing military defeat, deposition or expulsion from territories often ruled for generations, could scarcely fail to dent the prestige and authority of the rulers undergoing such traumas. Eighteenth-century warfare had been about bargaining and balancing off the recognized rights of adversaries. Revolutionary and Napoleonic conflict was about winner taking all. Some monarchies did not survive this more brutal atmosphere. The most hoary and illustrious victim was the Holy Roman Empire itself, along with many a smaller German principality. But those that did resurface were often barely recognizable, and as a result their rulers had to rebuild their shattered authority on new, more utilitarian foundations. Napoleon, as heir to the Revolution, forced all rulers with whom he came into conflict to do things his way, and create their own authority anew. Like him, they did it not by appealing to their prescriptive rights and ancient, God-given authority; but to the material interests of their subjects. They now needed to win support, to earn it, rather than assume it.

Only one monarchy survived these upsets unscathed, and that was of course the Crown of Great Britain. There were, certainly, republican stirrings after Paine's *Rights of Man* was published, and in Ireland in 1798 there was a full-scale rebellion in favour of republican independence. Once war with the ancestral enemy broke out, however, the British rallied to their monarchy and lent fraternity and assistance to the French pretender. But George III and his ancestors had ruled, ever since 1688, with the cooperation and consent of their greater subjects; and for at least a century there had been no absolute, divine right monarchy to challenge in the island state. And that was largely because the islanders had chopped off their own king's head a century and a half earlier.

Footnotes to this Chapter may be found on page 366.

12: Adam Bruce

"Nemo Me Impune Lacessit"; the kingdom of the Scots to 1603

DESPITE A RESURGENCE in the study of the history of Scotland, it is a common perception that it is one comprised entirely of tragic heroes and heroic failures. Recent attempts by Hollywood to make blockbusters of the lives of some of Scotland's heroes have been but modern manifestations of an ancient tradition, rendering the history of Scotland to fit contemporary circumstances. Ever since John of Fordun traced the origin of the Scots to the elopement of Scota, the Pharaoh's daughter, with Gathelus the Greek prince, Scotland's history has been a tool in the hands of the propagandist; a weapon wielded in the fight for political and cultural autonomy.

In the medieval quest for a national ancestor, Scotland stood alone. Despite an apparent attempt by John Barbour to trace Scotland's origins to the fall of Troy, Scotland's ancestor myth remains distinct from those of England and continental Europe. Medieval scholars across Europe sought to trace the origins of their kingdoms to the princes of Troy who had escaped its fall. England claimed descent from Brutus, the French from his brother Francion, and the Catholic kings of Spain sought to unify the history of their new kingdom by claiming common descent from the Trojan prince Hispanus.[1] In Scotland the national family tree bore distinct characters, mingling Scythian origins with the descent of the Scottish church from the Apostle Andrew. While European humanist scholars sought to debunk the medieval *mythistoires* of Geoffrey of Monmouth and the monks of St Denis, Scotland's mythological roots were dusted down and rewritten by Hector Boece, whose influence on Scottish historiography remains immense.[2] How else can you measure the significance of the late 20th-century relocation of the Stone of Scone from Westminster to Edinburgh?

In his colourful book on monarchy, *Blood Royal*, the late Sir Ian Moncrieffe collaborated with Don Pottinger to produce an artistic analysis of the descent of the Crown of Scotland. Starting with King Fergus the Great emerging from the clouds and descending to James VI and I, many of the crowned heads sit with daggers in their backs or swords in their front. Queen Mary sits headless.[3] However, Sir Ian's narrative is merely one in a long and picturesque counter history to the Galfridian legend of Brutus the Trojan. As we shall see later, the purpose of these elaborate national family trees was to lend credence to the claims by successive kings of England to sovereignty over Scotland and by the Scots in their rebuttal of those claims. The conjunction of propaganda with armed conflict was not an invention of the 20th-century.

A study of the monarchy of Scotland can be divided arbitrarily into three sections. The first an analysis of the origins of the kingdom of Scots, the second an appreciation of the medieval struggle to maintain the independence of the Crown of Scotland, and the third, a reappraisal of the character of the Scottish Crown, a mongrel institution or distinctly pedigree?

The "making" of the kingdom of Scots has been well documented[5]; less easy to identify is the making of the kingdom of the Picts. In his recent history of Scotland, Michael Lynch states that, "the history of the Picts can be likened to a mystery story with few clues and no satisfactory ending".[6] Whatever the origins of the Picts, or the mystery of their disappearance, their significance in understanding Scotland's history cannot be understated. The traditional view of their bloody end at the hands of Kenneth MacAlpin has been discredited.[7] What can be ascertained is that the Pictish kingdoms coexisted over a number of centuries with the Dalriadic Scots in Argyll and the Western Highlands, the Angles of Northumbria in the south, and the Britons of Strathclyde to the southwest. Early Scottish kingship appears to have followed the Irish pattern, with different "grades" of king. In a time when kingdoms lacked defined borders or even defined subjects, different degrees of monarchy and broader rules of succession made sense. Successors to the throne came from within the *derbfine* or kindred of the late monarch. The *rigdamna* or *tanaise* who was chosen as heir apparent was usually the choice of the largest faction within the *derbfine*. Previously held theories of matrilineal succession have given way to a better understanding of the complexities of early medieval power politics.[8]

The Picts appear to have been a substantial maritime nation. Their ships harried the Romans south of Hadrian's Wall, and great war fleets assembled from a chain of naval bases. Lynch points to an episode narrated in the *Annals of Tigernach* when in 729 some 150 Pictish warships were wrecked in a storm off a headland called Ross Cuissini.[9] At its maturity, the Pictish Confederation stretched from the Forth valley to Sutherland marching with the Norsemen in Caithness and the Scots, Britons, and Angles on the western and southern boundaries. Given their maritime record, it is likely that the Picts had an understanding of Scotland's coastal geography not matched until the early modern era. Echoes of their understanding of the sea can be found in King Robert I's amphibious operations off the western seaboard in the early 14th-century, and his commissioning of Scotland's first royal yacht.

The victory of King Bridei of the Picts over the Northumbrians at Dunnichen Moss in 685 marks the start of the Pictish consolidation of power in Scotland.[10] By the late seventh century, Pictish power was centred on the kingdom of Fortriu, and contemporary chronicles referred to Fortriu as the kingdom of the Picts. Bridei, victor at Dunnichen, was King of Fortriu and High King of the Picts. It would be wrong, however, to view the Picts in isolation from their neighbours. It is likely that the royal houses of Fortriu and Dalriada intermarried. But, to misquote Clauswitz, marriage was only one method of continuing diplomacy by other means; war was the second. In an uncanny prelude to later family feuds between the kings of Scots and England, the eighth and ninth century royal houses of Fortriu and Dalriada were as often at each others throats as in each others beds. By 741, Oengus, King of the Picts, had overwhelmed the Scots at Loch Awe and assumed overlordship of Dalriada. A century later, in 839, his descendant, King Eoganan, his brother Bran, and almost the entire Pictish *derbfine* were wiped out in battle with the Norsemen, marking the effective end of the kingdom of Fortriu. In the interim there had been a dual Scoto-Pictish monarchy under Eoganan, his uncle Constantine, and his father Oengus (II), kings of Dalriada and Fortriu.

A further difficulty arises in marking the demise of the kingdom of the Picts and the rise of "Alba": the kingdom of the Scots. The medieval chronicles state that remnants of the Pictish nobility were slaughtered to a man at a particularly gruesome banquet held in their honour by Kenneth MacAlpin who then assumed the throne. In all likelihood, Kenneth was already a member of the Picto-Scottish *derbfine* who emerged out of the carnage in 839. That he called his son Constantine is perhaps a mark of dynastic continuity, or at least a desire to achieve continuity. It was later chroniclers who referred to that Constantine as Constantine I, thus breaking the continuity and marking the "official" start of the kingdom of the Scots.

King Kenneth's sleight of hand in marketing old wine in new bottles unravelled two centuries later with the last great struggle within the house of MacAlpin for the throne of Scots. For 150 years after Kenneth's death in 858, the throne passed through his two sons, Constantine and Aed, and their respective male heirs. At each stage, the Crown seems to have passed to the best placed male candidate within the *derbfine*. On the death of Malcolm II in 1034 he was succeeded by his son Duncan, rather than by his elder nephew MacBeth. Duncan's attempt to win the support of his kinsmen in the extended royal house failed after a disastrous foray into Northumbria and County Durham in 1039. In 1040, he was defeated and killed in a coup instigated by MacBeth with the support of Thorfinn "the Headcleaver", Jarl of Orkney.

MacBeth's reign, far from being the bloody prelude to the victory of Malcolm III, was relatively long and remarkably stable – so much so that he was able to go on pilgrimage to Rome in 1050. The end of his reign came not in a final confrontation at Dunsinane, but in a series of skirmishes with Malcolm, culminating in MacBeth's defeat and death at Lumphanan in 1057.[11] His burial on the sacral Isle of Iona marked the end of what one 19th-century historian called the "uncharted age" of Scottish history.[12]

If MacBeth's death brought Scotland out of the Dark Ages, it was only because later chroniclers viewed the wife of his successor as the lady with the lamp. Queen Margaret, sister of Edgar the Aetheling, married Malcolm III as his second wife in 1070. The contrast between Queen Ingibjorg, who died before 1069, and Queen Margaret, cannot be more remarkable. The former, the widow, or perhaps the daughter, of Jarl Thorfinn of Orkney, represented Scotland's ties to the north and to its Norse and Celtic roots; the latter brought

Scotland into the Anglo-Norman world and all the trappings that went with
it. Later chroniclers hailed Margaret, latterly canonized and reburied in the
abbey built at Dunfermline by Durham masons, as the woman and saint,
who dragged Scotland out of the Dark Ages, jettisoning the relics of a
superstitious past as she went. In reality, her marriage to Malcolm was
probably seen by contemporaries as a brief interruption in Scotland's Celtic
progress. Her inheritance was not immediately secure, for when Malcolm
died he was succeeded first by his brother Donald Ban, then by Ingibjorg's
son Duncan; who between them "drove out all the English who were with
King Malcolm before".[13]

But Malcolm and Margaret's sons did not disappear. Three of them Edgar,
Alexander, and David, all ascended the throne, and in retrospect their reigns,
and the years that followed under David's immediate descendants do mark
a crucial development in Scottish history. There has been much debate,
some of it still under way, on the legacy of the "Margaretsons" especially
David I. David's own achievements are by any degree remarkable. The younger
son of a second wife without any real prospect of succeeding to the throne,
he was gathered up by his brother-in-law Henry Fitz William, another younger
son, ostracized by his elder brothers, William Rufus of England and Robert
of Normandy. Together they pooled around them men from the "unfashionable"
end of Normandy, from the Cotentin peninsula and the Breton marches; men
who had been overlooked in the great parcelling out of England that followed
the Battle of Hastings. David became an integral member of Henry's court
and when he moved north to share in the government of Scotland under his
brother Alexander I, he took with him a cadre of men most of whom had
lived within a day's riding of each other in Normandy. David's new men were
rewarded with extensive landholdings in the south of Scotland, often in
addition to estates given to them by Henry I in the north of England. By the
death of David's grandson, William the Lion in 1214, Scotland had undergone
an administrative and cultural revolution seen through by the descendants
of his Norman, Breton, and Flemish followers. Their achievement was to
bring that change about without the bloody intervention that was required
in England. An analysis of the itinerary of one of David's chief supporters
shows how almost impossible it is to identify them either as Scottish or
English, and why modern attempts to distinguish between 12th-century
Scotland and England are particularly difficult.[14]

Robert de Brius, the son of Adam of Brix (or Brius) in the Cotentin was
rewarded by Henry I with land in Yorkshire and Cleveland after the battle
of Tinchebrai, in addition to his estates in Normandy. In 1124, he was granted
the lands of Annandale by David I, to which he added manors in Cumbria
so that he could break his journey from Yorkshire to Scotland. Charter evidence
shows him in attendance on Henry I and on David I as well as attending to
his estates in Yorkshire and Scotland. On his death, his vast inheritance
was divided between his two sons with the younger, Robert II, inheriting
Annandale and the manors of Hart and Hartlepool in England.[15]

This apparent "middle kingdom" came to a definite end with the Scottish wars of independence. The descendants of the men who had done homage to the kings of Scots and to the kings of England had to decide between the two. Perhaps the greatest achievement of King Robert I (the Bruce), the descendant of Robert I of Annandale, was not in evicting the English from Scotland, but in uniting the disparate elements that made up the community of the realm in Scotland into one political community. In his own bloodline, Robert I combined the MacAlpin and MacMalcolm blood of his father's grandmother with the Norman and Flemish roots of his father, and the Celtic and Gallovidian stock of his mother. In the body of King Robert, Scotland had its first truly national monarch.

The history of the medieval Scottish monarchy can perhaps best be measured by its success at holding at bay the external and internal forces that beset it. Scotland's middle age compares well with that of England. As one 18th-century historian put it when comparing Scotland's liberty with the four conquests of England from Roman to Norman by way of Dane and Saxon.

> For our heretage was ever free,
> Since Scota of Egypt tuik the sea ...
> Thus four times thirled and overhauld
> You're the great refuse of all the world[16]

The constant theme that ran through this period, and that resurfaced in the debate over Union in 1707 was whether the Crown of England was an imperial crown whose authority bounded the entire British Isles. The claim of successive kings of England to feudal superiority over Scotland was prosecuted with varying degrees of success from the 11th to the 16th centuries. The Union of the Crowns of 1603 brought these military and diplomatic conflicts to a close, but academic conflict continued through the 17th century. In Sir Thomas Craig's *De Hominio*, translated in 1695 by the Scottish historian, George Ridpath, and published with the title *Scotland's Sovereignty Asserted*, it was argued that successive kings of Scots had publicly refused to do homage to kings of England. Further, and to undoubted English indignation, it was argued that Scotland's independence and freedom from conquest had been preserved in contrast to England's several defeats and subjugations by foreign powers, culminating in Craig's assertion that the English had principally been givers than receivers of homage.[17]

This trenchant defence of Scottish liberty followed in a long train of national *mythistoires* each one designed to combat the pan-British imperial history coming from England. The English claim to feudal superiority was first canvassed by Geoffrey of Monmouth in his *History of the Kings of Britain*. Later works, culminating in the 16th-century publications of Grafton and Holinshed, put forward one central argument to assert England's pre-eminence. They claimed Brutus the Trojan as the original *arriviste* whose three sons, Locrinus, Camber, and Albanactus, divided the British Isles between them.

Locrinus, the eldest, took England, Camber Wales, and Albanactus Scotland. This ancestral division of Britain served as the basis for subsequent claims advanced through the Middle Ages that Scottish kings had frequently paid homage to the kings of England, acknowledging the *de facto* sovereignty of the southern kingdom. That kings of Scotland did pay homage is not in question, but solely for the lands they held in England. The chronicle account of Alexander III's response to his being asked to do homage for his kingdom to Henry III of England does not mince its words.[18]

Edward I, Richard II, Henry IV, and Henry VIII of England all relied on the Galfridian legend to lend legal justification for their incursions into Scotland. Scotland's response, articulated by John of Fordun in the 14th century and by Hector Boece in the 15th, first found public voice in the early 14th century Declarations of St Andrews and Arbroath. But there were other voices looking to an eventual union, or reunion of the two kingdoms. In his *History of Greater Britain* published in 1521 the historian John Mair, or Major, later Provost of St Salvator's College at St Andrews, argued that there was little historical evidence to support either country's legends of descent. Major advocated the peaceful union of the two kingdoms under one crown. This desire for amicable union was set back by the last concerted effort by the English to establish a satellite state in Scotland. On the death of James V, the English embarked on a seven-year campaign to win over the Scots. The Treaty of Greenwich in 1543 saw the betrothal of young Mary, Queen of Scots, to Edward, Prince of Wales. A year before, Henry VIII had published his *Declaration* restating English sovereignty over Scotland. To re-enforce his claim and to encourage support for the royal nuptials, English troops engaged in a systematic harrying of the south of Scotland in what became known as the "Rough Wooing". The defeat of the Scots at the battle of Pinkie in 1547, led to Queen Mary being spirited away to France in July 1548. The following year brought decisive French intervention on the side of their old allies, and by 1551 the English had departed leaving a trail of sacked and looted abbeys and other religious houses throughout the borders. Just over half a century later, Henry's great-grand nephew, James VI of Scots, assumed the English throne left barren by his Tudor cousins.

The Union of the Crowns in 1603 provides us with an opportunity to reflect on the achievements of the Stewart dynasty which held sway in Scotland from the accession of Robert II in 1371 to the abdication of Queen Mary in 1567. James VI succeeded his mother as first monarch of the Stuart dynasty, taking his father's family name. The Lennox Stuarts had adopted the French spelling of their patronym after a period of service in France which saw them created seigneurs d'Aubigny. Queen Mary, as Queen of France, also had her family name deracinated.

The Stewart dynasty has been the victim of "concise" histories of Scotland that have written off the monarchs as weak, incompetent, and victims of a family death-wish that saw very few of them die in their beds. Around this has been woven the purple prose of successive romantic historians who have set up some of the monarchs as tragic heroes, and none more so than Mary Queen of Scots. But perhaps the greater injustice has been to her second husband Henry, whom Mary made her King Consort and before that Earl of Ross and Duke of Albany. In an attempt to underline his admittedly unhealthy character, successive historians who should know better, continue to refer to him, using English custom, as "Darnley". If they want to use his pre-marital style they could at least give him his vernacular title of Master of Lennox.[19] The Stewart dynasty which, to paraphrase the dying words of James V, came in with a lass and went out with a lass, is the most enduring feature of late medieval and early modern Scotland. The dynasty may not have been as dominant as the Bruces or as decisive as the MacAlpins, but its mark on the pages of Scottish history is indelible. A complete review of the dynasty is under way, with a volume planned for each crowned head.[20]

It was Robert I (the Bruce) who settled the Crown on the Stewarts. His daughter Marjorie had married Walter Stewart and in 1318 the Scottish Parliament ratified the King's decision to prefer his daughter's offspring to those of his deceased brother Edward.[21] Edward had been nominated Robert I's heir in 1315, but his own dynastic ambitions saw him crowned High King of Ireland, in an ill-fated attempt to create a Celtic confederation spanning the Irish Sea, that was to end with his death at the battle of Dundalk in October 1318. The birth of Prince David of Scots in 1324 saw the dynastic deckchairs rearranged once more, and on the death of David II in 1371 he was succeeded by his elderly nephew Robert Stewart, Earl of Carrick, as Robert II. The surviving Bruce male heir, the grandson of Edward of Ireland, was confirmed by Robert II in the barony of Clackmannan. It was the closing act of the ancient *derbfine*. From then on, primogeniture ruled.

The success of the Stewart monarchs is best observed in what appears their most obvious failing; the habit of dying prematurely. From the accession of James I to the death of Queen Mary, none of the crowned heads lived long enough to stamp their personalities on the reigns of their successors and the lives of their subjects. Some, notably James I and James IV, oversaw a considerable enhancement of royal authority and the curbing of the influence of over-mighty magnates. But neither managed to so tighten the screws of personal rule so as to spark the kind of dynastic upheaval seen at regular intervals in England. James I and James III may both have been assassinated, but these were more palace coups than changes of dynasty.

The English pattern of royal adventures overseas leading to demands of taxation, which in turn led to the rise of representative assemblies, and then saw attempts by the Crown to get round the strictures of those assemblies by improving royal administration in the localities, to improve the flow of fines and levies into the Exchequer, was not replicated in Scotland. Instead, Scotland developed an almost *laissez faire* regime where royal authority was restricted to supervising what has been termed a "loosely linked network of communities".[22] This is not to say that Scotland's institutions were any less robust or developed than in England. The parliamentary, noble, and religious counterbalances to royal authority have been described in sister volumes to this. The foundation of the Court of Session in 1532 is perhaps the most enduring of the steps taken by the Stewarts to enhance the administration of royal justice in Scotland.

It is apparent that Scotland, as a small northern European state, did not play a pivotal role in medieval *realpolitik*. However, it occasionally acted as an honest broker in continental disputes, and its enduring alliance with France bound it to the Catholic heartland of Europe. The Stewart kings married into the royal houses of England, France, Burgundy, and Denmark and their daughters found themselves betrothed to a veritable panoply of foreign princes. Tied into the continent by alliance and marriage, the Stewart kings still harboured ambitions out of keeping with their relative stature. James III thought about invading Brittany, James IV sought to lead a crusade against the Turks, James V was offered the kingship of Ireland, and James VI put himself forward as leader of a Protestant Europe.

The Stewarts were also prone to the grand gesture. James II and James IV spent considerable amounts on armaments; the former on artillery and the latter on his navy. James II took advantage of his access to Burgundian craftsmen through his wife Mary of Guelders to build a series of large artillery pieces. The most famous, Mons Meg, which still sits at Edinburgh Castle, was a gift from his uncle-in-law, the Duke of Burgundy for whom it had been made. James' use of artillery enabled him to overthrow the Earls of Douglas in 1455; three of their castles were overwhelmed by royal artillery and the Douglases succumbed in a campaign lasting only a few months. Emboldened by his domestic success, James set out to recapture the border town of Roxburgh. Taking advantage of the defeat of the Lancastrian regime in 1460 he marched south with a large army. In personal command of the artillery, he was killed when one of his bombards exploded. His army held its ground and recaptured Roxburgh.

James IV's naval ambitions saw him embark on maritime manoeuvres with the Danes against the Swedes, and were the springboard for his alliance with France and the termination of the Treaty of Perpetual Peace with England in 1513. James IV's flagship, the "great" *Michael* launched in 1511 with a complement of more than 300 was the largest warship in northern Europe. The *Michael* was captained with success by Sir Andrew Wood, defeating an English fleet off the River Forth. Henry VIII is thought to have used the *Michael's* specifications when commissioning his own flagship, *Henri Grace à Dieu* in 1512, in one example of the Anglo-Scots arms race. On James IV's death, the *Michael* was sold to the French and renamed *La Grande Nef D'Ecosse*. James IV's expenditure on his navy was colossal. On the assumption that total Crown revenue in any one year was about £30,000 (Scots), it is estimated that the costs of the royal navy over his reign came to more than £100,000 (Scots).[23]

The six Jameses were very different characters in many ways, but their reigns are marked by distinctive similarities. They all succeeded as minors. James I was sent by his father to France for safety only to be captured by pirates and imprisoned in the Tower of London for 18 years. James II was seven when he succeeded his father, and James III only nine when James II was killed at Roxburgh. James IV was party to the coup that overthrew James III and saw his accession aged 15. James V was still an infant when his father was slain at Flodden in 1513. James VI and his mother Mary acceded to the throne as minors. In other countries, these constant changes from major to minor might have brought about a change in dynasty. In Scotland it probably saved the dynasty, not that there were many other families waiting in the wings.

Each monarch had enough time to check the rise of any over-mighty local nobles without upsetting the delicate balance of power between the centre and the localities. However, when the Crown did build up sufficient power to overthrow a territorial magnate it often lacked the resources to maintain central authority in that area. Whenever the Stewart kings struck, the resultant settlement saw the Crown unable to maintain its hold over the area it had subdued. In seeking to bind the country to their rule, James II and IV pursued a different course of administration from James III and V. James IV relied on his territorial magnates to bind the localities to the centre, as did James II after the overthrow of the Douglas family. James III and V by contrast preferred to rule through a circle of trusted administrators. James III so alienated his traditional supporters in the localities that he faced two coup attempts, one in 1482 and one in 1488 which resulted in his death at the battle of Sauchieburn.

It might be said, reviewing the reigns of the five Jameses, that they each lived lives that were nasty, brutish, and short. Each displayed such a particular vindictiveness against perceived domestic enemies that it can be regarded as a malevolent Stewart gene. James II's slaying of the 6th and 8th Earls of Douglas fits into a pattern of family pique that can be seen in the sacking of Elgin Cathedral by his great-uncle the Wolf of Badenoch, the murder of Robert III's heir, David Duke of Rothesay by his uncle the Duke of Albany or in the later extermination of the Master of Glamis and his mother by James V.

Yet for all their flaws, the Stewart kings were remarkably successful. They built up a distinct system of royal administration. They sustained a regular system of taxation, admittedly rudimentary. Law reform under James I, II and V saw advances in land tenure, parliamentary representation, and the administration of justice. Each of the Jameses was renowned for his piety. Royal patronage of the arts was sustained in each of the reigns and each king oversaw the development or rebuilding of royal palaces at Falkland, Dunfermline, Linlithgow, Stirling, and Edinburgh. James IV has been held to be an "ideal medieval king".[24] It is perhaps his court that has a reputation for being the most cultured. Characters such as the alchemist Damian who threw himself from the walls of Stirling Castle in an effort to demonstrate the principles of flight mixed with the domestic talent of the musician, Carver and the poet, Dunbar. James IV followed the tradition set by his grandfather in holding tournaments, the most famous being held at Holyrood in 1508 in which the King himself participated, in defence of the "lady with the meikle lippis".[25] The other advantage enjoyed by the Stewarts, particularly when compared to the descendants of Edward III, was that except for the Douglases there was no one single noble family strong enough to challenge the Crown. Those families that did rise to prominence usually did so, like the Boyds, as a result of having control of the king during his minority, but they usually fell when the king came of age.[26] The great families of the 16th century and beyond spent most of the late Middle Ages bedding down their authority in the localities. By the 16th century, with a queen overseas, or later with a king gone south, the Campbells, Gordons, and Hamiltons came out to play.

What was the legacy left by James VI and his predecessors as kings and queens of Scots? The institution of monarchy proved itself strong enough to withstand the charged circumstances of the Stewart era. The history of the Scottish monarchy in the medieval and early modern eras is one of dynastic continuity and stable royal administration. It drew its strength from the different peoples that settled in the country, with the royal family receiving regular infusions of new blood. In terms of status, or wealth, or military strength, the Royal House of Scotland did not compete in the same league as the Valois, Habsburg, or Plantagenet dynasties. But, in terms of sheer longevity, it outlived every other medieval dynasty. Compared to other European kingdoms, it is a remarkable record. In order properly to examine the institution it is vital to breach the surface gloss of romantic myth and legend that has bedevilled the study of Scottish history. The complex characters and achievements of the different crowned heads can only be properly assessed by a detailed analysis which this chapter cannot provide.

As monarch of the United Kingdom of Great Britain and Northern Ireland, the Queen is by right Queen of Scots. She still maintains a Household in Scotland, and her Officers of State attend her on her annual visits to Edinburgh, where they are protected by the Hereditary Lord High Constable, (the Earl of Errol), maintained by the Hereditary Master of the Household, (the Duke of Argyll), marshalled by the Lord Lyon King of Arms, (Sir Malcolm Innes of Edingight), and guarded by Members of the Royal Company of Archers. The ceremonial that marks the Queen's residence at Holyrood, and that of her Lord High Commissioner during the sitting of the General Assembly of the Church of Scotland, can be traced straight back to pre-Union pageantry; although the Royal Company's claim to be the sovereign's bodyguard is of more recent vintage.[27] Pre-Union ceremonial can be seen at the dissolution of the United Kingdom parliament, when the official proclamation declaring the dissolution is announced in Edinburgh two days after it has been issued in London, to record its historic carriage by an equestrian courier.

These colourful differences between the two kingdoms reflect one remarkable fact; that Scotland has sustained and protected its monarchy without interruption for longer than any other nation in western Europe. Tear away the myths and legends of Scota and Gathelus and you still retain the core; that the Crown of Scots has outlived all its rivals and has taken to itself the other kingdoms of the British isles. It may be considered an anachronistic platitude to state that the monarch is a non-political and classless focus of national unity; but our monarch, as Queen of Scots, is a mirror for Scotland. She is a dynamic link between the myths of our past and the legends yet to come. In a time of national uncertainty and institutional denigration it is vital to reassert the Crown's distinct Scottish pedigree. It is the mark of our mature democracy that it can nurture and sustain its monarchy while political institutions rise and fall. No country can hope to fashion its future if it ignores its past. At a time of change in the constitutional framework of the United Kingdom, the ancient motto of the Kings of Scots is more relevant than ever. *No one provokes me with impunity.*

Footnotes to this Chapter may be found on pages 366–67.

13: David Starkey

The modern monarchy:
rituals of privacy and their subversion

FOR THE BRITISH monarchy, the 20th century has been both the best of times and the worst of times. Total war and social revolution, which brought down most other European thrones, left it unscathed, while the long decline of Britain's political power and its economic might seemed only to strengthen the monarchy's place in popular affection. The culmination of all this was the great national street-party of the Queen's Silver Jubilee in 1977: an unpretentious nation sang happy birthday to its modest Queen. Fifteen years later, however, in 1992, the Queen confronted her "annus horribilis": Windsor Castle, her favourite residence, was badly damaged by fire and the marriage of the Prince and Princess of Wales lay in very public ruins.

But, of course, the surprising thing is not that the monarchy is doing badly at the end of the 20th century, but that it exists at all. And its exists thanks to the idea of the Family Monarchy. The monarchy's embodiment of this idea carried it to its triumphs in the earlier 20th century; its failure to live up to it brought about its later decline. The idea of the Family Monarchy is new, new at any rate in its details. But its essentials go back to the fundamentals of monarchy itself.

All monarchy is a form of deeply personal authority, in which the actual royal person is given major public status. The great variable, therefore, lies in the relationship between the particular person and the power of the public office. At one extreme, in the purest forms of absolutism, there is no distinction between the two: "L'etat, c'est moi", as Louis XIV is supposed to have said. At the other, in modern constitutional monarchy, the personal will of the sovereign is allowed no part in the discharge of the public office: the monarch is a royal automaton whose levers are pulled by others. Royal ritual alters to reflect this changing relationship between the personal and the public. During the age of real royal power in England (though not in France) access to the monarch's person was jealously guarded. There was a succession of apartments that led to the inner or privy chambers of the monarch. Fewer and fewer people were allowed into each successive room and only a handful were permitted – as a mark of especial favour – to penetrate the inmost sanctum of the Closet, where they could exercise the most direct personal influence over the monarch and reap commensurate rewards in terms of public power and wealth.

With the monarch's loss of personal political power, this pattern of regulated access and the rituals based upon it faded way. Its last vestige was the presentation of debutantes at Court, which was abolished in the present reign. It was replaced by a new pattern in which the monarch's seclusion was guarded even more jealously than before. But this was a tribute to royal powerlessness, not royal power. It also had a different meaning. Real monarchs know no privacy and have no private capacity: "kings are not as privates are", as Shakespeare's Henry V soliloquizes. But as our monarchs lost public power, they gained what their great predecessors had never enjoyed: privacy. I shall first address the succession of decisions which develop this private identity in the 19th century and then examine its dramatic redeployment in the 20th.

The monarchy's loss of public political power and its acquisition of a private identity occur simultaneously and the watershed in both is the latter part of the reign of George III. This is when the King goes mad and starts talking to trees, and making abusive remarks about Shakespeare. A monarch in this state could neither rule the country, nor even look after his own affairs. His short-comings in his public capacity were dealt with formally by the creation of the Regency and, in practice, by the rapid transfer of power to the political élite; his personal incompetence also required the appointment of others to act on his behalf. But they could act only if their sphere of competence were defined: in other words, if the public and private capacities of the sovereign were formally distinguished. This is what happened.

The most important step was the creation of the position of private secretary. Hitherto, the King had handled nearly all his own correspondence, writing it himself in a rapid, vigorous roundhand. In so far as he received official assistance, it came from the Secretary of State for the Home Department himself. With the King's blindness, this arrangement became impossible and Colonel Herbert Taylor was appointed his private secretary. Despite the evident need for the post, the institution of the private secretaryship was highly contentious. Was it appropriate, it was immediately asked, for the monarch to have a private secretary as opposed to the actual secretary of state? The reason for the furore is clear: the political élite feared that, as so often in the past, the monarch would use this new personal instrument to impose his will more effectively on the public political process. The fears show that the monarch's loss of political power was recent and – conceivably – reversible. But, in the event, the fears proved groundless. Far from being means of reestablishing royal absolutism, the private secretaryship was to become the key to the establishment of the new constitutional monarchy and to its subsequent management. This is due above all to the first holder of the post. Under George III, Sir Herbert, as he became, was a model of loyalty and discretion to his rapidly failing master. But he also had sufficient *nous* to sense the direction of the political tide. When he was reappointed private secretary to William IV, he made it his business to inculcate the King in these new realities. The King, as a life-long Tory Ultra, was passionately opposed to the Great Reform Bill. Taylor persuaded him that it was his duty, as a constitutional sovereign, to subordinate his private political judgment to the public will of the nation. In so doing, he certainly avoided a political crisis. He also probably saved the monarchy – though at the price of transforming it into a form of kingship that would have been anathema to all previous holders of the crown and was not much liked by William IV's successor, Queen Victoria.

The second change was legally even more significant: the monarch was given the right to make a private will. Of course, monarchs had always made wills. But the standard rule was that each royal will was repudiated by the testator's successor. The reasons varied: the bequests might be too expensive; the regency council inappropriately structured or the rules of succession be impracticable (as was the case with the will of Henry VIII). But the underlying realities were the same. Because each monarch succeeded to the plenitude of royal power and acquired absolute control of the royal assets, each could simply ignore the will of his predecessor. For uniquely, and unlike the will of the king's meanest subject, the royal will had no legal force whatever. It was not subject, for example, to ordinary probate, and it belonged, as anyone who has used the Public Records Office will know, to a separate class of documents. The act of parliament which empowered the monarch to make a private will put an end to these anomalies. But only at the price of a further assimilation of the king to his subjects. For a private will required that royal property – or at least some aspects of royal property – be defined as private and subject to private property law. The result was a new-found distinction between the public property of the Crown and the private property of the monarch. This distinction was capitalized on (in both senses of the word) during the reign of Queen Victoria. At the beginning of her reign, the monarchy was relatively poor and several of the dukes had resources, estates, and a manner of life that equalled or even exceeded hers: "I am coming from my house to your palace", the Queen famously remarked to the Duchess of Sutherland, her first Lady of the Bedchamber. Victoria, vigorously aided and abetted by the Prince Consort, embarked on a deliberate and successful strategy to redress the balance by increasing her private wealth. The royal couple were none too choosy about the means. They tightened up the management of the royal estates; they imposed strict economies on the royal household (all those missing dusters and purloined candle-ends); above all, they saved as much as possible from the Civil List. By these means, they built up a huge private fortune and a large private landed estate. The two chief properties were Balmoral in Scotland and Osborne on the Isle of Wight. The two properties altered upper-class life-style; what matters here, however, is they were properties held privately by the monarch and nowhere publicly accounted for.

The accumulation of privacy goes further than just private secretaries, wills, and estates. Victoria, in particular, created private palaces. At Osborne, there was a single concession to the fact that Victoria was monarch: a council chamber. There was no throne room, in which to display her state; no withdrawing-room in which to receive her Court. Instead, Osborne was deliberately designed to offer the same accommodation as a very grand private house. At Balmoral, things went even further: there is nothing to indicate the owner's regal status. Not even a council chamber. It was absolutely private and was recognized as such.

But, above all else, Victoria created a private royal death. This, I would argue, was the most dramatic change. At Westminster Abbey, there are the great funerary monuments of the medieval English kings. They are vast public statements which ensure that kings and queens die as they have lived – publicly. The tombs, in fact, completed the royal life cycle. Their reign had begun in this place when they were crowned in front of the shrine of their greatest ancestor (greatest at least in the Middle Ages) Edward the Confessor. It ended when they were buried here in the gigantic two-tiered tomb chests which surround the Confessor's shrine. Death was the most public of royal rituals in the medieval and early modern period. Victoria, however, changed all this when she founded a private mausoleum for her beloved Albert at Frogmore in Windsor Great Park. Albert had a prone public monument in the Memorial Chapel at Windsor and a magnificently erect one in the Albert Memorial in Hyde Park. But his body is at Frogmore, where Victoria herself would be reunited with him after her own death. With succeeding monarchs and their consorts some concession was made to earlier practice: all are buried at St George's Chapel, Windsor. But other members of the Royal Family are interred at Frogmore, which is open to the public only one day a year, on the anniversary of the death of Victoria. The ritual for a modern royal death observes the same distinction: there is a public lying-in-state and a state funeral, but the actual interment is utterly private.

All this amounts to a revolution in the nature of monarchy. The most public office that an individual can hold had become private. The development was intensified by Victoria's withdrawal into her self-imposed purdah of grief: from the death of Albert in 1861 to the end of the 1880s, she was deeply reluctant to discharge her ordinary public duties. For example, at the state opening of parliament of 1866, her first since Albert's death, she appeared veiled, in black widow's weeds, crownless and silent, leaving her Lord Chancellor to read the Speech. Indeed, the state opening had withered so far by the end of Victoria's reign that everybody thought it was going to be abolished. Victoria was also invisible in her own capital: a frequent visitor at Balmoral and Biarritz she became something of a stranger in Buckingham Palace. The result was predicable. Republicanism rose to its highest point in the 1870s and reached into the highest quarters: at least one member of the Liberal Cabinet was a closet republican. The monarch had virtually disappeared from public view; the danger evidently was that the monarchy itself would disappear as well. That it did not was due to an astonishing process of reinvention. For a hundred years, the monarchy had been on the defensive: first against the aristocratic Georgian élite; then against the broader Victorian middle class. The rise of "our new masters, the people" threatened to topple it completely. In fact, the opposite proved to be the case. The monarchy not only adapted to the coming age of mass democracy; it positively throve in it. This is only one of the many ironies involved. Another is the role of privacy.

Privacy had been the last redoubt of the monarchy into which it had retreated as it was driven out of the sphere of public, political power. But now the tables were turned and it was the private face of monarchy that was used as the basic instrument to repopularize it – and, in so doing, to win for itself a larger place on the public stage than it had ever occupied before, even in the days of its greatest power.

But this is to anticipate somewhat. In the late 19th century, the essential instruments of the royal revival were not privacy, but history and spectacle. The 1880s and 1890s were the overture to the Edwardian age. The Edwardians loved grand gestures: musically this is the age of Elgar's Pomp and Circumstance Marches, while architecture was dominated by the theatrical gestures of Blomfield and Lutyens ("Potsdam classical", as Osbert Lancaster rather unkindly called Blomfield's Regent Street). Both the music and the building were also consciously revivalist, which meant that, at their best, their grandiosity was softened with a plangent nostalgia. More straightforward examples of the spirit of the age were, on the one hand, the collectors of English folk songs or the founders of the National Trust with their rural sentimentalisms, and, on the other, the new variety theatres which mounted ever more daring and lavish spectaculars.

The application of this heady mixture to the staid body of the British monarchy took place in Victoria's two Jubilees: her Golden Jubilee in 1887 and her Diamond Jubilee in 1897. The two events were intended to celebrate Victoria's reign; in fact, they represented a sharp reversal of the royal style that had characterized her youth and maturity. At first sight, this assertion will appear strange, for the pictorial record of the two events conveys an immediate sense of familiarity. Here are the ancestors of the royal processions that have marked the highs and lows of 20th-century British history. Vast, exceedingly well-organized, well-rehearsed processions through the streets of central London with large numbers of soldiers and policemen, all standing (interestingly) with their backs to the crowd. They are there for show, not for use against the assassin or rioter. In the procession, tall soldiers dressed in red uniforms and with bear-skins on their heads march very straight in perfect time and to beautifully played music. Finally, and nicely off-setting the disciplined uniformity of the British contingent, there is a multitude of exotic costumes and peoples representing various bits of the Empire. It is, in short, the sort of thing the British do so well. Or rather, it is the sort of thing that the British *came* to do so well. For hitherto they had been rather bad at it. Moreover, they were proud of doing it badly. Doing things badly was just as much a part of being British as doing things well. The things we were most proud of doing badly were anything that savoured of the militarized continental monarchies. Marching in time was not British. It was Prussian. Large-scale ritualized public ceremony was Romanov. The use of historicist gestures was Austro-Hungarian.

The last great public ceremony before 1887 was Victoria's own coronation.

It was the nadir of the coronation ceremony. Indeed it was clear that the officiating clergy neither knew nor cared what they were doing. Large portions of the medieval *ordo* were simply omitted. The use of the various instruments of the coronation was heavily abbreviated, and the annointing – the climax of the ceremony – became a mockery because of Victorian prudery. The monarch was supposed to be annointed on the breasts and – as we all know – Victoria did not have such appendages. But not only was there a drastic paring down of the coronation rite, there was, amazingly, no rehearsal at all. The inevitable result was that the solemnities descended into farce. The Archbishop of Canterbury apparently started without his spectacles; service books were held upside down; Victoria's hand had not even been measured for the coronation ring. Unfortunately, the goldsmiths had erred on the small side. Nevertheless, the ring was forced by the half-blind Archbishop onto Victoria's finger. She had to soak her hand in iced water for half an hour afterwards to get it off.

How, the question has to be asked, did they get away with it? The answer lies in the nature of the audience in Westminster Abbey. This was overwhelmingly aristocratic: Victoria was crowned in the presence of her peers, who *understood*. Here it becomes important to understand the changing audience for royal ceremonies. Coronations and funerals had always been more or less public. The same was true in the later Middle Ages for royal marriages and christenings as well. The *Royal Book*, the handbook of ceremony in use under the Yorkists and early Tudors, laid down that the font in which a royal infant was christened should be placed on a high wooden platform so that the baptism could be clearly seen by the people. A similar platform was used for the marriage of Prince Arthur, first-born son of Henry VII, to Catherine of Aragon. This wedding took place in St Paul's, like the wedding of Prince Charles and Lady Diana. And, like that wedding, it was a carefully choreographed public event. Arthur and Catherine even turned to the crowd before entering the gates of the Sanctuary to hear Mass, and the crowd duly went wild.

But from the end of the 17th century, royal weddings and christenings become private, or at least restricted, occasions. They take place at Court, in the Chapel Royal, never publicly in Westminster Abbey or St Paul's Cathedral, and, away from the public eye, the iron discipline which had characterized Tudor ceremony was relaxed. The royal infant now squalls away while a soprano from the Italian opera warbles behind a screen. The whole thing is shambolic, and, as with Victoria's coronation, it does not matter because the aristocratic audience of courtiers is complicit. Court ritual is something that goes on within the circle of those who know and understand and who are brought up to it. It is not public performance. It is not treated as public performance. It is rather something that you are born to and that you do because it comes naturally. This breeds a certain casualness.

All this had changed by the end of the 19th century. The new royal processional rituals that were pioneered in Victoria's two Jubilees did not take place behind the closed doors of the Palace but in the streets of London, and their audience consisted of men and women in the street too. This was the audience which went to the Palace of Varieties: it expected just as good a performance from the stars of the new royal show as well. And it got it: out went Hanoverian muddle and improvization; in came exhaustive rehearsals and clockwork perfection.

A change of this magnitude has two different components: the macro and the micro. On the one hand, it was a product of the broad historical shift towards mass society and democracy. The political system had begun its adaptation to the new age with Disraeli's Reform Act of 1867. Victoria, Disraeli's "fellow author", had always sworn that she would never be Queen of a democracy. However, the Jubilees of 1887 and 1897 revealed that the monarchy had become popular, if not yet democratic. But historical tides do not operate of themselves; an individual pilot has to spot the drift of things and alter the direction of the ship of state. The pilot who set the monarchy on a new course was Reginald Brett, Viscount Esher. Brett's father was a successful lawyer who had served as Master of the Rolls and been ennobled. But his mother was French. This meant that Brett was both inside and outside the English Establishment. He had been educated at Eton and then at Trinity College, Cambridge – those great nurseries of the Establishment. But he completed his studies abroad. His dual nationality was complemented by his bisexuality. He married and fathered several children, but also had a series of crushes on senior boys at Eton. The most passionate of them seems to have been with his own second son. We do not know whether any of these relationships was consummated. He was also on the fringes of the series of homosexual scandals that shook the Establishment in the aftermath of Oscar Wilde's fall. But somehow he always emerged smelling of roses (but not too much).

He was in short a very remarkable man and not only for how he lived, but for what he did. Not only did he invent the modern monarchy; he was also the most influential member of the committee on Imperial Defence which reorganized the British army after the débâcle of the Boer War. He was offered the Garter, an earldom, the vice-royalty of India, and the secretaryship of state for war. He turned them all down. Instead, he contented himself with two modest positions: at the start of his career he was briefly a parliamentary private secretary and then, in his maturity, he became Constable of Windsor Castle. The reason for the self-denial of an otherwise indulgent man is simple: Esher preferred behind the scenes to centre stage. He avoided the spotlight and was a "creature of the dark": a backstairs intriguer, a negotiator, a spin-doctor. He was to the late 19th century what Peter Mandelson is to the late 20th: Mandelson invented New Labour; Esher the New Monarchy. Both took a moribund institution and adapted it to the modern world. Mandelson, however, shows a dangerous fondness for publicity; Esher was wiser and knew that you must not shine too much daylight onto the magic of spin-doctoring, any more than onto the magic of monarchy itself. A spin-doctor, of course, is primarily concerned with image. Here Esher's very Edwardian fascination with the stage made him a natural. In another age, he could have been a successful film director. But the great spin-doctors, and Esher was of the greatest, are as interested in the message as in the medium. Here Esher's peculiar contribution was his interest in history and its application to the present – and not only British history. His French ancestry alerted him to the importance of the French Revolution. This he regarded as an object lesson in how not to bring about political change. He was determined that Britain should never experience the same trauma. Finally, Esher was an obsessive hoarder of paper and he accumulated a huge archive, now deposited at Churchill College, Cambridge. Thanks to this collection, we can assess the public contribution of this most private of men.

Looking at even the printed extracts of Brett's papers, I am struck by his awareness and his self-awareness. He was aware of what he was doing. He was aware of why he was doing it. He was aware, above all, of broad patterns of historical change. He says with utter frankness: "our great problem is democracy", and, of course, it was. Democracies are great levellers. They are impatient of the past and unconcerned about the future. How can a constitution which had begun life in a feudal society survive into democracy? How can a democracy sustain an empire? How can one have a peerage in a democracy? Most of all, how can one have a monarchy in a democracy? Esher was not alone in his recognition of the problem. We always think of the Victorians as confident, assertive, knowing where they were going. But this does not apply to the later Victorians. Look at a photograph of Matthew Arnold: the worry on his face, and the intensity of the lines. Or one of Tennyson, seemingly with agonies on his brow. Both are worried about the consequences of popular rule. Arnold feared for culture and wanted a new class, the clerisy, to protect it. Tennyson thought that chivalry and faith and pageantry would disappear. What was unusual about Esher was that he had a practical solution to offer. His aim was to use the monarchy to educate democracy: to teach it about tradition and to make it respect time-honoured ways of conducting politics. But, as the people were in their political infancy, they had to be taught like young children with pictures.

To do this, Esher went back to first principles. Democracy, from the Greek *demos*, is the rule of the people. In a democracy, therefore, royal ritual must be popular, even vulgar (from the Latin *vulgus* "the people"). Esher unashamedly used the world "vulgar" to describe the ceremonial of Victoria's Jubilee of 1897. He had designed it to be big, bold, brassy, and instantly comprehensible by the common man. But Esher not only devised the ritual language appropriate for democracy; he reshaped the fabric of central London to accommodate this new type of royal ceremony. His opportunity came with the death of Victoria. He had been very close to Victoria; he was even closer to Victoria's successor, Edward VII. This made him a natural choice as chairman of the commission charged with the construction of the national monument to Victoria. Characteristically, he fulfilled the task of commemorating the great 19th-century Queen by creating the stage set for the rituals of the 20th-century British monarchy. The architect to the scheme was Sir Aston Webb. They layout of the Mall was regularized. At one end there was the triumphal Admiralty Arch, and, at the other, the great roundabout in front of Buckingham Palace, with the statue of Queen Victoria at its centre. Finally, as the climax of the whole composition, the front of Buckingham Palace was refaced.

Buckingham Palace had been built in several stages. Originally, the town residence of the dukes of Buckingham (whence its name, Buckingham House) it had been bought by George III as a private royal residence to supplement his official quarters at St James's. His son, George IV, rebuilt it entirely. His architect, John Nash, designed a U-shaped building looking up the Mall. Marble Arch was placed in the centre as the triumphal entrance to the Palace. Later developments, however, forced the removal of the arch to its new site at the top of Park Lane. These developments were the responsibility of Queen Victoria. Victoria, with her rapidly growing family, decided that Buckingham Palace was too small. She employed the architect Edward Blore to create more space by filling in the U-shape with a new block. Blore was chosen largely because he was cheap (this, in reaction to the extravagancies of the Regency, was the age of economical government). His new building justified his reputation and its public façade on to the Mall was unkindly described as a cross between a railway station and a minor German princely palace. The imperial Indian Summer of Edward VII's reign demanded something grander.

Aston Webb's façade, which is modelled on the north side of the Place de la Concorde, supplied the necessary pomp and circumstance. But more than aesthetics were involved. The architects of the Regency had created a series of arches to serve as a triumphal way between Buckingham Palace and Hyde Park. But – with their casual indifference to such matters – the Victorians had destroyed the sequence with the removal of Marble Arch and the realignment of the Quadriga Arch at Hyde Park Corner. The Esher-Webb scheme created a new triumphal way. But it was differently aligned, linking the Palace to the City via Trafalgar Square and Strand, and to the Palace of Westminster via Whitehall. It also envisaged a different relationship between monarch and people. The Prince Regent's carriage had been greeted as often with stones as with cheers. Esher, however, was confident that the monarchy could now expect only cheers – and from larger and larger crowds. Hence the great roundabout in front of the Palace. When the roundabout was proposed, the ladies of the royal family objected: "the people will be able to get so close," they said with distaste. Esher replied that that was the whole idea. He had laid out a huge outdoor theatre; it remained only to construct the stage. This was supplied by the balcony in the middle of the new façade of the Palace. The result was scenes unprecedented in the history of the monarchy, in which the Royal Family on the balcony was hailed by a vast, wildly cheering crowd. It looked back to the acclamation of the Roman emperors – or forward to the mass adulation of the 20th-century dictators.

The creation of a popular royal ceremonial, with an appropriate ritual and theatre, was Esher's great contribution to the reinvention of the monarchy for mass society. But it was only half of the story. It was implicit in Esher's scheme that the monarchy should be popular. But, save for the fact that royal processions now supplied spectacular entertainment, it was hard to see why. Esher, for all his ad-man's gifts, had launched a campaign without a slogan. The slogan was not found until towards the end of the First World War, in 1917, the year of revolution. The Russian Revolution of 1917 has had a switchback ride among historians. As a Cambridge undergraduate in the 1960s, I was taught that it was the central event of the 20th century. Now it looks like only one of the long sequence of disasters that the Slavic peoples have inflicted upon themselves. At the time, however, no one was in doubt about its importance. Above all, it seemed to presage the end of empires, perhaps of monarchy itself. The imperial throne of the Romanovs fell. So soon after did those of Austria-Hungary and Germany. The Balkan monarchies were also tottering. George V, who had succeeded as King of Great Britain and Emperor of India just before the First World War, was well aware of these events. He was the first cousin of the Romanovs and bore the closest physical resemblance to Tsar Nicholas. But it was he, and not his Liberal Prime Minister, David Lloyd George, who was responsible for refusing to give Nicholas and his wife Alexandra sanctuary in Britain. He feared that by giving refuge to the fallen tyrant (as popular British opinion regarded the Tsar) he might expose himself to the same fate. Once again, then, the monarchy changed through fear. The changes before the First World War happened as a result of moves to mass society and democracy and the alarm they engendered. The even greater changes in the aftermath of the First World War were the result of the spectre of red revolution.

There were two significant changes in 1917. The first, which has been widely discussed, is the change in the name of the dynasty. It was not very clear what the royal house of Great Britain was called, but it was probably something like Saxe-Coburg-Gotha. This was unfortunate if the kingdom over which you reigned happened to be engaged in a life-and-death conflict with Germany. After a great deal of heart-searching, the name was changed to the house of Windsor. The choice of Windsor was a masterstroke. It was mere English, with overtones of Shakespeare, the Garter, and the romance of chivalry. Two men, who were both masters of language in their way, were responsible: Brett and Lord Stamfordham, the King's private secretary. The second and consequential change is less discussed but was actually more important in shaping the modern monarchy. The royal house had not only been German in name; it had also practised the full rigour of German dynastic customs, particularly with regard to marriage. With the change of name, these customs too were replaced with English ones.

In a German dynasty, the heirs had to marry women of their own rank: Serene Highness had to be joined with Serene Highness. Failure to do so led to *dérogeance*: in other words, the issue from the marriage took the mother's inferior rank and became ineligible to inherit. Positively applied, these rules also led to the idea of "morganatic marriage". This was a private marriage for a public figure. The marriage was valid and the children were legitimate. But the wife did not assume her husband's status, nor were the children able to inherit his royal or princely titles. The British monarchy also had its rules. These were established in the Glorius Revolution of 1688–89, which put William and Mary on the throne, and in the Act of Settlement of 1701, which gave the succession to the House of Hanover. These British rules had a single purpose: to prevent the succession of a Roman Catholic. Finally, the Royal Marriages Act of 1772 required that, for a marriage to be valid, the formal consent of the sovereign had to be given.

The marriages of the British royal house were thus subject to a double limitation: on the one hand, its princes were required to marry princesses of equivalent rank; on the other, they were forbidden to marry Roman Catholics. Apply both of these positive and negative rules and there were very few people whom you could actually marry. This is why the British royal house constantly married into miniscule German dynasties, that happened to be both Protestant and of the appropriate social rank. A good example of this was Princess Mary of Teck, later Queen Mary. She was originally intended for Edward VII's elder son, the Duke of Clarence. But he died in his 20s. After his death, Mary was passed on, like so many goods and chattels, to the next brother George, Duke of York, later George V. That was how royal marriages were handled. It was a straightforward dynastic arrangement and there was no pretence that it was anything else. Romantic love did not enter into it (however close the couple might become after they were married).

In 1917, however, George V changed these rules as well. He was the first monarch since Elizabeth I to feel himself "mere English" and probably the first ever to speak only English. His family was now English by name; he determined that it should be English by blood and behaviour as well. Instead, therefore, of German princelings, he decreed that his children would be able to marry English men and English women. On the day that the necessary Order in Council was issued, he noted in his diary: "This was an historic day." It was historic indeed. A couple of princesses had previously married British subjects, as had several of the sons of George III. But the princesses were remote from the succession; while the marriages of George III's sons were hole-in-corner affairs of doubtful legitimacy. A British marriage for a British prince in the direct line would be a tremendous novelty, for emotions were involved as well as nationality. "Love and marriage," the song goes, "go together like a horse and carriage." Royal marriages had hitherto been a great exception to this rule, as a marriage to the daughter of a German princely house was, of necessity, dynastic. But a marriage to a British lady, met in the course of the London season, might be the result of romantic love;

at least, it could be presented that way. Add to the love-interest the actual horses and carriages, and all the King's horses and all the King's men, of Brettian royal ceremony and the mixture was powerful indeed. Royal marriages became gigantic love affairs of the nation: the couple fell in love with each other and the nation fell in love with the result.

The nation did not have to wait long for this new sensation. For the first of the new style royal marriages took place on 26 April 1923, when George V's second son, Prince Albert, Duke of York, was married to Lady Elizabeth Bowes-Lyon, daughter of the Earl of Strathmore, at Westminster Abbey. The bride was pretty, if a little on the plump side; the bridegroom was shy and stuttering. But the crowds cheered themselves silly anyway. They have not stopped cheering since. The British family monarchy had been invented.

Walter Bagehot, in his classic account of *The English Constitution*, first published in 1867, anticipates much of the essence of the family monarchy:

> A *family* on the throne is an interesting idea also. It brings down the pride of sovereignty to the level of petty life... The women – one half of the human race at least – care fifty times more for a marriage than a ministry... A princely marriage is the brilliant edition of a universal fact, and, as such, it rivets mankind.

But aphorisms, however brilliant, do not make a reality, and it is a mistake to draw, as many commentators have done, a straight line from Bagehot's account to the family monarchy of the 20th century. The marriage of Victoria and Albert had begun as another arranged union. But it had quickly blossomed into a passionate love affair *after* their wedding. They had also worked hard to present an image of sober, happy family life after the profligacy and debauchery of the Queen's "wicked uncles". But this connubial bliss had ended with Albert's premature death in 1861 – at the beginning of the very decade in which Bagehot wrote. The publication in 1868 of Victoria's *Leaves from the Journal of Our Life in the Highlands* gave their married happiness the immortality of a royal best-seller. The book also showed the "friendly footing" on which she lived with her Highland servants. This suggestion "that all are on the same footing" did the Queen's reputation no harm at all among the middle classes. Against this warm after-glow of Victoria's married life, however, there have to be set three hard facts: the prolonged seclusion of her widowhood; the foreign marriages of most of her children, and, above all, the fact that Edward, Prince of Wales, showed every sign of taking after his "wicked uncles" rather than his dutiful and uxorious father. Not only did his behaviour help to kill Albert, as Victoria thought, it also killed, or at least put into cold-storage, the idea of a family monarchy.

But the idea was triumphantly revived in 1923, and with the new idea royal ritual was transformed. It was a case of off with the old and on with the new. The grand ceremonies of the state opening of parliament and the coronation, with their novel overlay of Brettian populist glitz and glamour, survived and thrived. But the rituals and etiquette of the Court withered away. This was a symptom of a wider change: as the monarchy embraced the people it repudiated the aristocracy. Relations between individual peers and peeresses and the Royal Family remained close, but they did so on a purely personal footing. On the other hand, the nobility, as a class, no longer formed the natural royal *milieu*. This shift had already been signalled by the King's behaviour in 1910–11 during the passage of the Parliament Act, which removed the legislative veto of the House of Lords. Class-analysis would have required the Crown to die at the last ditch to preserve the structure of hereditary power of which it was the apex. Instead, the monarchy gallantly kicked the peerage in the teeth to protect its own position. It had no choice if it were to survive. On the ruins of the old, there arose a new style of royal ritual. This focused on what anthropologists call the *rites de passage* of family life: the births, marriages, and deaths. These now became the key occasions of royal ceremony. Added to them were a series of other important moments in the family year, like going on holiday or Christmas. The English Christmas had largely been invented by two men: the novelist, Charles Dickens, and Prince Albert, the Prince Consort. In the 1930s, mass communications and the monarchy came together once more to invent the ritual of the royal Christmas broadcast. It was very simple and very artful. Everything was done to emphasize the informality and spontaneity of the occasion. It was a typical family Christmas, at which grandpa chose to make a speech. The setting, of course, was Sandringham and grandpa was the King-Emperor George V. But the new medium of radio gave the impression that he had just got up from a rather heavy lunch and ambled into his study to say a few words to his peoples. The truth was that the first broadcast was written by Rudyard Kipling and the second by the Archbishop of Canterbury. They were highly staged, but they were staged intimacy.

It is easy to see why the 20th-century monarchy worked. It worked because its rituals were not really royal at all. The form, of course – the crowns and golden coaches – was royal, though it was the royalty of fairy-tale. But the substance – the moments, big and small of family life – was universal. Everybody had a family so everybody could identify with the Royal Family: rich or poor, Labour, Tory, or even Liberal. It was the perfect means by which monarchy could be adapted to democracy. The monarchy, now transmuted into the Royal Family, represented everybody and it belonged to everybody, from the grandest and richest to the poorest and meanest – and especially, indeed, to those at the bottom of the pile. It was a sort of pathetic fallacy. The pathetic fallacy is the literary device which attributes human feelings to the impersonal forces of nature; the pathetic fallacy of the family monarchy was to attribute the democratic unction of ordinariness to the most extraordinary family of all. It reached its *ne plus ultra* in the Archbishop of Canterbury's address at the marriage of Princess Elizabeth, then heir to the throne, to her handsome, sea-faring cousin, Prince Philip of Greece, in 1947. The ceremony, the Archbishop declared, was exactly the same as it would be for any cottager who might be married this afternoon in some small country church in a remote village in the Dales: the same prayers are offered; the same blessings are given.

It was indeed the same, apart from the 12 wedding cakes at the reception and the 2,666 wedding presents, including a solid gold coffee set and a 54 carat pink diamond, which, if not as big as the Ritz-Carlton Hotel, was at least unique. But the imputed ordinariness made the ostentatious wealth somehow all right: it was like a welcome shaft of sunlight amid the grey austerity of postwar Britain. The result was that, while other thrones tottered and fell, the British monarchy seemed impregnable. "Soon", one of the growing multitude of former monarchs, ex-King Farouk of Egypt, prophesied, "there will only be five kings left: the King of England, The King of Spades, the King of Clubs, the King of Hearts, and the King of Diamonds."

But the family monarchy was more than a national fairy-story, in which the British, like children or poets, willingly suspended disbelief. Its effectiveness required a medium and a message. The medium was the media. First came the press. Here the early 20th century saw fundamental changes in demand and supply: universal primary education created a new mass market, while technology made printing and illustration cheaper than ever. The result was a new, popular press, which was written, as Lord Salisbury sniffily remarked of *The Daily Mail*, "by office boys for office boys". Actually, office girls were at least as important, both as a market for the "yellow press" and, consequently, in setting its tone. And their appetite for royal stories was insatiable. Buckingham Palace, which was then much faster on its feet than it subsequently became, was quick to embrace the new developments and had a press office as early as the 1920s. Not that there was much need for spin-doctoring as the press fell over itself to present a picture of the monarchy that was at once respectful and enthusiastic. This was even more true of radio. Radio in Britain was made into a state monopoly: it was felt to be too dangerous to be anything else. Indeed, John Reith, the first director-general of the British Broadcasting Corporation, was determined to go further, and turn this potentially subversive medium into a source of national uplift. The monarchy, as we shall see, was central to his plans. Once again, the alliance was cemented early, with the King's Christmas Broadcasts. The press and broadcasting were the big stories. But lesser developments also played their part, like the brilliance and controllability of electric light. This was already being used to good effect for the state opening of parliament in the 1930s. It is an autumn day and little natural light filters into the heavily-gilded House of Lords. Suddenly, as the trumpets sound to announce the King's imminent arrival, all the lights are switched off. Then, as the King enters, the lights come up, focusing on the imperial crown. The great jewels flash and glitter. This is an extraordinarily precocious use of technology; it should also give us pause about the conventional distinction made between the 20th-century dicatorships and the surviving monarchies. The dictatorships, it is argued, consciously emphasized their modernity with their employment of the new technologies while the monarchies played the card of tradition. But the British monarchy, which arguably was the most successful of the lot, did both.

It owed its success, however, not only to its presentation, but to its message. For the family monarchy was more than a good slogan for the house of Windsor. It takes us to the very heart of Britishness. It is generally accepted that the monarchy became a surrogate for nationalism in Britain and took the place in the nation's affections that, in most other countries, was occupied by political symbols like the flag or cultural icons such as language, national costume, or folklore. But if the monarchy were a substitute for nationalism, then the family monarchy became the touchstone of a national morality. Bagehot had anticipated this idea as well. "We have come," he wrote, "to regard the Crown as the head of our *morality*." But he had the good sense to emphasize the fragility of this position: to assume that all monarchs would be virtuous, he continued, was "to expect grapes from thorns and figs from thistles", and the thorns and thistles bore an abundant crop of their natural fruits under Edward VII. But, with the three principal reigns of the 20th century (George V, George VI, and Elizabeth II), there occurred a return to the stolid family virtues – or, at least, to a convincing appearance of them. The result was that we came not only to expect virtue in our monarch, we made a religion of it – arguably indeed the only religion that the British had.

The particular relationship between the Crown and religion went back to Henry VIII, who had made himself Supreme Head on Earth of the Church of England. His successors were not quite so presumptuous, but all monarchs after Elizabeth I styled themselves Supreme Governors of the Church. Despite the lesser title, however, they wielded the same power: just as socialism was what the Old Labour Party said it was, so the faith of the Church of England was what the king ordained. Until, that is, the reign of James II. His Catholicism clashed irreconcilably with the Protestantism of the political nation and, after his flight and the ensuing Glorious Revolution, the old position was reversed. Instead of the people having the same religion as their king, the king was required to adhere to the religion of his people. Subsequent monarchs had to make a declaration against transubstantiation and to swear, as part of their coronation oath, to maintain "the Protestant Reformed religion established by law". But though they had to be Protestant, nobody expected them to be virtuous. The fact was highlighted by George I, the king who secured the Protestant succession. He was not only divorced from his wife, Sophia Dorothea (whom he kept imprisoned in a castle in his German lands, just to make sure); he also had two official mistresses of astonishing ugliness: one of whom was unusually tall and thin and the other remarkably short and fat. And so it continued, with the most voluble defender of the Protestant establishment being the gluttonous and debauched George IV. He was happy enough to enter into an illicit marriage with a Catholic, but threatened to die in the last ditch rather than agree to Catholic Emancipation. The threat was not too serious – his threats never were, and, in any case, it would have been difficult to find a ditch big enough to accommodate his swollen frame.

Once again, the first decades of 20th century marked a sharp break. The key event was the wedding of the Duke and Duchess of York in 1923. The address at the wedding was given by Cosmo Gordon Lang, then Archbishop of York and later Archbishop of Canterbury. Not for Lang the banalities of Archbishop Runcie at the marriage of Charles and Diana, when he burbled about their "fairy-tale marriage". Instead, Lang's address was solemn, even intimidating. "You cannot," he told the young couple, "swear that your marriage will be happy. But you can and will vow that it shall be noble." In other words, Lang, like Bagehot, recognized the vagaries of human nature. But, unlike Bagehot, he expected that those vagaries would be hidden by a public façade: whatever the reality of their marriage, the Yorks were required to keep up appearances. First the monarch had been required to adhere to the religion of his people; now he and his family had to practise – or appear to practise – the morality of their most respectable subjects. The result was to turn "duty" into the watchword of the house of Windsor: it was duty which required private happiness to be subordinate to public appearance; duty which demanded a protocol as rigid and unbending as Queen Mary's ramrod back; duty which had to crush the butterfly of the personal expressiveness and indulgence of an Edward VIII.

Lang's 1923 wedding address was not a one-off, however impressive. Instead it represented his harnessing of the monarchy to a project to impose a public morality on Britain. The project, like the reformed monarchy itself, was a response to change and the fear of change. For two great institutions were under threat: the Church and the family. In the 19th century, the Church of England had lost the moral high ground and the leadership of progressive public opinion to the assertive, self-confident nonconformist churches. Lang, who himself came from a Presbyterian background, was reluctant to accept the eclipse of the Established Church; he was even less willing to bend before the wind of 20th-century atheism and indifference which threatened the hold of all varieties of Christianity. Lang was also concerned about the loss of the Church's hegemony in one particular area: the family. The law of England on marriage corresponded more or less to the Church of England's teaching on the indissolubility of Christian marriage. This meant that divorce was difficult, expensive, and subject to profound social stigma. Pressure to reform what many felt to be impossibly restrictive laws grew in the late 19th century. Lang set himself to resist the pressures to the best of his very considerable abilities. In 1909, he was made a member of the Royal Commission on Matrimonial Causes, whose task was to consider the liberalizing of the divorce laws. The majority of the commissioners duly recommended liberalization. But Lang was one of the three signatories to the minority report which opposed any substantive change. The matter was pushed to one side by domestic political crisis and the upheavals of the First World War and it was not until 1920 that a bill based on the majority report was finally submitted to parliament. The intervening years had not softened Lang's stance: he made a powerful and influential speech against it and the bill failed.

Even more effective, however, was Lang's wedding address of 1923. Its effect was to turn the family monarchy into the figurehead of his campaign. Once, Christian kings had led crusades to recover the Holy Land from the infidel; now the Royal Family would lead the defence of the Christian, British family. Traditionally, the king had not seen death; now divorcées became equally invisible to the royal eyes. They were not received at Court and could not enter the Royal Enclosure at Ascot: divorce became social death, while the maintenance of a conventional family life became the central tenet of a new public morality.

Lang's invention of the ideology of the family monarchy was as important as Brett's popularization of royal ceremony. Indeed, there were striking resemblances between the two men. Lang, as a Scot and a Presbyterian, was also an outsider. He too had a fast-track at Court. He had first encountered Victoria at her retreat at Osborne, while he was vicar of Portsea. He quickly became a firm favourite with the old Queen and managed to retain his position under her son and grandson. With Edward VII, it was a shared passion for pomp and circumstance that held them together. Edward, a confirmed dandy, suggested that the clergy should wear their "best clothes" at the service of thanksgiving for his recovery from his serious illness at the beginning of his reign. Lang, a confirmed ritualist, was happy to oblige and scandalized the Archbishop of Canterbury by arranging for the bishops to wear copes. With George V, however, it was Lang's moral earnestness, on the one hand, and his high view of kingship, on the other, that provided the basis for a relationship that blossomed into a genuine friendship. Nor was Lang's fondness for ceremony limited to the liturgical: he had an actor's magnificent speaking voice and a flair for theatre that, again, he shared with Brett.

Finally, and above all, Lang's sexuality, like Brett's, was unconventional. What prostitutes were to Gladstone, boys were to Lang: choir-boys at Magdalen and St Paul's, street-boys at Leeds. But whatever the social variety, the gender remained the same. For a man of these passions, the Church, then as now, provided a sympathetic home. He first encountered Anglican high campery when, on the eve of his decision to seek ordination, he went to be confirmed by the Bishop of Lincoln. He was seated next to the bishop at supper, at the head of a table of earnest young men in cassocks. Sensing his guest's unease, the Bishop, as Lang himself remembered, "put... his hand on my thigh [and] whispered to me: 'They're not half as good as they look and I'm the naughtiest of them all.' " In his prime, or rather primacy, the Archbishop would have given the bishop a good run for his money in the naughtiness stakes. He developed a series of passionate relationships with his favourite chaplains and secretaries. One of these was Dick Shepherd, later Dean of Canterbury. When Lang was made Archbishop of York, Shepherd wrote him a letter of congratulation from one "who finds he loves you even more than he loves the East End boy". Now there are important *caveats* to enter here. The first is our change of attitude. With the increased acceptance of homosexuality, which is an almost unmitigated good thing, there has also come an increased knowingness about it, which is sometimes a bad one. This in turn has altered the frontier between "normal" and "abnormal" behaviour. The instances I have cited strike us as overtly sexual. But they appear in Lang's highly laudatory official biography and, to the Archbishop's contemporaries, would have seemed entirely proper examples of close male friendship. The second follows. There is no evidence at all that Lang's feelings ever turned themselves into acts. He was a man who quickly learned to put a firm grip on his inner lift and, amidst the redecorated splendours of his archiepiscopal palaces, slept (or rather dozed, for he was a chronic insomniac) in a little iron bedstead. He knew from hard, personal experience the sacrifice he demanded from the young Duke and Duchess of York when he enjoined them to put duty above happiness.

Lang's most powerful ally in his determination to elevate public life by an "*active* warfare against evil, specially drunkenness, impurity and infidelity" was John Reith. Lang spoke from the pulpit of the established Church; Reith, yet more resonantly, controlled the output of the transmitters of the BBC. Like Lang, he was a son of the Scottish manse, and, like Lang, he made it to the top early, as director-general of the fledgling BBC. There his regime of high moral didacticism has given the word "Reithian" to the language. Reith's was explicitly a national crusade, and he deliberately put himself shoulder to shoulder with Lang by having his son christened by the Archbishop as head of the National Church – even though Reith remained loyal to the Presbyterianism of his forebears. He was rigorous too in maintaining the purity of his beloved corporation: applicants were asked, "do you accept the fundamental teachings of Our Lord Jesus Christ?" and when the chief engineer of the BBC was divorced he was summarily dismissed. Finally, Reith's insistence on the public pieties was equally at variance with the baroque unconventionality of his private life. Unlike Lang, he did marry. But the grand passion of his life was not his wife, whom he hated as often as he loved her, but a young man, Charlie Bowser, who was seven years his junior.

The result of these tensions meant that Reith was always an actor, and, as an actor, he was the perfect impresario to the Family Monarchy. He invented the new radio rituals for the royal life cycle; made them suitably portentious and clothed them in sonorous language. Once the heralds had announced the death and accession of kings: now it was the BBC. Reith's role was particularly important at the death of George V. Two months previously, he had attended a meeting at the Cabinet Office to consider "arrangements for the demise of the Crown". With the event, he moved swiftly. On the evening of 20 January 1936, Stuart Hibberd, the chief announcer of the BBC, broadcast the first bulletin: "The King's life is moving peacefully to its close" (as indeed it was, thanks to an injection of morphine). The announcement was then repeated at 15 minute intervals until, just after midnight, Reith himself read the final bulletin: "Death came peacefully to the King at 11.55 p.m." The next evening, the Prime Minister, Stanley Baldwin, was to broadcast to the nation from Downing Street. Reith, invited to dinner with Baldwin, was asked to comment on the script and made crucial alterations: "bringing in the moral authority, honour and dignity of the throne". In short, Reith, long before Richard Dimbleby, was the first gold microphone in waiting.

But "the moral authority, honour and dignity of the throne", so central to the Reithian and Langian enterprise of national moral renewal, depended not only on presentation but, crucially, on the personality of the incumbent. The new King, Edward VIII, was not good moral rearmament material. Reith was well aware of the gossip about his affair with Mrs Simpson and it was his idea that Baldwin's broadcast should include the words: "God guide him aright." God, however, proved deaf to the Prime Minister's prayers and the result was the Abdication Crisis. The Abdication Crisis is the most picked-over episode in the history of the 20th-century monarchy, apart from the break-up of the marriage of Charles and Diana and its recent, tragic dénouement. The two events are closely linked: both derive their magnitude from the idea of the Family Monarchy whose origins and development have been sketched in this essay. But, because they are big, they are typically described as constitutional crises. That is the last thing they are. If they had been, life would have been much simpler, as the experience of Clive Wigram, the King's private secretary, showed. In early 1936, shortly after Edward VIII's accession, Wigram had consulted the Lord Chancellor "about the Marriage Laws of a sovereign". He had expected to be told that marriage with a divorced woman, like Mrs Simpson, was explicitly excluded. Instead, he must have been informed that the laws spoke only of marriage with a Roman Catholic and were silent on the subject of a union with a divorcée. So the law could not stop Edward VIII; only public opinion could do that. But, at the high noon of the Family Monarchy, public opinion, combined with Edward VIII's own doubts about his royal role, was quite strong enough to force the Abdication. Reith and Lang could breathe again, confident that in George VI they had a king who would play his appointed part. And the present Queen Elizabeth II was equally sure about what she should do when she succeeded in 1952: in her speech to her Accession Council she pledged herself to maintain the monarchy as it had been under her father and grandfather.

But if Queen Elizabeth II would not change, the times did, and in the 1960s they changed with unprecedented rapidity: Britain escaped a political revolution; it had a social one instead. And though the Queen remained aloof, her children and still more their future spouses were creatures of the new world. This was a world in which men and women, and women perhaps even more than men, were less inclined to submit themselves to the iron laws of duty; instead, they demanded their own happinesses and satisfactions and, when their marriages failed to supply them, they turned, as more and more of the Queen's subjects did, to the divorce courts. It was also a much less deferential world, in which journalists were more inclined to ask whether an image of happy family life corresponded to the reality. Despite these warning signals, however, the propaganda machine of the Family Monarchy continued to turn. It was like the sorcerer's apprentice, and, like the sorcerer's apprentice, it all ended in tears when the "fairy-tale" marriage of Charles and Diana turned into nightmare.

It was back to 1936, but with a different outcome and a crucially different balance of forces. For instead of the united front of 1936, both public opinion and the Establishment spoke with forked tongues. Separation and even divorce would present no constitutional barrier to Prince Charles' accession, the Prime Minister said. Even the Archbishop of Canterbury temporized. Nevertheless, there was widespread unease. There was a feeling that the "rules" (even if they were only unwritten conventions) had been broken and that Prince Charles had somehow "broken his compact with the nation" (as the *Sun* put it). Public opinion also decided, as public opinion tends to, that an older, rather unattractive man was in the wrong and a young and pretty woman was in the right. Finally, the War of the Wales, in which Charles and Diana slugged it out in public, and traded scandal for scandal, brought the house of Windsor into widespread question. Back in 1936, Edward VIII had no direct heirs, whereas his younger brother, Prince Albert, had two daughters. It was thus easy (as well as sound dynastic policy) to shunt Edward off the throne and replace him with his brother. This is why the Abdication Crisis was over almost as quickly as it had happened. For the Royal Family it was a terrible trauma; for the nation at large it was a nine-day wonder. Now, however, it is not so simple, as Charles has at least done his duty by providing two sons. That makes him virtually immovable. However flawed he may be, the monarchy is most likely stuck with him.

The house of Windsor is therefore stuck also with the failure of the Family Monarchy, of which Charles was the symbol. He resents the role and makes clear to his official biographer, Jonathan Dimbleby, that he regards the whole idea of the Family Monarchy as having been a mistake. His resentment is understandable, but it should not blind us to realities. The Family Monarchy was an extraordinarily effective sales pitch; indeed, it is difficult to think of anything else that could have carried a great imperial monarchy through this turbulent century. It was good for Britain as well. In a fairly benign way, it promoted social and ideological cohesion and this unity in turn helped Britain to survive the strains of the Depression and the Second World War. We paid a price in too much cosiness and conformity. But we have more than made up for it since. Moreover, it is not clear even now that there is any real alternative – least of all the "alternative" monarchy that Charles himself appears to support. No doubt ecology, multiculturalism, and oecumenism are all good causes. But outside *Guardian*-reading circles they have little popular resonance, and popularity is the *sine qua non* of a democratic monarchy.

What must be most galling of all for Prince Charles is that here again his late wife was more successful. What she came up with was not so much an alternative to the Family Monarchy, as its continuation and culmination in the cult of royal celebrity. A celebrity was once defined as someone who is famous for being famous. The later 20th century is more exacting. Coriolanus had to strip to show his wounds to be elected by the Roman plebs and revolted at the thought. Modern celebrities have to strip off in a deeper sense and parade their private lives for public delectation. Few of them seem to balk at the task. Nor, in one of her moods, did Diana. In Andrew Morton's book she describes in detail her upper colonic lavages at one end and her being sick into the lavatory at the other. Royal toilet ritual has always been arcane but this goes beyond even early-modern monarchs who gave audience while using their close-stools. But, bizarre though it is, it was hugely popular. It is also a clear continuation of the Family Monarchy. The Family Monarchy too depended on turning private life into public symbol, but it was a carefully edited privacy. It was also different in its effects. It was designed to reinforce rules and stiffen upper lips. Diana's royal celebrity, on the other hand, was all about doing your own thing and letting it all hang out.

The anticipation, and later the acceptance, of celebrity marks the difference between the British monarchy and the continental monarchies. It has nothing to do with being a bicycling monarch, or much to do with being rich or poor. Some continental monarchs are richer. Queen Beatrix of the Netherlands, for instance, owns personally and directly a substantial slice of Royal Dutch Shell. There is no debate about whether she can sell off the odd Van Dyke or the occasional Holbein drawing; instead she owns tradable stock. The real difference is that the British monarchy is the only one to have played the family card, the celebrity card. The result was its earlier triumphant success; its later débâcle and its present impasse.

14: J Enoch Powell

Monarchy is the expression of the Nation

THE BRITISH public has recently been going through one of its recurrent spells of agony about the future of the hereditary monarchy. The historical origin of an institution being hereditary has no necessary connection with the reasons for its survival. In the case of the hereditary monarchy and hereditary peerage, the origin is connected with the hereditary descent of landed property. The laws governing the descent of peerage derive from those governing the descent of land. Under feudal rules, the tenant of land was under obligation to obey a summons to give counsel and certain other assistance to the owner; and this obligation to obey a writ of summons for that purpose would naturally be inherited when the land passed according to the law governing inheritance.

Monarchy is much older than the feudal system; but there is no reason to doubt that the succession to it has been seen in Britain as comparable to the descent and inheritance of the realm by inheriting land. For instance, when a sovereign leaves more than one female heir and no male heir, parliamentary authority is necessary for succession to the realm, which is treated as an "impartible hereditament", that is, as an inheritance not liable (as land would feudally be liable) to division between co-heiresses. Parliamentary sovereignty, that is, the obligation of the sovereign to rule in accordance with the will of a parliamentary majority, has long since superseded the concept of the realm as the sovereign's property; but there are profound reasons why the hereditary principle has continued to prevail in relation to the House of Lords and to the monarchy itself.

In the last resort, a constitution is that order of things under which the people are content to be governed; and the British, in this as in other important matters, are creatures of habit. There is no enactment (nor could there be) which requires that a parliament can only create law by means of a bill duly passed by both Houses, nor is there any enactment which prescribes the composition of the Upper House. The Upper House is such as that by which along with the predominant Lower House the people of this country have in course of time come to be content to be governed. In a single word, the authority of the House of Lords as at present constituted rests upon "prescription", upon the notion, that is to say, that "it has come to be so".

In the case of the monarchy, its descent, apart from being regulated by the Act of Settlement of 1701, is also dependent upon prescription: we have a monarchy as the functioning mainspring of our constitution "because it has come to be so" – in other words, because we are the sort of people that we are. There is an argument in a circle, but it is a wide and comprehensive circle; for it is by inheritance that we have come to be the people that we are: we were born into it. The status of British citizens, though it can be acquired by a prescribed legal process, is overwhelmingly secured by being born. It is hereditary, and the hereditary monarchy, light years away from the world of feudal thinking, reflects the hereditary nature of the nation itself: we were born into it, and we are what we are by descent. We possess our goods, we possess our political and legal rights, in the same manner and by the same title as that by which the Queen wears her crown.

The Crown, with its duty to rule upon the advice tendered on behalf of a parliamentary majority, is the result of the same historical process as that which shaped and formed the British nation. A seamless garment has been woven by history; we can no more step out of an hereditary monarchy than we can step out of ourselves. It is this fact which inspires and secures the affection and respect in which the wearer of the crown is held and which enables that wearer to "represent", in the full sense of that term, the nation over which he or she rules. Other countries have other histories; but from our history, the history of our monarchy cannot be detached without falsification. The long process of discovering and exploiting ministerial responsibility and thereby parliamentary government has proceeded by means of the monarchy until we accept it unreflectingly as if it were a work of nature. It is not: it is the work of the people, equipped with the resource of an hereditary monarchy, which in the modern world we share with few others. The unbroken evolution of the rights and duties of the British citizen is balanced by the unbroken evolution of the rights and duties of an hereditary monarch: the one goes with the other.

There is a practical aspect to all this. Those who might wish to advocate abolition of the hereditary descent of the monarchy are obliged to specify by what alternative means the head of state would then fall to be identified. When we begin to address that question, we become aware how fortunate we are in that with which history has endowed us. The only alternative available is some form of election, which, in modern times, must surely mean popular election.An insurmountable disadvantage, however, accompanies the popular election of the head and representative of a state. This disadvantage is devastatingly illustrated by the example of the head of state in the United States. No mechanism can cope, or even begin to cope, with change in the political opinion of the electorate, resulting in a contradiction at the heart of government itself, when the executive can at any time be at variance with the legislature or political elective choice of the people. This opens up the reason of the superficially paradoxical fact that in Britain hereditary monarchy has not only been consistent with the evolution of parliamentary democracy but was instrumentally essential to its rise: an hereditary head of state is the ideal accompaniment of government through an elected assembly, because it and it alone resolves the tension between the continuity of policy and of the state itself and the continuing electoral expression of the majority will of the people.

We are in Britain happy in our circumstances. We find ourselves endowed

– no doubt in part because of our situation and our character – with a source of sovereignty, that is to say, with a source of authority which endures, irrespective of electoral fluctuations and to which obedience is owed continuously by all within the nation irrespective of their status or function. The rule of law itself is thus seen as inseparable in origin and in operation from the hereditary monarchy. Not infrequently, the British can look without envy – indeed, with a modicum of conscious pride – upon the predicament of others who have endeavoured to construct viable constitutions without the aid of an inherited and hereditary monarchy. We ought to be thankful for the advantages which we continue to enjoy at the small expense of continuing to be ourselves.

To a certain extent, a similar consideration applies to the hereditary element in the constitution of the Upper House of Parliament. The Lower House, being elected by popular vote, has for more than a century claimed with justice the upper hand in forming the laws and the composition of government. In the absence of the hereditary principle, some other means has to be found for constituting the membership of an upper or second chamber, supposing such to be desirable. Whatever device is adopted must differ from that which determines from time to time the composition of the lower house; if it were not different, unacceptable results would follow: an upper chamber which claimed to be as good a representative of the people as the lower house would be either an unnecessary encumbrance or an insurmountable obstacle. So we arrive at the paradoxical, but unavoidable, conclusion that the hereditary peerage has been, and continues to be, essential to the supremacy of the elected House of Commons – a companion piece, even if not so important, to the function of an hereditary monarchy in relation to the supremacy of parliament.

So long as the observation of the law relating to the Church is observed by the monarch, no constitutional complaint can be lodged against the way the royal supremacy is exercised by a monarch who is in breach of sexual or other moral requirements. The existence of a libertine holder of the Crown is constitutionally perfectly feasible. Only disloyalty on the monarch's part to the constitutional settlement of the Church of England can afford an arguable case for treating the monarch's role as incompatible with his position as Head of the Church; and it is unlikely that behaviour of that kind by the Crown would occur.

It is with a view to make the monarch safe from the only constitutional temptation to which he might be liable, namely, to abandon Protestantism, that special precautions are taken in the coronation service and otherwise. This, and nothing else, is the purpose of the restrictions placed on royal marriages. It would be a mistake, General Synod or no General Synod, to undertake anything which could be understood as a move towards renewing submission to Rome. The momentous consequences of the secession from Rome in which 16th century retain to this day something of their validity.

Being historical and constitutional, the attachment, whatever it may be, of the British public to the monarchy owes precious little to the constitutional indispensability of the monarchy being morally untouched.

The exposure to adverse publicity of the Royal Family by the media has naturally raised the question whether, and how, the law might be brought in to prevent such intrusion. This is a question to which I am obliged to offer a personal answer. I say, therefore, that for myself I can only declare that I would view with grave alarm any attempt to prevent lawful exposure of behaviour which involves no disaffection to any part of the constitution.

What is called British parliamentary democracy is based on these theoretical propositions for the practical workaday life of central management. Down to the secretary of a party branch in the most obscure constituency, all who take part in organizing and ensuring the democratic process are links in a chain which ultimately finds its anchor in the monarchy. The Americans are fond of using the term "democracy" to classify constitutions of which they choose to approve. Well, if Britain is a democracy, that is what we mean by it. As the keystone of this arch there is a person, not an abstraction nor an elected president with a political past. The person of the sovereign is the single indispensable piece in the political set-up of this country. Without the monarchy, the entire structure would collapse. When people ask, "but what does the monarchy *do*?", the literally correct answer has to be: "The monarchy does everything". To remove the monarchy, it would be necessary to recreate the whole structure, to abolish the entire constitutional history of England – which is as much to say, the entire history of England.

It may be that we are suffering from the long reign of Queen Empress Victoria, a reign which coincided with parliament and its power temporarily expanding with British rule and influence in the world. To this the Commonwealth affords a barely sustainable postscript – barely sustainable or compatible, because it is a function of the Crown in the constitution of the United Kingdom to govern on the advice of a responsible minister. When the Queen is Head of the Commonwealth and speaks as such, upon whose advice, and responsibly to whom, can she do it? In this respect, the Crown has been affected: the royal assent for conventional and publicity causes has to be the rule of the sovereign as Head of the Commonwealth. It was the salve which the British people applied to the wound left by the loss of Empire and imperial power: would self-deception still be able to wipe out the consequences with the consolation of a future for the Commonwealth?

Much of the criticism heard today relates to members of the Royal Family who are unlikely to become the sovereign. "The Royals" have become an industry. This view is a constitutional misconception. The duty of complying with the legitimate advice is peculiar to the actual ruling sovereign: it does not extend to those who are not even members of the court of the monarch. While, therefore, it is only natural and well established for the monarchy to refrain from disagreeing visibly with the advice which emerges, this obligation rests upon no other member of the sovereign's family. In the tendering and receipt of advice lies the principal constitutional benefit of having a person, not an abstraction, as sovereign.

The interaction of the Crown and its ministers, the intervention of the monarch, though rarely exposed, is no mere act of state. It is the explanation and discussion of the brief by the chief minister of the Crown which counts. The very act of giving advice and information imposes upon all governments considerations thitherto unrealized. The sovereign is not entitled to decline this advice, but has the right to understand it and receive answers to its questions. That is a practice which may induce reflection and a new direction to the political ball game in cases where there is public controversy. In these circumstances, the advice of ministers can undergo subtle alteration – a safeguard against political aberration.

The personality and individuality of the monarch are of little significance so long as they do not interfere with, or bring into question, the kernel conception of his or her constitutional duty. Being human, it must be expected that monarchs will behave as human beings do behave; for the vulgar this may be a cause of wonder and hilarity – a whole industry is based upon feeding that curiosity – but for the lover of England, of English history, and of England's constitution there can be no such occasion. The question, and the only question, is whether the Crown is disabled from behaving in a constitutional manner. If the answer is No, then *cadit questio*.

There is too much loose talk about the present monarch being succeeded not by the eldest son, but the eldest son's elder son. This ignores a vital fact about the monarchy: the monarchy is subject to the law of England, and the law of England decides the succession. The law of England knows no succession to the Crown other than by the eldest son. For anyone else to succeed, it would be necessary for the reigning sovereign to have already assented to an act of parliament to that effect, passed in both Houses. Until that has happened, the eldest son succeeds at the moment of the monarch expiring and is proclaimed as such by a proclamation which Privy Councillors have signed. When people talk of an alternative successor to the throne, they are talking about passing through parliament a bill to disinherit the lawful heir and replace him by somebody else, an action highly improbable in the absence of evidence of public demand. Such an action would amount to revolution – the alteration of a fundamental principle of the law of the land. The likelihood of this revolution taking place suddenly in that way may reasonably be regarded as extremely remote, especially remembering that it has to take place before the event. In any case, the monarchy is integrated firmly and securely in the constitutional practice of England. As long as the sovereign – and there is no evidence against this – acts only on the advice of an elected minister resting on the majority of the House of Commons, the power of the British monarch is secure against disturbance.

15: David Williamson

Why the monarchy will survive

IN RECENT YEARS, the prophets of gloom and doom have taken a perverse delight in predicting the end of the British monarchy and the establishment of a republic after the death of Her Majesty Queen Elizabeth II. When pressed to give reasons for such a prediction, the woolliness of their thought processes soon becomes apparent. They cite the loss of popularity and confidence in the monarchy resulting from the matrimonial tribulations of the Queen's three married children and follow this up with references to the "cost to the taxpayer" that maintaining the monarchy allegedly involves. This last is an enduring myth which lives on no matter how many times it is pointed out that the monarchy costs the taxpayer nothing, being maintained by the revenues from the Crown Lands, which, since the reign of King George III, every sovereign has voluntarily surrendered to the government in exchange for a Civil List and whereby the government has gained the better bargain since the revenues far exceed the expenses of the monarchy and its trappings.

Characteristically, those who predict the end of the monarchy venture no suggestions of how this is to be effected. Will it be abolished by act of parliament, which the monarch of the day would be called upon to ratify, or will it follow a referendum? Imagination boggles at the thought of the cumbersome machinery and legislation which would be required to dismantle the present monarchical system and set up a republic with an elected head of state in its place. Fortunately, this country tried republicanism and got it out of its system more than 300 years ago, long before the rise of republics elsewhere.

For the first 500 years after the Norman Conquest, monarchs were accepted without question as the natural rulers ordained by God. There were good kings and bad kings, but on the few occasions when one was deposed he was always replaced by another, any other form of government being not only unthinkable but unknown. It cannot really be said that any medieval kings were popular since little more than their names was known to the majority of the people. With the advent of the Tudors, things began to change and the introduction of realistic portraiture on the coinage ensured that the monarch's true likeness became known at last to the people. The first sovereign who can be said to have been popular was Queen Elizabeth I. Her royal progresses about the country made her known to far more of her subjects than any of her predecessors had been, and towards the end of her reign she was able to claim that she counted as its greatest glory the fact that she had reigned with her people's love.

Elizabeth's successor, the alien James I, although unprepossessing in appearance and often uncouth in manner, nevertheless managed to attain a measure of popularity, occasioned partly by his general air of affability and bonhomie and partly by recognition of his skilled statecraft. It was not for nothing that he was called "the wisest fool in Christendom". Under James, too, England experienced the presence of a young royal family. It was a tragedy that the godlike Henry Frederick, Prince of Wales, was cut off in his prime in 1611 and that Princess Elizabeth married and left the country to live abroad, leaving only the sickly "Baby Charles" to take on the burden of royalty after the death of their father. He did so convinced of his "divine right" to rule and, despite his many mistakes which were to lead to the Civil War and the temporary abolition of the monarchy, managed to inspire an all-consuming devotion in his followers. His trial and execution dismayed far more than those who condoned them and it is recorded that when his head was severed from his body a great groan went up from the crowd surrounding the scaffold outside the Banqueting House in Whitehall, and many surged forward to dip handkerchiefs in the royal blood, thus initiating the cult of the "Martyr King" which has persisted in one form or another to the present day. Nearly 150 years were to elapse before another European sovereign (Louis XVI of France) was destined to meet a like fate at the hands of his subjects.

The eleven years that followed Charles I's death saw Britain's first and only experiment with a republican form of government, destined to become a virtual dictatorship under Oliver Cromwell, who assumed many of the trappings of the old monarchy, even to the extent of being seated in the Coronation Chair (moved from Westminster Abbey to Westminster Hall for the purpose) for his installation as Lord Protector. On Cromwell's death, his son and successor, Richard Cromwell, proved to be less than half the man his father had been, so paving the way for the restoration of King Charles II in 1660. The new monarch was received with great enthusiasm on all sides. Young, good-looking, and possessed with the Stuart charm in full measure, he won all hearts and soon proved himself to be an astute ruler well able to maintain his position. Unfortunately, his brother and successor, James II, lacked Charles's charm and was tainted by his bigoted obsession to restore the country to Roman Catholicism. This was something the people would not tolerate and the so-called Glorious Revolution brought about James' downfall and replacement by the joint sovereigns, William III and Mary II. Mary, as James's daughter, was able to command the loyalty which her family had so long inspired, while her husband and cousin William (a Stuart on his mother's side) remained an uninspiring figure accepted as the champion of Protestantism and, after Mary's early death, was endured without enthusiasm until his own death brought Mary's sister Anne to the throne.

Anne's popularity mirrored that of Elizabeth I. She possessed the Stuart charisma in abundance and her tragic failure to rear any of her numerous children only served to endear her even more to her subjects. She would have liked the succession to revert to her Stuart half-brother, but the Act of Settlement had ensured the Protestant succession and Anne's death in 1714 brought the first Hanoverian monarch from Germany to claim the throne.

George I and George II were tolerated rather than loved and neither could be described as a popular monarch. George I's command of English was almost non-existent, while George II's, although fluent, was so heavily accented as to be well-nigh unintelligible. The reigns of both were further marred by the unedifying quarrels which both pursued with his heir apparent.

With the accession of George III in 1760, a new phase in the history of the royal family began. The young King, as he himself said in his first speech to parliament, "gloried in the name of Briton", having been born and bred in England with English as his first language. The young German princess whom he married in the year after his succession soon adapted herself to her new country and the simple, uncomplicated tastes of the King and Queen and their fast growing young family endeared them to the British public in a way which none of their predecessors had achieved. The royal family adopted a lifestyle more in keeping with that of the emerging middle class rather than that of the old aristocracy, with whom they had little in common. Plain fare was served at the royal table and a plain style of dress was affected by the sovereigns, although they could rise to the occasion for court functions and great state ceremonies, which were not to their natural inclination. It was probably because of their austere upbringing that George III's sons did their best to reverse the situation by their louche and often flamboyant behaviour.

George IV, as Regent and King, brought about a brief return of royal magnificence and grandeur with his self-importance and great sense of showmanship. It is only today that we have come to realize how much we owe to his exquisite taste and connoisseurship in the arts. In his day, he was one of our most unpopular sovereigns, reviled for the scandals in his private life as much as for his extravagance. The brief reign of his brother and successor, William IV, a bluff and hearty sailor whose wilder eccentricities were tempered by the gentle influence of Queen Adelaide, paved the way for the accession of Queen Victoria, in whose reign royal popularity was to reach its zenith.

Although Victoria had to weather some anti-monarchical demonstrations during the early years of her reign, she won through with Albert's guidance and despite her later years of seclusion as "the Widow of Windsor" was to end it as the most loved monarch this country has known. "Well done, old girl," the spontaneous exclamation of a bystander at her Diamond Jubilee procession, was music to her ears and greatly appreciated by her.

The short reign of Edward VII which followed that of Victoria again brought Britain a sovereign whose lifestyle and love of splendour emulated that of George IV to some extent, yet "King Teddy" enjoyed a personal popularity second to none and his subjects were willing to turn a blind eye to his extramarital peccadilloes as was his wife, the beautiful Queen Alexandra.

Under King George V and Queen Mary, the Royal Family returned to the humdrum, though much admired, domesticity effected by George III and Victoria. At his Silver Jubilee in 1935 King George felt able to record in his diary after the overwhelming demonstration of popular affection he had received, "I'd no idea they felt like that about me. I am beginning to think they must really like me for myself."

The Abdication Crisis of 1936, far from weakening the monarchy as many predicted, only served to give it a new boost of popularity as King George VI and Queen Elizabeth continued the pattern set by King George V and Queen Mary, and the accession of a young and attractive Queen in 1952 was the occasion of further popular acclaim. Throughout her long reign, Queen Elizabeth II has maintained her personal popularity and on the occasion of her Silver Jubilee in 1977 the atmosphere which could be felt by anyone who mingled with the crowds testified to this a thousandfold. It is unfortunate that the matrimonial troubles experienced by the Queen's three married children have brought about a certain disillusionment in them and consequent loss of popularity, although Princess Anne appears to have suffered the least from this and a recent survey named her as the first choice for president should this country become a republic.

The monarchy will survive because history has shown it to be the most stable form of government where the head of state is above politics and provides continuity whatever governments may come and go, thus remaining the true representative of all the people. I am confident that when Queen Elizabeth II celebrates her Golden Jubilee in 2002 she will experience a demonstration of her people's love and affection exceeding that of 1977. Over the past 500 years, as I have tried to demonstrate, the popularity of our sovereigns and royal family has waxed and waned and it will continue to do so. If the Queen matches her mother's longevity the next reign may be comparatively short, but I venture to predict that the monarchy will enjoy a new golden age under the future King William V.

16: Hugo Vickers

The legacy of Diana, Princess of Wales

ON 6 SEPTEMBER 1997, a solemn and magnificent funeral took place at Westminster Abbey. Let us suppose there was someone with a certain knowledge of protocol and heraldry who turned on the television set without knowing who had died. Let us suppose also that this person had not been following recent events for a year or two. What would he see?

Looking at the coffin, he would observe the standard of a Royal Highness (the Royal Standard with the ermine patterned border that is traditionally used by those princesses who have married into the Royal House). He would see the Royal Family on the one side and the Spencers on the other. Presently, he would deduce that the coffin was that of the Princess of Wales. Interestingly, and significantly, there would be nothing to indicate that she was divorced from Prince Charles. In death, for the ceremonial royal funeral, Diana returned to her position within the royal fold. Had she looked down on the service, she would no doubt have experienced ambivalent feelings. On the one hand, she would have been reassured that her esteem in the hearts of the nation was secure; on the other, she may well have felt that this was everything from which she longed to escape.

It is a challenge − thought not an impossible one − to put Diana, Princess of Wales into perspective. Queen Elizabeth II came to the throne in 1952 and moved into Buckingham Palace with her two children, Prince Charles (born in 1948) and Princess Anne (born in 1950). Later the family expanded to include Prince Andrew (born in 1960) and Prince Edward (born in 1964).

There were times in the late 1950s and early 1960s when interest in the monarchy was fairly mute. Interest focuses on members of the family at the times when they are being born, growing up, getting married, and having babies. There is also a more solemn interest in the older ones and sadness when they die. Therefore, the Royal Family attracted more attention than hitherto towards the end of the 1960s as Prince Charles emerged from his shy chrysalis into a charming, rather articulate young man. After leaving Cambridge, he began to travel, he undertook training at RAF College, Cranwell, obtaining his wings, making a solo jet flight in a Jet Provost, and co-piloting a supersonic Phantom jet. During these years, he was seen engaging in a great number of activities, including such dramatic endeavours as undertaking a parachute jump into the sea. Then he entered the Royal Navy. He responded to whatever demands were put to him in the interests of making him a well rounded heir to the throne. In 1977, he left the Royal Navy to oversee the Silver Jubilee Appeal and to take part in the various celebrations. It was after that year that pressure grew about his choice of a bride.

The Prince did not make matters easy for himself by declaring at a much younger age, when presumably it all seemed a long way off, that the age of 30 would be a good one at which to take a wife. As his 30th birthday approached in November 1978, so too the pressure from the media increased. The Prince's choice of bride was interesting in many ways. He had given his yardstick in an important interview with Kenneth Harris in *The Observer* in June 1974. The gist of it was as follows:

> Whatever your place in life, when you marry you're forming a partnership which you hope will last, say, fifty years ... I've been brought up in a close-knit happy family and family life means more to me than anything else. So I'd want to marry someone who had interests which I understood and could share ... A woman not only marries a man; she marries into a way of life in which she's got a contribution to make. She's got to have some knowledge of it, some sense of it, or she wouldn't have a clue about whether she's going to like it and if she didn't have a clue it would be risky for her, wouldn't it? If I'm deciding on whom I want to live with for fifty years – well, that's the last decision in which I would want my head to be ruled entirely by my heart. It's nothing to do with class; it's to do with compatibility.

There were a number of options open to the Prince of Wales. One was to marry a bride from a foreign royal house, who would therefore understand the problems of royal life. In a sense, this would follow the well established line of arranged royal unions. In the 1970s, this was complicated by a lack of candidates and the Catholic issue. A great number of them were Roman Catholics and if he had married a Catholic, he would have lost his rights to the throne. A second option was the "executive" woman. In the late 1970s, the influence of his father and Lord Mountbatten might perhaps have steered him to an executive girl, someone highly qualified who had made a mark on life through her own merit. In this context Queen Silvia of Sweden comes to mind. The daughter of a businessman, university educated, and further trained at interpreters' school, Silvia Sommerlath had worked in the Argentinian consulate in Munich and her most senior post before marriage was as deputy head of protocol on the Organizing Committee of the Winter Olympics at Innsbruck. She has proved an admirable Queen of Sweden, probably more in touch with modern times than the King himself. But Prince Charles eschewed the world of foreign princesses or career girls, and in his choice of a bride, he veered back to the world so beloved by King George VI and Queen Elizabeth The Queen Mother – the world of Sandringham, of winter shoots, Wellington boots, and thick jackets to keep out the cold.

Lady Diana Spencer was a resident of Park House, Sandringham, where she spent her first fourteen years, until the death of her grandfather in 1975. Thus she was a neighbour of the Royal Family and a youthful playmate of Prince Andrew's. The Spencers had been settled in Northampton at Althorp since 1506. They were sheep farmers. Then, while their Spencer-Churchill cousins were warriors, they became patrons of the arts and courtiers. Lady

Diana's great-grandfather, the 6th Earl Spencer, was Lord Chamberlain to Edward VII and George V. Both her grandmothers and no less than four great-aunts had served the Queen Mother as ladies-in-waiting, and some of these were close personal friends. Her sister Jane was married to Robert Fellowes, who had joined The Queen's household in 1977 and would eventually become the Queen's Private Secretary.

That was one version of the story. There were, however, other elements. Lady Diana's mother had left the family when they were all very young. With her brother, Lady Diana had trailed from her father's home to her mother's during family holidays. There was further dissension in the family in that during the divorce, Ruth, Lady Fermoy, Lady Diana's maternal grandmother, had sided against her daughter, and assisted her son-in-law, Lord Spencer, to gain custody of the children. Lord Spencer then remarried, his second wife being Raine, Countess of Dartmouth, born a McCorquodale, the daughter of Barbara Cartland, the romantic novelist. There was further divorce in that family. This introduced a rather different element into the story, and for many years, there was a certain *froideur* between Lady Diana and her step-mother.

Prince Charles and Lady Diana were said to have met in a ploughed field on the Sandringham estate, and the courtship was conducted discreetly at Balmoral. She was assisted in her romantic quest, for such it clearly was, by her sister, Lady Jane Fellowes, who knew the Prince of Wales's whereabouts during his holiday. Presently, young Diana was being included in more and more of the Prince's activities. Here there was a definite sense of a campaign to brighten his existence with a youthful companion. If his heart was not stirred to love, it was at least stirred. Lady Diana was not a girl of academic achievement, nor did she show any particular flare or style. She was a kindergarten teacher, sharing a flat in Earls Court with three other girls. Therefore, it is clear that it was her Spencer origins that stood her in good stead, combined with her readiness to accept the challenge. The Prince of Wales was reassured in his choice of bride. He proposed early in 1981 and they were married at St Paul's Cathedral in a magnificent, happy ceremony in July 1981.

One of the reasons that made the wedding memorable was an element of poignancy and concern – the feeling that matters between the Prince and his bride were not entirely resolved. While it would be wrong to say that many predicted that the affair would end in disaster, even the bride herself was aware that she had not yet won Prince Charles's heart. She was aware of the presence in the background of Camilla Parker-Bowles, who had been the Prince's girlfriend and was married to the very Household Cavalry officer, who was in charge of the Sovereign's Escort at the wedding. To what extent Mrs Parker-Bowles was a threat to the happiness of the bride we shall probably never know, but she was enough of one to make the new Princess of Wales extremely insecure. Again, most of this we know with hindsight. But the hints of it, circulating at the time, were enough to make many feel protective of the young princess. The Royal Wedding heralded a new age of royalty. The Prince of Wales, who had appeared a slightly lonely figure in the year or so before his marriage, now emerged with his young bride at his side. If he changed at all, it was imperceptible, but she did. The shy Lady Diana, previously noted for hanging her head, blossomed into the role of Princess of Wales. Then, during the 15 years or so of the marriage, she underwent several transformations or reinventions.

At first she was youthful, coltish, and gauche. The world waited and watched, fascinated to see how she would cope. She coped very well. Her friendly shyness endeared her to the crowds, and in the early years of her marriage, she fulfilled the sternest expectations of any dynastic family, by producing not one son, but two. Prince William was born in 1982 and Prince Harry two years later.

Then she blossomed into an icon of style. She grew ever more lovely, wore striking clothes, and became a great boost to the British fashion industry. In those heady early days of marriage, the couple were wanted everywhere and there was something rather touching about the fact that the Princess was just as excited to meet stars such as Elizabeth Taylor as they were to meet her. The quality that particularly endeared her to the general public was the one that has traditionally made princesses popular since the beginning of time. Naturally, the glamour and physical beauty helped to a large extent, but there are many vapid beauties who hold little appeal for the crowd. More so, it was that she possessed a good heart. This gave her a natural affinity with young people and the old and an almost mystical identification with the sick. These are gifts that cannot be faked and others have looked uncomfortable when trying to emulate her performance. Children were drawn to her and she cheered many an old person whose life had become sad. Her care for the sick was directed to the great plague of modern times, Aids and HIV. When this disease first became a phenomenon in the early 1980s, there were many who shied away from the victims, treating them as lepers. But the Princess reached out to them, and with that simple gesture, redirected the general awareness of the public to a more humane understanding of their suffering. This humanitarian attitude was also directed to poor and starving children, to the war wounded, and leprosy sufferers.

Those fortunate enough to see the Prince and Princess of Wales in the early days of their marriage can testify to their appearance of happiness together. It is easy to negate the good times, but good times there were, and everywhere they went they caused so much happiness and joy that much of it reflected on them. But there were downsides to this too. The Prince of Wales was so trained for duty that he found much of the hype embarrassing and tiresome. It is said that he resented the crowd's wish to see his wife and their disappointment if they drew him instead. It is impossible not to sympathize with him when he was trying to make an important point in a speech and get his message over, when next day he found the headlines preoccupied solely with Diana's latest outfit. The gradual drawing apart of the Prince and Princess has been well chronicled. The marriage could possibly have survived publicly, if not privately, had the scrutiny of the press not been so intense. They were subjected to gross invasions of privacy. Both had telephone conversations tapped on a regular basis, and the most damaging and embarrassing results broadcast to the world. The Princess caused her rooms at Kensington Palace to be swept regularly and bugs were sometimes found. She felt the need to post her letters in miscellaneous boxes and to talk on her mobile telephone in the garden for fear that her calls were being monitored. Nothing merited such treatment and yet it continued. The press, of which there are too many rival representatives working in Britain, then chose to dwell on what it called "the war of the Waleses" emphasizing rivalries between two opposing camps. There was clearly some evidence for this, but it is hard to sift the truth from the mass of innuendo.

Both parties were aware of some of the unpleasant revelations that could emerge, notably the tapes later dubbed "Squidgygate" and "Camillagate". In a fevered atmosphere of paranoia, the Princess embarked on a misjudged campaign of damage limitation, authorizing friends to talk to a journalist called Andrew Morton, who produced a highly revelatory book called *Diana – Her True Story*. In a similar and equally misjudged attempt, Prince Charles cooperated with Jonathan Dimbleby on a documentary about his life, shown on television in the summer of 1994, and followed by an authorized book. While this book had considerably more merit than Morton's in style and content, it too fuelled the tabloids. In both film and book, Prince Charles revealed that, on the irretrievable breakdown of his marriage, he had been unfaithful. The ruffled feathers settled in time, only to be stirred again by the Princess of Wales undertaking a deeply frank interview with *Panorama* on BBC1 in the autumn of 1995. At that point, The Queen decided that enough was enough. Detecting a reluctance on either side to be the first one to instigate divorce proceedings, she instructed the Waleses to do just that. Thereafter, the divorce proceeded relatively smoothly and was finalized in August 1996. The Princess of Wales lost the title of Royal Highness and became known as Diana, Princess of Wales. She had declared a wish to be some kind of roving ambassador for Britain and set about creating this role for herself. She lived exactly a year following the divorce, and it seemed that she was beginning to find her feet. Though she had no official role, she continued to do her bit for Britain mainly in support of a handful of charities. She travelled to Bosnia and Angola. She raised the question of land mines, which was treated more seriously after her death than during her lifetime. She raised astonishing sums in a sale of her dresses at Christie's in New York, donating the money to the Aids Crisis Trust.

On the one hand, she developed the humanitarian side of her life, and on the other she retreated into a form of private life. Britain was the country that made her feel most unwelcome, yet this was her home. She carried out relatively few official engagements in Britain, reserving her more formal and glamorous engagements for overseas. This country was the loser. Our enduring image of her in the last year or so was of a figure in a track suit on her way to a strenuous workout at the Harbour Club. The contradictions continued. She claimed that she wanted a role, yet she dropped out of working for a great number of her charities after her divorce. No longer a Royal Highness she resigned as colonel of the regiments that held her in esteem. She was a loose cannon and no one could be sure which way she would next turn. From time to time, fears were expressed for her health and sanity, and yet she could still charm any who met her, and certainly in the last summer of her life, she looked the picture of Californian health, and had lost none of her sparkle or wit or gentle conspiratorial way of talking to strangers and making them feel immensely special.

History may well choose to judge that in the last few months of her life, she was spiralling into a dangerous form of chaos. Whatever the merits of character possessed by Mr Dodi Fayed, he came from one of the most controversial dynasties operating in Britain today. Had she proceeded to marry him, there would have been considerable embarrassment for the Royal Family, and surely a great falling away of her many supporters. It was said, too, that she intended to drop out of official life, to cease her humanitarian activities. She might even have ended up as mistress of the house in the Bois de Boulogne where the Duke and Duchess of Windsor eked out their last years in self-imposed exile. It would have been no more than a phase, ultimately damaging to her. She might have done none of these things, for those incessant holidays of the last weeks, punctuated by her attendance at the murdered Gianni Versace's funeral and a highly publicized Red Cross trip to Bosnia, did not necessarily presage marriage. Frightened by the Establishment and its ways, and virtually driven from these shores by the relentless harassment of the media, the Princess sought a different kind of happiness. She could have been better protected – indeed one would have thought that the Fayeds would have ensured more than adequate protection, given their predilection for body guards and guard dogs – yet, for whatever exact reason, late on an August night, she fled the paparazzi in a car driven by a man called back on duty when he had thought it safe to drink, and as a result she was involved in a desperate car accident in the tunnel de l'Alma in Paris, and may have spent her last conscious moments in the familiar, but merciless blitz of paparazzi flashes.

The effect of the death of Diana, Princess of Wales, moved all but the soulless. Britain lived through an extraordinary week in the aftermath of her death. Shock and disbelief grew into anger and the wish to blame – frequently a part of grief, especially where he or she who grieves feels an element of guilt. The anger was directed first at the paparazzi photographers and the press in general, then at the driver of the car (particularly when it was learnt that he was three times over the legal alcohol limit), and then towards the Royal Family. It may be logical to suppose that it was a long week and that newspapers had to fuel the flames to keep interest at fever pitch until the funeral on

Saturday, but there was clearly an undercurrent of resentment towards The Queen who remained silent at Balmoral while mass hysteria grew in London.

The grieving soon became a cult. Those who left their flowers and messages were doing more than mourn Diana. It was as though her sudden, tragic death had unleashed a semi-religious fervour. Each who laid flowers was laying them for their own private sorrow as much as for her. We have had massacres and tragedies over the years that have shocked the country (Newbury and Dunblane, for example) but no major national figure has died who has inspired national mourning on a grand scale. Possibly the last to inspire such feelings was Earl Mountbatten of Burma, brutally murdered by the IRA in 1979. In Diana's case, the mourning was more emotional and unrestrained. Mythology and the rewriting of history abounded that week. The Diana who had been ruthlessly attacked in the week before for interfering in politics was now thought of only as a saintly humanitarian figure. It seemed that a secular saint was being created, and her death, like those of Evita Peron, Marilyn Monroe, Elvis Presley, and even Princess Grace of Monaco, inspired what virtually amounted to the worship of a graven image, fulfilling a deep need of the soul that was not found in traditional religion. That there were tiny candles and that the flowers came wrapped in cellophane was indicative of that kind of Catholic fervour found in peasant villages on the continent. It was, somehow, very un-English.

Looking back on the week from a position of modest perspective which the passing of even a little time can give, several things become clear. The new government, in power for three heady months, possibly well meaning or possibly not, was inexperienced and appeared to respond to different feelings from those traditionally associated with Britain. Mr Blair hailed her as "The People's Princess" which struck a popular chord with most people, though a note of caution in others. Then the journalists were largely so young as to be ignorant of any of the ground-rules that apply on such occasions. Unnecessary trouble was therefore fuelled over what were perceived as slights such as the Union Flag not flying at half-mast over Buckingham Palace. The Royal Family were presented as distant and remote figures, hiding on their estate in Scotland, while the Londoners mourned in the streets. It is clear that direct statements from the Palace will be needed often in the future. The nation needs to be nursed more than hitherto, and even the most obvious of facts need to be publicly stated before tabloid newspapers promote the opposite. Thus we needed a spokesman to explain the simple fact the Queen was staying at Balmoral to look after her two grandsons, whose mother had been tragically killed in a car accident. The Princess of Wales would have expected nothing less, after all.

By the middle of the week, the Queen was unfairly the focus of the anger. Much of this abated when her press secretary, Geoffrey Crawford, emerged from Buckingham Palace to announce that she would return early and make a statement. The Queen was very much "on trial" before her live, televized statement, but the hostility dissolved the moment she arrived in London and stepped out of her car to look at the flowers. Her statement that evening wholly fulfilled the needs of media and nation and her appeal for unity was heard. Alas, some of the good done was undone the next day when Lord Spencer used his otherwise excellent eulogy to deliver a lightly veiled attack on the Royal Family. Thereafter, the so-called debate on the monarchy was reopened. Since Diana's death, acres of newspaper space has been filled with predictions whether the monarchy will survive and how it will change. For some years, certain vociferous republicans have emerged from relative obscurity. In a media-run age, there is a better living to be made from attacking old institutions such as the monarchy than by defending them. The call for change, the continual undermining, the reinterpretation of events, the inspiring of conflict and debate is what keeps radio and television thriving. The Royal Family have been made the victims of much of this, and in years when human failings have been unearthed in the younger ones, there has been much on which to feed.

The power of the press has been shown in full measure in the weeks since Diana's death. The Queen's tour of India was described as a "disaster", a "catastrophe", and as "The Queen's unhappy tour". It did not seem any of those things in India at the time. Indeed, the Queen and Prince Philip could be forgiven for thinking they were on a wholly different trip from that reported in the British press. Then much has been made of the success of the Prince of Wales, with young Prince Harry, in Africa in late October and November. The Prince was hailed as a new man, which, quite clearly, he is not. More likely he is emerging from the protective shell in which he has hidden in recent years, without fear of being upstaged by his late wife. The true conclusion is that for the first time in many years the press decided to give the Prince an easy ride.

At the time of Diana's funeral, the people appeared to clamour for informality and the common touch and for emotion to be shown. Yet, on the other hand, none could fail to be impressed by the well rehearsed procession to the abbey, the cortège arriving on the dot of 11am, and also by the restrained composure of the Princess's two young sons as they walked behind their mother's coffin. Thus there are contradictions in the air. The same contradictions caused the entire crowd in Hyde Park to stand at the playing of the National Anthem, and yet to clap and cheer Lord Spencer when he said of his sister that she "proved in the last year that she needed no royal title to continue to generate her particular brand of magic". There is danger in the fast-moving global media that everyone is only as good as their last "sound-bite". Events are flashed onto screens all over the world the moment they happen. We can assess these events as they take place and before the participants have finished performing them. Lacking historical perspective, or the ability to put these events into some kind of context, we make instant responses. Inevitably, this is dangerous for figures such as members of the Royal Family, who have been trained not to react and respond but to keep their own counsel.

They risk appearing as remote figures living under a veil of mystique, custom, and ritual. As we saw perhaps more acutely than ever before in connection with this death, the "sound-bite" is all important. Yet it must also be emphasized that the slick "sound-bite" is not everything. There is value in continuity, reliability, acquired experience, the absolute attributes of a good, constitutional monarch, trained for life for the job.

The Princess of Wales had a natural way with people and had developed into a living icon, quick to be photographed, her every effort rewarded with media coverage, often complimentary. But there were other aspects to her character, which led to criticism. She was accused of hogging the cameras, manipulating the press and, worst of all, airing her grievances against her husband in public. She was unpredictable, self-destructive, and wayward in her friendships. She had a considerable turnover in staff, which is never a good sign. She had even quarrelled with Andrew Morton about possession of the tapes she had given him. Any rounded portrait of the Princess would have to address these negative aspects of her character.

The Queen, at the age of 71, cannot compete with the Diana image in her appeal to photographers and journalists. But the Queen's qualities, some of which may appear old-fashioned, are of considerable value. For more than 45 years she has served this country dutifully. She has dealt with governments of every political persuasion, remained unswerving through crises large and small, and a number of small wars, and has visited more or less every country in the world, even Russia and China, which appeared impossible at the outset of the reign. She has met, entertained, and been entertained by a host of historical figures, from Khrushchev to Yeltsin, Truman to Nixon, de Gaulle to Emperor Hirohito of Japan. She is most adept at dealing with heads of state. Her first British Prime Minister, Sir Winston Churchill, was a man born in 1874, who had served as a junior minister to Queen Victoria. Her present Prime Minister, Tony Blair, was not even born when she came to the throne. This wealth of absorbed experience, the day to day study of state papers, and being well informed at a high level for nearly half a century, is exactly what makes a constitutional monarch increasingly valuable.

There have been times of instability, moments of political unrest, and times when governments are in crisis, but always there has been the Queen, unchanging and undeterred, waiting to work with whoever emerges from the fray. The Queen is above politics, but no longer above the demands of the global media. She will need a certain awareness to deal with this problem, a certain flexibility, though not too much. It is unfair to expect her to change radically. She is at an age when most people are already retired and yet this she cannot and will not do, being anointed as Queen for life. She has only ever made four or five trips abroad for pleasure, always in connection with a professional interest in horses, racing, and breeding. She is not to be found on the yachts of dubious millionaires.

The monarchy is said to reinvent itself regularly and to have often done so in the past. This is true. Sometimes it happens by the natural process of the passing of time and sometimes by design. The next generation will no doubt be different, and will do things in a different way. They have been brought up with other values and new demands on them. If we wind the clock forward, we can picture how the Royal Family might look in 25 years' time. It will be considerably diminished in size. More than likely the lone figure of King Charles will be on the throne, with his two boys, grown up and possibly married with young families of their own. The Duke of York and Prince Edward are likely to be supporting figures, but it is possible that they will be somewhat marginalized. The Duke of York's two daughters may well have married into private or semi-private life. The Princess Royal, on the other hand, would be a formidable figure in the background. The others would be very old and thus on the sidelines. Winding the clock forward further still, the focus will be on King William and his brother, and any off-spring they may have. They will embody the tradition of their father's family, tempered by all they absorbed from their mother. They will be the ultimate, living legacy of Diana.

17: Robert Smith

The Royal Prerogative

THIS COUNTRY is no different from any other in its use of ritual as a binding agent of national unity. French ritual centres on the French Revolution; American on their War of Independence and the Constitution; Chinese ritual centres on the 1949 Revolution; Russian ritual used to centre on the 1917 Revolution. We are all bound up in the ritual of our countries, our outward symbols of maturity and nationhood. As nations, we all appeal to some historical "beginning", some event, some date. The further back in time the "originating" date, the greater the legitimacy the authority of the state seems to have. Rulers have long understood the importance of this – that their rights become "hallowed by time". Assyrian king lists were augmented with legendary kings to make their dynasties appear to be as ancient as those of pharaonic Egypt. More recently, the Conservative party likes to trace its antecedents to Edmund Burke; the Labour party, until recently, to the Tolpuddle Martyrs or Keir Hardie. It remains to be seen if, in losing its traditional roots, New Labour can thrive.

The principal difference between Britain and most other countries is that our ritual centres on an ancient monarchy, dating back, depending on your historical viewpoint, to Egbert, King of Wessex, or William the Conqueror. So we speak of a timescale of at least nine centuries of more or less continuous legitimacy that is perhaps only trumped by the Empire of Japan whose rulers claim descent from Amaterasu more than 2,000 years ago.

One of the ventricles at the heart of the British monarchy is the Royal Prerogative, a subject that arises whenever the pundits think that there might be a hung parliament. I want to address it by drawing my conclusion at the beginning, which is that the Royal Prerogative, for all practical purposes, is completely misunderstood, and spoken of almost always wrongly, by defenders and opponents of the monarchy alike, to support their cases.

The Crown

But first, we must define the most important of our terms which occurs throughout this book and this is "the Crown". This is a very lazy expression, often used by historians and constitutional folk to mean the monarch, the monarch's prerogative, the Royal Family, the Royal Yacht, Trooping the Colour, the Royal Train, and everything else. In fact, the crown is a lump of gold, studded with gems and lies in the Jewel House of the Tower of London. The abstract of "the Crown" is everything from the law courts, the Queen's secretaries of state, to local authorities, and even the gas board, which latter enjoys some statutory powers. Clearly, the statutory powers of the gas board to enter your house to read the meter are hardly powers one associates with the Queen's Prerogative.

We need a brief historical guide to that seamless garment, the British constitution, which jurists, like de Tocqueville, thought did not exist, but others of us, with Anson, would say does exist and that if only one could find it, it would be a monument to political sagacity. Our unwritten, or uncodified, constitution is a gradual adaptation of rules to suit convenience; it is original and spontaneous, and we need to go back to the old feudal monarchy to try to understand it. As suggested by Professor Smyth at chapter 2, the Anglo-Saxon kings were very like tribal chiefs. William the Conqueror was, perhaps, only the most successful of these medieval warlords, and he effectively owned the kingdom and was everyone's landlord. Kings also owned, in a very real sense, the justice of the kingdom and made great profits in administering it. The Crown itself was much like a piece of real property which William the Conqueror claimed was bequeathed to him by Edward the Confessor. The Anglo-Norman monarchy tended towards absolutism, but an absolutism tempered with a kind of public acclamation at coronations, no doubt encouraged by troops with swords and spears, and a coronation oath, promising to govern by the laws of King Edward. William II may have been assassinated for not ruling in accordance with these laws (whatever they may have been, as Edward, though sometimes known as a lawgiver, has left us no laws of his own). It was accounted of some importance by the baronage that William's brother and successor, Henry I, swore to uphold the ancient laws at his coronation. Additionally, the matter-of-factness of feudal land ownership, which treated even the Crown as private property, was further tempered by the personal bond of fealty and commendation: ie that in return for service, the man doing homage received, among other things, protection. The implication was that there was a contract, binding on both parties, as King John was to discover at Runnymede in 1215 when Magna Carta was forced on him.

Dr Carpenter shows at chapter 5 that as government became more complex and costly during the 13th century, so kings of England felt obliged to summon the more substantial men of the kingdom and the high clergy to a parliament, the purpose of which was not just to grant taxes (or supplies, as taxes are still called), but to obtain the opinions of the important persons in the kingdom, particularly to make sure that they supported royal policy. In the course of the 14th century, it became customary for parliament to lay petitions before the king and, quite soon, individuals began to lay petitions before parliament: precursors perhaps of lobbyists today. With the accession of Henry IV, at the end of the 14th century, government − mainly the law courts − had become so busy and complex that it was not only impossible for the king to deal with any business himself, except of the gravest nature, but even his officials could no longer cope. The Lord High Steward, the Lord High Treasurer, the Marshal − really only grand-sounding names given to officers who could be found on any reasonable sized estate − were inadequate to the task, and power, while emanating originally from the king, was no longer in the king's hands, which is not to say that kings were powerless (after all, the Tudors lay in the future), but kings were simply unable to deal with matters except of first importance. With the disintegration of the feudal system, from the 13th century onwards, a new idea of kingship developed, especially after the Reformation, when the pope was excluded and the Holy Roman emperor's powers relied more on his Habsburg demesne lands than on being emperor. This was the concept of the Divine Right of kings. The kingdom was still property, but now it was held of God, according to this theory, and Tudor and Stuart kings claimed only to be answerable to Him. This was opposed by an increasingly important group of people – not just restricted to the well off – whom we might loosely call puritans, who saw the king as the exponent of the wishes of the nation, by which they meant their wishes.

The puritans, we might say, won the last battle in 1688–9, when a convention parliament declared the throne vacant; altered the succession by offering the Crown jointly to William III and Mary II; and passive obedience, which had been at the heart of divine monarchy, was superseded by attaching conditions to the tenure of the Crown. We call it the Glorious Revolution, but in many ways, the importance of parliament in 1689 had been prefigured by Henry VIII. Locke wrote of our natural rights; Hobbes that the state existed to restrain lawlessness; the utilitarians that it existed for the common good. The years 1688–9 were when the state came to be set up for our advantage (or at least our advantage eventually) and the king was simply part of the state, though an important part. It would be unwise to imagine that William III was a cipher. Parliament gave him a great deal of money – far more than had ever been given to any British-born king – and left him with powers of veto, for example, which he was expected to use, and did. But he was, at it were, chairman and chief executive, with co-directors and shareholders in parliament whose good will was critical if he were to discharge his functions and, indeed, keep his job. The historian Walter Bagehot called it the "secret republic", and it is the basis of our present constitutional arrangements.

The Privy Council

But in the last 300 years, a curious thing has happened. Power appears to be vested in the hands of people who never exercise it; while power is actually exercised by people who are not recognized by the law. Since the Glorious Revolution, the Cabinet has evolved, but I think I am right in asserting that the Cabinet has no legal standing. I also believe I am correct in asserting that the law does not recognize the office of prime minister. From very earliest days, English and Scots kings had a council, or great council, of the most important men in the kingdom. But the great council was unwieldy and only summoned for the gravest of matters, such as that called in 1085 when Domesday Book was commissioned, or to rubber-stamp such rules as the king and his close officials had already decided. The Norman kings' high officers ran his household, which was not just his court, purveyances, and other necessities of life, but administered his laws, the lands he held directly himself. Officials included the Lord Steward, the Chief Butler, the Marshal, in themselves menial posts, but urgently sought by the highest noblemen in the realm for the close proximity they gave to the person of the king. Almost at once, these offices became hereditary and almost simultaneously they ceased to have any power. Norman kings were well aware that the officials who administered their estates and their courts had to be answerable and thus removeable. The great noblemen expected their offices to be hereditary, like their other titles and lands, and the Norman kings dealt with this by appointing complementary officials to discharge the functions of the hereditary officials, who enjoyed all the social status without any of the day-to-day power. This lay in the hands of others, often low-born men, who could be removed at will.

The modern cabinet enjoys some similarities: the monarch has the outward symbols of power, but the cabinet can only be removed at a general election. The monarch can only be removed by revolution.

The judicial system is the keystone of any organized state, and by controlling the judicial system the medieval king controlled the state, so the first of this new breed of officer, as early as the first years of the 12th century, was the justiciar, who headed the royal courts and was wholly dependent on the king for his place. He quickly became so important that in their long absences in their French dominions, Angevin kings of England almost always appointed the justiciar chief governor of the kingdom, or regent. We can count some of the hereditary officers even today: the office of Lord Great Chamberlain belongs to whoever shall be Marquess of Cholmondeley, but he does nothing, except attend the State Opening, and is not paid. His ancient functions are administered by the Lord Chamberlain, presently the Earl of Airlie, who is appointed, paid, and can be sacked. The Lord Treasurership merged in the monarch on the accession of Henry IV, and has remained in the person of the monarch ever since. We shall revert to some of these officials presently.

We must now return to the Great Council to see how law was administered. From about the reign of Henry III in the 13th century, this council comes to be known as the Privy Council for the very good reason that, while many men might claim a place on it and, from time to time, be summoned to it, essentially it becomes the council of the king's key servants: his private advisers. The Privy Council is very well known to the law and from quite early times the members of the Council, such as the Chancellor (who superseded the Justiciar in the 13th century) dispensed the king's powers. The king could, of course, dispense these powers himself had he been able to discharge the growing business of government, but it was obviously much more convenient for the king's powers to be delegated, say, to what was soon to be the Court of King's Bench, staffed by trained lawyers. Before long, it is impossible for the king to preside because he does not know the law, so while his judges are interpreting the king's law and exercising the delegated power of the king in his courts, it would be quite improper for the king to attend these courts himself and to insist on judging. I believe I am correct in thinking that the last king to preside at a trial was Edward IV in the 1470s.

The law courts

This is not to say that kings ceased to take an interest in their courts. On the contrary, they took a keen interest and one of the bones of contention between parliament and executive until 1701 was the king's claim that judges only held their office during pleasure – *bene placido*, to use the legal expression – like all other officers. Stuart kings in particular guarded their right to dismiss judges, upon whom Charles I had hoped to rely in the legal contest with parliament, most notably the Lord Chief Justice, Sir Edward Coke, who failed to bring in judgments to the king's liking. The Act of Settlement of 1701 finally established that the king could no longer sack judges, who were to hold henceforth on good behaviour and could only be removed on an address to the sovereign by both Houses of Parliament. The situation has not changed, although county court judges, established in 1846, who are appointed by the Lord Chancellor, can be dismissed without reason.

Control over appointments to and, formerly, removal from the bench, of judges is of the greatest importance, but to propose, as some do, that the royal link with the judiciary gives the sovereign, and thus the executive, special privileges in respect of the law is nonsense. Of course, governments in this country and elsewhere no doubt still try to influence the outcome of legal processes and inquiries by choosing people they might consider favourable to their cause. Two recent prominent examples spring to mind: the Scott and Nolan inquiries, certainly thought before they reported to be safe hands, but who turned out to be, we might say, less than satisfactory from the government's angle. US presidents also tend to try to appoint to the Supreme Court judges who, they think, are of their political persuasion – hence the present Democratic White House has a bench of Supreme Court judges of a largely conservative cast of mind who were appointed by Ronald Reagan.

By the same token, can the sovereign create new courts? The old prerogative courts of Star Chamber and High Commission, which enjoyed considerable support in their early years, were finally abolished in 1641. The answer is that the Queen in Parliament can create new courts and did so most recently in the 1970s with the Industrial Relations Court. The Queen's power to establish courts, however, is limited, firstly, by the fact that she cannot make triable offences (a) either unknown to the law or (b) try cases already cognizeable in existing courts; and, secondly, if she did create new courts, how would she pay for them? In other words, while there is, I think, no statute barring the Queen from erecting new courts, practically, there would be no point because parliamentary consent would be required to identify offences and to pay for their administration. In the context of the administration of justice, we should ask whether the Queen has power to suspend or dispense with law. On the whole, statutes directed at curbing the Royal Prerogative have not told monarchs that such and such an act is illegal. Perhaps out of a sense of respect laws telling a king what he cannot do are rare. On the whole, laws tell kings what they can do, the implication being that everything else is illegal. Not so the Bill of Rights in regard to the power to suspend the law. The clause runs: "The pretended power of suspending of laws, or the execution of laws by regal authority, without the consent of parliament, is illegal." It could not be clearer. The clause in the Bill referred to James II's attempt to suspend the penal laws against Roman Catholics and to have his proclamation to this effect announced from the pulpits of the Church of England – since it was more or less against the law not to attend church on Sunday, the pulpit was the most effective way of announcing royal orders to the people. As recalled by Professor Miller at chapter 9, seven bishops, including the two archbishops, refused to have the proclamation read out in their dioceses and were accordingly arrested and brought to trial. They were acquitted and shortly afterwards King James fled the country.

The case hinged on whether the king had authority to abrogate his own laws. It is a nice point, is it not: if you are the king and make and administer the law, why should you not suspend it when fancy took you? But Charles II had conceded in 1672 that his Declaration of Indulgence to Roman Catholics (ie suspending the penalties against them) was unlawful, and the only other time the suspending power had been attempted was in the reign of Richard II and even that proud king did not seem to imagine that he had so huge a power. The case against the seven bishops failed because the precedents were extremely weak. As Home Secretary, Michael Howard failed to exercise the Prerogative successfully in respect of increasing certain sentences already handed down by the courts.

The dispensing power was different, in that it had been routinely used in individual cases: such as, after the Reformation, granting a foreign ambassador the right to have a private chapel for the Catholic Mass. No one really opposed this prerogative power until the Bill of Rights, and only then because of James II's attempt to extend the dispensing power into a suspending power. Kings had always exercised the right to pardon individuals and had always exercised the right as to whether they would prosecute a case. Royal clemency, when we had the death penalty, was exercised on the advice of the Home Secretary. Almost the first task of the present Queen, as Princess Elizabeth, when she was made a Councillor of State in the absence of the King in North Africa in 1943, was to countersign a death warrant: the Secretary of State (Home Department) had not recommended clemency. The Attorney-General can still enter a *nolle prosequi*, effectively ending a prosecution, as happened in 1975 in the trial of Leila Khaled, a Palestinian terrorist. (Undoubtedly, the government of John Major would have suffered less had the Attorney-General entered a *nolle prosequi* in the case of the Matrix Churchill directors). These are examples of the dispensing power which is specific. The suspending power, which was general, was illegal. The Queen can exercise these powers, on the advice of the relevant minister, but, crucially, the minister in question can be confronted in the House of Commons.

Taxation

Having touched on the law and its administration, we need to look at how
the law is made and by whom, and how everything is paid for. I have already
introduced the Privy Council and mentioned some of the great officers who
staffed it in the Middle Ages. Many of these officers still staff the Privy
Council, but are now formed into something we know as the Cabinet, although
the Cabinet is unknown to the law. "The Cabinet" was originally a very private
room in the palace, part of the king's personal apartments. Here the king
met his chief ministers, received their opinions, approved their course of
action, or gave them new orders. By the reign of Charles II, in the 1670s, the
Cabinet, as a political expression, had gained common currency. It comprised
the king and his chief ministers, but with one very important condition: the
ministers, or the ministry as it came to be known, had to be able to manage
parliament, and parliament had to be managed because parliament found
the money for the conduct of the king's business. As already observed,
parliaments had been needed from the 13th century for at least two reasons:
the voting of supply and as a soundboard of the "political nation", if we can
use that term in the Middle Ages. While medieval kings, on the whole, could
survive on their traditional revenues (the feudal aids) and their estates,
they found it increasingly hard to conduct an aggressive foreign policy from
the 13th century. Almost all calls for taxation, from the Welsh and Scottish
campaigns of Edward I to the French war in the 1620s, were occasioned by
the needs of war. Charles I was forced to summon the Short Parliament in
1640 to resist a Scottish incursion, known as the Bishops' War.

As long ago as 1345, I think, the king had accepted the principle that he could
only collect taxes as granted by parliament, but old habits die hard and, given
the necessities of politics, crises tend to happen quickly, while the summoning
and persuading of parliaments take a lot longer. From time to time, therefore,
kings resorted to what were late described as "illegal" uses of the Prerogative
to raise cash. Henry VII resorted to benevolences, or forced loans, and
indentures for good behaviour, mercilessly extracted by John Morton. Elizabeth
and James I resorted to monopolies. Charles I was only granted the Customs
for the first year of his reign, but went on collecting them anyway, together
with all manner of dubious exactions, such as ship money, resistance to which
was to be an important contributory factor to the contest between king and
parliament in the 1640s.

But no king, since Edward I in 1297, had attempted to collect what we might
loosely call an income tax, known then as tenths or fifteenths – sometimes
eighths – of moveable property; not even Henry VIII, who came closest to
being an absolute monarch and obtained a statute from parliament which
enabled him to legislate without parliament, ever collected taxes without
parliamentary consent. Indeed, he adroitly used men, like Thomas Wolsey
and Thomas Cromwell, whose expertise lay in managing parliaments, quite
often by bribery and coercion, but never illegally.

The Restoration of 1660 finally settled the so-called Prerogative taxes in favour of parliament but there was still a necessary step – the appropriation of the money. Parliament had sought, from the Middle Ages, to get the king to account for the money they granted, and I believe that Henry IV was the first king to render an account, admittedly reluctantly. The appropriation of a tax (that is to say, earmarking it for a specific purpose before collection) happened for the first time in 1665, when Charles II was granted more than a million sterling for the war against the Dutch. However, the 1660 Act granted the king what are known as the "hereditary taxes" (certain taxes on cider and fortified wines, among other commodities) and these still belong to each monarch on accession, except that monarchs have forsworn them. The Queen forswore them in 1952 and because of a quirk in the system at the accession of Queen Victoria Customs men actually started to collect them in 1837.

Nevertheless, Charles II managed to reign for almost the last five years of his life without calling parliament, and had his brother, James II, been a cleverer man, it has been suggested, parliament, like the French States General, might not have been called for a hundred years. Royal financial problems almost always involved a war – a costly business and nothing changes in this regard: the First World War almost bankrupted the British Empire, the Second World War did bankrupt us, as surely as arms spending bankrupted the old Soviet Union and may yet bankrupt the United States. Charles II ended his reign without parliament by a number of expedients. Firstly, the Cavalier Parliament had granted him the Customs for life in 1660, together with the hereditary revenue; by the Treaty of Dover, in 1670, Charles received a pension (as the bribe was called) from Louis XIV of France, although this was never very much; and his ministers used the Prerogative carefully to revoke and re-grant corporate charters in return for cash and compliance. The City of London's charter only dates from 1683, and the last use of the Prerogative to grant parliamentary representation was in favour of Newark in 1674.

The Commons as senior partner

This all came to an end with the Bill of Rights, which William III accepted in 1689. We have already dealt with the appointment of judges and the administration of the courts. After the Glorious Revolution, parliament was to be summoned at least once every three years (the Triennial Act of 1694); all the loopholes for extraparliamentary revenue were closed; a standing army could not be maintained in time of peace without the consent of parliament (a consent easily withheld by not voting supplies). The Army Act and the Mutiny Act were renewed annually by parliament, so jealously did members guard against the possible pretensions of an overweening executive. Interestingly, though not surprisingly, the Mutiny Act has been repealed and the Army Act is now voted every five years. Did this occur under the rule of Henry VIII or the last of our kings to claim to rule by Divine Right, James

II? No it did not. It happened six years ago under the rule of Mr John Major. I am utterly convinced that the kind of democracy we have devised in the West will eventually become the most perfect form of tyranny.

But as we have already noticed, William III was still left with considerable executive powers, powers he was expected to use, provided parliament were in agreement with him. As described in our book on the House of Commons, the country was run a bit like a company. The king and his ministers, the board of directors, with parliament, the shareholders, all had the same objects – it was the means of achieving them that sometimes differed. We still speak of government on the one hand and parliament on the other, as if somehow the two are separate in our constitutional monarchy. Perhaps they ought to be, but they are not. We even speak of government money, which is a stupid description of our own money as taxpayers. To some extent, we speak of the government as a separate entity for historical reasons. Much is done by government that cannot be done by parliament, as being simply impracticable. It is, in fact, the Queen's government, but this is simply a legal formula. Ultimately, government can only be carried on with the support of parliament, particularly the House of Commons. Ministers must come to the Commons for money, and they must account to the Commons for their actions, and today, if a minister loses the support of a majority of the Commons, not even the Queen can keep him in office, but we shall come to this later when we speak of the appointment of a prime minister. Day-to-day government is carried on by the ministry, all appointees of the sovereign, and it used to amuse me to hear that arch-royalist Margaret Thatcher frequently refer to "my government" and "my minister". At the end of the 17th century, as we know, William III was his own chief executive. He presided in Cabinet and left management of the Commons to Danby. William used his veto on numerous occasions, and maintained ministers through a system of patronage which we shall deal with under the first two Georges.

Parliament tried on a number of occasions to widen the number of active privy councillors, the last attempt being in 1700, so as to exercise greater control over the executive, but this was bound to fail as many political decisions are taken on the hoof, so to speak, and cannot be left to argument among a larger group of men. So long as the minister responsible for an action could be called to account before the House, this was a sensible compromise. For this reason, ministers were not permitted to sit in the Commons, and the Act of Settlement specifically excluded them from the House, the fear being that a king could overawe, or even subborn, parliament with grants of office to key members. It was also felt that, as a member of the Commons, a minister could not, somehow, be brought to book before the House, while a minister in the Lords could be impeached. Fortunately for Cabinet government and subsequently party organization, this Place Bill clause was repealed in 1705, though with some curious consequences: until 1926, a backbench MP who took a cabinet post had to stand for re-election. With the exception that the Presidency is not hereditary, this is essentially how the US Constitution is devised: no member of the Congress can hold government office, except that he must resign his seat in the House of Representatives or the Senate. Interesting academic argument has emerged recently in the United States to the effect that a more parliamentary form of government might, in fact, be the only way to reduce the government deficit. America would be unwise to take this course. The US Constitution is a series of checks and balances, based to some extent on the early 18th century British constitution. British checks and balances, however, are now much less effective under party government, for vastly more power is concentrated in the hands of a prime minister today than an American president, and most of this power is derived from a prime minister's control of the Commons and the Privy Council.

The Cabinet, therefore, is the inner circle of the Privy Council, so that the king's business can be done expeditiously, and it does not matter that the title, prime minister or home secretary, is not recognized by the law; they are all Privy Councillors, who are recognized by the law, while the prime minister since the end of the last century holds the office of First Lord of the Treasury, an office recognized by the law, and the home secretary is a secretary of state, another office recognized by the law. I think I am right in believing that Danby was the first chief minister to be referred to as a prime minister in the 1670s, though perhaps not in exactly the same context as Sir Robert Walpole, who always disliked the style and denied it.

Privy Councillors

Now this title of Privy Councillor is considerably more important than implied in the case of Jonathan Aitken who resigned the post in 1997, it being merely described as an "honour". It is also an honour, but it is only as a Privy Councillor that a Cabinet minister can exercise most of his or her powers, which are largely statutory. History is fairly clear for once: the inner circle, the Cabinet, emerges because the king needed to take advice, although, in law, there was no requirement on him (or, I think, still is on the Queen) to take any advice on the exercise of royal powers. In practice, of course, kings did take advice, and they could seek it from anyone of their choosing – invariably, such advisers were Privy Councillors. From the reign of William III, kings tended to seek advice from men who could be relied on to manage the Commons, or who, like Marlborough, were great generals, though Marlborough, like Wellington, was better on the field than in the debating chamber, rather as Eisenhower made a better general than President, or Al Haig was a better head of Nato than Secretary of State – politics and the military seldom seem to emulsify. The shape of the Council and the officers who still staff it today grew under the Tudors: the Lord President of the Council emerges as an important figure and his post became more or less permanent in the 17th century. Lord Whitelaw held this job for Margaret Thatcher in the 1980s, and I once visited him in the Privy Council Office, at the House of Lords. Besides being a magnificent, gilded private office and council chamber, it is arranged in exactly the same way as 450 years ago, the largest chair always left vacant in case the monarch wishes to preside. Private secretaries or clerks spring up from about the reign of Henry VIII between the king and the Chancellor, who in the early Tudor period acts as the king's chief minister. Eventually, one of the king's secretaries becomes Keeper of the Privy Seal, the Lord Privy Seal today. The office of Chancellor, while still important so far as the law is concerned, is gradually confined to the administration of the law and justice, and he gains a deputy in the person of the Master of the Rolls. The King's Secretary, by 1601, had effectively become the chief minister and is known as Principal Secretary of Estate.

Offices of state

The office of Lord High Treasurer is entirely honorific and the government's finances were managed by one or as many privy councillors and clerks as were deemed necessary on an *ad hoc* basis. The office of Lord High Treasurer is routinely in commission, having passed back into the Crown with Henry IV, which means that commissioners were appointed at pleasure to run the king's finances, as commissioners still are. The distinction between "at pleasure" for ministers and "during good behaviour" for judges is an important one. Governments should be removed if they lose the confidence of the House of Commons, whereas judges should not be removed if they lose the confidence of the House of Commons. Other great officers of state, such as Master of the Horse, or Falconer were still appointed, but they were often titular, their holders being Privy Councillors whose government functions were quite other than looking after the royal stables. But these great and prestigious offices were recognized by the law and enjoyed their own social precedence. As an interesting aside only, the Lord High Admiralship has been in commission since 1827, when the Duke of Clarence, the future William IV, resigned the post. Until the functions of the Admiralty, therefore, were taken over by the Ministry of Defence, there were commissioners of Admiralty and older people will recall that we used to have a First Lord of the Admiralty, always a member of the Cabinet and, unusually for modern government, not necessarily a member of parliament, although the Second Lord Commissioner was an MP.

The prime minister

Finally, we come to the First Lord of the Treasury, or the Prime Minister, which latter title, we have noted, is not known to the law, although Edward VII did issue Letters Patent in 1905 granting the Prime Minister, by that style, precedence after the Archbishop of Canterbury. The law does, however, recognize the Lord High Treasurer and when the Treasury is in commission, as it has been for almost 300 years, it also recognizes the Lords Commissioners of the Treasury. The Prime Minister is simply the First Lord Commissioner. In 1721, George I appointed Sir Robert Walpole First Lord and he has been described as Britain's first Prime Minister. King George was not very interested in his new kingdom of Great Britain and could not speak English. His interest lay in his German principality of Hanover. George and his successor and namesake, who also could hardly speak English and was, like his father, more interested in Hanover, ceased to preside at Cabinet meetings, and it is from the first half of the 18th century that the conception of modern Cabinet government springs up.

Political parties

Now we have to touch on political parties to see how the powers of the king gradually come to be exercised by an executive totally dependent on a majority in the Commons. The terms Whig and Tory appear in the reign of Charles II, and by the 1720s and 1730s governments are being formed by Walpole based on "affinities". We cannot probably yet call these governments party-based and perhaps party government cannot be said to establish itself until after the Second Reform Act of 1867, but it had become essential by the 1720s for the conduct of business that the king's government could rely on a Commons majority.

As we have said, the inner circle of the Privy Council, the Cabinet, meets without the king from the reign of George I, but this does not mean that the king is not consulted. Indeed, in matters of particular interest to the first two Georges, especially the French wars which impacted on Hanover and led to George II being the last King of Great Britain to lead his troops into battle (at Dettingen in 1743), the government could not ignore them. Orders in Council, those most vital means of day-to-day government action, had to be signed by the king, or they would have been unlawful and could not have been laid before parliament. We shall return to Orders in Council, or Statutory Powers presently. Unless he was absent abroad, or ill – when councillors of state would act for him – the king always presided at meetings of the Privy Council for the approval of Orders. These meetings became formal, in the sense that they were not debates in front of the king, any more than they are debates today in the presence of the Queen. The Orders were a forgone conclusion, but the prime minister, or some other minister would have consulted the king's wishes beforehand either informally at one of the many social meetings around London in the 18th century, or at formal audiences, much as the Prime Minister today attends the Queen every Tuesday early evening. Likewise today, the Queen's Private Secretary is almost certainly in daily touch with the Cabinet Secretary, but we shall come to this later too.

A further reason, if there were no legal ones, why Walpole and his immediate successors had to consult the king was because the king's influence was still considerable. Like any other great landowner, the king controlled what historians have been pleased to call "rotten boroughs", and he was able to nominate men as candidates for election to the Commons whose affinity was in accord with that of his government. The king also had considerable patronage through the Church of England, 26 of whose archbishops and bishops sat in the Lords (and still do), and in the creation of peers, though Hanoverian kings were never excessive in peerage creations as, once in the House, he might have created a line of hereditary opponents to his policies. In the peerage, however, the king could bribe existing peers with promotions to higher ranks, and quite a few earls and dukes today owe their rank to just such arrangements. The Hanoverian monarchs also exercised considerable influence – one might almost say had final refusal – over the Secret Service funds voted by parliament. As its name implies, the fund was for intelligence purposes and was secret. Parliament accepted, as it still largely does, save a few siren voices, that you cannot conduct foreign policy always in the teeth of open, political debate. Intelligence is often sensitive and of necessity secret, and money from the Secret Service fund was routinely directed as pensions to members of both Houses of Parliament in return for their votes. The king also had in his gift numerous offices, such as victualling the Navy, which his prime minister might well grant to a syndicate, whose members included parliamentarians, provided, of course, that the MPs' votes could be relied upon. Such things today seem utterly corrupt to us, but it is a serious mistake to judge the past by present standards. In the 18th century, it was entirely normal and by no means as corrupt as many other courts in Europe. Indeed, if you exceeded even the generous limits of the period – as Sir Robert Sutton did in the 1730s with a charity – you could could expect no mercy, and the Commons showed him none.

To recap: we see that government quite early on is far too complex for the king, or chief minister, or Lord Chancellor to conduct as an individual or as a tiny group. *Ad hoc* groups of Privy Councillors emerge at which the king will preside if the matter is urgent enough for him. Not long into the 18th century, an inner circle of Privy Councillors form the Cabinet at which the king does not preside, but whose wishes are consulted. The Cabinet enjoys support in the Commons, although this support is often fluid. Party government has probably not arrived, but there are affinities in the House, which is now the paramount, though not the only, power in the land. Orders in Council are the daily routine of government and we should remember that by the reign of the first two Georges Britain has become, to all intents and purposes, a modern state, possibly the first of its kind: there is a Bank of England, which enjoys special privileges in respect of government financing, such as a National Debt with associated Sinking and Consolidated Funds, a Bank whose paper is backed by parliamentary supply, so that people can lend to the government with absolute confidence. So important was the Bank that it enabled 18th century British governments, as Douglas Hurd might put it, to punch above their weight, for Britain was essentially a medium economic and military power, though an increasing mighty financial one.

The seals of office

How were all of these matters drawn together so that some one did not run off with the money in the Consolidated Fund, for example? We go back to the Tudor period and the answer centres on the king's seals and, therefore, who controls them. As early as the reign of Elizabeth, I think we can say, the royal power was already fairly circumscribed. While she could no doubt have ordered a stuffed partridge for dinner by word of mouth, her word was not enough in matters of state and even she probably realized this, for it probably saved her life when the Governor of the Tower of London was sent a death warrant from Bishop and Chancellor Gardiner when, as the Lady Elizabeth, she was a prisoner there. She asked to see the warrant and when shown it is said to have laughed. Not only was it not signed by her half-sister, the Queen, it was not sealed even with the Privy Seal. She dared the Governor to carry out the execution in full knowledge that Bishop Gardiner would certainly have him arrested, blamed, and executed for compassing the death of the heir to the throne, the warrant, of course, being denounced as a forgery.

Warrants, whether for death until 1965 or obtaining funds from the Bank of England, needed the sovereign's signature, the signature of a secretary of state, or other high official, and the Privy or Great Seal, which was in the charge of a third official. We still speak of in-coming ministers kissing hands and taking up their seals of office, or resigning and surrendering their seals of office. In endorsing an Order in Council, two of the three signatures or seals were not enough. All three were, and still are, necessary. Mr Tony Blair's government cannot get a penny out of the Bank of England, for instance, without a warrant signed and sealed as described. In 1830, George IV had the utmost difficulty in using his writing-hand, and an Act was rushed through parliament for the king to sign, empowering him to use a stamp for the sign manual. The Queen must sign many hundreds of these warrants alone every year. It is really no different in the United States where a bill from Congress becomes an act only on signature by the President, the relevant departmental secretary, and the affixing of the President's Seal: if one of the three is missing, the bill is not law.

We can see now that the king must have ministers, first, because he cannot discharge the business of government alone and, by the 16th century, because seals and countersignatures are required, or a warrant drawn on, say, the Treasury will not be honoured. We have remarked how, by the beginning of the 18th century, the king must really select his ministers from among men who have a following in parliament. Towards the end of his tenure of office, not even Sir Robert Walpole could be maintained in office simply because this was the king's wish; just as Lord Bute could not be maintained long in office simply because this was the will of George III. The king's wishes and his control over parliamentary constituencies certainly helped leaders, like Pitt the Younger, to stay in office and, undoubtedly, it was very hard for a ministry to remain in office in the 18th century against the king's wishes, but Pitt also needed his own following. The king's support was not enough. During the 18th century, therefore – although we may not be able to speak of a party system – we can begin to speak of political unanimity in a Cabinet, of responsibility of ministers to parliament in a Cabinet, and of a Cabinet's submission to a prime minister. Ministries tend to become, as it were, "party-based", though this was not always the case, as with Lord Shelburne. Early in the century, a minister would resign if defeated on a policy in parliament, but not the whole ministry necessarily. This gradually changed until, in 1782, Lord North and his entire government were forced to resign, despite the wishes of the king, because the ministry could no longer command a majority in the Commons. By this time, too, ministers in the Commons − so disliked in the late 17th and early 18th centuries − are now wanted there because members can question them, eyeball to eyeball, across the Dispatch Box. (I digress, but it seems to me that circular debating chambers do not permit the proper cut and thrust of debate because at least half the opposition in such chambers are looking at the back of the minister's head. At Westminster, government and opposition can look at one another, which is how the rest of us conduct our conversations or arguments with other people.)

By the early 19th century, it is more or less settled convention that the monarch can only act on the advice of ministers, whether in drawing warrants on the Bank of England, or in signifying the Royal Assent to a bill. This has come about because it is the government, as supported by the tax-granting Commons, who make all the decisions. For the king to withhold his assent − and there is no law which says he may not withhold it − would result, by the 19th century, in a constitutional crisis. The government would resign and, no matter that the king called the leader of the opposition to form a government, if the resigning government had a healthy majority in the Commons, no alternative government could be formed and the king's business could not be carried on.

This was particularly the case after 1832 and the passing of the Great Reform Act. By this Act, although the franchise was not vastly increased, many of the really rotten "rotten boroughs" were abolished and, while landlords could still influence some voters through poll books because the ballot was not secret until 1872, it was very much more difficult for the aristocracy, and the king, to return their own people to parliament by, as it were, nomination: until 1832, Old Sarum, for example, had returned two members although there were no electors. From the 1830s, the king's power over individual constituencies came to an end and, with it, any direct power over members of the House of Commons.

We mentioned the great patronage enjoyed by the first two Georges through the Secret Service fund, and through the granting of government contracts. George III also enjoyed these powers for the first 20 years of his reign, but his government's mismanagement of the American colonies − a policy very much driven by the king himself − and his increasing incompetence, due to worsening bouts of insanity, weakened his grasp of these areas of government, so that by the reign of William IV, and certainly the accession of the 18-year-old Victoria, this form of royal patronage had passed into the hands of the prime minister of the day. Additionally, after the American War of Independence, there was an outcry against "government corruption" and, while among any group of people holding power there is always some corruption, the old army and navy contracts, and other *douceurs*, could not be used to the same degree as bribes to influence members of the House of Commons. British government started to become honest and this coincided with the growth of a professional Civil Service, in an age bursting forth with the industrial revolution, dissenting philanthropy, the work ethic, religiosity, and "family values", which has come to be personified here and in the United States as the Victorian Age.

Three years after the Great Reform Act, Sir Robert Peel launched the Conservative party with his Tamworth Manifesto, while the Whigs, in a manner of speaking, had become the Liberals by the 1850s, and party government was born, although it was not to take on its full-fledged modern form until after the Representation of the Peoples Act (Second Reform Act) of 1867, and the Ballot Act. What the queen thought, or some great landowner thought, politically was of only marginal significance after 1867. The parties, especially the Conservative Party, built up what we now call "grassroots" organizations in the constituencies and from then on, the people chose the government of the day and the queen merely rubber-stamped the electorate's decision. Although Queen Victoria, under Prince Albert's tutelage, exercised considerable beneficial influence in putting together government coalitions in the 1850s and early 1860s, because neither party tended to have overall control of the Commons, this was an interlude and nothing much to do with the Royal Prerogative. What is important about this period is the conception by Queen Victoria, again under Albert's guidance (the Prince Consort has been a much maligned gentleman), that the monarch should be above politics, some one to whom politicians could turn for independent consultation, or, as Walter Bagehot put it, the right of the sovereign to be informed, to encourage, and to warn.

Appointing governments

The idea that the sovereign might veto a bill, or dismiss a government by the Royal Prerogative because she might happen to have a bee in her bonnet about something is all but impossible because such an action would put her into politics. The point about ministerial responsibility is that ministers take the blame for the acts of the sovereign, which acts monarchs make on the advice of ministers. The present Queen found herself very nearly being asked not only to choose a prime minister in 1957 and 1963, but also a leader of the Conservative party. This came to an end in 1965, when the parliamentary party was empowered to hold elections to find a leader and, consequently, a potential prime minister. I do not think that this difficulty has occurred in the Labour party who have always elected their leaders. Of course, things could change in a hung parliament, and very likely would be in a permanent state of flux if we had proportional representation, for the only time this century that any party has gained more than 50% of the vote was in 1935. In this situation, the Queen would be required to find a government and there are many precedents for this, including Buckingham Palace Conferences, as in 1914, 1923, and 1931. But it would be up to the political parties to try to form a government and to convince the Queen that a government, either as a minority (often the case on the continent) or as a coalition, could govern. Only then could the Queen appoint a prime minister – or, at least, only then would it be sensible for the Queen to appoint a prime minister. Her aim would always be to remain above politics and the moment she appeared to take any side, she would be seen to be equally to blame for any of the mistakes that then ensued, bringing the monarchy into danger.

It is for this reason that several think tanks and some MPs, including Tory MPs, have considered various possibilities to keep the Queen out of this danger. They range from vesting these powers in the Speaker, or in a panel of senior Privy Councillors, even in a presidency, when the latter idea emanates from a republican group. But it seems to me that none of these proposals is any better than the system we would have available, in the event of a hung parliament, and there is no evidence that such reforms are likely to improve matters and, in fact, evidence from other countries suggests that changes of this sort would be a lot worse. In Sweden, according to Vernon Bogdanor, under the Instrument of Government (1974) the Speaker of the Riksdag, and not the king, nominates the prime minister, and this has led to all sorts of political skulduggery, as in 1979, when the Speaker who chose the "wrong" political leader as prime minister was promptly unelected as Speaker by the successful prime ministerial candidate's grouping in the Riksdag. Presidents are always nominated on party tickets, and this would be no different in Britain, than in France, or Germany, or the United States, whether the election were, as Mr Tony Benn suggests, by MPs or by the whole electorate, as the Liberal Democrats suggest. Nor is depriving the Queen of the right, on the advice of the prime minister, to dissolve parliament and instituting fixed-term parliaments likely to be of any help. The Federal German parliament is supposedly fixed for four years, but in 1983, Chancellor Kohl – who was rising in the opinion polls – arranged for some really contentious legislation to be introduced into the Bundestag which, he knew, would bring a motion of no confidence from the opposition SPD. All he needed to do was to have a few members of his own party abstain to defeat his own government, so forcing the President of the republic to dissolve parliament at a time to suit the CDU/CSU coalition electorally. In Britain, the monarchy, and certainly the present Queen, has no political history. If it turns out in the future that a monarch does let his or her personal feelings intrude then we can think again.

Dissolving parliament

We now come to the dissolution of parliament, a clear Prerogative power within the five-year plan laid out in the 1911 Parliament Act. Suppose that, in May 1979, when Margaret Thatcher won the general election, Jim Callaghan, who was still prime minister, asked the Queen for another dissolution in hopes of getting a better result for Labour (I make no political point – it could just as well have been Conservatives in May 1997). If she refused Mr Callaghan's putative dissolution, she would be breaking convention that the monarch only acts on the advice of ministers, but I think that everyone would agree that the Queen would have been quite right not to have granted a dissolution, and would have been quite right to have used her Prerogative powers to dismiss the government and invite Mrs Thatcher to form one, an act of royal fiat not used since 1834 when William IV sacked Earl Grey's government.

We now come nearer our own time: in 1993, Mr Major threatened Tory Eurosceptics over the Maastricht Bill that if the government were defeated he would call a general election. Now the question that arises is this: since Mr Major still had a reasonable overall majority, would the Queen have been right in granting a dissolution? It would have depended on whether Mr Major had the support of his Cabinet in requesting a dissolution. If he had not, and it is quite likely that several members would not have supported him, then would the Queen have been correct in not granting a dissolution? We have to go back to 1916, when H H Asquith, having lost the support of members of his Cabinet and a considerable number of backbenchers, asked the king for a dissolution. After consultation with Lord Rosebery, a previous Liberal prime minister and various other senior, retired politicians, George V concluded that he could not grant a dissolution since there was likely to be another government available which could gather sufficient support for its programme in the existing House of Commons, as turned out to be the case. The king was, anyway, reluctant to authorize a general election in the middle of a world war. The same would, I think, have been the case in 1993: the Conservatives could have formed another government without putting the country to the trouble and expense of another election and all that this entailed for confidence in the currency. Of course, all these are matters of political judgment and, depending on your political view, you will agree or disagree with the course that might have been taken by the sovereign. Essentially, however, the sovereign, it seems to me, is likely to be less biased than anyone else, and I would prefer to leave these residual powers in her hands than in the dirtier hands of politicians, which remark is intended as no disrespect to politicians, but they are politicians.

Royal veto

Now we come to the Royal Veto (*la reine s'avisera*). The last time this was used was in 1707, by Queen Anne, over the Scottish Militia Bill, and some historians, including even the great Dicey, have suggested that the Royal Veto has fallen into desuetude and could no longer be used. Now it seems to Professor Bogdanov and I agree, that this must be wrong on two counts. Firstly, there could be a situation where the monarch is advised to veto a bill by her ministers. Occasions are likely to be rare, but might include a bill for the abolition on the nuclear deterrent, just as hostilities, say, broke out between France and Germany. Secondly, just because a royal power has not been used for almost 300 years does not necessarily mean that it cannot be used today. The Veto is, in essence, a last resort and ought only to be used rarely, so just because it is used rarely does not mean that it should not be used at all. To argue that the Veto has fallen into desuetude is topsy-turvy. Again, we cannot escape politics, but then neither can a president, nor a speaker. There may be occasions when the monarch, especially one with years of experience and knowledge – and the heart of successful constitutional monarchy is hard work with the red boxes – feels that an act is a step too far for a government with perhaps even 45% of the popular vote half way through a parliament. Such an occasion, perhaps, could occur if the government of the day sought radically to attenuate the sovereign powers of the House of Commons. With the knowledge we now have of the Treaty of Rome, to which we acceded in 1972 and which parliament ratified in 1973, in the teeth of some of the worst political bribery and chicanery this century, perhaps the Queen could have invited the prime minister to hold a referendum. This did eventually happen, in 1975, though for different reasons, but no one really understood what was happening in 1972–3, although Sir Edward Heath has since been on television almost boasting how he really understood the implications of this treaty, and how it was necessary that the public should not have them drawn to its attention.

Now that we do all know so much more and are so much better informed, it could be that, without an overwhelming Commons majority and a manifesto pledge, the Queen could be right in inviting the prime minister of the day to hold a referendum on a single currency, failing which a Royal Veto would be forthcoming. These are just two examples of matters of such importance where it might be correct for the monarch to threaten the Veto if the government failed to ballot the people. It seems to me that the European Union presents potential danger for the monarchy, for those not in favour of a single currency might applaud a move by the Queen to force a government with a parliamentary majority to hold a referendum. Pro-Europeans would not agree, of course, and would undoubtedly see the use of her powers in this way as a negation of the Queen's independence of politics. For the Queen to exercise her powers in this or that way, independently of the advice of her ministers, would require the most extreme and unusual circumstances. In the case of the single currency, there would have to be a most vocal and demonstrable opposition in the country, as expressed through the media, in opinion polls, in marches, and so forth. Additionally, a government would probably have to be some reasonable way through a parliament, perhaps have reneged on a manifesto pledge to hold a referendum, and be losing the support of backbenchers, even of Cabinet ministers.

There is another difficulty too: parliament has passed laws in the last 30 years which, if put to a referendum, would almost certainly have to be repealed: the law decriminalizing sexual acts between two consenting adults of the same sex, abolition of the death penalty, possibly the Commission for Racial Equality. Perhaps the difference here is that, unlike a single currency, none of these laws actually affects the power of parliament to take future, remedial steps. So much of what the Queen might be called upon to do in critical situations does not depend on laws, but depends on rules which are not rules of law. In politics, by its very nature, laws governing constitutional crises cannot really be framed, because events are so different and what might have suited in 1931 when Britain came off the Gold Standard, may not suit the year 2010. A speaker of parliament, or a president would be in no different a position, except that they would be de-electable, and therein lies another problem for an official elected to administer these residual powers: do they want to be re-elected?

War and peace

We should touch on that great matter, the making of war and its corollary peace. Only the sovereign can declare war which was last done, I think, in 1939 when George VI, on the advice of the prime minister, declared war on Germany. Parliament was not consulted, in the sense that in America the Congress must authorize the president to declare war, though Neville Chamberlain would have been pretty foolish had he not understood that, if there had been a vote, a majority of the House of Commons would have backed him. War is one of those Prerogative powers over which parliament has almost no control, in the sense that Parliament may oppose a war, but may be able to do nothing about it once hostilities have broken out. While the other Prerogative powers, such as establishing new courts of law, can be reined in, if necessary, by the simple expedient of not voting supplies, once your army has invaded the territory of another country it may be very hard to get out of the situation, and supply will have to be granted to save the lives of troops at the very least.

Despite the War Powers Act (1973), the US Congress has little effective control over the president's ability to wage war as Vietnam showed, and the War Powers Act also demonstrates clearly how unsatisfactory such a law can be, as when Mr Clinton was authorized to send an intervention force to Somalia for six months only. If war is, as Clausewitz said, merely an extension of foreign policy, then how can you limit this form of belligerent diplomacy without it having a deleterious effect on your general policy, as Somalia revealed. After war comes peace and it is often thought that the making of treaties is an act under the Royal Prerogative. I doubt this very much. Suppose that the Queen wanted to sell the Channel Islands, or Kent to the French, as Professor Maitland put it: she simply could not make a treaty to do this, any more than John Major could have got the Queen to sign the Maastricht Treaty if the Commons had voted it down – there was talk at the time of using the Prerogative to override the Commons. It was a close-run thing, but I can find nothing in the precedents to suggest that anyone would have to obey rules and regulations not authorized by an act of parliament. If the Queen made a treaty with the President of France to interdict the export of Cheddar cheese to that country, shippers would be breaking no British law if they ignored the ban.

The best example may be the American War of Independence. George III and Lord North had been defeated by 1781 and, reluctantly, had to give way to the colonists. Parliament empowered the king by an act to make a peace treaty with the Americans, ceding the colonies and repealing all previous acts of parliament passed in regard to the colonies since they were planted. This was not something the king could have done by fiat, any more than it was something Mr Major could have caused the Queen to do by fiat on Maastricht because it would have been perfectly legal for anyone to have ignored the regulations contained in that treaty, as only parliament can deal with matters affecting the laws of the land and the appropriation of money.

Statutory powers

We come to the Statutory Powers of the monarch, which people so frequently confuse with the Prerogative powers. The Statutory Powers really date from the 19th century, before which parliament, other than in matters of foreign policy, is essentially involved in private matters: for example, private enclosure awards, or rules regulating the paving of the streets of Truro. From the early 19th century, by contrast, we start to get public bills which need to be administered: public health, factory acts, acts affecting trade unions, education acts, police acts – a whole plethora of acts which we now understand to be modern government. As we have observed, parliament cannot administer the laws it passes. The most it can do is to maintain an overview of the application of the acts members pass, and in this respect Margaret Thatcher should be congratulated for extending select committees. These acts literally bristle with Statutory Powers which are delegated sometimes to the home secretary, as in the appointment of chief constables; but many of the acts delegate statutory powers to the Queen in Council, by the words: "it shall be lawful for the Queen in Council to do such and such…" The Council, of course, is the Privy Council, that absolutely crucial organ of government without which the whole machinery would break down. Since the Privy Council's meetings are secret, no one has ever actually decided what a quorum should be; but it seems to be taken to mean: the Queen, three Privy Councillors, and the Clerk. All three must sign the Order which is then laid on the table of both Houses of Parliament. If no objection is raised in 20 days, I believe, then the Order can be carried out as if it were a law, although an important difference between an Order in Council and a Statute is that the courts can ignore an Order, but not the terms of a Statute.

We are now at the end, when I must try to sum up the powers of the monarch. Firstly, it seems to me that many of the Prerogative powers of the Queen are now Statutory Powers. This is not to say that the Queen and her predecessors have been deprived of their powers, merely that they are exercised in a different way, sometimes even by a secretary of state.

Secondly, some of the Prerogative powers might actually be unlawful. For instance, when we had the Gold Standard, I do not think that, in theory, it would have been illegal for the king to have debased the currency. Hale and Blackstone both thought the king could debase the currency, although a king is likely to have been driven from the throne for doing so. The fact is that there are statutes which say exactly how pure gold and silver coins shall be, so while the king may have the Prerogative power of debasing the currency, he would certainly have been breaking statute law.

Thirdly, the Queen must, by convention, act on the advice of her ministers. Not to do so could court the gravest of dangers for the monarchy, although I have mooted one or two possibilities where the Queen might act independently.

The power of the monarchy, it appears to me, has been replaced by influence and at the heart of this influence are three things:

1: That the monarch is above politics;
2: That she is as well informed as all of her ministers;
3: That her role is to facilitate her government, of whatever party, in the conduct of her business.

There have been exceptions to this in the past. There may be exceptions in the future, particularly if we adopt proportional representation when the Queen may well find herself embroiled in facilitating either minority governments or coalitions. Conditions of this sort wrapped up with some controversial legislation about Europe, say, could bring her into politics as an arbiter. Insofar as precedents exist, and provided she follows them, there ought to be no real danger to the monarchy. Whether she would act better than a party political president or speaker of parliament in facilitating governments or dealing with crises seems obvious to me from the one or two examples already given.

The Queen has certain powers in respect of dominions of which she is head of state, but I do not intend to deal with these. She is also supreme governor of the Church of England, again of peripheral interest in the context of this chaper, although I might echo a member of parliament who thought that the Church of England had been invented to protect us from Christianity. Recent royal divorces and the death of Diana, Princess of Wales, do not fit in here.

The central aspect of the Prerogative is that it is hard to say where it begins and ends, which is why, as I have observed, defenders and detractors misunderstand it. In the examples I have given, I think it is clear that its use cannot be set down sensibly on paper. What might have suited between 1909 and the Parliament Act of 1911 would not have suited the circumstances surrounding the Reform Act of 1832, though there were many similarities. Even if the dissolution of parliament and the appointment of a prime minister could be practically reduced to written regulations, there are potentially many other situations that could require fine judgment, not necessarily based on what happened 85 years ago, but on a set of circumstances and individuals, within a public opinion about which, now, we have absolutely no inkling. The question, if such it is, is whether we want these powers transferred to a politician, or as some have suggested to senior members of the Privy Council (for which read retired politicians). But excellent elected officials, like Mary Robinson, are few and far between.

Further reading to this chapter may be found on pages 367–68.

KINGS OF KENT (CONT)

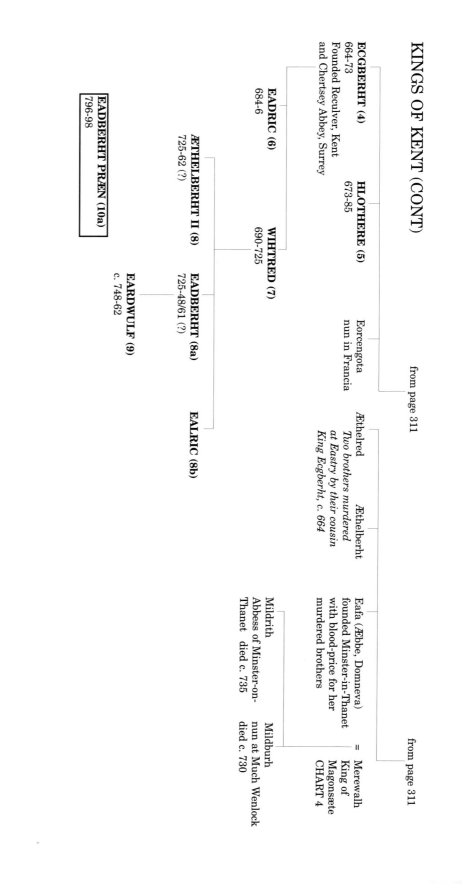

from page 311

from page 311

ECGBERHT (4)
664-73
Founded Reculver, Kent
and Chertsey Abbey, Surrey

HLOTHERE (5)
673-85

Eorengota
nun in Francia

Æthelred   Æthelberht
Two brothers murdered
at Eastry by their cousin
King Ecgberht, c. 664

Eafa (Æbbe, Domneva)   =   Merewalh
founded Minster-in-Thanet   King of
with blood-price for her   Magonsæte
murdered brothers   CHART 4

EADRIC (6)
684-6

WIHTRED (7)
690-725

Mildrith   Mildburh
Abbess of Minster-on-   nun at Much Wenlock
Thanet died c. 735   died c. 730

ÆTHELBERHT II (8)
725-62 (?)

EADBERHT (8a)
725-48/61 (?)

EALRIC (8b)

EARDWULF (9)
c. 748-62

EADBERHT PRÆN (10a)
796-98

CHART 1   KINGS OF KENT

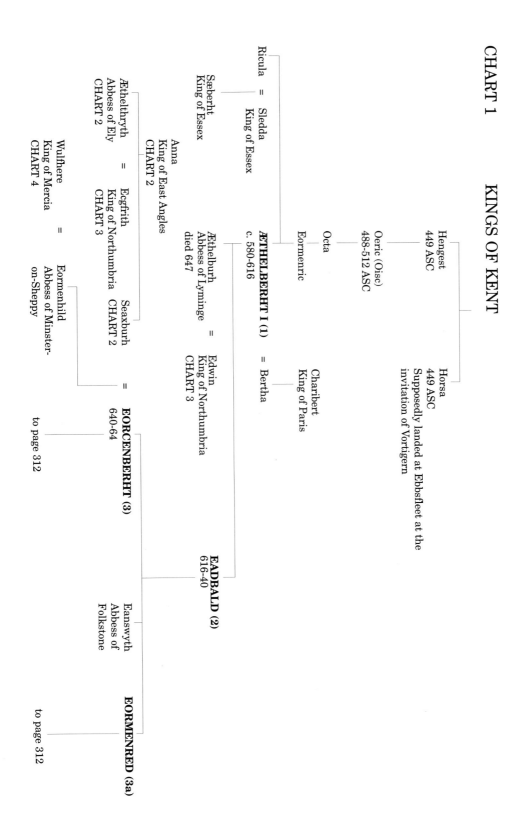

Hengest
449 ASC

Horsa
449 ASC
Supposedly landed at Ebbsfleet at the
invitation of Vortigern

Oeric (Oisc)
488-512 ASC

Octa

Eormenric

Charibert
King of Paris

ÆTHELBERHT I (1)
c. 580-616   =   Bertha

Ricula   =   Sledda
King of Essex

Saeberht
King of Essex

Æthelburh
Abbess of Lyminge   =   Edwin
died 647   King of Northumbria
                                    CHART 3

Anna
King of East Angles
CHART 2

Æthelthryth   =   Ecgfrith   Seaxburh
Abbess of Ely   King of Northumbria   CHART 2
CHART 2   CHART 3

                                    =   **EORCENBERHT (3)**
                                         640-64

EADBALD (2)
616-40

Wulfhere   =   Eormenhild
King of Mercia   Abbess of Minster-
CHART 4   on-Sheppy

Eanswyth
Abbess of
Folkstone

EORMENRED (3a)

to page 312

to page 312

CHART 2

KINGS OF THE EAST ANGLES

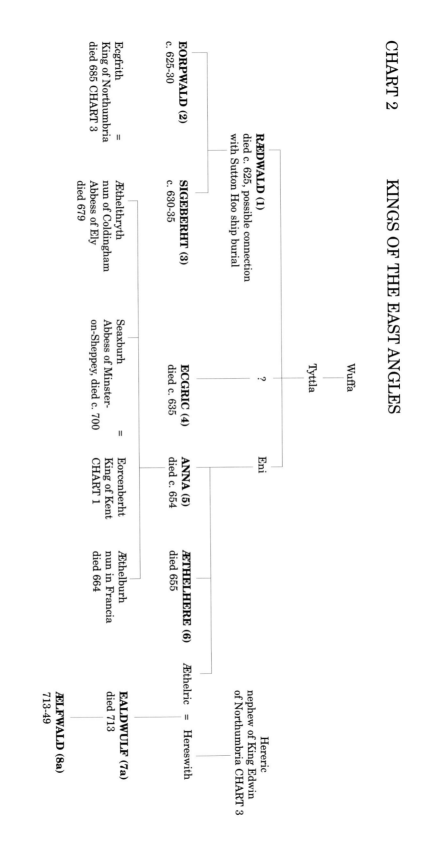

Wuffa

Tyttla

RÆDWALD (1)
died c. 625, possible connection
with Sutton Hoo ship burial

?

Eni

Hereric
nephew of King Edwin
of Northumbria CHART 3

EORPWALD (2)
c. 625-30

SIGEBERHT (3)
c. 630-35

ECGRIC (4)
died c. 635

ANNA (5)
died c. 654

ÆTHELHERE (6)
died 655

Æthelric = Hereswith

Ecgfrith
King of Northumbria
died 685 CHART 3

=

Æthelthryth
nun of Coldingham
Abbess of Ely
died 679

Seaxburh
Abbess of Minster-
on-Sheppey, died c. 700

=

Eorcenberht
King of Kent
CHART 1

Æthelburh
nun in Francia
died 664

EALDWULF (7a)
died 713

ÆLFWALD (8a)
713-49

It is not clear how many kings ruled between Æthelhere (**6**) and Ealdwulf (**7a**)

The native English kings of East Anglia continued to rule that kingdom until the slaying
of King Edmund by Danish invaders in 869.

CHART 3   KINGS OF NORTHUMBRIA

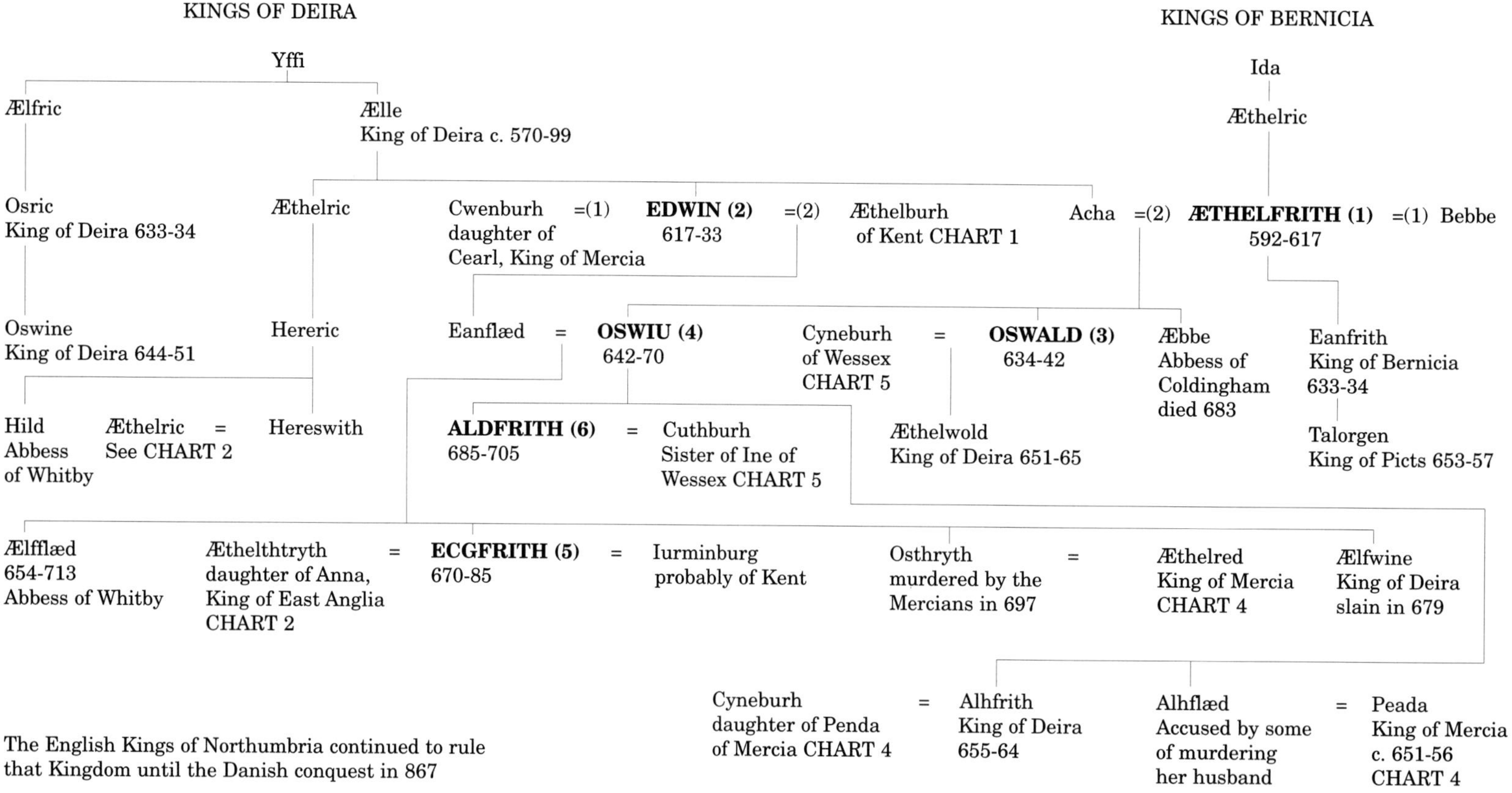

KINGS OF DEIRA

KINGS OF BERNICIA

Ælfric

Yffi

Ida

Ælle
King of Deira c. 570-99

Æthelric

Osric
King of Deira 633-34

Æthelric

Æthelric

Oswine
King of Deira 644-51

Hereric

Æthelric   =   Hereswith

Hild
Abbess
of Whitby

Æthelric   See CHART 2

Eanflæd   =

Ælfflæd
654-713
Abbess of Whitby

Æthelthryth
daughter of Anna,
King of East Anglia
CHART 2

ECGFRITH (5)
670-85

=   Iurminburg
probably of Kent

ALDFRITH (6)
685-705

=   Cuthburh
Sister of Ine of
Wessex CHART 5

OSWIU (4)
642-70

Cyneburh
of Wessex
CHART 5

=

Cwenburh   =(1)
daughter of
Cearl, King of Mercia

EDWIN (2)
617-33

=(2)   Æthelburh
of Kent CHART 1

Acha   =(2)   ÆTHELFRITH (1)   =(1) Bebbe
592-617

Osthryth
murdered by the
Mercians in 697

Æthelwold
King of Deira 651-65

OSWALD (3)
634-42

Æbbe
Abbess of
Coldingham
died 683

Eanfrith
King of Bernicia
633-34

=

Alhfrith
King of Deira
655-64

Æthelred
King of Mercia
CHART 4

Ælfwine
King of Deira
slain in 679

Talorgen
King of Picts 653-57

Cyneburh
daughter of Penda
of Mercia CHART 4

=

Alhflæd
Accused by some
of murdering
her husband

=   Peada
King of Mercia
c. 651-56
CHART 4

The English Kings of Northumbria continued to rule
that Kingdom until the Danish conquest in 867

from page 315

KINGS OF MERCIA (CONT)

Alhflaed daughter of Oswiu, King of Northumbria CHART 3	=	Peada King of Middle Angles 651-56

Eafa daughter of Eormenred of Kent CHART 1	=	Merewahl King of Magonsæte (Hereford and Shropshire) died 685

Eormenhild	=	**WULFHERE (2)**
daughter of	685-75	675-704
Eorcenberht		
King of Kent		
CHART 1		

ÆTHELRED (3) = Osthryth
675-704   daughter
of King
Oswiu
CHART 3
murdered
697

Mildrith
Abbess of Minster-in-Thanet
died c. 735

Mildburh
Abbess of Much Wenlock
died c. 730

COENRED (4)
704-09
retired as a monk
to Rome, 709
founded Evesham, Worcs

Wærburh
died c. 700
founded Hanbury,
Staffs

COELRED (5)
709-16

BEORNWULF (11)

BEORHTWULF (14)
840-52

?   ?

BURGRED (15) = Æthelswith
852-74   daughter of King
retired to Rome   Æthelwulf of Wessex
CHART 5
died 888

Beorhtfrith

CHART 4   KINGS OF MERCIA

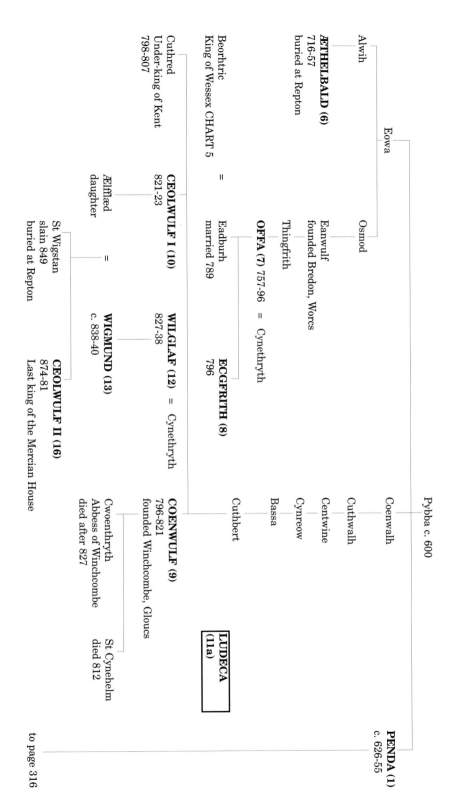

Pybba c. 600

PENDA (1)
c. 626-55

Coenwalh

Cuthwalh

Centwine

Cynreow

Bassa

Cuthbert

COENWULF (9)
796-821
founded Winchcombe, Gloucs

Cwoenthryth
Abbess of Winchcombe
died after 827

St Cynehelm
died 812

**LUDECA
(11a)**

Alwih

Eowa

Osmod

Eanwulf
founded Bredon, Worcs

Thingfrith

OFFA (7) 757-96 = Cynethryth

ÆTHELBALD (6)
716-57
buried at Repton

Beorhtric
King of Wessex CHART 5

=

Eadburh
married 789

ECGFRITH (8)
796

Cuthred
Under-king of Kent
798-807

CEOLWULF I (10)
821-23

WILGLAF (12) = Cynethryth
827-38

Ælfflæd
daughter

=

WIGMUND (13)
c. 838-40

St Wigstan
slain 849
buried at Repton

CEOLWULF II (16)
874-81
Last king of the Mercian House

CHART 5

KINGS OF WESSEX

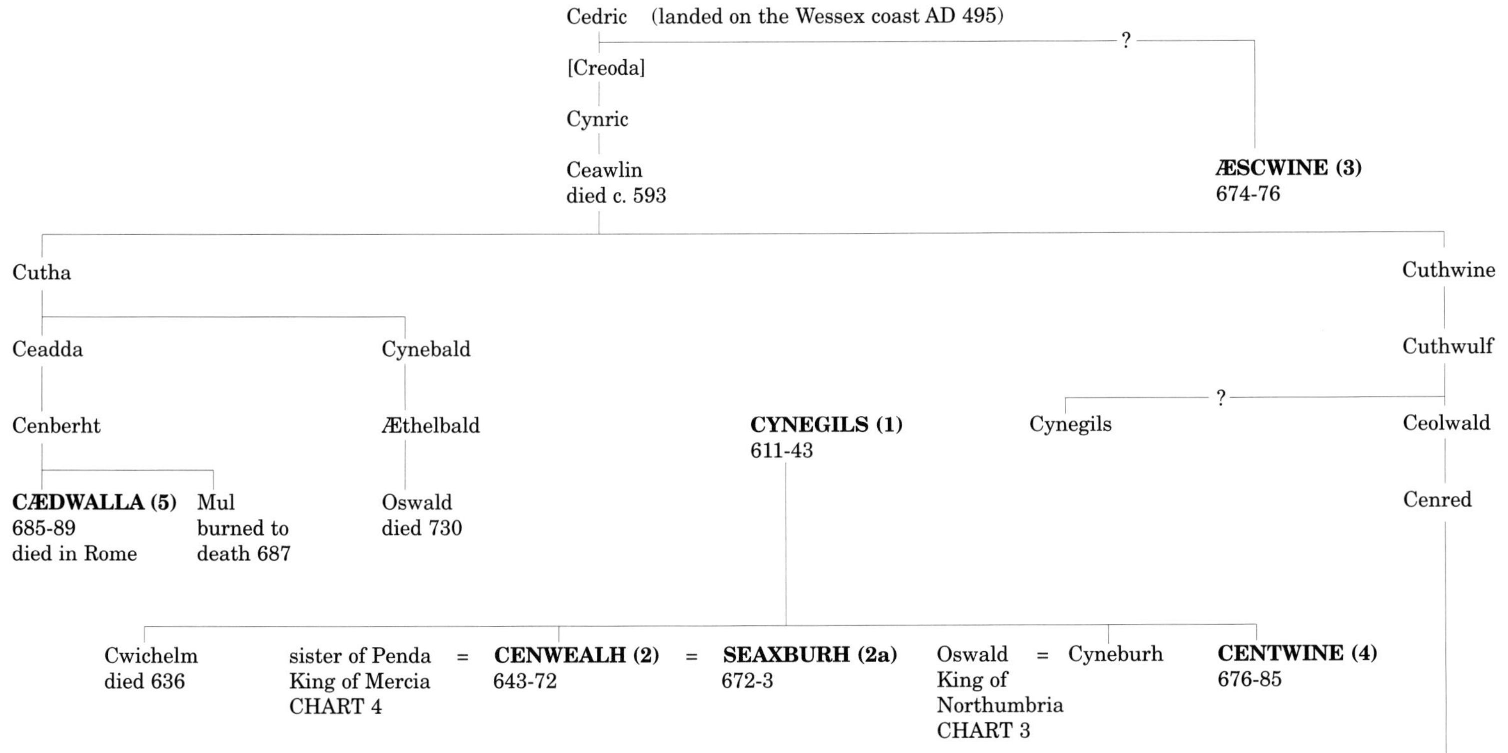

Cedric (landed on the Wessex coast AD 495)

[Creoda]

Cynric

Ceawlin
died c. 593

Cutha

Ceadda

Cenberht

CÆDWALLA (5)
685-89
died in Rome

Mul
burned to
death 687

Cynebald

Æthelbald

Oswald
died 730

Cwichelm
died 636

sister of Penda
King of Mercia
CHART 4

=

CENWEALH (2)
643-72

=

SEAXBURH (2a)
672-3

CYNEGILS (1)
611-43

Cynegils

ÆSCWINE (3)
674-76

?

Oswald
King of
Northumbria
CHART 3

=

Cyneburh

CENTWINE (4)
676-85

Cuthwine

Cuthwulf

Ceolwald

Cenred

?

to page 318

Aldfrith
King of Northumbria
685-705

=

Cuthburh
founded Wimborne
nunnery, Dorset

INE (6)
688-726

Inglid

Cwenburh
co-founder of
Wimborne nunnery

Eoppa

Eafa

Ealhmund
under-king of Kent, 784

ECGBERHT (12)
802-39

ÆTHELWULF (13)
839-58

The genealogy of the following kings is uncertain:

ÆTHELHEARD (7)	726-40
CUTHRED (8)	740-56
SIGEBERHT (9)	756-57
CYNEWULF (10)	757-86
BEORHTRIC (11)	786-802

ATHELSTAN (13a)	**ÆTHELBALD (14)**	**ALFRED THE GREAT (17)**	**ÆTHELBERHT (15)**	**ÆTHELRED (16)**
839-c. 852	858-60	871-99	860-65	865-71
under-king of Kent				

Genealogy of King Alfred the Great

The generations between Alfred's grandfather (King Eggberht) and Cenred (the father of Ine) may not be accurate. The dates for Cerdic's and Ceawlin's 'reigns' are notional figures supplied by the Anglo-Saxon Chronicle. [With acknowledgements to Professor D P Kirby]

Notes

A FULL reference to each work appears on its first mention in each chapter; later references in the same chapter appear under the author(s)'s surname(s) and a short title. The following abbreviations have been used:

BL	British Library, London	chap(s)	chapter(s)
col(s)	column(s)	*Cp*	Compare
ed(s)	editor(s)	edn	edition
esp	especially		
et al	and others (where there are more than two authors or editors).		
et seq	and the pages following.	fol(s)	folio(s)
Ibid	The same book or article as in the preceding note.		
idem	The same author or editor as in the preceding entry.		
MS	manuscript	n(n)	note(s)
no(s)	number(s)	NS	new series
OS	old series	p(p)	page(s)
PRO	Public Record Office, Kew	pt	part
r	recto (front of page)	repr	reprinted
rev	revised	ser	series
sub anno	under the year	v	verso (back of page)
vols	volumes		

The titles of some books, journals and series have also been abbreviated:

BAR	*British Archaeological Reports*
Econ Hist Rev	*Economic History Review*
EHD, vol I	D Whitelock, ed, *English Historial Documents, 500–1042* (London, 2nd edn, 1979)
EHD, vol II	D C Douglas, G W Greenaway, eds, *English Historical Documents, 1042–1189* (London, 2nd edn, 1981)
Eng Hist Rev	*English Historical Review*
Hist Jnl	*Historical Journal*
MGH	*Monumenta Germaniae Historica*
PRS	*Pipe Roll Society Publications*
RS	*Rolls Series*
Settimane	*Settimane di studio del Centro Italiano di studi sull'alto medioevo*
Trans Roy Hist Soc	*Transactions of the Royal Historical Society*

Introduction (Pages 1–29)

1   R Smith, J S Moore, eds, *The House of Lords: a thousand years of British Tradition* (London, 1994), esp Introduction and chaps 1–2; F Liebermann *The National Assembly in the Anglo-Saxon Period* (Hallé (Germany), 1913, repr New York (USA), 1961); T J Oleson, *The Witenagemot in the reign of Edward the Confessor*

(London and Toronto (Canada), 1995); G B Adams, *The King's Council in the Middle Ages* (Cambridge, 1913); J E Powell, K Wallis, *The House of Lords in the Middle Ages* (London, 1968).

2 R Smith, J S Moore, eds, *The House of Commons: seven hundred years of British Tradition* (London, 1996), esp Introduction and chaps 1–2, and references cited, pp 182–201.

3 *Ibid*, chaps 3–8, and references cited, pp 201–9. The remark that "the king reigns but does not rule" was made by the Polish Chancellor Jan Zamoyski (1541–1605) in a speech in the Polish *Seym* in 1605.

4 M Kishlansky, *A Monarchy Transformed: Britain, 1603–1714* (London, 1996).

5 J H Plumb, *The Growth of Political Stability in England, 1675–1725* (London, 1967); P Earle, *The World of Defoe* (London, 1976), pp 45–242; I R Christie, *Stress and stability in late 18th-Century England* (Oxford, 1985). The pre-conditions for political stability included sound government finance, the acceptance by the executive of the rule of law, and moderate economic growth: on these factors, see P G M Dickson, *The Financial Revolution in England: a study in the development of Public Credit, 1688–1756* (London, 1967); A Babington, *The Rule of Law in Britain from the Roman Occupation to the Present Day* (Chichester, 1978), pp 152–214; M Collison, *Public Order and the Rule of Law in England, 1688–1720* (Keele, 1987); B I Anderson, 'Law, finance and economic growth in England: some long-term influences', in B M Ratcliffe, ed, *Great Britain and Her World, 1570–1914* (Manchester, 1975), pp 99–124; J Brewer, *The Sinews of Power, War, Money and the English State, 1689–1763* (London, 1989). For the text of *The Vicar of Bray*, see T Paulin, ed, *The Faber Book of Political Verse* (London, 1986), pp 191–3; the passage quoted is on p 193.

6 P Langford, *A Polite and Commercial People: England, 1727–1783* (Oxford, 1989), p vii.

7 M Malia, 'The dead weight of Empire' (*Times Literary Supplement*, no 4916 (20 June 1997), p 8).

8 Lord Boyd-Orr, *As I Recall* (London, 1966), p 199. There is, therefore, no basis whatever for the attribution of this saying to an unnamed Egyptian pasha in J Archer, *A Quiver Full of Arrows* (London, 1980), p 152.

9 See for further details R Oresko, G C Gibbs, H M Scott, eds, *Royal and Republican Sovereignty in Early Modern Europe* (Cambridge, 1997).

10 See above, p 235.

11 See the admirable study by the late S E Finer, *The Man on Horseback: the role of the military in politics* (Boulder (USA), 3rd edn, 1988).

12 L Mair, *African Kingdoms* (Oxford, 1977); B Roberts, *The Zulu Kings* (London, 1974).

13 J Milton, 'On the New Forces of Conscience under the Long Parliament' (1646–7), line 20, printed in J Carey, A Fowler, eds, *The Poems of John Milton* (London, 1968), pp 296–8.

14 S Webb, B Webb, *Soviet Russia: a new civilisation?* (London, 2 vols, 1935; 2nd edn, 1937; 3rd edn, 1944) [The question mark in the title disappeared after the first edition: doubtless it was thought to diminish Stalin's perfection]; *idem, The Truth about Soviet Russia* (London, 1942; 2nd edn, 1944); H J Laski, *Communism* (London, 1927); J Strachey, A Bevan, G Strauss, *What we saw in Russia* (London, 1931); J Strachey, *What are we to do?* (London, 1938); *idem, A programme for progress* (London, 1940); *idem, A faith to fight for* (London, 1941).

15 G B Shaw, *The Intelligent Woman's guide to socialism, capitalism, sovietism and fascism* (London, 1928).

16   B Russell, *The Practice and Theory of Bolshevism* (London, 1920; 2nd edn, 1949).

17   N Wood, *Communism and British Intellectuals* (London, 1959); D Caute, *The Fellow-Travellers* (London, 1973).

18   A W Wright, *G D H Cole and Socialist Democracy* (Oxford, 1979), esp chaps IX–X).

19   E H Carr, *A History of Soviet Russia* (London, 14 vols, 1950–78), *The New Society* (Boston (USA), 1957); *idem, The Russian Revolution: from Lenin to Stalin, 1917–29* (London, 1979); R W Davies, *The Industrialization of Soviet Russia* (London, 4 vols, 1979–96, in progress).

20   E J Hobsbawm, *On History* (London, 1997), p. 239. In this belated recognition, Hobsbawm finally caught-up with Engels: "History has proved us, and those who thought like us, wrong."

21   A Koestler, *The God that failed: six studies in communism* (London, 1950).

22   R Conquest, *The harvest of sorrow: Soviet collectivization and the terror-famine* (London, 1986); *idem, The Great Terror: Stalin's purge of the Thirties* (London, 3rd edn, 1990). See also M Malia, *The Soviet Tragedy: A history of socialism in Russia, 1917–1991* (Oxford and New York (USA), 1994).

23   P Laslett, *The World We have Lost* (London, 2nd edn, 1971), p 74; *idem, The World we have Lost further explored* (London, 1983), p 71.

24   P Collinson, *The Religion of Protestants: The Church in English Society, 1559–1625* (Oxford, 1982); J Scarisbrick, *The Reformation and the English People* (Oxford, 1984); R Hutton, 'The Local Impact of the Tudor Reformation', in C Haigh, ed, *The English Reformation Revisited* (Cambridge, 1987), pp 114–38; P Collinson, *The Birthpangs of Protestant England: religious and cultural change in the sixteenth and seventeenth centuries* (London, 1988); R Whiting, *The Blind Devotion of the People: popular religion and the English Reformation* (Cambridge, 1989); R N Swanson, *Church and Society in Later Medieval England* (Oxford, 1989); E A Duffy, *The Stripping of the Altars: traditional religion in England, c.1400–c.1580* (New Haven (USA), 1992); A Pettegree, *The Reformation of the Parishes: the ministry and the Reformation in town and countryside* (Manchester, 1993); A Walsingham, *Church Papists* (Woodbridge, 1993); R Serton, ed, *The Reformation in National Context* (Cambridge, 1994), chap 5; S Canley, W J Shiels, eds, *A History of Religion in Britain* (Oxford, 1994), chap 9; B A Kumin, *The Shaping of a Community: the rise and reformation of the English parish, c.1400–1560* (London, 1996); D Rosman, *From Catholic to Protestant: religion and the people in Tudor England* (London, 1996).

25   B Smalley, *The study of the Bible in the Middle Ages* (Oxford, 3rd edn, 1983); *idem, The Gospels in the schools, c.1100–c.1280* (London, 1985).

26   H Eaton, *Kingship and the Psalms* (London, 1976); B C Birch, *The rise of the Israelite Monarchy: the growth and development of I Samuel, 7–15* (Missoula (USA), 1976); T Ishida, *The royal dynasties in ancient Israeli: a study in the formation and development of royal-dynastic ideology* (Berlin (Germany), 1977); G E Gerbrandt, *Kingship according to Deuteronomistic history* (Atlanta (USA), 1986).

27   J R Porter, *Moses and Monarchy* (Oxford, 1963); S Herrmann, *A History of Israel in Old Testament Times* (Philadelphia (USA), 1981), pts 2–3; H Jagersma, *A History of Israel in the Old Testament period* (London, 1982), chaps 7–12; *idem, A History of Israel from Alexander the Great to Bar Kochba* (London, 1985), chaps 8–18; J H Miller, J H Hayes, *A History of ancient Israel and Judah* (London, 1986), chaps 4–12; N P Lemche, *Ancient Israel a new history of Israelite Society* (Sheffield, 1988), chaps 4–5; J A Soggin, *A History of Israel from the beginnings to the Bar Kochba revolt, AD 135* (London, 2nd edn, 1993), pts 3–4; W I Toews,

Monarchy and religious institutions in Israel under Jeroboam I (Atlanta (USA), 1993).

28 (All references to Biblical texts use abbreviated titles of books, with chapter numbers in bold figures and verse numbers in ordinary figures.) *Daniel*, **2**, 47; *I Timothy*, **6**, 15; *Revelations*, **17**, 14, and **19**, 16.

29 *Matthew*, **6**, 9, and **12**, 28.

30 *Matthew*, **3**, 2; **4**, 17; **5**, 3, 10, 18–20; **7**, 21; **8**, 11; **10**, 7; **11**, 11–12; **13**, 11, 24, 31, 33, 44–5, 47, 52; **16**, 19; **18**, 1, 3–4, 23; **19**, 14, 23; **20**, 1; **22**, 2; **23**, 13; **25**, 14.

31 *Matthew*, **6**, 33; **19**, 24; **21**, 31, 43; *Mark*, **1**, 14–15; **4**, 11, 26, 30; **9**, 47; **10**, 14–15, 23–5; **12**, 34; **14**, 25; **15**, 43; *Luke*, **4**, 43; **6**, 20; **7**, 28; **8**, 1, 10; **9**, 2, 11, 27, 60, 62; **10**, 9, 11; **11**, 20; **12**, 31; **13**, 18, 20, 28-9; **14**, 15; **16**, 16; **17**, 20–21; **18**, 16–17, 24–5; **19**, 11; **21**, 21; **22**, 16, 18; **23**, 51; *John*, **3**, 3, 5; *Acts*, **8**, 12; **14**, 22; **19**, 8; **20**, 25; **28**, 23, 31; *I Corinthians*, **4**, 20; **6**, 9–10; **15**, 24, 50; *Galatians*, **5**, 21; *Ephesians*, **5**, 5; *Colossians*, **4**, 11.

32 *Psalms*, **11**, 4; **47**, 8; *I Kings*, **22**, 19; *II Chronicles*, **18**, 18; *Isaiah*, **6**, 1; *Matthew*, **5**, 34; **23**, 22; *Acts*, **7**, 49. There are also unlocalised references to the "throne of God" (*Hebrews*, **1**, 8; **12**, 2; *Revelations*, **4–7**; **14**, 5; **22**, 1).

33 *I Saul*, **12**, 3, 5; **15**, 17; **16**, 6; **24**, 6, 10; **26**, 9, 11, 16, 23; *II Saul*, **1**, 14, 16; **2**, 4, 7; **3**, 39; **5**, 3, 17; **12**, 7; **19**, 21; *1 Kings*, **1**, 39, 45; **5**, 1; *2 Kings*, **9**, 3, 6, 12; **11**, 12; **23**, 30; *I Chronicles*, **11**, 3; **14**, 6; **16**, 22; *Psalms*, **2**, 2; **18**, 50; **20**, 6; **28**, 8; **45**, 7; **84**, 9; **89**, 20, 38, 51; **92**, 10; **105**, 15; **132**, 10, 17; *Isaiah*, **45**, 1; *Lamentations*, **4**, 20.

34 *John*, **5**, 18; **6**, 27; **8**, 41–2; *Romans*, **1**, 7; *I Corinthians*, **1**, 3; **8**, 6; *II Corinthians*, **1**, 2–3; **9**, 31; *Galatians*, **1**, 1, 3; *Ephesians*, **1**, 2–3; **4**, 6; **6**, 23; *Philip*, **1**, 2; **2**, 11; **4**, 20; *Colossians*, **1**, 2–3; *I Thessalonians*, **1**, 1, 3; **3**, 11; *II Thessalonians*, **1**, 1–2; **2**, 16; *I Timothy*, **1**, 2; *II Timothy*, **1**, 2; *Philemon*, 3; *II Peter*, **1**, 17; *II John*, 3; *Jude*, 1.

35 *Matthew*, **5**, 16.

36 *Matthew*, **6**, 9.

37 *Luke*, **33**, 34; *John*, **14**, 2.

38 *Exodus*, **20**, 12; *Deuteronomy*, **5**, 16; *Matthew*, **15**, 4; **19**, 9; *Mark*, **7**, 10; *Luke*, **18**, 20; *Ephesians*, **6**, 1–2; *Colossians*, **3**, 20.

39 *I Peter*, **3**, 1, 7; *Ephesians*, **5**, 22–3, 33; *Colossians*, **3**, 18. A further passage, "A wife hath not power of her own body" (*I Corinthians*, **7**, 4), could easily be misinterpreted if it were taken out of context, though in fact St Paul was enjoining mutual respect for husbands and wives. For Eve as made from Adam's rib, see *Genesis*, **2**, 21–3, and for 'the business of the apple' see *Genesis*, **3**, 6–20.

40 *I Timothy*, **2**, 11–14.

41 *Colossians*, **3**, 22; *Ephesians*, **6**, 5.

42 *Matthew*, **22**, 21; *Romans*, **13**, 1.

43 *I Peter*, **2**, 13–18.

44 *Hebrews*, **13**, 17; *Titus*, **3**, 1.

45 *Proverbs*, **8**, 15.

46 The serious study of literacy before 1754 begins with D Cressy, *Literacy and the Social Order: Reading and Writing in Tudor and Stuart England* (Cambridge, 1980), whose findings are summarised in D Cressy, 'Levels of Illiteracy in England 1530–1730', in H J Graff, ed, *Literacy and Social Development in the West* (Cambridge, 1981), chap 6, and R O'Day, *Education and Society, 1500–1800* (London, 1982), chap 2; see also K Thomas, 'The Meaning of Literacy in Early Modern England', in G Baumann, ed, *The Written Word: Literacy in Transition* (Oxford, 1986), chap 4.

47 S L Greenslade, ed, *The Cambridge History of the Bible. The West from the Reformation to the Present Day* (Cambridge, 1963), esp chaps IV–V; F F Bruce, *History of the Bible in English* (Guildford, 3rd edn, 1979), esp chaps 5–8; G Hammond, *The Making of the English Bible* (Manchester, 1982).

48 M Spufford, *The World of Rural Dissenters, 1520–1675* (Cambridge, 1995); J Morgan, *Godly learning; Puritan attitudes towards reason, learning and education, 1560–1640* (Cambridge, 1986); C Hill, *The English Bible and the seventeenth-century Revolution* (London, 1993), esp chap 1; N H Keeble, *The literacy culture of nonconformity in later seventeenth-century England* (Leicester, 1987); D Davie, *A Gathered Church: the literature of the English dissenting interest, 1700–1930* (London, 1978); M R Watts, *The Dissenters*, vol I (Oxford, 1978).

49 M G Jones, *The Charity School movement: a study of eighteenth-century Puritanism in action* (Cambridge, 1938); R W Unwin, *Charity Schools and the defence of Anglicanism: James Talbot, Rector of Spofforth, 1700–08* (York, 1984).

50 F Adams, *History of the Elementary School contest in England* (London, 1882, repr Brighton, 1972); C K F Brown, *The Church's part in Education, 1833–1941, with special reference to the work of the National Society* (London, 1942); G Sutherland, *Elementary education in the nineteenth century* (London, 1971); S Hurt, *Elementary schools and the working classes, 1860–1918* (London, 1979); B Gardner, *The lost elementary schools of Victorian England* (London, 1984).

51 *Book of Common Prayer*, Articles of Religion, XXIV.

52 Both the *Sermon of 'Wolf' to the English* and the *Institutes of Polity* are translated in M J Swanton, *Anglo-Saxon Prose* (London, 1975; 3rd edn, 1993), pp 116–22, 125–38.

53 P E Szarmach, B F Huppé, eds, *The Old English homily and its backgrounds* (Albany, (USA), 1978), esp pp 1–74; the passage quoted is on p 18. Nevertheless, M McCGatch, *Preaching and Theology in Anglo-Saxon England: Ælfric and Wulfstan* (Toronto (Canada), 1977), does not touch on the political context or content of the homilies by Ælfric and Wulfstan.

54 W A Chaney, *The Cult of Kingship in Anglo-Saxon England* (Manchester, 1970).

55 See also W Ullmann, *The Carolingian Renaissance and the Idea of Kingship* (London, 1969); R W Southern, *Western Society and the Church in the Middle Ages* (London, 1969); J M Wallace-Hadrill, *Early Germanic Kingship in England and on the Continent* (Oxford, 1971).

56 For the coming of the Friars, see M D Knowles, *The Religious Orders in England*, vol I (Cambridge, 1962), pt 2; A Hinnebusch, *The Early English Friars Preachers* (Rome (Italy), 1952); A Gwyn, *The English Austin Friars* (Oxford, 1940); F Roth, *The English Austin Friars, 1249–1538* (New York (USA), 2 vols, 1961–6); R B Brooke, *The Coming of the Friars* (London, 1975); C H Lawrence, *The Friars: the impact of the early mendicant movement on Western society* (London, 1994). For the 'triumph of English', see B Cottle, *The Triumph of English, 1350–1400* (London, 1969), and N Blake, ed, *The Cambridge History of the English Language, II: 1066–1476* (Cambridge, 1992), esp. chaps 1–2, 6. For the associated decline of Norman-French and Latin, see M K Pope, *From Latin to modern French, with special consideration of Anglo-Norman* (Manchester, 2nd edn, 1952); M D Legge, 'Anglo-Norman as a spoken language' (*Proceedings of the Battle Abbey Conference on Anglo-Norman Studies*, vol II (1980), pp 108–17); *idem, Anglo-Norman Literature and its background* (Oxford, 1963, repr Westport (USA), 1978); and A G Rigg, *A history of Anglo-Latin literature, 1066–1422* (Cambridge, 1992); F A C Mantello, A G Rigg, *Medieval Latin: an introduction and bibliographical guide* (Washington (USA), 1996). For medieval preaching, see G R Owst, *Literature*

and Pulpit in Medieval England (Cambridge, 1933; 2nd edn, 1961); J W Blench, *Preaching in England in the late Fifteenth and Sixteenth Centuries* (Oxford, 1964); H L Spencer, *English Preaching in the Late Middle Ages* (Oxford, 1993).

57 Owst, *Literature and Pulpit in Medieval England*, pp 72–3.

58 *Ibid*, p 129.

59 *Ibid*, p 159.

60 Blench, *Preaching in England in the late Fifteenth and Sixteenth Centuries*, p 273.

61 I Morgan, *The Godly Preachers of the Elizabethan Church* (London, 1965), p 3.

62 *Certain sermons or homilies, appoynted by the Kynges majestie to be declared, and redde, by all persones, vicars or curates, every Sundaye in their churches, where they have cure* was first issued in 1547 (STC 13638.5); it was reissued in 1559 (STC 13468), and was augmented by *The seconde tome of homelyes containing XX discourses* in 1563 (STC 13663). A further *homelie against disobedience and wylfull rebellion* was issued in 1570 or 1571 (STC 13679.2) after the Revolt of the Northern Earls in 1569.

63 A Hart, *Shakespeare and the Homilies* (Melbourne (Australia), 1934, repr New York (USA), 1971), pp 9–76.

64 *Richard II*, Act I, Scene II, lines 40–1; Act IV, Scene I, lines 126–7.

65 *Hamlet*, Act IV, Scene V, lines 119–20.

66 *Henry V*, Act IV, Scene I, lines 123–6, 165.

67 In addition to Hart, *Shakespeare and the Homilies*, pp 9–76, see S Lee, C T Onions, eds, *Shakespeare's England*, (Oxford, 2 vols, 1916), esp vol I, chaps I–II; E M W Tillyard, *The Elizabethan World Picture* (London, 1943), chap 2.

68 A Lovejoy, *The Great Chain of Being* (Cambridge (USA), 1936); Tillyard, *The Elizabethan World Picture*, chaps 1–7.

69 *Troilus and Cressida*, Act I, Scene III, lines 85–126.

70 Paulin, ed, *The Faber Book of Political Verse*, p 191.

71 J N Figgis, *The Divine Right of Kings* (Cambridge, 2nd edn, 1914, repr New York (USA), 1965, Gloucester (USA), 1970); P Laslett, ed, *Patriarcha and other works of Sir Robert Filmer* (Oxford, 1949). At this point, monarchy and patriarchy again converged: G J Schochet, *Patriarchialism in Political Thought: the authoritarian family and political speculation and attitudes, especially in seventeenth-century England* (Oxford, 1975).

72 G Every, *The Byzantine Patriarchate, 451–1204* (London, 2nd edn, 1962), chap 1; S Runciman, *The Byzantine Theocracy* (Cambridge, 1977), chaps 1–2; J M Hussey, *The Orthodox Church in Byzantium* (Oxford, 1986), esp pt II, chap 2; J H Burns, ed, *The Cambridge History of medieval political thought, c.350–c.1450* (Cambridge, 1988), chap 4.

73 J Godfrey, 'The defeated Anglo-Saxons take service with the Eastern emperor' (*Proceedings of the Battle Abbey Conference on Anglo-Norman Studies*, vol I (1979), pp 63–74, 207–9); S Blöndel, B S Benedikz, *The Varangians of Byzantium: a military history* (Cambridge, 1978), pp 141–52, 158, 167–80, 187–8).

74 C H Haskins, *The Normans in European History* (London, 1916), chaps VII–VIII; J J Norwich, *The Normans in the South, 1016–1130* (London, 1967); *I Normanni, Settimani*, vol XVI (1969), pp 15–35, 439–552; D C Douglas, *The Norman Achievement, 1050–1100* (London, 1969); *idem, The Norman Fate, 1100–1154* (London, 1976), esp chaps 2–3, 9–11; D Matthew, *The Norman Kingdom of Sicily* (Cambridge, 1992).

75 For the '(Norman) Anonymous of York (Rouen)', see G H Williams, *The Norman Anonymous of A.D 1100: towards the identification and evaluation of the so-*

called Anonymous of York (Cambridge (USA), 1951): his work is printed in K
Pellens, ed, *Die texte des Normannischen Anonymous* (Wiesbaden (Germany),
1966), and is discussed in E H Kantorowicz, *The King's Two Bodies: a study in
medieval political theology* (Princeton (USA), 1957), esp pp 42–61, and in Burns,
ed, *The Cambridge History of medieval political thought, c.350–c.1540*, pp 172,
241–2, 681. See also R Nineham, 'The so-called Anonymous of York' (*Journal
of Ecclesiastical History*, vol 14 (1963), pp 31–45).

76 Burns, ed, *The Cambridge History of medieval political thought, c.350–c.1450*,
    p 172.

77 C Morris, *The Papal Monarchy. The Western Church from 1050 to 1250* (Oxford,
    1989).

78 W L Warren, *King John* (London, 2nd edn, 1978), chaps 5, 7; R V Turner, *King
    John* (London, 1994), chaps 6, 8. See also J E Sayers, *Innocent III: leader of
    Europe, 1198–1216* (London, 1994).

79 C H Haskins, *The Renaissance of the Twelfth Century* (Cambridge (USA), 1927,
    repr Cleveland (USA), 1957); C N L Brooke, *The Twelfth-Century Renaissance*
    (London, 1969); R L Benson, G Constable, eds, *Renaissance and Renewal in the
    Twelfth Century* (Cambridge (USA), 1982); T Stiefel, *The Intellectual Revolution
    in Twelfth-Century Europe* (London, 1985); C Morris, *The Discovery of the
    Individual, 1050–1200* (London, 1972, repr Toronto (Canada), 1987).

80 C J Nederman, ed, *John of Salisbury: Policraticus. Of the Frivolities of Courtiers
    and the Footprints of Philosophers* (Cambridge, 1990). John's letters are printed
    in W J Millor, H E Butler, C N L Brooke, eds, *The Early Letters of John of
    Salisbury* (London, 1955), and W J Millor, C N L Brooke, eds, *The Later Letters
    of John of Salisbury* (Oxford, 1979). He also wrote a history of the Papal court
    (M M Chibnall, ed, *Historia Pontificalis. Memoirs of the Papal Court* (London,
    1956).).

81 A P D'Entrèves, *The medieval contribution to political thought* (London, 1939,
    repr New York (USA), 1959); B Smalley, *Trends in medieval political thought*
    (Oxford, 1965); Burns, ed, *The Cambridge History of medieval political thought,
    c.350–c.1450*, pt V.

82 E E Barker, *The Political Thought of Plato and Aristotle* (London, 1906, repr
    New York (USA), 1959); D Kagan, *The great dialogue: history of Greek political
    thought from Homer to Polybius* (New York (USA), 1965); T A Sinclair, *A history
    of Greek political thought* (London, 2nd edn, 1967); A Oldfield, *Ordered cities,
    ordered souls: an introduction to Greek political thought* (London, 1995).

83 J W Allen, *A history of political thought in the sixteenth century* (London, 2nd
    edn, 1941); J H Burns, M Goldie, eds, *The Cambridge, History of Political
    Thought, 1450–1700* (Cambridge, 1991), pts II–III, esp chaps 6–10.

84 B Tierney, *Foundations of the Conciliar Theory* (Cambridge, 1955); A Black,
    *Monarchy and Community: political ideas in the later conciliar controversy,
    1430–1450* (Cambridge, 1970); E F Jacob, *Essays in the Conciliar Epoch*
    (Manchester, 2nd edn, 1973); C M D Crowder, *Unity, Heresy and Reform,
    1378–1460: The Conciliar Response to the Great Schism* (London, 1977);
    A Black, *Council and commune: the conciliar movement and the fifteenth-century
    heritage* (London, 1979). The deposition by the Council of Pisa of two men bearing
    the title 'Pope' in 1409 (Benedict XIII and Gregory XII) and its election of a new
    pope (Alexander V), the deposition of John XXIII by the Council of Constance
    in 1415 and the deposition of Eugenius IV by the Council of Basle in 1439 dispose
    of Catholic claims to an unbroken succession of 'true' popes and to the superiority
    of popes over Church councils as matters of historical fact.

85 Smith and Moore, eds, *The House of Lords: a thousand years of British Tradition,* esp Introduction and chaps 5, 7; *idem,* eds, *The House of Commons: seven hundred years of British Tradition,* esp Introduction and chaps 5–6.

86 Smith and Moore, eds, *The House of Lords: a thousand years of British Tradition,* esp Introduction and chaps 8–9; *idem,* eds, *The House of Commons: seven hundred years of British Tradition,* esp Introduction and chaps 7–8.

87 The last Emperor, Pu Yi, was, however, restored as Emperor of the Japanese puppet-state of Manchukuo from 1933 to 1945.

88 For the tribal areas of pre-Roman Britain, see L Laing, *Celtic Britain* (London, 1979, repr 1981), chap 2; P Salway, *Roman Britain* (Oxford, 1981), pt I; T C Darvill, *Prehistoric Britain* (London, 1987), chaps 6–8; B Cunliffe, *Iron Age Communities in Britain* (London, 3rd edn, 1991), chaps 4–10. The 'Peoples of Roman Britain' series unfortunately seems to have been discontinued: it included B Cunliffe, *The Regni* (London, 1973); M Todd, *The Coritani* (London, 1973); R Dunnett, *The Trinovantes* (London, 1975); G Webster, *The Cornovii* (London, 1975); H Ramm, *The Parisi* (London, 1978); A Detsicas, *The Cantiaci* (Gloucester, 1983); K Branigan, *The Catuvellauni* (Gloucester, 1985); N Higham, B Jones, *The Carvetii* (Gloucester, 1985); B R Hartley, R L Fitts, *The Brigantes* (Gloucester, 1988). For the evidence of coinage, see R P Mack, *The coinage of ancient Britain* (London, 3rd edn, 1975); D F Allen, *The coins of the ancient Celts* (Edinburgh, 1980), esp chaps 1, 5; C Haselgrove, 'Iron Age coinage in south-east England' (*BAR, British Ser,* vol 174, 1987); R Reece, *Coinage in Roman Britain* (London, 1987); R D Van Arsdell, *Celtic Coinage of Britain* (London, 1989); R Hobbs, *British Iron Age Coins* (London, 1996).

89 J Morris, *The Age of Arthur: a history of the British Isles from 350 to 650* (London, 1973, repr Chichester, 3 vols, 1977), vol I, pp 29, 44.

90 *Ibid,* pp 38 (Vortigern), 57, 84 (Council).

91 *Anglo-Saxon Chronicle,* sub anno 577 (*EHD,* vol I, p 157).

92 *Anglo-Saxon Chronicle,* 'E' text, sub anno 605 (*EHD,* vol I, p 159). The date can be established from Welsh and Irish sources as between AD 613 and 616 (F M Stenton, *Anglo-Saxon England* (Oxford, 3rd edn, 1971), p 78).

93 Chaney, *The Cult of Kingship in Anglo-Saxon England*; Stenton, *Anglo-Saxon England,* esp chaps II–III, VII–VIII, X–XI. XV; S Bassett, ed, *The Origins of Anglo-Saxon Kingdoms* (Leicester, 1989), D P Kirby, *The Earliest English Kings* (London, 1991); B Yorke, *Kings and Kingdoms in Early Anglo-Saxon England* (London, 1992).

94 E A Thompson, *The Early Germans* (Oxford, 1965), esp chaps 1–2; Wallace-Hadrill, *Early Germanic Kingship in England and on the Continent.*

95 *Anglo-Saxon Chronicle* sub anno 455, 477, 488, 519 (*EHD,* vol I, pp 154–5).

96 *Anglo-Saxon Chronicle* sub anno 547 (*EHD,* vol I, p 156).

97 *Anglo-Saxon Chronicle* sub anno 495, 519 (*EHD,* vol I, p 155).

98 See above, pp 50–51.

99 See above, p 52. In fact, the best-known Old English king to be elected who was not of royal descent was also the last: Harold Godwineson.

100 Morris, *The Age of Arthur,* vol I, pp 88–93; vol II, pp 249–51.

101 See above, p 77.

102 Stenton, *Anglo-Saxon England,* pp 321–2; P Stafford, *Unification and Conquest. A political and social history of England in the tenth and eleventh centuries* (London, 1989), pp 24, 40–2, 115.

103 See above, p 78.

104 For the subsequent development of English local government see H M Jewell,

English local administration in the Middle Ages (Newton Abbot, 1972). For the later period, the old work of S Webb, B Webb, *English Local Government from the Revolution to the Municipal Corporations Act* (London, 7 vols, 1906–29). has still not been superseded.

105 Stafford, *Unification and Conquest. A political and social history of England in the tenth and eleventh centuries*, chaps 8, 11.

106 H P R Finberg, *The Early Charters of the West Midlands* (Leicester, 1961), p 11. In earlier centuries the Mercian archives were more probably kept at Repton or Tamworth.

107 H R Loyn, *The Governance of Anglo-Saxon England, 500–1087* (London, 1984), chap 5; C R Hart, The *Codex Wintonensis* and the King's *Haligdom'*, in J Thirsk, ed, *Land, Church and People. Essays presented to Professor H.P.R. Finberg* (Reading, 1970), pp 7–38; S D Keynes, *The Diplomas of Æthelred 'The Unready', 978–1016* (Cambridge, 1980), esp pp 14–19, 45–6, 67–76, 115–20, 134–5, 146–53; *idem*, 'Regenbald the Chancellor (*sic*)' (*Anglo-Norman Studies*, vol X (1988), pp 185–222).

108 For monasteries drafting charters, see Keynes, *The Diplomas of Æthelred 'The Unready' 978–1016*, esp pp 19–30, 79–83, 115–25; Loyn, *the Governance of Anglo-Saxon England, 500–1087*, pp 106–18. For outright forgery, see in general L C Hector, *Palaeography and Forgery* (York, 1959); N P Brooks, *History and myth, forgery and truth* (Birmingham, 1986). For forgery at Westminster Abbey, see E Mason, *Westminster Abbey and its people, c.1050–c.1216* (Woodbridge, 1996), pp 8, 21, 25, 28, 41–3, 47–8, 60, 73, 89, 101–5, 111, 117–23, 149, 158–60, 163, 179–80, 184, 222–3, 233, 261–4, 266, 294–304; D Bates, 'The prosopographical Study of Anglo-Norman Royal Charters', in K S B Keats-Rohan, ed, *Family Trees and the Roots of politics. The prosopography of Britain and France from the tenth to the twelfth century* (Woodbridge, 1997), pp 90–1. *Cp*, for Winchester Cathedral, H P R Finberg, *The Early Charters of Wessex* (Leicester, 1964), chap VII.

109 Keynes, *The Diplomas of Æthelred 'The Unready', 978–1016*, pp 151–2.

110 H R Loyn, *Anglo-Saxon England and the Norman Conquest* (London, 2nd edn, 1991), pp 93–100, 118, 157.

111 *Ibid*, pp 335–6; E Miller, J Hatcher, *Medieval England: Towns, Commerce and Crafts, 1086–1348* (London, 1995), pp 13–16, 41–2, 181–210. English overseas trade before the later 13th century, when the customs records start (E M Carus-Wilson, O Coleman, *England's Export Trade, 1275–1547* (Oxford, 1963).), is a topic much in need of research combining fragmentary mentions in literary sources and inadequate documentary records with the evidence of coins, archaeology, and architectural history; it is a subject totally ignored by R W Finn, *The Norman Conquest and its effects on the economy, 1066–86* (London, 1971), which concentrates solely on the evidence of the Domesday survey.

112 P Sawyer, '1066–1086. A Tenurial revolution?', in *idem*, ed, *Domesday Book: a reassessment* (London, 1985), pp 71–85; R Fleming, 'Domesday Book and the Tenurial Revolution' (*Anglo-Norman Studies*, vol IX (1986), pp 87–102); D Roffe, 'From Thegnage to Barony: Sake and Soke, Title and Tenants-in-chief' (*Anglo-Norman Studies*, vol XII (1989), pp 157–76).

113 For Richard the young man, see *DB, Gloucs*, fol.167b, *34*, 8; for Wigot of Wallingford's son-in-law and grandson, see I J Sanders, *English baronies: a study of their origin and descent, 1086–1327* (Oxford, 1960), p 93 and n 2.

114 R Fleming, *Kings and Lords in Conquest England* (Cambridge, 1991), esp pp 145–214.

115 For recent emphasis on the continuing importance of Anglo-Saxon *antecessores*, see A Williams, 'A West-Country Magnate of the Eleventh Century', in Keats-Rohan, ed, *Family Trees and the Roots of politics*, pp 45–6; C P Lewis, Joining the Dots', in *ibid*, pp 82–7.

116 W Stubbs, ed, 'Memoriale Walteri de Coventria' (*Rolls Ser*, vol 58, 2 pts (1872–3), pt II, p 227). For the castle in England after 1066, see J H Round, *Feudal England* (London, 1895), pp 225–314; E S Armitage, *Early Norman Castles of the British Isles* (London, 1912); A Hamilton-Thompson, *Military Architecture in England during the Middle Ages* (London, 1912); S Painter, 'English Castles in the Early Middle Ages' (*Speculum*, vol X (1935), pp 321–32); J Beeler, *Warfare in England, 1066–1189* (Ithaca (USA), 1966); D F Renn, *Norman Castles in Britain, 1066–1216* (London, 2nd edn, 1973); R A Brown, *English Castles* (London, 3rd edn, 1976); C Platt, *The Castle in Medieval England and Wales* (London, 1982); D J C King, *Castellarium Anglicanum* (New York (USA), 2 vols, 1983); R A Brown, 'The Castles of the Conquest', in A Williams, R W H Erskine, eds, *Domesday Book Studies* (London, 1987), reprinted in R A Brown, *Castles, Conquest and Charters* (London, 1987), pp 65–74; N J G Pounds, *The Medieval Castle in England and Wales: a social and political history* (Cambridge, 1990); M W Thompson, *The Rise of the Castle* (Cambridge, 1991); R Higham, P Barker, *Timber Castles* (London, 1992).

117 For later medieval castles, especially as residences, see Brown, *English Castles*, esp. chap 8; K Mertes, *The English Noble Household, 1250–1600* (Oxford, 1988); King, *The Castle in England and Wales*, pp 2–5, 7–9; Pounds, *The Medieval Castle in England and Wales*, chaps 2–6; Thompson, *The Rise of the Castle*, vii, 86–108; *idem, The Decline of the Castle* (Cambridge, 1987).

118 A Williams, 'A bell-house and a burh-geat: lordly residences in England before the Norman Conquest', in C Harper-Bill, R Harvey, eds, *Medieval Knighthood*, vol IV (1992), p 221.

119 H Ellis, ed, *Liber Censualis Vocati Domesday Book*, vol IV, *Additamenta* (London, 1816), pp 1–528, *passim*. This rather poor edition remains the only complete printed text of the Exon Domesday.

120 For the use of dismounted knights at battles such as Tenchebrai, Brémule, Bourgthéroulde and the Standard, see A L Poole, *Obligations of Society in the XII and XIII Centuries* (Oxford, 1946), pp 37–8; C W Hollister, *The Military Organization of Norman England* (Oxford, 1965), pp 125–9, 229–30; M Strickland, ed, *Anglo-Norman Warfare: studies in late Anglo-Saxon and Anglo-Norman military Organization and warfare* (Woodbridge, 1992), pp 187, 189–93; S Morillo, *Warfare under the Anglo-Norman Kings, 1066–1135* (Woodbridge, 1994), pp 151–62, 169–70, 171–4.

121 J Schlight, *Monarchs and Mercenaries* (Bridgeport (USA), 1968), esp chaps I–II; M Chibnall, 'Mercenaries and the *Familia Regis* under Henry I' (*History*, vol LXII (1977), pp 15–23); Strickland, *Anglo-Norman Warfare*, pp 84–127, 143–60, 182–207; Morillo, *Warfare under the Anglo-Norman Kings, 1066–1135*, pp 11, 17, 30, 52, 55, 76–7, 178.

122 D Bates, 'The Origins of the Justiciarship' (*Anglo-Norman Studies*, vol IV (1982), pp 1–12); F J West, *The Justiciarship in England, 1066–1232* (Cambridge, 1966).

123 Loyn, *The Governance of Anglo-Saxon England, 500–1087*, chaps 5, 7; W L Warren, *The Governance of Norman and Angevin England, 1086–1272* (London, 1987), chaps 2–3, 5–7; G B Adams, *The King's Council in the Middle Ages*; C W Hollister, 'The origins of the English Treasury' (*Eng Hist Rev*, vol XCIII (1978), pp 262–75); R L Poole, *The Exchequer in the Twelfth Century* (Oxford,

1912); D M Stenton, *English Justice between the Norman Conquest and the Great Charter, 1066–1216* (London, 1965); B Wilkinson, *The Chancery under Edward III* (Manchester, 1929).

124 For the use of 'castle treasuries', see J E A Jolliffe, 'The Chamber and the Castle Treasuries under King John', in R W Hunt, W A Pantin, R W Southern, eds, *Studies in Medieval History ... presented to ... F M Powicke* (London, 1957), pp 117–42; R A Brown, '"The Treasury" of the late twelfth century' in J C Davies, ed, *Studies presented to Sir Hilary Jenkinson* (London, 1957), pp 35–49; H G Richardson, G O Sayles, *The Governance of Medieval England* (Edinburgh, 1963), pp 235–8. For the Wardrobe, see T F Tout, *Chapters in the administrative history of medieval England* (Manchester, 6 vols, 1920–33).

125 F Pollock, F W Maitland, *History of English Law before the time of Edward I* (Cambridge, 2 vols, 2nd edn, 1923); G W Keeton, *The Norman Conquest and the Common Law* (London, 1966); S F C Milsom, *Historical Foundations of the Common Law* (London, 2nd edn, 1981); R C Van Caenagem, *The birth of the English Common Law* (Cambridge, 2nd edn, 1988). *Cp*, for Scotland, H L MacQueen, *Common Law and Feudal Society in medieval Scotland* (Edinburgh, 1993).

126 For royal taxation of the peasantry, see S K Mitchell, *Studies in Taxation under John and Henry III* (New Haven (USA), 1914), pp 159–69; *idem, Taxation in Medieval England* (Yale (USA), 1951, repr New York (USA), 1971), esp chaps III–IV (both these works are much in need of updating); F A Cazel, A P Cazel, eds, 'Rolls of the Fifteenth ... and Rolls of the Fortieth' (*Pipe Roll Society*, NS vol XLV (1983), pp v, viii–ix, 54, 58, 66, 69, 85, 99). For the taxation of merchants' goods, see D M Stenton, ed, 'Pipe Roll of 5 John' (*PRS*, NS vol XVI (1938), pp xii–xiii, 11–12); *idem*, ed, 'Pipe Roll of 6 John' (*PRS*, NS vol XVIII (1940), pp xliii–v, 218–20); N S B Gras, *The Early English Customs System* (Cambridge (USA), 1918), chaps I–II, VII–XV; Carus-Wilson and Coleman, *England's Export Trade, 1275–1537*. For the 'assize of arms', see Pollock and Maitland, *History of English Law before the time of Edward I*, vol I, pp 421–2; Poole, *Obligations of Society in the XII and XIII Centuries*, p 33; M Powicke, *Military Obligation in Medieval England* (Oxford, 1962), pp 48, 54–6, 82–90, 119–21, 139.

127 Smith and Moore, eds, *The House of Lords: a thousand years of British Tradition*, esp Introduction and chaps 2–3; *idem*, eds, *The House of Commons: seven hundred years of British Tradition*, esp Introduction and chaps 1–2.

128 See below, p 132.

129 Smith and Moore, eds, *The House of Commons: seven hundred years of British Tradition*, pp 5, 9–10, 61.

130 G Chaucer, *The Canterbury Tales, Prologue*, lines 124–6. For the success of vernacular English, see Cottle, *The Triumph of English, 1350–1400*, and Blake, ed, *The Cambridge History of the English Language, II: 1066–1475*, esp chaps 1–2, 6.

131 See above p 136.

132 C G A Clay, *Economic expansion and social change: England, 1500–1700* (Cambridge, 2 vols, 1984), vol II, pp 105–6, 117–18, 182–4.

133 The concept of a 'Tudor Revolution' was first advanced by G R Elton, *The Tudor Revolution in Government* (Cambridge, 1953). It aroused a controversy which still continues among historians: for recent views, see C Coleman, D Starkey, eds, *Revolution reassessed: revisions in the history of Tudor government and administration* (Oxford, 1986).

134 For these developments see Smith and Moore, *The House of Lords: a thousand*

years of British Tradition, esp Introduction and chap 7; idem, *The House of Commons: seven hundred years of British Tradition*, esp Introduction and chaps 5–6.

135 Dockson, *The Financial Revolution in England: a study in the development of Public Credit, 1688–1756*; Anderson, 'Law, finance and economic growth in England: some long-term influences'; Brewer, *The Sinews of Power, War, Money and the English State, 1689–1763*.

136 Smith and Moore, *The House of Lords: a thousand years of British Tradition*, p 18.

137 *Ibid*, pp 6, 8–9, 12, 102, 115, 117, and references cited, p 181, n 22.

138 See above.

139 Smith and Moore, *The House of Commons: seven hundred years of British Tradition*, Introduction and chap 8.

Chapter 1 (pages 31–45)

1 Einhard's work is that of a man who owed his career advancement to his benefactor Charlemagne. After being educated at the monastery of Fulda, where he acquired his great familiarity with classical Latin authors, he spent some years at court: the architecture of Charlemagne's palace at Aachen is credited to him. He and his wife Emma retired to estates granted to him by Charlemagne and by his son Louis the Pious and founded the churches of Steinbach and Seligenstadt.

2 O Holder-Egger, ed, 'Einhard: Vita Karoli' (*MGH, Scriptores rerum germanicarum*, vol 25 (1911), chaps 22–5); English translation by L Thorpe, *Two Lives of Charlemagne* (London, 1969) pp 76–9, from the version in Bibliothèque Nationale (Paris), MS Lat 10,758 edited by P Jaffé in 1867.

3 E Dümmler, ed, 'Theodulf, Carmina' (*MGH, Poetae*, vol I (1880), p 483); English translation by P Godman, *Poetry of the Carolingian Renaissance* (London, 1985), p 151. For a survey of poetic accounts of Charlemagne, see D Schaller, 'Karl der Grosse in der Dichtung in Mitellateinsche Literatur' (*Lexikon des Mittelalters*, vol 5 (1991), cols 961–2). See also M Garrison, 'The emergence of Carolingian Latin literature and the court of Charlemagne (780–814)', in R McKitterick, ed, *Carolingian Culture: emulation and innovation* (Cambridge, 1994), pp 111–40.

4 On the work of Einhard and its date of composition in the context of Carolingian historiography, see the recent assessment by M Innes and R McKitterick 'The writing of history', in McKitterick, ed, *Carolingian Culture*, pp 193–220.

5 J L Nelson, 'Kingship and Empire', in *ibid*, pp 52–87.

6 On the coinage see P Grierson, M Blackburn, *Medieval European Coinage with a catalogue of the coins in the Fitzwilliam Museum, Cambridge, Vol I, The Early Middle Ages (5th–10th centuries)* (Cambridge, 1986), pp 209–10 and Plate 34, no 749.

7 R McKitterick, 'Charles the Bald and the image of kingship in the early middle ages' (*History Today*, vol 38 (1988), pp 29–36).

8 E Sears, 'Louis the Pious as *miles Christi*. The dedicatory image in Hrabanus Maurius' *De laudibus sanctae crucis*', in P Godman, R Collins, eds, *Charlemagne's Heir. New perspectives on the reign of Louis the Pious* (Oxford, 1986), pp 605–28.

9 Grierson and Blackburn, *Medieval European Coinage*, pp 329–30 and Plate 34, nos 750–1.

10 Bibliothèque Nationale (Paris), MS Lat 266, fol lv, illustrated in J Hubert, J Porcher, W Volbach, *Carolingian Art* (London, 1970), p 145.

11   Bibliothèque Nationale (Paris), MS Lat 1, fol 423r, illustrated in Hubert *et al*, *Carolingian Art*, p 139.

12   *Ibid*, p 138. See also H Kessler, 'A lay abbot as patron: Count Vivian and the First Bible of Charles the Bald' (*Committenti e produzione artistico-letteraria nell'alto medioevo occidentale. Settimane di Studio del Centro Italiano di studi sull'alto medioevo*, vol XXXIX (1992), pp 647–76).

13   R Deshman, 'The exalted servant: the ruler-theology of the prayerbook of Charles the Bald' (*Viator*, vol XI (1980), p 417).

14   Illustrated in Hubert *et al*, *Carolingian Art*, p 152.

15   *Ibid*, p 149. See also E H Kantorowicz, 'The Carolingian king in the Bible of San Paolo fuori le mura', in K Weitzmann, ed. *Late classical and medieval studies in honor of Albert Mathias Friend, Jnr* (Princeton (USA), 1955), pp 287–300, and W J Diebold, 'The ruler portrait of Charles the Bald in the S Paolo Bible' (*The Art Bulletin*, vol 76 (1994), pp 6–18).

16   L Nees, *A tainted mantle: Hercules and the classical tradition at the Carolingian court* (Philadelphia (USA), 1991).

17   Hubert *et al*, *Carolingian Art*, p 149.

18   See the comments in W J Diebold, '*Nos quoque morem ilius imitari cupientes.* Charles the Bald's evocation and imitation of Charlemagne' (*Archiv für Kulturgeschichte*, vol 75 (1993), pp 271–300).

19   Gospel Book of Otto III: Bayerische Staatsbibliothek (Munich), Clm 4453, fol 24r; Sacramentary of Henry II: Bayerische Staatsbibliothek (Munich), Clm 4456, fol IIv. See also H Mayr-Harting, *Ottonian Book Illumination* (London, 1992), for discussion, other examples and illustrations.

20   BL Cotton MS Vespasian A VIII, fol 2v, and see R Deshman, '*Benedictus monarcha et monachus.* Early medieval ruler-theology and the Anglo-Saxon reform' (*Frühmittelalterliche Studien*, vol 22 (1988), pp 204–40, with illustrations).

21   '*Liber de rectoribus christianis*', in S Hellmann, ed, *Sedulius Scottus* (Munich, 1906), p 22; English translation in E G Doyle, *Sedulius Scottus: On Christian Rulers and the Poems* (Binghampton (USA), 1983), p 52.

22   '*De institutione regia*', chap 4, in J Reviron, ed, *Les idées politico-religieuses d'un évêque du IXe siècle: Jonas d'Orléans et son 'De institutione regia'* (Paris, 1930); English translation in R W Dyson, *A ninth-century politicasl tract: The De institutione regia of Jonas of Orléans* (Smithtown (USA), 1983), p 20.

23   J L Nelson, 'The earliest surviving royal ordo', in B Tierney, P Linehan, eds, *Authority and Power, Studies on medieval law and government presented to Walter Ullmann on his seventieth birthday* (Cambridge, 1980), pp 29–48, and 'The Lord's anointed and the people's choice: Carolingian royal ritual', in D Cannadine, S Price, eds, *Rituals of royalty: Power and Ceremonial in traditional societies* (Cambridge, 1987), pp 137–80.

24   Text and translation in J L Nelson, 'Kingship and Empire', in McKitterick, ed, *Carolingian Culture*, p 58.

25   *MGH, Leges, Capitularia regum Francorum* [hereafter *MGH, Capitularia*], vol I (1883), no 28; English translation in P D King, *Charlemagne. Translated Sources* (Kendal, 1987), pp 224–30.

26   *MGH, Capitularia*, vol I, nos 26–7; English translation in King, *Charlemagne. Translated Sources*, pp 205–8, 230–2.

27   *MGH, Capitularia*, vol I, nos 33 (802), 50 (808); English translation in King, *Charlemagne Translated Sources*, pp 233–42, 261–3.

28   *MGH, Capitularia*, vol I, no 22; English translation in King, *Charlemagne. Translated Sources*, p 209.

29   See R McKitterick, *The Carolingians and the Written Word* (Cambridge, 1989), pp 22–75.

30   R McKitterick, *The Frankish Church and the Carolingian Reforms (789–895)* (London, 1977).

31   For a fuller discussion see McKitterick, ed, *Carolingian Culture.*

32   L D Reynolds, *Texts and Transmission. A survey of the Latin classics* (Oxford, 1983).

33   R McKitterick, 'Royal patronage of culture in the Frankish kingdoms under the Carolingians: motives and consequences' (*Settimane*, vol XXXIX (1992), pp 93–130).

34   W Gundlach, ed, 'Remigius' (*Corpus Christianorum, Series latina*, vol 117 (1957), pp 408–9).

35   On the Franks, see E James, *The Franks* (Oxford, 1988), and I Wood, *The Merovingian Kingdoms, 450–751* (London, 1993).

36   Aspects of early medieval kingship are discussed in P Sawyer, I Wood, eds, *Early Medieval Kingship* (Leeds, 1977), and J M Wallace-Hadrill, *Early Germanic Kingship in England and on the Continent* (Oxford, 1971).

37   J M Wallace-Hadrill, *The Frankish Church* (Oxford, 1983).

38   For recent analyses of late Merovingian politics see R A Gerberding, *The Rise of the Carolingians and the Liber Historiae Francorum* (Oxford, 1987), and Wood, *The Merovingian Kingdoms.*

39   J Hanig, *Consensus fidelium. Frühfeudale interpretationen des Verhältnisses von Königtum und Adel am Beispiel des Frankenreiches (Monographien zur Geschichte des Mittelalters*, vol 27, 1982).

40   *Annales regni francorum*, sub anno 775, in R Rau, ed, *Quellen zur karolingische Reichsgeschichte*, vol I (Darmstadt, 1974), p 30; English translation in B W Scholz *Carolingian Chronicles* (Ann Arbor, 1970), p 51.

41   *MGH, Capitularia*, vol I, no 23, chap 18.

42   *Ibid*, no 25, chaps 1–2; English translation in King, *Charlemagne. Translated Sources*, p 223.

43   *MGH, Capitularia*, vol I, no 33, chaps 2–9; English translation in King, *Charlemagne. Translated Sources*, pp 234–5. The text of the oath is given in *MGH, Capitularia*, vol I, no 34, chap 19; English translation in H R Loyn, J Percival, *The Reign of Charlemagne* (London, 1975), pp 81–2. For a fuller discussion see C E Odegaard, 'Carolingian oaths of fidelity' (*Speculum*, vol 16 (1941), pp 284–94) and *idem*, 'The concept of royal power in the Carolingian oaths of fidelity' (*Speculum*, vol 20 (1945), pp 279–89).

44   See R McKitterick, *The Frankish kingdoms under the Carolingians, 751–987* (London, 1983), pp 372–3, Map 3.

45   On the history of the Carolingians see *ibid*, esp pp 169–99 on Charles the Bald. See also J L Nelson, *Charles the Bald* (London, 1992).

46   T Reuter, *Germany in the early middle ages, 800–1056* (London, 1991) and E Hallam, *Capetian France, 987–1328* (London, 1980).

47   'Charlemagne to Offa of Mercia', in E Dümmler, ed, '*Alcuini Epistolae*' (*MGH, Epistolae Karoli Aevi*, vol II (1895), no 100; English translation in *EHD*, vol I, pp 848–9.

48   On the early political development of England see S Basset, *The origins of the Anglo-Saxon kingdoms* (Leicester, 1989) and D P Kirby, *The earliest English kings* (London, 1991).

49   See below, chap 4.

50   There is, however, room for the view that English initiatives may also have

played a role on the continent in the period (C R E Cubitt, *Anglo-Saxon Church Councils in the eighth century* (Leicester, 1995).).

51 S Keynes, M Lapidge, eds, *Alfred the Great. Asser's Life of King Alfred and other contemporary sources* (London, 1983), p 254, n 139.

52 J L Nelson, 'The political ideas of Alfred of Wessex', in A J Duggan, ed, 'Kings and kingship in medieval Europe' (*King's College, London Medieval Studies*, vol X (1993), pp 125–58) and D Pratt, 'Wisdom, warfare and wealth: the political thought of Alfred, Angul-Saxonum rex' (unpublished BA History dissertation, University of Cambridge, 1994).

53 H M Cam, *Local Government in Francia and England* (London, 1912).

54 J Yver, 'Les premiers institutions du duché de Normandie', in *I Normanni e la loro espansione in Europa nell'alto medioevo. Settimane di Studio del Centro Italiano di studi sull'alto mediaevo*, vol XVI (1969), pp 299–366, and M Fauroux, ed, *Recueuil des Actes des ducs de Normandie, 911–1066* (Caen (France), 1961). On the historical background and political formation of Normandy before the Conquest, see D Bates, *Normandy before 1066* (London, 1982); E Searle, *Predatory kinship and the creation of Norman power, 840–1066* (Berkeley (USA), 1988); E M C Van Houts, ed, *The Gesta Normannorum Ducum of William of Jumièges, Orderic Vitalis and Robert of Torigni*, vol I (Oxford, 1992).

55 See, for example, the discussions in J Campbell, 'Observations on English government from the tenth to the twelfth century' (*Trans Roy Hist Soc*, 5th ser, vol 25 (1975), pp 39–54) and *idem*, 'The significance of the Anglo-Norman state in the administrative history of western Europe', in W Paravicini, K-F Werner, eds, *Histoire comparée de l'administration* (Munich, 1980), pp 117–34; repr in Campbell, *Essays in Anglo-Saxon History* (London, 1986), pp 155–90; P Sawyer, ed, *Domesday Book: a reassessment* (London, 1985); J C Holt, ed, *Domesday Studies* (Woodbridge, 1987).

56 I should like to thank the Manorial Society of Great Britain for its hospitality at its conference on 'Monarchy' in Oxford in September, 1993, and members of the audience for their many useful comments and questions on that occasion.

Chapter 2 (pages 46–77)

1 For a survey of the barbarian settlements, see J M Wallace-Hadrill, *The Barbarian West, 400–1000* (London, 3rd edn, 1967).

2 The classic survey of the end of Roman Britain is still that by R G Collingwood, J N L Myres, *Roman Britain and the English Settlements* (Oxford, 2nd edn, 1945), now supplanted by P Salway, *Roman Britain* (Oxford, 1981) and J N L Myres, *The English Settlements* (Oxford, 2nd edn, 1989). See also P Salway, *The Frontier People of Roman Britain* (Cambridge, 1967) and M Todd, *Roman Britain, 55 BC–AD 400: the province beyond the Ocean* (Brighton, 1981).

3 D P Kirby, *The Earliest English Kings* (London, 1991), p 14 and n 74.

4 Collingwood and Myres, *Roman Britain and the English Settlements*, pp 337, 341. See further for the Frisians G C Homans, 'The Frisians in East Anglia' (*Econ Hist Rev*, 2nd ser, vol X (1958), pp 189–206) and for the Juto-Frankish element in Kent J E A Jolliffe, *Pre-Feudal England: the Jutes* (Oxford, 1933); K P Witney, *The Jutish Forest: a study of the Weald of Kent from 450 to 1380* (London, 1976); A M Everitt *Continuity and Colonization: the evolution of Kentish settlement* (Leicester, 1986).

5 Kirby, *The Earliest English Kings*, pp 21–2, points out that the geographical or territorial tags of 'East', 'West', 'South' and 'Middle' as applied to the Saxons

may not have been much older than the records of *c* 700 in which they first appear.

6   For detailed studies on early English royal genealogies, see D M Dumville, 'The Anglian Collection of Royal Genealogies and Regnal Lists' (*Anglo-Saxon England*, vol 5 (1976), pp 23–50); *idem*, 'Kingship Genealogies and Regnal Lists', in P Sawyer, I N Wood, eds, *Early Medieval Kingship* (Leeds, 1977), pp 72–104; K Sisam, 'Anglo-Saxon Royal Genealogies' (*Proceedings of the British Academy*, vol XXXIX (1953), pp 287–346).

7   For England's earliest kings and kingdoms, see B Yorke, *Kings and Kingdoms in Early Anglo-Saxon England* (London, 1992); Kirby, *The Earliest English Kings*; F M Stenton, *Anglo-Saxon England* (Oxford, 2nd edn, 1967); S Bassett, ed, *The Origins of Anglo-Saxon Kingdoms* (Leicester, 1989), as well as the bibliographies in these works for detailed studies on regional dynasties such as B Yorke, 'The Kingdom of the East Saxons' (*Anglo-Saxon England*, vol 14 (1985), pp 1–36). See also D Hill, *An Atlas of Anglo-Saxon England* (Oxford, 1961).

8   The term *Bretwalda* ('Ruler of Britain') is found in the Anglo-Saxon Chronicle alongside a variant form *brytenwealda* ('wide ruler'): the latter may well be the earlier form.

9   J Morris, ed, *Nennius: British History and Welsh Annals* (Chichester, 1980), p 35.

10   J W Ab Ithel, *Annales Cambriae* (London, 1860), p 4 (sub anno 537).

11   For the early historical background to Arthurian legend and to Arthur's Britain generally, see J Morris, *The Age of Arthur: a history of the British Isles from 350 to 650* (London, 1973, repr Chichester, 3 vols, 1977). *Cp* L Alcock, *Arthur's Britain: History and Archaeology, AD 367–634* (London, 1971), and D M Dumville, 'Sub-Roman Britain: History and Legend' (*History*, vol LXII (1977), pp 173–92).

12   Morris, ed, *Nennius: British History and Welsh Annals*, pp 26, 28–9, 31–2, 66–7, 68–70, 72–3.

13   Gildas does not associate Ambrosius Aurelianus personally with the British victory at *Mons Badonicus*, but he does imply that Ambrosius was responsible for rallying his people in a counter-offensive which culminated in the victory at *Mons Badonicus* (J Morris, ed, *Gildas: The Ruin of Britain and Other Works* (Chichester, 1978), pp 28, 98).

14   For the archaeological significance of South Cadbury see L Alcock, '*By South Cadbury is that Camelot ...*' *The Excavations of Cadbury Castle, 1966–70* (London, 1972). See also L V Grinsell, *The Archaeology of Wessex* (London, 1958), pp 304–5.

15   For the history of relations between the Northumbrians and their Celtic neighbours in what is now Scotland, see A P Smyth, *Warlords and Holy Men: Scotland, AD 80–1000* (London, 1984), pp 1–83.

16   For studies of English kingship see J M Wallace-Hadrill, *Early Germanic Kingship in England and on the Continent* (Oxford, 1971), and W A Chaney, *The Cult of Kingship in Anglo-Saxon England* (Manchester 1970).

17   See pp 53–4, 57–8, 70–71 and n 40 below.

18   D Wright, ed, *Beowulf: a prose translation* (Harmondsworth, 1965), p 51.

19   *Anglo-Saxon Chronicle*, see anno 937, in *EHD*, vol I, p 200.

20   Wright, ed, *Beowulf: a prose translation*, p 48.

21   B Colgrave, R A B Mynors, eds, *Bede's Ecclesiastical History of the English People* (Oxford, 1969), pp 268–9.

22   *Ibid*, pp 192–3.

23   Translation based on H L Hargrove, ed, *King Alfred's Old English Version of St Augustine's Soliloquies* (New York (USA), 1904), p 27.

24   *EHD*, vol I, p 502; W de G Birch, ed, *Cartularium Saxonicum: a collection of*

charters relating to Anglo-Saxon history (London, 6 vols, 1883–99), vol II, p 236.

25 Colgrave and Mynors, eds, *Bede's Ecclesiastical History*, pp 74–5.

26 *EHD*, vol I, p 361.

27 For the Sutton Hoo ship burial, see R L S Bruce-Mitford, *et al, The Sutton Hoo Ship Burial: I. Excavations, Background, the Ship, Dating and Inventory* (London, 1975); *The Sutton Hoo Ship Burial: II. Arms, Armour and Regalia* (London, 1978); *The Sutton Hoo Ship Burial: a Handbook* (London, 1979); C Chase, ed, *The Dating of Beowulf* (Toronto (Canada), 1981); D M Wilson, 'Sweden-England', in J P Lamm, H A Nordstrom, *Vendel Period Studies* (Stockholm (Sweden), 1983), pp 163–6; M O H Carver, 'Sutton Hoo in Context' (*Angli e Saxoni al di qua e al di la del mare, Settimani di Studio del centro Italiano di studi sull'alto medioevo* (1984), vol I, pp 77–177); R L S Bruce-Mitford, 'The Sutton Hoo Ship Burial: Some Continental Connections' (*Ibid*, vol I, pp 14–210); R Cramp, 'Beowulf and Archaeology' (*Medieval Archaeology*, vol I (1957), pp 55–77).

28 D Whitelock, *The Audience of Beowulf* (Oxford, 1951); W W Lawrence, *Beowulf and Epic Tradition* (Cambridge (USA), 1928); D Whitelock, *The Beginnings of English Society* (Harmondsworth, repr 1963), pp 204–22; F Klaeber, ed, *Beowulf and the Fight at Finnsburh* (London, 1951).

29 Wright, ed, *Beowulf: a prose translation*, p 53.

30 A P Smyth, *King Alfred the Great* (Oxford, 1995), pp 551–2.

31 Colgrave and Mynors, eds, *Bede's Ecclesiastical History*, pp 182–5.

32 For the significance of Columba's mission to Scotland, see Smyth, *Warlords and Holy Men*, pp 84–140.

33 *Ibid*, p 97.

34 Colgrave and Mynors, eds, *Bede's Ecclesiastical History*, pp 220–1.

35 *Ibid*, pp 296–7.

36 Smyth, *Warlords and Holy Men*, p 121.

37 A Williams in A Williams, A P Smyth, D P Kirby, eds, *Biographical Dictionary of Dark Age Britain* (London, 1991), p 39; Stenton, *Anglo-Saxon England*, pp 88-9.

38 For detailed discussion and bibliography on Offa's coinage, see C E Blunt, 'The Coinage of Offa', in R H M Dolley, ed, *Anglo-Saxon Coins: Studies Presented to F M Stenton* (London, 1961), pp 39–62, and B H I H Stewart, 'The London Mint and the Coinage of Offa', in M A S Blackburn, ed, *Anglo-Saxon Monetary History: Essays in Memory of Michael Dolley* (Leicester, 1986), pp 27–44.

39 An introduction to the subject of Offa's Dyke will be found in J Campbell, E John and P Wormald, eds, *The Anglo-Saxons* (Oxford, 1982), pp 120–1. Detailed studies include C Fox, *Offa's Dyke* (London, 1955); M Gelling, ed, 'Offa's Dyke Reviewed by Frank Noble' (*BAR: British Series*, vol 114, 1983); D Hill, 'The Relationship of Offa's and Wat's Dykes' (*Antiquity*, vol XLVIII (1974), pp 309–412); *idem*, 'Offa's and Wat's Dykes: Some Aspects of Recent Work' (*Transactions of the Lancashire and Cheshire Antiquarian Society*, vol LXXIX (1977), pp 21–33).

40 Wright, ed, *Beowulf: a prose translation*, pp 72–3.

41 Colgrave and Mynors, eds, *Bede's Ecclesiastical History*, pp 234–5.

42 M Biddle, ed, *Winchester Studies: I* (Oxford, 1975).

43 *Anglo-Saxon Chronicle*, sub anno 682, in *EHD*, vol I, p 155.

44 *Anglo-Saxon Chronicle*, sub anno 757, in *EHD*, vol I, p 162–3.

45 For the identification of the leaders of the Great Army of Danes and for the progress of the Danish invasion of England, see A P Smyth, *Scandinavian Kings in the British Isles, 860–880* (Oxford, 1977), in which I take a pessimistic view

of the effect of the earliest Scandinavian raiders. For a more optimistic approach, see P H Sawyer, *The Age of the Vikings* (London, 2nd edn, 1971).

46 Smyth, *Scandinavian Kings in the British Isles*, p 211.

47 For the reign of Alfred, see A P Smyth, *King Alfred the Great* (Oxford, 1995).

48 For a study of how and when the English first came to regard themselves as being 'English', see A P Smyth, 'The Origins of English Identity', in A P Smyth, ed, *Medieval Europeans. Studies in Ethnicity and National Perspectives in Medieval Europe* (Basingstoke, forthcoming).

Chapter 3 (pages 78–100)

1 See, for instance, P Sawyer, *Anglo-Saxon Charters* (London, 1968), nos 134, 168, 186.

2 For a translation of the *Burghal Hidage*, see S Keynes and M Lapidge, *Alfred the Great* (Harmondworth, 1983), pp 193–4; there is a full study of both the document and the burhs themselves in D Hill and A R Rumble, eds, *The Burghal Hidage* (Manchester, 1996).

3 D N Dumville, The treaty of Alfred and Guthrum', *Wessex and England from Alfred to Edgar* (Woodbridge, 1992), p 7, n 37.

4 For Alfred's royal titles, see Keynes and Lapidge, *Alfred the Great*, pp 38–9. It was perhaps for Edward's consecration in 900 that the Second English *Ordo* (the first to prescribe the use of a crown in the ceremony) was composed; it refers to the kingship of 'both peoples', presumably West Saxons and Mercians, subsequently emended to West Saxons, Mercians and Northumbrians (J L Nelson, 'The Second English *Ordo*', in *Politics and Ritual in early medieval Europe* (London, 1986), pp 365–6).

5 Asser, *Life of Alfred*, chapter 80; see Keynes and Lapidge, *Alfred the Great*, pp 96, 262–3.

6 Compare the accounts of the battle of Farnham and the siege of Thorney in 893: the *Anglo-Saxon Chronicle* merely records the triumph of the 'English army', whereas Æthelweard names the commander as the Ætheling Edward, assisted by 'King Æthelred of the Mercians' (A. Campbell, ed, *The Chronicle of Æthelweard* (London, 1962), pp 50–1).

7 In his earliest surviving charter (in 883) Æthelred, described as 'endowed and enriched with part of the Mercian kingdom', makes a grant to Berkeley Abbey 'with the leave and cognisance of King Alfred'; but a charter issued in the following year as 'lord of the Mercians' contains no such reference to Alfred's permission (Sawyer, *Anglo-Saxon Charters*, nos 218–9; see Dumville, 'The treaty of Alfred and Guthrum', p 7). For the meeting places of the Mercian *witan* in Æthelred's time, see D Hill, *An atlas of Anglo-Saxon England* (Oxford, 1981), p 47.

8 Campbell, ed, *Chronicle of Æthelweard*, pp 49–50; *cp* the *Anglo-Saxon Chronicle*'s description of Mercia as 'that part [of Alfred's kingdom] for which Æthelred … was responsible' (Keynes and Lapidge, *Alfred the Great*, p 116). Irish sources also call Æthelred a king and his wife Æthelflæd a queen (J N Radner, ed, *Fragmentary Annals of Ireland* (Dublin, 1978), pp 169, 181; W M Hennessy, B MacCarthy, eds, *Annals of Ulster, otherwise Annals of Senat* (London, 4 vols, 1888–1901), vol I, sub anno 918).

9 *Anglo-Saxon Chronicle*, sub anno 910. For Æthelred's participation, see Campbell, ed, *Chronicle of Æthelweard*, p 52; according to the *Mercian Register*, however, it was Æthelflæd, not her husband, who fortified *Bremesbyrig* (unidentified, but possibly near Bromsgrove, Worcs) later in the same year (for the *Mercian Register*, see n 12 below).

10 There is an excellent account of Edward's campaigns in the east midlands in P Stafford, *The East Midlands in the early middle ages* (Leicester, 1985), pp 111–14. For Æthelflæd, see n 12 below.

11 *Anglo-Saxon Chronicle*, 'A' text, sub anno 914. *Hold* was a Scandinavian title, applied to men of particularly high status.

12 For Æthelflæd's career, see F T Wainwright, 'Aethelflæd, Lady of the Mercians', in his *Scandinavian England* (Chichester, 1975), pp 305–24. The *Mercian Register* is preserved both in the 'B' text of the *Anglo-Saxon Chronicle*, compiled between 977 and c 1000, and in the 'C' text, written-up at Abingdon c 1045 (S Taylor, *The Anglo-Saxon Chronicle: a collaborative edition. 4: MS B* (Cambridge, 1983), pp xxiii, xxxiv, xliv–vii, and (for the text) pp 49–51). The surviving (incomplete) text of the annals for 911–24 is translated in D Whitelock, D C Douglas and S I Tucker, eds, *The Anglo-Saxon Chronicle* (London, 1965), pp 62–8.

13 *Mercian Register*, sub anno 917. The 'borough which is called Derby' was probably not Derby itself, but the refurbished Roman fort at Little Chester (R A Hall, 'The Five Boroughs of the Danelaw: a review of present knowledge' (*Anglo-Saxon England*, vol 18 (1989), pp 159–61).).

14 For Ragnall's career, and the Irish background generally, see A P Smyth, *Scandinavian York and Dublin*, vol 1 (Dublin (Eire) 1975), pp 60–74, 93–116.

15 *Mercian Register*, sub anno 918.

16 *Anglo-Saxon Chronicle*, 'A' text, sub anno 918. The Mercians' submission was accompanied by that of the Welsh kings, who had presumably been tributary to Æthelflæd. Edward had already detached London and Oxford and their districts from Mercian control on the death of Æthelred in 911.

17 Smyth, *Scandinavian York and Dublin*, vol I, pp 110–2; A P Smyth, *Warlords and Holy Men: Scotland, AD 80–1000* (London, 1984), pp 198–201. Ealdred of Bamburgh and his brother Uhtred had received lands from Edward and Æthelred, subsequently confirmed by Athelstan (Sawyer, *Anglo-Saxon Charters*, nos 396–7, and see P Sawyer, ed, *Charters of Burton Abbey* (Oxford, 1979), pp 5–7).

18 *Historia Regum* (see below), sub anno 920; *Mercian Register*, sub anno 921; F M Stenton, *Anglo-Saxon England* (Oxford, 3rd edn, 1971), p 330. For the northern annals preserved in the 12th-century *Historia Regum*, see *EHD*, vol 1, pp 239–54.

19 William of Malmesbury explains his presence in the area as a response to a rising by the men of Chester, with Welsh support; Edward subdued the town and replaced the garrison (W Stubbs, ed, 'Willelmi Malmesburiensis de Gesta Regum' (*RS*, vol 90, 2 pts (1887–9), pt I, pp 144–5); Stenton, *Anglo-Saxon England*, p 339).

20 Her name, Eadgyth, is recorded only by the 13th-century historian, Roger of Wendover, who identified her with St Edith (Eadgyth) of Polesworth, Warwickshire (H O Coxe, ed, *Rogeri de Wendover Chronica sive Flores Historiarum* (English Historical Society, 1841), vol I, p 385. Since Athelstan is said to have had a daughter called Eadgyth (E O Blake, ed, 'Liber Eliensis' (*Camden Soc*, 3rd ser, vol 92 (1962), p 292).), Sigtrygg's bride may have been Athelstan's full sister, a daughter of Edward the Elder's first wife, Ecgwynn.

21 M Lapidge, 'Some Latin poems as evidence for the reign of Athelstan' (*Anglo-Saxon England*, vol 9 (1981), pp 91–2, n 140).

22 Stubbs, ed, 'Willelmi, Malmesburiensis de, Gesta Regum', pt I, 147–8, translated in *EHD*, vol I, pp 280–1, no 8. Two royal charters of 928 (Sawyer, *Anglo-Saxon Charters*, nos 399–400) were issued 'in the royal hall' (*in arce Regis*) at Exeter.

23 *Anglo-Saxon Chronicle*, sub anno 934. The northern annals preserved in the 12th-century *Historia Regum* (*EHD*, vol I, p 252) claim that the land-force

ravaged as far as Dunnotar (Fordun, Kincaidshire), while the fleet raided the coasts as far as the Norse settlements in Caithness.

24 The name means 'the fortified place of *Brun*'. Professor Alfred Smyth (*Scandinavian York and Dublin*, vol II, pp 41–55) has argued for a location in the ancient forest of *Bruneswald* on the Northants/Hunts borders, commemorated in the place names Leighton Bromswold (Hunts) and Newton Bromswold (Northants); M Wood, 'Brunanburh revisited' (*Saga Book of the Viking Society* vol 20, pt 3 (1980), pp 200–17) makes a case for Brinsworth (Yorks, WR), in which case Olaf and Constantine were on their way home when Athelstan's force attacked.

25 For the casualties, see Smyth, *Scandinavian York and Dublin*, vol II, pp 39–40. On the English side, Ælfwine and Æthelwine, the sons of Edward the Elder's brother Æthelweard, were killed.

26 Campbell, ed, *Chronicle of Æthelweard*, p 54.

27 Lapidge, 'Some Latin poems as evidence for the reign of Athelstan', pp 83–93; C E Blunt, 'The coinage of Athelstan, 924–39: a survey' (*British Numismatic Journal*, vol 42 (1974), p 56).

28 This is the estimate of William of Malmesbury (Stubbs, ed, 'Willelmi Malmesburiensis de Gesta Regum pt I, pp 143–52, translated in *EHD*, vol I, p 281).

29 Eadgifu's marriage to King Charles had taken place in her father's reign, probably in 919. Arnulf of Flanders (918–65) and Adelolf of Boulogne were the sons of Alfred's daughter Ælfthryth and Baldwin II, himself the son of Alfred's onetime stepmother and sister-in-law Judith, daughter of Charles the Bald (D Nicholas, *Medieval Flanders* (London, 1992), pp 16–20, 39–43).

30 K Leyser, 'The Ottonians and Wessex', in T Reuter, ed, *Communications and power in medieval Europe* (London, 1994), pp 73–104.

31 Ælfweard's full brother Edwin, the younger son of Edward the Elder and his second wife, Ælfflæd, was already dead, drowned at sea in 933.

32 *Anglo-Saxon Chronicle*, sub anno 878.

33 He was the son of Sigtrygg *Caech*, though not by King Athelstan''s sister.

34 Ragnall was also baptized, with Edmund's sponsorship, later in the same year. A certain Sigtrygg, who is otherwise unknown, was also minting coins at York at this time (C E Blunt, B H I H Stewart, C S S Lyon, *Coinage in Tenth-century England* (London, 1989), p 211; Smyth, *Scandinavian York and Dublin*, vol II, p 124, n 40).

35 D N Dumville, 'Learning and the church in the England of King Edmund I, 939–46', *Wessex and England from Alfred to Edgar*, p 184. The *Anglo-Saxon Chronicle* records the name of his killer, Leofa, and the 12th-century historian, John of Worcester, says that the man was a convicted outlaw, and that Edmund had intervened to save the life of his seneschal, whom Leofa had attacked (P McGurk, R R Darlington, eds, *The Chronicle of John of Worcester*, vol II, (Oxford, 1995) [hereafter cited as John of Worcester], pp 398–9.

36 Osulf succeeded his father Ealdred as lord of Bamburgh in 934 and died in 963; he attests royal charters as 'high-reeve' of Bamburgh (D Whitelock, 'The dealings of the kings of England with Northumbria in the tenth and eleventh centuries', in P Clemoes, ed, *The Anglo-Saxons, Studies ... presented to Bruce Dickins* (London, 1959), p 77).

37 For the chronological contradictions, see P Sawyer, 'The last Scandinavian rulers of York' (*Northern History*, vol 31 (1995), pp 39–44). The following interpretation is based on discussion with Marios Costambeys, who is preparing a study of

Erik Bloodaxe's career, and I should like to thank Dr Costambeys for his assistance in unravelling this knotty problem. Any errors of interpretation are, of course, my own.

38 Olaf's expulsion is recorded under the year 952 by the 'E' text of the *Anglo-Saxon Chronicle*, but the true date is likely to be 949, for in charters of 949–50 Eadred is described as 'king of the Northumbrians, pagans [ie Danes] and Saxons' and he must have had control of York in these years. For the same reason, the formal submission to Eadred by Archbishop Wulfstan and the men of York, which the 'D' text records in 947, is probably also to be dated to 949. Neither 'D' nor 'E' is contemporary for these years, and some degree of temporal dislocation in their entries is to be expected.

39 *Anglo-Saxon Chronicle*, 'D' text, sub anno 952. The 'D' text of the *Anglo-Saxon Chronicle* places Eadred's expedition in 948, but the *Historia Regum* in 950; the same source records, sub anno 952, that 'the kings of the Northumbrians came to an end' (*EHD*, vol I, no 3, pp 253–4).

40 The details of Erik's fate are recorded by the 13th-century historian, Roger of Wendover, who places his death in 950 (*EHD*, vol I, p 257). Roger was using the same northern annals employed by the compiler of the *Historia Regum*. The Old Norse *Lay of Eric*, recording his triumphant arrival in Valhalla, is translated in W H Auden and P B Taylor, *Norse Poems* (London, 1983), pp 60–1. He is nevertheless commemorated in the *Liber vitae* of Durham Cathedral.

41 Sawyer, *Anglo-Saxon Charters*, no 1515 (my italics).

42 *Life of Dunstan* by 'B', in W Stubbs, ed, 'Memorials of Saint Dunstan, archbishop of Canterbury' (*RS*, vol 63 (1874), p 31). He is also said to have suffered from 'a weakness of the feet', possibly gout (Herman of Bury, in T Arnold, ed, 'Memorials of St Edmund's Abbey, Bury' (*RS*, vol 96, 3 pts, 1890–6), pt I, p 29): I owe this reference to Simon Keynes).

43 *EHD*, vol I, nos 234, 238, pp 900–1, 920; Campbell, ed, *Chronicle of Æthelweard*, p 55.

44 The *Anglo-Saxon Chronicle* is also ambiguous; the 'B' and 'C' texts have Edgar succeeding to the Mercian kingdom in 957, whereas the 'D' text records that when Eadred died, Eadwig received Wessex and Edgar Mercia.

45 For Edgar's charters as King of the Mercians, see Sawyer, *Anglo-Saxon Charters*, nos 667, 673, 674, 675, 676, 676a, 677, 678, 679.

46 The *Anglo-Saxon Chronicle*, sub anno 973, mentions six kings, but Ælfric the homilist has eight (*EHD*, vol I, p 853) and this is the number given by John of Worcester, who names the participants (John of Worcester, vol II, pp 422–3; see also Stubbs, ed, 'Willelmi Malmesburiensis de Gesta Regum', pt I, p 165). For the identifications, see Stenton, *Anglo-Saxon England*, pp 369–70.

47 E John, *Orbis Britanniae* (Leicester, 1966), pp 1–63, 276–89; J L Nelson, 'Inauguration rituals', in P H Sawyer, I Wood, eds, *Early medieval kingship* (Leeds, 1977), pp 63–71.

48 Smyth, *Warlords and Holy Men*, pp 215–38, esp pp 232–3. Edgar's 'cession of Lothian' is recorded by Roger of Wendover, sub anno 975 (*EHD*, vol I, p 258 and n 2).

49 *Anglo-Saxon Chronicle*, 'D' and 'E' texts, sub anno 975; the translation is that of M Swanton, *The Anglo-Saxon Chronicle* (London, 1996), p 121. The 'A' and 'C' texts have a longer poem, couched in more general terms.

50 The law codes are printed, with translations, by F L Attenborough, *The laws of the earliest English kings* (Cambridge, 1922) and A J Robertson, *The laws of the kings of England from Edmund to Henry I* (Cambridge, 1925).

51   II and III Edgar 'seems to have formed a single act of legislation', dealing with ecclesiastical and secular matters respectively (*EHD*, vol I, no 40, p 394). I Edgar is the *Hundred Ordinance*.

52   IV Edgar, clause 15, 1.

53   For his career, see C R Hart, 'Athelstan "Half-King" and his family' (*Anglo-Saxon England*, vol 2 (1973), pp 115–44).

54   *Ibid*, p 122; Blake, ed, 'Liber Eliensis', pp xiv, 111. Thurferth, Scule, and Halfdane are all Danish names; Thurferth indeed might be the Danish jarl who submitted to Edward the Elder in 917. Those Danish magnates who submitted to Edward were allowed to retain their lands; the lands of those who did not were confiscated (*Ibid*, pp xi, 98–9).

55   I Edgar. The ordinance is largely concerned with the judicial aspect of the hundred, whose court met every four weeks, but it had military functions too; Æthelweard the Chronicler, who, as ealdorman of the Western shires (West Wessex) was in a position to know, describes the shire levies as 'hundreds' (*centurias*), and in the 11th century the men of Swineshead (Hunts), 'paid geld in the hundred and went with [the men of the hundred] against the enemy' (Campbell, ed, *Chronicle of Æthelweard*, p 28; *Domesday Book, Huntingdonshire*, fol 208b, *D*, 14). See also H R Loyn, 'The hundred in England in the tenth and eleventh centuries', in H Hearder, H R Loyn, eds, *British government and administration* (Cardiff, 1974), pp 1–15; repr in Loyn, *Society and peoples: studies in the history of England and Wales, c 600–1200* (London, 1992), pp 111–34. The association of the king's reeve and the local court is found in the legislation of Edward the Elder (II Edward, clause 8), and the reeves, hundred-men and tithing men are already functioning in the arrangements made for implementing Athelstan's laws by the Londoners (VI Athelstan, clause 8, 1).

56   Other such 'shipsokes' are known, but it is difficult to say how many there were; the known examples all relate to ecclesiastical land, but this is probably a function of the surviving sources. A 12th-century legal collection says that the shires are divided into 'hundreds and shipsokes' (L P Downer, ed, *Leges Henrici Primi* (Oxford 1972), p 97 (section 6, clause 1b); see N Hooper, 'Some observations on the navy in late Anglo-Saxon England', in C Harper-Bill, C Holdsworth, J L Nelson, eds, *Studies in medieval history presented to R Allen Brown* (Woodbridge, 1989), pp 203–13.

57   H R Loyn, *The Governance of Anglo-Saxon England* (London, 1984), pp 146–7.

58   III Æthelred (the Wantage Code); *cp* IV Edgar clause 12, 15. The 'Five Boroughs' of the northeast (Lincoln, Stamford, Nottingham, Derby and Leicester) were constituted, probably from Eadred's time, as a confederacy, an arrangement superseded in the 11th century by the shires of Lincoln (with Stamford), Nottingham, Derby and Leicester (D Roffe, 'The origins of Derbyshire' (*Derbyshire Archaeological Journal*, vol 106 (1986), pp 110–5).

59   Another set of 'local' customs is the *Ordinance concerning the Dunsæte*, which probably dates from Athelstan's time; it regulates relations between Welsh and English in the border regions. The text is printed, with translation, by F Noble in M Gelling, ed, 'Offa's Dyke reviewed' (*BAR, British series*, vol 114 (1983), pp 103–9).

60   Ælfric, *Life of St Æthelwold*, translated in *EHD*, vol I, no 235, p 835.

61   See, for instance, the case of Thorney Abbey (C R Hart, *The early charters of eastern England* (Leicester, 1966), pp 165–89).

62   See D J V Fisher, 'The anti-monastic reaction in the reign of Edward the Martyr' (*Cambridge Historical Journal*, vol X (1950–2), pp 254–70).

63 Ælfthryth's elder son, Edmund, died in 970 or 971. There is debate whether Edgar had actually married Wulfthryth, the mother of his daughter, St Eadgyth. Eadgyth was the lady who, when reproached by St Æthelwold for her fine clothes, retorted that as true a heart beat beneath her gold embroidery as beneath his tattered furs (N E S A Hamilton, ed, 'Willelmi Malmesburiensis de Gestis Pontificum' (*RS*, vol 52 (1870), p 189).

64 *Vita Oswaldi*, in J Raine, ed, 'The historians of the Church of York and its archbishops' (*RS*, vol 71, 3 pts, 1879–94), pt I, p 448 (*EHD*, vol I, no 236, p 841).

65 For Ælfhere, see A Williams, '*Princeps Merciorum gentis*: the family, career and connexions of Ælfhere, ealdorman of Mercia, 956–83' (*Anglo-Saxon England*, vol 10 (1982), pp 143–72).

66 *Vita Oswaldi* (*EHD*, vol I, no 236, p 542).

67 For the murder and its ramifications see S Keynes, *The diplomas of Æthelred II, 'the Unready', 978–1016* (Cambridge, 1980), pp 163–76. The hiding of the corpse was part of the definition of 'murder' (*murdrum*, 'concealment') in this period.

68 The 'A' text, which presents a different picture, has only a few entries for this period (see also next note).

69 S Keynes, 'The declining reputation of King Æthelred the Unready', in D Hill, ed, 'Ethelred the Unready' (*BAR, British series*, vol 59 (1978), pp 227–53).

70 S Keynes, 'A tale of two kings: Alfred the Great and Æthelred the Unready' (*TRHS*, 5th ser, vol 36 (1986), p 213); see also *idem, The diplomas of Æthelred II, 'the Unready', 978–1016*, esp pp 154–231.

71 In the 'A' text this entry is placed against the year 993, and the entry may be conflating the Maldon campaign of 991 with Olaf's later depredations (J M Bately, 'The 'Anglo-Saxon Chronicle' in D Scragg, ed, *The Battle of Maldon, AD 991* (Oxford, 1991), pp 37–50; S Keynes, 'The historical background of the battle of Maldon', in *ibid*, pp 88–93). In the Old English poem (*The Battle of Maldon*) which commemorates the event, none of the Vikings is named.

72 *Anglo-Saxon Chronicle*, 'C', 'D' and 'E' texts, sub anno 994. The terms of the truce are preserved in the document known as II Æthelred, a treaty between Æthelred and the leaders of the Viking army, named as Olaf [Tryggvason], Josteinn and Guthmund (see Keynes, 'The historical background of the battle of Maldon', pp 91–2, 103–7).

73 *Anglo-Saxon Chronicle* 'C', 'D' and 'E' texts, sub anno 1011.

74 His reign lasted until his defeat at the sea-battle of Svold (999), when, rather than submit to his enemies, he leapt from the deck of his ship, the *Long Serpent*, 'and never came back again to his kingdom in Norway' (S Laing, J Simpson, eds, *Snorri Sturluson, Heimskringla: the Olaf sagas*, vol I (London, 1964), pp 97–8).

75 Its leaders are never named, but may have included the Tostig with whom Ulv of Borresta (Sweden) first took service; Ulv's memorial stone claims that he 'took three gelds in England', first from Tostig, then from Thorkell (the Tall, between 1009 and 1012), and finally from Cnut (1015–18); se N Lund, 'The armies of Swein Forkbeard and Cnut: *leding* or *lið*?' (*Anglo-Saxon England*, vol 15 (1986), pp 118–19).

76 Ælfgifu is overshadowed by her formidable mother-in-law, Ælfthryth, who lived until 1002. Ælfgifu was probably the daughter of Thored, ealdorman of Northumbria, exiled in 992. The *Anglo-Saxon Chronicle* records the death of her brother Athelstan at the battle of Ringmere in 1010.

77 *Anglo-Saxon Chronicle*, sub anno 1002; only the massacre at Oxford is recorded elsewhere (Sawyer, *Anglo-Saxon Charters*, no 909).

78 Keynes, 'The historical background of the battle of Maldon', pp 90–1.
79 For the 300-hide shipsokes, see above, p 186 and n 56. The weapons and armour were for the crews which manned and fought the ships.
80 See below, n 106.
81 *Anglo-Saxon Chronicle*, sub anno 1009.
82 *Anglo-Saxon Chronicle*, sub anno 1012. The murder of the archbishop and Thorkell's remorse are also recorded, in a garbled form, by the German chronicler, Thietmar of Merseberg (translated in *EHD*, vol I, no 27, p 221).
83 *Anglo-Saxon Chronicle*, sub anno 1010.
84 For Thorkell's relations with Swein, see A Campbell, ed, 'Encomium Emmae Reginae' (*Camden Soc*, 3rd ser, vol 72 (1949)), pp 10–11, 73–82).
85 *Anglo-Saxon Chronicle*, sub anno 1013.
86 *Anglo-Saxon Chronicle*, sub anno 1014.
87 Ælfgifu had reason to be hostile to King Æthelred, for her father had been murdered in 1006, with the king's connivance (*Anglo-Saxon Chronicle*, sub anno 1006).
88 *Anglo-Saxon Chronicle*, sub anno 1016. The site is still disputed (C R Hart, 'The site of *Assandune*', in his *The Danelaw* (London, 1992), pp 553–65).
89 The most recent studies of Cnut's reign are M K Lawson, *Cnut: the Danes in England in the early eleventh century* (London, 1993) and the articles collected in A R Rumble, ed, *The reign of Cnut* (Leicester, 1994).
90 He did not, however, repudiate his first wife Ælfgifu, whom he later made regent of Norway for their son Swein; her rule was so unpopular that in later years, the Norwegians were accustomed to dismiss bad patches in their history as better than 'Ælfgifu's time' (P Sawyer, 'Cnut's Scandinavian Empire', in Rumble, ed, *The reign of Cnut*, p 21).
91 In Cnut's letter of 1027 to the English people, he is described as 'king of all England, and of Denmark, and of the Norwegians, and of part of the Swedes' (*EHD*, vol I, no 49, pp 416–18).
92 The coronation, and the negotiations which Cnut carried on with pope and emperor for the benefit of English merchants and travellers, are described in his letter of 1027 to the English people (see previous note). The marriage of Henry and Gunnhild took place in 1036, after her father's death, and she herself died two years later.
93 R Frank, 'King Cnut in the verse of his skalds', in Rumble, ed, *The reign of Cnut*, pp 106–24; for the earlier Danish kings, see Sawyer, 'Cnut's Scandinavian empire', *ibid*, pp 10–14.
94 I and II Cnut, printed in Robertson, *Laws of the kings of England from Edmund to Henry I*, pp 154–74; extracts are translated in *EHD*, vol I, no 50, pp 419–30.
95 S Keynes, 'Cnut's earls', in Rumble, ed, *The reign of Cnut*, pp 43–88.
96 N Hooper, 'The housecarls in the eleventh century' (*Anglo-Norman Studies*, vol 7 (1985), pp 161–76); idem, 'Military developments in the reign of Cnut', in Rumble, ed, *The reign of Cnut*, pp 88–100. For the assimilation of English and Danes see A Williams, '"Cockles amongst the wheat": Danes and English in the west Midlands in the first half of the eleventh century' (*Midland History*, vol II (1986), pp 1–22).
97 Hooper, 'Some observations on the navy in late Anglo-Saxon England', in Harper-Bill *et al*, eds, *Studies in medieval history Presented to R Allen Brown*, pp 203–13.
98 See T A Heslop, 'The production of *de luxe* manuscripts and the patronage of King Cnut and Queen Emma' (*Anglo-Saxon England*, vol 19 (1990), pp 156–62).

99 A R Rumble, R Morris, 'Osbern's account of the translation of St Ælfheah's relics from London to Canterbury, 8–11 June 1023', in Rumble, ed, *The reign of Cnut*, 283–93.

100 See, for example, the eulogy of Cnut and his sons in Henry of Huntingdon (T Arnold, ed, 'Henrici archidiaconi huntendunensi Anglorum Historia' (*RS*, vol 74 (1885), pp 188–90, 220).). It is Henry who tells the story of Cnut and the waves, as an example of the king's scornful contempt for the lying flatteries of his courtiers.

101 *Anglo-Saxon Chronicle*, 'C' text, sub anno 1037.

102 Campbell, ed, 'Encomium Emmae Reginae', pp 42–5.

103 *Anglo-Saxon Chronicle*, 'C', 'D' texts, sub anno 1040; this version adds that Harthacnut 'did nothing worthy of a king as long as he ruled'. The 'E' text is much less overtly hostile.

104 Edward's reign is fully covered by F Barlow, *Edward the Confessor* (London, 1970).

105 F Barlow, ed, *The life of King Edward who lies at Westminster* (London, 1962).

106 See above, note 80. Earl Godwine's career has been studied by D G J Raraty, 'Earl Godwine of Wessex: the origins of his power and his political loyalties' (*History*, vol 74 (1989), pp 3–19) and by R Fleming, 'Domesday estates of the king and the Godwinesons: a study in late Saxon politics' (*Speculum*, vol 58 (1983), pp 987–1007); *idem, Kings and lords in Conquest England* (Cambridge, 1991), pp 53–103.

107 See above, p 92. Ulf and Estrith were the parents of Swein Estrithson, King of Denmark (1047–76); he bears his metronymic because his mother was of higher status than this father.

108 Swein's earldom included, as well as Herefordshire, the shires of Berkshire, Somerset and Oxford, and Gloucestershire, once governed by his maternal uncle, Eilaf.

109 A Williams, 'The king's nephew: the family, career and connections of Ralph, earl of Hereford', in Harper-Bill *et al*, eds *Studies in medieval history presented to R Allen Brown*, pp 327–43. Ralph was the son of Edward's full sister Godgifu and Drogo, Count of the Vexin (D Bates, 'Lord Sudeley's ancestors; the family of the Counts of Amiens, Valois and the Vexin in France and England during the eleventh century', in Lord Sudeley, ed, *The Sudeleys, Lords of Toddington* (London, 1987), pp 34–48.

110 'Pentecost's castle and 'Robert's castle' (*Anglo-Saxon Chronicle*, 'E' text, sub anno 1051, 1052).

111 The 'D' text of the *Anglo-Saxon Chronicle* implies the existence of such a castle (A Williams, *The English and the Norman Conquest* (Woodbridge, 1995), p 15). Godwine may have had some particular association with Dover, for it was probably he who rebuilt the minster-church of St Mary at Dover, later St Mary-in-Castro (T Tatton-Brown, 'The churches of Canterbury diocese in the eleventh century', in J Blair, ed, *Minsters and parish churches: the local church in transition, 950–1200* (Oxford, 1988), p 110).

112 Eustace was the second husband of Edward's sister Godgifu, who died c 1049 (see n 109 above).

113 The implication is that they were expecting trouble.

114 Thus they committed the capital crime of *hamsocn*, attack on a man in his own house.

115 *Anglo-Saxon Chronicle*, 'D' text, sub anno 1051.

116 So says the *Anglo-Saxon Chronicle*: the *Vita Edwardi*, written for Queen Edith,

softens her treatment by having her withdraw to Wilton Abbey, where she had
been educated.

117 *Anglo-Saxon Chronicle*, 'C' text, sub anno 1053.

118 *Anglo-Saxon Chronicle*, 'C' text, sub anno 1055.

119 *Anglo-Saxon Chronicle*, 'D' and 'E' texts, sub anno 1063.

120 Harold's first wife was Edith (Eadgyth) Swanneck, mother of his elder children.
Since she is referred to as a concubine, the union was presumably a 'handfast
match' (*more Danico*), like the first marriage of Cnut to Ælfgifu of Northampton.
Such unions were not recognized by the Church, and remarriage, even in the
lifetime of the first spouse, was perfectly possible.

121 *Anglo-Saxon Chronicle*, 'D' text, sub anno 1065.

122 So says the *Anglo-Saxon Chronicle*, 'C' and 'D' texts, sub anno 1065), John of
Worcester, vol II, pp 600–1, and the *Vita Edwardi* (Barlow, ed, *The life of King
Edward who lies at Westminster*, p 74); Edward's designation of Harold is also
accepted by William of Poitiers, though of course he regards the previous promise
to William as having greater validity (R Foreville, ed, *Gesta Guillielmi* (Paris
(France), 1952), pp 172–5).

123 *Anglo-Saxon Chronicle*, 'C', 'D' texts, sub anno 1066.

124 *Anglo-Saxon Chronicle*, 'C' text, sub anno 1066.

125 *Anglo-Saxon Chronicle*, 'D' text, sub anno 1066.

126 M Wood, *In search of the Dark Ages* (London, 1981), p 218.

127 E Van Houts, ed, *William of Jumieges: Gesta Normannorum Ducum* (Oxford,
1996), vol II, pp 166–7.

128 Foreville, ed, *Gesta Guillielmi*, pp 207–8; for the clifftop burial, see C Morton,
H Munz, eds, *The Carmen de Hastingi Proelio of Guy, bishop of Amiens* (Oxford,
1972), pp 36–7.

129 L Watkiss, M Chibnall, eds, *The Waltham Chronicle* (Oxford, 1994), pp 50–7.

130 J L Nelson, 'The earliest royal *ordo*: some liturgical and historical aspects', in
her *Politics and ritual in early medieval Europe* (London, 1986), pp 356–8; see
also above, p 328, n 4. In the inauguration ritual, the significant element was
not so much the coronation but the consecration of the king with holy oil.

131 Downer, ed, *Leges Henrici Primi*, pp 96–7.

Chapter 4 (pages 101–115)

1 F Barlow, ed, 'The Letters of Arnulf of Lisieux' (*Camden Soc*, 3rd ser, vol 61
(1939), p 73, no 42. The first part of the translation follows that of W L Warren,
Henry II (London 1973), pp 628–9. For the context, F Barlow, *Thomas Becket*
(London 1986), pp 135–6. All translations in this chapter, with the exception of
those from the *Anglo-Saxon Chronicle*, are from Latin. Where a published
translation is cited it has been used, although minor changes have occasionally
been made where the sense of the Latin demands them.

2 C N L Brooke, R A B Mynors, eds, *Walter Map, De Nugis Curialum* (Oxford,
1983), pp 450–1.

3 J S Brewer, *et al*, eds, 'Giraldi Cambrensi Opera' (*RS*, vol 21, 8 pts (1861–91),
pt VIII, pp 317–20). Henry II's infidelities were noted by a number of chroniclers,
notably William of Newburgh, 'Historia Rerum Anglicarum', in R S Howlett,
ed, 'Chronicles and Memorials of the Reigns of Stephen, Henry II and Richard
I' (*RS*, vol 82, 4 pts (1884–90), pt I, p 283).

4 R W Southern, 'England's first entry into Europe', in his *Medieval Humanism
and Other Studies* (Oxford 1970), p 147. This chapter draws heavily on Southern's
brilliant essay, *ibid*, pp 135–57.

5   W Stubbs, ed, 'Willelmi Malmesburiensis de Gestis Regum Anglorum' (*RS*, vol 90, 2 pts (1887–9), pt II, p 360). The speaker is Odo of Bayeux.

6   *Anglo-Saxon Chronicle*, sub anno 1087, in *EHD*, vol II, p 163–4.

7   T Arnold, ed, 'Henrici Huntendunensis Historia Anglorum, (*RS*, vol 74 (1879), pp 255–6. The release from prison of Count Waleran of Meulan in 1129 was probably in return for the sexual favours of the count's sister, by whom Henry had at least one child (D Crouch, *The Beaumont Twins. The Roots and Branches of Power in the Twelfth Century* (Cambridge, 1986), p 25).

8   J Green, *The Government of England under Henry I* (Cambridge, 1986), p 1.

9   See especially M Chibnall, ed, *The Ecclesiastical History of Orderic Vitalis* (Oxford, 6 vols, 1969–81), vol II, pp 318–23; vol IV, pp 98–101.

10 B Thorpe, ed, *Florence of Worcester: Chronicon ex Chroniciis* (London, 2 vols, 1848–9), vol II, p 39; *Anglo-Saxon Chronicle*, sub anno 1096 (*EHD*, vol II, p 173); Chibnall, ed, *the Ecclesiastical History of Orderic Vitalis*, vol IV, pp 284–5.

11 Stubbs, ed, 'Willelmi Malmesburiensis de Gestis Regum', pt II, p 475; *cp* Chibnall, ed, *The Ecclesiastical History of Orderic Vitalis*, vol VI, pp 98–9 and n 2, who does say that Robert was given every comfort during his imprisonment. However, it was rumoured that William of Mortain was blinded while a prisoner (Henry of Huntingdon, 'Historia Regum Anglorum', p 255). The Bermondsey Annals, a late and unreliable source, alleged that he was released from the Tower of London in 1118, but this is not otherwise attested, and he probably remained a prisoner until he became a monk at Bermondsey in 1140 (H R Luard, ed, 'Annales Monastici' (*RS*, vol 36, 5 pts (1864–9), pt III, pp 432, 436).).

12 *Anglo-Saxon Chronicle*, sub anno 1125, in *EHD*, vol II, p 192; Arnold, ed, Henrici Huntendunensis Historia Anglorum', p 246. The opinion quoted is that of Eadmer in M Rule, ed, 'Eadmeri Historiae' (*RS*, vol 81 (1884), p 193). *Cp* Green, *The Government of England under Henry I*, pp 89–91.

13 Chibnall, ed, *The Ecclesiastical History of Orderic Vitalis*, vol VI, pp 522–3; Warren, *Henry II*, p 164, who says that the Welsh hostages were then hanged. However, both the *Annales Cambriae* (J Williams ap Ithel, ed, 'Annales Cambriae (*RS*, vol 20 (1860), p 50) and Gerald of Wales in his *Itinerarium Kambriae* (J S Brewer, *et al*, eds, 'Geraldi Cambrensis Opera', pt VI, p 143), only mention mutilation, while the Welsh *Brut y Twysogyon* said that Henry had four prince's sons and several others blinded (T Jones, ed, *Brut y Twysogyon or the Chronicle of the Princes. Peniarth MS 20 Version*, (Cardiff, 1952), pp 63–4; T Jones, ed, *Brut y Twysogyon: Red Book of Hergest version* (Cardiff, 1955), p 147). Warren may have confused this episode with King John's hanging of Welsh hostages in 1212.

14 C W Hollister, 'Royal acts of mutilation: the case against Henry I', in his *Monarchy, Magnates and Institutions in the Anglo-Norman World* (London, 1984), pp 291–301, at pp 296–8.

15 Chibnall, ed, *The Ecclesiastical History of Orderic Vitalis*, vol IV, pp 114–15.

16 *Ibid*, vol VI, pp 98–9.

17 H Waquet, ed, *Suger, Vie de Louis VI Le Gros*, (Paris (France), 2nd edn, 1964), p 100.

18 W Stubbs, ed, 'Radulfi de Diceto Opera Historica' (*RS*, vol 68, 2 pts (1876), pt I, p 371). The comparison with Henry I was made by William of Newburgh, 'Historia Rerum Anglicarum' (Howlett, ed, 'Chronicles and Memorials of the Reigns of Stephen, Henry II and Richard I', pt I, p 280), with reference especially to forest offences.

19 Chibnall, ed, *The Ecclesiastical History of Orderic Vitalis*, vols II, pp 230–3, IV, pp 94–5 (which has William repenting of his action on his deathbed, though this speech is an invention of Orderic's). However, the ravaging of Yorkshire may well have been only an exceptionally brutal example of fairly standard practice in medieval warfare: see J Gillingham, 'William the Bastard at war', in C Harper-Bill, C Holdsworth and J L Nelson, eds, *Studies in Medieval History Presented to R Allen Brown*. (Woodbridge, 1989), pp 141–58.

20 Chibnall, ed, *The Ecclesiastical History of Orderic Vitalis*, vol VI, pp 352–5, discussed by Hollister, 'Royal acts of mutilation', pp 291–2, 300. *Cp* Chibnall, ed, *The Ecclesiastical History of Orderic Vitalis*, vol VI, pp 18–19: 'He [Henry I] was implacable in his enmity to those who broke faith, and scarcely ever pardoned any of known guilt'.

21 Stubbs, ed, 'Willelmi Malmesburiensis de Gestis Regum', pt II, p 475.

22 K R Potter, R H C Davis, eds, *Gesta Stephani*, (Oxford, 1976), pp 4–5, 22–3.

23 *Anglo-Saxon Chronicle*, sub anno 1137, in *EHD*, vol II, pp 199–200.

24 E Searle, ed, *The Chronicle of Battle Abbey* (Oxford, 1980), pp 212–13.

25 Chibnall, ed, *The Ecclesiastical History of Orderic Vitalis*, vol VI, pp 522–3.

26 Potter and Davis, eds, *Gesta Stephani*, pp 10–11. The dispute was recorded by K R Potter, ed, *The Historia Novella of William of Malmesbury* (Edinburgh, 1955), p 4.

27 J T Appleby, ed, *The Chronicle of Richard of Devizes* (Edinburgh, 1963), p 32.

28 For Henry, see J B Robertson, ed, 'materials for the History of Thomas Becket, Archbishop of Canterbury,' (*RS*, vol 67, 7 pts 1882), pt VI, p 72 (epistle 253), part of which is translated in Warren, *Henry II*, p 183.

29 Barlow, ed, 'Letters of Arnulf of Lisieux', pp 164–70, nos 105–7; the quotation is from p 165, to Walter of Coutances; Gerald of Wales, '*Expugnatio Hibernica*, Book I, chap 46, in Dimock, ed, 'Geraldi Cambrensis, pt V, p 304, which continues that Henry 'rarely hated a man he once loved', but, as Barlow, 'Letters of Arnulf,' p lii, writes, this latter remark was hardly true in practice.

30 W Stubbs ed, 'Chronica Rogeri de Hoveden', (*RS*, vol 51, 4 pts (1868–71), pt III, p 238.

31 A Hofmeister, ed, 'Ottonis de Sancto Blasio Chronica', *MGH, Scriptores* (Hannover (Germany), 1912), p 61. *Cp* Suger, *Vie de Louis VI*, pp 246–7, for that ruler's vengeance inflicted upon the murderers of Count Charles of Flanders in 1127.

32 Walter Map, *De Nugis Curialum*, pp 476–7.

33 *Anglo-Saxon Chronicle*, sub anno 1079, in *English Historical Documents*, vol II, p 159; Chibnall, ed, *The Ecclesiastical History of Orderic Vitalis*, vol IV, p 167, vol VI, p 989. *Cp* also the still very valuable essay by F M Stenton, 'English families and the Norman Conquest' (*Trans Roy Hist Soc*, 4th Ser, vol 26 (1944), pp 1–12).

34 Appleby, ed, *The Chronicle of Richard of Devizes*, p xii.

35 A few random examples: in 1174 Henry II sent Roger of Howden (the chronicler) to southern Scotland to persuade the lords of Galloway to submit to his rule, in 1182 he forbade the consecration of Walter of Coutances as Bishop of Lincoln and ordered the Justiciar to inquire into the property left by the recently deceased Archbishop of York (W Stubbs, ed, 'Gesta Regis Henrici Secundi Benedicti Abbatis' [actually by Roger of Howden] (*RS*, vol 49, 2 pts, 1867), pt I, pp 80, 289, 299). Probably the best guide to the scale of this cross-Channel activity is L Landon, 'The Itinerary of Richard I' (*PRS*, NS vol 13, 1935).

36 Searle, ed, *The Chronicle of Battle Abbey*, pp 212–15.

37 Chibnall, ed, *The Ecclesiastical History of Orderic Vitalis*, vol II, pp 168–9; Stubbs, ed, 'Gesta Regis Henrici Secundi', pt I, p 285; *Cp* 'Pipe Roll, 28 Henry II' (*PRS*, vol 31 (1910), p 139), which records the expenses of his officials 'while they made a delay at Portsmouth before the king's crossing'.

38 There is a splendidly tendentious account in Chibnall, ed, *The Ecclesiastical History of Orderic Vitalis*, vol VI, pp 294–301, in which the disaster was ascribed to the drunkenness of the sailors in charge of the ship.

39 Stubbs, ed, 'Gesta Regis Henrici Secundi', pt I, pp 306, 381–2, pt II, p 5.

40 D L Douie, D H Farmer, eds, *Magna Vita Sancti Hugonis* (Oxford, 1985), pp 73–4.

41 Stubbs, ed, 'Radulfi de Diceto Opera Historica', pt I, pp 381–2. Warren, *Henry II*, p 127 suggests that Henry may have made a very brief visit to England to check on the situation there in the summer of 1173. He also suggests (*Ibid*, pp 132–3) that his enemies later hoped to lure him to England to leave Normandy open to them.

42 F J West, *The Justiciarship in England, 1066–1232* (Cambridge, 1966) is the standard work; see pp 16–23 for Roger of Salisbury, and Green, *Government of Henry I*, pp 44–8. For Odo as the king's representative, D R Bates, 'The origins of the Justiciarship', (*Anglo-Norman Studies*, vol IV (1981), pp 1–12), though this is an extreme statement of the case.

43 Stubbs, ed, 'Radulfi de Diceto Opera Historica', pt I, pp 367–9. In 1184 Ranulf Glanvill held a council of bishops which refused to permit papal envoys to levy a tax on the Church (Stubbs, ed, 'Gesta Regis Henrici Secundi', pt I, p 311).

44 *Ibid*, pt I, p 94; *cp ibid*, pt I, p 316, where Henry pardoned a knight whom Ranulf Glanvill had condemned to death; Warren, *Henry II*, pp 140, 154.

45 Green, *Government of Henry I*, pp 41, 50; C Johnson, H A Cronne, eds, *Regesta Regum Anglo-Normannorum*, vol II (Oxford, 1956), p 96, no 963.

46 G D G Hall, ed, *The Treatise on the Laws and Customs of England Commonly Called Glanvill* (Edinburgh, 1965), pp 2–3.

47 So his modern biographer sums him up (Warren, *Henry II*, esp pp 313–16). Walter Map suggested that his tendency to postpone decisions was deliberate and calculated policy (Walter Map, *De Nugis Curialum*, pp 484–5). For the 'Dialogue of the Exchequer' see below, n 64.

48 J Green, 'Lords of the Norman Vexin', in J Gillingham, J C Holt, eds, *War and Government in the Middle Ages. Essays in Honour of J.O. Prestwich* (Woodbridge 1984), pp 46–61.

49 According to Abbot Suger, 'for the defence of his land he [Henry I] garrisoned nearly all the march of Normandy, as far as his duchy extended, with many knights at great expense' (Suger, *Vie de Louis VI*, pp 110–12). The classic modern studies are by J O Prestwich, 'War and finance in the Anglo-Norman state' (*Trans Roy Hist Soc*, 5th Ser, vol 4 (1954) pp 19–43), and 'The military household of the Norman kings' (*Eng Hist Rev*, vol 96 (1981) pp 1–35). But see also M Chibnall, 'Mercenaries and the *familia regis* under Henry I' (*History*, vol 62 (1977), pp 15–23).

50 The Germans who accompanied Richard I back to England in 1194 were alleged to have been amazed at its wealth, and to have said that if the emperor had known of the country's riches then the king's ransom would have even higher than it was (William of Newburgh, 'Historia Rerum Anglicarum', pt I, p 406).

51 M Fauroux, ed, *Recueil des Actes des Ducs de Normandie, 911–1066* (Caen (France), 1961), pp 41–4.

52 S Harvey, 'Domesday Book and its predecessors' (*Eng Hist Rev*, vol 86 (1971), pp 753–73).

53 J Green, 'William Rufus, Henry I and the royal demesne' (*History*, vol 64 (1979), pp 337–52), recapitulated in her *Government of England under Henry I*, pp 55–65. But the Crown lands were still the most important source of revenue in 1130.

54 K Yoshitake, 'The Exchequer in the reign of Stephen' (*Eng Hist Rev*, vol 103 (1988), pp 950–9); *cp* J Green, 'Financing Stephen's war' (*Anglo-Norman Studies*, vol 14 (1992), pp 91–114).

55 William of Newburgh, 'Historia Rerum Anglicarum' (Howlett, ed, 'Chronicles and memorials of the Reigns of Stephen, Henry II and Richard I', pt I, p 282), suggested that Henry's financial demands only became burdensome with the Saladin tithe of 1188, but see here J C Holt, *Magna Carta* (Cambridge, 2nd edn, 1992), pp 41–3, and his 'The end of the Anglo-Norman realm' (*Proceedings of the British Academy*, vol 61 (1975), pp 223–65, esp pp 234–9). There is a useful discussion of royal finance in W L Warren, *The Governance of Norman and Angevin England, 1086–1272* (London, 1987), pp 144–60.

56 J Stevenson, ed, 'Radulphi de Coggeshall Chronicon Anglicanum' (*RS*, vol 66 (1875), pp 92–3).

57 Rule, ed, 'Eadmer Historiae', p 192.

58 Potter and Davis, eds, *Gesta Stephani*, pp 22–5.

59 D Greenaway, ed, *Charters of the Honour of Mowbray, 1107–1191* (London, 1972), pp 7–10, no 3, discussed by R W Southern, 'The place of Henry I in English History', in his *Medieval Humanism and Other Studies*, p 221. For another example of the restitution of stolen properly by one of Henry's *curiales*, see U Rees, ed, *The Cartulary of Shrewsbury Abbey* (Aberystwyth, 1975), pp 23–4, nos 22–3.

60 Walter Map, *De Nugis Curialum*, p 468.

61 See especially the famous passage in Chibnall, ed, *The Ecclesiastical History of Orderic Vitalis*, vol VI, pp 16–17, who went on to say that 'witnesses too are the men who, on trumped-up charges and unjust pretexts, have been oppressed by them'; *cp* Potter and Davis, eds, *Gesta Stephani*, pp 22–3, on the allegedly low birth of Henry's *curiales*. But see also C W Hollister, 'The rise of administrative kingship: Henry I' (*American Historical Review*, vol 83 (1978), pp 887–90) and Green, *Government of England under Henry I*, pp 171–93. Among Henry's *curiales* from Cotention families were Bishop Roger of Salisbury, William and Nigel d'Aubigny, Rualon d'Avranches, Robert de la Haye, Aubrey de Vere, Eustace and Payn Fitz John, and Geoffrey de Clinton, although not all of these were old enough to have been in his service before 1100.

62 Stubbs, ed, 'Radulfi de Diceto Opera Historica', pt I, p 434; Howlett, ed, 'Chronicles and Memorials of the Reigns of Stephen, Henry II and Richard I' pt I, p 283.

63 See generally R V Turner, *Men Raised from the Dust: Administrative Service and Upward Mobility in Angevin England* (Philadelphia (USA), 1988).

64 C Johnson, ed, *Dialogue de Scaccario* (Oxford, 2nd edn, 1983), p 76.

65 *Ibid*, p 120.

66 The classic examination is J E A Jolliffe, *Angevin Kingship* (London, 2nd edn, 1963), pp 50–109. Two excellent case studies from the reign of Henry I are C W Hollister, 'The misfortunes of the Mandevilles' (*History*, vol LVIII (1973), pp 18–28) and D Crouch, 'Geoffrey de Clinton and Roger, Earl of Warwick: new men and magnates in the reign of Henry I' (*Bulletin of the Institute of Historical Research*, vol LV (1982), pp 113–24).

67 Stubbs, ed, 'Gesta Regis Henrici Secundi Benedicti Abbatis', pt I, p 278; Robertson, ed, 'Materials for the History of Thomas Becket, Archbishop of Canterbury',

26   T Hog, ed, *Fratris Nicholai Triveti Annales'* (London, 1845), pp 279–80, My translation largely comes from Gransden, *Historical Writing in England*, p 506.

27   H Rothwell, ed, 'The Chronicle of Walter of Guisborough' (*Camden Soc*, vol LXXXIX (1957), p 212).

28   PRO C 47/3/44; E 101/349/30.

29   Hog, ed, *Fratris Nicholai Triveti Annales'*, pp 281–2; Gransden, *Historical Writing in England*, p 506.

30   K R Potter, ed, *The Historia Novella by William of Malmesbury* (London, 1955), p 16.

31   H R Luard, ed, 'Matthaei Parisiensis Chronica Majora' (*RS*, vol 57, 7 pts (1872–84), pt V, p 514).

32   These problems are discussed in J C Holt, *King John* (London, 1963), reprinted in his *Magna Carta and Medieval Government* (London, 1985), esp pp 86–92.

33   T D Hardy, ed, *Rotuli de Oblatibus et Finibus* (London, 1835), p 275.

34   Sidney Painter implies that the fine was made at Marlborough in December 1204 (S Painter, *The Reign of John* (Baltimore (USA), 1949), p 231), but there is no evidence of this. The entry is undated but is placed on the fine roll for John's sixth regnal year, June 1204 – May 1205.

35   So Painter, *The Reign of John*, pp 231–2. Holt, 'King John', in *Magna Carta and Medieval Government*, pp 88–9, is more sceptical.

36   'Pipe Roll 14 John' (*PRS*, NS, vol XXX (1954), p 45; T D Hardy, ed, *Rotuli de Liberate ac de Misis et Praestitis* London, 1844), p 209.

37   C Bémont, 'Rotulus finium retrouvé' (*Bulletin Philologique et Historique*, vol XXXVI (1924), pp 225–39, at pp 238–9). I am grateful to John Maddicott for bringing this source to my notice. The Emperor Otto about whom Henry dreamed was presumably Otto of Brunswick.

38   There are numerous references to Peter in the printed chancery rolls. He was particularly concerned with acquiring wine for the king.

39   The ridiculous nature of the debts extended to the selling of wine at £3 a cask in the last entry. The king normally paid about half as much for a cask of (non prisage) wine; for example *Calendar of Liberate Rolls, 1240–5* (London, 1930), pp 101–2.

40   For a speech of Henry III at the Exchequer in 1250, brought to light by Michael Clanchy, and an illuminating discussion of the sources for Henry's kingship and its nature, see M T Clanchy, 'Did Henry III have a policy?' (*History*, vol LIII (1968), pp 203–16).

41   The appearance of the sheriffs and other bailiffs at the Michaelmas and Easter Exchequer was described in the Memoranda Roll as the *Adventus Vicecomitum* (Appearance at the Exchequer). See M H Mills, *Adventus Vicecomitum, 1258–1272'* (*Eng Hist Rev*, vol XXXVI (1921), pp 481–96). I am most grateful to James Collingwood (who is completing a thesis on English royal finance 1255–1272), Paul Brand and David Crook for helping me with the problems of Exchequer practice discussed in the following pages.

42   Luard, ed, 'Matthaei Parisiensis Chronica Majora', pt V, pp 588–9.

43   Each year there were two sets of memoranda rolls, one kept by the lord treasurer's remembrancer (PRO E 368) and one kept by the king's remembrancer (PRO E 159). In this period they are very nearly identical. Henry's provision is found on both: E 368/32, m ld; E 159/30, m ld.

44   He also said the sheriffs were to appear in the octaves of Michaelmas rather than on the day after Michaelmas.

45 Paris says that the sheriffs were to be amerced on the first day at 5 marks (£3 6s 8d), on the second at 10 marks (£6 13s 4d) and on the third at 15 marks (£10) but he is probably here counting up the daily amercement of 5 marks.

46 Paris says that on the fourth day the sheriff would be held to ransom (*sit redimendus*). This was the equivalent of being amerced at the king's will.

47 See Vaughan, *Matthew Paris*, pp 14, 17–18.

48 For a diatribe on this subject soon after his account of this episode, see Luard, ed, 'Matthaei Parisiensis Chronica Majorca', pt V, pp 594–5.

49 PRO C 60/53, schedule attached to m 3.

50 *Calendar of Close Rolls, 1254–6* (London, 1931), p 293.

51 PRO C 60/53, schedule attached to m 3. The amercement is here described as being of a half mark of gold but that was the same as 5 marks of silver (£3 6s 8d).

52 See for example H Summerson, 'The king's *clericulus*: the life and career of Silvester de Everdon, Bishop of Carlisle, 1247–1254' (*Northern History*, vol XXVII (1922), pp 84–5).

53 Carpenter, 'Gold treasure', esp p 72.

54 In what follows I have largely confined myself to discussing the merits of Henry's ruling in respect of the sheriffs. There are problems with the evidence regarding the cities, boroughs, and manors, which makes the subject too long to discuss here.

55 PRO E 159/30, m 23.

56 PRO E 159/30, m ld, printed in T Madox, *History and Antiquities of the Exchequer* (London, 2nd edn, 2 vols, 1769), vol II, p 154, n 'f'.

57 PRO E 401/28.

58 PRO E 401/28. The receipt rolls officially recorded the money received day by day into the Exchequer. The proffer section on the memoranda rolls merely record the sums the sheriffs said they had brought. See the next note.

59 The proffer is thus a record of the money the sheriffs *said* they had brought, not a record of the money actually received and counted by the Exchequer. Thus, in the earliest surviving record of the proffer, that for Easter 1208, each individual sum of money brought by a sheriff is qualified by the statement 'as he says': R A Brown, ed, 'Memoranda Roll 10 John' (*PRS*, NS, vol XXXI (1955), pp 31–3). This formula is still found in the memoranda rolls of Henry III's reign but gradually falls out of use. In 1235 the bailiff of Kingston appeared on the day after Michaelmas at the Exchequer (of receipt), said he had brought £25 and caused it to be written down (it does indeed appear in the memoranda roll's record of the proffer), but he then went away without licence of the treasurer and paid nothing of the £25 (PRO E 159/14, mm 4, 1). In the record of the 1256 proffer some sheriffs are said to have come and brought no money, but money is later recorded as received from them on the receipt roll. This too suggest they may genuinely have appeared in person on 30 September, their money only arriving later. For the proceeds of the proffer see E F Jacob, *Studies in the Period of Baronial Reform and Rebellion, 1258–1267* (Oxford, 1925), table between pp 248–9. See also Mills, 'Adventus Vicecomitum'.

60 The sheriffs were those of of Oxfordshire, Lancashire and Cumberland, although the money brought by the last two, according to the memoranda roll, does not match exactly with the money recorded on the receipt roll, a common problem for which see Mills, 'Adventus Vicecomitum', p 491.

61 PRO E 159/30, m 23.

62 PRO E 159/30, m 23; E 159/29, m 30.

63 Carpenter, 'Gold treasure', p 76.

64 It should be stressed, however, that only a proportion of the king's annual revenue was expected every year at the formal proffers. The sheriffs were also summoned to pay in revenue at other times and individuals came with money throughout the Easter and Michaelmas terms. Hence the totals recorded on the receipt rolls were always much larger than those of the memoranda roll proffers.

65 PRO E 159/15, mm 11, 12. According to the memoranda roll heading, the amercement was for failing to appear on the day after the close of Easter, not for failing to appear in person, but it is noticeable that only those sheriffs who came through deputies were amerced. See also *Close Rolls, 1234–7*, (London, 1909), pp 438, 528.

66 Johnson, ed, *Dialogus de Scaccario*, pp 79–80. In 1255, when the sheriff of Surrey failed to turn up to account, he was amerced £5 for each of the first three days and then at the king's will (PRO E 368/31, m.7d; see also m 11 for the sheriff of Lincolnshire being treated in comparable fashion. An example from the 1230s is *Close Rolls, 1234–7*, pp 385, 390; PRO E 159/15, m 16.

67 PRO E 159/30, m lv; E 368/32, m lv (Madox, *History and Antiquities of the Exchequer*, vol II, p 154, n 'f'). The monetary penalty is only mentioned in PRO E 159/30 where it is cancelled, apparently because of the order to take the city into the king's hands. York was not punished entirely retrospectively for breach of the new ruling. It would have escaped had it sent a deputy with the money.

68 PRO E 401/30. Again the record of the proffer on the memoranda roll (PRO E 159/30, m 23v) has everyone coming on the day after Michaelmas.

69 PRO E 159/30, m.23v.

70 The bracket and gap is on the memoranda roll of the king's remembrancer only (PRO E 159/30, m 11v). It does not appear on the roll of the lord treasurer's remembrancer (PRO E 368/32, m 11v).

71 This conclusion is based on an examination of the pipe rolls which have no sign of such amercements. By contrast, the amercements imposed on the sheriffs at Michaelmas 1256 for failing to distrain for knighthood do appear. Quite a number of sheriffs in the 1250s were amerced £5, and sometimes several amounts of £5, for contempt *coram rege* which probably means the court *coram rege*. The sheriff of Lincolnshire left office in the summer of 1257, but considerably later than Easter. The sheriff of Bedfordshire and Buckinghamshire remained in office till 1258.

72 PRO E 159/31, m 23. For one year to the next, the same sheriffs (the more distant ones) tended to send deputies but this is not an invariable rule and the lists were never exactly the same. We cannot tell how many sheriffs proffered acceptable excuses for failing to appear at the Easter and Michaelmas proffers of 1257. Henry's provision, however, made no mention of excuses and was surely designed to do more than secure them.

73 This is to judge from a comparison of the memoranda roll and the receipt roll (PRO E 159/31, m 23; E 401/33).

74 PRO E 159/29, m 31; E 159/30, m 23v. These are the total proffers including the sums from the cities, boroughs and manors.

75 PRO E 159/30, m 23; E 159/31, m 23. For examples of the writs, see *Close Rolls 1254–6*, pp 417–8, 426.

76 PRO E 401/12; E 159/15, m 13.

77 Brown, ed, 'Memoranda Roll 10 John', pp 31–3. The number is 15, but the master of one of the deputies was present in his capacity as a baron of the exchequer (William Brewer).

78 Johnson, ed, *Dialogus de Scaccario*, pp 79–84.

79 For the change in the nature of the office, see my 'The decline of the curial sheriff in England, 1194–1258' (*Eng Hist Rev*, vol XCI (1976), pp 1–32).

80 Four journeys if they had to come up separately for the view of their account after Easter.

81 PRO E 368/81, m 8 (Madox, *History and Antiquities of the Exchequer*, vol II, p 155, n 'i').

82 This is clear from the subsequent Michaelmas proffers (PRO E 159/17, m 12 (ink); E 159/64, m 17 (ink).

83 Johnson, ed, *Dialogus de Scaccario*, p 81; the sheriff's clerk, however, long continued as his representative at the proffer: see *Calendar of Memoranda Rolls, 1326–7* (London, 1968), nos 1–27, 31–57.

84 Carpenter, *Minority of Henry III*, p 163.

85 H Hall, ed, 'The Red Book of the Exchequer' (*RS*, vol 99, 3 pts, (1897), pt III, pp 894–7). For actual practice after the Ordinance see *Calendar of Memoranda Rolls, 1326–27*, nos 1–57, 2118–97.

86 *Close Rolls, 1256–9* (London, 1932), pp 46–7.

Chapter 6 (pages 132–148)

1 E M Thompson, ed, *Chronicon Adae de Usk* (London, 1904), p 52.

2 One king whom Richard may have had in mind was King Leir, who figures in Geoffrey of Monmouth's *History of the Kings of Britain*.

3 P S Lewis, 'Two Pieces of Fifteenth-Century Political Iconography' (*Journal of the Warburg and Courtauld Institutes*, vol 27 (1964), pp 319–20). Ancient examples were drawn from Anglo-Saxon history.

4 J de Mata Carriazo, ed, *El Vitorial. Cronica de Don Pero Nino, Conde de Buelna, por su alferez Gutierre Diez de Gamez* (Madrid (Spain), 1940), p 183.

5 E Perroy, *The Hundred Years War* (London, 1951), pp 134–5.

6 M Brown, *James I* (Edinburgh, 1994), pp 186–8.

7 A Paz y Melia, ed, Alonso de Palencia, *Cronica de Enrique IV* (Madrid (Spain), 1973), p 168.

8 W H Dunham, S Pargellis, eds, *Complaint and Reform in England, 1436–1714* (Oxford, 1938), p 64.

9 *Ibid*, pp 64–5.

10 Berners' translation was made at the behest of Henry VIII; the first volumes were printed in 1523 and 1525.

11 C Allmand, *Henry V* (London, 1992), chap 20.

12 I am indebted to a lecture given by D A L Morgan on Edward III's historical reputation at the Anglo-American Conference of Historians in London in 1987.

13 Dunham and Pargellis, eds, *Complaint and Reform*, pp 8–10, 25–6.

14 A R Myers, ed, *The Household of Edward IV* (Manchester, 1959).

15 For the increasing importance of the knights of the Chamber in the 14th century, see C Given-Wilson, *The Royal Household and the King's Affinity, Service, Politics and Finance in England, 1360–1413* (London, 1986), pp 204–11.

16 R A Brown, H M Colvin, A J Taylor, eds, *History of the King's Works* (London, 6 vols, 1963–82), vol II, pp 934–5, 976.

17 T Johnes, ed, *The Chronicles of England, France and Spain … by Jean Froissart* (London, 2 vols, 1848), vol II, p 637. Froissart attributed the criticism to Gaunt's brother, Thomas of Woodstock, Duke of Gloucester, who, he says, also applied it to their brother Edmund of Langley, Duke of York.

18   M D Legge, ed, *Anglo-Norman Letters and Petitions* (Oxford, 1941), no 29.

19   Johnes, ed, *Chronicles of England, France and Spain*, vol II, pp 576–7.

20   *Ibid*.

21   P McNiven, 'The problem of Henry IV's health, 1405–1413' (*Eng Hist Rev*, vol C (1985), pp 241–2).

22   Margaret Galway convincingly identified John de Surrey as the son of Edward III and Alice Perrers: M Galway, 'Alice Perrers' Son John' (*Eng Hist Rev*, vol LXVI (1951), pp 242–3). It may well be that Alice's daughters, both of whom were called Joan, were Edward's too. The brass of one of them, the wife of the lawyer Robert Skerne, can be seen in the church of Kingston-upon-Thames (Surrey): she wears some prominent jewels. Alice Perrers' jewel collection was as infamous as Imelda Marcos's collection of shoes.

23   R A Griffiths, *The Reign of Henry VI* (London, 1981), pp 241–2.

24   N Orme, *From Childhood to Chivalry* (London, 1984), p 22.

25   F J Furnivall, I Gollancz, eds, 'Hoccleve's Works', vol 3 (*Early English Text Society*, vol LXXIII, 1897).

26   Colvin, *et al*, eds, *The History of the King's Works*, vol II, p 935.

27   D Knowles, *The Religious Orders in England*, vol II (Cambridge, 1955), pp 185–6. *Cp* N Orme, 'Medieval Hunting – Fact and Fancy', in B Hanawalt, ed, *Chaucer's England: Literature in Historical Context* (Minneapolis (USA), 1992), pp 133–53.

28   W A Baillie-Grohman, F Baillie-Grohman, eds, *The Master of Game by Edward, Second Duke of York* (London, 1909).

29   H T Riley, ed, 'Chronica Monasterii Sancti Albani' (*RS*, vol 28, 7 pts in 11 sections (1863–73), pt 1, section 2, p 183).

30   Colvin, *et al*, eds, *The History of the King's Works*, vol II, p 998.

31   G E Cokayne, V Gibbs, eds, *Complete Peerage* (London, 13 vols, 1910–29), vol VIII, pp 571–6; M Jones, 'Edward III's Captains in Brittany', in W M Ormrod, ed, *England in the Fourteenth Century* (Woodbridge, 1986), pp 101–2.

32   J M Hanna, 'The Royal Heart Preserved at St Margaret's Convent, Whitehouse Loan, Edinburgh' (*Proceedings of the Society of Antiquaries of Scotland*, 5th ser, vol III (1916–7), pp 16–23). I am grateful to the sisters of this now defunct house for having been allowed to examine the heart-shrine – a large, heavy, dull, pitted, and cracked metal container in a conventional heart shape.

33   Henry V's organs were buried at St-Maur des Fosses, Val-de-Marne (Allmand, *Henry V*, p 174).

34   B Wolffe, *Henry VI* (London, 1981), pp 51–3 and plate 4.

35   D Gordon, F Luard, eds, *Making and Meaning. The Wilton Diptych* (London, 1949), pp 51–2; Allmand, *Henry V*, p 106.

36   *Ibid*, p 106.

37   Carriazo, ed, *El Vitorial*, p 182.

38   L C Hector, B F Harvey, eds, *The Westminster Chronicle, 1381–1394* (Oxford, 1982), pp 188–91.

39   J M Steane, *The Archaeology of Medieval England and Wales* (London, 1984), pp 83–4.

40   There were 400–700 household servants in the 14th century, and more than 800 in 1450 (Given-Wilson, *The Royal Household and the King's Affinity*, p 259).

41   G Kipling, 'Richard II's "Sumptuous Pageants" an the idea of civic triumph', in D M Bergeron, ed, *Pageantry in the Shakespearean Theater* (Athens (USA), 1985), pp 83–103.

42   Allmand, *Henry V*, pp 411–3.

43   A Goodman, *John of Gaunt* (London, 1992), p 61.

44 A Goodman, *The Loyal Conspiracy. The Lords Appellant under Richard II* (London, 1971), p 7.

45 Hector and Harvey, eds, *Westminster Chronicle*, pp 308–11, 312–5.

46 Goodman, *John of Gaunt*, p 255.

47 J S Roskell, 'Sir Richard de Waldegrave of Bures St Mary, Speaker in the Parliament of 1381–2' (*Proceedings of the Suffolk Institute of Archaeology*, vol XXVII, pt 3 (1957), p 165).

48 For English urban chronicles of the 15th century, see D Hay, *Annalists and Historians* (London, 1977), pp 85–6.

49 G Holmes, *The Good Parliament* (Oxford, 1975).

50 R Knox, S Leslie, eds, *The Miracles of King Henry VI* (Cambridge, 1923), pp 79–80, 153.

51 Gordon and Luard, eds, *Making and Meaning*, p 82.

52 A H Gilbert, 'Notes on the Influence of the *Secretum Secretorum* (*Speculum*, vol 3 (1928), pp 84–98); M A Manzalaoui, ed, 'Secretum Secretorum. Nine English Versions' (*Early English Text Society*, vol I, 1937); C F Briggs, 'The English Manuscripts of Giles of Rome's *De Regimine Principum* and their Audience, 1300–1500' (PhD thesis, University of North Carolina at Chapel Hill, 1993). I owe thanks to Dr Briggs for allowing me to consult his instructive thesis, which demonstrates the wide diffusion of MSS of the work in England.

53 Orme, *From Childhood to Chivalry*, pp 93–7.

54 J F Goodridge, ed, *William Langland, Piers the Ploughman* (Harmondsworth, 1959), pp 115–6.

55 The 33 charges have been translated by C Given-Wilson, *Chronicles of the Revolution, 1397–1400* (Manchester, 1993), pp 172–84.

56 For a general survey, see R Frame, *The Political Development of the British Isles, 1100–1400* (Oxford, 1990).

57 J E Lloyd, *Owen Glendover* (Oxford, 1931), p 46.

58 H J Hewitt, *The Black Prince's Expedition of 1355–1357* (Manchester, 1958), pp 15–16.

59 For a survey of Welsh captains prominent in the war, see A D Carr, 'Welshmen and the Hundred Years' War' (*Welsh Historical Review*, vol 4 (1968–9), pp 21–46).

60 Johnes, ed, *Chronicles of … Froissart*, vol II, p 578, for Henry Cristeyde's dismal words about Irish terrain, part of the generally unfavourable account of Ireland and the Irish which he gave to the chronicler.

61 C T Allmand, *Lancastrian Normandy, 1415–1450* (Oxford, 1983).

62 J F Lydon, *Ireland in the later Middle Ages* (Dublin (Eire), 1973), pp 140–2.

63 Chaucer's vagueness about the geography of Northumberland may have had ironic overtones (*The Reves Tale*, lines 4013–4).

64 Colvin, *et al*, eds, *History of the King's Works*, vol II, pp 818–21.

65 C M Crowder, *Unity, Heresy and Reform, 1378–1460. The Conciliar Response to the Great Schism* (London, 1977), pp 108–26.

66 Lord Twining, *A History of the Crown Jewels of Europe* (London, 1960), p 127.

Chapter 7 (pages 149–166)

1 G R Elton, *England under the Tudors* (London, 1955); *idem*, 'Rapacity and Remorse' (*Hist Jnl*, vol I (1958), pp 21–39); *idem, The Tudor Constitution* (Cambridge, 1960, 2nd edn, 1982); R L Storey, *The Reign of Henry VII* (London, 1968); J R Lander, 'Attainder and forfeiture, 1453–1509' (*Hist Jnl*, vol IV (1961), pp 119–51); *idem, The Wars of the Roses* (London, 1965, 2nd edn, Gloucester, 1987).

2   J R Lander, *Crown and Nobility, 1450–1509* (London, 1976).

3   C Ross, *Edward IV* (London, 1974).

4   During his brief campaign in France in 1475, Edward had directed that his queen should act as regent in the event of his death, but that was far enough in the past to be ignored in 1483. The assertion that he named Richard on his deathbed seems to depend upon the unsupported testimony of Polydore Vergil. It is not certain that Edward left any specific instructions.

5   In *Rewards and Fairies*; not, admittedly, a work intended for students of history.

6   Privy Purse expenses of Henry VII (BL Add MS 7099, fol 42); D M Loades, *The Tudor Court* (London, 1986), pp 84–132.

7   S B Chrimes, *Henry VII* (London, 1972), pp 248, 251.

8   J R Lander, 'Bonds, coercion and fear; Henry VII and the peerage', in J G Rowe, W H Stockdale, eds, *Florilegium historiale: essays presented to Wallace K Ferguson* (Toronto (Canada), 1971), pp 328–67.

9   L Stone, *The Crisis of the Aristocracy, 1558–1640* (Oxford, 1965).

10 Chrimes, *Henry VII*, p 212.

11 *Ibid*, p 216.

12 Elton, *The Tudor Constitution*, pp 89–91; Chrimes, *Henry VII*, pp 149–52.

13 M K Jones, M G Underwood, *the King's Mother* (Cambridge, 1992), pp 66–92.

14 D Starkey, 'Intimacy and Innovation, the Privy Chamber, 1485–1547' in D Starkey, ed, *The English Court from the Wars of the Roses to the Civil War* (London, 1987), pp 71–118.

15 D M Loades, *The Tudor Navy* (Aldershot, 1992), pp 40–3.

16 M Condon, 'Ruling Elites in the reign of Henry VII', in C Ross, ed, *Patronage, Pedigree and Power in Later Medieval England* (Gloucester, 1979), pp 109–42.

17 He had been betrothed to Catherine soon after Arthur's death and had then denounced the arrangement on the eve of his 14th birthday. Doubts had already been expressed about the lawfulness of the dispensation which his father had obtained (Duque de Berwick y de Alba, *Correspondencia de Gutierre Gomez de Fuensalida* (Madrid (Spain), 1907), pp 518 *et seq*).

18 Henry, Lord Montague, was trapped, together with the Courtenays, in the so-called 'Exeter conspiracy' of 1538, when Henry was still apprehensive about the succession and determined to deter any possible resistance (M H Dodds, R Dodds, *The Pilgrimage of Grace and the Exeter Conspiracy* (Cambridge, 2 vols, 1915).

19 P J Gwyn, *The King's Cardinal* (London, 1990), pp 15–18.

20 B J Harris, *Edward Stafford, Third Duke of Buckingham, 1478–1521* (Stanford (USA), 1986), pp 180–202.

21 S J Gunn, *Charles Brandon, Duke of Suffolk, 1484–1545* (Oxford, 1988), pp 60–1.

22 *Acts of the Privy Council, 1550–1552* (London, 1891), pp 347–9, 29 August 1551.

23 D Loades, *Politics and the Nation, 1450–1660* (London, 1974), p 203. For a full discussion of Henry's relations with his peers, see H Miller, *Henry VIII and the English Nobility* (Oxford, 1986), and for an examination of noble power as it survived in the northern marches, S G Ellis, *Tudor Frontiers and Noble Power* (Oxford, 1995).

24 See particularly the Act in Restraint of Appeals (24 Henry VIII, chap 12), the Act in Restraint of Annates (25 Henry VIII, chap 20) and the Act of Supremacy (26 Henry VIII, chap 1) (A Luders, *et al*, *Statutes of the Realm* (London, 11 vols, 1810–28), vol III, pp 427–9, 462–4, 492–3).

25 J J Scarisbrick, *Henry VIII* (London, 1968), pp 33–5.

26   G L Harriss, P H Williams, 'A Revolution in Tudor History?' (*Past and Present*, vol 25 (1963), pp 1 *et seq*.).

27   M Dewar, ed, *Sir Thomas Smith, De Republica Anglorum* (Cambridge, 1982), pp 78–9.

28   The Royal Supremacy was, in effect, the jurisdiction of the pope transferred to the king. There was no such thing as a papal minority.

29   The Lady Mary to the Council, 22 June 1549 (J Foxe, *Actes and Monuments of matters most special and memorable* ... (London, 2 vols, 1583), vol II, p 1332).

30   Notably C Haigh, *English Reformations* (Oxford, 1993) and E Duffy, *The Stripping of the Altars* (New Haven (USA), 1992).

31   D MacCulloch, ed, The *Vitae Mariae Angliae Reginae* of Robert Wingfield of Brantham' (*Camden Soc*, 4th ser, vol XXIX (1984), pp 181–301).

32   The statute 1 Mary, stat 3, chap 1 (Luders *et al, Statutes of the Realm*, vol IV, p 222).

33   On the Earldom of Northumberland, see particularly P G Boscher, 'Politics, Administration and Diplomacy in the Anglo-Scottish Borders, 1550–1560' (Durham PhD dissertation, 1985).

34   S Adam, M J Rodriguez Salgado, eds, 'The Count of Feria's Dispatch to Philip II of 14 November 1558' (*Camden Soc*, 4th ser, vol XXIX (1984), pp 302–44).

35   Indictment of John, Lord Bray (*Calendar of Patent Rolls, Philip and Mary*, vol III (London, 1961), p 396).

36   The lords lieutenant were noblemen, but the effective work of mustering and leadership fell to the deputy lieutenants (C G Cruikshank, *Elizabeth's Army* (Oxford, 1966).

37   J Strype, ed, *Memorials of ... Thomas Cranmer* (Oxford, 2 vols, 3rd edn, 1840), vol I, pp 127–8.

38   This was on account of the removal of the mitred abbots after 1540. Unlike the bishops and the lay peers, the attendance of these abbots was still largely at the discretion of the king, but they had normally attended in numbers approximately equal to the bishops, who numbered 26.

39   G R Elton, *The Parliament of England, 1559–1581* (Cambridge, 1986). For a careful examination of how many of the misunderstandings about this 'opposition' arose out of the tangled politics of the Elizabethan council, see M A R Graves, *Thomas Norton: the Parliament Man* (Cambridge, 1995).

Chapter 8 (pages 167–181)

1   Quoted in C W Daniels, J Morrill, *Charles I* (Cambridge, 1988), pp 8–9.

2   Quoted in P Gregg, *King Charles I* (London, 1981), pp 438–9.

3   The best starting points for reassessing the historical reputation of James I are J Wormald, 'James VI and I; two kings or one?' (*History*, vol 68 (1983), pp 187–209); R C Munden, 'James I and "the growth of mutual distrust"; king, Commons and reform' in K Sharpe, ed, *Faction and Parliament: Essays in Early Stuart History* (Oxford, 1978), pp 43–72; and M Schwarz, 'James I and the historians: towards a reconsideration' (*Journal of British Studies*, vol 13, pt 2 (1973), pp 114–34). Recent critical views of Charles I are reflected in D Hirst, *Authority and Conflict: England 1603–58* (London, 1985), pp 137 *et seq*, and C Russell, *Causes of the English Civil War* (Oxford, 1990).

4   Quoted in Wormald, 'James VI and I', pp 190–1.

5   C Coleman, 'Professor Elton's revolution', in D C Coleman, D Starkey, eds, *Revolution Reassessed* (Oxford, 1986), pp 1–11.

6   D Starkey, ed, *The English Court from the Wars of the Roses to the Civil War* (London, 1987); C Russell, 'Perspectives in parliamentary history, 1604–29' (*History*, vol 61 (1976), pp 1–27); *idem, Parliaments and English Politics, 1621–29* (Oxford, 1979).

7   C Haigh, *Elizabeth I* (London, 1988) is the best reassessment of the queen's historical reputation. Neale's important books on the queen are *Queen Elizabeth* (London, 1934) and *Elizabeth and her Parliaments* (London, 2 vols, 1953, 1957).

8   A Hassell Smith, *County and Court: Government and Politics in Norfolk, 1558–1603* (Oxford, 1974).

9   J A Guy, 'The Tudor age', in K O Morgan, ed, *The Oxford Illustrated History of Britain* (Oxford, 1984), p 284. Professor Guy modifies this assessment considerably in his *Tudor England* (Oxford, 1988), pp 45–58.

10 C Russell, 'The British problem and the English Civil War' (*History*, vol 72 (1987), pp 395–415); A Hughes, *The Causes of the English Civil War* (Basingstoke, 1991), chap 2.

11 This view is reflected in D H Willson, *James VI and I* (London, 1962). Henry VI of France allegedly called James 'the wisest fool in Christendom', but Dr Wormald has failed to find any evidence that he ever did so (Wormald, "James VI and I', p 192, n 17).

12 G P V Akrigg, ed. *The Letters of King James VI and I* (Berkeley (USA), 1985), p 3.

13 Quoted in J P Kenyon, *The Stuarts* (London, 1958), p 33.

14 This is illustrated, for example, in the disapproving way in which a Cheshire gentleman, William Davenport of Bramhall, commented on scandals at the court of James I, like the Essex divorce and the Overbury murder, in his commonplace book (J Morrill, *Cheshire, 1630–1660: County Government and Society during the 'English Revolution'* (Oxford, 1974), p 21).

15 Quoted in R Lockyer, *The Early Stuarts: a Political History of England 1603–41* (London, 1989), p 162. For the opposition in both countries to James's union scheme, see B Galloway, *The Union of England and Scotland, 1603–8* (Edinburgh, 1980); B P Levack, *The Formation of the British State: England, Scotland and the Union 1603–1707* (Oxford, 1987); N Cuddy, 'Anglo-Scottish union and the court of James I, 1603–25' (*Trans Roy Hist Soc*, 5th ser, vol 39 (1989), pp 107–24).

16 J R Tanner, ed, *Constitutional Documents of the Reign of James I, 1603–25* (Cambridge, 2nd edn, 1960), p 262.

17 M Kishlansky, 'The emergence of adversary politics in the Long Parliament' (*Journal of Modern History*, vol 49 (1977), pp 617–40); Russell, *Parliaments and English Politics*. See R Cust, A Hughes, 'Introduction: after revisionism', in *idem*, eds, *Conflict in Early Stuart England: Studies in Religion and Politics, 1603–42* (Harlow, 1989), pp 1–46, for a critique of this view.

18 L L Peck, '"For a king not to be bountiful were a fault": perspectives in court patronage' (*Journal of British Studies*, vol 25 (1960), p 262).

19 *idem*, 'Goodwin v. Fortescue: the local context of parliamentary controversy' (*Parliamentary History*, vol 3 (1984), pp 33–56).

20 P Lake, 'Constitutional consensus and Puritan opposition in the 1620s: Thomas Scott and the Spanish Match' (*Hist Jnl*, vol 25 (1982), pp 805–25); T Cogswell, 'England and the Spanish Match' in Cust and Hughes, eds, *Conflict in Early Stuart England*, pp 107–33; T Cogswell, *The Blessed Revolution: English Politics and the Coming of War, 1621–24* (Cambridge, 1989).

21 K Fincham, P Lake, 'The ecclesiastical policy of King James I' (*Journal of British Studies*, vol 24 (1985), pp 169–235); *idem*, 'The ecclesiastical policies of James

I and Charles I' in K Fincham, ed, *The Early Stuart Church, 1603–42* (Basingstoke, 1993), pp 23–49.

22 P Collinson, 'The Jacobean religious settlement: the Hampton Court conference', in H Tomlinson, ed, *Before The English Civil War* (London, 1983), p 39.

23 The best recent introduction to James's record as king of Britain is K Brown, *Kingdom or Province?: Scotland and the Regal Union, 1603–1715* (Basingstoke, 1992), chap 4.

24 Fincham and Lake, 'The ecclesiastical policy of James I'.

25 Cogswell, 'The Spanish Match'; Cogswell, *The Blessed Revolution*; and L Reeve, *Charles I and the Road to Personal Rule* (Cambridge, 1989) are detailed accounts of the tangled diplomatic manoeuvres that culminated in Charles's decisions to declare war on Spain and on France.

26 R Cust, *The Forced Loan and English Politics, 1626–28* (Oxford, 1987).

27 J P Kenyon, ed, *The Stuart Constitution: Documents and Commentary* (Cambridge, 2nd edn, 1986), p 45.

28 Cust, *Forced Loan*, pp 27–36.

29 J A Guy, 'The origins of the Petition of Right reconsidered' (*Hist Jnl*, vol 25 (1982), pp 289–312).

30 K Sharpe's view of the 1630s is in his 'The personal rule of Charles I', in H Tomlinson, ed, *Before the Civil War* and his *The Personal Rule of Charles I* (New Haven (USA), 1992). For a different view see, for example, P Lake, 'The collection of ship money in Cheshire during the 1630s: a case study of relations between central and local government' (*Northern History*, vol 17 (1981), pp 44–71); K Fincham, 'The judges' decision on ship money in February 1637: the reaction of Kent' (*Bulletin of the Institute of Historical Research*, vol LVII (1984), pp 230–7); A Hughes, 'Thomas Dugard and his circle in the 1630s: a parliamentary-puritan connection?' (*Hist Jnl*, vol 29 (1986), pp 771–93); J Fielding, 'Opposition to the personal rule of Charles I: the diary of Robert Woodford, 1637–41' (*Hist Jnl*, vol 31 (1988), pp 769–88).

31 Quoted in J Richards, '"His nowe Majestie" and the English monarchy: the kingship of Charles I before 1640' (*Past and Present*, vol 113 (1986), p 78).

32 This is currently a very controversial topic among early 17th-century English historians. For the views reflected in my lecture see N Tyacke, 'Puritanism, Arminianism and counter-revolution', in C Russell, ed, *The Origins of the English Civil War* (London, 1973), pp 119–43; N Tyacke. *Anti-Calvinists: the Rise of English Arminianism, c 1590–1640* (Oxford, 1987); P Collinson, *The Religion of Protestants: The Church in English Society, 1559–1625* (Oxford, 1982) and P Lake, 'Calvinism and the English Church' (*Past and Present*, vol 114 (1987), pp 32–76). For an alternative interpretation see P White, 'the rise of Arminianism reconsidered' (*Past and Present*, vol 101 (1983), pp 34–54); P White, *Predestination, Policy and Polemic* (Cambridge, 1992); Sharpe, *Personal Rule*; and G Bernard, 'The Church of England, c 1529–1642' (*History*, vol 75 (1990), pp 183–206).

33 D Stevenson, *The Scottish Revolution, 1637–44: The Triumph of the Covenanters* (Newton Abbot, 1973); M Lee, *The Road to Revolution: Scotland under Charles I, 1625–37* (Urbana (USA), 1985); A I MacInnes, *Charles I and the Making of the Covenanting Movement, 1625–41* (Edinburgh, 1991); P Donald, *An Uncounselled King: Charles I and the Scottish troubles, 1637–41* (Cambridge, 1990).

34 P H Donald, 'New light on the Anglo-Scottish connections of 1640' (*Historical Research*, vol LXII (1989), pp 221–9).

35 C Hibbard, *Charles I and the Popish Plot* (Chapel Hill (USA), 1983).

36 Kenyon, *Stuart Constitution*, p 200.

37 Their last child, Henrietta, was born in 1644.

38 This is reflected in the subtitles of books like R Ashton, *The English Civil War: Conservatism and Revolution, 1603–49* (London, 1976, 2nd edn, 1989) and J Morrill, *The Revolt of the Provinces: Conservatives and Radicals in the English Civil War, 1630–50* (London, 1976, 2nd edn, 1980).

39 See my *Oliver Cromwell* (London, 1991), pp 57–65 for a suggested explanation why Charles's actions pushed army leaders like Cromwell and Henry Ireton, who had worked assiduously for a monarchical settlement in 1646–7, to decide to put the king on trial at the end of 1648.

Chapter 9 (pages 182–202)

1 M Bloch, *The Royal Touch* (London, 1973); R O Bucholz, *The Augustan Court* (Stanford (USA), 1993), pp 210–2, 223–4.

2 See J N Figgis, *The Divine Right of Kings* (New York (USA), 1965).

3 It has recently been suggested that the term 'Exclusion Crisis' is misleading (J Scott, *Algernon Sidney and the Restoration Crisis, 1677–83* (Cambridge, 1991), pp 9–25). It is certainly clear that exclusion played a less important role in the 1679 Parliament and in elections than used to be thought, but it is also clear that exclusion *was* a major issue (as was religion) and the term has the merits of being succinct, in common usage, and easily understood (M Knights, 'Politics and Opinion during the Exclusion Crisis' (unpublished Oxford DPhil thesis, 1989), chaps 2, 4; M Goldie, 'Danby, the Bishops and the Whigs', in T Harris, P Seaward, M Goldie, eds, *The Politics of Religion in Restoration England* (Oxford, 1990), pp 78–80; T Harris, *Politics under the Later Stuarts* (London, 1993), pp 80–2. Harris' book is the best general introduction to the politics of this period.

4 G R Elton, *The Tudor Constitution* (Cambridge, 1960), p 15.

5 Figgis, *Divine Right of Kings*, pp 137–8.

6 J P Kenyon, *The Stuart Constitution* (Cambridge, 2nd edn, 1986), p 349; R L'Estrange, *The Holy Cheat* (?London, 1662, repr 1682), pp 27–9; M Nedham, *A Pacquet of Advices to the Men of Shaftesbury* (London, 1676), pp 42–3; J R Western, *Monarchy and Revolution* (London, 1972), pp 13–14.

7 K G Feiling, *History of the Tory Party, 1640–1714* (Oxford, 1924), pp 362–3, 409–10 (quoted); J P Kenyon, *Revolution Principles: The Politics of Party, 1689–1720* (Cambridge, 1977), chap 5.

8 This was true even in London: see G De Krey, *A Fractured society: The Politics of London in the First Age of Party, 1688–1715* (Oxford, 1985).

9 P Monod, *Jacobitism and the English People, 1688–1788* (Cambridge, 1989), pp 255–66. Note the parallel with Monmouth (R Clifton, *The Last Popular Rebellion* (London, 1984), p 137).

10 Elton, *Tudor Constitution*, p 15.

11 P Laslett, ed, *Two Treatises of Government by John Locke* (New York (USA), 1965), p 470. For the Jesuits, see J J Scarisbrick, *Jesuits and Princes, 1600–1700* (London, 1993), pp 2–4.

12 See C Hill, *Change and Continuity in Seventeenth-Century England* (London, 1974), chap 8; B Manning, *The English People and the English Revolution, 1640–9* (London, 1976). Manning's work is marred by a tendency to see all popular activity in terms of class conflict, but it remains the fullest study of this subject.

13 See M A Judson, *The Crisis of the Constitution* (New Brunswick (USA), 1949); A Sharp, *Political Ideas of the English Civil Wars, 1641–9* (London, 1983).

14 M Goldie, 'John Locke and Anglican Royalism' (*Political Studies*, vol XXI (1983), pp 61–85); *idem*, 'The Political Thought of the Anglican Revolution', in R Beddard, ed, *The Revolutions of 1688* (Oxford, 1991), pp 102–36; J Spurr, *The Restoration Church of England, 1646–89* (New Haven (USA), 1991), pp 88–100.

15 J Miller, 'Charles II and his Parliaments' (*Trans Roy Hist Soc*, 5th ser, vol XXXII (1982), p 4).

16 E S de Beer, ed, *The Diary of John Evelyn* (Oxford, 6 vols, 1955), vol III, p 246.

17 Kenyon, *Stuart Constitution*, p 349.

18 See I M Green, *The Re-establishment of the Church of England 1660–3* (Oxford, 1978); Spurr, *Restoration Church of England*, pp 29–52.

19 J Miller, 'The Crown and the Borough Charters in the Reign of Charles II' (*Eng Hist Rev*, vol C (1985), pp 59–63).

20 A Luders, *et al, Statutes of the Realm* (London, 11 vols, 1810–28), vol V, pp 433, 524, 556, 577.

21 Wardship would therefore have been restored to the king in 1661 – had the Convention not already abolished it.

22 See C D Chandaman, *The English Public Revenue, 1660–88* (Oxford, 1975).

23 H M Margoliouth, ed, *The Poems and Letters of Andrew Marvell* (Oxford, 3rd edn, 2 vols, 1971), vol II, p 315.

24 *Journals of the House of Commons*, vol VIII, p 104; vol IX, p 276; C Robbins, ed, *Diary of J Milward* (Cambridge, 1938), pp 189–90; for a threat to withhold money in 1662 see E Berwick, ed, *Rawdon Papers* (London, 1819), p 138. More generally, see J Miller, 'Charles II and his Parliaments'; D Hirst, 'The Conciliatoriness of the Cavalier Commons Reconsidered' (*Parliamentary History*, vol VI (1986), pp 221–35).

25 See Chandaman, *English Public Revenue*; J Miller, *Charles II* (London, 1991).

26 Historical MSS Commission, *5th Report*, p 184.

27 Bodleian Library, Oxford, Carte MS 232, fol 20; Historical MSS Commission, *Report on the Ormonde MSS*, NS vol III, p 306.

28 P Seaward, *The Cavalier Parliament and the Reconstruction of the Old Regime, 1661–7* (Cambridge, 1989), pp 193–4; Spurr, *Restoration Church of England*, pp 39–42.

29 See Miller, *Charles II*.

30 The Compton Census was intended to show how few Dissenters there were (A Whiteman, *The Compton Census of 1676* (Oxford, 1986), pp xxiv–xxix). For an earlier rough census, in 1669, with the same objective, see BL, Harleian MS 7377, fol 6.

31 BL, Egerton MS 2539, fol 170.

32 Robbins, ed, *Diary of J Milward*, pp 220–2, 248–50; A Grey, ed, *Debates in the House of Commons 1667–94* (London, 10 vols, 1769), vol I, pp 127–32.

33 E Newton, *The House of Lyme* (London, 1917), pp 242–3.

34 *Ibid*, p 252; Margoliouth, ed, *The Poems and Letters of Andrew Marvell*, vol II, pp 314–5.

35 Miller, *Charles II*, chap 7.

36 M Bond, ed, *Diaries and Papers of Sir E Dering* (London, 1976), pp 125–6; G Burnet, *History of my Own Time* (Oxford, 6 vols, 1823), vol II, p 1.

37 W D Christie, ed, 'Letters addressed from London to Sir Joseph Williamson, 1673–4' (*Camden Soc*, NS vol 8–9 (1874), vol 9, p 142).

38 See W Temple, *Memoirs of what passed in Christendom from the war begun in*

1672 ... to the peace concluded 1679 (?London, 1692), pp 153–4; A Browning, *Thomas, Early of Danby* (Glasgow, 3 vols, 1951), vol II, p 70.

39 *Calendar of State Papers, Domestic Series, 1680–1* (London, 1921), p 660; N Luttrell, *Brief Historical Relation of State Affairs, 1678–1714* (Oxford, 6 vols, 1851), vol I, p 199.

40 PRO PC 2/71, p 1 (my italics).

41 BL Add MS 63057B, fol 22; Burnet, *History of my own Time*, vol II, pp 27, 428n.

42 See J Miller, *James II: A Study in Kingship* (London, 1989), chaps 9–12.

43 See J R Jones, *The Revolution of 1688 in England* (London, 1972), chap 6.

44 J Gutch, *Collectanea Curiosa* (London, 2 vols, 1781), vol I, p 436; A F Havighurst, 'James II and the Twelve Men in Scarlet' (*Law Quarterly Review*, vol LXIX (1953), pp 522–46).

45 Kenyon, *Stuart Constitution*, p 410. James seems to have seen no difference between the dispensing and suspending power (BL Egerton MS 2543, fol 270).

46 Miller, 'Crown and Borough Charters', pp 70–84. The first charter giving the king the power to nominate, as distinct from removing, members of the corporation was that for Exeter in March 1688 (*Calendar of State Papers, Domestic Series, 1687–9* (London, 1972), no 855). The state papers make it clear that James was installing members of corporations even where he had no legal right to do so.

47 A Coleby, *Central Government and the Localities: Hampshire, 1649–89* (Cambridge, 1987), p 220; J Bloxam, 'Magdalen College and James II' (*Oxford Historical Society*, OS vol VI, 1886); Spurr, *Restoration Church of England*, pp 93–8.

48 G H Jones, *Convergent Forces: Immediate Causes of the Revolution of 1688 in England* (Ames (USA), 1990), chap 3; Spurr, *Restoration Church of England*, pp 94–7.

49 J R Jones, 'James II's Whig Collaborators' (*Hist Jnl*, vol III (1960), pp 65–73); M Goldie, 'James II and the Dissenters' Revenge: The Commission of Enquiry of 1688' (*Historical Research*, vol LXVI (1993), pp 53–88).

50 Miller, *James II*, pp 175–7.

51 On the Whigs, see R Beddard, 'The Unexpected Whig Revolution of 1688', in Beddard, ed, *The Revolution of 1688*, chap 1; on the Tories, see J Miller, '"Proto-Jacobitism"? The Tories and the Revolution of 1688–9', in E Cruickshanks, J Black, eds, *The Jacobite Challenge* (Edinburgh, 1988), chap 1.

52 H C Foxcroft, ed, *Life and Letters of Halifax* (London, 2 vols, 1898), vol II, p 204; Burnet, *History of my Own Time*, vol III, p 374; R J Frankle, 'The Formulation of the Declaration of Rights' (*Hist Jnl*, vol XVII (1974), pp 265–79).

53 See J Brewer, *The Sinews of Power: War, Money and the English State* (London, 1989); J H Plumb, *The Growth of Political Stability in England, 1675–1725* (London, 1967), chap 4.

54 Burnet, *History of my Own Time*, vol III, p 374. See also J Miller, "The Glorious Revolution: "Contract" and "Abdication" Reconsidered' (*Historical Journal*, vol XXV (1982), pp 541–56); J P Kenyon, 'The Revolution of 1688: Resistance and Contract', in N McKendrick, ed, *Historical perspectives: Studies in English Thought and Society in Honour of J H Plumb* (London, 1974), chap 3; H Horwitz, '1689 (and all that)' (*Parliamentary History*, vol VI (1987), pp 23–32).

55 See Kenyon, *Revolution principles*.

56 Frankle, 'Formulation of the Declaration of Rights', pp 275–9. But see also the very different interpretation advanced by L G Schwoerer, *The Declaration of Rights, 1689* (Baltimore (USA), 1982).

57 Grey, *Debates in the House of Commons*, vol IX, p 36; vol X, p 10; C Roberts, 'The Constitutional Significance of the Financial Settlement of 1690' (*Hist Jnl*, vol XX (1977), pp 59–76).

58 See G Holmes, *British Politics in the Age of Anne* (London, rev edn, 1987), pp 102–3.

59 C Brooks, 'The Country Persuasion and Political Responsibility in the 1690s' (*Parliaments, Estates and Representation*, vol IV (1984), pp 135–46); D Hayton, 'The Country Interest and the Party System, 1689–c1720', in C Jones, ed, *Party and Management in Parliament, 1660–1784* (Leicester, 1984), pp 37–85.

60 See Holmes, *British Politics in the Age of Anne*; H Horwitz, *Parliament, Policy and Politics in the Reign of William III* (Manchester, 1977).

61 E Gregg, *Queen Anne* (London, 1980).

62 See G C Gibbs, 'The Revolution in Foreign Policy', in G Holmes, ed, *Britain after the Glorious Revolution* (London, 1969), pp 66–76; Gibbs, 'Laying Treaties Before Parliament in the Eighteenth Century', in R M Hatton, J S Bromley, eds, *Essays in Diplomatic History in Memory of D.B. Horn* (London, 1970), chap 7.

63 Bucholz, *The Augustan Court*, chaps 6–7.

64 W C Costin, J S Watson, eds, *The Law and Working of the Constitution* (London, 2 vols, 1951), vol I, p 376.

65 J B Owen, *The Rise of the Pelhams* (London, 1957), pp 298–9.

Chapter 10 (pages 203–227)

1 J Watkins, *A Biographical Memoir of His Late Royal Highness Frederick Duke of York and Albany* (London, 1827), pp 307–8, cited in D Gates, *The British Light Infantry Arm, c1790–1815* (London, 1988), p 37; 'Evolutions of the Squadron under the command of Commodore Goodall when viewed by His Majesty, 18 August 1789 off Plymouth' (BL Add MS 71206); J A Houlding, *Fit for Service: The Training of the British Army, 1715–1795* (Oxford, 1981), p 71; *Maggs Catalogue*, no 1161, p 36, George III to Anon, 23 Oct 1798. None of the letters of George III cited in this piece appears in the published editions of his correspondence.

2 Hull University Library, DDHo/4/22, Buckinghamshire to Sir Charles Hotham, 12 July 1783.

3 BL Add 379334, fol 32, Anon to Anon [1742]. The most important reevaluation of the king is provided by J Owen, 'George II reconsidered', in A Whiteman, J S Bromley, P G M Dickson, eds, *Statesmen, Scholars and Merchants* (Oxford, 1973), pp 113–34.

4 PRO SP 35/24/75, 35/6/66; *Pickering and Chatto List*, no 40, September 1984, item 109; B van Muyden, ed, *A foreign view of England in the reigns of George I and George II* (London, 1902), pp 60, 229, 233; Pulteney to Swift, 2 December 1736 (BL Add MS 4806, fol 178); J Brooke, ed, *Horace Walpole, Memoirs of King George II* (New Haven (USA), 3 vols, 1985), vol I, pp 118–19.

5 Hertfordshire Record Office, Hertford, Panshanger papers D/EP F204, fol 16, Lady Paulet to Lady Cowper, 4 August 1716.

6 BL Add MS 32686, fol 108, Sunderland to Duke of Newcastle, 1 October 1717.

7 BL Add MS 32686, fol 193, Carteret to Newcastle, 27 August 1721.

8 BL Add MS 9152, fol 3, Newcastle to Horatio Walpole, 21 May 1724.

9 J Simon, ed, *Handel. A Celebration of his Life and Times, 1685–1759* (London, 1985), p 251. For an earlier emphasis on the king as political redeemer, see M Schonhorn, *Defoe's Politics. Parliament, power, kingship, and 'Robinson Crusoe'* (Cambridge, 1991).

10 P D Brown, K W Schweizer, eds, 'The Devonshire Diary. William Cavendish,

Fourth Duke of Devonshire, Memoranda on State of Affairs, 1759–1762' (*Camden Society*, 4th ser, vol 27 (1982), pp 54, 60).

11 Paris, Archives des Affaires Etrangères, Correspondance Politique, Angleterre, 450, fol 337.

12 BL RP 2149, George III to Bishop of Lichfield, 2 June 1776.

13 BL Add MS 70956, George III to Richard Grenville, 29 December 1780, 6 February 1781. For the same theme with reference to the future William IV, BL RP 2283, George III to Sir Samuel Hood, 13 June 1779.

14 BL Add MS 70956, George III to Grenville, 29 October, 23 November 1781 (quoted), 29 July, 12 August 1783.

15 BL Add MS 70956, George III to Grenville, 30 April 1782.

16 BL Add MS 70956, George III to Grenville, 29 November 1782.

17 BL Add MS 70956, George III to Grenville, 1, 15 July 1783.

18 BL Add MS 2382, George III to Prince William, 13 February 1784; BL Add MS 70956, George III to Grenville, 29 July 1783, 13 February 1784, 29 August 1786; Bedfordshire Record Office, Lucas papers L30/14/326/2, Reynolds to Lord Grantham, 20 July 1773. I would like to thank Lady Lucas for permission to quote from the letter.

19 BL Add MS 70990, fol 8, George III to Robinson, 6 September 1780.

20 F O'Gorman, 'Pitt and the 'Tory' Reaction to the French Revolution, 1789–1815', in H T Dickinson, ed, *Britain and the French Revolution, 1789–1815* (London, 1989), p 29.

21 L J Colley, 'The Apotheosis of George III: Loyalty, Royalty and the British Nation, 1760–1820' (*Past and Present*, vol 102 (1984), pp 94–129), and *Britons. Forging the Nation, 1707–1837* (New Haven (USA), 1992), pp 206–30.

22 L G Mitchell, *Charles James Fox* (Oxford, 1992), p 194.

23 J J Sack, *From Jacobite to Conservative. Reaction and orthodoxy in Britain, c1760–1832* (Cambridge, 1993), p 134.

24 R O Bucholz, *The Augustan Court, Queen Anne and the Decline of Court Culture* (Stanford (USA), 1993), p 251.

25 G Finley, *Turner and George the Fourth in Edinburgh 1822* (London, 1981); J Prebble, *The King's Jaunt: George IV in Scotland, August 1822* (London, 1989).

26 Catalogues of exhibitions at the Queen's Gallery, Buckingham House: *Carlton House: The Past Glories of George IV's Palace* and *George IV and the Arts of France*. For George's patronage of Nash, see D J Olsen, *Town Planning in London: The Eighteenth and Nineteenth Centuries* (New Haven (USA), 1982).

27 J M Beattie, *The English Court in the Reign of George I* (Cambridge, 1967).

28 N Gash, *Pillars of Government and Other Essays on State and Policy, c1770–c1880* (London, 1986), p 106.

29 I would like to thank Eveline Cruikshanks, John Derry, Grayson Ditchfield, David Eastwood, Bill Gibson, Robert Harris, Nicholas Henshall, Brian Hill, John Plowright and Philip Woodfine for commenting on earlier drafts of this essay.

Chapter 11 (pages 228–236)

1 F Furet, *Revolutionary France, 1770–1880* (Oxford, 1993), first published in France in 1988; S Schama, *Citizens, A Chronicle of the French Revolution* (New York (USA) and London, 1989).

2 J Hardman, *Louis XVI* (New Haven (USA) and London, 1993).

3 J Merrick, *The Desacralization of the French Monarchy in the eighteenth century* (Baton Rouge (USA) and London, 1990); L Hunt, *The Family Romance of the French Revolution* (Berkeley and Los Angeles (USA), 1992).

4 Hardman, *Louis XVI*, pp 121, 144.

5 M Roberts, 'The Dubious Hand: the history of a Controversy', in his *From Oxenstierna to Charles XII* (Cambridge, 1991), pp 144–203.

6 Hardman, *Louis XVI*, chap 14.

7 See D P Jordan, *The King's Trial, Louis XVI versus the French Revolution* (Berkeley and Los Angeles (USA), 1979), chaps IX-XI; and, more generally M Walzer, *Regicide and Revolution. Speeches at the Trial of Louis XVI* (Cambridge, 1974).

8 Hunt, *The Family Romance of the French Revolution*, chap 4.

9 See I Collins, *Napoleon and his Parliaments, 1800–1815* (London, 1979).

Chapter 12 (pages 237–247)

1 B Guenee, *States and Rulers in Later Medieval Europe* (Oxford, 1965), pp 60–2.

2 H Boece, *Scotorum Historiae a prima gentis origine* (Paris, 1574); C Kidd, *Subverting Scotland's Past* (Cambridge, 1993). *Cp* R Mason, 'Scotching the Brut', in J Wormald, ed, *Scotland Revisited* (London, 1991).

3 I Moncrieffe, D Pottinger, *Blood Royal* (Edinburgh, 1956), p 42.

4 A H Williamson, *Scottish National Consciousness in the Age of James VI* (Edinburgh, 1979).

5 A A M Duncan, *The Making of the Kingdom* (Edinburgh, 1979).

6 M Lynch, *Scotland: A New History* (Edinburgh, 1992), p 12.

7 *Ibid*, pp 21 *et seq*.

8 B O'Corrain, 'Irish Regnal Succession: A Re-Appraisal' (*Studia Hibernica*, vol XI (1971), pp 7–39).

9 Lynch, *Scotland: A New History*, p 16.

10 G Donaldson, ed, *Scottish Historical Documents* (Edinburgh, 1974), p 3.

11 Lynch, *Scotland: A New History*, p 50.

12 J Hill-Burton, *The History of Scotland* (Edinburgh, 8 vols, 1876).

13 A O Anderson, ed, *Scottish Annals from English Chroniclers* (London, 1908), p 118.

14 *Cp* the difference in approach between G W S Barrow, *The Anglo-Norman era in Scottish History* (Oxford, 1980) and K J Stringer, *Earl David of Huntingdon* (Edinburgh, 1985).

15 A Bruce, 'The Bruce Family, 1100–1203: A Study in the Norman Settlement of Scotland' (unpublished Oxford BA dissertation, 1989).

16 G Steele, *Robert III of Scotland: His Answer to a Summons sent by Henry IV of England* (Edinburgh, 1700). *Cp* Kidd, *Subverting Scotland's Past*, p 45.

17 T Craig, *Scotland's Sovereignty Asserted* (London, 1695).

18 Donaldson, ed, *Scottish Historical Documents*, pp 36–7; but see the terms of submission of the claimants to the Scots throne to Edward I in 1291 (*ibid*, pp 43–4).

19 H Montgomery-Massingberd, ed, *Lord of the Dance: a Moncreiffe miscellany. Diverse writings of Sir Iain Moncreiffe of that Ilk* (London, 1988), p 49, in which the late Sir Ian Moncreiffe argued that referring to King Henry as 'Darnley' would be like describing the Duke of Edinburgh as Lt Philip Mountbatten.

20 N MacDougall, *James III* (Edinburgh, 1982); *James IV* (Edinburgh, 1989); other volumes in this series edited by Dr MacDougall are in preparation.

21 Donaldson, ed, *Scottish Historical Documents*, p 33.
22 J Wormald, 'The House of Stewart and its Realm', in *idem*, ed, *Scotland Revisited*, pp 12 *et seq*.
23 N MacDougall, 'The Kingship of James IV of Scotland', in *ibid*, p 33.
24 *Ibid*, p 25.
25 Lynch, *Scotland: A New History*, p 160.
26 *Ibid*, p 166.
27 Montgomery-Massingberd, ed, *Lord of the Dance*, pp 98–102.

Chapter 13 (pages 248–268)

There are no Notes or Further Reading to this chapter.

Chapter 14 (pages 269–273)

There are no Notes or Further Reading to this chapter.

Chapter 15 (pages 274–277)

There are no Notes or Further Reading to this chapter.

Chapter 16 (pages 278–287)

Further Reading:

F Barlow, *William I and the Norman Conquest* (London, 1965).
C N L Brooke, *The Saxon and Norman Kings* (London, 1963).
Burke's Guide to the Royal Family (London, 1972).
J Harvey, *The Plantagenets* (London, rev edn, 1959).
R Hatton, *George I – Elector and King* (London, 1978).
C Hibbert, *George IV, Regent and King* (London, 1973).
H Hobhouse, *Prince Albert: His Life and Work* (London, 1983).
E Longford, *Victoria RI* (London, 1964).
P Magnus, *King Edward the Seventh* (London, 1964).
H Nicolson, *King George V: His Life and Reign* (London, 1952).
J Pope-Hennessy, *Queen Mary, 1867–1963* (London, 1959).
J W Wheeler-Bennett, *King George VI: his life and reign* (London, 1958).
D Williamson, *Kings and Queens of Britain* (London, 1991).
D Williamson, *Brewer's British Royalty* (London, 1996).
A King's Story. The Memoirs of HRH The Duke of Windsor (London, 1951).
P Ziegler, *King William IV* (London, 1971).

Chapter 17 (pages 288–310)

Further Reading:

F W Maitland, *Constitutional History of England* (Cambridge, 3rd edn, 1961), esp pp 281–327.

W Anson, *Law and Custom of the Constitution* (Oxford, 2nd edn, 1892), pt 1, esp pp 286–345.

W Bagehot, *The English Constitution* (London, 7th edn, 1963; 8th edn, 1964; 9th edn, 1993).

V Bogdanor, *The Monarchy and the Constitution* (Oxford, 1995), esp pp 145–82.

Index